T0122173

# Lecture Notes in Computer Science 13198

More information about this series at https://link.springer.com/bookseries/558

Carmelo Ardito · Rosa Lanzilotti ·
Alessio Malizia · Marta Larusdottir ·
Lucio Davide Spano · José Campos ·
Morten Hertzum · Tilo Mentler ·
José Abdelnour Nocera · Lara Piccolo ·
Stefan Sauer · Gerrit van der Veer (Eds.)

# Sense, Feel, Design

## INTERACT 2021 IFIP TC 13 Workshops
## Bari, Italy, August 30 – September 3, 2021
## Revised Selected Papers

Springer

*Editors*
Carmelo Ardito
Polytechnic University of Bari
Bari, Italy

Rosa Lanzilotti
University of Bari Aldo Moro
Bari, Italy

Alessio Malizia
Computer Science Department
University of Pisa
Pisa, Italy

Marta Larusdottir
Reykjavik University
Reykjavik, Iceland

José Campos
Department of Information
University of Minho
Braga, Portugal

Lucio Davide Spano
University of Cagliari
Caglieri, Italy

Tilo Mentler
Fachbereich Informatik
Trier University of Applied Sciences
Trier, Germany

Morten Hertzum
Department of Communication
University of Copenhagen
Copenhagen, Denmark

José Abdelnour Nocera
ITI/Larsys
University of West London
London, UK

Lara Piccolo
Knowledge Media Institute
Open University
Milton Keynes, UK

Stefan Sauer
University of Paderborn
Paderborn, Germany

Gerrit van der Veer
Faculty of Sciences, Department of Computer Science
Vrije Universiteit
Amsterdam, The Netherlands

ISSN 0302-9743 ISSN 1611-3349 (electronic)
Lecture Notes in Computer Science
ISBN 978-3-030-98387-1 ISBN 978-3-030-98388-8 (eBook)
https://doi.org/10.1007/978-3-030-98388-8



This Springer imprint is published by the registered company Springer Nature Switzerland AG
The registered company address is: Gewerbestrasse 11, 6330 Cham, Switzerland

# Preface

This volume presents a series of revised papers selected from workshops organized by IFIP TC 13 Working Groups (WGs) during the 18th IFIP TC 13 International Conference on Human-Computer Interaction, INTERACT 2021, held in September 2021 in Bari, Italy. The University of Bari Aldo Moro organized INTERACT 2021 in cooperation with ACM and ACM SIGCHI.

Seven IFIP TC 13 workshops were held at INTERACT 2021. They had various aims, which are listed below.

- WG 13.1 Workshop on Human-centred Technology for Sustainable Development Goals: Challenges and Opportunities (HCT4SDG)—to build an agenda defining challenges and opportunities for the design of interactive technologies addressing one or more United Nations' Sustainable Development Goals.
- WG 13.2 Workshop on Human-Centered Software Engineering for Changing Contexts of Use—to share knowledge and experiences that address how to deal with evolving contexts of use in today's and future application domains and the influence on human-centered socio-technical system design and development practices.
- WG 13.4/2.7 and WG 13.1 Joint Workshop on HCI Engineering Education for developers, designers and more (HCI-$E^2$)—to identify, examine, structure, and share educational resources and approaches to support the process of teaching and learning human-computer interaction engineering (HCI-E).
- WG 13.5 Workshop on Control Rooms in Safety Critical Contexts: Design, Engineering and Evaluation Issues—to share experiences in designing, implementing, and evaluating interactive systems in control rooms.
- WG 13.6 Workshop on Pilot Implementation: Testing Human-Work Interaction Designs (PILOT4HWID)—to help mature and formulate the research agenda on the pilot implementation technique for evaluating human-work interaction designs during the process of their development and implementation.
- WG 13.7 Workshop on Wearables, Humans, and Things: Addressing Problems in Education—to discuss new ideas on how wearable or even implantable devices can be used in an educational context (collocated with HCI-$E^2$).
- WG 13.8 Workshop on Geopolitical Issues in Human Computer Interaction—to explore, address, and discuss geopolitical issues in human-computer interaction as a field of knowledge and practice.

The chapters in this volume are the outcome of a thorough and competitive selection process that started with selecting workshops for INTERACT 2021. The IFIP TC 13 WGs organizers were encouraged to propose workshops for extending the work of the working groups. The workshops could be in diverse formats, including paper and poster presentations followed by forum discussions or collaboration sessions with participants. All the workshops were held both on-site and online. The workshop selection process was juried by the INTERACT 2021 workshop co-chairs.

The workshop organizers selected the technical programs, and also picked which workshop papers were eligible for being extended to chapters in this volume. For the selected papers, authors were requested to revise their contributions taking into account the comments and remarks they received during the event. To ensure the quality of these post-proceedings, we requested that the proposed chapters were peer-reviewed by the workshop organizers. In addition, workshop organizers were invited to write a summary chapter for their workshop, reporting on the aims and outcomes of the workshops. We received summary chapters from five workshops, which were reviewed by the INTERACT 2021 workshop co-chairs.

The selected chapters in this volume show the state of the art of research according to the aims of the workshops and demonstrate the maturity of the work performed by IFIP TC 13 WGs. In total, 45 chapters are published in this volume, which are organized into seven sections corresponding to the IFIP TC 13 workshops held at INTERACT 2021.

Interested readers of this volume should note that IFIP TC 13 WGs are open to new members. The full list of IFIP TC13 WGs is available at http://ifip-tc13.org/working-groups/. Please contact the officers of the WGs for further information on how to get enrolled in WG activities such as the workshops organized at the INTERACT conference.

January 2022

Carmelo Ardito
Rosa Lanzilotti
Alessio Malizia
Marta Larusdottir
Lucio Davide Spano
José C. Campos
Morten Hertzum
Tilo Mentler
José Abdelnour Nocera
Lara Piccolo
Stefan Sauer
Gerrit van der Veer

# Organization

## INTERACT 2021 Technical Program Co-chairs

| | |
|---|---|
| Carmelo Ardito | Polytechnic University of Bari, Italy |
| Rosa Lanzilotti | University of Bari Aldo Moro, Italy |
| Alessio Malizia | University of Pisa, Italy |

## INTERACT 2021 Workshop Co-chairs

| | |
|---|---|
| Marta Larusdottir | Reykjavik University, Iceland |
| Lucio Davide Spano | University of Cagliari, Italy |

## INTERACT 2021 Workshop Organizers

### WG 13.1 Workshop on Human-centred Technology for Sustainable Development Goals: Challenges and Opportunities (HCT4SDG)

| | |
|---|---|
| Lara Piccolo | The Open University, UK |
| Vânia Neris | Federal University of São Carlos, Brazil |
| Kamila Rodrigues | University of São Paulo, Brazil |
| Masood Masoodian | Aalto University, Finland |

### WG 13.2 Workshop on Human-Centered Software Engineering for Changing Contexts of Use

| | |
|---|---|
| Carmelo Ardito | Polytechnic University of Bari, Italy |
| Regina Bernhaupt | Eindhoven University of Technology, The Netherlands |
| Stefan Sauer | Paderborn University, Germany |

### WG 13.4/2.7 and WG 13.1 Joint Workshop on HCI Engineering Education for Developers, Designers and More (HCI-E$^2$)

| | |
|---|---|
| Konrad Baumann | FH Joanneum University of Applied Sciences, Austria |
| José C. Campos | Universidade do Minho, Portugal |
| Alan Dix | Swansea University, UK |
| Laurence Nigay | University of Grenoble Alpes, France |
| Philippe Palanque | University of Toulouse III – Paul Sabatier, France |
| Jean Vanderdonckt | Université catholique de Louvain, Belgium |

| | |
|---|---|
| Gerrit van der Veer | Vrije Universiteit Amsterdam, The Netherlands |
| Benjamin Weyers | University of Trier, Germany |

### WG 13.5 Workshop on Control Rooms in Safety Critical Contexts: Design, Engineering and Evaluation Issues

| | |
|---|---|
| Tilo Mentler | Trier University of Applied Sciences, Germany |
| Philippe Palanque | Université Toulouse III – Paul Sabatier, France |
| Susanne Boll | University of Oldenburg, Germany |
| Chris Johnson | Queen's University Belfast, UK |
| Kristof Van Laerhoven | University of Siegen, Germany |

## WG 13.6 Workshop on Pilot Implementation: Testing Human-Work Interaction Designs (PILOT4HWID)

| | |
|---|---|
| Morten Hertzum | University of Copenhagen, Denmark |
| Torkil Clemmensen | Copenhagen Business School, Denmark |
| Barbara Rita Barricelli | Università degli Studi di Brescia, Italy |
| Pedro F. Campos | University of Madeira, Portugal |
| Frederica Gonçalves | University of Madeira, Portugal |
| José Abdelnour Nocera | University of West London, UK |
| Ganesh Bhutkar | Vishwakarma Institute of Technology, India |
| Arminda Guerra Lopes | Polytechnic Institute of Castelo Branco, Portugal |

### WG 13.7 Workshop on Wearables, Humans, and Things: Addressing Problems in Education

| | |
|---|---|
| Gerrit van der Veer | Vrije Universiteit Amsterdam, The Netherlands |
| Achim Ebert | University of Kaiserslautern, Germany |
| Nahum Gershon | The MITRE Corporation, USA |
| Peter Dannenmann | RheinMain University of Applied Sciences, Germany |

### WG 13.8 Workshop on Geopolitical Issues in Human Computer Interaction

| | |
|---|---|
| José Abdelnour Nocera | University of West London, UK, and ITI/Larsys, Portugal |
| Torkil Clemmensen | Copenhagen Business School, Denmark |
| Zhengjie Liu | Dalian Maritime University, China |
| Anirudha Joshi | IIT Bombay, India |
| Xiangang Qin | Beijing University of Posts and Telecommunications, China |
| Judy van Biljon | University of South Africa, South Africa |
| Isabela Gasparini | Santa Catarina State University, Brazil |
| Leonardo Parra-Agudelo | University of los Andes, Colombia |

# IFIP TC 13

Established in 1989, the Technical Committee on Human–Computer Interaction (IFIP TC 13) of the International Federation for Information Processing (IFIP) is an international committee of 34 member societies and 10 Working Groups, representing specialists of the various disciplines contributing to the field of human–computer interaction. This includes (among others) human factors, ergonomics, cognitive science, and multiple areas of computer science and design.

IFIP TC 13 aims to develop the science, technology, and societal aspects of human–computer interaction (HCI) by

- encouraging empirical, applied, and theoretical research,
- promoting the use of knowledge and methods from both human sciences and computer sciences in design, development, evaluation, and exploitation of computing systems,
- promoting the production of new knowledge in the area of interactive computing systems engineering,
- promoting better understanding of the relation between formal design methods and system usability, user experience, accessibility, and acceptability,
- developing guidelines, models, and methods by which designers may provide better human-oriented computing systems, and
- cooperating with other groups, inside and outside IFIP, to promote user-orientation and humanization in system design.

Thus, TC 13 seeks to improve interactions between people and computing systems, to encourage the growth of HCI research and its practice in industry, and to disseminate these benefits worldwide.

The main orientation is to place the users at the center of the development process. Areas of study include

- the problems people face when interacting with computing devices;
- the impact of technology deployment on people in individual and organizational contexts;
- the determinants of utility, usability, acceptability, accessibility, privacy, user experience…;
- the appropriate allocation of tasks between computing systems and users, especially in the case of automation;
- engineering user interfaces, interactions, and interactive computing systems;
- modelling the user, their tasks, and the interactive system to aid better system design; and
- harmonizing the computing system to user characteristics and needs.

While the scope is thus set wide, with a tendency toward general principles rather than particular systems, it is recognized that progress will only be achieved through both general studies to advance theoretical understanding and specific studies on practical issues (e.g., interface design standards, software system resilience, documentation, training material, appropriateness of alternative interaction technologies, guidelines, integrating computing systems to match user needs and organizational practices, etc.).

In 2015, TC 13 approved the creation of a Steering Committee (SC) for the INTERACT conference series. The SC is now in place, chaired by Anirudha Joshi, and is responsible for

- promoting and maintaining the INTERACT conference as the premier venue for researchers and practitioners interested in the topics of the conference (this requires a refinement of the topics above);
- ensuring the highest quality for the contents of the event;
- setting up the bidding process to handle the future INTERACT conferences (with decisions made at the TC 13 level);
- providing advice to the current and future chairs and organizers of the INTERACT conference;
- providing data, tools, and documents about previous conferences to the future conference organizers;
- selecting the reviewing system to be used throughout the conference (as this affects the entire set of reviewers, authors, and committee members);
- resolving general issues involved with the INTERACT conference; and
- capitalizing on history (good and bad practices).

In 1999, TC 13 initiated a special IFIP award, the Brian Shackel Award, for the most outstanding contribution in the form of a refereed paper submitted to and delivered at each INTERACT. The award draws attention to the need for a comprehensive human-centered approach in the design and use of information technology in which the human and social implications have been taken into account. In 2007, IFIP TC 13 launched an Accessibility Award to recognize an outstanding contribution in HCI with international impact dedicated to the field of accessibility for disabled users. In 2013, IFIP TC 13 launched the Interaction Design for International Development (IDID) Award that recognizes the most outstanding contribution to the application of interactive systems for social and economic development of people in developing countries. Since the process to decide the awards takes place after papers are sent to the publisher for publication, the awards are not identified in the proceedings. Since 2019, a special agreement has been in place with the International Journal of Behaviour and Information Technology (BIT), published by Taylor and Francis with Panos Markopoulos as editor in chief. In this agreement, authors of BIT papers whose work is within the field of HCI are offered the opportunity to present their work at the INTERACT conference. Reciprocally, the authors of a selection of papers accepted for presentation at INTERACT are offered the opportunity to extend their contributions to be published in BIT.

IFIP TC 13 also recognizes pioneers in the area of HCI. An IFIP TC 13 pioneer is one who, through active participation in IFIP Technical Committees or related IFIP groups, has made outstanding contributions to the educational, theoretical, technical, commercial, or professional aspects of analysis, design, construction, evaluation, and use of interactive systems. IFIP TC 13 pioneers are appointed annually and awards are handed over at the INTERACT conference.

IFIP TC 13 stimulates working events and activities through its Working Groups (WGs). Working Groups consist of HCI experts from multiple countries who seek to expand knowledge and find solutions to HCI issues and concerns within a specific domain. New Working Groups are formed as areas of significance in HCI arise.

Further information is available at the IFIP TC13 website: http://ifip-tc13.org/.

# IFIP TC13 Members

## Officers

**Chairperson**

Philippe Palanque, France

**Vice-chair for Awards**

Paula Kotze, South Africa

**Vice-chair for Communications**

Helen Petrie, UK

**Vice-chair for Growth and Outreach**

Jan Gulliksen, Sweden

**Vice-chair for Working Groups**

Simone D. J. Barbosa, Brazil

**Vice-chair for Development and Equity**

Julio Abascal, Spain

**Treasurer**

Virpi Roto, Finland

**Secretary**

Marco Winckler, France

**INTERACT Steering Committee Chair**

Anirudha Joshi, India

## Country/Society Representatives

### Australia

Henry B.L. Duh
Australian Computer Society

### Austria

Geraldine Fitzpatrick
Austrian Computer Society

### Belgium

Bruno Dumas
IMEC – Interuniversity Micro-Electronics Center

### Brazil

Lara S. G. Piccolo
Brazilian Computer Society (SBC)

### Bulgaria

Stoyan Georgiev Dentchev
Bulgarian Academy of Sciences

### Croatia

Andrina Granic
Croatian Information Technology Association (CITA)

### Cyprus

Panayiotis Zaphiris
Cyprus Computer Society

### Czech Republic

Zdeněk Míkovec
Czech Society for Cybernetics and
Informatics

**Finland**

Virpi Roto
Finnish Information Processing Association

**France**

Philippe Palanque and Marco Winckler
Société informatique de France (SIF)

**Germany**

Tom Gross
Gesellschaft fur Informatik e.V.

**Ireland**

Liam J. Bannon
Irish Computer Society

**Italy**

Fabio Paternò
Italian Computer Society

**Japan**

Yoshifumi Kitamura
Information Processing Society of Japan

**The Netherlands**

Regina Bernhaupt
Nederlands Genootschap voor Informatica

**New Zealand**

Mark Apperley
New Zealand Computer Society

**Norway**

Frode Eika Sandnes
Norwegian Computer Society

**Poland**

Marcin Sikorski
Poland Academy of Sciences

**Portugal**

Pedro Campos
Associacão Portuguesa para o Desenvolvimento da Sociedade da Informação (APDSI)

**Serbia**

Aleksandar Jevremovic
Informatics Association of Serbia

**Singapore**

Shengdong Zhao
Singapore Computer Society

**Slovakia**

Wanda Benešová
The Slovak Society for Computer Science

**Slovenia**

Matjaž Debevc
The Slovenian Computer Society INFORMATIKA

**Sri Lanka**

Thilina Halloluwa
The Computer Society of Sri Lanka

**South Africa**

Janet L. Wesson and Paula Kotze
The Computer Society of South Africa

**Sweden**

Jan Gulliksen
Swedish Interdisciplinary Society for Human-Computer Interaction
Swedish Computer Society

**Switzerland**

Denis Lalanne
Swiss Federation for Information
Processing

**Tunisia**

Mona Laroussi
Ecole Supérieure des Communications De Tunis (SUP'COM)

**UK**

José Abdelnour Nocera
British Computer Society (BCS)

**United Arab Emirates**

Ahmed Seffah
UAE Computer Society

**ACM**

Gerrit van der Veer
Association for Computing Machinery

**CLEI**

Jaime Sánchez
Centro Latinoamericano de Estudios en Informatica

## Expert Members

Julio Abascal, Spain
Carmelo Ardito, Italy
Nikolaos Avouris, Greece
Kaveh Bazargan, Iran
Ivan Burmistrov, Russia
Torkil Torkil Clemmensen, Denmark

Peter Forbrig, Germany
Dorian Gorgan, Romania
Anirudha Joshi, India
David Lamas, Estonia
Marta Kristin Larusdottir, Iceland
Zhengjie Liu, China
Fernando Loizides, UK/Cyprus
Ochieng Daniel "Dan" Orwa, Kenya
Eunice Sari, Australia/Indonesia

## Working Group Chairpersons

### WG 13.1 (Education in HCI and HCI Curricula)

Konrad Baumann, Austria

### WG 13.2 (Methodologies for User-Centered System Design)

Regina Bernhaupt, The Netherlands

### WG 13.3 (HCI, Disability and Aging)

Helen Petrie, UK

### WG 13.4/2.7 (User Interface Engineering)

José C. Campos, Portugal

### WG 13.5 (Human Error, Resilience, Reliability, Safety and System Development)

Chris Johnson, UK

### WG 13.6 (Human-Work Interaction Design)

Barbara Rita Barricelli, Italy

### WG 13.7 (HCI and Visualization)

Peter Dannenmann, Germany

### WG 13.8 (Interaction Design and International Development)

José Adbelnour Nocera, UK

## WG 13.9 (Interaction Design and Children)

Janet Read, UK

## WG 13.10 (Human-Centred Technology for Sustainability)

Masood Masoodian, Finland

# IFIP TC 13 Working Groups

**WG 13.1 - Education in HCI and HCI Curricula**

The Working Group 13.1 aims to improve HCI education at all levels of higher education, coordinate and unite efforts to develop HCI curricula, and promote HCI teaching.

**Chair**

Konrad Baumann — FH Joanneum University of Applied Sciences, Austria

**Vice-chairs**

Jean Vanderdonckt — Université catholique de Louvain, Belgium
Carlo Giovannella — University of Rome Tor Vergata, Italy

**Secretary**

Konrad Baumann — FH Joanneum University of Applied Sciences, Austria

**WG 13.2 - Methodology for User-Centred System Design**

The Working Group 13.2 aims to foster research, dissemination of information, and good practice in the methodical application of HCI to software engineering.

**Chair**

Regina Bernhaupt — Eindhoven University of Technology, The Netherlands

**Vice-chair**

Carmelo Ardito — Polytechnic University of Bari, Italy

**Secretary**

Stefan Sauer — Paderborn University, Germany

**WG 13.3 - HCI, Disability and Aging**

The Working Group 13.3 aims to make HCI designers aware of the needs of people with disabilities and encourage development of information systems and tools permitting adaptation of interfaces to specific users.

**Chair**

Helen Petrie — University of York, UK

**Vice-chair**

Gerhard Weber — Technical University Dresden, Germany

**Secretary**

David Sloan — University of Dundee, UK

## WG 13.4/WG 2.7 - User Interface Engineering

The Working Group 13.4 (also WG 2.7) investigates the nature, concepts, and construction of user interfaces (UIs) for software systems, using a framework for reasoning about interactive systems and an engineering model for developing UIs.

**Chair**

José C. Campos — Universidade do Minho, Portugal

**Vice-chair**

Gaëlle Calvary — Laboratoire d'Informatique de Grenoble, France

**Secretary**

Judy Bowen — University of Waikato, New Zealand

## WG 13.5 - Resilience, Reliability, Safety and Human Error in System Development

The Working Group 13.5 seeks a framework for studying human factors relating to systems failure, develops leading edge techniques in hazard analysis and safety engineering of computer-based systems, and guides international accreditation activities for safety-critical systems.

**Chair**

Christopher Johnson — University of Glasgow, UK

**Vice-chairs**

Michael Feary — NASA, Ames Research Center, USA
Asaf Degani — General Motors R&D, Israel

**Secretary**

| | |
|---|---|
| Philippe Palanque | ICS-IRIT, University of Toulouse III - Paul Sabatier, France |

## WG 13.6 - Human-Work Interaction Design

The Working Group 13.5 aims at establishing relationships between extensive empirical work-domain studies and HCI design. It promotes the use of knowledge, concepts, methods, and techniques that enable user studies to procure a better apprehension of the complex interplay between individual, social, and organizational contexts and thereby a better understanding of how and why people work in the ways that they do.

**Chair**

| | |
|---|---|
| Barbara Rita Barricelli | Università degli Studi di Milano, Italy |

**Vice-chairs**

| | |
|---|---|
| Pedro Campos | University of Madeira, Portugal |
| Torkil Clemmensen | Copenhagen Business School, Denmark |
| José Abdelnour Nocera | University of West London, UK, and ITI/Larsys, Portugal |
| Arminda Guerra Lopes | Polytechnic Institute of Castelo Branco, Portugal |
| Ganesh Bhutkar | Vishwakarma Institute of Technology, India |
| Xiangang Qin | Beijing University of Post and Telecommunications, China |
| Judith Ann Molka-Danielsen | Molde University College, Norway |

**Secretary**

| | |
|---|---|
| Frederica Gonçalves | University of Madeira, Portugal |

## WG 13.7 - Human–Computer Interaction and Visualization

The Working Group 13.7 aims to establish a study and research program that will combine both scientific work and practical applications in the fields of human–computer interaction and visualization. It will integrate several additional aspects of further research areas, such as scientific visualization, data mining, information design, computer graphics, cognition sciences, perception theory, or psychology, into this approach.

**Chair**

| | |
|---|---|
| Peter Dannenmann | RheinMain University of Applied Sciences, Germany |

**Vice-chairs**

Gerrit van der Veer — Vrije Universiteit Amsterdam, The Netherlands
Nahum Gershon — The MITRE Corporation, USA

**Secretary**

Achim Ebert — University of Kaiserslautern, Germany

### WG 13.8 - Interaction Design and International Development

The Working Group 13.8 aims at supporting and developing the research, practice, and education capabilities of HCI in institutions and organizations based around the world taking into account their diverse local needs and cultural perspectives; promoting application of interaction design research, practice, and education to address the needs, desires and aspirations of people across the developing world; and developing links between the HCI community in general and other relevant communities involved in international development and cross-cultural aspects of ICT development.

**Chair**

José Abdelnour Nocera — University of West London, UK, and ITI/Larsys, Portugal

**Vice-chairs**

Andy Dearden — Sheffield Hallam University, UK
Torkil Clemmensen — Copenhagen Business School, Denmark
Christian Sturm — Hamm-Lippstadt University of Applied Sciences, Germany

**Secretary**

Anirudha Joshi — IIT Bombay, India

### WG 13.9 - Interaction Design and Children

The Working Group 13.9 aims to support practitioners, regulators, and researchers to develop the study of interaction design and children across international contexts.

**Chair**

Janet Read — University of Central Lancashire, UK

**Vice-chair**

Panos Markopoulos — Eindhoven University of Technology, The Netherlands

**Secretary**

Matthew Horton — University of Central Lancashire, UK

**WG 13.10 - Human-Centred Technology for Sustainability**

The Working Group 13.10 aims to promote research, design, development, evaluation, and deployment of human-centered technology to encourage sustainable use of resources in various domains.

**Chair**

Masood Masoodian — Aalto University, Finland

**Vice-chairs**

Elisabeth André — University of Augsburg, Germany
Nuno J. Nunes — Instituto Superior Técnico, Universidade de Lisboa, Portugal

**Secretary**

Thomas Rist — University of Applied Sciences Augsburg, Germany

# INTERACT 2021 Partners and Sponsors

**Partners**

International Federation for Information Processing

In cooperation with ACM

In cooperation with SIGCHI

**Sponsors**

EULOGIC

exprivia

openwork
Just solutions

# Contents

**Pilot Implementation: Testing Human-Work Interaction Designs**



**Wearables, Humans, and Things – Addressing Problems in Education**

**Sociocultural Issues in Human-Computer Interaction**

# Human-Centred Technology for Sustainable Development Goals: Challenges and Opportunities

# Human-Centred Technology for Sustainable Development Goals - Workshop Results

Kamila Rios da Hora Rodrigues[1], Vânia Paula de Almeida Neris[2](✉), Lara Piccolo[3], and Masood Masoodian[4]

[1] Institute of Mathematical and Computer Sciences, University of São Paulo (ICMC/USP), São Carlos, Brazil
[2] Department of Computing, Federal University of São Carlos (UFSCar), São Carlos, Brazil
vania.neris@ufscar.br
[3] Knowledge Media Institute (KMi), Open University, Milton Keynes, UK
[4] School of Arts, Design and Architecture, Aalto University, Espoo, Finland

**Abstract.** This paper presents the results of the workshop on Human-centred Technologies for Sustainable Development Goals (HCT4SDG) - Challenges and Opportunities. The workshop was part of the 18th International Conference promoted by the IFIP Technical Committee 13 on Human-Computer Interaction (Interact 2021). Nine papers were presented by authors from several different countries and discussed in the workshop. Six of these papers were extended in this proceedings. After discussion, seven challenges and eight research opportunities were listed as expression of the participants' views on HCT4SDG.

**Keywords:** Sustainability · Sustainable development goals · Human-centred design · Human-centred technologies

## 1 Introduction

The 2030 Agenda for Sustainable Development adopted by the United Nations (UN) Members calls for global partnerships to achieve significant advances in fairness and prosperity in the world. This includes equal access to, and management of resources such as water, energy, climate, oceans, urbanization, transport, science and technology. These themes are addressed as a set of 17 UN Sustainable Development Goals (SDGs)[1] intended to be achieved by the year 2030. These goals should be achieved uniformly across the nations, dissolving the well-established dichotomy of *developed* and *developing* contexts [2].

In line with this agenda, we understand *sustainability* more broadly, beyond the environmental aspects related to solutions that do not harm the environment, to include also the social aspects related to human rights, respecting differences,

[1] https://sdgs.un.org/goals.


Published by Springer Nature Switzerland AG 2022
C. Ardito et al. (Eds.): INTERACT 2021, LNCS 13198, pp. 3–9, 2022.
https://doi.org/10.1007/978-3-030-98388-8_1

and the dissemination of values that are the basis of the continuance of life in society for future generations [3–5].

According to Blevis [1], sustainability can, and should be, a central focus of interaction design. The author believes that for a perspective of sustainability, "design is defined as an act of choosing among or informing choices of future ways of being. This perspective of sustainability is presented in terms of design values, methods, and reasoning".

Addressing technology design for sustainable development goals with a human-centred approach demands rethinking the way technological solutions are developed and consumed, and considering the situated design solutions and their impact in the social, economic and environmental aspects. As stated in Neris, Rodrigues e Silva [3], this should be used by designers as an opportunity to establish a bridge between the real-life, with its inequalities and injustices, and the ideal world, as aspired by the UN SDGs.

### 1.1 Objectives

With this broad perspective of *sustainability* in mind, the objective of this workshop was to build an agenda which aims to define challenges and opportunities for design of interactive technologies that address one or more SDGs with a holistic view.

Topics of interest included:

- IoT and smart communities;
- Environmental monitoring;
- Design solutions that support sustainable behaviour;
- Green computing;
- Ethical aspects of green computing;
- Equality and fairness in access to technology;
- Sustainable design;
- Design for sustainability.

The workshop engaged the participants in sharing research on the theme, in a broad sense considering several different UN SDGs, and discussing challenges and obstacles related to creating human-centred technology towards advancing the sustainable development goals (HCT4SDG).

## 2 Workshop Activities and Participants

This one day workshop was structured to be engaging, practice-oriented, hands-on, and participatory. The workshop started with the participants' presentations, focusing on their main research interest and design approaches to advance the SDGs.

The papers selected were divided into 3 main groups for presentation, namely: 1) Behaviour and Awareness, 2) Technology and 3) Education and Beyond Technology - SDGs 3 and 5 (Health and Gender).

The works added in the group *Behaviour and Awareness* were:

- Extreme Citizen Science Contributions to Sustainable Development Goals: Challenges and Opportunities of a Human-Centred Design Approach
- An Action-Management Video Game to Foster Sustainability Through Garbage Recycling
- Envirofy: Behaviour Change Wheel based Tool for Sustainable Online Grocery Shopping
- Striving to increase self-sufficiency: design and evaluation of a smart energy dashboard for prosumers with solar panels

In the group *Technology and Education* were presented the following works:

- Internet of Things in Education for Sustainable Development
- Interactive Map Visualizations for Supporting Environmental Sustainable Development Goals
- Guidelines for the Sustainable Development of Computing Technology

In the group *Beyond technology - SDGs 3 and 5 (Health and Gender)* were presented the following works:

- An Informatics-based Approach for Sustainable Management of Factors Affecting the Spread of Infectious Diseases
- Women Techno-education and Sustainability

Authors had about 15 min to present each paper, followed by 5 min for discussion. More details on the workshop program are available at the workshop website[2].

A Padlet supported the discussions on each paper. Participants were invited to write questions and comments about the paper that was being presented. The posts included clarification questions, suggestions for future work and also some preliminary challenge and opportunities closely related to the topics being discussed. Figure 1 illustrates some of the questions and comments that raised from the paper presentations.

After all presentations, a discussion was carried out as presented in Sect. 4. Finally, for wrapping up, a round of thoughts was conducted and some publication plans were announced.

In the next section, the six papers extended to this proceedings are presented.

## 3 Papers Extended

The works presented in the workshop were invited for extension and possible publications in two different means of publication: a journal and this extended proceedings. Authors of six papers accepted the invitation to extend their work and publish here. The works are:

[2] https://lifes.dc.ufscar.br/HCT4SDG.

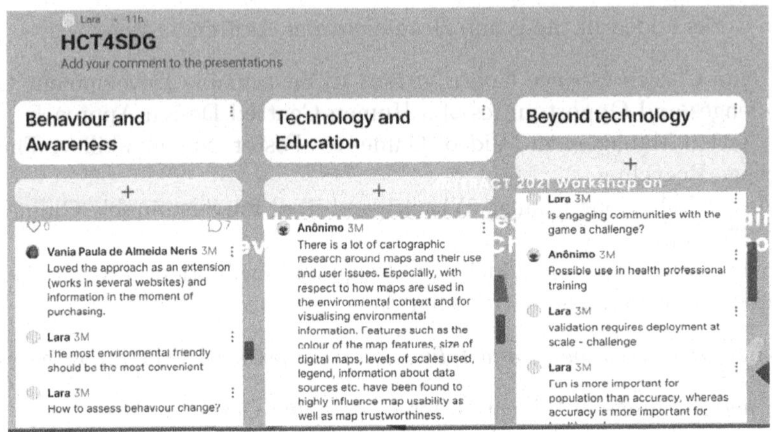


**Fig. 1.** Part of the Padlet with some questions and comments from the participants.

**An Action-Management Video Game to Foster Sustainability Through Garbage Recycling:** It is proposed video game offers to post-adolescent players educational contents about garbage recycling, implementing a gameplay that merges the Action and Management game genres with a pixel-art inspired graphic style. A preliminary user-based evaluation has been performed with three players using the Thinking Aloud technique. Comments about the game mechanics were generally positive and the sustainability topic was perceived well-integrated and non-invasive, proving the need of further experimentation and evaluation.

**Extreme Citizen Science Contributions to Sustainable Development Goals: Challenges and Opportunities for a Human-Centred Design Approach:** The authors focus on Extreme Citizen Science, which includes a set of situated, bottom up practices, used for environmental monitoring purposes and for recording local indigenous knowledge, mainly in the Global South. They present and discuss in this paper the human-centered approach that the implementation of extreme citizen science requires, they identify and present the challenges they face as well as the opportunities that extreme citizen science initiatives create for contributing to Sustainable Development Goals.

**Interactive Map Visualizations for Supporting Environmental Sustainable Development Goals:** The authors present a summary overview of the main factors that need to be considered when designing interactive map visualizations in support of the SDGs. They also provide a few example of the use of interactive maps in web-based information systems, decision support systems, and computer games that focus on environmental issues.

**An Informatics-Based Approach for Sustainable Management of Factors Affecting the Spread of Infectious Diseases:** The paper presents an informatics-based approach to the management and monitoring of infectious diseases, in the context of one of these SDGs focusing on the eradication of vector-borne diseases such as malaria, Zika and other neglected tropical diseases. The authors outline the challenges faced by many conventional approaches to ecoepidemiological modelling and proposes a distributed interactive architecture for teamwork coordination, and data integration at different levels of information, and across disciplines. This approach is illustrated by an application to the surveillance of leishmaniasis, a neglected tropical disease, in remote regions.

**Guidelines for the Sustainable Development of Computing Technology**: The authors has formalized a set of recommendations to guide the designers in the creation of computational solutions, and thus allow the sustainability factors in design to be considered. The guidelines were applied in an academic scenario and three specialists evaluated the solutions made with and without them. The results suggest that the guidelines supported the sustainable development of Computing technologies.

**Internet of Things in Education for Sustainable Development:** The authors discuss some potential roles of technology, more specifically the Internet of Things (IoT), with a human-centred design perspective to be applied in Education for Sustainable Development (ESD). They propose some preliminary guidelines to apply IoT-based projects to educate and empower students related to environmental Sustainable Development Goals and illustrate these guidelines with a practical project on ultraviolet radiation measurement.

## 4 Challenges and Opportunities on HCT4SDG

After the presentation of the papers, we had a discussion section about the participants' views on challenges and opportunities for HCT4SDG. This activity was supported by another Padlet with only two columns: one for the challenges and another one for the opportunities. The board was shown on sharing screen and one organizer was responsible for filling in the board while the discussion was happening.

Seven challenges were written on the board. They are:

- Think beyond research questions. Consider impact.
- Compromise when making environmental decisions.
- Consider sustainability as a transdisciplinary issue.
- Trigger trust.
- Involve different stakeholders, including policy makers.
- Not misinform people by showing a single perspective (or a slice of the problem) trivializing issues.

On the other hand, opportunities to be explored were also mentioned and discussed. Eight opportunities were written on the board. They are:

- Address misinformation on SDGs.
- Fill knowledge gaps.

- Consider trustfulness between people (people may trust more other people than institutions).
- Propose sustainable development guidelines for developers.
- Consider personalization and emotions for improving engagement and awareness.
- SDGs are generic, but we have to address individual needs.
- Build tools to support decision-making "in real life". Bridging willingness with reliable data.
- Develop serious games and/or educational tools.

## 5 Final Remarks

This paper presented the results of the HCT4SDG workshop that was part of the Interact 2021 program. In this one-day workshop, nine papers were presented and participants discussed several challenges and opportunities for improving the state-of-the-art in this field. It is interesting to highlight that researchers from several countries submitted papers and joined the workshop, emphasizing that research on this theme is globally needed. Moreover, different research contributions were presented including games and maps visualizations, but also guidelines and approaches, for instance.

A participatory approach was adopted and Padlets were used to support discussions. From the authors' experiences and perspectives, research challenges and opportunities in this field were listed. The challenges ranged from involving different stakeholders to triggering trust and considering the impact of the research. Several and broad opportunities towards human-centred technology for the SDGs were also discussed, including addressing individuals' needs, considering trustfulness between people, and also the development of guidelines for developers.

**Acknowledgement.** This workshop was supported by the IFIP Working Group 13.10 on Human-Centred Technology for Sustainability. For more information please visit: 4se.hs-augsburg.de/wg13-10/.

## References

1. Blevis, E.: Sustainable interaction design: invention & disposal, renewal & reuse. In: Proceedings of the SIGCHI Conference on Human Factors in Computing Systems, CHI 2007, pp. 503–512. Association for Computing Machinery, New York (2007). https://doi.org/10.1145/1240624.1240705
2. Kumar, N., et al.: HCI across borders and sustainable development goals. In: Extended Abstracts of the 2020 CHI Conference on Human Factors in Computing Systems, CHI EA 2020, pp. 1–8. Association for Computing Machinery, New York (2020). https://doi.org/10.1145/3334480.3375067. https://doi-org.libezproxy.open.ac.uk/10.1145/3334480.3375067

3. Neris, V., Rodrigues, K., Silva, J.: The future, smart cities and sustainability. In: I GranDIHC - BR Grand Research Challenges in Human-Computer Interaction in Brazil. Human-Computer Interaction Special Committee (CEIHC) of the Brazilian Computer Society (SBC) (2015)
4. Neris, V.P., Rodrigues, K.R., Silva, J.: Futuro, cidades inteligentes e sustentabilidade. GranDIHC-BR-Grandes Desafios de Pesquisa em Interação Humano-Computador no Brasil, pp. 16–18 (2012)
5. de Santana, V.F., Neris, V.P.A., Rodrigues, K.R.H., Oliveira, R., Galindo, N.: Activity of Brazilian HCI community from 2012 to 2017 in the context of the challenge 'future, smart cities, and sustainability'. In: Proceedings of the XVI Brazilian Symposium on Human Factors in Computing Systems. IHC 2017, Association for Computing Machinery, New York (2017). https://doi.org/10.1145/3160504.3160562

# An Action-Management Video Game to Foster Sustainability Through Garbage Recycling

Fabrizio Balducci(✉) and Paolo Buono

University of Bari 'A. Moro', via E. Orabona 4, 70125 Bari, Italy
{fabrizio.balducci,paolo.buono}@uniba.it

**Abstract.** The proposed video game offers to post-adolescent players educational contents about garbage recycling, implementing a gameplay that merges the Action and Management game genres with a pixel-art inspired graphic style. A preliminary user-based evaluation has been performed with three players using the Thinking Aloud technique. Comments about the game mechanics were generally positive and the sustainability topic was perceived well-integrated and non-invasive, proving the need of further experimentation and evaluation.

**Keywords:** Video game · Sustainability · Recycling · Management · Educational

## 1 Introduction and Related Works

Lindley[1] defines a game as *a goal-directed and competitive activity conducted within a framework of agreed rules* thus the act of play involves to learn mechanics in a closed world that can be implemented as interactive systems. The learning concept is therefore inherent in the game definition so it is possible to define rules and mechanics (the gameplay) in order to teach aspects on peculiar topics, such as the environmental sustainability and garbage recycling.

Dos Santos et al. propose there is a survey about serious games for sustainability and, through the analysis of 45 games, a taxonomy is proposed with design strategies for the development of effective sustainability games [11]. Heterogeneous aspects about this topic have already been addressed through video games, for example in [12] the mobile game *LifeTree* uses bubbles with a set of power to combat mutants and prevent specific pollutions to occur teaching about green sustainability and tree safety while Lameras et al. [7] present simple mini-games that introduce the process of urban planning with sustainable spaces and citizens participation.

[1] C. Lindley, https://www.gamasutra.com/view/feature/131205/game_taxonomies_a_high_level_.php, last visit: 2021-05-01.


Published by Springer Nature Switzerland AG 2022
C. Ardito et al. (Eds.): INTERACT 2021, LNCS 13198, pp. 10–19, 2022.
https://doi.org/10.1007/978-3-030-98388-8_2

Piccolo et al. [9] developed a game-with-a-purpose to engage people with climate change inviting to adopt sustainable lifestyle choices by statistically analyzing game strategies. The topic of waste sorting is approached by Gaggi et al. [4] and for kids through a 3D game in [6] where enemies are depicted as aggressive personifications of human pollution and every item recycled provides points useful to clean the environment, fertilise plants using compost and to repair a spaceship; the social robot Pepper is exploited in [3] as an engaging interface of a serious game that by challenging and teaching children how to recycle waste materials makes them well disposed towards such processes.

The work of Menon [8] exploits a motion sensing input device like Microsoft Kinect to train people in recycle trash quickly, in fact while a particular waste drops down from the top of the screen the trainee has to it with the help of a ball controlled by its the movements and drag the waste into the correct bin. In Calvi et al. [10] a collaborative VR game inquires through a presence questionnaire the relationship about player immersion and its empathy for the marine environment sustainability while *ReLife* is a casual mobile game developed by [5] that educate about reuse practices and when players complete tasks to reduce the volume of wasted materials they are also given information on how to produce crafts from them. Al-Hammadi et al. [1] developed *City of Life*, a mobile AR game that teaches students about tasks (including recycling) to achieve the U.N. goals while the educational parts uses mini-games to entertain and verify the player's educational knowledge.

This paper is organized as the following: Sect. 2 describes game design concepts with the target audience and Sect. 3 presents the developed game features and mechanics. Section 4 reports a preliminary evaluation while conclusions and future work are in Sect. 5.

## 2 Game Design and Motivations

This work is inspired to the *Millennium Goal 7* of the *United Nations* and, more specifically, the *Target 7.A*[2] which aims to *'Integrate the principles of sustainable development into country policies and programmes and reverse the loss of environmental resources.* The topic of *garbage recycling* has been chosen to foster the players' awareness about sustainability and about the advantages of recycling materials, highlighting the risks that their indiscriminate accumulation or incorrect disposal can cause to the environment and to people health.

A correct management of waste and its disposal is nowadays also a social problem for many countries of the world, where abuses on the landscape and the exploitation of poor populations by criminal organizations are raising. This game emphasizes the management and the importance of some types of waste and their sustainability showing how obtain new objects by saving money and materials. This topic also fits with the educational efforts being made in the Italian context in which, unfortunately, garbage accumulation crises periodically break out and

[2] Millennium Goals, http://www.un.org/millenniumgoals/environ.shtml, last visit: 2021-05-01.

the illegal disposal ruled by eco-mafias causes detriment of communities and territories. The Recycle process addresses the climate change problem that is influenced by atmospheric pollution, in fact the Energy used for the production of goods implies harmful emissions to the atmosphere and the ozone layer.

The name chosen for the game is *The (H)ill* and it is a way to associate the physical place where a pile of garbage is created (the hill) with the harmful state that this situation has entailed (ill). The game allows the indirect control of the hill that polluting the surrounding land risks to become an environmental disaster; the main goal is to remove the accumulated garbage coming from the outer land by exploiting a set of Recycle Units since through their managing the player will exploit the materials facing the cost/reward aspects of the process.

The target audience is post-adolescent people (over 18 years old) due to the fact that, being out from school educational paths, they are hard to involve in awareness campaigns but usually they are video games passionate.[3] In this way, the purely educational content consisting of static information about the recycling subject was voluntarily introduced in indirect ways so that it could be perceived as non-invasive and always contextual to the game mechanics (gameplay) and to the actions performed in the virtual environment. Obviously, the game can be interesting for older age groups while the younger ones may have some difficulty in appreciating the managerial part of the gameplay.

Considering that young adults (and older) are fond of 70s–90s retro-gaming and old-style games like *Minecraft*[4] it has been developed a graphic style inspired to the pixel art. Regarding the game mechanics, it is proposed a fusion of two distinct game genres: *Action* (inspired to classic arcade game like *Tetris*[5]) and *Management* (inspired to awarded simulation games like *SimCity*[6]).

To implement at best this mixture, the game loop has been conceptualized as a continuous switching between two main game phases, inspired by the dynamics of an *American baseball* match in which attack phases alternate with defensive ones. During the frenzy action phase in fact, the player will experience the pressing danger of garbage that accumulates constantly and randomly while, in the managerial phase, he must strategically administrate the recycling processes and its monetization looking for upgrades and investments in new recycling units taking into account opportunities and dynamic situations.

## 3 Game Development

When starting the video game, from the initial menu the player begins a gaming session or selects one of the three available difficulty levels: to quickly explore the game features "Easy" level is appropriate while, for more challenge, the 'Medium' or 'Hard' settings are suggested since the type of garbage blocks, as far as their spawn and falling speed, vary with respect to such levels.

[3] IIDEA Game Reports, https://iideassociation.com/dati/mercato-e-consumatori.kl, last visit: 2021-05-01.

[4] Minecraft, https://www.minecraft.net/it-it, last visit: 2021-05-01.

[5] Tetris, https://tetris.com/play-tetris, last visit: 2021-05-01.

[6] SimCity, http://wiki.laptop.org/go/SimCity, last visit: 2021-05-01.

**Fig. 1.** The *General Panel* located at the top of the game screen featuring at the left all general information and in-game messages, at the right the Recycle Unit buttons and at center the "M" button for the mission list.

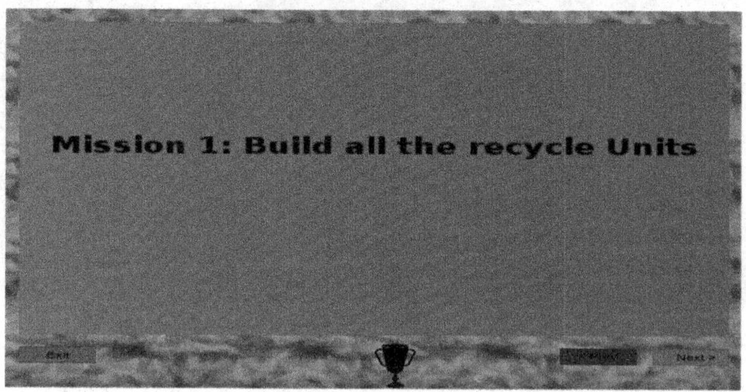


**Fig. 2.** The first game mission depicted in the *Missions panel* featuring the "Next", "Prev" and "Exit" navigation buttons. The *cup icon* denotes if this mission has been or not accomplished (black colored) by the player.

The *General Panel* in Fig. 1 is placed at the top of the screen: in the left part it shows general information such as actual *Difficulty level*, elapsed *Gaming Time*, *SunnyPoints* earned and the dynamic in-game *messages* while in the right one there are buttons about the Recycle Units featuring their build cost (when it can be paid by the player they are enabled otherwise a icon is red colored and interaction is prevented). At the center of the panel there is a yellow "M" button used to display the *Missions panel* (Fig. 2): to navigate in such list the "Next" and "Prev" buttons at the bottom-right are available as far as the "Exit" one at bottom-left. At the bottom center there is a *cup icon* which is black-colored until the mission has not yet been completed. To complete the game three missions have to be accomplished: i) build all the Recycle Units, ii) earn at least 100 SunnyPoints and iii) produce 3 golden objects (maximum unit upgrade) from *Ewaste Recycling Unit* (the most expensive).

In the UI there are two icons to indicate the type of currency points: for the SunnyPoints (earned by the player) it is used a stylized *orange sun* while to indicate the UnitPoints (earned by each Recycle Unit) there is a *black shovel.* In Fig. 1 the orange sun icon is present in the left for the total earned SunnyPoints and on the right under each Recycle Unit icon meaning the required build cost; moreover, in Fig. 4) the same icon is placed in the *Unit Menu* under each object that can be produced by a Recycle Unit meaning the SunnyPoints amount that the player will earn by such recycle process. SunnyPoints are the measure of

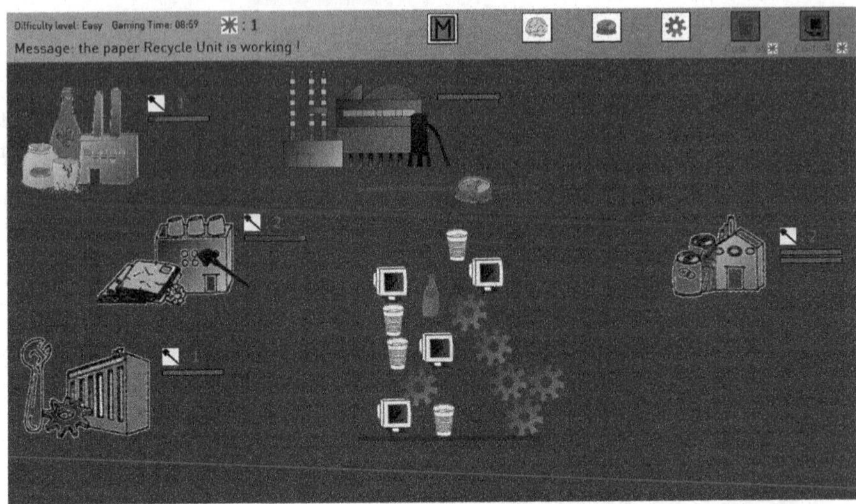


**Fig. 3.** The screen during an action game phase with garbage blocks randomly falling. At the top stands the *General Panel* while four Recycle Units (Glass, Paper, Steel and Plastic) plus the Incinerator are located around the central garbage Hill. Next to each Unit there are working red bars and the amount of the gained UnitPoints.

the garbage recycled by the player during a gaming session, and therefore, how many resources he has saved avoiding polluting.

On the contrary, the black shovel icon is displayed next to each Recycle Unit on the playfield to indicate its current UnitPoints and in the *Unit Menu* (Fig. 4) where in the left stands for the total UnitPoints earned by the Unit during the garbage accumulation, in the center for the upgrade cost and, under each object thumbnail on the right part, meaning the cost that the player has to pay in such Recycle Unit for the production of the new object.

### 3.1 Action Gameplay

The mechanics related to the *Action* genre and introduced in this video game concern the acts of *recognize*, *grab* and *drag* blocks that appear and accumulate constantly over time starting from its base (schematized by the blue line on such area). At the center of the screen in fact there is *the Hill* representing a dump area where *Garbage Blocks* continuously and randomly fall stacking on the top of each other (Fig. 3).

To avoid a 'Game Over' it is necessary to prevent that the accumulated blocks exceed the upper limit of the Hill (schematized by the red line). There are six block types which are (in increasing order of build cost and SunnyPoints provided in the recycling process): *Glass*, *Paper*, *Aluminum*, *Steel*, *Plastic* and *Ewaste*. It should be noticed that, in the gaming fiction, it has been inserted the *Nuclear* block, considered highly polluting and not recyclable, that could appear in later stages of a gaming session with a frequency depending by the

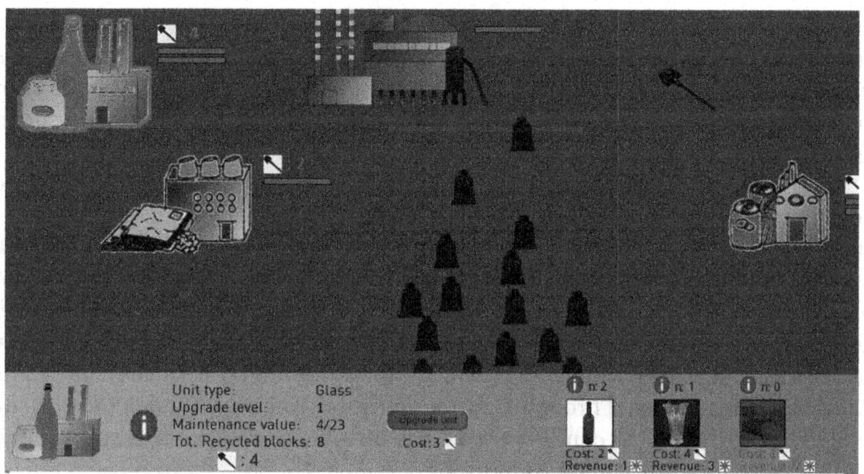


**Fig. 4.** The *Unit Menu* related to a yellow-highlighted Recycle Unit is located at the bottom of the game area during a managerial phase. The garbage Hill and its blocks are blacked out since the player has to focus on evaluating the statistics, increasing the Unit efficiency with an upgrade or producing profitable objects from the collected garbage material. (Color figure online)

chosen difficulty level. The player can grab, drag and release a garbage block on a compatible *Recycle Unit* located in the area all around the Hill. To add frenzy to the gaming action, while dragging a block if more than 3 s pass the player will lose his hold and its block will automatically return into the Hill.

### 3.2 Management Gameplay

The mechanics related to the *Management* genre concern the *building*, *upgrade* and *maintenance* of Recycle Units and their *monetization*. A Recycle Unit can be built using *SunnyPoints* credits earned and their build cost increases in relation to the garbage blocks order described above (the Glass Unit has 0 cost, Ewaste Unit the maximum one). It is possible to build only one Unit for each garbage material and, once built, it cannot be removed from the playing field.

At the beginning of a gaming session the player only owns the Glass Recycle Unit (whose garbage block is identified by a green broken bottle) while the others must be built in a strategic way taking into account i) the number and the type of blocks present at the moment into the Hill and ii) their positioning and their accumulation patterns. In their random falling in fact, garbage blocks may create local heaps that rise in different parts of the Hill (or that are joined by some of them): being able to remove a specific type of block helps to lower the height of the Hill leaving enough time to accumulate credits for the building of more expensive missing Recycle Units.

When the player selects a Recycle Unit on the playfield, it will be highlighted with a yellow outline and the associated *Unit Menu* (Fig. 4) will appear in the lower part of the screen. This selection act clearly separates the action gaming phase from the managerial one and, for this reason, the fall of new blocks will be interrupted and the Hill (with all its blocks) will be temporarily blacked out preventing the player from interacting with it; by de-selecting the Unit resumes the falling and makes blocks visible and interactive again.

To remove the hazardous Nuclear blocks the only possibility available to the player is dropping them in the *Incinerator* and paying a fixed amount of SunnyPoints. It is a special Unit located on the playfield just above the Hill useful in emergency cases to remove blocks of types whose Recycle Unit is not currently available. No upgrades are possible for this unit and its use provokes the emission of pollution that darkens the whole screen for a few moments, obstructing the player from seeing which blocks fall and where they are going to position themselves. Through the *Power Up* button in the Incinerator Menu (enabled only if the cost can be payed) it is possible to remove from the Hill all the blocks resting directly on its bottom.

### 3.3 Educational Contents

A Recycle Unit can only be in state "free" or "occupied": when the player drags a block onto the suitable unit if that unit is in the "free" state the block will be accepted, the unit will enter in the "occupied" state and the progress bar(s) positioned at the right side will fill in red indicating the beginning of a recycling process. Each Unit has a different speed with which red bars gradually empty depending on the complexity of the recycling process associated with the garbage type and at the completion the Recycle Unit earns *UnitPoints*.

A *Unit Menu* shows all the information associated with the selected Recycle Unit: *Unit type*, *upgrade level*, *maintenance value*, *UnitPoints amount* and *number of garbage blocks* recycled so far. The Unit Menu can be used to perform two actions (both costing UnitPoints) as i) upgrade the Unit and ii) produce new objects from the contained garbage. When having enough UnitPoints, the *Upgrade button* positioned at the menu center will be active so that paying the fixed cost will add a new bar (up to 3) increase the recycling capacity through parallel processes. In such way, the *Maintenance value* specifies how many blocks at most can still be recycled before losing a bar previously obtained with an upgrade. The incoming risk of missing a bar is signaled after exceeding a threshold value by the appearance of a 'triangular danger sign' under the unit bar group, however there will always remain at least one bar, similarly to the building state.

By producing new objects through a Recycle Unit, the player exploits the material coming from the garbage blocks: in the right part of a Unit Menu in fact, there are from 1 to 4 buttons featuring the thumbnail of the object that can be produced, which vary according to the material that the unit is able to recycles and to their number depending by the upgrade level (there is always one object, the second level reaches three objects and the last four).

Each object is denoted by a cost (in UnitPoints) and a revenue (in SunnyPoints) so that, when there are enough UnitPoints to pay, the visible object

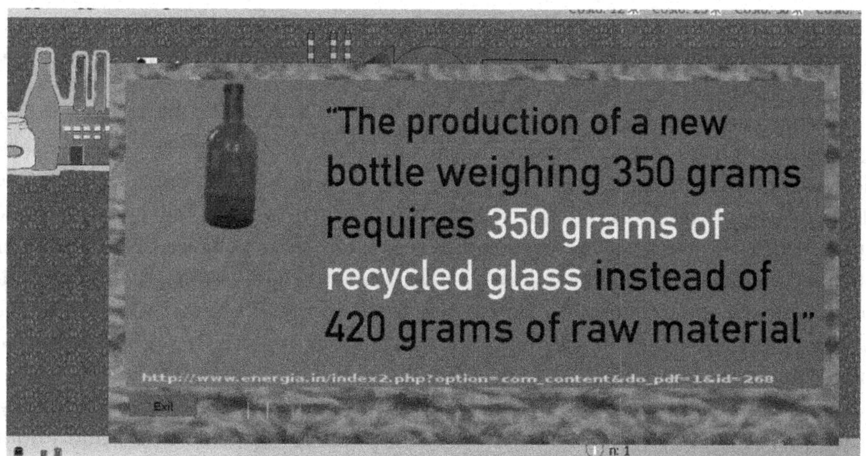


**Fig. 5.** An educational panel that shows information about the recycling process when a specific object is created for the first time by a Recycle Unit (the first object of the Glass Unit in this example).

thumbnail will be active (otherwise it will be red colored). The cost-reward relationship is incrementally so that at the basic level producing an object yields less than the production cost while with Unit upgrades this ratio is progressively reversed in favor of earning more SunnyPoints (for example, in Fig. 4 a glass bottle features a cost of 2 UnitPoints and a revenue of 1 SunnyPoint while for a glass tiles (that appears after the first unit upgrade) the cost is 6 UnitPoints but the revenue is 7 SunnyPoint).

When a object is produced for the first time, an information panel will appear providing useful educative information related to the recycling process as in Fig. 5; the player can always view such information later through the green circular icon featuring an 'i' (for Info) placed under each thumbnail; next to the 'i' icon there is how many instances of that object have been produced up to that moment. In this way the educational content can be presented to the player in a dynamic and reasoned way but never repetitive or unwanted (details-on-demand), helping to motivate the player towards environmental sustainability and the recycling processes of garbage materials, acquiring the awareness that the actions performed in the virtual world and the consequent advantages for survival in the game can also be realized in its real world.

## 4 User-Based Evaluation

A preliminary user-based evaluation has been performed with the aim to investigate the goodness of the implemented game mechanics. After a brief but complete introduction about the goals and the gaming phases, three users (1 female and 2 male, avg.age 30, university education and interest in generic but non-educational video games) played both the Easy and Hard difficulty level of the game following the *Thinking Aloud* technique in a comfortable quiet room. It is allowed to play up to three times each level since some gaming session were too short to explore all the features provided.

During each gaming session players commented aloud their thoughts and feelings about outcomes, mistakes, uncertain and, in general, the user experience provided with the UI and the gameplay mechanics. Comments were generally positive, all users found the video game easy to understand and fun while the recycling theme was perceived well-integrated and never intrusive. The User Interface and the interactions allowed in the game were immediately understandable thanks to the explanatory labels and to their visual organization while the natural learning achieved through the carried out sessions resulted useful to understand the relationship between Sunnypoints and UnitPoints.

Some critics however were raised about the difficulty balance (some game sessions became early too difficult due to the type of blocks generated) and about the not very clear cost/reward relationship in objects creation which requested the experimenter's suggestion on using a long-term strategy rather than immediately producing only low-yielding objects.

## 5 Conclusions and Future Work

The decisions made at the design level proved worthy of further experimentation. By creating a video game that blends two very different genres it was possible to 'blur' the fact that it was an educational game, making it more attractive for players that may be less interested in the educational aspects.

This study can be expanded to cooperative play introducing new materials, groups of Recycle Units and different environmental settings also exploiting IoT sensors and multiple interaction modes. Heterogeneous IT technologies like mobile and web could be considered and integrated as well as the development of advanced difficulty management techniques through deep learning and Dynamic Difficulty Adjustment (DDA) techniques.

Great attention must be given to the evaluation through a larger and stratified subject sample to better evaluate both the game mechanics and how the educational content is able to penetrate the players culture changing their approaches to sustainability. In order to reach a wider audience, it would be useful to develop the game using commercial video game level editors [2] or sandbox systems such as *Minecraft* itself, in order to exploit technological infrastructures and assets already familiar to the gamers.

**Acknowledgments.** Authors thank Claudia Balducci for the help with graphic assets and Andrea Maiellaro for his help in the development of the early prototype.

## References


1. Al-Hammadi, F.Y., Aldarwish, A.F., Alasmakh, A.H., Zemerly, M.J.: Augmented reality in educational games: city of life (COL) Emirati sustainability-edutainment interactive game. In: Advances in Science and Engineering Technology International Conference (ASET), pp. 1–7 (2018)
2. Balducci, F., Grana, C.: Affective classification of gaming activities coming from RPG gaming sessions. In: Tian, F., Gatzidis, C., El Rhalibi, A., Tang, W., Charles, F. (eds.) Edutainment 2017. LNCS, vol. 10345, pp. 93–100. Springer, Cham (2017). https://doi.org/10.1007/978-3-319-65849-0_11
3. Castellano, G., De Carolis, B., D'Errico, F., Macchiarulo, N., Rossano, V.: Pepperecycle: improving children's attitude toward recycling by playing with a social robot. Int. J. Soc. Robot. **13**(1), 97–111 (2021)
4. Gaggi, O., Meneghello, F., Palazzi, C.E., Pante, G.: Learning how to recycle waste using a game. In: GoodTechs 2020, pp. 144–149. Association for Computing Machinery, New York (2020)
5. Ibrahim, N., Wen, A.B., Hooi Khee, C.: Casual gaming to encourage reuse of waste materials for environmental sustainability. In: 2nd International Sustainability and Resilience Conference: Technology and Innovation in Building Designs, pp. 1–3 (2020)
6. Ishoj-Paris, Y., et al.: AXO: a video game that encourages recycling to preteens. In: Extended Abstracts of the 2021 Annual Symposium on Computer-Human Interaction in Play, CHI PLAY 2021, pp. 350–355. Association for Computing Machinery (2021)
7. Lameras, P., Petridis, P., Dunwell, I.: Raising awareness on sustainability issues through a mobile game. In: International Conference on Interactive Mobile Communication Technologies and Learning (IMCL 2014), pp. 217–221 (2014)
8. Menon, B.M., R, U., Muir, A., Bhavani, R.R.: Serious game on recognizing categories of waste, to support a zero waste recycling program. In: 2017 IEEE 5th International Conference on Serious Games and Applications for Health (SeGAH), pp. 1–8 (2017)
9. Piccolo, L., Fernández, M., Alani, H., Scharl, A., Föls, M., Herring, D.: Climate change engagement: results of a multi-task game with a purpose. In: Proceedings of the International AAAI Conference on Web and Social Media, vol. 10 (2016)
10. dos Santos, A.D., Strada, F., Bottino, A.: The design of an augmented reality collaborative game for sustainable development. In: Bottino, R., Jeuring, J., Veltkamp, R.C. (eds.) GALA 2016. LNCS, vol. 10056, pp. 15–23. Springer, Cham (2016). https://doi.org/10.1007/978-3-319-50182-6_2
11. Diniz dos Santos, A., Strada, F., Bottino, A.: Approaching sustainability learning via digital serious games. IEEE Trans. Learn. Technol. **12**(3), 303–320 (2019)
12. WaiShiang, C., Wei, T.Z., Kee, B.H., Mohamad, F.S.: Interactive mobile game for learning about sustainablity education. In: International Conference on Informatics and Creative Multimedia, pp. 168–173 (2013)

# Extreme Citizen Science Contributions to the Sustainable Development Goals: Challenges and Opportunities for a Human-Centred Design Approach

Artemis Skarlatidou[1](✉), Dilek Fraisl[2,3], Yaqian Wu[1], Linda See[2], and Muki Haklay[1]

[1] Department of Geography, University College London (UCL), London, UK
a.skarlatidou@ucl.ac.uk
[2] International Institute for Applied Systems Analysis (IIASA), Laxenburg, Austria
[3] University of Natural Resources and Life Sciences Vienna (BOKU), Vienna, Austria

**Abstract.** Citizen science has been recognized for its potential to contribute to the UN Sustainable Development Goals in multiple ways (e.g., for defining and monitoring indicators, data production, etc.). In this paper, we focus on Extreme Citizen Science, which includes a set of situated, bottom-up practices, used for environmental monitoring purposes and for recording local indigenous knowledge, mainly in the Global South. Here we present and discuss the human-centered approach that the implementation of extreme citizen science requires, and we identify and discuss the challenges that we face as well as the opportunities that extreme citizen science initiatives can create for contributing to the Sustainable Development Goals.

**Keywords:** Extreme citizen science · Sustainable Development Goals · Human-centered design

## 1 Introduction

Citizen science is defined as the 'scientific work undertaken by members of the general public, often in collaboration with or under the direction of professional scientists and scientific institutions' [1]. Citizen science projects have recently gained increased momentum, mainly as a result of technological developments including the availability and increasing use of mobile devices. There is a plethora of citizen science activities that cover a wide range of topics from pollution monitoring to bird watching and other ecological monitoring activities to astronomy [2]. Apart from contributing to scientific discovery, citizen science activities are also used for advocacy purposes and volunteer-initiated participatory action to address issues of local concern [3].

Since 2017, the contributions of citizen science to the Sustainable Development Goals (SDGs) at the goal and/or target level have been the subject of several workshops. Moreover, it has been recognised that citizen science has the potential to contribute to

The original version of this chapter was revised: this chapter was previously published non-open access. The correction to this chapter is available at
https://doi.org/10.1007/978-3-030-98388-8_46


C. Ardito et al. (Eds.): INTERACT 2021, LNCS 13198, pp. 20–35, 2022.
https://doi.org/10.1007/978-3-030-98388-8_3

the SDGs by: explicitly contributing to the indicators and transforming the SDGs so that their measurement is better aligned to people's experiences; acting as a spatial proxy for monitoring indicators with specified methodologies and engaging citizens in data production; and implementing the interventions and actions based on evidence as well as providing mechanisms to accelerate the achievement of the targets [4, 5].

This paper discusses the role of a particular form of public participation in research, called extreme citizen science [22], where participants have more control over the design and implementation process than in citizen science projects more generally. To date, these initiatives have focused on environmental monitoring and capturing traditional ecological knowledge, mainly in the Global South. Due to the contextual conditions and the characteristics of the communities that are engaged in extreme citizen science, a human-centred design approach is required for the application of the methods. It is also required for the development of the technological infrastructure, which is used to assist local communities in data collection and analysis so that they can identify locally appropriate solutions to tackle local issues. Here we emphasise the challenges that we face in applying extreme citizen science and the opportunities that this brings in achieving the Sustainable Development Goals (SDGs).

## 2 Citizen Science and Its Role in Sustainable Development

### 2.1 The Sustainable Development Goals (SDGs)

The United Nations Sustainable Development Goals (SDGs) consist of a set of goals that aim to tackle a range of social, environmental and economic issues, as well as a set of metrics that are used to track their progress in order to achieve a sustainable world by 2030. Tracking SDG progress in a timely, accurate and efficient way is essential for ensuring their successful delivery. Conventional data, which are commonly used to monitor SDG progress such as household surveys, are important for providing reliable and useful insights, but they are expensive, resource-intensive, and inadequate for tracking all 231 unique indicators in the SDG framework [6–8]. Citizen science - defined as public participation in scientific research and knowledge production - can support the monitoring of SDGs as a new data source to provide timely, relevant and reliable information with a higher temporal and spatial resolution, which can either be used on their own or for complementing more conventional data sources [6, 7, 9].

The potential offered by citizen science for SDG monitoring and their implementation has been widely discussed in the more recent academic literature [6, 7, 10–13]. In fact, evidence - from a comprehensive review of SDG indicators and citizen science initiatives at the local, regional and global levels - suggests that citizen science data are already contributing or have the potential to contribute to the monitoring of 33% of the SDG indicators [6]. The authors also demonstrated that the SDGs that could benefit most from citizen science data include: SDG 15 Life on Land; SDG 11 on Sustainable Cities and Communities; SDG 3 on Good Health and Wellbeing and SDG 6 on Clean Water and Sanitation [6]. The greatest contributions of citizen science to SDG monitoring are, therefore, to the environmental SDG indicators. It is also important to highlight that 58% of the 92 environmental SDG indicators lack data, and thus the role of citizen science data in monitoring the SDGs becomes even more crucial. For example, at the indicator level, the contributions from citizen science to SDG monitoring may cover areas such as marine litter (indicator 14.1.1b), rural access (9.1.1), threatened species (15.5.1), post disaster damage (1.5.2), air quality (3.9.1), water quality (6.3.2), land use and land cover (15.1.1, 15.2.1) and sexual violence (16.1.3), among others.

There have been ongoing efforts at the UN level to include citizen science in the methodologies for SDG monitoring. For example, the global methodology for SDG indicator 14.1.1b on plastic debris density explicitly mentions the use of citizen science approaches, particularly for the monitoring of beach litter [15, 16]. UNEP has also been providing financial and operational support to citizen science initiatives, with the aim to improve their methodologies and match them to the monitoring requirements of SDG indicator 14.1.1b [14].

It has been already mentioned that citizen science can complement SDG monitoring efforts at a national, regional, and global level. Citizen science can achieve this through the participation of volunteers and communities in data collection activities that focus on the local level. Capturing this local knowledge and local wisdom from volunteers and local communities provides an irreplaceable source of information that is essential for bridging community level initiatives with global monitoring efforts. Additionally, although not always possible as we discuss later, local citizen science initiatives may leverage the SDG framework to support their data collection activities and therefore, ensure that the data collected feeds directly into the official monitoring schemes.

Although citizen science in the context of sustainability and the SDGs has started to gain increasing recognition by the wider academic community more recently, it should be noted that the majority of citizen science efforts mainly concentrate on the advanced economies of the Global North, enabled by social trends such as access to education, exposure to science and the wide use of digital technologies. There is a more recent realization that citizen science can demonstrate significant local and global impacts and that it has the potential to contribute to the global sustainability agenda based on evidence from successful citizen science initiatives, which can also address issues in the Global South. For example, [17] discuss citizen science as an innovation mechanism and highlight that in opening up participation in science, "it is equally important to include indigenous and local knowledge as an added benefit to science, for example, in framing questions, designing projects, analysing results and understanding their possible impacts upon decision-making processes". Moreover, [18] demonstrate that "both ILK [indigenous local knowledge] and institutionally derived scientific understanding can be valuable in conservation planning activities. This knowledge inclusivity can bring specific expertise to citizen science projects and embed the results in the community affected" [18; 468].

We make the argument, and further discuss in this paper, that in line with the "leaving no one behind" principle of the 2030 Agenda for Sustainable Development, it is extreme citizen science activities that can operate in local indigenous environments in remote locations, provide insights into how people interact with their local environment, generate environmental data for areas where data gaps exist, and subsequently make the monitoring of SDGs more inclusive and impactful.

## 2.2 Citizen Science and Extreme Citizen Science

Several definitions and terms have been used to describe citizen science, capturing the disciplinary perspective or the unique cultural, geographical and scientific characteristics of the discipline and context in which citizen science is being implemented. Despite this potpourri of definitions, there is consensus that citizen science can be broadly described as the involvement of non-professional scientists in scientific research and knowledge production. Some scholars from the field of citizen science have provided in-depth theoretical and practical perspectives on how citizen science is currently being utilised through the lens of different hierarchies or taxonomies, for example, Shirk's five models of participation in scientific research [19]; Haklay's 4-level hierarchy [20]; and Cooper's 5Cs model of participation [21]. In Fig. 1, we present Haklay's [22] hierarchy.

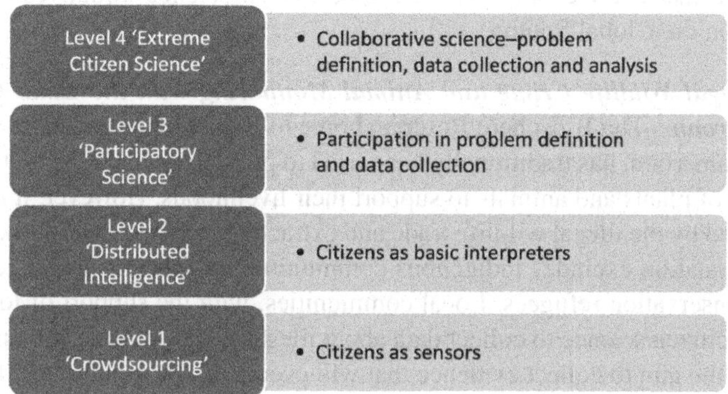


**Fig. 1.** Levels of engagement in citizen science [22].

Haklay's hierarchy (Fig. 1) includes four levels: level 1 'crowdsourcing', where participation happens at much larger scales, with activities that mainly focus on sharing resources (e.g., computer power) rather than requiring any significant cognitive effort; level 2 'distributed intelligence', where participants contribute to data collection or interpretation tasks and which, therefore, involve some cognitive effort; level 3 'participatory science', where participants contribute not only to data collection and interpretation but also in forming the research questions and problem definition; and level 4 'extreme citizen science', where participants can be involved at all stages of the scientific process. In other words, extreme citizen science gives any community the support they need to conduct collaborative science - including problem definition, data collection and analysis - for issues that matter to them and which they decide they want to tackle.

In UCL's Extreme Citizen Science (ExCiteS) group, they define extreme citizen science as a philosophy of situated, bottom-up practices that take local needs, practices and cultures into account and that work with broad networks of people in order to design and build new devices as well as knowledge creation processes that can make positive transformations in the world. In the next section, we present a set of extreme citizen science initiatives and their methods and tools in order to build a better understanding of how our work in extreme citizen science has the potential to promote sustainable development.

## 3 Extreme Citizen Science: Methods and Tools

Extreme citizen science initiatives use a set of methods and technologies that have been developed to support individuals and communities in the collection of traditional ecological knowledge, environmental data for monitoring and other data to address issues that communities want to tackle. Subsequently, communities or individuals engage in data collection processes that allow them to collect the evidence required to prove the existence of these specific local problems - for example, to local governmental authorities - and eventually to take the necessary steps to resolve them.

Below we list a few examples of extreme citizen science initiatives that mainly concentrate on the Global South:

***Tackling Illegal Wildlife Crime and Animal Monitoring with the Baka Communities in Cameroon.*** Dja Biosphere Reserve, home to Baka hunter-gatherers and Mbulu farmers of Cameroon, has traditionally been used to provide its local populations with a large variety of plants and animals to support their livelihoods. However, it is currently being depleted by the illegal wildlife trade and extractive industries, while existing conservation legislation excludes indigenous communities and their knowledge and turns them into conservation refugees. Local communities, with the support of local NGOs, use extreme citizen science to collect data about illegal wildlife crime and animal monitoring, with the aim to collect evidence that will eventually be used to inform effective forest management legislation [23].

***Collecting Data for Indigenous Plants with Maasai warriors in Kenya.*** One of the greatest threats that Maasai communities in Narok county, Kenya, face is the loss of traditional ecological knowledge and the increased deforestation in the Maasai Mara National Reserve. Therefore, local communities rely on extreme citizen science tools to collect indigenous plant data, with the aim to pass this knowledge onto future generations and preserve it. Since 2019, they have collected thousands of observations of the medicinal and other properties of local indigenous flora.

***Managing Natural Resources for New Conservation Legislation with Indigenous Communities in the Pantanal Wetlands, Brazil.*** The Pantanal is the largest wetland in the world, with local fishers being totally dependent on it for their daily livelihoods. Legislation for resource management and consumption in the area does not consider people's traditional practices, and this has resulted in their physical and economic displacement. Local communities have used extreme citizen science since 2014 to collect data on their fishing practices, which provide evidence to demonstrate that indigenous practices are indeed sustainable; as a result, the local people have been officially recognised as a "traditional community". This has legally given them the right to protect their livelihoods and continue using their traditional natural resource management practices [24].

***Managing Natural Resources and Fighting Illegal Cattle Invasions with the Ju /'hoansi in Namibia.*** The Nyae Nyae Conservancy in Namibia, officially registered in 1998, has come under threat since the local communities have come into contact with agricultural economies and due to the extensive cattle farming in traditional hunting and gathering grounds. As the primary custodians of the conservancy, the Ju/'hoansi use extreme citizen science methods and tools to collect data that can help them tackle the issues of illegal cattle invasions in their territory, and more recently, they also collect data that will eventually help them to manage their local community forest resources [25].

It has been already mentioned that in extreme citizen science, and the examples mentioned above, that each community identifies the problem(s) they want to tackle, and hence, the purpose and the cultural, contextual and environmental characteristics vary. Moreover, the majority of the extreme citizen science initiatives, including the ones described above, include communities with varying levels of literacy, with no access to technological infrastructure (e.g., electricity, Internet access, etc.) and without previous exposure to digital technology (e.g., smartphones, data collection apps, online maps, etc.). These are just a few of the challenges that we face in the majority of extreme citizen science projects. Therefore, despite the differences in contextual characteristics, all extreme citizen science initiatives follow a very similar methodological framework and utilise the same set of technologies (modified to fit each context), which are designed to support these communities, and which are constantly being improved to deal with additional challenges. Before we describe the opportunities and challenges in more detail, we introduce the extreme citizen science methodology and tools in the Sects. 3.1 and 3.2.

### 3.1 Engagement in Extreme Citizen Science

All extreme citizen science initiatives rely heavily on a participatory design approach methodology, informed by anthropological and Human-Computer Interaction methods. The same methodological steps are followed during the development and iterative design of extreme citizen science practices, and the development and adaptation of our tools to fit the context of each initiative.

As communities identify the problems to address, engagement is mostly initiated by the communities themselves (or local organisations that support these communities). A set of preliminary meetings with local communities, their trusted gatekeepers and local intermediaries then take place to identify or further discuss their local issues and to develop a mutual understanding of how extreme citizen science can be best utilised to support them. Once this is established, an engagement process is then applied as described below.

Free, Prior and Informed Consent Process (FPIC). The FPIC process aims to inform "the affected persons about planned activities and their impacts" and verify "that the information provided has been understood, before explicit consent can be negotiated" [26]. The consent is free and informed, highlighting the ability of communities to refuse an intervention, and it takes place prior to them being affected by any external actions [26]. While the FPIC process is a prerequisite for many studies that include human participants, here the process relies heavily on taking local cultural frameworks into account (e.g., local protocols, hierarchies, etc.) and communicating what constitutes consent. This process, which is explained in detail in [27] further sets the foundations for local capacity building [26, 28].

Establishment of a Community Protocol. Community protocols are used to establish the expectations of communities in the conduct of the initiative and formalise the terms collectively agreed. They are also crucial in sustaining each initiative over its lifetime. The community protocol documents a detailed plan capturing issues such as: who will be collecting the data, when will data collection take place, how will the data be stored, how will equipment be managed, issues of data security, access and sovereignty, support provision (e.g., technical, methodological, logistical) and others. Potential risks and other implications are explored collaboratively in community protocol designated meetings, which take place throughout the duration of the initiative, as terms need to be redefined when new concerns or issues arise or the situation changes (e.g., new actors are involved), and solutions are co-designed. In this process, as [27] explain, communities are encouraged to lead discussions, and particular care is taken to ensure that everyone feels encouraged to express their views without any criticism or judgment.

Participatory Design for the development and evaluation of locally appropriate and relevant technologies. Extreme citizen science initiatives target communities where education and literacy, access to technological infrastructure and familiarity with technology and local environmental conditions present various obstacles to their successful adoption and utilization, as we discuss in more detail in Sect. 4.1. Most of the communities we work with are either technically and/or textually illiterate or have low levels of literacy, and hence, research in the development and design of our tools and methods draws upon the fields of Human-Computer Interaction for Development (HCI4D), mainly with respect to the use of iconic interfaces, menu structures and information organisation (for further information see [28]).

Our main data collection tool, Sapelli Collector, which is discussed in more detail in the next section, uses a pictorial interface and a hierarchical decision tree to represent an ontology of data items for which information is collected. The pictorial icons (Fig. 2) used by Sapelli Collector are co-designed with the communities involved to ensure that local meanings and cultural conventions are taken into account and so that the icons are well understood. This is an iterative process; for example, if decision trees are shown to be too complex, we co-design alternative solutions, either by simplifying the project (e.g., see [30]), or even introduce alternative technologies such as Tap&Map [31]).

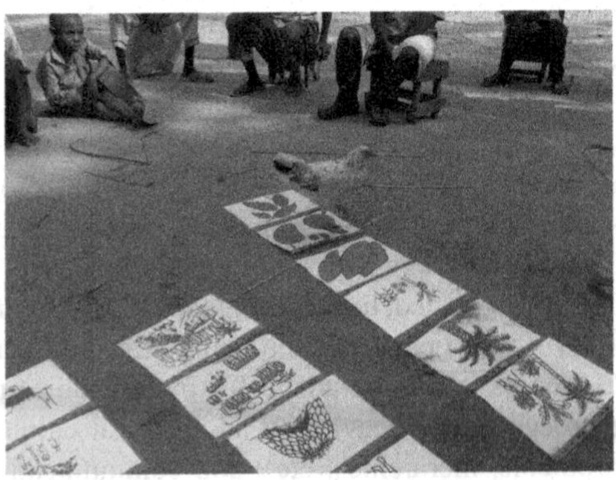

**Fig. 2.** Community workshop for designing Tap&Map pictorial icons for data collection [31].

Ethnographic observation is used to understand how technologies are used locally, paying particular attention to challenges and how use is shaped by contextual and environmental conditions, and social organisational structures. Human-computer interaction methods (usually modified to be locally appropriate) are also used to explore and improve interaction with extreme citizen science tools. In our participatory design process, emphasis is placed on reciprocity and giving back to the community (e.g., helping with daily activities; spending significant time to learn the local culture, language and participate in social activities; building friendships; and learning from each other and passing on new skills etc.). Our vision, similar to [32], is to "promote empowerment, through technology, enabling people to become better equipped so that they can innovate for themselves" [32;243], rather than focusing solely on innovation in the first place.

### 3.2 Extreme Citizen Science Tools

In the following, we provide a brief overview of the main technological tools used in extreme citizen science initiatives, which are mainly used for data collection for environmental monitoring purposes as well as for capturing local indigenous knowledge.

**Sapelli Collector.** Sapelli is an Android-based, open source mobile data-collection and -sharing application, designed with a particular focus on users with low or no literacy and little or no prior ICT experience. The application executes surveys, which take the form of pictorial decision trees (Fig. 3) based on hierarchical ontological structures that describe the data items being collected. The leaves represent specific answers or classifications, while in-between nodes represent categories of similar items. Users navigate the decision tree by repeatedly 'tapping' images to select child nodes until they reach a leaf node, which represents the data item being collected (i.e., audio, photos, geospatial coordinates, etc.).

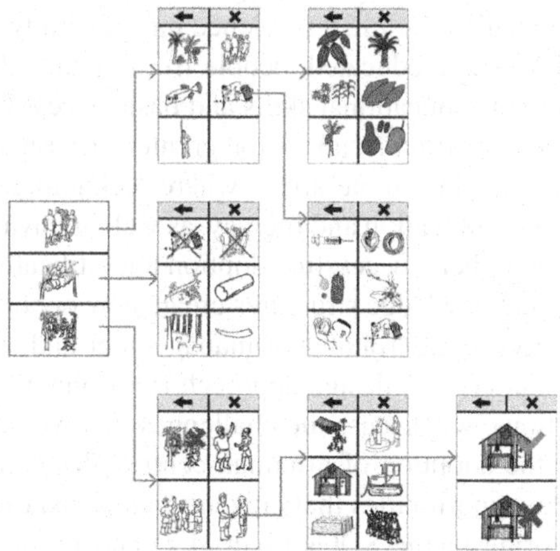

**Fig. 3.** Sapelli collector interface design and decision tree [31].

**Tap&Map.** Preliminary testing of Sapelli Collector in Congo has shown that local participants had difficulty navigating its hierarchical structure - a finding consistent with the wider HCI4D literature in terms of how people with low levels of literacy navigate hierarchical data structures [34, 35] – as well as other issues (e.g., fear of using technology, difficulties with the touchscreen, etc.) [31]. A more accessible user interface, Tap&Map, was developed to tackle these challenges. It consists of a series of physical cards, each with a pictogram representing the data item being collected and an Android application. Using cards with near field communication (NFC) tags, the user must identify the card for which information is being collected, and then they touch it on the phone while standing as close as possible to the actual location of the physical object so that the application registers the correct coordinates. Tap&Map then reads the user's location from the device's Global Positioning System (GPS) sensor and stores it, along with other necessary metadata recorded by the user (e.g., photos, audio).

**Sapelli Viewer.** A common expectation across communities involved in extreme citizen science initiatives is the need to view data instantly, or soon after the data are recorded. To support this need, we are currently developing Sapelli Viewer, which is a data visualisation application for Android devices (i.e., smartphones and tablets) that also includes basic (e.g., select and view all crop type 'A') and advanced data filtering options (e.g., view changes of crop 'A' in different time periods), enhancing the application's analytic capabilities, the types of spatial thinking that it will support and how this could potentially be used to develop and apply more effective local environmental management strategies.

## 4 Extreme Citizen Science for Environmental Monitoring in the Global South: Opportunities and Challenges

Citizen science attracts people of all ages, backgrounds and interests. Although this has its own massive design challenges, citizen science has generally focused on a limited demographic profile of Western, educated, people from industrialized, rich and democratic nations [36], where the educational skills and basic access to, and familiarization with, digital technologies are usually taken for granted. Extreme citizen science initiatives include communities in remote areas, where technological infrastructure and familiarity with technology, education and literacy, as well as environmental conditions, present various obstacles to their successful adoption and utilization. At the same time, local cultural contexts and knowledge structures create new opportunities to further our understanding with respect to environmental management and sustainability. It is for these reasons that a human-centred design approach is absolutely essential.

In the next two sections, we discuss the challenges that we face in extreme citizen science, which require the adoption of a human-centred design approach (Sect. 4.1). Secondly, we discuss the opportunities that citizen science and extreme citizen science can bring to the monitoring of the SDGs (Sect. 4.2) and to the global sustainability agenda, especially if they are to be implemented effectively and efficiently in a way that further empowers and protects local actors and their voices.

### 4.1 Challenges

The challenges posed by extreme citizen science depend on several contextual factors. If we take a step back, remove the unique contextual characteristics and the challenges that these create, and then look at the broader context of extreme citizen science, we can identify two major sets of challenges that are common and exist in the majority (if not all) of our initiatives. First, we have challenges that refer to data-related issues (e.g., data ownership, security, accuracy, etc.). Secondly, we face challenges that emerge mainly due to specific technological and educational barriers and that influence how extreme citizen science is being implemented and practiced in areas where these barriers exist. We discuss these challenges in more detail in the paragraphs that follow.

There is an ongoing debate in the broader academic literature of citizen science around data quality issues. For example, top-down citizen science projects, led by professional scientists, rely heavily on large numbers of volunteers collecting data at large scales, which then allows research questions to be explored using a spatial coverage that would otherwise be impossible and that improves the scientific understanding of the topic for which data are being collected (e.g., ecology and biodiversity citizen science projects such as the Christmas Bird Count). In this context, common data quality concerns may refer to the reliability and quality of the data collected, or they may be due to volunteer training and the skill of the "non-expert" as opposed to that of a professional scientist, as well as variations in the sampling efforts and the coverage, which may introduce further bias, among other issues.

With extreme citizen science initiatives, which have a much smaller geographic focus, the data collection is only possible by working directly with local communities in a bottom-up way. This allows for investigation into what these communities need and how professional scientists can support them through the provision of the appropriate local capacity building mechanisms and tools. In this way, communities can invest their time and effort in the activities appropriately that serve their specific aims. Although western beliefs about techno-scientific innovation and top-down approaches have long been proven to be problematic, and exclude local communities from the global environmental sustainability agenda, it is still 'difficult for people from "advanced" cultures to accept the idea that people from "primitive" cultures might know something scientifically significant' [37;14]. Subsequently, they may not challenge the data quality of these approaches on this basis. Considering the fact that these communities are integral to how their local environments are shaped, and they possess a wealth of local knowledge that is completely neglected by conventional scientists (e.g., not only in terms of the data that they collect, the cultural norms and meanings behind it, but also the way monitoring and data collection actually occurs), we need to rethink arguments about the scientific validity of these data and their assessment via conventional scientific standards of quality. This is particularly important not only when extreme citizen science data become the only available data source for remote geographic regions, but also that it is being used to complement other scientific data sources in terms of promoting equality, inclusiveness and ensuring that 'no one is left behind'. By bringing local knowledge and traditional expertise together, emerging collaborations can promote conservation and sustainable development.

Other data related challenges within the context of extreme citizen science that may further influence how efficiently this data source may be used in the context of sustainable development goals are data ownership and security issues. Communities in extreme citizen science, through the FPIC process (Sect. 3.1), take complete ownership of the project and the data being collected. However, there are cases in which communities may decide that they do not want to share their data because of data sensitivity and a lack of trust (e.g., unrecorded traditional ecological knowledge that indigenous communities do not wish to share with outsiders) or that extra measures for protection and security need to be taken into account due to adverse local conditions and local political power dynamics [38, 39].

Data-related challenges are not the only ones we face in extreme citizen science. The majority of these initiatives rely on an entire technological ecosystem, yet the presence of such an ecosystem cannot be taken for granted, especially if it is used to engage with communities in remote, rural areas. Lack of electricity and wireless coverage create various obstacles in engaging with extreme citizen science, which necessitates identifying creative solutions (e.g., for charging the devices that are used to support data collection or visualisation tasks, updating the software to continue with the current tasks over long periods of time, etc.). Moreover, lack of access and familiarity with the technological infrastructure means that communities usually face difficulties managing the equipment that is used (e.g., phones, tablets, cables, chargers, converters, etc.) and for which training and support are required over long periods of time.

Interaction with smartphones and tablet devices relies heavily on on-screen gestures (e.g., swipe, long tap, short tap, pinch) and knowledge of interface design metaphors, which cannot be assumed. For example, some communities may have never used such devices before, or they may be illiterate or have low levels of literacy. Considering that most western interface design creations assume a certain level of textual literacy, this means extensive training needs to be provided in the use of technological equipment as well as research and ongoing testing to understand how to design user-friendly interfaces that can be utilised successfully by the intended audience. Within that context, the above-mentioned technological tools cannot rely on ontological structures that are derived from western knowledge systems, as evidence shows that when systems "are organised according to an externally imposed exogenous structure, [they] will become graveyards of objects no longer accessible to the practices of indigenous knowledge traditions and that knowledge captured in such a way is more in danger of being lost or misunderstood" [33; 240]; therefore ongoing research - which is highly context specific - is further required to develop tools that are culturally appropriate and ideally match, from an ontological point of view, the local knowledge systems. Considering these complexities, these initiatives usually require additional funding to support local capacity building, technical training, regular environmental data monitoring, equipment maintenance, etc.

Having mentioned that context specific research is needed to develop culturally appropriate and user-friendly extreme citizen science tools to support data collection for environmental monitoring and local indigenous knowledge, it should be further noted that anthropological and HCI methods, which are traditionally used for this purpose, require adaptation. First, with respect to HCI methods, we have previously discussed how conventional HCI methods are not culturally universal, they rely on assumptions, and therefore, we need to identify and design experiments that are locally appropriate (e.g., group usability testing for egalitarian communities, proxy user testing, etc.) [28, 29]. Secondly, with respect to participatory methods, as [33] explain, these "must be considerably devised to ensure successful community engagement" (245). The authors propose that the implementation of culturally appropriate methods of engagement should answer questions such as "what will happen to the resulting knowledge, who really stands to benefit from the research, and how will the community benefit from the engagement" (243). They also suggest that instead of focusing on solutions "to overcome or compensate for something lacking", the emphasis should be on a "rhetoric of engagement, that promotes empowerment through technology" (243). Our methodological framework (i.e., with the FPIC, community protocol, etc.) aspires to the same vision and attempts to overcome these challenges; by placing reciprocity at the centre of our engagement approach, we attempt to establish familiarity, build mutual respect and establish trust with the communities with whom we work (e.g., see [39]). This is perhaps one of the greatest obstacles to be overcome, as past or even current projects that have engaged with the same communities have left a set of unfulfilled promises, resulting in a legacy of distrust [39].

Last but not least, the sustainability of extreme citizen science initiatives relies heavily on sustaining participant motivation and eventually 'closing the loop' by supporting communities to innovate themselves, or in other cases, expose the issues that they face (through the data collected and the analysis) and create some positive impact, as identified by the community itself. With respect to motivation, the majority of the initiatives are conceived by communities, and they are shaped around local issues; therefore, there is a high level of intrinsic motivation. Various challenges remain, and these concern, amongst others, the mobilisation of relevant stakeholders (when and if the community protocol supports it) whose involvement might be necessary for achieving change, the continuation of funding to support local communities, as well as questions about how to best take this body of local knowledge into account to more effectively address the environmental challenges we face.

## 4.2 Opportunities

The opportunities that extreme citizen science initiatives are offering in the context of SDG implementation and monitoring are many, and by using the examples described above, we can identify some of the ones that are potentially relevant within the 2030 agenda.

First, they offer a significant way to achieve the principle of "no one left behind". In a world in which literacy is very common, there is marginalisation and exclusion for people with little or no literacy. As a result, their knowledge and views about their environment are frequently excluded from statistical efforts including the SDG indicators. The education-related targets of SDG 4 aim to provide quality education and lifelong learning for all, especially for those who lack the skills to read or write. To achieve these targets, the UNESCO Institute for Statistics, in collaboration with the Global Education Monitoring (GEM) Report, have presented new data and policymaking tools to Member States that will help to produce and use indicators for monitoring and achieving SDG 4 at the national level. Yet within the national and local levels, we still need to identify culturally acceptable ways for all potential local communities to be part of the data collection and sharing efforts, so that they can gain representation and a voice within these larger scale processes, which are also linked to the access and distribution of resources.

Secondly, and which is now becoming widely recognised within UN reports such as the Global Environmental Outlook 6 or those produced by the Intergovernmental Science-Policy Platform on Biodiversity and Ecosystem Services (IPBES), traditional ecological knowledge is now accepted as a valuable source of environmental knowledge. The approaches that we describe here open up the possibilities for setting up mechanisms to collect and share such knowledge in a way that will ensure control over the data by the community and which also benefits the people who collect it. With the support of the United Nations Committee of Experts on Global Geospatial Information Management (UN-GGIM), the establishment of digital data infrastructure is encouraged to enable the integration, coordination, connectivity and expansion of local multi-source datasets. Such infrastructures for measuring, comparing and monitoring the inclusive progress of the SDGs can facilitate the registration and sharing of new global indicators. For example, cloud services with big data and artificial intelligence can revolutionize environmental and resource monitoring to track the SDGs. Google, Amazon and Alibaba have their own cloud computing products, which could help to archive environmental data, e.g.,, from gauging stations, Google Earth Engine (GEE), the Amazon Web Service (AWS) or the Alibaba Cloud. While this by itself will not solve the challenges of extractive and colonial science, it can create the conditions to address them.

Finally, the approach that we describe here can be extended with the use of sensors and other forms of data collection and sharing at the community level. Through cloud services, SDGs in any region of interest in the world can be monitored and tracked at any time and in any place. Appropriate sensors can be used to assess the quality of water resources, or record samples from the environment that can serve different SDG indicators. RiverWatcher is an example of such a model in China; since 2019, thousands of patrols from all over the country have provided regular monitoring along with rubbish clean ups through the Alipay mini program 'Xunhebao'. The fact that many of these communities live in a remote location opens up the possibility for improving the spatial and temporal coverage of different datasets. Here the FPIC and the community protocol can be used to ensure that equitable compensation is provided to those who collect the data, as well as improving their ability to find ways to utilize the information.

## 5 Conclusions

As noted previously, citizen science already contributes to the monitoring of 33% of the SDG indicators. Moreover, there are ongoing efforts at the UN level that are attempting to extend the utilisation of citizen science further in the context of SDG monitoring in order to improve the data coverage, especially for the 58% of the 92 environmental SDG indicators for which the data are not available. Citizen science has the potential to capture local knowledge and information that is often only available within local communities, and which provides an irreplaceable source of information essential for bridging community level initiatives with global monitoring efforts. Although the majority of current citizen science initiatives focus on the Global North, here we have discussed how extreme citizen science is currently being utilised in the Global South and that this work is important for several reasons. First, it brings us closer to realising the "leaving no one behind" vision of the 2030 Agenda for Sustainable Development. Secondly, an extreme citizen science approach is well suited to local indigenous environments in remote locations for which hardly any data exist, making, when possible, the monitoring of SDGs more inclusive and impactful. Thirdly, through extreme citizen science initiatives, we actually recognise the importance of traditional ecological knowledge that indigenous communities have relied on for millennia, and we make an effort to incorporate this knowledge into the global sustainability agenda.

Despite these potential benefits, the successful implementation of extreme citizen science initiatives to support environmental monitoring and the collection of local indigenous knowledge, in diverse cultural, environmental and infrastructural contexts, requires focusing attention on local specificities, and the careful consideration of how these specificities can inform the design of the tools and strategies for implementation. We found that anthropological and HCI methods are key in this process, as it is a participatory design process for the development and adaptation of extreme citizen science tools to a specific geographic and socio-cultural context. It is only through the human-centered design approach for implementing extreme citizen science initiatives that we can improve our ability to more effectively translate local knowledge into data sets that can be placed in dialogue with current scientific conservation and environmental management policy models and eventually contribute to the SDGs.

**Acknowledgments.** This work is supported by: the European Union's ERC Advanced Grant project European Citizen Science: Analysis and Visualisation (under Grant Agreement No 694767); the European Union's H2020 research and innovation programme EU-Citizen.Science (The Platform for sharing, Initiating and Learning Citizen Science in Europe) under Grant Agreement No824580; the European Union's coordination and support action TIME4CS (Sustainable institutional changes to promote public engagement inn science and technology) under Grant Agreement No 101006201; and the ERASMUS+ Programme of the European Union under Grant Agreement No 2020-1-UK01-KA226-he-094667. We would like to thank all volunteers and local communities, which participate in extreme citizen science initiatives.

## References

1. Oxford English Dictionary (OED) Online: Citizen Science. Oxford University Press. Accessed August 2014
2. Preece, J.: Citizen science: new research challenges for human-computer Interaction. Int. J. Hum. Comput. Interact. **32**(8), 585–612 (2016)
3. Theobald, E.J., Ettinger, A.K., Burgess, H.K., DeBey, L.B., Schmidt, N.R., Froehlich, H.E., et al.: Global change and local solutions: tapping the unrealized potential of citizen science for biodiversity research. Biol. Cons. **181**, 236–244 (2015)
4. Brissett, N., Mitter, R.: For function or transformation? A critical discourse analysis of education under the sustainable development goals. J. Crit. Educ. Policy Stud. **15**(1), 181–204 (2017)
5. Bio Innovation Service. Citizen science for environmental policy: development of an EU-wide inventory and analysis of selected practices. Final report for the European Commission, DG Environment under the contract 070203/2017/768879/ETU/ENV.A.3, in collaboration with Fundacion Ibercivis and The Natural History Museum (2018)
6. Fraisl, D., et al.: Mapping citizen science contributions to the UN sustainable development goals. Sustain. Sci. **15**(6), 1735–1751 (2020). https://doi.org/10.1007/s11625-020-00833-7
7. Fritz, S., et al.: Citizen science and the United Nations sustainable development goals. Nat. Sustain. **2**, 922–930 (2019). https://doi.org/10.1038/s41893-019-0390-3

8. MacFeely, S., Nastav, B.: "You say you want a [data] revolution": a proposal to use unofficial statistics for the SDG global indicator framework. Stat. J. IAOS **35**, 309–327 (2019). https://doi.org/10.3233/SJI-180486
9. Ajates, R., Hager, G., Georgiadis, P., Coulson, S., Woods, M., Hemment, D.: Local action with global impact: the case of the GROW observatory and the sustainable development goals. Sustainability **12**, 10518 (2020). https://doi.org/10.3390/su122410518
10. Campbell, J., et al.: The role of combining national official statistics with global monitoring to close the data gaps in the environmental SDGs. Stat. J. IAOS **36**, 443–453 (2020). https://doi.org/10.3233/SJI-200648
11. Head, J.S., Crockatt, M.E., Didarali, Z., Woodward, M.-J., Emmett, B.A.: The role of citizen science in meeting SDG targets around soil health. Sustainability **12**, 10254 (2020). https://doi.org/10.3390/su122410254
12. König, A., Pickar, K., Stankiewicz, J., Hondrila, K.: Can citizen science complement official data sources that serve as evidence-base for policies and practice to improve water quality? Stat. J. IAOS **1–16** (2020). https://doi.org/10.3233/SJI-200737
13. Laso Bayas, J.C., et al.: Crowdsourcing LUCAS: citizens generating reference land cover and land use data with a mobile app. Land **9**, 446 (2020). https://doi.org/10.3390/land9110446
14. UNEP: Measuring progress: towards achieving the environmental dimension of the SDGs (2020). https://wedocs.unep.org/handle/20.500.11822/27627
15. UN: Metadata for indicator 14.1.1 (2021). https://unstats.un.org/sdgs/metadata/files/Metadata-14-01-01.pdf
16. GESAMP: Guidelines for the Monitoring and Assessment of Plastic Litter in the Ocean (2019). http://www.gesamp.org/publications/guidelines-for-the-monitoring-and-assessment-of-plastic-litter-in-the-ocean
17. Hecker, S., Haklay, M., Bowser, A., Makuch, Z., Vogel, J., Bonn, A.: Citizen Science. Innovation in Open Science, Society and Policy. UCL Press, London (2018)
18. Danielsen, F., et al.: The value of indigenous and local knowledge as citizen science. In: Hecker, S., Haklay, M., Bowser, A., Makuch, Z., Vogel, J., Bonn, A. (eds.) Citizen Science: Innovation in Open Science, Society and Policy, pp. 254–268. UCL Press, London (2018)
19. Shirk, J.L., et al.: Public participation in scientific research: a framework for deliberate design. Ecol. Soc. **17**, 29 (2012)
20. Haklay, M.: Citizen science and volunteered geographic information: overview and typology of participation. In: Sui, D.Z., Elwood, S., Goodchild, M.F. (eds.) Crowdsourcing Geographic Knowledge: Volunteered geographic information (VGI) in theory and practice, pp. 105–122. Springer, New York (2013). https://doi.org/10.1007/978-94-007-4587-2_7
21. Cooper, C.: Citizen Science: How Ordinary People Are Changing the Face of Discovery. Overlook Press, New York (2016)
22. Haklay, M.: Geographic citizen science: an overview. In: Skarlatidou, A., Haklay, M. (eds.) Geographic Citizen Science Design: No one Left Behind. UCL Press, London (2021)
23. Hoyte, S.: Indigenous Baka hunters vs. The illegal wildlife trade (2017). https://simonhoyte.wordpress.com/2017/03/01/indigenous-baka-hunters-vs-the-illegal-wildlife-trade/
24. Chiaravalloti, R.: The displacement of insufficiently 'traditional' communities: local fisheries in the Pantanal. Conserv. Soc. **17**(2), 173–183 (2019)
25. Laws, M.: Sapelli to tackle illegal cattle invasions for the JuHoansi of NyaeNyae conservancy (2015). https://uclexcites.blog
26. Lewis, J.: How to implement free, prior informed consent (FPIC). In: Biodiversity and Culture: Exploring Community Protocols, Rights and Consent, p. 175. International Institute for Environment and Development, London (2012)
27. Fryer-Moreira, R., Lewis, J.: Methods in anthropology to support the design and implementation of geographic citizen science. In: Skarlatidou, A., Haklay, M. (eds.) Geographic Citizen Science Design: No one Left Behind. UCL Press, London (2021)

28. Pejovic, V., Skarlatidou, A.: Understanding interaction design challenges in mobile extreme citizen science. Int. J. Hum. - Comput. Interact. **36**, 1–20 (2019)
29. Skarlatidou, A., Moustard, F. Vitos, M.: Experiences from extreme citizen science: using smartphone-based data collection tools with low-literate people. In: Conference Proceedings of CHI 2020. Association for Computing Machinery (2020)
30. Chiaravalloti, R.: Representing a fish for fishers: geographic citizen science in the Pantanal Wetland, Brazil. In: Skarlatidou, A., Haklay, M. (eds.) Geographic Citizen Science Design: No one Left Behind. UCL Press, London (2021)
31. Vitos, M.: Lessons from recording traditional ecological knowledge in the Congo Basin. In: Skarlatidou, A., Haklay, M. (eds.) Geographic Citizen Science Design: No one Left Behind. UCL Press, London (2021)
32. Rogers, Y., Marsden, G.: Does he take sugar?: moving beyond the rhetoric of compassion. Interactions **20**(4), 48–57 (2013)
33. Brereton, M., Roe, P., Schroeter, R., Lee Hong, A.: Indigenous knowledge technologies. moving from knowledge capture to engagement, reciprocity and use. In: Bidwell, N.J., Winschiers-Theophilus, H. (eds.) At the Intersection of Indigenous and Traditional Knowledge and Technology Design. Informing Science Press, Santa Rosa (2015)
34. Chaudry, B., Connelly, K., Siek, K.,Welch, J.: Mobile interface design for low-literacy populations. In: 2nd ACM SIGHIT International Health Informatics Symposium, Miami, FL, pp. 91–100 (2012)
35. Lalji, Z., Good, J.: Designing new technologies for illiterate populations: a study in mobile phone interface design. Interact. Comput. **20**(6), 574–586 (2008)
36. Dourish, P.: Forward. In: Bidwell, N., Winschiers-Theophilus, H. (eds.) At the Intersection of Indigenous and Traditional Knowledge and Technology Design. ISP, California (2015)
37. Berkes, F.: Sacred Ecology. Routledge, Oxon (2012)
38. Vitos, M., Altenbuchner, J., Stevens, M., Conquest, G., Lewis, J., Haklay, M.: Supporting collaboration with non-literate forest communities in the Congo-Basin. In: Proceedings of the 2017 ACM Conference on Computer Supported Cooperative Work and Social Computing – CSCW 2017, pp. 1576–1590. Association for Computing Machinery (ACM), New York (2017). https://doi.org/10.1145/2998181.2998242
39. Hoyte, S.: Co-designing extreme citizen science projects in Cameroon: biodiversity conservation led by local values and indigenous knowledge. In: Skarlatidou, A., Haklay, M. (eds.) Geographic Citizen Science Design: No One Left Behind. UCL Press, London (2021)

# Interactive Map Visualizations for Supporting Environmental Sustainable Development Goals

Thomas Rist[1] and Masood Masoodian[2](✉)

[1] Faculty of Computer Science, University of Applied Sciences Augsburg, Augsburg, Germany
thomas.rist@hs-augsburg.de

[2] School of Arts, Design and Architecture, Aalto University, Espoo, Finland
masood.masoodian@aalto.fi

**Abstract.** Several of the Sustainable Development Goals (SDGs) of the United Nations have direct or indirect environmental concerns. These SDGs naturally require a greater involvement of ordinary people in achieving their targets. Data visualizations in general, and map visualizations in particular, can play an important role in assisting people to better understand environmental challenges the world is facing, and consequently change their behaviour towards a more sustainable future. In this paper we present a summary overview of the main factors that need to be considered when designing interactive map visualizations in support of these SDGs. We also provide a few examples of the use of interactive maps in web-based information systems, decision support systems, and computer games that focus on environmental issues.

**Keywords:** Sustainable Development Goals · Interactive maps · Map visualizations · Sustainability · Environment · Visualization

## 1 Introduction

The United Nations' 2030 Agenda for Sustainable Development [27] proposes 17 Sustainable Development Goals (SDGs). Several of these SDGs are targeted at the environmental concerns being faced by current and future generations across the globe. These include, for instance, SDGs number *7* ("ensure access to affordable, reliable, sustainable and modern energy for all"), *13* ("take urgent action to combat climate change and its impacts"), *14* ("conserve and sustainably use the oceans, seas and marine resources for sustainable development"), and *15* ("protect, restore and promote sustainable use of terrestrial ecosystems, sustainably manage forests, combat desertification, and halt and reverse land degradation and halt biodiversity loss") [27].


Published by Springer Nature Switzerland AG 2022
C. Ardito et al. (Eds.): INTERACT 2021, LNCS 13198, pp. 36–46, 2022.
https://doi.org/10.1007/978-3-030-98388-8_4

To achieve these types of SDGs within a short span of only a decade, all of us need to change our behaviour towards a more sustainable future. Data visualization tools and techniques are increasingly considered as "critical to driving sustainable change" [20]. Unfortunately however, most visualizations – other than simple graphs and charts – are often designed for experts with extensive knowledge of the data they are visualizing. This approach maybe useful in cases that deal with domain-specific visualizations, in which case their users are expected to have a deep understanding of the relevant data. Achieving environmental SDGs, on the other hand, requires a greater participation of ordinary people in targeting them through the use of available data, which can often be complex and beyond the understanding of non-experts.

In this context, maps [19] and "map-like" visualizations [10] could play an important role in supporting efforts towards achieving sustainability goals. In this paper, we provide an overview of interactive map visualizations that support users in their exploration of visualized data. To investigate the role of such maps in concrete application contexts, we consider three example domains: *web-based information systems* for interested citizens, *decision support systems* for professional users dealing with sustainability-related tasks, and *computer games* with educational value aimed particularly at younger people.

## 2 Map Visualizations

While various types of maps have been in use for centuries[1], the age of modern visualizations in the form of maps and statistical graphs really began around the beginning of the 19th century [5,17]. Maps have since become one of the most widely used forms of visualization. These days some of the best known visualizations – at least amongst visualization experts – are maps, and include, for instance, many of the visualizations designed by Charles Joseph Minard [1781–1870]. As Friday notes [5], many map-based visualization techniques, such as isolines by Edmund Halley [1656–1742] and continuous shading by Baron Charles Dupin [1784–1873], have also been in use for a long time.

The earliest uses of maps with some environmental aspects are perhaps disease maps [15], including the map of cholera epidemic in the Soho district of London in 1845 by John Snow [1813–1858], which showed that most of the deaths occurred in the neighbourhood of a water pump on Broad Street, and this led to the of discovery of the water-borne nature of cholera [5,15].

As mentioned, maps also have the benefit of being perhaps the most commonly used form of visualization by ordinary people – i.e., people who are not visualization or data domain experts. These include, for instance, the use of cartographic maps [16] and other less-cartographic maps such as tourist maps [12], illustrated tourist maps [1] and public transport maps, many of which now follow the example set by the London Underground map designed by Harry Beck [1902–1974] in 1931 [24].

[1] For a brief history of cartography, see for instance [17].

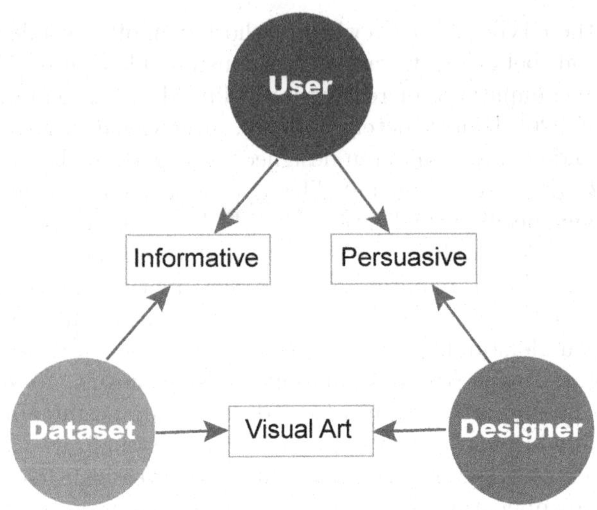


**Fig. 1.** Three categories of visualizations. *Adapted from* [11]

Maps, in their various forms [18], are essentially visualizations which aim to assist their users to better understand the underlying dataset represented in a map form. Therefore, the uses of maps are – as with all other visualizations – for either *exploration* or *explanation* of their datasets. Iliinsky and Steele [11] describe the role of *exploratory* visualizations as that of allowing the user to make sense of the data, while *explanatory* visualizations allow describing – visually – what is already known about the dataset. Static maps are designed primarily for explanation, with some level of support for exploration without interactivity.

Interactive maps, on the other hand, are designed to play a *hybrid* role with elements of both exploration and explanation. According to Iliinsky and Steele [11], such a hybrid visualization "involves a curated dataset that is nonetheless presented with the intention to allow some exploration" on the user's part. In these hybrid – as well as exploratory – interactive visualizations, the designer of the visualization plays an important role in facilitating the user's interaction with the underlying dataset. Figure 1 depicts the relationship between the designer, the user, and the dataset in creating three different categories of visualizations, defined by Iliinsky and Steele [11] as:

- **Informative:** This type of visualization provides "a neutral presentation of the facts" which aims to educate its users, rather than persuading them.
- **Persuasive:** This type of visualization aims to change the minds of its users through "a very specific point of view [of the dataset], and advocates a change of opinion or action" on their part.
- **Visual art:** This type of visualization "entails unidirectional encoding of information", which means that its users may not actually be able to "decode the visual presentation to understand the underlying information".

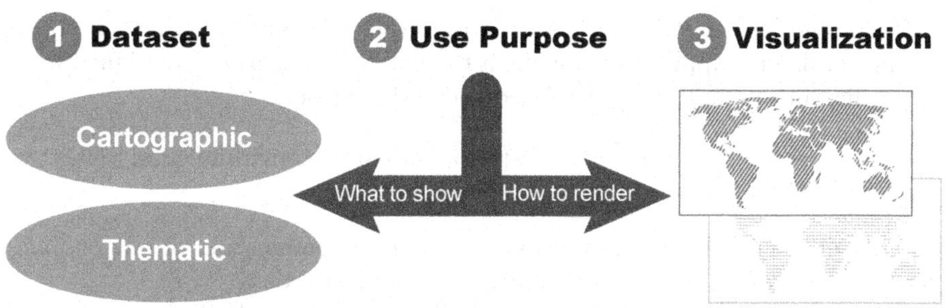


**Fig. 2.** Three factors affecting interactive map visualizations.

In using maps for supporting environmental SDGs, we would argue that while *informative* map visualizations can play an important role in educating ordinary people by providing them with valuable information about the underlying factors affecting different SDGs, it is perhaps the *persuasive* visualizations that have the most crucial role in supporting people in changing their behaviours. It is also important to mention that, as Iliinsky and Steele note, "While an informative visualization may not have an intentional point of view in the manner that a persuasive visualization does, all visualizations are going to be biased to some degree, based on the fact that designers are human and have to make choices." [11]. As for maps in the form of visual art, since these do not necessarily support decoding of their underlying coded datasets, their role in supporting environmental SDGs would generally be limited – except for perhaps raising general environmental awareness amongst people.

It is likely that interactive maps – when designed purposefully and effectively – would have better means of informing and persuading their users in changing their behaviours toward achieving environmental SDGs. Their success however, as shown in Fig. 2, depends largely on three factors:

1. **Dataset:** The underlying map dataset can be divided into two categories: i) *geographic data* (e.g., location, regions, terrains, etc.) and ii) *thematic data* (e.g., population, water usage, air quality, etc.). Most useful interactive maps provide access to one or more datasets from each of these two categories.
2. **Use purpose:** The use purpose of a map determines *what* dataset is needed and *how* that dataset is visualized. Decisions made regarding the purpose of a map largely influence its informative and persuasive values. Traditionally, map designers and domain experts have been making these decisions – which is why, as noted, all maps are subjective [17], and as such, biased to some extent. Increasingly however, automated "intelligent" systems are making such "mapping" decisions.
3. **Visualization:** Depending on the underlying dataset, and the purpose for which a map is designed, the visualization of the map itself can either be

*general-purpose* or *thematic*[2]. A general-purpose visualization may support a range of diverse applications, while a thematic visualization is designed for a specific purpose and using a related thematic dataset.

In the case of using interactive maps for supporting environmental SDGs, we would make the following three general assumptions:

1. **Dataset :** The underlying dataset is usually a combination of one or more sets of geographic data and thematic environmental data.
2. **Use purpose :** The use purpose is largely persuasive and informative, aimed at changing people's attitudes and behaviour.
3. **Visualization :** The visualization is usually thematic, with the possibility of combining or filtering different thematic datasets.

## 3 Interactive Map Visualizations

The term *interactive map* [25] visualization has multiple interpretations. It can refer to a computerized system for graphical map display – for example, as a webmap [26] or a standalone application – which enables the user to change parameters that drive and control map generation and display during its use. Interactivity can also refer to some graphical constituents of a map display, which might be part of a request to retrieve information. In simulation and gaming contexts, on the other hand, interactivity might refer to more complex user interventions aiming at composing or modifying maps.

In general, interactivity augments users' exploratory capabilities far beyond what is possible with static maps. While there is a great variety of interactive map systems, there are always some constraints in terms of which parameters can be manipulated, to what extend, and by which interactive means. In this paper, however, we focus on map interactivity in the context of three different application areas. As noted earlier, these are interactive *web-based information systems*, *decision support systems*, and *computer games*.

### 3.1 Interactive Maps in Web-Based Information Systems

Since sustainable behaviour often requires the user to know where to find the necessary information (e.g., location of compost sites or recycling centres), many communities and public agencies have set up web-based information portals for citizens interested in environmental SDGs. Such portals often use maps for showing useful location information within a geo-spatial reference frame.

Figure 3-a is a typical example of such an information system. It features a schematic base-map showing the topology of a town and provides several menus with check-boxes that allow users to display subject matters of interest.

[2] For a more detailed description of these and other map types, including *special-purpose* maps, see for instance [25,26].

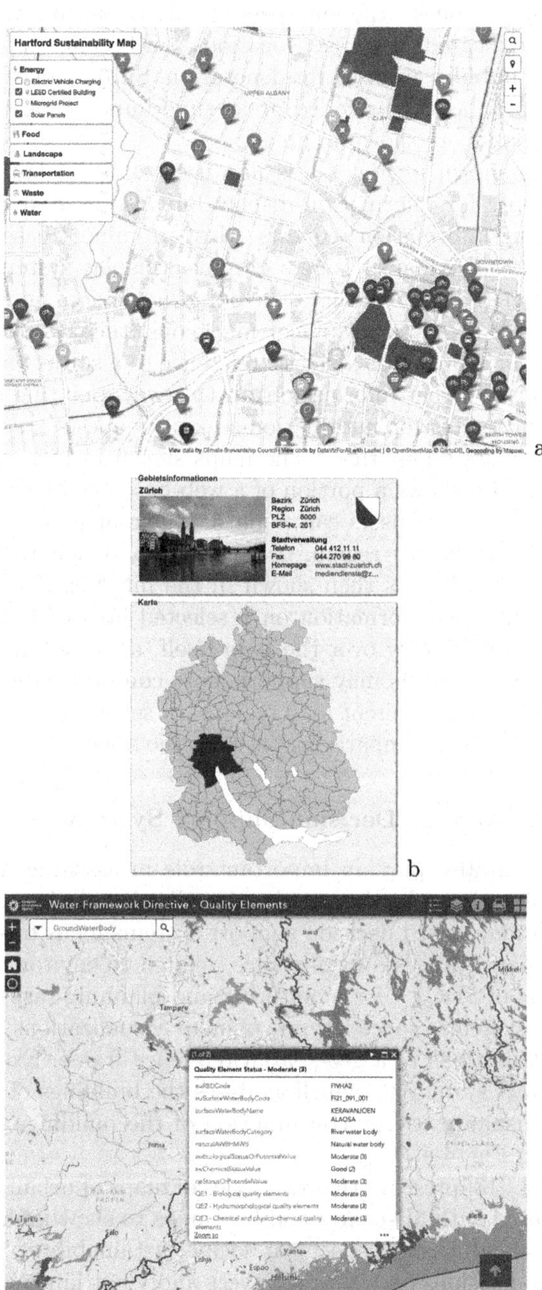


**Fig. 3.** Examples of information systems: a) a map showing locations of interest, b) a clickable map as part of a portal for citizens, and c) a portion of an interactive map for waste treatment. *Images are from* [8,14] , *and* [4] *respectively.*

In response to a user request, the map gets updated, showing where these subjects of interest are located. If subject locations can be pinpointed on the map, icons appearing in bubbles are used for denotation. Subject matters covering an area, however, appear as colour-coded areas superimposed on the base-map – e.g., area such as parks are shown in green.

While the map shown in Fig. 3-a is just used as a display medium, maps can be used not only for information display but also as part of the interface to allow formulating information requests. Most prominent cases of such maps are the so-called *clickable* maps. Using a graphical display system that supports direct manipulation (e.g., by means of a pointing device, or a touch screen) a user can point to displayed graphical map constituents. The target of the pointing is usually interpreted as a deictic reference to a subject about which the user wants to receive further information. In this way, pointing at map objects may be seen as surrogates for information-seeking requests – such as "what is this?" or "tell me more about this". The maps shown in Figs. 3-b and 3-c are of this type. Figure 3-b shows a portion of a web-based community information portal for citizens, in which users can point at different map regions, to either see the name of a particular region, or to select a region to receive further information about it, which is then shown in the info-box above the map. As an alternative, additional information on a selected area or location might be displayed in a pop-up window over the map itself, as shown in Fig. 3-c. More advanced information systems may support more complex interactive *graphical queries*, such as encircling different map regions, or selection of multiple regions, for the purpose of making comparisons between the selected regions.

### 3.2 Interactive Maps in Decision Support Systems

Interactive maps can also play an important role in assisting decision-making at the local neighbourhood level or at the city, district, national or even global levels. Many such map-based decision support systems focus on the integration of heterogeneous data sources – for instance, related to environmental or socio-economical aspects of SDGs – for monitoring and planning tasks.

In most such systems, special types of map visualizations are often used to show data distributions in a geo-spatial reference frame. Examples of these include the *CityBES* system [2], which analyses the buildings of a city and uses colour-coding to visualize energy consumption of the buildings and neighbourhoods, as shown in Fig. 4-a.

Johansson et al. [13] present other examples of maps of urban and rural areas which are augmented with 3D-charts and heatmaps to show information related to social values and different aspects of social sustainability. Such maps can influence political decisions on where to invest and what kinds of developments should be promoted. Another example of these types of maps is provided by Ruche et al. [23], who show land-use indicators on a topological base-map to assess the degree of connectivity of open spaces within an urban area. Yet another example is given by Herman and Řezník [9], who merge 3D terrain maps with localized noise data to visualize noise pollution.

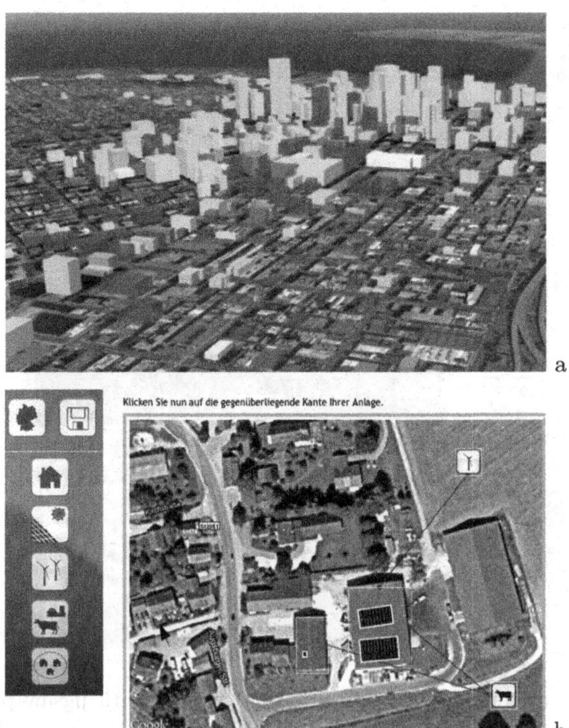


**Fig. 4.** Examples of decision support systems: a) a city map showing the energy use of selected buildings, and b) a web-based simulation tool for placement of renewable energy generators. *Images are from* [2], *and* [21] *respectively.*

Decision support can also be assisted by simulation tools that enable users to explore "what-if?" scenarios. Figure 4-b shows an example of such a system, called the *Micro-Grid* simulator [21]. This tool enables the user to select a portion of a terrain map – using Google map API [7] – on which a potential micro-grid of renewable energy generators can be placed. This placement information, together with a specified time period, are used for estimating potential future energy generation levels – based on real recorded weather data for the specified time period. This allows users to select their own buildings on the map, and use the simulator to evaluate the future pay-off potential of any possible investment in renewable energy generation.

### 3.3 Interactive Maps in Computer Games

Computer games can be used for educating people about environmental sustainability challenges. In such games, interactive maps can, for instance, form the playgrounds on which the players design and manage settlements and infrastructure in a sustainable manner. Among the many variants of such games are

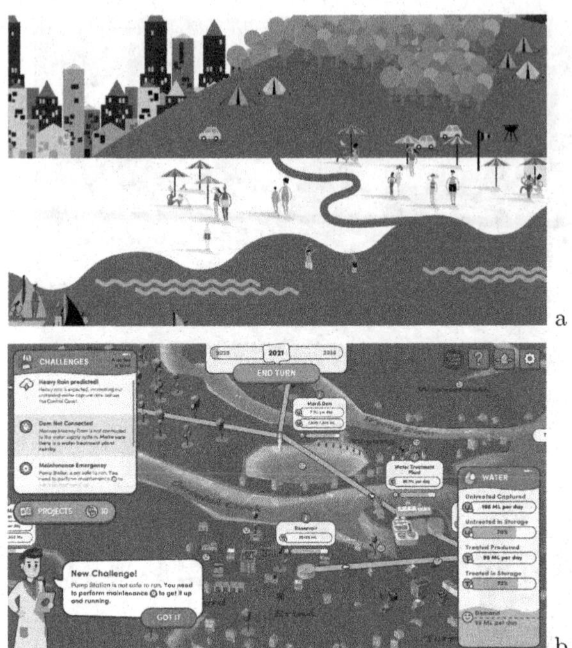


**Fig. 5.** Examples of computer games: a) a virtual map with jigsaw pieces, and b) a map of real-world terrain. *Images are from* [22] , *and* [28] *respectively.*

simple *tile-laying* games, in which the map itself is created by the player using map pieces. An example of this is the mobile game *Once Upon a Tile* [22], which allows the player to construct a virtual world map using matching resource tiles (see Fig. 5-a).

There are also more complex simulation games in which players create and expand different kinds of human settlements, and are subsequently forced to deal with environmental issues such as shortage of resources like energy and water, pollution, and so on. The aim of these types of simulation games is often to find a good balance between preserving the environment and creating economic growth. In these games, the world may be virtual – for instance, settlements evolve on maps of virtual terrain, as was the case in *EnerCities* [3] – or the map can refer to real-world terrain – for instance, in the game *Working With Water* [28], in which the map also serves as a dashboard for the virtual monitoring of water resources (see Fig. 5-b).

Other examples of sustainability-related games, some of which use maps as their basis, can be found on the Games4Sustainability blog [6].

## 4 Conclusions

In this paper, we have investigated the use of interactive map visualizations for supporting the United Nations' SDGs with environmental concerns. We have also presented a few examples of interactive maps that are included in web-based information systems, decision support systems, and computer games for such SDG-related purposes.

Interactive maps can, for instance, be used in web-based information systems to support not only answering information-seeking questions, but also to facilitate formulation of such questions interactively through visual means. In decision support systems, on the other hand, interactive map visualizations can help to link heterogeneous datasets to allow answering complex questions or making future predictions, as well as allowing users to specify simulation parameters. Alternatively, when used as part of computer games, interactive maps can provide high-levels of autonomy and agency which can help players learn through experimentation. They can also help players visualize the impact of their behaviour and see the consequences of their actions on the environment, both within and outside the games they play.

While the examples presented here have highlighted some of the roles that interactive maps can play, there are many other application areas in which interactive maps could be deployed as tools for raising awareness of environmental SDGs amongst their users, and support them in changing their behaviours towards achieving those SDGs.

Finally, it should also be noted that although an increasing number of interactive maps are being designed and used for supporting environmental SDGs, not many of them are in fact ever evaluated. Without such empirical evaluations, however, it remains unclear in which cases interactive maps are effective for purposes for which they are designed and deployed, and what the reasons for their success or failure might be.

## References


1. Airikka, M., Masoodian, M.: A survey of the visual design of cartographic and other elements of illustrated tourist maps. In: Proceedings of the 23rd International Conference in Information Visualization - Part II, pp. 7–13 (2019)
2. CityBES (2021). https://citybes.lbl.gov/. Accessed Dec 2021
3. EnterCities (2010). https://seriousgamessociety.org/2016/09/21/enercities/. Accessed Dec 2021
4. European Environment Agency (2021). https://www.eea.europa.eu/data-and-maps/explore-interactive-maps/water-framework-directive-quality-elements. Accessed Dec 2021
5. Friendly, M.: The golden age of statistical graphics. Stat. Sci. **23**(4), 502–535(2008)
6. Games4Sustainability (2021). https://games4sustainability.org/. Accessed Dec 2021
7. Google: Google map platform (2021). https://developers.google.com/maps. Accessed Dec 2021
8. Hartfort Usability Map (2021). https://hartfordclimate.github.io/climate-stewardship-map/. Accessed Dec 2021
9. Herman, L.S., Řezník, T.S.: 3D web visualization of environmental information - integration of heterogeneous data sources when providing navigation and interaction. Int. Arch. Photogram. Remote Sens. Spatial Inf. Sci. **XL-3/W3**, 479–485 (2015)

10. Hogräfer, M., Heitzler, M., Schulz, H.J.: The state of the art in map-like visualization. Comput. Graph. Forum **39**(3), 647–674 (2020)
11. Iliinsky, N., Steele, J.: Designing Data Visualizations: Representing Informational Relationships. O'Reilly Media, Sebastopol (2011)
12. Jancewicz, K., Borowicz, D.: Tourist maps - definition, types and contents. Polish Cartograph. Rev. **49**(1), 27–41 (2017)
13. Johansson, T., Segerstedt, E., Olofsson, T., Jakobsson, M.: Revealing social values by 3D city visualization in city transformations. Sustainability **8**(2) (2016)
14. Kanton Zürich (2021). https://www.zh.ch/de/politik-staat/gemeinden/gemeindeportraet.html. Accessed December 2021
15. Koch, T.: Disease Maps: Epidemics on the Ground. University of Chicago Press, Chicago (2011)
16. Kraak, M.J., Ormeling, F.: Cartography: Visualization of Spatial Data. 3rd edn. Guilford Press, New York (2011)
17. Lambert, N., Zanin, C.: Practical Handbook of Thematic Cartography: Principles, Methods, and Applications. CRC Press, London (2020)
18. Luz, S., Masoodian, M.: Readability of a background map layer under a semi-transparent foreground layer. In: Proceedings of the 2014 International Working Conference on Advanced Visual Interfaces, AVI 2014, pp. 161–168. Association for Computing Machinery, New York (2014). https://doi.org/10.1145/2598153.2598174
19. MacEachren, A.M.: How Maps Work: Representation, Visualization, and Design. Guilford Press, New York (2004)
20. Metabolic: Why data visualization is critical to driving sustainable change (2019). https://www.metabolic.nl/news/why-data-visualization-is-critical-to-driving-sustainable-change/. Accessed Dec 2021
21. Micro-Grid Simulator (2021). http://it4se.hs-augsburg.de/projectlist.html. Accessed Dec 2021
22. Once Upon a Tile (2021). https://www.wearemuesli.it/out/. Accessed Dec 2021
23. Rusche, K., Reimer, M., Stichmann, R.: Mapping and assessing green infrastructure connectivity in European city regions. Sustainability **11**(6) (2019)
24. Spence, R.: Information Visualization: An Introduction. 3rd edn. Springer, Cham (2014). https://doi.org/10.1007/978-3-319-07341-5
25. Tyner, J.A.: Principles of Map Design. Guilford Press, New York (2014)
26. Tyner, J.A.: The World of Maps: Map Reading and Interpretation for the 21st Century. Guilford Press, New York (2014)
27. United Nations: Sustainable development goals (2021). https://sdgs.un.org/goals. Accessed Dec 2021
28. Working With Water (2021). https://www.chaostheorygames.com/work/working-with-water. Accessed Dec 2021

# An Informatics-Based Approach for Sustainable Management of Factors Affecting the Spread of Infectious Diseases

Saturnino Luz[1] and Masood Masoodian[2](✉)

[1] The Usher Institute, Edinburgh Medical School, University of Edinburgh, Edinburgh, UK
s.luz@ed.ac.uk

[2] School of Arts, Design and Architecture, Aalto University, Espoo, Finland
masood.masoodian@aalto.fi

**Abstract.** Several of the United Nations' Sustainable Development Goals (SDGs) are directly or indirectly concerned with improving health and well-being of the world population. This paper presents an informatics-based approach to the management and monitoring of infectious diseases, in the context of one of these SDGs focusing on the eradication of vector-borne diseases such as malaria, Zika and other neglected tropical diseases. Here we outline the challenges faced by many conventional approaches to ecoepidemiological modelling and proposes a distributed interactive architecture for teamwork coordination, and data integration at different levels of information, and across disciplines. This approach is illustrated by an application to the surveillance of Leishmaniasis, a neglected tropical disease, in remote regions.

**Keywords:** Sustainable Development Goals · Agent-based modelling · Serious games · Mobile games · Game engines · Vector-borne diseases · Tropical neglected diseases

## 1 Introduction

The 17 Sustainable Development Goals (SDGs) of the United Nations [21], set as part of its 2030 Agenda for Sustainable Development, "are an urgent call for action by all countries - developed and developing - in a global partnership" towards achieving "peace and prosperity for people and the planet, now and into the future" [21]. Health and well-being clearly play important roles in this global vision of peace and prosperity. Therefore, it is not surprising that at least one of the 17 SDGs – Goal 3 – is related directly to health and well-being, aiming to "ensure healthy lives and promote well-being for all at all ages" [22]. Indeed,

Both authors contributed equally to this paper, and are listed in alphabetical order.


Published by Springer Nature Switzerland AG 2022
C. Ardito et al. (Eds.): INTERACT 2021, LNCS 13198, pp. 47–57, 2022.
https://doi.org/10.1007/978-3-030-98388-8_5

target 3.3 of this goal aims to "end the epidemics of AIDS, tuberculosis, malaria and neglected tropical diseases and combat hepatitis, water-borne diseases and other communicable diseases" by 2030.

Despite these ambitious future goals, the past decade has actually seen the (re)emergence of several vector-borne diseases [23], including malaria and most neglected tropical diseases [10]. The increased spread of such diseases is frequently associated with increased human mobility [1] and climate change [4,20], which is also related to various environmental factors targeted by several other UN SDGs.

Many neglected tropical diseases are zoonoses, and as such, they spread as a result of the complex interactions and through cycles of transmission between humans and a range of domestic or wild animals [20]. The effectiveness of their related control actions is, therefore, contingent on the availability of consistent, user-friendly and up-to-date epidemiological, environmental and socioeconomic data. However, obtaining and checking the quality of such spatial and temporal data remains challenging, particularly in the case of environmental data, known as Earth Observation [9].

In this paper, we argue that novel approaches to epidemiological surveillance, prevention and control of vector-borne diseases should be considered in order to address these challenges. These approaches should aim to better integrate models of transmission and hitherto fragmented data infrastructures. This paper discusses an informatics-based approach, underpinned by *agent-based modelling* (ABM) methods, which incorporate data gathering and simulations that encompass various *agents* – i.e., vectors, reservoirs, human susceptible populations – and environmental factors, such as micro- and macro-climatic variations, vegetation cover, and sanitation standards under a single platform.

## 2 Challenges of Dealing with Vector-Borne Diseases

As identified by the UN SDG number 3, eradication of vector-borne diseases such as malaria and other neglected tropical diseases is an important step towards global health and well-being. Similarly, in its recent roadmap 2021–2030, the World Health Organization (WHO) also sets global targets for prevention, control, elimination and eradication of neglected tropical diseases by 2030 [26]. Achieving these goals, however, remains a major challenge, as many such diseases are widespread in mostly less-developed parts of the world, with little access to adequate health resources [24].

The Zika crisis of 2017, which affected several developing countries, underscored this challenge. As the crisis unfolded, WHO emphasized the need for new and more efficient instruments to control Zika (re)emergence. Similarly, the Brazilian Association of Collective Health called upon health authorities and funding agencies to provide more support for environmental sanitation and epidemiological surveillance measures that had been neglected in the 2016 Zika emergency [2]. The Zika virus outbreak reached pandemic levels in Latin America and continued to spread in other parts of the world [25]. In these countries, traditional approaches to epidemiological surveillance methods and control strategies based on conventional modelling have long been insufficient to respond to such emergencies.

In Brazil, for instance, although a unified epidemiological surveillance system exists for Zika [18] and other arboviruses, access to up-to-date data is often difficult, with health-planning professionals having to rely on information aggregated at relatively coarse spatial resolutions (e.g., municipal level), and with significant time delays. In addition, relevant vector, climate, geographical and social data usually have to be obtained from separate sources, causing temporal and spatial resolution issues, and highlighting needed multidisciplinary teamwork. These challenges are common to resource-limited countries vulnerable to Zika [3] where, as in the Brazilian case, the available databases are often outdated and fragmented. Low spatial resolution is also a common problem, as is the lack of data on human-induced microgeographic factors influencing potential *Aedes aegypti* breeding habitats [11].

Researchers working with standard models of transmission of Zika and related arboviruses acknowledge that lacking or incomplete knowledge of the *A. aegypti* ecoepidemiology constitutes one of the greatest obstacles to effective surveillance and control actions [7]. In standard mathematical models, transmission dynamics is modelled as a system of ordinary differential equations which describe rates of change in measurable human and entomological population variables, as well as population and behaviour estimates. While these models enable researchers to explore how different epidemiological scenarios might develop under alternative parametrizations through numerical methods, their actual use in context is affected by difficulties in incorporating relevant data, such as their inability to accommodate high spatial resolutions, complex boundary conditions, and temporal constraints. Consequently, data which are currently gathered through geomonitoring, and (increasingly) citizen input and sensor networks, often remain underutilized in epidemiological work.

Novel approaches to epidemiological surveillance and prevention of vector-borne diseases are therefore needed – particularly those which move beyond traditional modelling frameworks [19] and fragmented data infrastructures. Such approaches could also prove relevant for the control of other infectious diseases, as illustrated by the increased interest in alternative methods during the COVID-19 pandemic, including large-scale agent based simulations [17].

## 3 Agent-Based Modelling Approach

Considering these challenges, we advocate an informatics-based approach underpinned by ABM, with support for data gathering, and simulations encompassing vectors, reservoirs, populations and environment under a single paradigm. The ABM approach differs considerably from other conventional approaches based on Differential Equations Modelling (DEM). Table 1 provides a summary comparison of the main characteristics of these two approaches.

Our research group has adopted an ABM approach in South-western Amazonia (see Fig. 1) to coordinate the actions of a multidisciplinary team working on

**Table 1.** A summary comparison of ABM and DEM used for modelling the spread of infectious diseases.

| | ABM | DEM |
|---|---|---|
| Granularity | Individual agent behaviour | System-level properties |
| Modelling units | Sets of rules, algorithms | Sets of differential equations |
| Geographical properties | Modelled as agents | Model only high level properties |
| Complex boundaries | Easily implemented | Non-trivial (e.g., multigrid) |
| Small populations | Easily modelled | Not suitable for small populations |
| Robustness to noise | May be affected by noisy data | Robust to noise |
| Interpretability | Interpretable but transition from local to global patterns often non-trivial | Interpretable at global level |
| Realism | Realistic simulations | Abstract simulations |

vector-borne neglected tropical diseases research. This work focused on American Cutaneous Leishmaniasis (ACL) which, in that region, presents complexities shared by several other vector-borne diseases, including:

- increased human mobility due to new roads linking Brazilian soy-beans producing regions to the Pacific ports of Peru;
- climatic changes in a region under intense land use and land cover changes;
- unplanned urbanization and rural occupation, leading to close coexistence of vectors, domestic and sylvatic animals, and infected and susceptible people;
- poor public and private sector support for appropriate preventative measures, with the consequent reliance on old and toxic drugs to mitigate transmission sources; and
- the unique geographical setting, which combines regional ACL hyperendemicity with increasing population vulnerability to Visceral Leishmaniasis, from the Brazilian North-eastern region towards the West, and Bartonellosis, From the Peruvian Western plateaus towards the East.

In this complex research context, our ABM approach has facilitated three broad lines of action:

1. the use of mobile devices for gathering and sharing of ecoepidemiological data from remote areas by local healthcare personnel [13];
2. health education through the use of "serious games" for improving community-level knowledge of transmission and prevention mechanisms; and
3. the use of spatiotemporal data visualization tools [5] to support the identification of critical points in the chain of transmission [16].

The tools that we have developed as part of these lines of action support a combination of online/offline access and database synchronization to overcome connectivity issues in remote areas [13].

**Fig. 1.** South-western Amazonia, where our multidisciplinary team working on vector-borne neglected tropical diseases has conducted its research.

An ABM describing the relevant environmental (climatic, geographical), entomological (vectors), zoological (reservoirs) and socioeconomic variables provided an infrastructure for incorporation of existing databases, newly gathered data, and expert knowledge, as well as a simulation mechanism for analysis purposes and for the health education application itself. The ABM also supported data validation by highlighting discrepancies between incoming data collected by local personnel and model predictions.

Therefore, in this informatics-based approach, the ABM functioned both as a predictive tool and as a database for integration of surveillance, population and spatiotemporal data. In the case of ACL, for instance, we were able to group municipalities according to statistical similarities – rather than the official grouping based on the river basins of the region – with implications to government policy and interventions. ABMs are better suited to such data-intensive analysis than other frequently used frameworks, even those supporting more detailed biological and environmental information, such as CIMSiM [15].

In the ABM framework, models are built by describing the behaviour of relevant "agents" (representing algorithmic abstractions of humans, vectors, and the environment), gathering data to instantiate their behaviour and characteristics through computer simulation, and exploring different scenarios by tracking system-level properties under varied parameters. These parameters can be set at the agent level – e.g., diversity in behaviours for male and female mosquitoes, in bloodmeal search by females according to lifecycle, in human exposure according to socioeconomic and neighbourhood-specific environmental factors – so that system-level properties emerge from the local interactions among heterogeneous agents. Therefore, modelling individuals along with spatial and temporal constraints becomes straightforward, allowing the incorporation of various data sources [12] and input from different disciplines and stakeholders. Homogeneity assumptions can also be relaxed or eliminated by, for instance, explicit specification of agent contact graphs [6], which can be defined using novel data sources, such as those accessible through the internet or collected using mobile devices.

Although ABMs are bottom-up models, they can incorporate features of top-down *Ross-MacDonald models* [19] through pattern-oriented modelling techniques now commonly employed in ecological research [8]. An overall informatics-based approach can thus be employed to support the work of personnel involved in the different facets of data gathering, in order to supply the model with the required information for use in context. Furthermore, a game-based ABM approach can support data gathering through community participation, with potential for feeding considerable amounts of population and environmental data into large-scale simulations. This could enhance modelling capabilities by interpolation and extrapolation from available data with increasing accuracy as more detailed local information is supplied.

It has been pointed out that agent-based models tend to have a large number of parameters, which could limit their analytic power [8]. However, while simpler models may lend themselves better to macro-level analyses under assumptions of population homogeneity and size, agent-based modelling provides greater realism and specificity, accounting for spatial and populational heterogeneity. In fact, at one extreme (still beyond the reach of current technological capabilities) one could conceive of a maximally realistic ABM as a detailed monitoring system capable of integrating data on households and public areas, and delivering information to epidemiological surveillance personnel in real time. Currently, these systems open up possibilities for gathering data through community participation, with potential for feeding considerable amounts of population and environmental data into large-scale simulations. This would enhance modelling capabilities by interpolation and extrapolation from available data with increasing accuracy as more detailed local information is supplied. In our view, these are characteristics of a promising tool for timely responses to public health emergencies such as the present Zika outbreak.

## 4 Serious Game Simulation

To investigate the feasibility of using and ecoepidemiological ABM as part of a game engine – to be deployed as a unifying mechanism for health promotion and data gathering by local citizens – we developed a module encompassing several variables that influence the spread of infectious vector-borne diseases. Table 2 gives an example of our ABM approach and a typical example of a DEM approach to allow their comparison.

Figure 2 provides an overview of the architecture of the overall game engine, which consists of the BADAGUA ABM simulator [14], a GUI-based game client, and a "gatekeeper" module that keeps track of the users and coordinates their

**Table 2.** Typical examples of ABM and DEM approaches to the modelling of infectious disease spread.

| | **Example** |
|---|---|
| **ABM** | Modelling an individual vector in Badagua/Mason: |

```
public static double DEFattToWater = .3;
public static double DEFattToLeaves = .4;
public static double DEFattToAnimal = .6;
public static double DEFattToSandfly = .7;

[...]
public double attractionToAnimal = 0;

public void step(SimState state) {
  Badagua bagua = (Badagua)state;
    if (age++ > longevity) {
      this.die(bagua);
      return;
    }
    if (this.isFemale()){
      Bag fb = bagua.map.getObjectsAtLocation(location.x, location.y);
      if (fb != null){
        Sandfly sf;
        Animal an;
        for (int i = 0; i < fb.numObjs; i++) {
          if (fb.objs[i] instanceof Sandfly){
            if ( this.isPregnant() )
            continue;
            sf = (Sandfly) fb.objs[i];
            if (sf.isMale()) {
              this.setPregnant(true);
              this.attractionToSandfly = 0;
              this.attractionToLeaves = 0;
              this.attractionToWater = 0;
              this.attractionToAnimal = DEFattToAnimal;
            }
          }
          else if (fb.objs[i] instanceof Animal) {
            an = (Animal) fb.objs[i];
            this.suckBlood(an);
          }
        } // end for
      } // end if fb != null
    } // end if this.isFemale()
    // [etc ...]
```

| | |
|---|---|
| **DEM** | Susceptible-Infective-Recovered (SIR) modelling |

Transmission dynamics modelled as a system of ordinary differential equations which describe rates of change in measurable human and entomological population variables, such as susceptible ($S$), infective ($I$), and recovered ($R$) individuals in a population of size $N$.
Let $S_t$, $I_t$, $R_t$ denote numbers at time $t$, and $s(t) = \frac{S_t}{N}$ etc, s.t. $s(t)+i(t)+r(t) = 1$
For parameters probabilities of transmission ($\beta$) and recovery ($\gamma$) a DEM could be set out as follows:

$$\frac{ds(t)}{dt} = -\beta s(t)i(t) \quad (1)$$

$$\frac{di(t)}{dt} = \beta s(t)i(t) - \gamma i(t) \quad (2)$$

$$\frac{dr(t)}{dt} = \gamma i(t) \quad (3)$$

There is an epidemic $\iff$ "reproductive number" $R_0 = \beta/\gamma > 1$

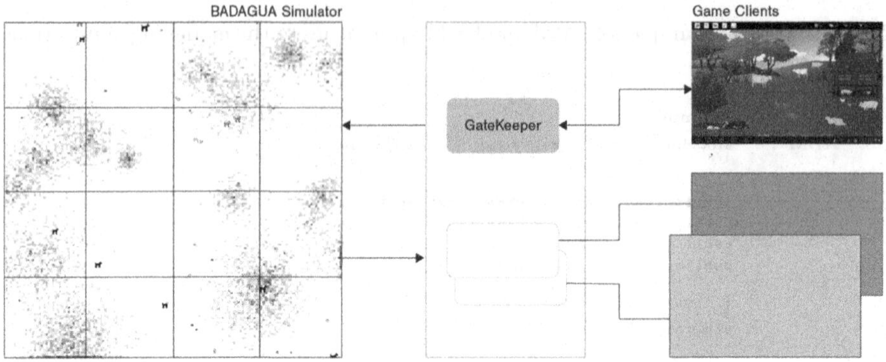


**Fig. 2.** Architecture of the BADAGUA serious game simulation.

access to different regions of the simulation, as well as game-specific tasks. This game setup combines features of two game genres, namely, life simulation and construction and management simulation. The underlying game mechanics leads players to manage virtual environments inhabited by avatars of themselves and, while doing so, receive information about disease prevention, and subsequently act on such information during the game. The simulator represents a physical environment in an area of interest for disease surveillance, consisting of human and animal habitats, and populated by humans, disease vectors and animals. Players can input information pertaining to the actual physical environment, and therefore, update the simulator running on a remote server.

The environment is represented as a sparse 2-dimensional grid where positions can be occupied by different agents – i.e., humans, vectors or animals. Each cell on the grid contains a score which determines the likelihood that an agent will move into that cell. Such scores can be specific to different types of agents. For instance, sand-flies in the Dr Ludens' LSG simulation [14] are attracted to accumulated leaves, water and rubbish, as well as nearby humans and animals. Each of these elements is modelled as an independent feature of the environment on a separate grid. Similarly, regularities in human behaviour can be modelled through superimposed grids with different attractiveness scores.

The simulator uses a discrete event schedule to control the activation of the various agents in the simulation as well as the dynamics of the environment. Disease spread thus emerges as a dynamic process that results from the interactions of several ABM variables, including population features, vector feeding behaviour, geographical distribution, and agent mobility patterns.

In addition to being useful as a health education tool, the game simulation facilitates the integration of ecoepidemiological information into a single platform. Such information could comprise the characteristics of the human, animal (i.e., reservoirs) and vector populations, and of the environment – initially specified by a multidisciplinary team of experts, and subsequently refined and validated as the simulation evolves and local information gets incorporated into the central system database.

## 5 Evaluation

We have conducted a preliminary evaluation of the proposed serious game among healthcare professionals, through questionnaires and interviews [14]. The overall perception was that the integration of a serious game and ABM has the potential to raise awareness of broader ecological issues implicated in the spread of Leishmaniasis and to promote behaviour change among community members. Perhaps not surprisingly, the respondents expressed concern regarding the need to balance the fun elements of the game component against the accuracy levels needed to make the ABM useful as a modelling and policy-informing tool. The study participants also highlighted a potential role for extending the game into a tool for training of health professionals as well.

## 6 Conclusions

In this paper, we outlined an approach to sustainable ecoepidemiological management based on ABM and informatics methods, and illustrated its use through the description of a serious game simulator used in the context of ACL monitoring. We argued that this approach is capable of simplifying the aggregation of the relevant vector, climate, geographical and social data continuously and at scale in a distributed, interactive environment, thus addressing temporal and spatial resolution, and multidisciplinary teamwork challenges involved in the eradication of vector-borne diseases. By doing so, we aim to assist healthcare professionals and local citizens in remote regions to work towards achieving one of the United Nations' SDGs.

## References

1. Aagaard-Hansen, J., Nombela, N., Alvar, J.: Population movement: a key factor in the epidemiology of neglected tropical diseases. Trop. Med. Int. Health **15**(11), 1281–1288 (2010). https://doi.org/10.1111/j.1365-3156.2010.02629.x
2. ABRASCO: Nota técnica sobre microcefalia e doenças vetoriais relacionadas ao aedes aegypti: os perigos das abordagens com larvicidas e nebulizações químicas - fumacê (2016)
3. Bogoch, I.I., et al.: Potential for Zika virus introduction and transmission in resource-limited countries in Africa and the Asia-Pacific region: a modelling study. The Lancet Infect. Dis. **16**(11), 1237–1245 (2016). https://doi.org/10.1016/S1473-3099(16)30270-5
4. Booth, M.: Climate change and the neglected tropical diseases. In: Rollinson, D., Stothard, J. (eds.) Advances in Parasitology, vol. 100, pp. 39–126. Academic Press (2018). Chap. 3. https://doi.org/10.1016/bs.apar.2018.02.001

5. Cesario, M., Jervis, M., Luz, S., Masoodian, M., Rogers, B.: Time-based geographical mapping of communicable diseases. In: Proceedings of the 16th International Conference on Information Visualisation, IV 2012, pp. 118–123. IEEE (2012). https://doi.org/10.1109/IV.2012.30
6. Eubank, S., et al.: Modelling disease outbreaks in realistic urban social networks. Nature **429**(6988), 180–184 (2004). https://doi.org/10.1038/nature02541
7. Fauci, A.S., Morens, D.M.: Zika virus in the Americas - yet another arbovirus threat. New Engl. J. Med. **374**, 601–604 (2016). https://doi.org/10.1056/nejmp1600297
8. Grimm, V., et al.: Pattern-oriented modeling of agent-based complex systems: lessons from ecology. Science **310**(5750), 987–991 (2005). https://doi.org/10.1126/science.1116681
9. Hamm, N.A.S., Magalhães, R.J.S., Clements, A.C.A.: Earth observation, spatial data quality, and neglected tropical diseases. PLoS Neglected Trop. Dis. **9**(12), 1–24 (2015). https://doi.org/10.1371/journal.pntd.0004164
10. Hotez, P.J., et al.: Control of neglected tropical diseases. New Engl. J. Med. **357**(10), 1018–1027 (2007). https://doi.org/10.1056/NEJMra064142
11. Jansen, C.C., Beebe, N.W.: The dengue vector Aedes aegypti: what comes next. Microbes Infect. **12**(4), 272–279 (2010). https://doi.org/10.1016/j.micinf.2009.12.011. Institut Pasteur
12. Karl, S., Halder, N., Kelso, J.K., Ritchie, S.A., Milne, G.J.: A spatial simulation model for dengue virus infection in urban areas. BMC Infect. Dis. **14**(1), 447 (2014). https://doi.org/10.1186/1471-2334-14-447
13. Luz, S., Masoodian, M., Cesario, M.: Disease surveillance and patient care in remote regions: an exploratory study of collaboration among health-care professionals in Amazonia. Behav. Inf. Technol. **34**(6), 548–565 (2015). https://doi.org/10.1080/0144929X.2013.853836
14. Luz, S., Masoodian, M., Cesario, R.R., Cesario, M.: Using a serious game to promote community-based awareness and prevention of neglected tropical diseases. Entertain. Comput. **15**, 43–55 (2016). https://doi.org/10.1016/j.entcom.2015.11.001
15. Magori, K., et al.: Skeeter buster: a stochastic, spatially explicit modeling tool for studying Aedes aegypti population replacement and population suppression strategies. PLoS Neglected Trop. Dis. **3**(9) (2009). https://doi.org/10.1371/journal.pntd.0000508
16. Masoodian, M., Luz, S., Kavenga, D.: Nu-view: a visualization system for collaborative co-located analysis of geospatial disease data. In: Proceedings of the Australasian Computer Science Week Multiconference. ACSW 2016. Association for Computing Machinery, New York (2016). https://doi.org/10.1145/2843043.2843374
17. Rockett, R.J., et al.: Revealing COVID-19 transmission in Australia by SARS-CoV-2 genome sequencing and agent-based modeling. Nat. Med. **26**(9), 1398–1404 (2020). https://doi.org/10.1038/s41591-020-1000-7
18. Secretaria de Vigilância em Saúde: Nota informativa - SVS/MS (2016)
19. Smith, D.L., Battle, K.E., Hay, S.I., Barker, C.M., Scott, T.W., McKenzie, F.E.: Ross, Macdonald, and a theory for the dynamics and control of mosquito-transmitted pathogens. PLoS Pathog. **8**(4) (2012). https://doi.org/10.1371/journal.ppat.1002588
20. Tidman, R., Abela-Ridder, B., de Castañeda, R.R.: The impact of climate change on neglected tropical diseases: a systematic review. Trans. Roy. Soc. Trop. Med. Hyg. **115**(2), 147–168 (2021). https://doi.org/10.1093/trstmh/traa192

21. United Nations: Sustainable Development Goals (2021). https://sdgs.un.org/goals/goal3. Accessed Dec 2021
22. United Nations: Sustainable Development Goals, No. 3 (2021). https://sdgs.un.org/goals/goal3. Accessed Dec 2021
23. Vanjani, R., Hotez, P., Diemert, D.J.: "emerging" neglected tropical diseases. In: Scheld, W.M., Grayson, M.L., Hughes, J.M. (eds.) Emerging Infections 9, pp. 273–285. John Wiley & Sons, Ltd. (2010). Chap. 14. https://doi.org/10.1128/9781555816803.ch14
24. World Health Organisation: Investing to overcome the global impact of neglected tropical diseases: third WHO report on neglected diseases 2015. World Health Organization (2015). https://apps.who.int/iris/handle/10665/152781. Accessed Dec 2021
25. World Health Organisation: Zika virus: an epidemiological update (2017). https://www.who.int/publications/i/item/10665-255010. Accessed Dec 2021
26. World Health Organisation: Ending the neglect to attain the sustainable development goals: a road map for neglected tropical diseases 2021–2030 (2020). https://www.who.int/neglected_diseases/Revised-Draft-NTD-Roadmap-23Apr2020.pdf?ua=1. Accessed Dec 2021

# Internet of Things in Education for Sustainable Development

Lara S. G. Piccolo[1(✉)], Luciano de Oliveira Neris[2], Luana Maria da Silva Menezes[2], and Vânia Neris[2]

[1] Knowledge Media Institute, The Open University, Milton Keynes, UK
lara.piccolo@open.ac.uk

[2] Department of Computing, Federal University of São Carlos, São Carlos, Brazil
{luciano,vania}@dc.ufscar.br, luana.menezes@estudante.ufscar.br

**Abstract.** Education for Sustainable Development (ESD), as stated by UNESCO, should empower learners towards new ways of thinking and acting for a more sustainable and just society for all. However, it is often narrowly interpreted and taught as scientific knowledge about the environment, failing to trigger relevant social changes. In this preliminary study, we visit the computer science literature to analyse some potential roles of technology, more specifically the Internet of Things (IoT), with a human-centred design perspective to be applied in ESD. Through these lenses, we propose some preliminary guidelines to apply IoT-based projects to educate and empower students related to environmental Sustainable Development Goals. We then apply these guidelines to set up an experimental study for students to sense and discuss the impact of ultraviolet (UV) radiation on their health.

**Keywords:** Sustainable Development Goals · Education for Sustainable Development · Internet of Things · Human-centred technology

## 1 Introduction

As a critical enabler for progressing towards the Sustainable Development Goals (SDGs), education is at the centre of the United Nations 2030 Sustainable Development Agenda [28]. For decades, UNESCO has been at the forefront of Education for Sustainable Development (ESD), supporting strategies and articulated actions to address sustainable development in education policies, teachers training and curricula across the world [26].

The current view of ESD encourages changes in knowledge, skills, values and attitudes to enable a more sustainable and just society for all [11]. However, as reported in [26], frequently ESD is still interpreted with a narrow focus, mostly associated with the teaching of scientific knowledge of the environment. This approach is rarely enough to empower learners towards new ways of thinking and acting, thus failing to reveal the real transformative power of education [26].


C. Ardito et al. (Eds.): INTERACT 2021, LNCS 13198, pp. 58–70, 2022.
https://doi.org/10.1007/978-3-030-98388-8_6

In this paper, we discuss some potential roles of user-centred technology, more specifically of Do-It-Yourself (DIY) projects, to empower learners while enabling them to better understand their own contexts regarding specific Sustainable Development Goals, in particular those related to the environment, relying on data as evidence.

Commonly applied in DIY projects, the Internet of Things (IoT) consists of connected objects (*things*) embedded with sensors, software, and other technologies [14]. IoT provides, among other features, 'simple' and affordable alternatives to sense and measure characteristics of the physical world, transforming aspects of the environment that are usually abstract into data, or even further, into a knowledge base. Beyond the most typical applications on environmental monitoring, i.e. measuring characteristics of water, soil or air, smart cities [4,19], healthcare [18], or smart home [22], IoT has also being applied in educational contexts in different ways [14,21].

In the next sections, we first introduce the concept of Education for Sustainable Development as adopted by UNESCO. Then, we present relevant characteristics of IoT, followed by an overview of IoT-based projects related to the environment being used in educational contexts. We then introduce as a preliminary set of guidelines some socio-technical criteria that should be considered when proposing a technology for ESD aiming at boosting learners' transformative power. After that, we put these criteria into practice in a project for sensing ultraviolet radiation.

## 2 Education for Sustainable Development

Beyond addressing key related concepts of Sustainable Develop Goals (SDGs), such as climate change, biodiversity, poverty, among others, ESD also aims at equipping learners with competencies to think and act as informed citizens towards a more sustainable society. As a holistic and transformational education, ESD shifts the focus of education from teaching to learning. It embraces elements such as collaboration, problem-orientation, inter and transdisciplinarity, self-directed learning, as well as the link between formal and informal learning. The ESD framework addresses pedagogy, learning environments, educational content and outcomes [11]. Other concepts intrinsic of ESD relevant to this research are:

**Humanist View.** Although education is typically connected with generating opportunities for economic development and employment of students, as highlighted in [25], for building the knowledge and skills needed for sustainable development, a more humanist vision of education that promotes inclusivity and universal ethical principles towards a common good is essential.

**Competences.** In [16], Rieckmann proposes approaching ESD with a competence perspective aiming at enabling individuals to participate in socio-political processes. Among other key competencies, the author highlights the importance of *problem-solving* to deal with complex sustainability problems, *self-awareness* as the ability to reflect on one's own role in the local community and (global) society; and *critical thinking* as the ability to question and reflect on values, norms, practices and opinions; and take a position in the sustainability discourse. Critical thinking is related to exploring and questioning 'the experts' views' and experimenting with the complexity and contradictions of sustainable living.

**Engaging the Youth.** For [29], typically, young people are not engaged as collaborators in decision making at political and policies levels. To change this, the engagement of young people with ESD and the SDGs has to foster reflexive, socially relevant and contextually situated learning and action, also helping learners to distinguish utopian perspectives from research-backed responsible actions.

For disseminating and boosting ESD worldwide, plentiful resources are currently available to support policy makers, educators or community leaders [27]. Yet, in academic research, contributions to ESD merging computer science and education are still emerging. This transdisciplinary perspective oriented by principles of human-centred design, socially-responsible technology and participatory design involving youth can potentially lead to technology-based educational projects suitable to different learning environments, respecting local and diverse cultures and values, and more effective in empowering learners towards transformations.

## 3 Internet of Things (IoT) for Education for Sustainable Development

### 3.1 IoT Technical Possibilities

The open-source platform Arduino[1] is the most popular for building electronics projects nowadays. First developed in Italy in 2005, it became popular due to its low cost, for running on different platforms (Windows, Mac, Linux), simplicity for programming it, and open-source extendable software and hardware. Arduino consists of both a physical programmable circuit board and an Integrated Development Environment (IDE), a software application for programming based on a simplified version of C++ programming language providing a standard way to perform micro-controller features, such as communicating with sensors and controlling hardware. There are a lot of Arduino clones boards in the market that support development with the Arduino IDE.

Raspberry Pi[2] is another popular platform created specifically for promoting computer science teaching to elementary school students. Until 2020, it was exclusively a Linux small single-board computer that boots up into a full operating system. In January 2021, the Raspberry Pi Foundation introduced the Pico version, a new form of the Raspberry Pi ecosystem which is itself a microcontroller, similar to Arduino.

In Table 1 we compare some characteristics of the two most popular platforms, Arduino and Raspberry, considering their cheapest boards with USB connection, which facilitates the development in practical aspects. There are many Arduino

[1] https://www.arduino.cc/.

[2] https://www.raspberrypi.org/.

boards below US$10.00 but without a USB port. The new Raspberry Pi Pico has better hardware and lower cost, thus it is more suitable to enhance the ESD in developing economies. As it is more popular worldwide, there are more DIY tutorials and projects available online for Arduino. However, with Arduino official support to the new Raspberry Pi RP2040 chip, much of this online material can now be ported to this version of Raspeberry Pi [1].

**Table 1.** Characteristics comparing Arduino and Raspberry Pi Pico

| | Arduino | Raspberry |
|---|---|---|
| Board | NANO EVERY | Pi Pico |
| Microcontroller | Atmel ATmega4809 | Raspberry RP2040 |
| Architecture | AVR RISC 8-bit | ARM Cortex-M0+ 32-bit |
| Speed | 20 MHz | 133 MHz |
| Data memory | 6 KB SRAM, 256B EEPROM | 256 KB SRAM |
| Program memory | 48 KB Flash | 2 MB Flash |
| Communication ports | 8 | 22 |
| Dimensions | 18 × 45 mm | 21 × 51.3 mm |
| Price | US$10,9 | US$4.00 |
| Programming language | C/C++ | C/C++/MicroPython |

There are many sensors compatible with both platforms including: ambient light, motion, temperature, magnetic fields, gravity, humidity, soil moisture, vibration, pressure, electrical fields, current, sound, position, smoke (MQ-2 gas), alcohol (MQ-3 gas), methane (Q-4 gas), toxic gases (MQ-135), ozone (MQ-131 gas), air quality level (PM2.5), flow, PH sensor, turbidity sensor, total dissolved solids, to name a few[3]. The number of available sensors extends the application range to be used in educational context, and the possibilities to match different SDGs, such as SDG 6 for treatment of wastewater or SDG 11 referring to the concentration of PM2.5 in the air.

## 4 Related Research

Aiming to find actual and representative examples in the literature on the topic of Internet of Things for Education for Sustainable Development, we searched for publications from 2016. The following keywords were used: kids, children, education, students, primary school, secondary school, elementary school, high school, low-cost sensors, eco-sensors, electronic sensors, Arduino, Raspberry Pi, IoT, water quality, air quality and environmental health. Searches with different sets of these keywords were made on Google Scholar and ranked in order of relevance.

[3] Examples extracted from https://www.sparkfun.com/categories/23.

From the selected articles in this first search, an iteration of backward snowballing [31] was performed to identify other relevant works. In this section, we present some of these works grouped according to the environmental aspect they address.

**Air Pollution.** Measuring the air quality was the target in [3,4,6]. Dutta et al. [4] investigated sensing air quality indoors and outdoors in an opportunistic approach, while people are on the move. The AirSense platform consists of the Air Quality Data Management (AQDM) circuit, a mobile application and cloud services to put data in a map named AQImap. The use of the solution can be made personal and collective. The authors argue the solution is low cost, low power and low weight to favor mobility.

Fjukstad et al. [6] adopted a citizen science approach with Norwegian students in secondary school (17–18 years old) using Arduino and the Air:bit[4] programmable sensor kit. Researchers offered a two-day workshops to teachers and provided a web application for the students and general public monitor the data collected over a 2 months period. According to the authors, the students enjoyed the interdisciplinary nature of the project and coding was considered the most difficult part.

Chen et al. [3] involved students in a 2-month voluntary monitoring campaign in schools in Las Vegas in the United States. Eight students of an environmental club performed indoor and outdoor measurements with a personal PM2.5 sensor. The initiative revealed the need to reduce both outdoor and indoor PM2.5 sources in the schools, as they can contribute significantly to the schoolchildren's exposure and health risks. According to the authors, low-cost sensors can be seen an opportunity to offer air quality monitoring into many schools by integrating the sensors into science projects with primary and secondary school students.

**Water Quality.** Tziortzioti et al. [24] proposed a set of game-based educational activities for primary and secondary students on aspects related to environmental impact of water usage. The games could be played individually or in teams. The activities involved measuring water temperature, acidity, alkalinity and turbidity observation, among others. The toolkit included Arduino Uno, a mobile application and cloud services. The study revealed issues with the low accuracy of the sensors.

**Energy.** Mylonas et al. [12] explored gamification and competitions to engage with teachers and students in order to perform energy-savings activities. This work uses the GAIA framework which includes and IoT plataform, a web application builder, an app to access data among others systems. The competition themes addressed activities to reduce energy consumption in class and at the school. Thirty educators from more than 20 schools in Greece and Italy observed that the competition approach increased the student's engagement.

**Temperature and Humidity.** Ga et al. [10] have adopted Arduino-based devices to deal with the monopoly in the process of data analysis in the school

[4] https://www.makekit.no/airbit.

environment. According to the authors, particular groups of students can take advantages of their competence with technology and privileged access to data. The authors argue that low-cost boards may optimize measuring methods and stimulate procedures for authentic scientific inquiry, i.e. getting closer to procedures that scientists engage in while conducting research.

## 5 IoT for SDGs Guidelines

Although restricted, this literature reviewed illustrates a range of possibilities for adopting IoT in primary and secondary education as part of citizen science initiatives [3,6,10], extended with game or gamification features [12,24], or as initiatives to measure and analyse their environment as part of sciences education [4]. These researches bring into discussion the adequacy of the IoT platforms and types of sensors, accuracy of the data collected, and some aspects of participants' engagement. However, studies with an educational and/or technology design perspective that also analyses the educational and technical resources for teachers, adequacy to specific age groups, and development of competences expected in ESD are still lacking.

Therefore, from this analysis we suggest a set of four socio-technical aspects to be considered to properly address strategic competences for ESD such as critical thinking, problem-solving and self-awareness, described as follows:

1. **Hardware choice:** Level of technical background and programming skills required; price and affordability in the context; availability of additional hardware resources; availability of supportive resources online.
2. **Relevance of the data collected in the context:** Consider different possibilities to experiment with the data collection within the context, such as trying different situations, locations, times in the day, etc. that could lead to a better understand of actual circumstances and possibilities to change towards SDGs; adequacy of the data visualisation; possibilities to contrast the data collected with other scenarios.
3. **Project design:** Level of complexity or "readiness" of the technical and educational resources provided tailored to age groups and typical skills within the groups; strategies to democratise the hardware development, preventing that only students with more technical skills monopolise the activity.
4. **Engagement:** Strategies to engage the students and their communities (family, friends, neighbourhood, etc.) with the initiative to discuss the impact related to SDGs.

## 6 Exploratory Study

Solar ultraviolet (UV) radiation conditions have been directly impacted by climate change and ozone depletion, thus affecting how people react to UV and eventual the consequences to their health [2].

While a certain level of exposure to UV radiation is essential for vitamin D production and calcium absorption for the formation of teeth and bones, exceeding exposure may reduce immune system activity, increase risks of developing problems including skin cancer and loss of vision. Even in areas where sunlight is abundant, such as in Brazil, vitamin D deficiency is still an issue also for children and adolescents [13]. Constant high temperatures and extreme heat actually may hold children from spending time playing outdoors. Therefore, raising awareness, monitoring and controlling UV exposure can directly benefit children's healthy growing [5,9,23].

### 6.1 UV Radiation

The Sun is the main source of energy on planet Earth and essential for most existing living beings. Created in the Sun's core by the thermonuclear fusion of hydrogen atoms to helium, this energy is transferred to Earth through electromagnetic radiation that travels in the form of waves at the speed of Light [33].

Considering the electromagnetic spectrum, the visible and near infrared regions contain the largest fraction of solar energy. Approximately 46% of solar radiation is concentrated in the near infrared, 46% in the visible (0.4 to 0.7 μm) and on the order of 8% at wavelengths smaller than those of the visible, where the ultra violet radiation is present. UV radiation is classified as UV-A (315–400 nm), UV-B (280–315 nm) and UV-C (200–280 nm). The fractions of solar energy above the atmosphere in the UV-B and UV-A ranges are approximately 1.5% and 7% respectively [5].

Atmospheric gases absorb very little UV-A radiation. Whoever, the oxygen and ozone gases absorb all UV-C radiation and prevent it from reaching the earth's surface. Absorption by ozone increases rapidly with decreasing wavelength in the UV-B range and causes surface radiation to fall off sharply with decreasing wavelength [5,7].

Radiation at progressively shorter wavelengths in the UV range increases energetically and becomes increasingly harmful to most biological species.

Sensing UV radiation is a topic still sparse in the IoT and education related literature. Contextualised in Brazil, this exploratory study targeted the creation of a DIY technology to be part of a lesson plan, therefore, properly communicating with teachers, tutors, parents and guardians with no or little expertise in technology and IoT developments.

As follows, we describe how the four socio-technical criteria proposed in Sect. 5 have influenced the project design technically.

### 6.2 Hardware Choices

The selection of adequate processing modules and UV sensor were driven by their *(low) cost, the availability of open-source developing tools, diversity of related libraries, good manageability and availability in the Brazilian market.*

Two microcontrollers that are supported by Arduino platform, therefore with plenty of resources available and with a large number of modules that incorporate them, were considered adequate in this context: the Atmega328P and RP2040. Among the various options of microcontroller board, two stand out for their low cost and ease of use (Table 2):

**Table 2.** Processing modules fitting the hardware choice criteria

| Board | Microcontroller | Interface | Cost |
|---|---|---|---|
| Raspberry Pi Pico [15] | RP2040A | USB | $4.00 |
| Nano V3.0 [8] | ATmega328P | USB | $6.48 |

Again, the criteria of low cost, related resources and availability were sought in the selection of the device for obtaining UV radiation. Thus, the UVM-30A and SI1145 UV sensor modules are the modules used in the initial experiment. The UVM-30A sensor offers only the amount of UV radiation obtained in the range of 200 to 370 nm in wavelength. This information is made available analogically by varying the voltage from 0 to 1 V on the module's output pin. This voltage must be digitized by the processing module and converted into the UV light index obtained [30]. In contrast, the SI1145 sensor is a digital sensor capable of providing, through an I2C communication port, the amount of ambient light, the UV radiation index and the indication of proximity to an object [20]. The technical characteristics of the selected UV sensors (UV UVM-30A) e (SI1145) are summarised in Table 3.

**Table 3.** UV sensors

| Modules | Output | Interface |
|---|---|---|
| UVM-30A | UV (200–370 nm) | Analogic (DC 0–1 V) |
| SI1145 | Infrared<br>UV index<br>Ambient light | Digital (I2C) |

Two ways of building the user interface were adopted in the initial experiment: using light-emitting diodes (LEDs), which allow the construction of simplified output interfaces for presenting data to the user; and through Node-RED, a visual tool that considerably lower the complexity of programming hardware [17]. Node-RED provides a browser-based flow editor that makes it easy to wire together flows using the wide range of nodes in the palette. It is a model that lends itself very well to a visual representation and makes it more accessible to a wider range of users. Originally developed by IBM's Emerging Technology Services team, Node-RED now is an open source tool part of the OpenJS Foundation [17].

Three construction options were considered allowing teachers and students to play around different the interpretation of the data collected:

1. **Absence or presence:** the use of a single LED makes it possible to indicate when a value or magnitude obtained reaches a previously defined threshold. Thus, it is possible to demonstrate to the child how to build a simple alarm when UV radiation is too high.
2. **Safe, beware, critical:** three LEDs allow you to build a signaling interface similar to a traffic light. Thus, it is possible to demonstrate to the child ways to experiment with different levels of radiation, classify data and the construction of state signaling devices.
3. **Range:** it is possible to display the amount of a magnitude in a previously defined range using a set of LEDs. The LEDs can be arranged sequentially forming a bar to indicate the amount of magnitude obtained.

Using the Node-RED tool, it is possible to build artifacts similar to the LED-based ones and using gauges, bars and other graphic elements provided.

### 6.3 Relevance of the Data Collected in the Context

The Ultraviolet Radiation Index (UVI) was introduced in Canada in 1992 and adopted internationally in response to growing concerns about the potential increase of UV radiation due to climate change and ozone reduction. The main goal was raise awareness and encourage the public to protect their skin from skin cancer. The UVI is also used in studies that investigate the impact of UV on other biological and photochemical processes [5,7].

The Table 4 describes UVI and respective recommended level of protection to mitigate the effects of prolonged exposure to UV radiation.

**Table 4.** UV radiation index [32]

| Index | Level | Protection |
|---|---|---|
| <2 | Low | No protection |
| 3 a 5 | Moderate | Some protection |
| 6 a 7 | High | Protection essential |
| 8 a 10 | Very high | Extra protection |
| >11 | Extreme | Stay inside |

Teachers and students can ground discussions on safe levels of UVI, and experiment with data throughout the school settings and different times in day to investigate where, when and for how long the students could have a beneficial exposure to UV.

### 6.4 Project Design

This project execution encompasses reading the data provided by the sensors and its presentation in the user interfaces. To this end, the most complex steps related to reading and presenting data in the two possible interfaces were encapsulated in C++ classes.

Encapsulation allows instructors with little computational knowledge to instruct children to build reading and data presentation software. The classes and methods created in the Arduino Integrated Development Environment for the proposed experiment are described in Table 5.

**Table 5.** C++ classes and methods

| Class | Method | Description |
|---|---|---|
| Sensor_UVM30A | Sensor_UVM30A(int pin)<br>measure_UVindex() | Constructor: pin assignment<br>Get UVI from UVM30 sensor |
| Sensor_SI1145 | Sensor_SI1145()<br>begin()<br>measure_UVindex()<br>measure_visible_light()<br>measure_infrared() | Constructor<br>Initialize I2C interface<br>Get UVI from SI1145 sensor<br>Get light value from SI1145 sensor<br>Get IR value from SI1145 sensor |
| LedBar | LedBar(int led_pins[], int n)<br>init()<br>show(int uv_index_value)<br>off_all()<br>on_until(int until) | Constructor<br>Pin assigment<br>Show UVI in LED bar<br>Tun off all LEDs<br>Turn on a number of LEDs |

An important step in creating interfaces using Node-RED is sending the collected data through a serial communication port connected to a PC. The received data is then extracted by a decoding node as illustrated in Fig. 1.

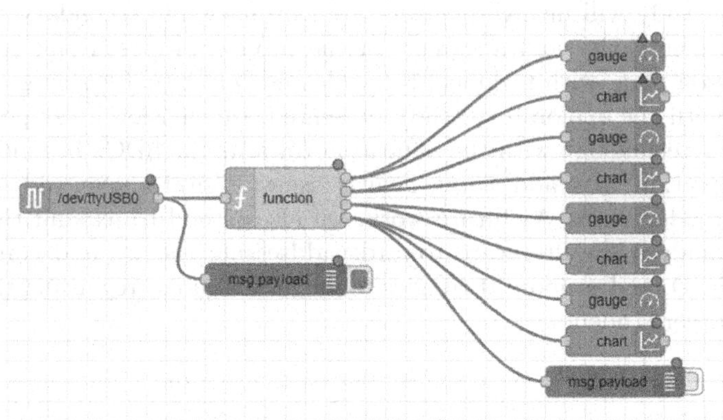


**Fig. 1.** Node_RED flow.

Thus, as in the software implementation of data reading in the collection hardware, the construction of the decoding node can be built together with the students or simply inserted from a model depending on their technological domain or age.

### 6.5 Engagement

As part of a lesson plan, teachers are invited to explore "That in my world" with the students, discussing the relationship of computational knowledge in the construction of the proposed artifacts with the data obtained and the child's world, seeking to present current problems and solutions to achieve a more sustainable development. Thus, an analogy of the contents presented to children with real situations in the world in which they live is presented.

They can discuss together levels of vitamin D deficiency in their area and contrast it with other ares in the planet (*self-awareness*), how they could change their habits to benefit from sunlight exposure (*critical thinking*), main technical challenges and limitations of the project (*problem solving*) and the need and strategies to raise awareness of parents and guardians to the benefits and risks of extreme sunlight exposure (*empowerment*).

## 7 Conclusion and Future Work

In this paper, we reviewed the literature on IoT projects within educational contexts through the lenses of human-centred technology and Education for Sustainable Development Goals. This preliminary analysis led to an initial set of guidelines for choosing the right hardware platform, analysing the adequacy of the data collected to the context, and for designing strategies to engage students and to democratise the hardware development. These guidelines were exemplified as criteria to define a project on sensing UV radiation. Next step in this exploratory study will involve teachers from primary and secondary schools to discuss the complexity and adequacy of the project proposed and co-create a detailed lesson plan, with technical tutorials and contextual learning activities.

In line with the exploratory study presented, we envision great potential to connect DIY technology with the education towards the SDGs beyond environmental protection, also addressing health issues, digital access and social justice in a broader sense. As future work, we also intend to expand this review to deeper analyse the literature towards addressing themes and competences related to ESD, and propose strategies to evaluate studies regarding the potential to empower students.

## References

1. Arduino: Arduino Mbed core for RP2040 boards (2021). https://blog.arduino.cc/2021/04/27/arduino-mbed-core-for-rp2040-boards/. Accessed 12 May 2021
2. Barnes, P.W., et al.: Ozone depletion, ultraviolet radiation, climate change and prospects for a sustainable future. Nat. Sustain. **2**(7), 569–579 (2019)

3. Chen, L.-W.A., Olawepo, J.O., Bonanno, F., Gebreselassie, A., Zhang, M.: Schoolchildren's exposure to $PM_{2.5}$: a student club–based air quality monitoring campaign using low-cost sensors. Air Qual. Atmos. Health **13**(5), 543–551 (2020). https://doi.org/10.1007/s11869-020-00815-9
4. Dutta, J., Chowdhury, C., Roy, S., Middya, A.I., Gazi, F.: Towards smart city: sensing air quality in city based on opportunistic crowd-sensing. In: Proceedings of the 18th International Conference on Distributed Computing and Networking, pp. 1–6 (2017)
5. Fioletov, V., Kerr, J., Fergusson, A.: The UV index: definition, distribution and factors affecting it. Can. J. Public Health. Revue canadienne de santé publique **101**, I5–19 (2010). https://doi.org/10.1016/j.atmosres.2012.01.005
6. Fjukstad, B., et al.: Low-cost programmable air quality sensor kits in science education. In: Proceedings of the 49th ACM Technical Symposium on Computer Science Education, SIGCSE 2018, pp. 227–232. Association for Computing Machinery, New York (2018). https://doi.org/10.1145/3159450.3159569
7. Heckman, C., Liang, K., Riley, M.: Awareness, understanding, use, and impact of the UV index: a systematic review of over two decades of international research. Prev. Med. **123**, 71–83 (2019). https://doi.org/10.1016/j.ypmed.2019.03.004
8. HK Shan Hai Group Limited: Nano v3.0 (2020). Original document from HK Shan Hai Group Limited. https://shorturl.at/huQTU
9. Holick, M.F.: Sunlight, ultraviolet radiation, vitamin D and skin cancer. In: Sunlight, Vitamin D and Skin Cancer, pp. 1–16. Springer, New York (2014). https://doi.org/10.1007/978-1-4939-0437-2_1
10. Hyun, S., Cha, H., Kim, J.: Adapting Internet of Things to Arduino-based devices for low-cost remote sensing in school science learning environments. Int. J. Online Biomed. Eng. **17**(2), 4–18 (2021)
11. Leicht, A., Heiss, J., Byun, W.J.: Issues and Trends in Education for Sustainable Development. UNESCO (2018)
12. Mylonas, G., Paganelli, F., Cuffaro, G., Nesi, I., Karantzis, D.: Using gamification and IoT-based educational tools towards energy savings - some experiences from two schools in Italy and Greece. J. Ambient Intell. Humaniz. Comput. (5), 1–20 (2021). https://doi.org/10.1007/s12652-020-02838-7
13. Peters, B.S.E., Dos Santos, L.C., Fisberg, M., Wood, R.J., Martini, L.A.: Prevalence of vitamin D insufficiency in Brazilian adolescents. Ann. Nutr. Metab. **54**(1), 15–21 (2009)
14. Ramlowat, D.D., Pattanayak, B.K.: Exploring the Internet of Things (IoT) in education: a review. In: Satapathy, S.C., Bhateja, V., Somanah, R., Yang, X.-S., Senkerik, R. (eds.) Information Systems Design and Intelligent Applications. AISC, vol. 863, pp. 245–255. Springer, Singapore (2019). https://doi.org/10.1007/978-981-13-3338-5_23
15. Raspberry Pi (Trading): Raspberry Pi Pico datasheet (2021). Original document from Raspberry Pi (Trading) Ltd. https://datasheets.raspberrypi.com/pico/pico-datasheet.pdf
16. Rieckmann, M.: Learning to transform the world: key competencies in education for sustainable development. Issues Trends Educ. Sustain. Dev. **39**, 39–59 (2018)
17. Rodger, L.: Node red programming guide. Node-RED: lecture (2016)
18. Selvaraj, S., Sundaravaradhan, S.: Challenges and opportunities in IoT healthcare systems: a systematic review. SN Appl. Sci. **2**(1), 1–8 (2020). https://doi.org/10.1007/s42452-019-1925-y

19. Shah, J., Mishra, B.: IoT enabled environmental monitoring system for smart cities. In: 2016 International Conference on Internet of Things and Applications (IOTA), pp. 383–388. IEEE (2016)
20. Silicon Laboratories Inc.: Si1145/46/47 (2020). Original document from Silicon Laboratories Inc. https://www.silabs.com/documents/public/data-sheets/Si1145-46-47.pdf
21. Silva, M.J., Lopes, J.B., Silva, A.A.: Using senses and sensors in the environment to develop abstract thinking-a theoretical and instrumental framework. Probl. Educ. 21st Century **53**, 99 (2013)
22. Stojkoska, B.L.R., Trivodaliev, K.V.: A review of Internet of Things for smart home: challenges and solutions. J. Clean. Prod. **140**, 1454–1464 (2017)
23. Turner, J., Igoe, D., Parisi, A.V., McGonigle, A.J., Amar, A., Wainwright, L.: A review on the ability of smartphones to detect ultraviolet (UV) radiation and their potential to be used in UV research and for public education purposes. Sci. Total Environ. **706**, 135873 (2020)
24. Tziortzioti, C., Andreetti, G., Rodinò, L., Mavrommati, I., Vitaletti, A., Chatzigiannakis, I.: Raising awareness for water polution based on game activities using Internet of Things. In: Kameas, A., Stathis, K. (eds.) AmI 2018. LNCS, vol. 11249, pp. 171–187. Springer, Cham (2018). https://doi.org/10.1007/978-3-030-03062-9_14
25. UNESCO: rethinking education: towards a global common good? (2015)
26. UNESCO: education for sustainable development: a roadmap. UNESCO (2020)
27. United Nations: education for sustainable development for 2030 toolbox (2021). https://en.unesco.org/themes/education-sustainable-development/toolbox. Accessed 10 June 2021
28. United Nations: the sustainable development agenda (2021). https://www.un.org/sustainabledevelopment/development-agenda/. Accessed 10 June 2021
29. Vallabh, P.: Youth on the move: intentions and tensions. In: Issues and Trends in Education for Sustainable Development 39 (2018)
30. Wiltronics: UV detection sensor (2021). Original document from Wiltronics Research Pty. Ltd. https://www.wiltronics.com.au/wp-content/uploads/datasheets/ARD2-2062.pdf
31. Wohlin, C.: Guidelines for snowballing in systematic literature studies and a replication in software engineering. In: ACM International Conference Proceeding Series, May 2014. https://doi.org/10.1145/2601248.2601268
32. World Health Organization: global solar UV index: a practical guide (2002)
33. Yung, Y.L.: An introduction to atmospheric radiation. Q. J. Roy. Meteorol. Soc. **129**(590), 1741–1741 (2003). https://doi.org/10.1256/003590003102695746. By K. N. Liou. Academic Press. Second edition, 2002. pp. xiv+583. ISBN: 0 12 451451 0

# Guidelines for the Sustainable Development of Computing Technology

Renata O. Rodrigues[1], Kamila Rios H. Rodrigues[2], and Vânia Paula A. Neris[1](✉)

[1] Department of Computing, Federal University of São Carlos, São Carlos, Brazil
vania@dc.ufscar.br

[2] Institute of Mathematics and Computer Sciences, University of São Paulo, São Carlos, Brazil
kamila.rios@icmc.usp.br

**Abstract.** When referring to sustainability, the expression must be understood in terms of environmental, social and economic factors, with an emphasis on the breadth of its scope. Computational solutions involve consumer goods and hence it should be responsibility of the software and hardware industry, (as well as its designers and developers), to ensure that there is an awareness of the need for sustainability. The literature includes several works that address the question of sustainable design. However, there are few studies that deal with sustainability in terms of design and its Computing technology is still in its early stages. In light of this, this paper has formalized a set of recommendations to guide the designers in the creation of computational solutions, and thus allow the sustainability factors in design to be considered. The guidelines were applied in an academic scenario and three specialists evaluated the solutions made with and without them. The results suggest that the guidelines supported the sustainable development of Computing technologies.

**Keywords:** Design for sustainability · Design sustainability · Sustainable computing · Guidelines

## 1 Introduction

Through Computing it is possible to include concepts of sustainability in people's lives, as pointed out by Spangenberg [14], as well as in the outside world, so that it is everyone's duty to assist in this task.

The increasingly available technology also raises concerns about how people use it and how its data can be generated. With this in mind, sustainability forms an integral part of the context of computational technology, which requires the production, use and correct disposal of computational solutions.

Baranauskas, Souza and Pereira [2] have drawn up a list of challenges in the research field of Human-Computer Interaction in Brazil. Challenge 1 draws attention to the consumer practices of the modern world and how we need to rethink what they involve and the design of interactive goods and services based


Published by Springer Nature Switzerland AG 2022
C. Ardito et al. (Eds.): INTERACT 2021, LNCS 13198, pp. 71–82, 2022.
https://doi.org/10.1007/978-3-030-98388-8_7

on new technological solutions that foster sustainability for both individuals and society. It is necessary to include renewal, reuse and disposal strategies for both hardware and software, as requirements of a sustainable design awareness, as per Neris, Rodrigues and Silva [1].

The area of technology generally has a direct influence on people's behavior, owing to its pervasive presence in modern society and, for this reason; it should be used as a facilitator of sustainable practices that are vital for ensuring the continuity of the world. This factor characterizes design for sustainability, which as already been discussed, (albeit in a tentative way), in the literature by Blevis et al. [5] and also by Neris, Rodrigues and Silva [1].

The other factor, which is the focal point of this work, underlines the value of sustainability in design, which encompasses environmental, economic and social issues in the creative process. It is worth reflecting on how designers and developers can merge sustainability with their creative skills, with the aim of establishing social equality, equity, environmental conservation and an equitable distribution of income.

In this work, we describe the procedure of formalizing a set of recommendations to guide designers in the sustainable development of Computing technology.

## 2 Sustainable Development

The idea of sustainable development originated with environmental movements a few decades ago. It has undergone a number of transformations since then, and become a broader concept that in addition to encompassing environmental, climate, clean energy and resource consumption patterns, also covers public health, social inclusion and poverty [13].

The United Nations (UN) report entitled "Transforming Our World: 2030 Agenda for Sustainable Development", addresses the objectives of sustainable development, by setting out a road map for the sustainable development of countries and lists 17 sustainability goals for those involved in this undertaking. These objectives include action plans for the next years in crucial areas, such as: people, the well-being of the world, prosperity, peace and partnership [11].

ICTs (Information and Communication Technologies) have come to be seen as engines of development both globally and regionally, which seek to reduce social and economic inequalities while, at the same time providing guidance on the correct way of obtaining benefits, without causing harm to other areas [12]. Gartner's report [10], on ICTs, states that their effect on sustainable development can be divided into 3 orders. The first order concerns the immediate impacts they can have on computational solutions, that is, the direct result of an existing situation. For example, the emission of air pollutants caused by computer solutions, or equipment that is not energy-efficient and the disposal of electronic waste after it is obsolescent. Second-order impacts include the indirect use of computational solutions, that is, they are caused by the use of ICTs, such as the holding of meetings by video link, transport load optimization, operational logistics and data center asset management. All of these processes have an indirect impact on solutions [12]. Third-order impacts occur as a result of the use of ICTs. For example, the reliance on ICT employees in the workplace, turning off monitors when they are not using the computer, turning off the lights and printing only what is necessary [13]. It takes a long time and a change in habits on the part of people who use ICTs, to implement these changes.

## 3 Related Works

Burnell [6] defends the incorporation of sustainability in the design of products and commercial artifacts, and examines the sustainability tripod model, according to the environmental, social and economic factors involved in the construction of the products. He handles sustainability in an integrative way, although he states that sometimes it becomes a utopian concept, because of the divergent opinions on the subject.

The author compares this design process with the one described by Waage [15], who also focuses on general design, that is, the design of any type of solution. The author believes that the design phase is the key feature when introducing the concept of sustainability, since decisions made in this phase determine 70% (seventy percent) of the costs that will be involved in product development.

In the opinion of Blevis [4], sustainability is both an ethical and practical issue, and this should be reflected in the design, so that it really corresponds to the author's values. He also discusses other perspectives such as the role of design in product innovation, economic growth and experience, and the aesthetic appeal of the design, but believes that these design perspectives are not exclusive and can coexist with the view that sustainability is fundamental to design.

The design put forward by Mann et al. [9], is regenerative, like that of Blevis [3]; this author has a theory centered on sustainable design that is linked to the environment, and establishes limits in favor of a prosperous future development. The authors believe that the relationship between Computing and regenerative design is difficult to understand, although they are closely linked. The view that there are viable alternatives to design as it is currently carried out, leads to regenerative sustainability.

The new regenerative design is concerned with looking at nature and the ecological system as a means of understanding the interaction between computing, society and biological systems [9]. The authors mention that this relationship must be based on the following features: inclusiveness, harmony, respect, integrity, mutuality, brotherhood, positive reciprocity, responsibility and humility.

## 4 A Methodological Approach

After conducting an analysis of the data presented in the literature, we carried out exploratory research into other areas that already have clear guidelines for testing sustainability, such as civil engineering. Thus, in the light of these techniques, it was possible to set out a list of recommendations for designers of the area of Computing. A rigorous search was also carried out in two databases, which were considered to be relevant to the area of Computing. After the application of the search string, and the inclusion and exclusion criteria, ten works were chosen that were returned from the mapping.

Following this, the opinions of the computing community on the subject were analyzed.

## 4.1 Survey with Computing Community

An online survey was carried out to find out the views of different people about sustainability and Computing.

The survey was answered by 128 people, including students, teachers and other professionals in the field of Computing. The preliminary analysis suggests the need to clarify and reflect more deeply on the aspects that make up the sustainability tripod. In particular, it emphasizes the role of the Brazilian Human Computer Interaction (HCI) community in the subject, particularly in the aspects of accessibility.

As for the profile of the survey respondents, the age range ranged between 20 and 66 years, with an average of 35, and 64% are male. Respondents' background was diversified.

The results suggest that the concern with the environment and the correct disposal of waste, when it comes to sustainability, is still what comes to the minds of respondents in the Brazilian Computing community. The fact that accessibility was not considered relevant to sustainability by half of the respondents reinforces the need for in-depth studies on the subject, which show that the exclusion of minorities does not contribute to a fairer, more egalitarian society that seeks to guarantee a future best everyone.

## 4.2 Affinity Diagram

The affinities diagram helps in the process of clarifying the dimension and extent of problems and grouping ideas and opinions on subjects that have similarities, that is, affinities with each other.

An affinity diagram was also used to illustrate the concept of sustainability in Computing. This diagram is used in complex situations that are not yet well defined and, helps to group ideas by finding similarities between them.

The profile of the participants was composed of students, who were masters and PhD students in the field of Computing in the Human Computer Interaction research line. The problem question to be solved in the affinity diagram was: What should the designer consider in building a sustainable solution?

The questions considered by the participants around sustainability in the area of computing were extracted from survey. They guided the related areas in which the affinity diagram was divided, the most similar ideas, or that could be considered part of a large area, were grouped and quantified.

The affinities were grouped by the areas of production, documentation, reuse, ecological, social and human, financial and aspects that were not considered.

Through the diagram of affinity it is understood that when we speak of sustainability the largest remembrance that people cling is still in the hardware of solutions. It is a minority that only considers the software as an integral part of the sustainable question.

## 5 Guidelines for Sustainable Computing Technology

By combining these studies, the literature, the survey of the Computing community and the affinity diagram, a set of guidelines could be created that cover the various stages of the design process. The result was that recommendations were made for computational solutions that could be created in a more sustainable way.

The guidelines were related to stages in the design process of Computing solutions, as these are not isolated. They were also related to the professionals involved in each stage of the design process.

As a result, it was found that 25 (twenty-five) guidelines in which the **phase of the design process** was observed, could be used: these included the categories *Analyze, Design, Prototyping and Implementation*, and also defined the possible professional who would be responsible for that particular guideline. There follows a description of how the roles of the professionals in the study were chosen.

**Responsibilities:** *Executive Board*: responsible for the company and employees, as well as making decisions about producing new goods and services, and handling financial matters; *Developer*: responsible for back-end solutions, and for making the software applications work; *Architect*: responsible for the hardware design of the solutions; *Designer*: responsible for the visual appearance, form and philosophy of the solution, whether it be hardware or software; *Analyst*: responsible for analyzing the scenarios and the link between the client and the company.

It was also decided to use different forms of relationship (**levels**) with the solution: *a direct relationship with the product* or *process and an indirect relationship or external factors.*

The **guidelines** follow: 1) choosing materials that are suitable for finding computational solutions; 2) adopting fair wage policies that are compatible with the IT market; 3) fostering an awareness of the relationship between suppliers and service providers of technology companies; 4) Improving the relationship between technology companies and the government; 5) reducing incidents that involve civic responsibilities; 6) Optimizing consumption, and the reuse of water; 7) Improving cost control techniques, and having fair operating practices; 8) Creating solutions with good usability principles; 9) Adopting participatory design techniques; 10) Creating an accessible interface; 11) an equitable use of resources; 12) An use simple and intuitive of the interfaces, with easily available information; 13) Requiring a limited physical effort; 14) Creating scalable solutions (both hardware and software); 15) Reducing gas emissions in the atmosphere; 16) Involving the surrounding community, by forming close relationships and exchanging knowledge; 17) Making the features of sustainability publicly available through documentation and including them in the solution; 18) Flexibility of use; 19) Support for future releases and compatibility; 20) Encouraging ethical practices and respect for human and minority rights; 21) Prioritizing regional labor and culture; 22) The design of the solutions must clearly show their usefulness and include error tolerance; 23) Obtaining and correctly disposing of the computational solution, whether it be hardware or software; 24) Gender equality and; 25) The use of clean energy resources.

In the resulting set of guidelines there is also a brief explanation of how they could be used and what could be addressed by each guideline in question. Finally, mention is made of the reference used in deciding how to plan and draw up the guidelines.

Tables 1, 2, 3, 4 and 5 illustrate details on the guidelines.

**Table 1.** Guidelines for the design of computational solutions for sustainability awareness.

| | Phases of design process | Personnel responsible | Level | Guidelines | Subsidiary guidelines | Reference |
|---|---|---|---|---|---|---|
| 1 | Analysis | Designer<br>Architect<br>Board<br>Analyst | 1 | 1 | 1.1 Choosing suitable materials that take into account the time and amount of the material that has to be reused, after the product or process has reached the end of its usefulness<br>1.2 Prioritizing the use of materials with productive cycles in accordance with the principles of sustainability.<br>1.3 Prioritizing materials that are easily absorbed from [OR in ?] the environment at the end of their useful life | Computational<br>ISO 14004<br>Survey applied to the community |
| 2 | Analysis | Board | 2 | 2 | 2.1 Designing a job and salary structure based on principles of meritocracy<br>2.2 Setting up a wage subsidy scheme compatible with the job market in the region and size of the company | Affinity Diagram |
| 3 | Analysis | Board<br>Analyst<br>Architect | 2 | 3 | 3.1 Prioritizing consumer goods from companies that respect the environment and its operations.<br>3.2 Prioritizing the workforce of a company that has social and fiscal responsibilities<br>3.3 Attempting to establish a close relationship with these companies and thus be in a position to suggest improvements in their processes so that they can become more sustainable | ISO 14004 |
| 4 | Analysis | Board<br>Analyst<br>Designer<br>Programmer<br>Architect | 2 | 4 | 4.1 Complying with legislation applicable to the business sector<br>4.2 Being innocent of tax evasion<br>4.3 Finding solutions that do not leave loopholes for corruption | ISO 14004 |

**Table 2.** Guidelines for the design of computational solutions for sustainability awareness.

| | Phases of design process | Personnel responsible | Level | Guidelines | Subsidiary guidelines | Reference |
|---|---|---|---|---|---|---|
| 5 | Analysis of Design prototyping Implementation | Board Analyst Designer Programmer Architect | 2 | 5 | 5.1 Meeting the standards required to ensure a healthy environment for employees 5.2 Meeting the safety standards for the supply of equipment 5.3 Using PPE's 5.4 Ensuring there is a suitable environment for work practices, such as activity tables or chairs with armrests, which are designed for the health of employees | ISO 14004 |
| 6 | Analysis | Board Analyst Designer Programmer Architect | 2 | 6 | 6.1 Prioritizing input suppliers that have water optimization policies 6.2 Designing solutions with a view to reuse and the avoidance of water waste | ISO 14004 |
| 7 | Analysis of Design | Board | 1 | 7 | 7.1 Having a fair profit margin, compatible with the market 7.2 Ensuring transparency in the production chain with practices that are profitable without exploitation | ISO 14004 ISO 26000 |
| 8 | Analysis of Design | Designer Analyst | 1 | 8 | 8.1 Solutions that serve the needs for which they were designed 8.2 Solutions that are easy for the user to understand, thus avoiding any misuse of the product or stress being caused | Affinity Diagram with a Survey applied to community computing |
| 9 | Design | Designer | 1 | 9 | 9.1 Respect for the users' preferences and limitations. 9.2 Giving the users the right to choose by allowing them to be involved | Mocigemba (2005) Baranaukas (2008) |
| 10 | Design | Analyst Designer | 1 | 10 | 10.1 Creating interfaces that are accessible to different types of users. | W3C Design/Socially Conscious and Universal Design |
| 11 | Design | Analyst Designer | 1 | 11 | 11.1 Being useful to people with different skills 11.2 Providing the same (or similar) user experience to different types of users, whenever possible. | Universal Design |

## 5.1 Application and Preliminary Assessment of Guidelines

The set of guidelines was used by undergraduates in the Computer Science course, on the class of "Topics in Informatics". The students were invited, as volunteers, to apply the guidelines in their projects. They signed a consent form with these specifications and were divided into groups. They were asked to develop web applications: two of the groups had to follow the guidelines produced by this work, and the other two had to develop their solutions without the aid of the guidelines.

After the end of the development of the solutions following the guidelines, a questionnaire was applied to students with the in order to gather evidence of how the guidelines have been accepted and used.

**Table 3.** Guidelines for the design of computational solutions for sustainability awareness.

| | Phases of design process | Personnel responsible | Level | Guidelines | Subsidiary guidelines | Reference |
|---|---|---|---|---|---|---|
| 12 | Design | Designer | 1 | 12 | 12.1 Eliminating unnecessary complexity.<br>12.2 Having a wide range of language skills and levels of instruction.<br>12.3 Adopting different ways of displaying essential information<br>12.4 Being compatible with a wide range of technical equipment, as well as speeding up and simplifying communication | Universal Design |
| 13 | Design | Designer | 1 | 13 | 13.1 Reducing the need for physical effort by having fewer repetitive operations.<br>13.2 Allowing the user to be in a comfortable position when finding the solution | Universal Design |
| 14 | Analyze Prototyping Implementation | Analyst Programmer Architect | 1 | 14 | 14.1 Creating solutions that support hardware upgrades by reusing much of the original design<br>14.2 Creating solutions that support software upgrades, with the aim of optimizing the hardware, and avoiding the need to program obsolescent solutions<br>14.3 Finding portable solutions for different computing platforms, by expanding the range of their users | Affinity Diagram and a Survey applied to community computing |
| 15 | Analysis/ Prototyping | Board Analyst Designer Programmer Architect | 2 | 15 | 15.1 Avoiding the emission of air pollutants, through the solutions designed<br>15.2 Avoiding, whenever possible, using fossil fuels for transport<br>15.3 Using technology as a means of bringing people together, in meetings for example, avoiding unnecessary displacements | ISO 14020 Affinity Diagram Raghavan and Pargman, (2007) + a Survey applied to community computing |
| 16 | Analysis/ Implementation | Analyst Designer | 2 | 16 | 16.1 Concern about the company's surroundings when establishing a community t<br>16.2 Listening to the community and its needs with regard to the technology solutions created | ISO 26000 |
| 17 | | Designer | 1 | 17 | 17.1 Helpful Information for the solution.<br>17.2 Information about how to present the solution | Affinity Diagram |

The responses to the questionnaire showed that after contact with the guidelines, the view on sustainability has changed. All respondents considered having their thinking changed after the contact the guidelines.

At the end of the research project, the solutions generated by the 4 groups were evaluated, in a preliminary way, by 2 specialists in the design area who already had contact with the design literature on sustainability, and followed the evaluation guidelines recommended by Junior [7].

**Table 4.** Guidelines for the design of computational solutions for sustainability awareness.

| | Phases of design process | Personnel responsible | Level | Guidelines | Subsidiary guidelines | Reference |
|---|---|---|---|---|---|---|
| 18 | Design/Implementation | Designer Programmer | 1 | 18 | 18.1 Adapting user preferences, allowing the user to make a choice (for example color, font size) 18.2 Adapting to the user's work rhythm, (taking time outs to prevent the user experiencing stress) | Universal Design + Survey applied to community computing |
| 19 | Design/Prototyping/ Implementation | Designer Architect Programmer | 1 | 19 | 19.1 Making the solution compatible with the versions of different manufacturers 19.2 Ensuring functionality in future versions. 19.3 Updating the solution in accordance with the dictates and requirements of the current market | ISO 26000 Universal Design + Survey applied to community computing |
| 20 | Design/Prototyping/ Implementation | Board Analyst Designer | 1 | 20 | 20.1 Computational solutions must prevent unethical, corrupt or any kind of discriminatory activities? 20.2 The product design cannot discriminate against any beliefs or cultures, and must ensure that people are shown respect through the solution | ISO 26000 Universal Design + Survey applied to community computing |
| 21 | Design/Prototyping/ Implementation | Board Analyst Designer Programmer Architect | 2 | 21 | 21.1 Whenever possible, there is a need to take advantage of labor in regionalized solutions, and thus foster local development. 21.2 Prioritizing regional suppliers 21.3 Respecting the culture and customs of different kinds of people | Mucigemba, (2005) |

This meant that it was possible to determine whether the solutions created by the students who followed the guidelines, became more sustainable than the solutions of the students who did not follow them; specialists in the area were invited to assess the solutions. Three specialists on sustainability in the area of Computing analyzed the prototypes of the projects carried out by the students. Their academic qualifications consisted of a Ph.D student, a MSc. student and a MSc.; all the researchers in the field of Human-Computer Interaction were aged between 30 and 40. In making their evaluation, the specialists used the guidelines recommended in this work and the guidelines employed in the work of Junior [7], which consist of sustainability guidelines in the area of Software Engineering.

In the opinion of the specialists, the solutions created without the support of the guidelines did not have many traces of sustainable solutions. One factor that must be taken into account is that as it was about academic solutions, business matters, such as wages or questions that largely depended on the decisions of the board of directors could not be determined, since they were characterized as "Not applicable". The results suggest that the solutions obtained from following the guidelines were more sustainable than those that did not follow them. The concern of the groups that used the guidelines in making their solutions was remarkable when compared with the attitudes of the others.

**Table 5.** Guidelines for the design of computational solutions for sustainability awareness.

| | Phases of design process | Personnel responsible | Level | Guidelines | Subsidiary guidelines | Reference |
|---|---|---|---|---|---|---|
| 22 | Design/Prototyping/ Implementation | Analyst Designer | 1 | 22 | 22.1 There should be clear and concise solutions to help the users and give them a feeling of well-being when they reach the goal of the solution 22.2 The systems must predict possible errors that the user may make, by displaying error alerts, and help buttons; this can enable him to do what he wants in the solution with the minimum effort | ISO 14020 ISO 14001 |
| 23 | Design/Prototyping/ Implementation | Designer Programmer Architect | 1 | 23 | 23.1 Creating a life cycle policy in which the company is responsible for the solution from its creation to its correct disposal 23.2 There is a need to ensure that the software embedded in the hardware also has a) its share of recycling with regard to new models and b) its scalability 23.3 Creating the reverse logistics mechanism for the hardware after its useful life 23.4 Finding a destination for the components when the obsolete solution returns to its origin | ISO 14020 ISO 14001 |
| 24 | Analysis of Design/ Prototyping/ Implementation | Board Analyst Designer Programmer Architect | 2 | 24 | 24.1 Different genres must not show any distinction or signs of discrimination when developing a design product 24.2 The remuneration of different genders must also not be influenced by this factor | Kannabiran, (2014) Mucigemba, (2005) |
| 25 | Analysis of Design Prototyping/ Implementation | Board Analyst Designer Programmer Architect | 2 | 25 | 25.1 Prioritizing the use of solar or wind energy in solutions. 25.2 Prioritization of rechargeable batteries | Affinity Diagram and Survey applied to the community |

It was clear from the data and opinions collected from the students who took part in the study, that there is a need to strengthen other sustainable issues, especially those that are not most common (e.g. those related to the environment). A broader dissemination of information about sustainability and instructions for its practice could help to heighten awareness of this topic among the public.

## 6 Final Remarks

The work developed by Kim et al. [8] applies sustainability indicators to specific hardware. The creation of the guidelines suggested here broadens the view on hardware and also evolves the eight guidelines outlined by Zeid [16]. Both studies focus on the environmental issue. There is, therefore, a need to also guide other processes that encompass the term sustainability.

Our preliminary results suggest that the guidelines set out here can assist designers in creating more sustainable computing technologies.

Future work should include the use and evaluation of the guidelines outside an academic context, in the business environment, from the design of a product, whether software or hardware.

## References


1. de Almeida Neris, V.P., da Hora Rodrigues, K.R., Lima, R.F.: A Systematic review of sustainability and aspects of human-computer interaction. In: Kurosu, M. (ed.) HCI 2014. LNCS, vol. 8512, pp. 742–753. Springer, Cham (2014). https://doi.org/10.1007/978-3-319-07227-2_71
2. Baranauskas, M.C.C., Souza, C.d., Pereira, R.: I grandihc-br—grandes desafios de pesquisa em interaçao humano-computador no brasil. Relatório Técnico. Comissão Especial de Interação Humano-Computador (CEIHC) da Sociedade Brasileira de Computação (SBC), pp. 27–30 (2014)
3. Blevis, E.: Sustainable interaction design: invention & disposal, renewal & reuse. In: Proceedings of the SIGCHI Conference on Human Factors in Computing Systems, pp. 503–512. ACM, New York (2007)
4. Blevis, E.: Seeing what is and what can be: on sustainability, respect for work, and design for respect. In: Proceedings of the 2018 CHI Conference on Human Factors in Computing Systems, CHI 2018, pp. 370:1–370:14. ACM, New York (2018). https://doi.org/10.1145/3173574.3173944, http://doi.acm.org/10.1145/3173574.3173944
5. Blevis, E., Knowles, B., Clear, A.K., Mann, S., Håkansson, M.: Design patterns, principles, and strategies for sustainable HCI. In: Proceedings of the 2016 CHI Conference Extended Abstracts on Human Factors in Computing Systems, CHI EA 2016, pp. 3581–3588. ACM, New York (2016). https://doi.org/10.1145/2851581.2856497, http://doi-acm-org.ez31.periodicos.capes.gov.br/10.1145/2851581.2856497
6. Burnell, E.: Design for survivability: a participatory design fiction approach to sustainability. In: Proceedings of the 2018 Workshop on Computing Within Limits, LIMITS 2018, pp. 6:1–6:4. ACM, New York (2018). https://doi.org/10.1145/3232617.3232628, http://doi.acm.org/10.1145/3232617.3232628
7. Junior, N.G.: Diretivas para a Avaliação da Sustentabilidade em Soluções Computacionais. Master's thesis, Universidade Federal de São Carlos (2017)
8. Kim, S., Moon, S.K., Oh, H.S., Park, T., Choi, H., Son, H.: A framework to identify sustainability indicators for product design. In: 2014 IEEE International Conference on Industrial Engineering and Engineering Management, pp. 44–48. IEEE (2014)
9. Mann, S., Bates, O., Forsyth, G., Osborne, P.: Regenerative computing: de-limiting hope. In: Proceedings of the 2018 Workshop on Computing Within Limits, LIMITS 2018, pp. 1:1–1:10. ACM, New York (2018). https://doi.org/10.1145/3232617.3232618, http://doi.acm.org/10.1145/3232617.3232618
10. Mingay, S.: Green it: the new industry shock wave. Gartner RAS Research Note G 153703(7) (2007)
11. ONUBR, N.U.n.B.: Transformando nosso mundo: a agenda 2030 para o desenvolvimento sustentável **15** (2015), acesso em 4 June 2020

12. Pereira, D.M., Silva, G.S.: As tecnologias de informação e comunicação (tics) como aliadas para o desenvolvimento. Cadernos de Ciências Sociais Aplicadas **10**, 151–174 (2010)
13. Rising, L., Rehmer, K.: Patterns for sustainable development. In: Proceedings of the 17th Conference on Pattern Languages of Programs. PLOP 2010, pp. 13:1–13:11. ACM, New York (2010). https://doi.org/10.1145/2493288.2493301, http://doi.acm.org/10.1145/2493288.2493301
14. Spangenberg, J.H.: Design for sustainability (Dfs): interface of sustainable production and consumption. In: Kauffman, K.-M. Lee (eds.) Handbook of Sustainable Engineering, pp. 575–595. Springer, Dordrecht (2013). https://doi.org/10.1007/978-1-4020-8939-863
15. Waage, S.A.: Re-considering product design: a practical "road-map" for integration of sustainability issues. J. Clean. Prod. **15**(7), 638–649 (2007)
16. Zeid, A.: CAD tools for sustainable design. In: 2015 International Conference on Industrial Engineering and Operations Management (IEOM), pp. 1–5. IEEE (2015)

# Human-Centered Software Engineering for Changing Contexts of Use

# Workshop Report for IFIP WG 13.2's HCSE@INTERACT 2021

## International Workshop on Human-Centered Software Engineering for Changing Contexts of Use

Regina Bernhaupt[1], Stefan Sauer[2(✉)], and Carmelo Ardito[3]

[1] Eindhoven University of Technology, Eindhoven, The Netherlands
r.bernhaupt@tue.nl
[2] Paderborn University, Paderborn, Germany
sauer@uni-paderborn.de
[3] Politecnico di Bari, Bari, Italy
carmelo.ardito@poliba.it

## 1 General Workshop Setting

The context of use plays an important role in Human-Centered Software Engineering (HCSE) and Human-Computer Interaction (HCI) research. Typically, user, environment, and platform are considered to make up the core aspects of the context of use. Changing the context of use, for example due to unplanned circumstances like the current pandemic situation, has significant impact on how we use systems, and how we adapt and adopt them even if the systems were not designed for such usages.

The HCSE full-day workshop at INTERACT 2021 was organized around presentation of position papers and working activities in small groups. In the morning sessions, the selected position papers were presented and further position statements, comments to propositions and related experiences could be contributed by the workshop participants. The accepted papers were clustered according to four themes: A) Humans in Changing Contexts, B) Work Contexts at Change, C) Security and Privacy in the Context of Use, and D) Models for Context Adaptation, where A to C comprised two papers each, and D three papers. Position papers and statements together were then used to support the discussion that followed in the interactive working sessions during the afternoon, where participants were engaged to work in small groups.

The complete description of the workshop, its aim, topics as well as a detailed list and brief description of contributions is available in [1]. Revised versions of accepted workshop papers are included in this volume (ordered according to the above themes).

The International Workshop on HCSE for Changing Contexts of Use was organized and held in a way very close to the research topic it was focusing on: "Changing Contexts of Use". Held finally in a hybrid format, with about half of the participants on site and the other half joining virtually, the workshop delivered in the morning session a set of inspiring presentations with some lively Q&A sessions and in-depth discussions.


Published by Springer Nature Switzerland AG 2022
C. Ardito et al. (Eds.): INTERACT 2021, LNCS 13198, pp. 85–87, 2022.
https://doi.org/10.1007/978-3-030-98388-8_8

## 2 Interactive Working Sessions

Main goal of the afternoon was to support the activities and needs of the IFIP Working Group 13.2 members and the workshop participants to allow for easier collaborations and coordinated support when it comes to having new ideas for research projects to be set-up or to help doctoral candidates (PhD students) to get some informal feedback from other researchers.

We asked all workshop participants to perform a group activity to describe their current research projects that would likely have an overlap with others (based also on the presentations in the morning session). All workshop participants were split up in four groups (two groups working virtual, two groups in the premises on site). The list of research projects was gathered for each sub-group. To order the different projects by priority, the groups identified possible PhD topics that could be co-supervised by at least two participants of the sub-group. For each research topic, at least two PhD descriptions were generated and summarized. Supported by an online idea generation platform (Miro, see Fig. 1), the results of the group work were presented in a plenary session.

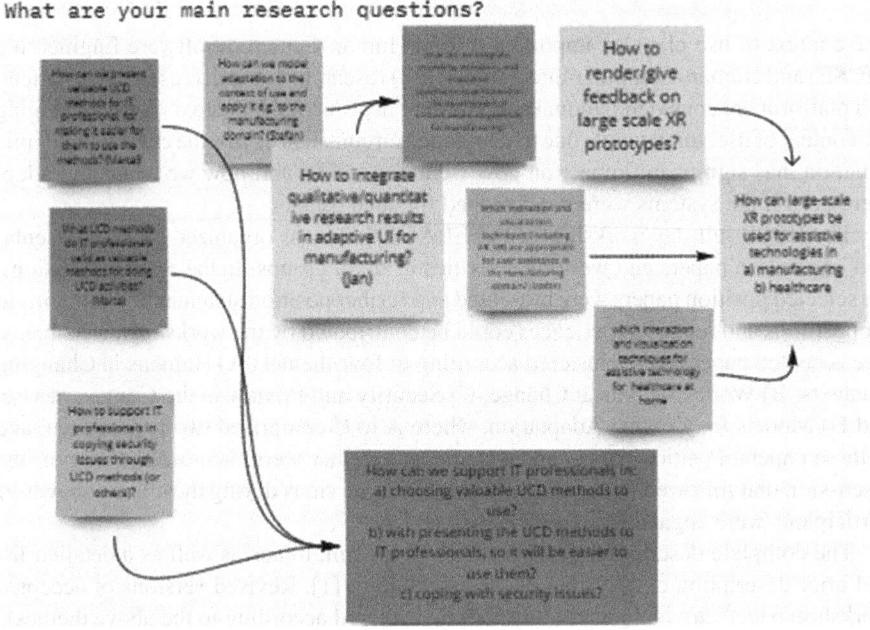


**Fig. 1.** Work Impressions from a hybrid workshop: Group work based on Miro, identifying a research question for a PhD on large scale XR prototyping

The workshop participants identified a set of largely diverse topics from the broad range of themes the Working Group 13.2 is typically considering. A possible research topic for a PhD would be the identification of a framework enabling to handle usability and security as two main software qualities in a development process. Key challenge especially was how to quantify or make measurable the conflict or trade-off between usability and security in such a framework, allowing for more objective decision making during design and development processes.

Key research topics for future PhD projects were identified from a more technological viewpoint (a) investigating how XR prototyping would be beneficial in the context of industry 4.0 and possible challenges for the development and usage of digital twins in such environments, and (b) how to use artificial intelligence approaches to support software developers during coding.

From a more human-centered perspective the need to support developers in their choice of user-centered design methods to improve the overall value was proposed as an important research project.

Combined, the seven different research projects developed showed the need to discuss further how context should be represented in design and development processes today, especially when it comes to different software properties like usability or security. Important topics are also how to face the new challenges of industry 4.0, the need to understand how to unify (or keep separate) virtual and real world and how to enhance and improve the way we support software designers when it comes to user-centered design and development methods.

For the future, we seek to continue to broaden the traditional scope of the workshop series of IFIP Working Group 13.2. We focus on the study of context of use, its long-term evolutionary trends as well as its short-term design and management in a user-centered design process, from a social and user-centered methodological viewpoint as well as from a technical viewpoint.

The long-term perspective of this workshop is to foster the development of theories, methods, tools and approaches for dealing with the changing context of use and its impact on HCI and collaboration that should be taken into account when developing interactive and socio-technical systems.

Workshop date: August 31, 2021.

Workshop organizers: Stefan Sauer, Regina Bernhaupt, Carmelo Ardito.

## Reference

1. Sauer, S., Bernhaupt, R., Ardito, C.: Human-centered software engineering for changing contexts of use. In: Ardito, C., et al. (eds.) INTERACT 2021. LNCS, vol. 12936, pp. 548–552. Springer, Cham (2021). https://doi.org/10.1007/978-3-030-85607-6_75

# How to Identify Changing Contexts of Use with Creativity Workshops – An Experience Report

Wasja Brunotte[1,2(✉)], Lukas Nagel[1,2], Kurt Schneider[1,2], and Jil Klünder[1,2]

[1] Leibniz University Hannover, Software Engineering Group, Leibniz, Germany
[2] Leibniz University Hannover, Cluster of Excellence PhoenixD, Leibniz, Germany
{wasja.brunotte,lukas.nagel,kurt.schneider, jil.kluender}@inf.uni-hannover.de

**Abstract.** Several software systems struggle with different contexts of use, e.g., due to a huge variety of end-user groups or various application scenarios. In some cases, the use of software systems may change due to external factors such as a pandemic. However, in other cases, software systems are known to be used in various contexts even before they are developed. In this case, it is crucial to consider as many different contexts of use as possible right from the beginning in order to avoid costly changes later on and, above all, user dissatisfaction. However, even when it is known that the software system will be used in different contexts, these contexts are often neither obvious nor easy to identify.

We propose to use workshops with stakeholders as a mean to identify different contexts of use. These workshops can be conducted at different points in time, but in this paper, we present a workshop conducted before starting the development phase, that is, during the requirements elicitation phase (to identify the different contexts of use as early as possible). We conducted such a workshop in a large interdisciplinary research project with different institutions from research and practice. In this paper, we present the workshop structure and its results, our experiences, as well as take-aways highlighting how (online) workshops might support the requirements elicitation when different contexts of use are to be expected.

**Keywords:** CrowdRE · Elicitation workshop · Creativity techniques · Context of use · Pandemic · Stakeholder identification

## 1 Introduction

The end-users influence *how* and *in which contexts* a software system will be used. Therefore, it is crucial to understand the context of use from the beginning, such as end-user goals, tasks, and characteristics of the environment [9]. Moreover, an increasing number of end-user groups has an impact on the number


C. Ardito et al. (Eds.): INTERACT 2021, LNCS 13198, pp. 88–97, 2022.
https://doi.org/10.1007/978-3-030-98388-8_9

of contexts of use of said software systems [1]. However, user requirements as well as the contexts of use are often not sufficiently considered when designing the software [5,12]. This is aggravated by the fact that the context of use of a software might change. For example, since no one can foresee future contexts of use [5], or due to unexpected external factors such as the pandemic situation the world faces these days.

Nevertheless, there are also cases in which the software system is known to be used in various contexts due to a large user group [8]. If this is known (or likely to be true) at the beginning of the development phase, taking this knowledge into account can improve the applicability of the software in the end, and it can reduce the necessity of future adjustments to different contexts.

As workshops have been proven to be meaningful for the requirements elicitation [7], we assume that workshops can also help identifying different contexts of use during the requirements elicitation phase. In addition, workshops are also an appropriate means of identifying (further) stakeholders. Following this line of thought we have conducted a workshop in the context of the cluster of excellence *PhoenixD*[1] in which optical systems, design and simulation tools are merged with production technologies. One of our tasks in this cluster of excellence is to develop a software that allows to connect different contributors in two means [8]: (1) to interact and collaborate with each other, and (2) to exchange different kind of data and knowledge.

In this paper in hand, we present our experience conducting an online workshop during the pandemic. The goal of this workshop was to elicit requirements from the crowd of different end users in order to identify as many contexts of use as possible.

*Outline.* The rest of the paper is structured as follows: Sect. 2 presents related work. In Sect. 3 we present the used methodology including the workshop structure. Section 4 summarizes our results which we discuss in Sect. 5. We conclude our paper in Sect. 6.

## 2 Related Work

The idea of using workshops to collect ideas is not new in scientific contexts. Ørngreen and Levinsen [10] discuss workshops as research methodology. They analyze five studies on teaching through video conferencing and argue that workshops are suited for domains that concern prospective subjects. The elicitation of requirements is one such domain, as the discussed project is not fully defined yet. A number of papers present workshop designs for such requirements elicitation processes.

Scherr et al. [11] evaluate the use of Amazons Echo Show device by elderly people through multiple different methods. An initial interview was conducted following the first interactions of participants with the device, before intermediate interviews were performed every three months. Additionally, the researchers

[1] https://www.phoenixd.uni-hannover.de/en/.

organized group meetings akin to workshops. Due to constraints related to the Covid-19 pandemic the intermediate interviews were conducted using video calls at a later stage of the experiment. The three methods lead to clear insights into the relationship of elderly users and the installed Alexa devices as well as information on requirements specific to their context of use.

An experience report by Haase and Herrmann [4] presents a workshop design for requirements engineering purposes in virtual settings. Their workshop makes use of the *6-3-5 method* as well as the six hats of de Bono [2]. A separate prioritization workshop was then conducted to prioritize the gathered requirements using the Hundred Dollar Test[2] as well as the Kano model [6].

Edwards and Sridhar [3] conducted an exploratory research study with 24 virtual teams consisting of university students based in Canada and India. Each team was paired with another group from the other university and tasked with the definition of requirements regarding a business information system. After the project phase participants were asked to fill out a survey. The researchers found indications for the importance of a good structure and ease of use of technologies regarding the efficiency, effectiveness and quality of virtual team projects.

In this paper we present a design for creative requirements elicitation workshops in the context of a virtual meeting that strives to identify different contexts of use as a by-product of the requirements elicitation phase. With in person meetings not being feasible due to Covid-19 restrictions, well designed processes and a thoughtful selection of supporting tools are required to increase the chance of a successful and satisfying workshop. Our design looks to identify further relevant stakeholders and to elicit requirements from end-users with different contexts of use (e.g., lab data exchange, knowledge exchange, data exchanges between machines, etc.) participating in an online meeting.

## 3 Methodology

We conducted the research presented in this paper in the context of the cluster of excellence *PhoenixD*. The main objective of *PhoenixD* is the creation of optical devices for different contexts of use. Several researchers from different universities (mainly Hannover and Braunschweig), as well as the Laser Zentrum Hannover and the Max Planck Institute for Gravitational Physics are involved in the project.

### 3.1 Case Project

The Software Engineering Group of the Leibniz University Hannover is also involved in the cluster of excellence. The large team of researchers and practitioners needs to exchange different kinds of data and knowledge. Working on such a project requires a close collaboration, an interactive exchange of information, and especially a well structured requirements engineering process. The

[2] In the Hundred Dollar Test participants are given 100 fictional dollars to spend on different ideas, thereby prioritizing the elicited requirements.

challenge here is not only to design a software system for different contexts of use (e.g., data exchange, collaboration, different requirements of the various scientific disciplines) that is tailored to the needs of many end-users, but above all to create an infrastructure for data exchanges within the cluster [8]. However, the contexts of use can be subsequently divided into several other contexts of use, which are not completely known. Therefore, this software system is a meaningful case project to which we applied our idea of using workshops with creativity techniques to identify as many different contexts of use as possible as a by-product of the requirements elicitation process.

### 3.2 Objective of the Workshop

The workshop aimed to collect requirements from as many end-user groups as possible, as well as to identify different contexts of use to allow for a widespread use of the software afterwards. Therefore, the workshop aimed at discussing the data exchange in the research project, as well as at answering two questions:

1. What kind of data needs to be exchanged, i.e., what defines the data exchange?
2. What is needed for the data exchange, e.g., on the infrastructure level?

### 3.3 Workshop Agenda

The workshop lasted one morning and consisted of several parts which are described in the following. Table 1 presents an overview of the different parts of the workshop.

**Table 1.** Overview of the workshop structure

| | Topic | Duration |
|---|---|---|
| | Welcome | 5 min |
| | Keynotes of PIs | 30 min |
| | Project Presentation | 10 min |
| | Introduction (Workshop Objective) | 5 min |
| Creative Task No. 1 | 6-3-5 method | 55 min |
| | Prioritization | 5 min |
| | Break | |
| Creative Task No. 2 | Walt-Disney method | 60 min |
| | Break | |
| | Summary and Outlook | 10 min |

### 3.4 Creativitiy Techniques Used

We opted for two different creativity techniques (Creative Task No. 1 and No. 2 in Table 1) to extract as many different requirements as possible - both must-have and nice-to-have requirements. We started with the *6-3-5 method*: a brainstorming technique in which six participants write down three ideas and then develop existing ideas or write down three more ideas five times. In contrast to the classic brainstorming, ideas are not collected in a central place like a flip chart. Instead, each participant is given a single sheet of paper to write on. After each iteration the sheets are passed around the table, which means that each participant contributes to every sheet once. The method thereby allows every participant to present their most important ideas while also letting them contribute to other lines of thought. To simulate the *6-3-5 method* in a virtual setting, we set up virtual sheets of paper that were accessible through static URLs. For this, we used an instance of OnlyOffice[3] hosted by our university. After each iteration we provided participants with the URL of the next sheet.

The second creativity technique used was the *Walt-Disney method.* Each participant runs through three roles: *Dreamer*, *Realist*, and *Critic.* Within these roles they are asked to voice hopes, general comments and concerns. In the *Walt-Disney method*, all participants work simultaneously. Results are collected in a central place and written down by the moderators. For the virtual setting of the presented workshop, we used an online whiteboard.

We chose the *6-3-5 method* at the beginning because this creativity technique is well suited for finding ideas in connection with concrete questions. The subsequent *Walt-Disney method* is already well suited for smaller groups. It also serves to generate ideas and refine them. We used the *Walt-Disney method* to refine the results of the *6-3-5 method.* Note that participants in this workshop had very little to no previous experience in using creativity techniques.

### 3.5 Data Collection

In the beginning of the workshop, the participants were asked for their agreement to record the workshop. We guaranteed to only use internal university servers for the data storage. As every single participant agreed to the data collection, we video-recorded the workshop.

In addition to these video-recordings, we used notes made during the workshop and - due to the pandemic situation - the online-setting of the workshop allowed to collect data in a digital format using a whiteboard and digital paper sheets.

### 3.6 Conducting the Workshop

We conducted the workshop as described above on Feb 24, 2021. Due to the pandemic situation, the workshop took place entirely online using BigBlueButton[4]

[3] https://www.onlyoffice.com.
[4] https://demo.bigbluebutton.org/gl.

for the workshop itself and Mural[5] as the whiteboard. In total, six researchers from five institutions participated in the workshop.

From the author team of this paper, two researchers conducted and moderated the workshop. In the background, two other researchers (who did not participate in the workshop) helped by clustering and processing the results. After having started the workshop with a welcome as presented in Table 1, we continued with the *6-3-5 method* regarding the questions presented in Sect. 3.2. Hereafter, the data was processed and clustered (while the participants could refresh in a coffee break).

Subsequently, participants were given 15 minutes to read the clustered results of the *6-3-5 method* and prioritize the aspects that were most important to them. For this, each participant had a total of 3 votes, without prioritization within their own votes. That is, a participant could also have rated one item with three votes, even though this did not happen. The voting was conducted across the clusters. After the 15 min had elapsed, the aspects that had just been rated were sorted in descending order of their rating.

Based on this rated data, the *Walt-Disney method* was conducted. To do this, all participants as a group took on one of the three roles in turn and advanced the vision of data exchange. Finally, each participant was asked to formulate a personal conclusion about the insights and points of the workshop that were most important to them.

## 4 Results and Interpretation

Using the results from the *6-3-5 method*, a total of 63 ideas were collected. Afterwards, we assigned these ideas to the following clusters: *Technical Solution*, *Types of Data*, *Collaboration Partners*, *Problems so far*, *Restrictions*, and *Types of Exchange*. In the subsequent prioritization by participants, 12 ideas were highlighted and deemed particularly important. The three highest rated ideas were used as the basis for the *Walt Disney method*. When adopting the role of the dreamer, participants produced eight refinements of ideas which were analyzed in terms of their feasibility by the role of the realist. In the role of the critic, participants examined their proposals constructively and critically.

From the results of both methods, we were finally able to identify the following first contexts of use: Data Diversity, Unified Data Annotations, Long Term Use of the Data, Devices and Platform, Data Exchange, and Data Authority. The context of use *Data Diversity* includes the consideration of different types of data, e.g. lab data, simulation data, measurement data, data for production as well as specific parameter information or knowledge of persons involved. *Unified Data Annotations* refers to a unified approach to annotating data. It is important that the data is searchable and easy to find. Simultaneously, it is critical that the source of the data and the data itself are comprehensible over the long term. This is to be achieved by designing a uniform concept for embedding metadata. The latter aspect connects directly to the context of use *Long Term Use*

[5] https://www.mural.co/.

*of the Data.* Until now, data has often only been usable in combination with an analog lab book. This will no longer be necessary in the future, as the data, including all dependencies, will be available digitally. In addition, data must also be understood by subsequent researchers, and a link from raw data to the corresponding publications must be ensured. Another context of use was identified as *Devices and Platform.* The system to be developed, or the emerging platform, must adapt to different end devices. This means, for example, that only certain information is provided depending on the performance of an end device. In order to enable data exchange between different researchers and disciplines, various aspects such as conversion of units, filtering of data, transmission of data, etc. have to be considered. These aspects belong to the context of use *Data Exchange.* The final context of use identified in the workshop was named *Data Authority.* It is intended to ensure that there is a superordinate instance that monitors the efforts or constraints surrounding data exchange within the cluster of excellence and ensures that operations are as error-free as possible.

In addition to the aforementioned results of the workshop, we were also able to identify other stakeholder groups for future iterations of the workshop. The final feedback from all participants was very positive. They expressed that the creativity techniques used during the workshop made it easier to envision the goals and requirements around the planned data management system. Based on this feedback we plan to conduct further editions of the workshop.

## 5 Discussion

Based on the insights we gained during the workshop, we can point to some advantages and disadvantages of such kinds of workshops both related to the workshop itself as well as to the online-setting due to the ongoing pandemic. We present these insights in the following and discuss their limitations.

### 5.1 Advantages and Disadvantages Due to the Pandemic

The workshop was conducted in the beginning of 2021, when there was the worldwide Corona pandemic. This required some adjustments compared to a non-pandemic situation.

Of course, an online workshop has disadvantages compared to a workshop in person. For example, interactions are way more difficult, in particular, if they are bi-directional and do not affect the whole group. In addition, the quality of the workshop and, consequently, of the results, depend on the technical equipment of the participants. For example, a low bandwidth complicates interactions and communication, and may lead to misunderstandings or lost information.

Nevertheless, according to the experiences we made during the workshop, meeting virtually also has some advantages. For example, results can be easily collected on a whiteboard that is accessible for all participants at the same time, and everybody can contribute to the data collection (without the problem of unreadable handwriting on a physical whiteboard). In addition, it appears to be easier to motivate people to participate in the workshop as they only need to be available for the real workshop time (and not, e.g., for traveling). This also facilitates to find appointments where as many participants as possible can join the workshop.

Summarizing, despite the fact that the pandemic shall end as soon as possible, we all - researchers and practitioners - can benefit to some extent from the experiences made when meeting virtually. There will be cases, when having such an online workshop is more practical even when the pandemic is over.

### 5.2 Take-Aways for Researchers

Given the experiences we made and the advantages and disadvantages we faced due to the online setting of our workshop, we have four take-aways that will influence our future research:

**1) Creativity workshops with end-users are a suitable method to find different contexts of use.** Considering the number of requirements we elicited during the workshop, we would encourage other researchers, requirements engineers, etc. to conduct such a workshop when different contexts of use should be taken into account. During the workshop, we got to know different viewpoints at the same time, and participants were able to extend or correct statements made by others.
**2) Include creativity techniques in online settings.** Creativity techniques are at the core of most workshops as they allow for interactions. Interactions are also possible in online-settings, but they need to be planned. Simply using creativity techniques from "normal" workshops often does not work in online-settings. Nevertheless, there are possibilities to increase the amount of interactions in online workshops.
**3) Think about creativity techniques when deciding which tool to use.** The selection of tools for an online-workshop should be thoughtful. However, the chosen creativity techniques have an influence on the choice of the tools to be used: Is there a need for a whiteboard? What about breakout rooms in which smaller groups of participants can converse without interruption? Surveys? On-the-fly video recording? Besides the requirements of the concrete workshop, it is meaningful to look at tools the participants are familiar with. The effort for the participants to join the workshop should be as small as possible.
**4) Think twice whether a workshop in person is necessary.** Given the advantages described above, it is meaningful to ask whether a workshop would benefit more from a meeting in person or from more participants being able to join. We expect that a meeting in person is not always the best choice.

### 5.3 Limitations

The insights we present in this paper emerge from only one workshop with six participants. Therefore, our results need to be taken with care and must not be over-generalized. Nevertheless, the results of the workshop are promising and motivate the further use of workshops to elicit requirements for different contexts of use from a crowd of end-users. We plan to expand the single workshop into a series of workshops throughout the software system development process to continuously engage end-users and collect as many insights and ideas as possible.

## 6 Conclusion

Workshops are frequently used during the requirements elicitation phase. This is a meaningful point in time to identify different contexts of use as this can help facilitate the further process and might help to improve the acceptance as well as the usability of a system. In this paper, we present the results of such a workshop conducted in the beginning of a software project of which we knew in advance that there will be a wide variety in the contexts of use.

Using two creativity techniques, namely the *6-3-5 method* and the *Walt-Disney method*, we identified different contexts of use with only six participants from a large end-user group participating in the workshop.

Besides, we also experienced advantages and disadvantages when this kind of workshop needs to take place online, e.g., as in our case, due to an ongoing pandemic.

Despite the limited generalizability and credibility of our results, the insights we gained during the workshop motivate future work striving to improve the workshop structure to identify as many contexts of use as possible before starting the development phase of a software project.

**Acknowledgment.** This work was funded by the Deutsche Forschungsgemeinschaft (DFG, German Research Foundation) under Germany's Excellence Strategy within the Cluster of Excellence PhoenixD (EXC 2122, Project ID 390833453).

## References

1. Bevan, N.: Using the common industry format to document the context of use. In: Kurosu, M. (ed.) Human-Computer Interaction. Human-Centred Design Approaches, Methods, Tools, and Environments. pp. 281–289. Springer, Heidelberg (2013). https://doi.org/10.1007/978-3-642-39232-0
2. De Bono, E.: Six Thinking Hats. Penguin, London (2017)
3. Edwards, H.K., Sridhar, V.: Analysis of software requirements engineering exercises in a global virtual team setup. J. Glob. Inf. Manag. **13**(2), 21–41 (2005)
4. Haase, C., Herrmann, A.: Virtual requirements engineering. In: Proceedings of the "Fachgruppentreffen Requirements Engineering" (2020)
5. Hadad, G.D., Litvak, C.S., Doorn, J.H., Ridao, M.: Dealing with completeness in requirements engineering. In: Encyclopedia of Information Science and Technology, 3rd edn, pp. 2854–2863. IGI Global, Hershey (2015)
6. Kano, N.: Attractive quality and must-be quality. Hinshitsu (Qual. J. Jpn Soc. Qual. Control.) **14**, 39–48 (1984)
7. Karras, O., Kiesling, S., Schneider, K.: Supporting requirements elicitation by tool-supported video analysis. In: 2016 IEEE 24th International Requirements Engineering Conference (RE), pp. 146–155. IEEE (2016)

8. Klünder, J., Brunotte, W., Schneider, K.: When you don't know with whom to collaborate: towards an interactive system connecting contributors in a research project. In: CEUR Workshop Proceedings 2503 (2019), vol. 2503, pp. 122–129. RWTH, Aachen (2019)
9. Maguire, M.: Context of use within usability activities. Int. J. Hum. Comput. Stud. **55**(4), 453–483 (2001). https://doi.org/10.1006/ijhc.2001.0486, https://www.sciencedirect.com/science/article/pii/S1071581901904860
10. Ørngreen, R., Levinsen, K.: Workshops as a research methodology. Electr. J. E-learn. **15**(1), 70–81 (2017)
11. Scherr, S.A., Meier, A., Cihan, S.: Alexa, tell me more-about new best friends, the advantage of hands-free operation and life-long learning. In: Mensch Computer 2020-Workshopband (2020)
12. Schneidewind, L., Hörold, S., Mayas, C., Krömker, H., Falke, S., Pucklitsch, T.: How personas support requirements engineering. In: 2012 First International Workshop on Usability and Accessibility Focused Requirements Engineering (UsARE), pp. 1–5 (2012). https://doi.org/10.1109/UsARE.2012.6226786

# Contextual Personas - A Method for Capturing the Digital Work Environment of Users

Marta Lárusdóttir[1(✉)], Ruochen Wang[2], and Åsa Cajander[2]

[1] Reykjavik University, Menntavegur 1, 101 Reykjavik, Iceland
marta@ru.is

[2] Uppsala University, P.O. Box 256, 751 05 Uppsala, Sweden

**Abstract.** It can be hard to understand the context in which a software system is used and how the whole work environment affects the usage of a particular system. In this project, we modified the Persona method to include aspects of the digital work environment and the context to extend the understanding of these aspects during software development. The modified version of the Persona method is based on the traditional Persona method, on theories on healthy work and research on the digital work environment. The objective of proposing the modifications of the method is to give software developers more insights into the complexity of the digital work environment. University students tried the modified Contextual Persona method in a user-centred software development course. Students worked on designing a new system for 12 weeks using the Contextual Persona method during the fourth week of software development. The students gave feedback on what positive and negative aspects they experienced while using the modified Contextual Persona method and their thoughts on how the method could be improved. In the paper, we analyse reports from 30 students and summarise the feedback gathered. We conclude by summarising the possible improvements to the method based on our findings.

**Keywords:** Persona method · Context of use · Usability · User-centred design · HCI methodology

## 1 Introduction

Software systems have become mobile, portable, wearable, and ubiquitous and thus are used in a more dynamic contextual setting than 20 or 30 years ago [1]. Hence, understanding the context of use while developing software systems has become more critical and has raised awareness in practice and research [1–4]. Software systems are often used in multi-contextual settings where the usage is more dynamic, heterogeneous and unpredictable than the usage of systems used in a single context of use with stationary computing systems [1]. Hence many factors affect the analysis of the context of use for systems being developed, such as the dynamics of business environments, organizational culture, organizational strategy, project type, the background of team members and more [1].


Published by Springer Nature Switzerland AG 2022
C. Ardito et al. (Eds.): INTERACT 2021, LNCS 13198, pp. 98–112, 2022.
https://doi.org/10.1007/978-3-030-98388-8_10

The term digital work environment has been used to explain using software systems in the context of work situations. Digitalization in work situations has developed lately by automating working processes, assisting decision-making, and sharing knowledge within the organizations [5]. However, digitalizing work situations has also resulted in negative consequences such as productivity loss, health problems, and privacy breaches [6]. One approach to address health problems caused by poorly designed software systems is to improve the usability and the user experience of the software systems by considering the human factors and the contextual factors of the systems when developing those.

The Persona method is a user-centred design (UCD) method applied frequently and extensively in the development of software systems to gain empathy for users and to extend the understanding of the users, their tasks and their context of use. The Persona method is often used for enriching the communication between designers and developers with this purpose [7]. When constructing a persona, a name and a portrait are selected to depict the persona. Additionally, a narrative form to describe the persona is written to make the persona like a natural person and provide a clear and detailed story concerning the goals and needs of the target users in the context of the designed products [8]. The narrative usually starts with a description of the type of individual, occupations, hobbies and more. The specific needs and personal goals in the product context are also described [8]. The Persona method can help designers and developers to put themselves in users' way of improving the user experience of the developed system [9, 10].

Based on the idea of including health aspects related to the work environment into the Persona method, a new method called the Contextual Persona method was proposed in 2015 [11]. Although it looks like the traditional Persona method, the Contextual Persona method focuses on describing users' physical environment, social environment, and technological environment. The Contextual Persona method gained positive feedback from users and researchers in a case study [11]. Unlike the traditional Persona method, which mainly describes the end users' behaviour, goals and motivation, the Contextual Persona method also considers the context or environment-related factors when end-users use the system.

In this study, we build on previous work on the Persona method and the Contextual Persona method. We suggest modifications to the Contextual Persona method to include several digital work environment aspects and study how university students experience the modified Contextual Persona method.

In this paper, we state the following research questions:

1. What are the positive and negative aspects that students experience from using the modified Contextual Persona method?
2. What improvements do the students suggest for future usage of the modified Contextual Persona method?

## 2 Background

In this section we describe briefly the related work on the concept of context of use, the concept of digital work environment and the Persona method.

## 2.1 The Concept of Context of Use

The concept of context of use in HCI research has been defined and developed by several researchers. It includes defining a framework of the context of use [12], the taxonomy of context of use components [13], defining contextual dimensions [14], and defining a user experience context scale [15]. Maguire describes the main contextual factors to be considered in the context of user analysis [12]. According to his framework, the main contextual factors should be 1) users, 2) tasks, and 3) environments such as technical environment, the physical environment and social or organizational environment. Alonso-Rios et al. provided a context of use taxonomy for usability studies [13]. The first level of the taxonomy consists of users, tasks, and environments, similar to Maguire's main contextual factors [12]. The taxonomy provided a more precise definition of context of use components. To simplify the representation of context and structure the contextual factors, Bradley and Dunlop suggested the following contextual dimensions: 1) task context, 2) physical context, 3) social context, 4) temporal context, 5) application context, 6) cognitive context [14]. Additionally, Lallemand and Koenig recently developed a user experience context scale (UXCS), to incorporate contextual dimensions in the UX assessment questionnaire [15]. Their work strives to understand and assess the influence of context factors in user experience.

## 2.2 The Concept of Digital Work Environment

Work environment refers to "work conditions at the workplace, which may encourage or discourage employees to work" [16]. They also stated that the work environment includes the physical environment as well as the social relationships at the workplace. Additionally, Wright and Davis stated that the work environment consists of two components: job characteristics and work context [17]. Job characteristics refers to how a job affects the employee's critical psychological states, such as "the meaningfulness of the work" and "employee's spirit, growth and development". The work context refers to the organizational settings such as organization's rewarding systems and organizational goals in their definition.

Digital work refers to employees' work using information and communications technology (ICT) [18]. Dittes and Smolnik conceptualized the digital work environment as "the online representation of the working conditions that the employees require to do their work" [19]. Williams and Schubert [20] argued that such work conditions should enable people to be productive and fulfil their requirements in data, information and knowledge. The term digital work environment is defined as "the working environment, with its problems and opportunities of physical, organizational, social and cognitive nature, which is the result of digitalization of the work support systems and tools." [21].

## 2.3 The Persona Method

The Persona method is a user-centred design (UCD) method applied frequently and extensively in the development of software systems. Cooper [22] was the first to introduce the concept of a persona and described that personas "are hypothetical archetypes of actual users". Although Cooper argues that personas as hypothetical and imaginary, he emphasises that personas are defined with significant rigour and precision [22]. To illustrate this, Cooper et al. [23] stated that just like physicists use models to describe the behaviour of particles, HCI researchers should use the Persona method as a model to describe the behaviour of end-users and the context in which they work and life. In this paper, we refer to this method as the traditional Persona method. An example of describing one persona using the traditional Persona method is shown in Fig. 1.

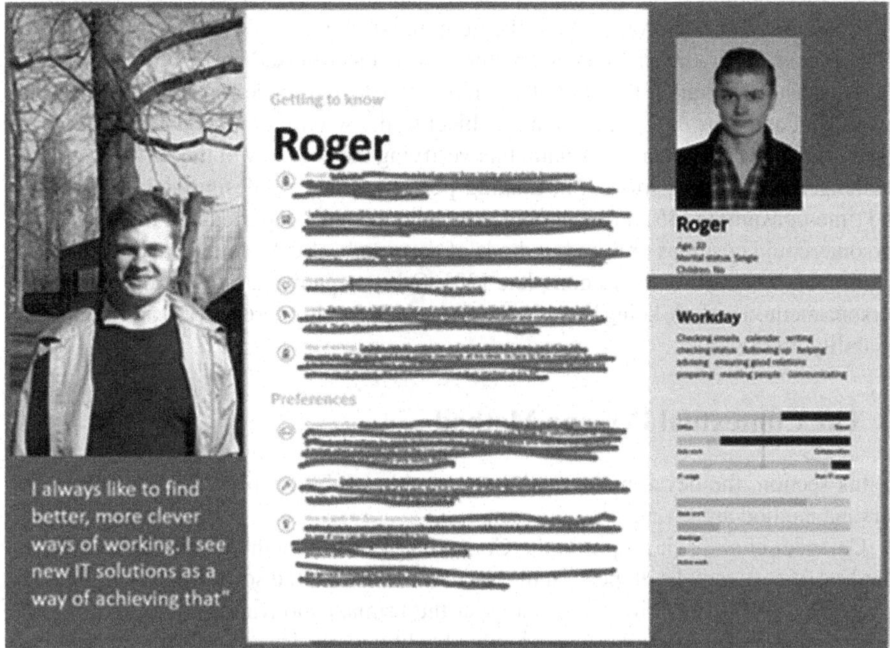


**Fig. 1.** An example of describe a persona by using the traditional Persona method

The personas are typically used to communicate between designers and developers to extend the empathy for users [7]. The traditional Persona method can help designers and developers put themselves in users' shoes that are useful for improving user experience using the developed system [9, 10]. When constructing a persona, a name and a portrait are selected to depict the persona, and a narrative form will be adopted to describe the persona [8]. The narrative usually starts with a description of the type of individual, occupations, hobbies, etc. The personas' specific needs and personal goals in the product context are described [8]. The narrative should be concise enough to express the design requirements accurately [24]. Typically, a persona is created through four steps [25, 26]: 1) collecting data from actual users, 2) grouping and segmenting the collected data, 3) analysing the grouped data, and 4) constructing a persona based on the information derived from the raw data. Qualitative data and quantitative data can be the source to create a persona [27].

The traditional Persona method offers several benefits in product design. One of the benefits is to facilitate communication among designers and stakeholders and to enable designers to put themselves in the users' shoes and extend empathy for the users [22, 28–31]. Elaborating upon previous research, Miaskiewicz and Kozar [8] concluded that the five most significant benefits of personas are the ability to: 1) focus the product design teams on the actual goals of the target users; 2) prioritise the product requirements and help to determine whether the designers are solving the correct problems; 3) prioritise the most critical audience; 4) challenge the long-standing and often incorrect assumptions about the users, and 5) prevent the self-referential design.

However, the traditional Persona method has been criticised for being not scientific. Chapman and Milham [32] argue that it is impossible to reproduce a specific persona from given data, and thus the process is not subject to the scientific method of reproducible research. Some researchers also claim that verifying the accuracy of the persona remains challengeable [33–35]. Moreover, making personas during a design activity is costly and time-consuming [35]. For example, An and colleagues reported that the creation of personas could cost tens or even hundreds of thousands of U.S. dollars, and the persona creation also takes months to complete [33]. Other negative aspects of the traditional Persona method include being biased by creators [35], being overused [24] and neglecting disability groups [9].

## 3 The Contextual Persona Method

In this section, the development and a description of the template for the Contextual Persona method are given.

Cajander et al. [11], proposed the Contextual Persona method to extend the understanding of software developers on the context of use that the software system they are developing will be used in. They state that the primary motivation for suggesting the Contextual Persona method was to promote healthy work. The original Contextual Persona method was based on the Demand-Control-Support model developed by Theorell and Karasek [36]. The model is used to analyse psycho-social work conditions and their effect on health. According to this model, high job demand with little control at work and little support at work will lead to stress and cause very adverse effects on health. The original Contextual Persona method includes sections for demand at work, control at work and support at work. These sections were meant to help developers consider the factors that cause health issues in designing their software system. In Fig. 2, an example of one Contextual Persona using the original version of the Contextual Persona method.

The Contextual Persona method received positive feedback in a case study, and the respondents thought the contextual personas truly reflected their work situation [11].

The modified Contextual Persona method suggested in this paper considers the concept of the context of use in addition to the other aspects covered in the original Contextual Persona method. Based on the ISO 9241-210 [37] standard definition of the context of

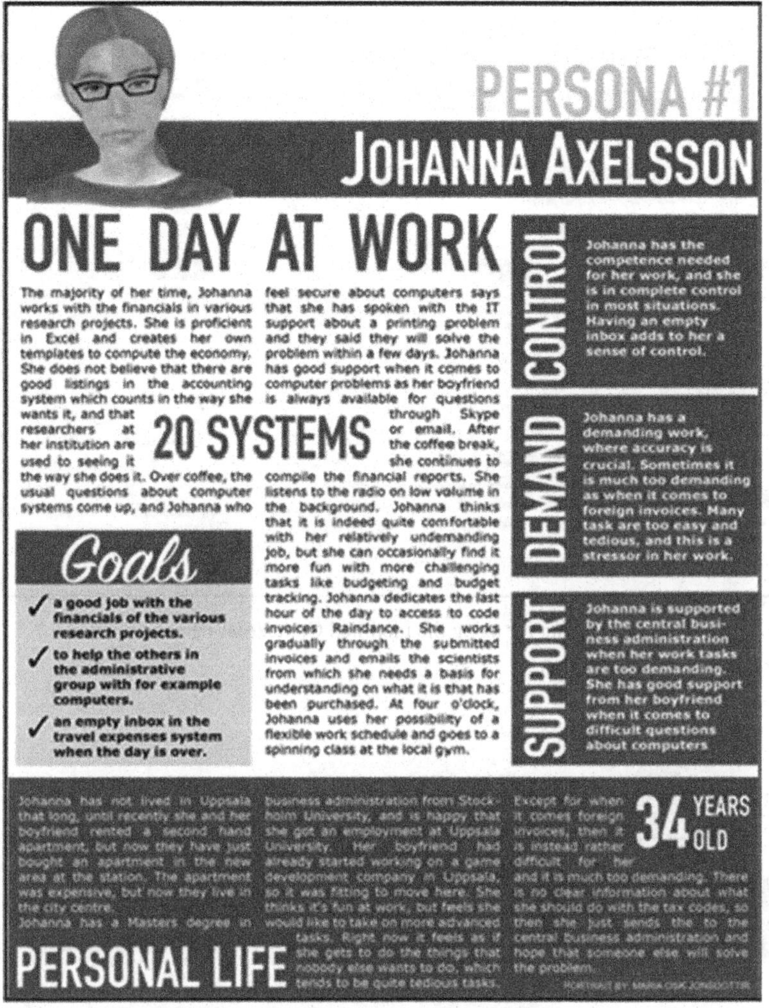


**Fig. 2.** An example of one contextual persona

use and Maguire's components of context of use [12], sections were added to describe the digital work environment of the personas. The aspects are: 1) physical work environment aspects, 2) organisational work environment aspects, 3) social work environment aspects and 4) the cognitive load aspect. A template for describing a persona using the modified Contextual Persona method is shown in Fig. 3.

In Fig. 4, we show one example of using the template, describing the same persona as described and shown in Fig. 2.

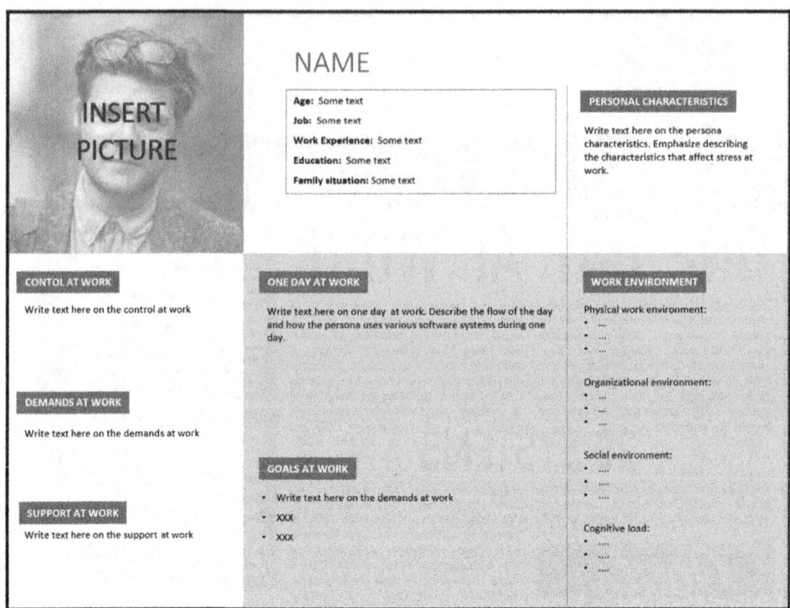


**Fig. 3.** A template for using the modified Contextual Persona method

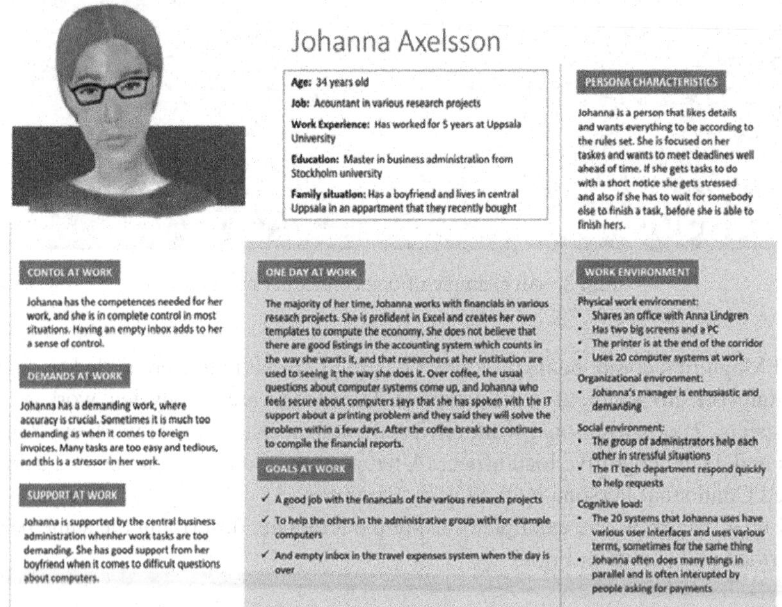


**Fig. 4.** One example describing a persona with the modified Contextual Persona method.

## 4 Method

The findings presented in this paper derive from 30 student reports from a user-centred software development course given in Spring 2020 at Reykjavik University. In that course, students were asked to use the modified Contextual Persona method in their design work. They provided us insightful feedback on the following topics: the positive aspects of the Contextual Persona method, the negative aspects of the Contextual Persona method, and what can be improved about the method. At the end of the course, each wrote a report on using the Contextual Persona method. We analysed their reports with the thematic analysis method.

### 4.1 Data Collection

Computer science students at Reykjavik University used the modified Contextual Persona method during a 12-week user-centred software development course. Students worked on designing a new system of their choice during the whole course. The new system was to be used in some work environment of the students' choice. The students attended the course on-site at the university one morning each week. The schedule combined lectures, hands-on training on site, and projects between the course occasions. During the course, one of the first activities was to conduct contextual interviews in a work environment to gather ideas for improving the digital work environment for potential users.

Students used the Contextual Persona method during the fourth week of the course. The students got a 40 min introduction lecture on personas in general and contextual personas particularly. They were shown some examples of contextual personas and got hands-on training in defining 3–5 contextual personas for 80 min. The contextual personas were based on the data gathered during the contextual interviews. The students got the template shown in Fig. 1 to fill in.

The students gave feedback on what positive and negative aspects they experienced while using the modified Contextual Persona method in the design project and their thoughts on how the method could be improved. To gain a deeper understanding of the usage of the Contextual Persona method, we analysed 30 student reports from Reykjavik University. Students answered a series of reflective questions in their reports: 1) What are the positive aspects of the Contextual Persona method? 2) What are the negative aspects of the Contextual Persona method? and 3) Is there anything that you think could be improved in the Contextual Persona method?

All the reports were thoroughly constructed, except that one student handed in an unfinished report. The contents of students' answers were heterogeneous, which enabled us to gain diverse perspectives from their reflections. Some students provided long and detailed reflection, while some students' answers were short. The aim of the research is not to focus on identifying the unique and idiosyncratic meanings and experiences. In the analysis, we strive to find common themes in their answers and we therefore, adopted the thematic analysis method to analyse the reports [38].

### 4.2 Data Analysis

The data were analysed following [38]. Reports were first read to familiarise with the data, and answers were extracted question by question. The answers to one specific question were analysed together. The initial codes were gathered by finding short segments that could answer the question clearly and explicitly.

After the initial coding, patterns and potential themes were identified. In most cases, several relevant codes were combined to form an overarching theme. In some cases, codes could become themes in their own right. Some codes, however, were discarded because they were too vague or not relevant enough to the specified question. Moreover, some codes that did not belong anywhere were grouped under a theme called "miscellaneous". These codes were revisited in the next stage to decide whether they should be combined, refined, or discarded.

Based on the potential themes, a thematic map was constructed. All the candidate themes were revisited to make sure that the themes were accurate representations of the data. The first step was to read all the extracted codes for each theme and consider whether those codes appeared to form a coherent pattern that is that all relevant codes under a theme fitted the theme. If codes did not fit the existing theme, that code was redefined to a suitable theme. If the codes were irrelevant or too vague, these were discarded from the analysis. The relationship between the candidate themes and the data set was validated by comparing the data set with candidate themes to confirm that the candidate themes were accurate representations of the data set. The categorisation into themes was finished when there was no missing information or nothing substantial that could be added to the candidate themes. After all candidate themes were validated, a thematic map was developed for each question by grouping relevant themes together.

The thematic maps are a hierarchical structure that consists of main overarching themes and sub-themes for each of the three questions analysed. Each central overarching theme has one or several related sub-themes. The thematic maps depict the relationship of all the themes.

## 5 Results

This section presents our findings by listing or narrating the themes identified from the 30 reports. Most respondents think that the Contextual Persona method will be valuable in the future and should be used at the beginning of the development. Moreover, six respondents particularly mentioned that the method should also be used throughout the whole design process. The presentation of the findings starts with showing the positive aspects and negative aspects of the Contextual Persona method. Additionally, we describe the possible improvement that the students suggested to the method.

### 5.1 Positive Aspects of the Modified Contextual Persona Method

The positive aspects of the Contextual Persona method extracted from the student reports include three themes described below.

**Help to Understand the Users and their Work Environment.** Almost all students described that the Contextual Persona method helps deepen their understanding of the users' needs and the users' work environment. Compared to the traditional Persona method, they reflect that the Contextual Persona method gives more relevant information about the context. For example, one of the students made such reflections: "It allows the team to get in sync with not only the Personas but also the work environment and the task that the design needs to be able to handle."

**An Excellent Tool to Facilitate the Design/Development Work.** Another important positive aspect is the efficiency that the Contextual Persona method brings to the design work. The Contextual Persona method is regarded as an efficient tool for collecting data, assisting communication and collaboration among the design group members, helping the design team make important decisions, and saving time for the design projects. Some respondents also reported that the Contextual Persona method is easy to use, and the layout of the Contextual Persona is easy to navigate.

**Help with the Scope and the Focus of the Design Work.** The respondents experience that Contextual Persona enables them to see the scope of the design work and help them focus on the critical tasks and features which matter most to the users. Just as one of the respondents said in her report: "By getting a more detailed context we get a better idea of what should be included in the implementation and how it should be handled."

## 5.2 Negative Aspects

The negative aspects of the Contextual Persona method extracted from the student reports were mainly focused on two themes: 1) The limitations in revealing users' needs and their working environment and 2) the inconvenience of using the Contextual Personas in the design activity.

**Limitations in Revealing Users' needs and their Working Environment.** First, Contextual Persona might encourage us in using stereotypes, and makes us focused on one type of user but ignores other types of users. For example, some respondents reflect that Contextual Persona might provide us with a stereotypical representation of elderly and non-tech savvy people. Second, although some respondents made multiple Contextual Personas, they reflected that their Personas were too similar and thus, lacked diversity. However, they did not explain in the report how they made those Personas and thus we cannot infer why they end up having Contextual Personas that look very much alike. Third, Contextual Personas are fictional and influenced by designers' Personal bias, affecting the system design and development work. Regarding this point, one respondent made such reflections: "Because the Persona is technically made up and fictional, when creating the Persona, we can become biased on how the Persona should be like which can greatly affect the outcome of the system if we were to base it on the Persona."

Fourth, the Contextual Persona method can lower the need to have frequent face-to-face conversations with real users. One respondent described this phenomenon as "the bigotry" of the designers. Another respondent pointed out that "this method could endanger the Persona by reinscribing existing stereotypes and following more of an I-methodological than a user-centred approach.

**Inconvenience in the Design Work Activity.** First, some respondents describe that once the Persona is made, it is difficult to change it. Thus, the wrongly made Persona would finally affect the whole process and the final product. Second, most respondents reported that making Persona is time-consuming, which will consequently slow the progress. Third, respondents also mentioned a phenomenon that developers might not keep the Contextual Persona that they made in mind, and thus the Contextual Persona turned out to be useless. One respondent described this phenomenon as follows: "A team could put time into making these Personas, and then not utilize them when designing the software, resulting in wasted time." Fourth, developers might have a different interpretation of the Persona details, which might lead to a different understanding or even misunderstanding of the Persona.

### 5.3 Possible Improvements of the Contextual Persona Method

Students also provided insightful ideas on how the Contextual Persona method could be improved. In total, seven themes were analysed.

**Layout and Content.** The first central theme identified from the reports is the improvements regarding the layouts and contents of the Contextual Persona. The first suggestion is that the Contextual Persona should be accurate and reliable. To achieve that, possible actions could be using analytic methods to get reliable information, building Persona based on actual users, and picking up the right end-users for an interview.

**Reducing Background Details.** The second suggestion is reducing the irrelevant background details in the Contextual Persona. They think such details do not help the team make decisions. "I also think that the Persona does not need a backstory, it does not improve the system to know if the Persona has three kids and loves tennis."

**Add Subsections on Work-Related Information.** The third suggestion is to add more subsections that care about work-related information. For example, the respondents suggest adding a subsection regarding the overall technical skills of the Persona. Besides, a respondent suggests adding a subsection describing the Persona's current anger points at work and a subsection describing what the Persona are not capable of at work.

**Multiple and Diverse Personas.** The fourth suggestion is to make multiple but diverse contextual personas. The respondents believe the diverse Personas could help them gain a broader picture of the end-users and their needs. One informant stated:

"I also think that making multiple personas for each user group would be beneficial as each user group could have users with different needs and one persona per user group might not catch all those needs."

**Stakeholders Involved in Making Personas.** Students suggested that the stakeholders should be involved in reviewing the contextual personas. They argued that the perspectives from outside stakeholders could avoid bias and thus help them get a more accurate understanding of users.

**Use Contextual Personas More Frequently during the Design Process.** The respondents commented that they think Contextual Persona could be used in a variety of ways, not just keeping it in mind. "Another thing that could be improved is to use the contextual personas for something else, other than simply keeping them in mind. For example, they could be used in user stories."

**Simplifying the Contextual Persona Description.** One respondent suggested that the method description should be simplified. Here is his reflection: "[I]n the beginning, when I didn't have any previous knowledge of using the Contextual Persona method, I found it fairly difficult to implement as I needed help from my teachers on how to implement it correctly, so I solely think that method description should be simplified with the goal of receiving larger groups of people, that want to implement the method."

## 6 Possible Improvements to the Method

Based on our results, we have made a list of possible improvements to the Contextual Persona method and the guidance that will be given out for using the method.

**The Credibility of the Contextual Persona Could Be Extended.** When introducing the Contextual Persona, the conductors of the method could be encouraged to involve actual users in contextual interviews. In doing so, they could make sure that the source of the Contextual Personas is more credible, and the Personas that they make represent the end-users well.

**The Contextual Persona Should Be Straight to the Point.** Conductors of the Contextual Persona method should be advised to write concise description and pertinent. They should avoid using lengthy paragraphs but instead, use shorter paragraphs or bullet points.

**The Focus in the Background Information Should Be Work-Related.** Conductors of the Contextual Persona method should be advised to focus on the background information on work-related topics and not focus as much on information regarding more personal details. Questions like: What do your users want to achieve at work? What hinders them? What are the stressors? How much control do they have? What kind of support can they get at work? should be answered. That will extend the understanding of users through the Contextual Persona. Additionally, conductors of the method should be advised to describe the users' work environment that **affect** usability and user experience. For example, they might want to describe the noise, lightning, and temperature of the work environment in their Persona. Before doing that, they need to think about whether such details affect the usage of the system. If not, they should leave such details out.

**The Contextual Persona Should Be Reviewed by Stakeholders.** Conductors of the Contextual Persona method should be advised to ask end-users and other stakeholders to review their Contextual Personas with stakeholders. Their feedback could make the Contextual Persona more credible and accurate.

## 7 Discussion

The Contextual Persona method is a relatively new HCI method, so it is still unclear how software developers perceive it. In this study, we have gathered feedback from students using the modified Contextual Persona method to gain insights into how they perceive the new method. Some improvements suggested by the students are in line with previous literature. For example, the proposed improvement concerning making multiple contextual personas, prioritising them and focusing on the primary persona share the same idea as Alan Cooper and colleagues describe in their book [23].

Several factors defining the digital work environment are incorporated the modified Contextual Persona method to support software developers during their design process. Previous research regarding the context of use, such as the framework from Maguire [12] of the context of use, Alonso-Rios et al. [13] description of the taxonomy of context of use components, Bradley and Dunlop [14] description of contextual dimensions and Lallemand and Koenig [15] description of user experience context scale (UXCS), does not discuss how the context of use or contextual factors can be reflected in design processes. The previous studies focus on discussing the context of use from its definition, components and dimensions. However, such discussions separate the context of use concept from the design processes. The Contextual Personas method provides software developers with a tool to consider the context of use during their design process.

One limitation of this study is that the data is collected from students' reports rather than feedback from designers or developers using the Contextual Persona method in real-life situations. We need to be aware of the differences between gathering feedback from students in a university course and collecting data in real-life situations. Designing or developing IT systems is a complex social activity that happens in a dynamic and inter-organizational context [1], which is quite different from doing the same things in a university course. Hence, further research can be conducted to investigate the usage of the Contextual Persona method in real-life situations.

The Contextual Persona method was described as a valuable tool to help students consider the digital work environment using the software system being designed. From the students' feedback on their own experience using the Contextual Persona method, we report the positive and negative aspects and what can be improved.

**Acknowledgments.** We would like to thank AFA Insurance in Sweden for the financial support to conduct this research project under the name STRIA - Software Development for a Better Work Environment (grant number 180250). Also, we would like to thank all informants in the study that took their time to participate in the study.

## References

1. Eshet, E., Bouwman, H.: Context of use: the final frontier in the practice of user-centered design? Interact. Comput. **29**(3), 368–390 (2017)
2. de Groot, B., van Welie, M.: Leveraging the context of use in mobile service design. In: Paternò, F. (ed.) Mobile HCI 2002. LNCS, vol. 2411, pp. 334–338. Springer, Heidelberg (2002). https://doi.org/10.1007/3-540-45756-9_34

3. Kim, J., Chang, Y., Chong, A.Y.L., Park, M.-C.: Do perceived use contexts influence usage behavior? An instrument development of perceived use context. Inf. Manage. **56**(7), 103155 (2019)
4. Yang, S., Lu, Y., Gupta, S., Cao, Y.: Does context matter? The impact of use context on mobile internet adoption. Int. J. Hum. Comput. Interact. **28**(8), 530–541 (2012)
5. Brahma, M., Tripathi, S.S., Sahay, A.: Developing curriculum for industry 4.0: digital workplaces. High. Educ. Skills Work Based Learn. **11**(1), 144–163 (2020). https://doi.org/10.1108/HESWBL-08-2019-0103
6. Hicks, M.: Why the urgency of digital transformation is hurting the digital workplace. Strateg. HR Rev. **18**(1), 34–35 (2019). https://doi.org/10.1108/SHR-02-2019-153
7. Matthews, T., Whittaker, S., Moran, T., Yuen, S.: Collaboration personas: a new approach to designing workplace collaboration tools. In: Proceedings of the SIGCHI conference on human factors in computing systems, pp. 2247–2256 (2011)
8. Miaskiewicz, T., Kozar, K.A.: Personas and user-centered design: how can personas benefit product design processes? Des. Stud. **32**(5), 417–430 (2011)
9. Goodman-Deane, J., Langdon, P., Clarkson, J.: Key influences on the user-centred design process. J. Eng. Des. **21**(2–3), 345–373 (2010)
10. Haag, M., Marsden, N.: Exploring personas as a method to foster empathy in student IT design teams. Int. J. Technol. Des. Educ. **29**(3), 565–582 (2018). https://doi.org/10.1007/s10798-018-9452-5
11. Cajander, Å., Larusdottir, M., Eriksson, E., Nauwerck, G.: Contextual personas as a method for understanding digital work environments. In: Abdelnour Nocera, J., Barricelli, B.R., Lopes, A., Campos, P., Clemmensen, T. (eds.) HWID 2015. IAICT, vol. 468, pp. 141–152. Springer, Cham (2015). https://doi.org/10.1007/978-3-319-27048-7_10
12. Maguire, M.: Context of use within usability activities. Int. J. Hum Comput Stud. **55**(4), 453–483 (2001)
13. Alonso-Ríos, D., Vázquez-García, A., Mosqueira-Rey, E., Moret-Bonillo, V.: A context-of-use taxonomy for usability studies. Int. J. Hum. Comput. Interact. **26**(10), 941–970 (2010)
14. Bradley, A.N., Dunlop, M.D.: Toward a multidisciplinary model of context to support context-aware computing. Hum. Comput. Interact. **20**(4), 403–446 (2005)
15. Lallemand, C., Koenig, V.: Measuring the contextual dimension of user experience: development of the user experience context scale (UXCS). In: Proceedings of the 11th Nordic Conference on Human-Computer Interaction: Shaping Experiences, Shaping Society, pp. 1–13 (2020)
16. Shravasti, R., Bhola, S.S.: Study on working environment and job satisfaction of employees in respect to service sector: an analysis. Rev. Res. **4**(4) (2015)
17. Wright, B.E., Davis, B.S.: Job satisfaction in the public sector: the role of the work environment. Am. Rev. Public Admin. **33**(1), 70–90 (2003)
18. Davison, R., Ou, C.: Digital work in a pre-digital organizational culture (2014)
19. Dittes, S., Smolnik, S.: Towards a digital work environment: the influence of collaboration and networking on employee performance within an enterprise social media platform. J. Bus. Econ. **89**(8–9), 1215–1243 (2019). https://doi.org/10.1007/s11573-019-00951-4
20. Williams, S.P., Schubert, P.: Designs for the digital workplace. Procedia Comput. Sci. **138**, 478–485 (2018)
21. Sandblad, B., Gulliksen, J., Lantz, A., Walldius, Å., Åborg, C.: Digitaliseringen och arbetsmiljön. Studentlitteratur, Lund (2018)
22. Cooper, A.: The inmates are running the asylum: Why high-tech products drive us crazy and how to restore the sanity. Sams Indianapolis, (2004)
23. Cooper, A., Reimann, R., Cronin, D.: About Face 3: The Essentials of Interaction Design. John Wiley & Sons, New York (2007)

24. Pruitt, J., Grudin, J.: Personas: practice and theory. In Proceedings of the 2003 Conference on Designing for User Experiences, pp. 1–15 (2003)
25. Wöckl, B., Yildizoglu, U., Buber, I., Diaz, B.A., Kruijff, E., Tscheligi, M.: Basic senior personas: a representative design tool covering the spectrum of European older adults. In: Proceedings of the 14th International ACM SIGACCESS Conference on Computers and Accessibility, pp. 25–32 (2012)
26. Zhu, H., Wang, H., Carroll, J.M.: Creating persona skeletons from imbalanced datasets-a case study using US older adults' health data. In: Proceedings of the 2019 on Designing Interactive Systems Conference, pp. 61–70, (2019)
27. Mulder, S., Yaar, Z.: The User is Always Right: A Practical Guide to Creating and Using Personas for the Web. New Riders, Indianapolis (2006)
28. Cooper, A., Reimann, R., Dubberly, H.: About Face 2.0: The Essentials of Interaction Design. John Wiley & Sons, Inc., New York (2003)
29. Grudin, J., Pruitt, J.: Personas, participatory design and product development: an infrastructure for engagement. In: Proceedings PDC (2002)
30. Long, F.: Real or imaginary: the effectiveness of using personas in product design. In: Proceedings of the Irish Ergonomics Society Annual Conference, vol. 14, pp. 1–10 (2009)
31. Ma, J., LeRouge, C.: Introducing user profiles and personas into information systems development. In: AMCIS 2007 Proceedings, vol. 237 (2007)
32. Chapman, C. N., Milham, R. P.: The personas' new clothes: methodological and practical arguments against a popular method. In: Proceedings of the Human Factors and Ergonomics Society Annual Meeting, pp. 634–636 (2006)
33. An, J., Kwak, H., Jung, S., Salminen, J., Admad, M., Jansen, B.: Imaginary people representing real numbers: generating personas from online social media data. ACM Trans. Web (TWEB) **12**(4), 1–26 (2018)
34. Pruitt, J., Adlin, T.: The Persona Lifecycle: Keeping People in Mind throughout Product Design. Elsevier, New York (2010)
35. Spiliotopoulos, D., Margaris, D., Vassilakis, C.: Data-assisted persona construction using social media data. Big Data Cogn. Comput. **4**(3), 21 (2020). https://doi.org/10.3390/bdcc4030021
36. Theorell, T., Karasek, R.A.: Current issues relating to psychosocial job strain and cardiovascular disease research. J. Occup. Health Psychol. **1**(1), 9 (1996)
37. International Standard Organization: Ergonomics of human-system interaction - 9241-210 (2019)
38. Braun, V., Clarke, V.: Using thematic analysis in psychology. Qual. Res. Psychol. **3**(2), 77–101 (2006)

# MyLYL: Towards Flexible Interaction Design for Operator Assistance Systems

Jan Van den Bergh(✉) and Florian Heller

Expertise Centre for Digital Media, Hasselt University - tUL - Flanders Make, Hasselt, Belgium
jan.vandenbergh@uhasselt.be

**Abstract.** Assistive systems in industrial assembly, such as cranes, hoists, and robotic arms are installed to reduce the ergonomic stress operators are exposed to. Whether such a system is suitable for a certain assembly step is currently evaluated based on ergonomic criteria. This does not seem sufficient as operators often choose not to use the assistive system. It is therefore important to ask why this is the case and what can be done to minimize the chances that support tools are not used.

To address the why-question, we ran contextual inquiries at three large production companies and used the results to design a simple scoring sheet to evaluate and compare the usability aspects of assistive systems in industrial assembly. This scoring sheet represents a design space: it provides an overview of different attention points relevant to the operators. As a first evaluation, we retroactively compared the (then) current to the desired situations in the visited companies. Further research is necessary to evaluate the design space and its representation.

## 1 Introduction

The manufacturing industry has long sought to automate and where that was not possible, provide tools that assist users in their tasks. One major driver for the latter are the negative health effects of physical stress on the worker due to handling of heavy loads or repetitive handling of (slightly) less heavy loads in the production process [6,9,10].

While such efforts frequently led to hoists and robots that assist workers in handling loads, such tools are regularly underused. Several usability factors lead potential users, in the remainder called *operators*, to not use these tools, even when knowing their use is beneficial to their health. One of the contributing factors is the sometimes large number of additional non-value added actions that are associated with hoist systems, as noted by a.o. Papetti et al. [8]. They propose a human-centered process for the design of human-centered manufacturing equipment. Within this process quantification of, among others, the number of tasks and ergonomics plays an important role. Virtual environments provide a

Florian Heller—affiliated with Hasselt University - tUL - Flanders Make at the time of research.


Published by Springer Nature Switzerland AG 2022
C. Ardito et al. (Eds.): INTERACT 2021, LNCS 13198, pp. 113–122, 2022.
https://doi.org/10.1007/978-3-030-98388-8_11

means to test potential technology before its actually made. El Makrini et al. [5] also demonstrated the benefits of a human-centered process for the introduction of assistive technology – a cobot for a gluing application – in manufacturing while they put more emphasis on qualitative research. In both these cases a large and diverse cooperative team led to success.

However, such a large team with deep knowledge on a large set of domains is not always available. For example, updating existing installations due to changing requirements, or transferring knowledge to work cells with similar tasks for different products may be such cases where it may be useful to have a view on what is possible and what are important points of attention. In this paper we want to address the questions of how to find out why current situations should be adapted and how this can be done; which design options are desirable in the specific situation.

Contextual inquiry [1] is a method to gain qualitative insight in the work experiences related to a specific goal. We used this method to investigate the operator's needs related to the repetitive handling of loads in their work environment at specific work cells in three large production companies. We then tried to generalize the outcome using a design space. Design spaces have been used for a long time to characterize possible design options. Buxton [2] and Card et al. [4] were among those that provided characterizations for input devices for computing systems decades ago. Card and Mackinlay [3] proposed a design space for information visualization. These design spaces use a set of variables (and associated values) to define the range of design options that are possible. These focus on the technical aspects of both input and output of computing systems. In contrast, our focus is on how the user, the operator, experiences the usage of the interactive system, the (smart) hoist.

In an effort to generalize the knowledge gained from the contextual inquiry, we identified six variables with three potential values each that characterize the interaction with an assistive system for industrial assembly. These characteristics can be used to assess the current situation in which operators work and to identify potential solutions in terms of desired qualitative values for these variables. We noticed that these variables can be applied to actions that relate to manipulating the load. These characteristics are the base of a simple sheet to assess the current situation and determine characteristics of the desired situation in terms of user needs, without prescribing specific solutions. The sheet contains spider diagrams that visualize the values for the different variable-action combinations in two situations. In this paper we discuss the contextual inquiry, the resulting design space, and its application.

## 2 Contextual Inquiries

In the context of a research project aimed at introducing smart hoists (or collaborative robots) to assist operators in the manipulation of heavy or large objects, we performed contextual inquiries in three companies. We obtained ethical approval for the approach before the start of the observations. We did one contextual inquiry in each of the companies. All inquiries were done by the same researcher, who used a camera to make movie clips and pen and paper to write down the operators' comments. The people involved in the inquiry and the timing were determined by the involved companies. During each visit, we observed and talked with two to three operators working in the same environment. Table 1 provides more details on characteristics of the sites, including the number of hoists available in the observed work cells. The questions were focused on understanding their current working environment. Each of the environments already had at least one hoist installed. The approach was approved by the relevant ethical committee of Hasselt University.

**Table 1.** Observed operators and how they work

| Company | Operators | Team | Hoists |
|---|---|---|---|
| A | 2 | separate work cells | 1, 2 |
| B | 2 | team along conveyor belt | 1 |
| C | 3 | team in one work cell | 1 |

In company A, operators pick a gear from a bin (Fig. 1, lower left), put it in a machine (Fig. 1, right), get it out, do a check, and put it in a sink. Operators work in teams across work cells and switch work cells during the day to increase diversity in tasks. One hoist is available to move the gear in and out of the machine (Fig. 1, center inset and right) and, in one work cell where the heaviest gears are manipulated, one for the other movements (Fig. 1, left). The hoists have different characteristics and, therefore, cannot be interchanged for all tasks. One hoist is used for movements from/to the machine, the other for the remaining movements. Operators experienced issues with ergonomics regarding the inertia of the hoists, specifically when rotating, or starting/stopping hoist movement. There was no clear labeling/instructions on one essential hoist control which reportedly had an effect on the memorability of when to use the control. This in turn led to harmful incidents. Picking products from a relatively low box involved several additional non-value-added actions because it was impossible to pick the products in the position they were delivered.

The operators in company B, have to do an assembly in which a pressure vessel is a central component and the heaviest one to manipulate. A hoist is available for transporting the heaviest pressure vessels over a relatively long distance to a turntable for a smaller sub-assembly and a short distance to the main assembly on the conveyor belt (Fig. 2, left). Operators in this case work in a team along a conveyor. The team decides on task distribution. One person in a team is responsible for transport using the hoist. It was this person that took part in the contextual inquiry for two different teams. In case of incidents, tasks are dynamically redistributed. Difficulties mentioned by the operators were the slowness of using the hoist, hindrance of the hoist during other actions and difficulty with coupling and decoupling of the pressure vessels.

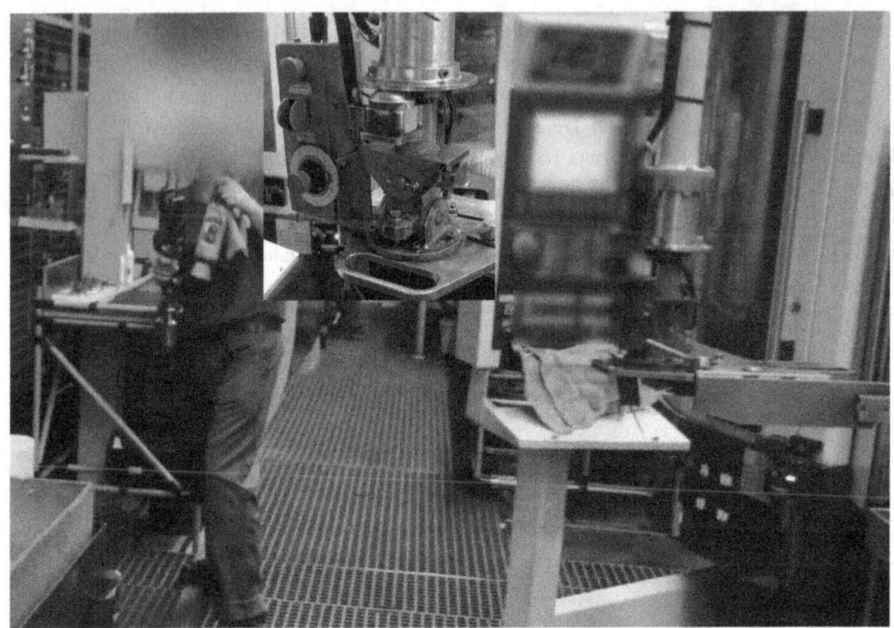

**Fig. 1.** Hoists in company A: chain hoist (left) and second hoist center and right.

**Fig. 2.** Hoist in company B (left) and company C (right).

In company C, the operators primarily build an enclosure consisting of poles, doors, and panels, around an existing sub assembly. A hoist (Fig. 2, right) is available to transport the top panels. There is no hoist[1] available to manipulate

[1] A new hoist has been installed since the visit that supports almost all panels and doors.

the other panels and doors. These can be handled without a hoist, although it is not ideal. The operators mentioned no issues with using the hoist. The researchers observed that the overall process of using the hoist was completely manual, relatively slow, it was not easy to correctly balance the top panel, and the process required the presence of two operators to guide the hoist to the top of the assembly. The height of the assembly necessitates operators to use stairs for mounting and fixing the top panel. Other panels need to be rotated and some sides consist of two panels, which were assembled before integration in the full assembly.

Despite significant differences in the settings, some common themes emerged: The observed operators were aware of the importance of ergonomic behavior for their self interest. Meeting or beating expected production goals was at least as important. Implicit social pressure heavily influences decisions on among others using the hoist. Task allocation was dynamic to meet a shared goal. Dragging and turning induce physical stress.

More specifically for hoists the following requirements were observed or explicitly mentioned by the operators:

- It should be easy to attach and detach loads, and to start and precisely stop movement.
- Hoists should not impact other actions and not make meeting production goals more difficult.
- Operators would appreciate if hoists would also support other actions (e.g. assembly or inspection) but should minimize additional actions.

These conclusions, together with video's of actual operator use of the hoists was presented to stakeholders. This type of qualitative information was appreciated and a reduced version, video recordings by the companies themselves were adopted to document operator practices.

## 3 Usability of Hoists in Changing Contexts of Use

ISO 9241-110:2020 [7] defines usability as the

> extent to which a system, product or service can be used by specified users to achieve specified goals with effectiveness, efficiency and satisfaction in a specified context of use

The context of use in this definition includes the user, goals and tasks, environment and resources. In the situations discussed before, the goals and tasks can be considered mostly static, changes in the physical environment are also limited. Users, in this case operators, can change quickly (and thus also the social environment); at one of the companies none of the operators participating in the contextual inquiry still work there. Resources change the most as there is a significant variety in products being treated.

This means that in order to be usable, it should be easy to learn using the hoist system and to remember how to use the hoist system with specific resources. It is thus essential that the system provides good affordances and a clear feedforward [11], it is clear what *function* will be performed when activating a control. One option to do that is to provide clear labels. The hoist in the middle of Fig. 1 has clear labels for the two top-most controls. The lower control was however missing a clear label and operators provided a fix. Such a fix is temporary and ideally a signal to provide a more permanent solution and not a reason to mark the issue as resolved. Sometimes control usage might be more complex and instructions may be needed.

Effectiveness can only be achieved when tasks are successfully completed. In the case of hoists this means (at least) attaching, moving, and detaching loads at the correct location. A precise view of the target location is crucial to achieve this result and thus feedback is important, especially when the load or the hoist itself hinder the view on the target location. In the observed cases, viewing the target location was still possible, although the associated posture was far from ideal. Another aspect of effectiveness is the potential to recover from use errors.

User satisfaction is the aspect that might be most easily overlooked in designing hoist systems as we saw that it relates to aspects that are not always directly related to the execution of the tasks. Things like control position when not using the hoist or rotation limitations when the product is attached to the hoist during assembly tasks impact user satisfaction, but do not directly relate to hoist operation tasks.

Efficiency is very important in the manufacturing industry. The fact that hoist usage often implies additional actions or reduces operational efficiency due to inertia or safety considerations (e.g., limited speed on button-controlled movement). Computer-controlled systems can alleviate the task for the user, as they allow to implement more user-centered controls. This can be, for example, continuous speed control[2], combined movement, or automated directional mapping based on the user's orientation. Our proposed design-space and evaluation sheet allows you to compare and assess different implementations of such improvements.

## 4 MyLYL Design Space

We compared available industrial control solutions as well as existing human-machine design guidelines. We then looked how these could inform the design of hoist-action controls. We identified six dimensions that can be controlled for a set of actions:

**speed** the flexibility with which speed can be controlled. This can impact both efficiency and user satisfaction,

**load** physical strain on the operator directly impacts operator satisfaction (and harm),

[2] An example of continuous speed control is available at https://www.youtube.com/watch?v=GTKRwtfGzCo.

**place** where the action can be controlled; this may impact user satisfaction as it influences the ease with which controls can be reached and potentially whether controls hinder other actions or require additional movement and thus efficiency,
**function** the way functionality of controls is observable through the system,
**effect** feedback when controls are used,
**instructions** task-specific documentation on how controls should be used or combined to complete specified tasks.

To ease usage of these dimensions, we determined three qualitative levels for each of the dimensions that indicate the level of support for an operator on that dimension. A higher value indicates more support for the operator on that dimension for a specific action. Whether more or less support on a specific dimension is needed, should be determined on a case-by-case level. Table 2 gives an overview of the design space dimensions and values. The additional 0 value is shared across all dimensions and thus mentioned only once in the overview.

The stated characteristics of the dimensions and the proposed values allow to quickly get a rough idea on the level of support offered by one or more solutions for a specific set of actions. We made a first version of a supporting tool by building a spreadsheet that allows to compare the support offered to operators by current and envisioned hoists to perform certain actions. The spreadsheet provides space for in two actions with the gripper and two movement actions with two (potential) hoists (see Fig. 3).

Supporting discussion on advantages and disadvantages of potential solutions without the need for deep technical or knowledge and consideration of aspects that might otherwise be overlooked are some of the drivers behind the research.

## 5 Application of the Design Space

For each of the company cases, discussed in the Sect. 2, we could identify two actions related to the gripper and two actions related to hoist movement for which we identified a current and desired value.

For Company A, the actions that needed a change in support were *horizontal* and *vertical* movement, as well as *rotation* and *taking products* with the available gripper(s). More specifically, the operator load was problematic for horizontal movement due to inertia of the hoists. The effect of hoist movements was hard to see during precise positioning. This led to ergonomically straining postures during this action. The lack of information on the load compensation control on the primary hoist was a problem for vertical movement; there was no information on control function and effect, nor instructions on the hoist. This hoist did not support gripper rotation (around horizontal axis) leading to the need for a second hoist and several additional actions for some of the heaviest objects. Taking objects with this primary hoist was also difficult because the hoist limited the visibility and thus hampered the required precision. This could be solved by more explicit information on how the controls function and their effect.

**Table 2.** Dimensions and values of the proposed hoist control design space. *Speed*, *Load* and *Place* document the functional aspect of the provided hoist control. *Function*, *effect*, and *instruction* specify the level information provided by the hoist

| Dimension | Value | Name | Explanation |
|---|---|---|---|
| *all* | 0 | N/A | Not applicable, no support provided |
| Speed | 1 | Binary | speed of operation is determined by hoist only control: on/off |
| | 2 | Discrete | operator can choose from predefined speeds |
| | 3 | Continuous | operator determines speed of operation |
| Load | 1 | Problematic | operator perceives execution of action as problematic |
| | 2 | Limited | input of operator during entire execution of the action execution of action is not considered to be problematic |
| | 3 | None | no load on operator *during* execution of action activation of the action or function by the operator might still be needed |
| Place | 1 | Handler | controller moves with hoist |
| | 2 | Product | operator uses the product to execute an action |
| | 3 | Operator | controller moves with operator |
| Function | 1 | None | no explicit indication is present |
| | 2 | Basic | basic indicator is present |
| | 3 | Detail | detailed information is provided for this variable |
| Effect | 1 | None | no explicit indication is present |
| | 2 | Basic | basic indicator is present |
| | 3 | Detail | detailed information is provided for this variable |
| Instruction | 1 | None | no explicit indication is present |
| | 2 | Basic | basic indicator is present |
| | 3 | Detail | detailed information is provided for this variable |

The actions that deserved more attention were similar for the work cell in Company B. The dimensions that needed attention differed, however. For vertical movement the place of control caused problems because it hindered the assembly actions of the operators or took too much time to put aside. For taking products it was the load that caused problems, due to the force needed to open the used hook. Rotation (around vertical axis) of the product was also hindered by the hoist, leading to unnecessary, load on the operators. It led operators to adapt the work procedure. The main issue with horizontal movement was similar to that in Company A, although additional load due to product stability issues was also mentioned.

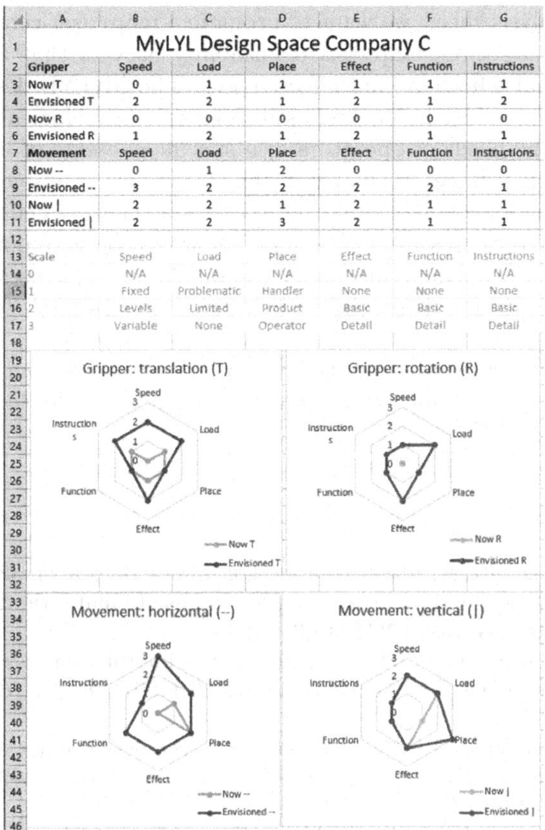

MyLYL Design Space Company C

| Gripper | Speed | Load | Place | Effect | Function | Instructions |
|---|---|---|---|---|---|---|
| Now T | 0 | 1 | 1 | 1 | 1 | 1 |
| Envisioned T | 2 | 2 | 1 | 2 | 1 | 2 |
| Now R | 0 | 0 | 0 | 0 | 0 | 0 |
| Envisioned R | 1 | 2 | 1 | 2 | 1 | 1 |
| **Movement** | **Speed** | **Load** | **Place** | **Effect** | **Function** | **Instructions** |
| Now -- | 0 | 1 | 2 | 0 | 0 | 0 |
| Envisioned -- | 3 | 2 | 2 | 2 | 2 | 1 |
| Now \| | 2 | 2 | 1 | 2 | 1 | 1 |
| Envisioned \| | 2 | 2 | 3 | 2 | 1 | 1 |

| Scale | Speed | Load | Place | Effect | Function | Instructions |
|---|---|---|---|---|---|---|
| 0 | N/A | N/A | N/A | N/A | N/A | N/A |
| 1 | Fixed | Problematic | Handler | None | None | None |
| 2 | Levels | Limited | Product | Basic | Basic | Basic |
| 3 | Variable | None | Operator | Detail | Detail | Detail |



**Fig. 3.** Spreadsheet supporting usage of the design space with visualisations using spider graphs for the situation in company C

In the observed work cell in company C, the actions that needed change in support (Fig. 3) resembled those in the other companies. However, the dimensions that needed to be addressed were different. To better support horizontal movement, load reduction as well as information for precise positioning were mentioned. For vertical movement the place of control needed change as both hands were needed for product control and thus no hand was available near guardrail to safely walk up stairs near large assembly. Rotation of the gripper was requested, which made usage of the hoist more complex and thus additional information might be necessary.

## 6 Conclusion and Outlook

Hoist, lifts, cranes, and robotic arms help operators in handling components of various weights in order to reduce ergonomic stress. As such, their purpose is human-centered, but the interaction side is still very technology-centered. With our proposed analysis sheet, we want to promote a more user-centered approach to control that puts more emphasis on usability aspects that affect adoption other than optimal efficiency and effectiveness. The MyLYL design space and supporting sheet give insight in the possibilities for technological support using hoists based on the needs of operators in a specific contexts of use. In the specific manufacturing cells, each change in the manipulated products but also the technological choices for hoists and other aspects of the work cell has a potential impact on the needs of operators. The sheet allows to compare potential changes in order to opt for the optimal solution. We applied it for some uses cases. Further research remains warranted to validate it in more diverse settings.

**Acknowledgments.** Supported by the ICON project SmartHandler (grant number: HBC.2018.0251), funded by Flanders Make, the strategic center for the manufacturing industry in Flanders, Belgium.

## References

1. Beyer, H., Holtzblatt, K.: Contextual design. Interactions **6**(1), 32–42 (1999)
2. Buxton, W.: Lexical and pragmatic considerations of input structures. ACM SIGGRAPH Comput. Graph. **17**(1), 31–37 (1983)
3. Card, S.K., Mackinlay, J.: The structure of the information visualization design space. In: Proceedings of VIZ 1997, pp. 92–99 (1997). https://doi.org/10.1109/INFVIS.1997.636792
4. Card, S.K., Mackinlay, J.D., Robertson, G.G.: The design space of input devices. In: Proceedings of CHI 1990, pp. 117–124. ACM, New York (1990). https://doi.org/10.1145/97243.97263
5. El Makrini, I., et al.: Working with Walt: how a cobot was developed and inserted on an auto assembly line. IEEE Robot. Autom. Mag. **25**(2), 51–58 (2018)
6. Hignett, S., McAtamney, L.: Rapid entire body assessment (REBA). Appl. Ergon. **31**(2), 201–205 (2000). https://doi.org/10.1016/S0003-6870(99)00039-3
7. IEC International Electrotechnical Commission: DIN EN ISO 9241-110:2020 ergonomics of human-system interaction - part 110: Interaction principles. https://www.iso.org/obp/ui/#iso:std:iso:9241:-110:ed-2:v1:en
8. Papetti, A., Ciccarelli, M., Brunzini, A., Germani, M.: Design of ergonomic manufacturing equipment by a human-centered methodology. Int. J. Interact. Des. Manuf. (IJIDeM) **15**, 1–5 (2020). https://doi.org/10.1007/s12008-020-00734-0
9. Schaub, K., Caragnano, G., Britzke, B., Bruder, R.: The European assembly worksheet. Theoret. Issues Ergon. Sci. **14**(6), 616–639 (2013)
10. Schneider, E., Irastorza, X.: OSH in figures: work-related musculoskeletal disorders in the EU—Facts and figures. Publications Office of the European Union (2020). https://doi.org/10.2802/10952
11. Vermeulen, J., Luyten, K., van den Hoven, E., Coninx, K.: Crossing the bridge over Norman's gulf of execution: revealing feedforward's true identity. In: Proceedings of CHI 2013, pp. 1931–1940 (2013)

# Creating a Post-sedentary Work Context for Software Engineering

Martin Hedlund[1(✉)], Cristian Bogdan[1], and Gerrit Meixner[1,2]

[1] KTH Royal Institute of Technology, Stockholm, Sweden
marthed@kth.se

[2] UniTyLab, Heilbronn University, Heilbronn, Germany

**Abstract.** Software engineers are sedentary and need technological help for a more healthy life. Current software engineering tasks are mostly confined to the standard sedentary desktop user interface. We believe that software engineering should be restructured so that it offers a non-sedentary alternative. In this paper, we describe a new research approach, called Post-sedentary Software Engineering. Our ambition with this approach is to provide an alternative, healthier work context without decreasing productivity. We take a spatial approach to post-sedentary tool design, starting from the assumption an interactive 3D environment with appropriate metaphors is necessary for full body movement. We discuss available technologies for achieving this goal and outline four studies that incorporate the software engineering phases of code comprehension, code creation and debugging in a non-sedentary context.

**Keywords:** Sedentary · Post-sedentary · Spatial · Metaphor · Software engineering

## 1 Introduction

Software engineers are sedentary and need technological help for a more healthy life. Current software engineering tasks are mostly confined to the standard sedentary desktop user interface. We believe that software engineering, like all forms of sedentary work activities involving digital technologies, should be restructured so that they offer a non-sedentary alternative. The research interest in sedentary behavior has grown rapidly in recent years [60]. Ergonomics researchers are investigating potential solutions such as sit-stand desks, software for nudging, active work stations (e.g. thread mills and bikes) and increasing the work time spent in non-work physical activity [58,61]. Our vision is to change the work activities themselves.

In this paper, we are describing a new research approach, which we call post-sedentary Software Engineering. We expect this research to extend the software engineering work context, i.e. the context of use for software engineering tools, by outlining a healthier work environment for software engineers. In other words, we are exploring alternative means of interacting with and representing software


C. Ardito et al. (Eds.): INTERACT 2021, LNCS 13198, pp. 123–138, 2022.
https://doi.org/10.1007/978-3-030-98388-8_12

that reduce sedentary behavior. In addition to health benefits, the interaction and movement incorporated in our tools could potentially improve cognitive functioning and learning ability [26,30]. Furthermore, our aspiration with this research is also to improve the software engineering work context by incorporating more efficient means of completing tasks in different phases of the software engineering process. In other words, we are not satisfied with studies that indicate health benefits but with a substantial drop in productivity.

We take a *spatial approach* to post-sedentary design. That is, we are starting from the assumption that stimulating movement can be done by defining various kinds of three-dimensional spaces. In order to accomplish a task, the software engineers need to physically move their bodies and arms to interact with the artifacts in the 3D space. Nowadays software engineers navigate the large space of a software project through a small, static view-port: the computer screen. The approach we propose is to make that navigation bodily-dynamic, at most stages of the software engineering process. For that, we will need to use or define new *spatial metaphors* for programming, debugging, code comprehension and other engineering activities.

To explore the potential of post-sedentary software engineering, we will initially address the following research questions:

- What type of non-sedentary interaction can be used for software engineering?
- What phases of the software engineering process can be supported in a post-sedentary way?
- What type of metaphors can be used in post-sedentary working spaces?
- What are the benefits and drawbacks of spatially oriented software engineering?
- How much does post-sedentary software engineering affect physical activity?
- What are the qualities of a motivating and learning-aiding post-sedentary software engineering tool?

## 2 Background

We will start this section by reviewing the literature on potential benefits of pursuing research in Post-sedentary software engineering. Next up we look at technologies we believe have the best potential of realizing our new work context. Finally, we look at potential spatial metaphors that can be used to represent software in a three-dimensional space.

### 2.1 Why Post-sedentary?

In this section we look at the potential benefits of a non-sedentary approach, the way we see it.

**Health and Sedentary Behavior:** The evidence is overwhelming that routine physical activity reduces the risk for premature mortality and is an effective primary and secondary preventive strategy for at least 25 chronic medical conditions [64]. Perhaps contrary to expectation, the greatest benefits occurs at relatively low physical activity volumes [64]. A recent long-term study with 2100 participants, and mean follow-up of 10.8 years, compared steps per day with mortality rate [40]. Participants who took >7000 steps/d had a 50–70% lower mortality rate. This relationship was true regardless of the step intensity. Along similar lines, one meta-analysis suggests that low doses of physical activity is associated with lower risk of mental illness [59]. However, the type of physical activity may play a role, where work-related physical activity might have the opposite effect. The enjoyment of, and motivation for the physical activity is likely impacting the mental health outcomes [3,68].

In the research field of Ergonomics, Straker & Mathiassen called for a shift in focus to account for the rise of sedentary occupations and the conjoining health implications [53]. The research interest in sedentary behavior has grown rapidly over the years [60]. But the evidence is currently inconclusive whenever current workplace interventions, for example sit-stand desks, nudging software, active work stations (e.g. thread mills and bikes) and increasing the work time spent in non-work physical activity, are effective at reducing sitting at work are effective [50,58]. Such interventions could also have potential drawbacks such as decreasing the work performance. An example of this is Straker et al. study that found active computer workstations (e.g. threadmills, bikes) decreased performance when using mouse and keyboard [52].

**Multimodal Learning:** Technologies used in Post-sedentary software engineering could potentially afford the concept of multimodal learning [30], the idea that an embodied learning situation which engages multiple sensory and action systems of the learner is beneficial for learning. This could mean that utilizing technologies that engages more sensory systems (e.g. direct hand manipulation, body movement), could be beneficial for learning in our post-sedentary work context. The idea of multimodal learning can be traced back to the philosophy of Montessori [28], which claims that motor behavior and cognition are closely intertwined and that physical movement can enhance thinking and learning.

**Movement and Cognition:** More recently, Leisman et al. argue that data supports the notion that motor and cognitive processes possess dynamic bidirectional influences on each other [26]. Furthermore, they conclude that "because of the linkage between motor and cognitive function that we represent here, it is our contention that inactivity has an effect of rendering an individual's cognitive as well as motor performance less efficient or utilizing significantly decreased modes of functional and effective connectivities and exercise has the converse effect" [26]. In other words, user movement could potentially not only afford increased ability to learn, but also support cognitive function in general. However, one potential drawback could be the loss of concentration due to overt body movement [26]. For example, Park et al. found that visual search was improved under physical effort, but made participants more affected by distracting stimuli [42].

## 2.2 Interaction Technologies

We will now visit a few interactive technologies that we believe have the potential to bring non-sedentary interaction to the software engineering work. For each of these technologies we will discuss the *affordances* that make them suitable for our purpose, and the novel possibilities they open. For example; a mouse, a keyboard or a desktop screen are inherently sedentary technologies. We are therefore exploring beyond such traditional interactive technologies.

**Virtual Reality:** Virtual Reality (VR) offers the possibility of bringing software engineering tasks into a 3D context. For navigating in this 3D context, there exist many different techniques. We are especially interested in locomotion-based VR navigation (e.g. walk-in-place, thread mills, natural walking) [8], as that would emphasize full body movement and attain to our post-sedentary goals. We will further discuss locomotion techniques in VR in a following subsection. Elliot et al. [12] suggest three affordances of VR for software engineering; (1) spatial cognition, (2) manipulation and motion and (3) feedback. Spatial cognition enhances the perception of depth and presence, "being there". Previous studies have suggested that this could be positive for user (software engineer) focus and learning [21]. Spatial navigation cognition can be stimulated when a user is moving around "as normal" in a virtual world. This could for example help software engineers better recollect the location of artifacts such as code modules. By manipulating artifacts physically, retention and perception can be improved. For example, turning book pages instead of reading on a computer monitor increases comprehension and recall. The development feedback loop could be improved with VR if the time it takes between an action and the results is shortened. This would especially be the case for using VR itself to develop VR applications, since the developer does not have to switch between the desktop and virtual environment. Riva et al. [44] found that VR could improve executive functioning and visual-spatial ability among users. The improved visual-spatial ability is in line with, and roughly equivalent with previously mentioned findings on Spatial cognition in VR [12,16]. Executive functioning refers to higher-level abilities in the following areas: planning, problem-solving, attention, mental flexibility, initiation, judgment, inhibition, and abstract reasoning [49]. Improved executive functioning from VR usage is arguably highly beneficial for software engineering.

**Augmented Reality:** Much of affordances of VR translate to Augmented Reality (AR), with the key difference that user does not get immersed in a different environment. This will have drawbacks related to the cognitive benefits of immersion [21]. AR instead provides a number of other benefits. For example, AR gives the option of working in enjoyable environments, for example outdoors, something that has been showed to positively effect sense of vitality and well-being [43,47]. This could also allow for more space to be utilized compared to an indoor office. Augmented Reality can be used in physical spaces to provide collaboration with non-immersed colleagues and non-immersed objects such as a physical table or board used for project planning, architecture discussions etc. AR technology, such as Microsoft Hololens [33] have been used to create tangible block programming environments for children [18]. Similar tangible programming environments have been proposed, although not utilizing AR [56,62]. AR has an advantage over VR when combining digital information with tangible material, since the user can view both types of artefacts simultaneously. The idea of combining tangible physical material with AR is an interesting concept that could be explored further for non-sedentary software engineering.

**Interaction Controllers:** There currently exist a variety of interaction technologies that can be utilized in a post-sedentary software engineering environment. We will test some of them in our studies. Popular VR systems such as HTC Vive and Oculus Rift utilize their own hand-held controllers [55]. Other approaches include multi-touch tablets [54], and different tangible interaction devices [25,27]. Using the arms to grasp and manipulate creates movement, which would make the hand-held controllers more suitable for our aims. However, tasks such as labeling, searching and filtering typically require some form of textual input. This could be achieved using these controllers, but are inefficient compared to a keyboard. Voice control could be a viable option for these tasks [51]. If some sort of portable keyboard is to be included, for example TAP [57], the user hands need to be free. For that, several options are available. Virtual hands can be tracked through optical senors, image recognition or with the use of gloves [13,19,48]. Gesture interaction [17] has been tested for programming environments [2,39] and could be useful for full body movement. However, a study by Onshi et al. [39] found using a VR controller more useful compared to Leap Motion gestures for programming in VR (Fig. 1).

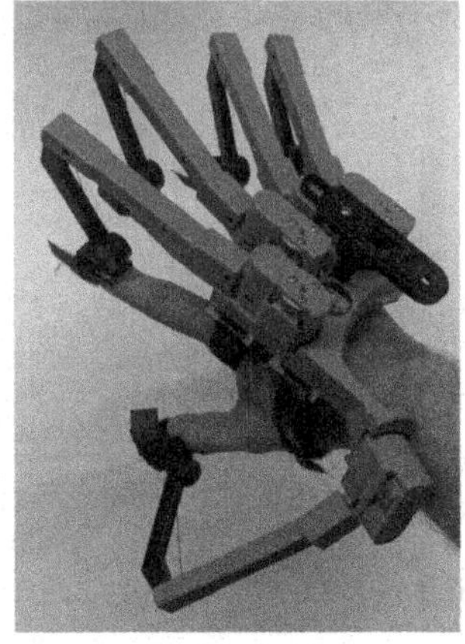

(a) SenseGlove

(b) Oculus Quest 2 controller

**Fig. 1.** Examples of interaction controllers.

**Locomotion Techniques:** The type of locomotion technique used is highly relevant for creating a post-sedentary work context. There currently exists a wide range of options [8], however we are primarily interested in those that affords more movement. Normal, natural walking, with a 1:1 mapping of physical travel to virtual travel is arguably the most straightforward solution. Findings from a recent study also suggests that this type of locomotion in VR could increase learning efficiency in STEM subjects. This was not the case for [35]. The drawback however, is of course the amount of physical space needed. Nilsson et al. [36] suggests a taxonomy for three types of solutions to the problem of walking in limited space, 1) Repositioning systems, 2) Proxy gestures, and 3) Redirected walking. Repositioning systems counteracts the forward movement of the user, thereby ensuring the user stays in a relatively fixed position. Examples include threadmills such as the Virtuix Omni [38] and Cyberith Virtualizer [9]. Proxy gestures requires the user to perform gestures that act as proxies for actual steps. The most common approach is the so-called walk-in-place technique [22], where the user performs step like movements on the spot or swings his or her arms as typically done when walking. The Redirected walking technique manipulates the virtual environment or the users perception in order to facilitate natural walking [36]. This is done, for example, by amplifying the distance traveled in virtual space compared to the physical space, or mapping a curved trajectory in physical space to a straight trajectory in virtual space (Fig. 2).

(a) Virtuix Omni

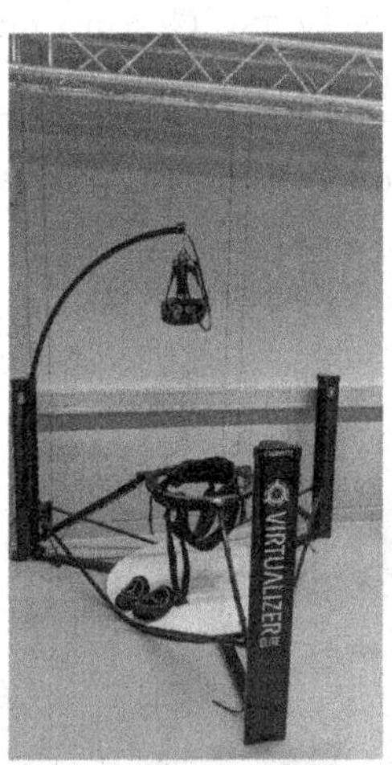


(b) Cyberith Virtualizer

**Fig. 2.** Examples of repositioning systems.

### 2.3 Spatial Metaphors in Software Engineering

Following the logic of our *spatial approach*, the digital representations also need to be translated into a 3D space. That is to say; we need to explore how inherent linear or 2D representations such as text, could be represented for intuitive motion-based interaction. In the following section, we look at some metaphors we believe have the potential to fit in our context.

**Spatial Metaphors in Current Software Engineering Practice:** It is important to reflect on the spatial aspects currently existing in software engineering. For example, many code bases are represented as *trees*. Graphical user interfaces are often represented internally as trees as well, and can be explored and navigated starting from that representation. The questions is how well these are adaptable to a three-dimensional space. The most powerful pattern recognition mechanisms of the brain works in 2D, not 3D [65]. Cone graphs are one example of tree graphs translated into 3D [45], and the author claims that as many as 1000 nodes could be displayed simultaneously without visual clutter. However, we do not see all those nodes at the same time and a user would need to rotate the tree to reveal them. Other 2D methods have been proven more efficient [24,65]. Using different interaction techniques might reduce this inefficiency. For example, moving your body to reveal other nodes might be more intuitive compared to mouse and keyboard interaction in a 3D context.

Unlike trees, other code bases or information could better be represented as node-like structures that don't follow the parent-child relationship of trees. These cannot be represented in 2D without some edges crossing, and thus might fit better in a 3D context. Ware & Frank found this to be the case. The amount of complexity that could be viewed was up to three times greater for these types of graphs in 3D compared to 2D [65,66].

Spatial metaphors for post-sedentary engineering could also be built on existing metaphors from software visualization research. Although many software visualization metaphors are poorly evaluated [32], the *city metaphor* is one of the most explored [41,46,67]. The city metaphor is used for program comprehension of large-scale software projects. It visualizes code as city with roads and buildings clustered in blocks. A recent experimental study by Romano et al. [46] evaluated participants comprehension of a Java code base visualized as a code city in VR. They found that participants were faster, and more correct on answering the comprehension questions compared to the desktop IDE (Eclipse) control group.

The *linear space of programming code rows* will be familiar to most programmers. Developer tools also present ordered spaces, for example *priority hierarchies* like programming variable *scopes* or style cascading representations. Other linear representations are *call stacks*, i.e. the order in which methods called other methods to get to the currently debugged method. Some of these spaces can just be explored (like scopes) while others can be actively navigated by the programmer. For example, the call stack can be used to exit a method context and move to another. Test suites are also typically hierarchical lists that can be navigated and selected by the engineer. Each of these linear"vectors" can become a dimension in a 3D representation designed to support post-sedentary software engineering. Our intention is to explore such combinations of dimensions further.

**Visual Programming:** One strand of existing metaphors that is inherently spatial is visual programming languages (VPL) [6,34]. A VPL makes use of direct manipulation for creating and editing code statements instead of textually typing them. A main advantage of VPLs is the ease of use, especially for beginner programmers [31]. The affordances of the visual code metaphors (e.g. shape and color) provide programmers with cues on how they can be used. A VPL typically also include a menu of possible constructs to choose from. The programmer can then depend more of recognition rather than recall to determine what constructs to use [31]. Unfortunately, this makes interaction slower compared to text-based interaction [5] (at least in mouse and keyboard comparison). Too many options in a menu will also decrease efficiency; some type of search and filter functionality is probably needed. Furthermore, more screen space is needed to convey the same information, and when the project scales it becomes cluttered [31,34]. However, in a post-sedentary paradigm this could be an advantage as it may create opportunities for navigation by physical movement. Also, the screen space in VR is typically larger than a desktop monitor which, provided that the screen resolution is sufficient [65], could mitigate this problem.

Continuing on the topic, VPLs have previously been implemented in VR. For example, FlowMatic [69] is a flow-based [29] environment for creating VR applications, while Cubely [63] makes use of blocks for teaching programming. HackVR [20] combines the flow-based approach with the object oriented paradigm, which they argue has a natural translation to VR applications. Another interesting aspect of VPLs is their usage in end-user development [23], which could open the potential advantages of post-sedentary software engineering to a much broader set of users.

## 3 Proposed Studies at Various Software Engineering Stages

We are currently designing several studies to advance our research for different stages in software engineering processes. We are exploring most phases of a classic engineering process: requirements, design/architecture, construction, testing, maintenance [4]. We are consciously not trying to find a holistic solution for *all* software engineering work but we are exploring individual phases for now, in order to study them in isolation and to make more rapid progress. It is well possible that our post-sedentary view applies to different extents to various software engineering phases, and conducting separate studies for different phases will allow us to detect this. In most studies, we aim to measure the participant travel distance, arms movement, heart rate and calories burned, but also work-related differences compared to a sedentary setup: task performance time, comprehension of work artifact spaces, etc. We expect to present at the workshop the results from at least one of these studies.

### 3.1 Code Exploration by Moving in VR

Program comprehension is an important area of software engineering which this study aims to address. VR for program comprehension has been explored in a number of studies [7,10,11,14,15,37,46], although with limited evaluation of its efficiency [32]. Different metaphors have been utilized to visualize code structure [1], none of which with the explicit goal of creating user movement. This study will visualize a code base, using different metaphors, which participants then explore in a post-sedentary manner. This could mean walking to different locations of the code base, and using arm movements to interact with it, for example zooming in and out of areas in the code repository and selecting objects of interest. After the exploration an interview is conducted to evaluate their comprehension of the code base. A control group may perform the same tasks with the regular textual code base using keyboard and mouse.

### 3.2 Programming by Moving in VR

An experimental study will be conducted for programming in a non-sedentary context using VPL based representations. Participants will be presented with some form of menu with primitives and operations too choose from. Using the objects in the menu, they then need to complete programming tasks by assembling the objects. The assembly, or "code", can be executed (see the debugging study below) and participants can view the result and potential error messages. Many independent variables could be incorporated. Spatial distance for fetching objects from the menu and connecting them to produce the code is probably the most important for making the participants move. Representation of operations and primitives could also influence the degree of movement. For example, declaring a string variable requires specifying the type, name and value. This requires some form of interaction with varying degrees of arm movement. Affordances such as shape and color of primitives can be varied which could influence the ease of use [31]. Finally, the choice of block- or flow based VPL [29] could influence the degree of space used, which indirectly would impact the degree of user movement. Dependent variables in this experiment could be task completion time and error rate.

### 3.3 Labeling, Filtering and Searching by a Post-sedentary Engineer

This experiment will address the disadvantage of not using a standard keyboard for text input in VR [5]. Labeling provides information about variable, component or module function. Filtering and searching becomes increasingly important as a code base grows. Therefore, finding an appropriate keyboard substitution is needed. We aim to compare voice controls [51], text input by a hand device such as TAP [57] and regular VR controllers. The text input from regular VR controllers will be a virtual display of a keyboard, using the pointers to choose letters. Participants will be presented with a code base and coding task in VR in which they need to label, filter and search for components. Dependent variable in this experiment is completion time and error rate.

### 3.4 Debugging by Moving in VR

This study is aimed at the troubleshooting stage of software engineering by setting up a post-sedentary way of performing debugging. The three dimensions that create the space are (1) the code modules (2) lines of code within the code modules and (3) the call stack with e.g. a virtual elevator. The interactive metaphor proposed is that the user/programmer can walk in a room to advance the code execution in dimension (2), walk to the side along dimension (1) to "step into" a certain method, and travel up and down the call stack along dimension (3) using various gestures to manipulate the elevator, or simply climbing gestures. Throughout, the VR environment can be used creatively to display the current state of the program.

This study can be designed around a defective code example, in which each subject needs to get immersed and spot the problem within a given amount of time. Also several users can be immersed in the same code space to try to spot the problem together. A series of experiments can be performed, to test for various VR designs as independent variables and e.g. task completion time as dependent variable.

## 4 Conclusion

In this paper we have outlined our upcoming research on Post-sedentary Software Engineering. We argue that this research area could potentially benefit the software engineering work context, by increasing physical activity, utilize multimodal learning and improve cognitive functioning. Our initial explorations spark questions for how to progress beyond the current desktop environment and allow for full body movement in software engineering, without decreasing task performance. With technologies such as VR or AR, it is possible to add a spatial dimension to the software engineering work context, which lets the engineer move and interact in 3D. Spatial metaphors based on Visual programming, node-structures and visualization metaphors such as code cities could be exported to this new 3D environment. Additionally, new spatial metaphors will be sought and tested. A number of interaction tools can be used for this new context, and further studies will investigate which ones are most suitable for our purpose. We have outlined studies on program comprehension, programming, debugging, and non-keyboard text input in a non-sedentary context. The design space of this research area is huge. These initial studies will provide evidence on challenges and benefits of post-sedentary software engineering, as well as indicate a direction for future studies.

## References


1. Averbukh, V., et al.: Metaphors for software visualization systems based on virtual reality. In: De Paolis, L.T., Bourdot, P. (eds.) AVR 2019, Part I. LNCS, vol. 11613, pp. 60–70. Springer, Cham (2019). https://doi.org/10.1007/978-3-030-25965-5_6
2. Baćíková, M., Maričák, M., Vančík, M.: Usability of a domain-specific language for a gesture-driven IDE. In: 2015 Federated Conference on Computer Science and Information Systems (FedCSIS), pp. 909–914, September 2015. https://doi.org/10.15439/2015F274
3. Bennie, J.A., Teychenne, M.J., De Cocker, K., Biddle, S.J.H.: Associations between aerobic and muscle-strengthening exercise with depressive symptom severity among 17,839 U.S. adults. Prev. Med. **121**, 121–127 (2019). https://doi.org/10.1016/j.ypmed.2019.02.022. https://www.sciencedirect.com/science/article/pii/S0091743519300611
4. Bourque, P., Fairley, R.E. (eds.): SWEBOK: Guide to the Software Engineering Body of Knowledge, version 3.0. IEEE Computer Society, Los Alamitos (2014). http://www.swebok.org/
5. Brown, N.C.C., Kolling, M., Altadmri, A.: Position paper: lack of keyboard support cripples block-based programming. In: 2015 IEEE Blocks and Beyond Workshop (Blocks and Beyond), pp. 59–61. IEEE, Atlanta, October 2015. https://doi.org/10.1109/BLOCKS.2015.7369003, http://ieeexplore.ieee.org/document/7369003/
6. Burnett, M.M., Baker, M.J.: A classification system for visual programming languages. J. Vis. Lang. Comput. **5**(3), 287–300 (1994). https://doi.org/10.1006/jvlc.1994.1015. https://www.sciencedirect.com/science/article/pii/S1045926X84710159
7. Castelo-Branco, R., Leitão, A., Brás, C.: Program comprehension for live algorithmic design in virtual reality. In: Conference Companion of the 4th International Conference on Art, Science, and Engineering of Programming, <Programming> 2020, pp. 69–76. Association for Computing Machinery, New York, March 2020. https://doi.org/10.1145/3397537.3398475
8. Cherni, H., Métayer, N., Souliman, N.: Literature review of locomotion techniques in virtual reality. Int. J. Virtual Real. **20**(1), 1–20 (2020). https://doi.org/10.20870/IJVR.2020.20.1.3183. https://ijvr.eu/article/view/3183
9. Virtual Reality Locomotion - Cyberith Virtualizer VR Treadmills. https://www.cyberith.com/
10. Dominic, J., Tubre, B., Houser, J., Ritter, C., Kunkel, D., Rodeghero, P.: Program comprehension in virtual reality. In: Proceedings of the 28th International Conference on Program Comprehension, ICPC 2020, pp. 391–395. Association for Computing Machinery, New York, July 2020. https://doi.org/10.1145/3387904.3389287
11. Drogemuller, A., Cunningham, A., Walsh, J., Thomas, B.H., Cordeil, M., Ross, W.: Examining virtual reality navigation techniques for 3D network visualisations. J. Comput. Lang. **56**, 100937 (2020). https://doi.org/10.1016/j.cola.2019.100937. https://research.monash.edu/en/publications/examining-virtual-reality-navigation-techniques-for-3d-network-vi
12. Elliott, A., Peiris, B., Parnin, C.: Virtual reality in software engineering: affordances, applications, and challenges. In: 2015 IEEE/ACM 37th IEEE International Conference on Software Engineering, pp. 547–550. IEEE, Florence, Italy, May 2015. https://doi.org/10.1109/ICSE.2015.191. http://ieeexplore.ieee.org/document/7203009/

13. Gu, X., Zhang, Y., Sun, W., Bian, Y., Zhou, D., Kristensson, P.O.: Dexmo: an inexpensive and lightweight mechanical exoskeleton for motion capture and force feedback in VR. In: Proceedings of the 2016 CHI Conference on Human Factors in Computing Systems, CHI 2016, pp. 1991–1995. Association for Computing Machinery, New York, May 2016. https://doi.org/10.1145/2858036.2858487
14. Hasselbring, W., Krause, A., Zirkelbach, C.: ExplorViz: research on software visualization, comprehension and collaboration. Softw. Impacts **6**, 100034 (2020). https://doi.org/10.1016/j.simpa.2020.100034. https://www.sciencedirect.com/science/article/pii/S2665963820300257
15. Heidrich, D., Schreiber, A.: Visualization of a software system in virtual reality. In: 2019 Proceedings of Mensch und Computer, MuC 2019, pp. 905–907. Association for Computing Machinery, New York, September 2019. https://doi.org/10.1145/3340764.3345378
16. Irani, F.: Visual-spatial ability. In: Kreutzer, J.S., DeLuca, J., Caplan, N. (eds.) Encyclopedia of Clinical Neuropsychology, pp. 2652–2654. Springer, New York (2011). https://doi.org/10.1007/978-0-387-79948-3_1418
17. Jantz, J., Molnar, A., Alcaide, R.: A brain-computer interface for extended reality interfaces. In: ACM SIGGRAPH 2017 VR Village, SIGGRAPH 2017, pp. 1–2. Association for Computing Machinery, New York, July 2017. https://doi.org/10.1145/3089269.3089290
18. Jin, Q., Wang, D., Deng, X., Zheng, N., Chiu, S.: AR-maze: a tangible programming tool for children based on AR technology. In: Proceedings of the 17th ACM Conference on Interaction Design and Children, IDC 2018, pp. 611–616. Association for Computing Machinery, New York, June 2018. https://doi.org/10.1145/3202185.3210784
19. Jörg, S., Ye, Y., Mueller, F., Neff, M., Zordan, V.: Virtual hands in VR: motion capture, synthesis, and perception. In: SIGGRAPH Asia 2020 Courses, SA 2020 pp. 1–32. Association for Computing Machinery, New York, November 2020. https://doi.org/10.1145/3415263.3419155
20. Kao, D., et al.: Hack.VR: A Programming Game in Virtual Reality. arXiv:2007.04495 [cs], November 2020
21. Ke, F., Lee, S., Xu, X.: Teaching training in a mixed-reality integrated learning environment. Comput. Hum. Behav. **62**, 212–220 (2016). https://doi.org/10.1016/j.chb.2016.03.094. https://www.sciencedirect.com/science/article/pii/S0747563216302655
22. Kim, W., Xiong, S.: User-defined walking-in-place gestures for VR locomotion. Int. J. Hum. Comput. Stud. **152**, 102648 (2021). https://doi.org/10.1016/j.ijhcs.2021.102648. https://www.sciencedirect.com/science/article/pii/S1071581921000665
23. Kuhail, M.A., Farooq, S., Hammad, R., Bahja, M.: Characterizing visual programming approaches for end-user developers: a systematic review. IEEE Access **9**, 14181–14202 (2021). https://doi.org/10.1109/ACCESS.2021.3051043
24. Lamping, J., Rao, R., Pirolli, P.: A focus+context technique based on hyperbolic geometry for visualizing large hierarchies. In: Proceedings of the SIGCHI Conference on Human Factors in Computing Systems, CHI 1995, pp. 401–408. ACM Press/Addison-Wesley Publishing Co., USA, May 1995. https://doi.org/10.1145/223904.223956
25. Lee, J., Sinclair, M., Gonzalez-Franco, M., Ofek, E., Holz, C.: TORC: a virtual reality controller for in-hand high-dexterity finger interaction. In: Proceedings of the 2019 CHI Conference on Human Factors in Computing Systems, CHI 2019, pp. 1–13. Association for Computing Machinery, New York, May 2019. https://doi.org/10.1145/3290605.3300301

26. Leisman, G., Moustafa, A.A., Shafir, T.: Thinking, walking, talking: integratory motor and cognitive brain function. Front. Pub. Health **4**, 94 (2016). https://doi.org/10.3389/fpubh.2016.00094. https://www.ncbi.nlm.nih.gov/pmc/articles/PMC4879139/
27. Li, S., He, W., Zhang, L., Hu, Y.: Physicalizing virtual objects with affordances to support tangible interactions in AR. In: 26th ACM Symposium on Virtual Reality Software and Technology, VRST 2020, pp. 1–2. Association for Computing Machinery, New York, November 2020. https://doi.org/10.1145/3385956.3422117
28. Lillard, A.S.: Montessori: The Science Behind the Genius. Oxford University Press, Oxford (2016)
29. Mason, D., Dave, K.: Block-based versus flow-based programming for naive programmers. In: 2017 IEEE Blocks and Beyond Workshop (B&B), pp. 25–28. IEEE, Raleigh, October 2017. https://doi.org/10.1109/BLOCKS.2017.8120405. http://ieeexplore.ieee.org/document/8120405/
30. Massaro, D.W.: Multimodal learning. In: Seel, N.M. (ed.) Encyclopedia of the Sciences of Learning, pp. 2375–2378. Springer, Boston (2012). https://doi.org/10.1007/978-1-4419-1428-6_273
31. McGuffin, M.J., Fuhrman, C.P.: Categories and completeness of visual programming and direct manipulation. In: Proceedings of the International Conference on Advanced Visual Interfaces, AVI 2020, pp. 1–8. Association for Computing Machinery, New York, September 2020. https://doi.org/10.1145/3399715.3399821
32. Merino, L., Ghafari, M., Anslow, C., Nierstrasz, O.: A systematic literature review of software visualization evaluation. J. Syst. Softw. **144**, 165–180 (2018). https://doi.org/10.1016/j.jss.2018.06.027. https://www.sciencedirect.com/science/article/pii/S0164121218301237
33. HoloLens 2-Overview, Features, and Specs—Microsoft HoloLens. https://www.microsoft.com/en-us/hololens/hardware
34. Myers, B.A.: Taxonomies of visual programming and program visualization. J. Vis. Lang. Comput. **1**(1), 97–123 (1990). https://doi.org/10.1016/S1045-926X(05)80036-9. https://www.sciencedirect.com/science/article/pii/S1045926X05800369
35. Nersesian, E., Vinnikov, M., Lee, M.J.: Travel kinematics in virtual reality increases learning efficiency. In: 2021 IEEE Symposium on Visual Languages and Human-Centric Computing (VL/HCC), pp. 1–5, October 2021. https://doi.org/10.1109/VL/HCC51201.2021.9576317. iSSN: 1943-6106
36. Nilsson, N.C., Serafin, S., Steinicke, F., Nordahl, R.: Natural walking in virtual reality: a review. Comput. Entertain. **16**(2), 8:1-8:22 (2018). https://doi.org/10.1145/3180658
37. Oberhauser, R., Lecon, C.: Virtual reality flythrough of program code structures. In: Proceedings of the Virtual Reality International Conference - Laval Virtual 2017, VRIC 2017, pp. 1–4. Association for Computing Machinery, New York, March 2017. https://doi.org/10.1145/3110292.3110303
38. Omni by Virtuix - The leading and most popular VR motion platform. https://www.virtuix.com/
39. Onishi, A., Nishiguchi, S., Mizutani, Y., Hashimoto, W.: A study of usability improvement in immersive VR programming environment. In: 2019 International Conference on Cyberworlds (CW), pp. 384–386, October 2019. https://doi.org/10.1109/CW.2019.00073. ISSN: 2642-3596
40. Paluch, A.E., et al.: Steps per day and all-cause mortality in middle-aged adults in the coronary artery risk development in young adults study. JAMA Netw. Open **4**(9), e2124516 (2021). https://doi.org/10.1001/jamanetworkopen.2021.24516

41. Panas, T., Berrigan, R., Grundy, J.: A 3D metaphor for software production visualization. In: 2003 Proceedings on Seventh International Conference on Information Visualization, IV 2003, pp. 314–319, July 2003. https://doi.org/10.1109/IV.2003.1217996
42. Park, H.B., Ahn, S., Zhang, W.: Visual search under physical effort is faster but more vulnerable to distractor interference. Cogn. Res. Princ. Implic. **6**(1), 17 (2021). https://doi.org/10.1186/s41235-021-00283-4
43. Pritchard, A., Richardson, M., Sheffield, D., McEwan, K.: The relationship between nature connectedness and eudaimonic well-being: a meta-analysis. J. Happiness Stud. **21**(3), 1145–1167 (2020). https://doi.org/10.1007/s10902-019-00118-6
44. Riva, G., Mancuso, V., Cavedoni, S., Stramba-Badiale, C.: Virtual reality in neurorehabilitation: a review of its effects on multiple cognitive domains. Expert Rev. Med. Devices **17**(10), 1035–1061 (2020). https://doi.org/10.1080/17434440.2020.1825939
45. Robertson, G.G., Mackinlay, J.D., Card, S.K.: Cone trees: animated 3D visualizations of hierarchical information. In: Proceedings of the SIGCHI Conference on Human Factors in Computing Systems, CHI 1991, pp. 189–194. Association for Computing Machinery, New York, March 1991. https://doi.org/10.1145/108844.108883
46. Romano, S., Capece, N., Erra, U., Scanniello, G., Lanza, M.: On the use of virtual reality in software visualization: the case of the city metaphor. Inf. Softw. Technol. **114**, 92–106 (2019). https://doi.org/10.1016/j.infsof.2019.06.007. https://www.sciencedirect.com/science/article/pii/S0950584919301405
47. Ryan, R.M., Weinstein, N., Bernstein, J., Brown, K.W., Mistretta, L., Gagné, M.: Vitalizing effects of being outdoors and in nature. J. Environ. Psychol. **30**(2), 159–168 (2010). https://doi.org/10.1016/j.jenvp.2009.10.009. https://www.sciencedirect.com/science/article/pii/S0272494409000838
48. SenseGlove—Make the Digital Feel Real. https://www.senseglove.com/
49. Shannon, C.R., Thomas-Duckwitz, C.: Executive functioning. In: Kreutzer, J.S., DeLuca, J., Caplan, B. (eds.) Encyclopedia of Clinical Neuropsychology, pp. 991–992. Springer, New York (2011). https://doi.org/10.1007/978-0-387-79948-3_1435
50. Shrestha, N., Kukkonen-Harjula, K.T., Verbeek, J.H., Ijaz, S., Hermans, V., Pedisic, Z.: Workplace interventions for reducing sitting at work. Cochrane Database Syst. Rev. (6) (2018). https://doi.org/10.1002/14651858.CD010912.pub4. Wiley
51. Sin, J., Munteanu, C.: Let's go there: voice and pointing together in VR. In: 22nd International Conference on Human-Computer Interaction with Mobile Devices and Services, MobileHCI 2020, pp. 1–3. Association for Computing Machinery, New York, October 2020. https://doi.org/10.1145/3406324.3410537
52. Straker, L., Levine, J., Campbell, A.: The effects of walking and cycling computer workstations on keyboard and mouse performance. Hum. Factors **51**(6), 831–844 (2009). https://doi.org/10.1177/0018720810362079. SAGE Publications Inc
53. Straker, L., Mathiassen, S.E.: Increased physical work loads in modern work - a necessity for better health and performance? Ergonomics **52**(10), 1215–1225 (2009). https://doi.org/10.1080/00140130903039101
54. Surale, H.B., Gupta, A., Hancock, M., Vogel, D.: TabletInVR: exploring the design space for using a multi-touch tablet in virtual reality. In: Proceedings of the 2019 CHI Conference on Human Factors in Computing Systems, CHI 2019, pp. 1–13. Association for Computing Machinery, New York, May 2019

55. Suznjevic, M., Mandurov, M., Matijasevic, M.: Performance and QoE assessment of HTC Vive and Oculus Rift for pick-and-place tasks in VR. In: 2017 Ninth International Conference on Quality of Multimedia Experience (QoMEX), pp. 1–3, May 2017. https://doi.org/10.1109/QoMEX.2017.7965679. ISSN: 2472-7814
56. Tada, K., Tanaka, J.: Tangible programming environment using paper cards as command objects. Procedia Manuf. **3**, 5482–5489 (2015). https://doi.org/10.1016/j.promfg.2015.07.693. https://www.sciencedirect.com/science/article/pii/S2351978915006940
57. Discover the Tap Strap 2. https://www.tapwithus.com/
58. Taylor, W.C., Williams, J.R., Harris, L.E., Shegog, R.: Computer prompt software to reduce sedentary behavior and promote physical activity among desk-based workers: a systematic review. Hum. Factors, 00187208211034271 (2021). https://doi.org/10.1177/00187208211034271. SAGE Publications Inc
59. Teychenne, M., White, R.L., Richards, J., Schuch, F.B., Rosenbaum, S., Bennie, J.A.: Do we need physical activity guidelines for mental health: what does the evidence tell us? Ment. Health Phys. Act. **18**, 100315 (2020). https://doi.org/10.1016/j.mhpa.2019.100315. https://www.sciencedirect.com/science/article/pii/S1755296619301632
60. Tremblay, M.S., et al.: Sedentary Behavior Research Network (SBRN) - terminology consensus project process and outcome. Int. J. Behav. Nutr. Phys. Act. **14**(1), 75 (2017). https://doi.org/10.1186/s12966-017-0525-8
61. Tudor-Locke, C., Schuna, J.M., Frensham, L.J., Proenca, M.: Changing the way we work: elevating energy expenditure with workstation alternatives. Int. J. Obes. **38**(6), 755–765 (2014). https://doi.org/10.1038/ijo.2013.223. https://www.nature.com/articles/ijo2013223, bandiera_abtest: a Cg_type: Nature Research Journals Number: 6 Primary_atype: Reviews Publisher: Nature Publishing Group
62. Turchi, T., Malizia, A.: Fostering computational thinking skills with a tangible blocks programming environment. In: 2016 IEEE Symposium on Visual Languages and Human-Centric Computing (VL/HCC), pp. 232–233, September 2016. https://doi.org/10.1109/VLHCC.2016.7739692. ISSN: 1943-6106
63. Vincur, J., Konopka, M., Tvarozek, J., Hoang, M., Navrat, P.: Cubely: virtual reality block-based programming environment. In: Proceedings of the 23rd ACM Symposium on Virtual Reality Software and Technology, VRST 2017, pp. 1–2. Association for Computing Machinery, New York, November 2017. https://doi.org/10.1145/3139131.3141785
64. Warburton, D.E., Bredin, S.S.: Health benefits of physical activity: a systematic review of current systematic reviews. Curr. Opin. Cardiol. **32**(5), 541–556 (2017). https://doi.org/10.1097/HCO.0000000000000437
65. Ware, C.: Chapter seven - space perception. In: Ware, C. (ed.) Information Visualization, 4th edn. Interactive Technologies, pp. 245–296. Morgan Kaufmann, January 2021. https://doi.org/10.1016/B978-0-12-812875-6.00007-4. https://www.sciencedirect.com/science/article/pii/B9780128128756000074
66. Ware, C., Franck, G.: Evaluating stereo and motion cues for visualizing information nets in three dimensions. ACM Trans. Graph. **15**(2), 121–140 (1996). https://doi.org/10.1145/234972.234975
67. Wettel, R.: Visual exploration of large-scale evolving software. In: 2009 31st International Conference on Software Engineering - Companion Volume, pp. 391–394, May 2009. https://doi.org/10.1109/ICSE-COMPANION.2009.5071029

68. White, R.L., Olson, R., Parker, P.D., Astell-Burt, T., Lonsdale, C.: A qualitative investigation of the perceived influence of adolescents' motivation on relationships between domain-specific physical activity and positive and negative affect. Ment. Health Phys. Act. **14**, 113–120 (2018). https://doi.org/10.1016/j.mhpa.2018.03.002. https://www.sciencedirect.com/science/article/pii/S1755296617301801
69. Zhang, L., Oney, S.: FlowMatic: an immersive authoring tool for creating interactive scenes in virtual reality. In: Proceedings of the 33rd Annual ACM Symposium on User Interface Software and Technology, pp. 342–353. ACM, Virtual Event USA, October 2020. https://doi.org/10.1145/3379337.3415824

# Coping with Changing Contexts: A Healthcare Security Perspective

Bilal Naqvi[1(✉)] and Carmelo Ardito[2]

[1] LUT Software, LENS, LUT University, 53850 Lappeenranta, Finland
syed.naqvi@lut.fi

[2] Dipartimento di Ingegneria Elettrica e dell'Informazione (DEI), Politecnico di Bari, Bari, Italy

**Abstract.** With the fourth industrial revolution, there is a digitization wave going on for the transformation of existing systems into modern digital systems. This has opened the window for many opportunities, but at the same time, there is a multitude of cyber-security threats that need to be addressed. This paper considers one such threat posed by phishing and ransomware attacks to the healthcare infrastructures. Phishing has also been the most prevalent attack mechanism on the healthcare infrastructures during the ongoing COVID-19 pandemic. The paper proposes two intervention strategies as a step towards catering to the challenges posed by phishing and ransomware attacks in the context of healthcare infrastructures.

**Keywords:** Healthcare · Phishing · Ransomware · Security · Usability · Usable security

## 1 Introduction

The fourth industrial revolution (referred to as Industry 4.0) involves automation of the existing infrastructures and brings in many opportunities and avenues for digitization of existing mechanisms including healthcare. From a healthcare perspective, some of these avenues include the use of telemedicine, artificial intelligence (AI)-enabled medical devices for scanning and procedures, blockchain-based health records, among others [1]. Although each of these avenues refers to limitless opportunities for improvements, yet several challenges emerge and are imperative to be addressed. One such challenge is the consideration of human factors associated with the deployment of these digitized solutions.

Human factors are about considering human abilities, limitations, and characteristics in the design of tools, devices, systems, and services. One prevalent mechanism aimed at exploiting the human limitation of distinguishing between original and fake content is known as phishing [2]. Phishing occurs when the attacker persuades the victim into doing something which is not beneficial for the victim or the system. Prevalent ways to initiate phishing include emails, advertisements, among others. With increased phishing, there have been instances of phishing attacks ultimately taking the form of ransomware attacks, where the attacker encrypts the systems' files and asks for money to decrypt


Published by Springer Nature Switzerland AG 2022
C. Ardito et al. (Eds.): INTERACT 2021, LNCS 13198, pp. 139–146, 2022.
https://doi.org/10.1007/978-3-030-98388-8_13

them. The implications of such attacks in healthcare infrastructures are not limited to monetary losses, but there are risks including (but not limited to) safety of patients, breach of the privacy of the medical records, etc. The recent trends show that phishing attacks are used as a common vector for launching ransomware attacks. Some of the recent incidents include:

1. Various malicious emails attempting to spread ransomware to several individuals were identified. The target was a Canadian government health organization actively engaged in the COVID-19 pandemic response efforts, as well as a Canadian university that is conducting COVID-19 research[1].
2. Hackers broke into computers at Hammersmith Medicines Research, a London-based company that was carrying out clinical trials for new medicines against the COVID-19 pandemic. The hackers then asked for ransom to let the professionals use their systems[2].

The case considered in this paper has relevance with the ongoing COVID-19 pandemic since the two incidents just discussed have occurred recently. However, this problem existed before COVID-19 and has ramifications even after. For instance, a ransomware attack on Victorian Regional Hospitals in Australia, where successful phishing led to ransomware on patient health care records[3]. Many surgeries were delayed due to the non-availability of the records. Furthermore, Europol, the European Union (EU) law enforcement agency has received reports of intensifying cyber-attacks in almost all its 27 member countries. The ransomware attacks come amid an increase in other cyber-attacks related to the pandemic. They have included a rash of "phishing" emails that attempt to use the crisis to persuade people to click on links that download malware or ransomware onto their computers.

This paper considers the challenges posed by phishing and ransomware attacks to the healthcare personnel and infrastructures and aims to shed light on the following research question:

RQ: *How to cope with changing contexts while considering the threats posed by phishing and ransomware attacks in the context of healthcare infrastructures?*

To answer this question, this position paper presents two intervention strategies, (1) educational intervention, and (2) design intervention. The remainder of the paper is organized as follows. Section 2 presents and background. Section 3 presents the intervention strategies to cater to the changing context, and Sect. 4 concludes the paper.

## 2 Background

The state of the art concerning digitization in healthcare shows that the industry has to do a lot to catch up to the pace of Industry 4.0. For instance, survey results [1] show that

[1] https://blog.malwarebytes.com/cybercrime/2020/10/fake-covid-19-survey-hides-ransomware-in-canadian-university-attack/.

[2] https://www.computerweekly.com/news/252480425/Cyber-gangsters-hit-UK-medical-research-lorganisation-poised-for-work-on-Coronavirus.

[3] https://www.abc.net.au/news/2019-10-01/victorian-health-services-targeted-by-ransomware-attack/11562988?nw=0.

seven percent of healthcare and pharmaceutical companies have gone digital as compared to 15% of companies in other industries, however, the ongoing COVID-19 pandemic has increased the pace of digitization of the healthcare industry. The results also identify seven key trends of digital transformation in healthcare in 2021. One of the trends is the rise in on-demand healthcare. Consumers are interested in healthcare services at a time of their convenience. It also identifies that the consumers use online means for finding doctors (47%), searching medical facilities (38%), and booking a medical appointment (77%). Furthermore, some other trends of digital transformation in healthcare include the use of big data and predictive analysis, the use of virtual reality for treating patients, use of wearable medical devices, among others [1]. These numbers identify both threats and opportunities. Opportunities could include, for example, the development of human-centric procedures, incorporating the elements of the UX in the systems and services, considering different age groups and impairments in the interface design; however, there is a multitude of threats, which could hamper all the merits of technology and digitization. Cyber-gangs and attackers have increasingly been using phishing and other attacks to cause damage to the existing healthcare systems and services and generate money using this means. Having said that, the focus needs to be not only on the development and deployment to keep up the pace with Industry 4.0 but also on contextual aspects and the human factors associated with these solutions.

From a healthcare perspective discussed in this paper, phishing is a common threat faced by healthcare personnel and a major cyber-security risk for healthcare infrastructures. A study was conducted in the United States to assess the anti-phishing preparedness of 5416 healthcare staff [3]. The participants of the study were sent 20 emails during the study. The results reveal that 65.3% of the participants clicked at least 2 phishing emails, with 772 participants clicking at least 5 emails. In another study [4], analysis of around 143 million Internet transactions revealed that 5 million among those were suspected phishing threats.

With such numbers and phishing attacks among the most prevalent vectors for launching ransomware attacks, it is vital to discuss and formulate intervention strategies to cater to this challenge. Ransomware is a type of malware designed to extort money from victims, who are prevented from accessing their systems [5]. The two most prevalent types of ransomware are encryptors and screen lockers. Encryptors, as the name implies, encrypt data on a system, making the content useless without the decryption key. Screen lockers, on the other hand, simply block access to the system with a “lock” screen, asserting that the system is encrypted.

One other aspect which needs to be considered is that while many of the healthcare organizations are adopting electronic means for patient records and other digital systems, the healthcare personnel seem to have limited awareness of the cyber-security threats. Moreover, most of the IT training content for healthcare staff is focused on how to use the software and applications, not the cyber-security attacks they could be exposed to. It is, therefore, pertinent to consider approaches to protect against cyber-security threats induced due to this evolving technological infrastructure. However, for this paper, we will limit to addressing the challenges posed by phishing and ransomware to the healthcare infrastructures.

## 3 How to Cope with Challenges in the Changing Context?

Having discussed the need for and importance of coping with the challenges posed by phishing and ransomware attacks, this section presents the intervention strategies to cope with these challenges. Broadly the intervention strategies can be classified into 2 categories:

1. Educational intervention strategies
2. Design intervention strategies

### 3.1 Educational Intervention Strategy

This strategy aims at educating the users of the system to be able to protect themselves against phishing and ransomware attacks. Three elements form the core of this intervention this strategy [13]:

- *Awareness*: the aim here is to catch people's attention and convince them that cyber security is worth their attention.
- *Education*: once people are aware and willing to learn, specialized information could be provided which helps to improve the security behavior and assists people to develop accurate mental models about cyber-security. To educate users, both traditional modes of education (i.e., conducting specialized courses) [14], and the use of gamification techniques have been proposed [15].
- *Training*: It is more specific and helps people to acquire skills, for instance, how to identify and report a phishing attack? It is relevant to consider the user's role in a system while planning and conducting such training, and thus requires preparation of the training manuals accordingly.

The following two approaches in line with the core elements just discussed are worth considering to support the educational intervention strategy.

**Training and Supporting Developers at Work**

Human factors and cyber-security have evolved as two different domains [7]. Expertise in both these domains (human factors and security) is hard to find in one person [8, 9], therefore, developers don't often consider the fact that the security systems and services without consideration of human factors despite being secure against known vulnerabilities could still be susceptible to users' mistakes leading to a breach. Therefore, there is a need for providing training on usability and usable security both at the educational institutions and work [10]. Such activities are expected to help the developers in understanding the unusable security mechanisms and realize that despite being secure against various attacks the systems will still be susceptible to user mistakes leading to malicious compromises.

Furthermore, design patterns can be effective to support the developers in handling security and usability issues [11]. Patterns can support the developers in assessing the usability of their security options, and vice versa. Each pattern expresses a relation between three things, context, problem, and solution. Patterns provide real solutions, not abstract principles by explicitly mentioning the context and problem and summarizing the rationale for their effectiveness. Since the patterns provide a generic "core" solution, its use can vary from one implementation to another. A usable security pattern encapsulates information such as name, classification, prologue, problem statement, the context of use, solution, and discussion on the right use of the pattern. Naqvi and Seffah [11] present more details on how a usable security pattern looks like. A challenge in this regard is collecting such patterns and making a catalog to be disseminated among the developers.

Training the developers and supporting them at work with the use of design patterns can assist in the development of user-centric security solutions that consider attributes of systems' users such as literacy and aptitudes, and thus are less likely to be susceptible to users' mistakes leading to security breaches.

**Initiating Cross-disciplinary Education and Training Mechanisms**
Another approach that could be adopted is initiating a cross-disciplinary forum to create educational content and new knowledge material. This forum can also be seen as a supportive mechanism for conducting usable security training for developers. Such a forum would include human factors and cyber-security researchers, and industry practitioners (see Fig. 1). The forum would exchange and understand viewpoints from academia and industry perspectives and identify the challenges that arise. The challenges are then assessed in a workshop/hackathon for identification of the new solutions. The solutions are then documented to create training manuals for the stakeholders. The two benefits of such a forum are:

1. A means for usable security knowledge sharing and dissemination between industry and academia. This would help in addressing the inconsistencies in perceptions between industry and academia about human factors in security.
2. A bidirectional mechanism in which the state of the art in research is closely connected with challenges and practices in the industry.

Other participants for this forum could include junior researchers, junior developers, and representatives from vocational training institutions. From the educational intervention perspective, the outcomes of the forum could be used for educating the participants such as:

- *junior researchers*, for advancing their research on the topic and trying to come up with solutions that address industry needs thereby creating an avenue for industry-academia collaboration;
- *junior developers*, for training purposes and addressing the multidisciplinary challenge posed by usable security. The outcomes could also be documented as design patterns for the developers to apply in specific contexts; and
- *vocational training institutions*, have a wider outreach in the society. They can use outcomes of the forum to create new courses and content focused on the training of health care personnel, senior students, and common citizens.

Furthermore, new content addressing the challenges can also be used in conventional educational activities such as at schools and colleges.

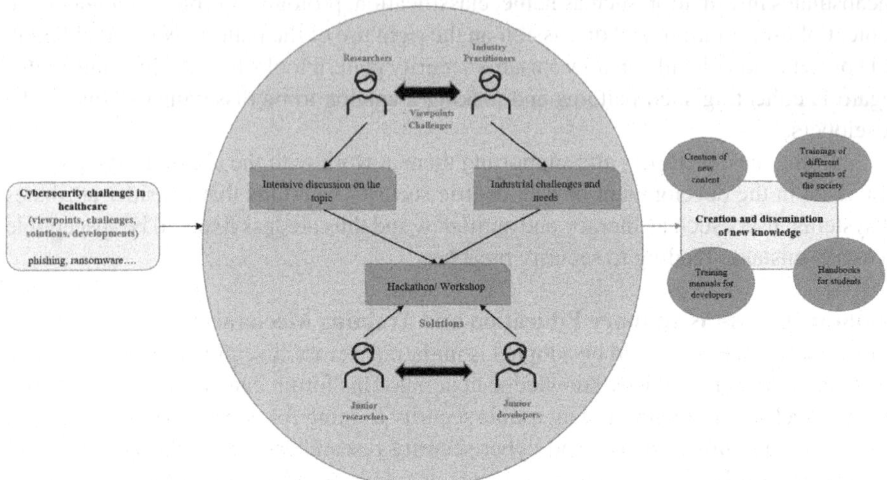


**Fig. 1.** Sequence of activities for initiating cross-disciplinary education and training mechanisms

One vital consideration while planning for initiating a cross-disciplinary education and training mechanism is to avoid creating silos. Thorough consideration needs to be put in for identifying similar forums and hackathons to synthesize their findings into a set of collective findings addressing the issue; such a synthesis could itself be very challenging especially in the case of domain-specific recommendations.

### 3.2 Design Intervention Strategy

This strategy refers to design choices that aim to support and guide users in developing accurate mental models concerning cyber-security. This involves the use of visual elements, color codes, highlights, among other visual techniques to supports user's decision-making abilities [16]. In the context of phishing attacks, it could also take the form of a tool that generates caution in case of a suspicious email and can be integrated with the email applications.

Furthermore, to facilitate the users in detecting and avoiding phishing attacks, existing HCI methods need to be considered, for instance, the use of task models for modeling interactions and identifying all possible scenarios that could lead to a successful phishing attack. One relevant approach here is the use of a polymorphic user interface to warn the users (healthcare personnel) against phishing. Aneke et al. [12] propose such a scheme, which addresses three main goals, (1) prevent user habituation, (2) provide an explanation of the attack, and (3) educate the user on cyber-attacks and risks. In addition, the prototype shows three panels to explain why a URL could be fake. However, there is a need to identify such implementations and work for their deployment after carefully analyzing any room for improvements.

## 4 Conclusion

In the era where the development is driven mainly to keep up the pace with Industry 4.0, this paper discusses an important challenge posed by phishing and ransomware attacks considering the case of healthcare personnel and infrastructures. The topic discussed in the paper is timely and important.

The paper advocates that there is a need to go beyond the traditional ways of development and adopt a multi-faceted approach for addressing the challenges posed by rapidly changing contexts. The paper proposes two strategies that need to be considered to cater to the challenges we face. Although we consider the healthcare perspective in this paper, the proposed strategies hold equally good for other domains. The educational intervention strategy aims at role-based educational activities, we also propose a cross-disciplinary forum for discussion of issues involving human factors in security, preparation of training manuals, and educational content. Moreover, the design intervention strategy aims at incorporating elements of human-computer interaction in the design of security systems and services. We believe that these strategies have the potential of contributing towards improvement in the state of the art, however, refinement to strengthen and improve these strategies would be considered as part of ongoing work on the topic.

## References


1. Reddy, M.: Digital Transformation in Healthcare in 2021: 7 Key Trends (2021). https://www.digitalauthority.me/resources/state-of-digital-transformation-healthcare/
2. Hong, J.: The state of phishing attacks. Commun. ACM **55**(1), 74–81 (2012)
3. Gordon, W.J., et al.: Evaluation of a mandatory phishing training program for high-risk employees at a US healthcare system. J. Am. Med. Inform. Assoc. **26**(6), 547–552 (2019)
4. Priestman, W., Anstis, T., Sebire, I.G., Sridharan, S., Sebire, N.J.: Phishing in healthcare organizations: threats, mitigation, and approaches. BMJ Health Care Inf. **26**(1). E10031 (2019)
5. Cartwright, E., Castro, J.H., Cartwright, A.: To pay or not: game theoretic models of ransomware. J. Cybersecur. **5**(1), 1–12 (2019)
6. HealthIT.gov. What are the advantages of electronic health records? (2019). https://www.healthit.gov/faq/what-are-advantages-electronic-health-records
7. Garfinkel, S., Lipford, H.R.: Usable Security History, Themes, and Challenges. Morgan and Claypool, USA (2014)
8. Naqvi, B., Clarke, N., Porras, J.: Incorporating the human facet of security in developing systems and services. Inform. Comput. Secur. **29**(1), 49–72 (2021)
9. Naqvi, B., Porras, J., Oyedeji, S., Ullah, M.: Towards identification of patterns aligning security and usability. In: Abdelnour Nocera, J., et al. (eds.) INTERACT 2019. LNCS, vol. 11930, pp. 121–132. Springer, Cham (2020). https://doi.org/10.1007/978-3-030-46540-7_12
10. Caputo, D.D., Pfleeger, S.L., Sasse, M.A., Ammann, P., Offutt, J., Deng, L.: Barriers to usable security? three organizational case studies. IEEE Secur. Priv. **14**(5), 22–32 (2016)
11. Naqvi, B., Seffah, A.: Interdependencies, conflicts, and trade-offs between security and usability: why and how should we engineer them?. In: 1st International Conference, HCI-CPT 2019 Held as Part of the 21st HCI International Conference, pp. 314–324. HCII 2019 Orlando, FL, USA (2019)

12. Aneke, J., Ardito, C., Desolda, G.: Designing an intelligent user interface for preventing phishing attacks. In: Abdelnour Nocera, J., et al. (eds.) INTERACT 2019. LNCS, vol. 11930, pp. 97–106. Springer, Cham (2020). https://doi.org/10.1007/978-3-030-46540-7_10
13. Sasse, A., Rashid, A.: The Cyber Security Body of Knowledge - Human factors knowledge area v 1.0. University of Bristol (2019). https://www.cybok.org/media/downloads/Human_Factors_issue_1.0.pdf
14. Turner, C.F., Taylor, B., Kaza, S.: Security in computer literacy- a model for design, dissemination, and assessment. In: Proceedings of the 42nd ACM Technical Symposium on Computer Science Education, pp. 15–20. Dallas, Texas, USA (2011)
15. Yang, C.C., Tseng, S.S., Lee, T.J., Weng, J.F., Chen, K.: Building an anti-phishing game to enhance network security learning. In: 12th IEEE International Conference on Advance Learning Technologies, pp. 121–123 (2012)
16. Franz, A., et al.: SoK: Still plenty of phish in the sea—a taxonomy of user-oriented phishing interventions and avenues for future research. In: USENIX Symposium on Usable Privacy and Security (SOUPS), Virtual Conference, pp. 339–357 (2021)

# Privacy Knowledge Base for Supporting Decision-Making in Software Development

Maria Teresa Baldassarre, Vita Santa Barletta(✉), Danilo Caivano, Antonio Piccinno, and Michele Scalera

Department of Computer Science, University of Bari Aldo Moro, Via Orabona 4, 70125 Bari, Italy
{mariateresa.badassarre,vita.barletta,danilo.caivano,antonio.piccinno, michele.scalera}@uniba.it

**Abstract.** Integrating security and privacy requirements at every stage of the software development cycle is critical to guarantee the confidentiality, integrity and availability of the system and consequently of the data. Developers need to be supported in this challenge, as many different skills are required to respond effectively to the growing number of cyber-attacks. In such a context, this research study endeavors to define the key elements that support decision-making in privacy oriented software development. A Privacy Knowledge Base (PKB) is defined to support developers' decisions in all software development phases, and a prototype (PKB-Tool) is developed to operationally integrate privacy and security requirements into the development of new systems and the re-engineering of legacy systems. An ongoing experimentation in the context of an industrial project is presented to validate the efficacy of the 5 key elements in supporting developers in integrating privacy and security requirements in the software life cycle.

**Keywords:** Privacy by design · Human-centered privacy · Privacy software application

## 1 Introduction

Nowadays, software development requires integration of security and privacy to address threats related to cyber-attacks [14]. The attacker's goal is to access and misuse confidential information by exploiting vulnerabilities within the code [9]. Therefore, for secure software development [7] it is required to stress concepts such as data and information security in project activities which deal with or target aspects such as integrity, availability, confidentiality, authenticity, non-repudiation and authorization [6]. Security should be a basic feature of smart project such as automatically enabling complex password building mechanisms rather than procedures for renewing passwords according to a time frame. Two


Published by Springer Nature Switzerland AG 2022
C. Ardito et al. (Eds.): INTERACT 2021, LNCS 13198, pp. 147–157, 2022.
https://doi.org/10.1007/978-3-030-98388-8_14

fundamental aspects come into play in this scenario: Security and Privacy. Security enables and protects activities and assets of both people and enterprises. Instead, Privacy respects and protects personal information [22]. So, it becomes imperative to support developers in privacy and security-oriented software development by identifying the key elements needed to support developers in assuming decisions during the software development process [8]. Accordingly, in this research work analysts, designers, and developers represent our potential end users.

The research work presents a knowledge base, called Privacy Knowledge Base (PKB), that formalizes the relationships between 5 key privacy elements: Privacy by Design, Privacy Design Strategies, Privacy Pattern, Vulnerabilities, and Context. The PKB is integrated within a prototype, called PKB-Tool, and supports the decision making in all the software development life cycle phases is shown. The tool is able to operationally support developers (our end users) by integrating privacy requirements, and consequently security in the software production process.

The paper is organized as follows. Section 2 discusses related works. Section 3 presents the Privacy Knowledge Base and Sect. 4 describes the Privacy Oriented Software Development. Section 5 describes an ongoing industrial case study that shows how to apply the privacy key elements in software development. Finally, conclusions are given in Sect. 6.

## 2 Related Works

In literature, the methodologies include two categories, Security-based adaptations, and Privacy-Friendly systems that aim to embed privacy into every step of the software development life cycle [3]. Therefore, several privacy requirement methodologies have been introduced in order to assist system designers and developers to analyze and elicit privacy requirements during the first phases of the software development [19]. PRIPARE introduces how privacy requirements should be incorporated into the software development life cycle [18]. LINDDUN [11] is a privacy threat modeling methodology that supports analysts in systematically eliciting and mitigating privacy threats in software architectures. The identified privacy threats are mapped with the existing privacy-enhancing technologies (PETs) [23]. RBAC [12] method considers privacy requirements as constraints on permissions and user roles in order to define access control policies. Security quality requirements engineering(SQUARE) methodology [17] supports the elicitation of privacy requirements at the early stages of software life cycle and consists of nine steps which include what techniques will be used to elicit security requirements then categorize, prioritize, and inspect the requirements. STRAP [15] is a light-weight structured analysis of privacy vulnerabilities into the software development cycle. Instead, STORE (Threat Oriented Requirements Engineering) [5] implements the processes to recognize the potential threats to privacy requirements, and P-STORES [4] examines each phase of the original process and demonstrates the legal enforcement issues that could arise in the process. Therefore, in today's environment, privacy needs to be integrated into software development to protect sensitive data in growing systems and to enhance software quality [7]. The principle of Full Functionality (positive sum "win-win") of the Privacy by Design underlines this need, as well as the need to integrate the privacy and security dimensions [10]. However, the literature analyzed deals with only one dimension, integrating privacy or security elements into software development. At the same time, they are not able to implement applicable solutions in real-world contexts, since they remain general in definition and are far from being operational [21].

Considering this need, the research work presents a Privacy Knowledge Base to support the development team in all phases of the software development life cycle.

## 3 Privacy Knowledge Base

Privacy Knowledge Base (PKB) identify the key elements for supporting decision-making in software development. The 5 key elements formalized in the PKB are the following: Context, Principles of Privacy by Design, Privacy Design Strategies, Privacy Patterns, and Vulnerabilities (Fig. 1). Each identified element is used in different phases of the system life cycle, and no relationship to vulnerabilities is established. For example, the privacy design strategies were developed because privacy patterns and privacy-enhancing technologies apply mostly to the design and development phase, while during the first two phases (conception and definition) important decisions are made that have a significant impact on the overall privacy properties of the system under development [13]. Therefore, PKB formalizes the relationships between key privacy elements and it is able to operationally support software development by integrating privacy requirements, and consequently security in the software production process. A decision table was used to formalize the knowledge. It is a tabular representation of a procedural decision situation, where the state of a number of conditions determines the execution of a set of actions [20].

- Context. In order to integrate security and privacy into software development, it is necessary to ensure three key properties: confidentiality, integrity and availability. Therefore, in accordance with security by design and privacy by design, in the PKB the context is identified by architectural requirements, use case and scenario, and PETs [23]. Respectively, the architectural requirements define the flow of data within the system, components, roles, and responsibilities; the use case case and scenario determine all interactions with the system in order to protect the information from unauthorized reading and manipulation; PETs help to protect the personal information handled by the applications.
- Privacy by Design (PbD) Principles [10]. PbD is based on 7 principles, each of which specifies action and responsibilities for evaluating "Privacy by Design Compliance":

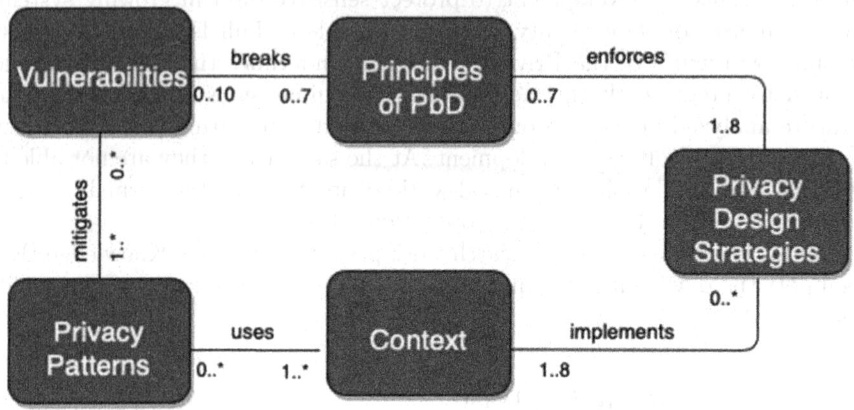


**Fig. 1.** PKB: relationship between the 5 key elements.

1. *Proactive not Reactive*: Anticipate and prevent privacy-invasive events before they happen and leverage architecture methods to guide the proactive implementation of security.
2. *Default setting*: Build privacy measures directly into any given software application, by default. Obviously, "Privacy by Default" does not exclude "Secure by default" policies, including least privilege, need-to-know, least trust, mandatory access control and separation of duties.
3. *Embedded into Design*: Privacy becomes a key requirement into design, system architecture and business logic. It should not be implemented in response to a given event.
4. *Positive-Sum*: PbD does not consider zero-sum approach that involves unnecessary trade-offs, but seeks to consider all legitimate interests and goals in a positive-sum "win-win" manner.
5. *End-to-End Security*: PbD ensures confidentiality, integrity and availability of data for all stakeholders. Therefore, it requires a secure life-cycle management of information, end-to-end.
6. *Visibility and Transparency*: Regardless of the business practice or technology involved, components and operations remain visible and transparent to users and providers. Moreover, it is necessary to strengthen security through open standards, well-known processes and external validation.
7. *Respect for the user*: Respect and protect interests of the individual, above all, and the interests of all information owners.

- Privacy Design Strategies. A design strategy describes a way to achieve a certain design goal with certain properties that distinguish it from other (basic) approaches for achieving the same goal [13]. Eight Privacy Design Strategies, based on the legal perspective of privacy, have been proposed: *Data-Oriented Strategies* focus on the privacy-friendly processing of the data (Minimize,

Hide, Separate, Abstract); and *Process-Oriented Strategies* focus on the process surrounding the responsible handling of personal data (Inform, Control, Enforce, Demonstrate).

- Privacy Pattern. A pattern describes both a process and a thing: the *things* is created by the *process*. For most software patterns - thus also for privacy patterns - *things* means a particular high-level design outline or code detail, including both static structure and intended behavior [16]. Therefore, Privacy Patterns provide the knowledge collected from experts in a structured, documented, and reusable manner and they contribute to build secure information system. Currently, in the literature such patterns are described theoretically and do not provide operational guidelines. So, in the PKB, they support documenting common solutions to privacy problems and can improve the re-engineering of existing systems, describing classes, collaborations between objects, and their purposes, and help designers identify and address privacy concerns. A privacy pattern represents an answer to the following questions: Which Privacy Design Strategies must be implemented? Which vulnerabilities are mitigated/eliminated with the privacy solution?
- Vulnerabilities. A vulnerability is a weakness an adversary could take advantage of to compromise the confidentiality, availability, or integrity of a resource. So, a weakness refers to implementation flaws or security implications due to design choices. For instance, being able to overrun an input validation while writing data to it introduces an SQL injection vulnerability.

The PKB defines which Principles of the PbD are violated by a specific vulnerability and which Privacy Design Strategies must be adopted to mitigate it, or given a specific context, which privacy design strategies to implement to ensure compliance with privacy by design principles using privacy patterns.

PKB-Tool was developed to provide an operational tool to support developer' decisions in each phase of the software. The architecture underlying PKB-Tool is Model-View-Controller: the model provides all the methods to access the elements of the PKB; the view visualizes the relations between the 5 elements and manages interaction with the developer; the controller receives user requests and fulfills them changing the status of the two components. Yii 2 MVC framework was used to developed PKB-Tool.

Below is an example to better understand how it works: starting from a specific vulnerability implemented of the OWASP Top 10 [2], the PKB-Tool gives a short description of the macro categories of vulnerabilities, an example that causes it and outlines how to mitigate it. For each vulnerability, the privacy patterns that help mitigate it and the principles of PbD violated are shown (Fig. 2).

In addition, developers have the benefit of understanding the privacy strategies implemented by the specific pattern in order to design a Privacy Software Architecture. Figure 3 shows an example of how privacy patterns implement privacy design strategies within the selected architecture and, also, considering specific use cases and scenarios. Figure 4 shows an example of a use case.

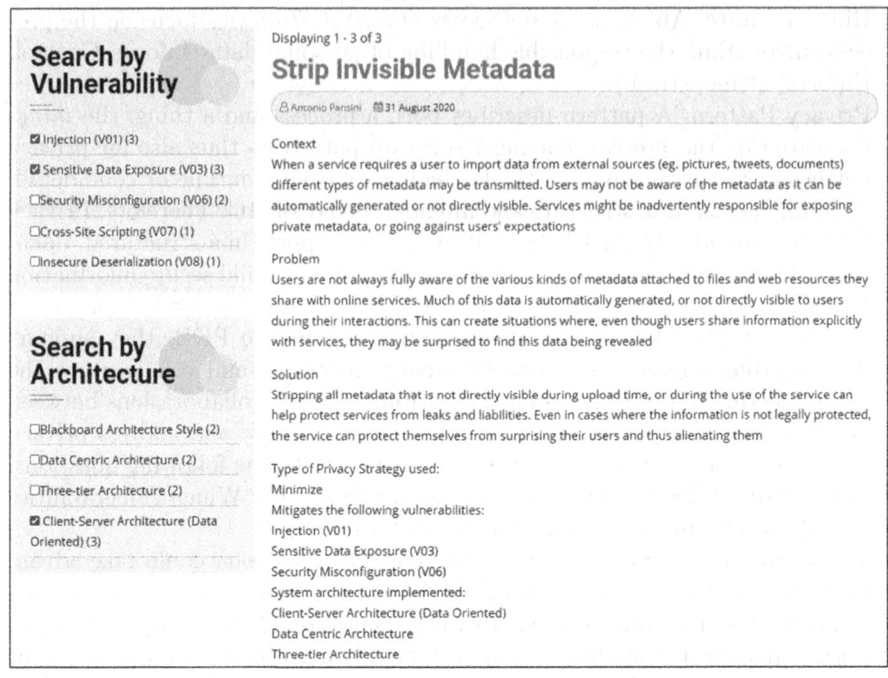


**Fig. 2.** PKB-Tool: vulnerability (strip invisible metadata) description example.

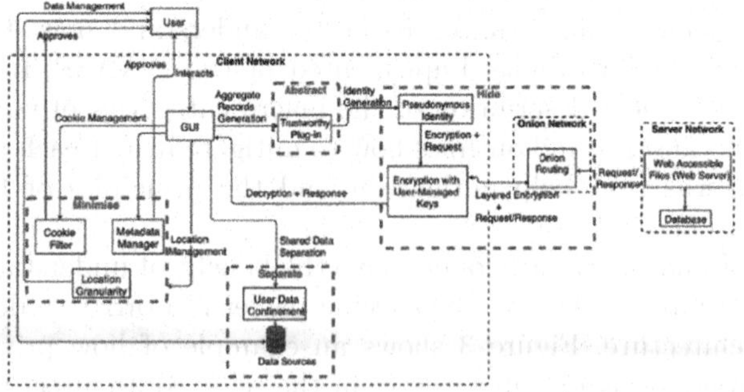


**Fig. 3.** PKB-Tool: privacy architecture example.

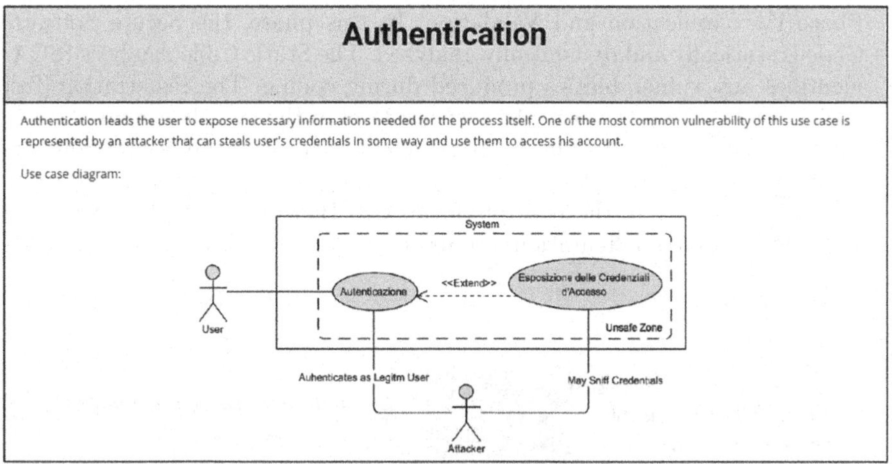


**Fig. 4.** PKB-Tool: use case example.

## 4 Privacy Oriented Software Development

An approach to integrate elements of PKB into any development process, has been proposed: Privacy Oriented Software Development (POSD). The Privacy Oriented Software Development (POSD) approach is inspired by the Software Development Life Cycle framework presented in [7]. The approach is briefly described below (Fig. 5).

- Phase I: Analysis. In the analysis phase, a Privacy Impact Analysis is carried out in order to define the development context, use cases and scenarios; delimit the system's privacy critical actors; identify architectural requirements. The output of this phase determines the Privacy Design Strategies and Privacy Patterns to be applied in the design phase.
- Phase II: Design. In the analysis phase, all the elements needed to design a Privacy Software Architecture are provided: Privacy Design Strategies, Privacy Patterns and Architectural Requirements. The use of privacy patterns provides a design solution to a recurring problem allowing the designer to add those data protection features to the solution starting to the design phase. While the adoption of privacy design strategies provides a greater level of abstraction by not imposing a specific structure but bind it to the achievement of certain objectives.
- Phase III: Coding. This phase defines the Privacy Enhancing Technologies to be used. The use of PETs enables us to contrast identity theft, fraud and discriminatory profiling. PETs together with the Software System Architecture, allow the development of the secure code, Secure Software Code. The objective of this phase on the one hand (Security) is to produce code without vulnerabilities; while on the other hand (Privacy) to ensure the protection and minimization of personal data at code level.

- Phase IV: Verification and Validation. In this phase, the Secure Software Code is statically and dynamically analyzed. The Static Code Analysis (SCA) identifies any vulnerabilities produced during coding. The Penetration Test (PENTEST) serves to verify the security level of the overall system.
- Phase V: Deploy. In this phase, after the deployment of the Secure Software Code in the operating environment, a Hardening phase is carried out to verify the correct setting of the base platform. CIS Benchmark [1], best practices for secure system configuration, are used.

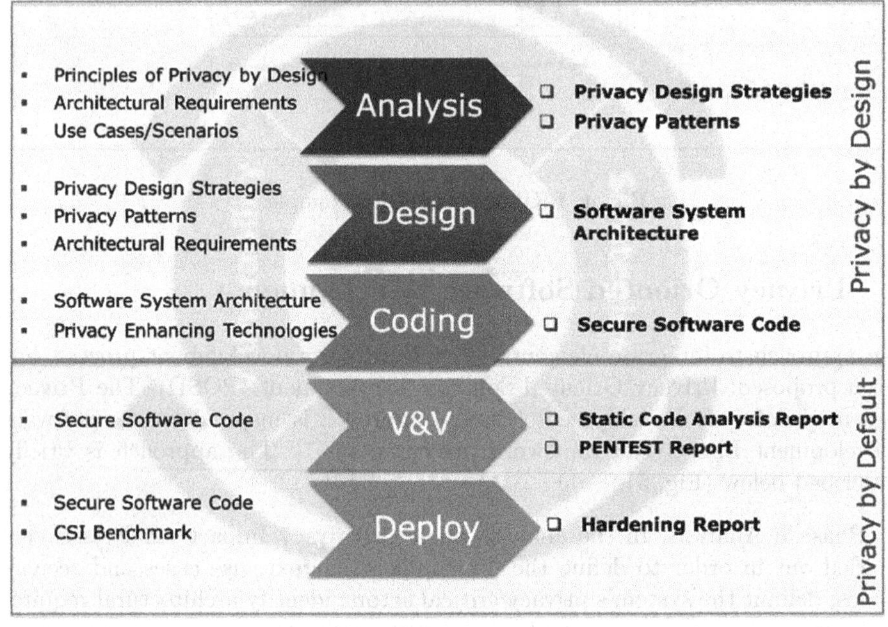


**Fig. 5.** Privacy oriented software development.

## 5 Case Study

This section presents an ongoing industrial case study that shows the preliminary results on how PKB provides the guidance needed for supporting developers in privacy-oriented software development. The system to be developed involves the analysis of textual and multimedia content in order to provide certain information about the analyzed resource. The two main functionalities of the system are acquisition and validation of the data of the subjects requesting the services and the recommendation of specific activities to be performed based on the data entered. The specific components to be developed are: Data Import Component, Web Scraping Component, Artificial Intelligence Component, Decision Support System Component. The development of the system involves a team of 4 people and started in April 2021. The end of the experimentation is scheduled in

August 2021 for a total of five months project duration. The people involved in the project were 3 junior developers and 1 senior developer with more than 3 years of experience in the filed but with no specific knowledge and competences on software security and privacy. The preliminary results obtained during the analysis phase are presented in the rest of the section. During the Analysis phase, privacy assessment was carried out by using PKB-Tool. Considering the use cases and architectural requirements selected by developers, the following Privacy Design Strategies (Table 1) and Privacy Pattern (Table 2) have been identified to design the system software architecture.

**Table 1.** Privacy design strategies to implement.

| Principles of PbD | Minimize | Hide | Separate | Abstract | Inform | Control | Enforce | Demonstrate |
|---|---|---|---|---|---|---|---|---|
| Proactive not Reactive | x | x | x | x | - | - | - | - |
| Default setting | x | x | x | x | - | - | - | - |
| Embedded into Design | x | x | x | x | x | x | x | x |
| Positive-Sum | x | x | x | x | x | x | - | - |
| End-to-End Security | x | x | x | x | - | - | - | - |
| Visibility and Transparency | - | - | - | - | x | x | x | x |
| Respect for the user | x | x | x | x | - | - | - | - |

**Table 2.** Privacy patterns that implement privacy design strategies.

| Privacy design strategies | Minimize | Hide | Separate | Abstract | Inform | Control | Enforce | Demonstrate |
|---|---|---|---|---|---|---|---|---|
| Trustworthy Privacy Plug-in | - | - | - | x | - | - | - | - |
| Unusual Activities | - | - | - | - | x | - | - | - |
| Protection against Tracking | x | - | - | - | - | - | - | - |
| Strip Invisible Metadata | x | - | - | - | - | - | - | - |
| Private link | - | x | - | - | - | - | - | - |
| Personal Data Store | - | - | x | - | - | x | - | x |
| Onion Routing | - | x | - | - | - | - | - | - |
| Minimal Information Asymmetry | - | - | - | - | x | - | - | - |
| Data Breach Notification Pattern | - | - | - | - | x | - | x | x |
| Informed Implicit Consent | - | - | - | - | x | - | x | x |
| Federated Privacy Impact Assessment | - | - | - | - | - | - | x | - |
| Sticky Policies | - | - | - | - | - | - | x | - |
| Access control | - | - | - | - | - | - | x | - |
| Use of logging and auditing | - | - | - | - | - | - | - | x |

## 6 Discussion

The preliminary results obtained show that PKB-Tool helps developers to integrate privacy and security requirements in software development. It allowed to identify the Privacy Design Strategies and Privacy Patterns required for system development in order to guarantee confidentiality, integrity, availability, authenticity, non-repudiation and authorization of data and system. The use of PKB-tool has allowed to share competences among the development team. The team was able to find privacy patterns after having understood the use cases and architectural requirements arising from the developer context. It allows to support the team during integration of the privacy elements by supporting its members in design decisions even though they did not have specific privacy skills. In addition, the use of POSD did not impact on the development process used within the organization. All the activities performed by the team, starting from the requirements provided by POSD, were carried out according to the software processes and procedures already used in the company without altering the modus operandi. In the future work to improve the privacy knowledge, an AI model will be developed. The integration of privacy elements is tested through static code analysis and penetration testing. This allows to validate the security of the system and consequently the privacy compliance. By training the A.I. model over the privacy existing solutions, it is possible to support team's decisions when, for example, new use cases and scenarios arise in the software development. Thus, the new privacy solutions obtained can be provided to the A.I. model to improve at various phases of software development the integration of privacy requirements and consequently support each decision of the development team.

## References


1. CIS benchmarks. https://www.cisecurity.org/cis-benchmarks
2. OWASP Top10 - 2017. Tthe ten most critical web application security risks. https://owasp.org
3. Al-Slais, Y.: Privacy engineering methodologies: a survey. In: 2020 International Conference on Innovation and Intelligence for Informatics, Computing and Technologies (3ICT), pp. 1–6 (2020). https://doi.org/10.1109/3ICT51146.2020.9311949
4. Ansari, M.T.J., Baz, A., Alhakami, H., Alhakami, W., Kumar, R., Khan, R.A.: P-STORE: extension of STORE methodology to elicit privacy requirements. Arab. J. Sci. Eng. **46**(9), 8287–8310 (2021). https://doi.org/10.1007/s13369-021-05476-z
5. Ansari, M., Pandey, D., Alenezi, M.: STORE: security threat oriented requirements engineering methodology. J. King Saud Univ. Comput. Inf. Sci. **34**(2), 191–203 (2018). https://doi.org/10.1016/j.jksuci.2018.12.005
6. Baldassarre, M., Barletta, V.S., Caivano, D., Raguseo, D., Scalera, M.: Teaching cyber security: the hack-space integrated model. In: CEUR Workshop Proceedings, vol. 2315 (2019)
7. Baldassarre, M.T., Barletta, V.S., Caivano, D., Scalera, M.: Integrating security and privacy in software development. Softw. Qual. J. **28**(3), 987–1018 (2020). https://doi.org/10.1007/s11219-020-09501-6
8. Baldassarre, M.T., Barletta, V.S., Caivano, D., Piccinno, A.: A visual tool for supporting decision-making in privacy oriented software development. In: Proceedings of the International Conference on Advanced Visual Interfaces. AVI 2020. Association for Computing Machinery, New York (2020). https://doi.org/10.1145/3399715.3399818

9. Baldassarre, M.T., Barletta, V.S., Caivano, D., Scalera, M.: Privacy oriented software development. In: Piattini, M., Rupino da Cunha, P., García Rodríguez de Guzmán, I., Pérez-Castillo, R. (eds.) QUATIC 2019. CCIS, vol. 1010, pp. 18–32. Springer, Cham (2019). https://doi.org/10.1007/978-3-030-29238-6_2
10. Cavoukian, A.: Operationalizing privacy by design: A guide to implementing strong privacy practices (2012)
11. Deng, M., Wuyts, K., Scandariato, R., Preneel, B., Joosen, W.: A privacy threat analysis framework: supporting the elicitation and fulfillment of privacy requirements. Requirements Eng. **16**(1), 3–32 (2011). https://doi.org/10.1007/s00766-010-0115-7
12. He, Q.: A framework for modeling privacy requirements in role engineering. In: Proceedings of REFSQ, vol. 3, pp. 137–146 (2003)
13. Hoepman, J.H.: Privacy Design Strategies (The Little Blue Book) (2020). https://www.cs.ru.nl/~jhh/publications/pds-booklet.pdf
14. Jang-Jaccard, J., Nepal, S.: A survey of emerging threats in cybersecurity. J. Comput. Syst. Sci. **80**(5), 973–993 (2014). https://doi.org/10.1016/j.jcss.2014.02.005, special Issue on Dependable and Secure Computing
15. Jensen, C., Tullio, J., Potts, C., Mynatt, E.D.: Strap: A structured analysis framework for privacy. Georgia Institute of Technology (2005). http://hdl.handle.net/1853/4450
16. Markus, S., Eduardo, F.B., Duane, H., Frank, B., Peter, S.: Security Patterns: Integrating Security and Systems Engineering. John Wiley & Sons, New York (2006)
17. Mead, N.R., Stehney, T.: Security quality requirements engineering (square) methodology. In: Proceedings of the 2005 Workshop on Software Engineering for Secure Systems-Building Trustworthy Applications, pp. 1–7. SESS 2005. Association for Computing Machinery, New York (2005). https://doi.org/10.1145/1083200.1083214
18. Notario, N., et al.: PRIPARE: integrating privacy best practices into a privacy engineering methodology. In: 2015 IEEE Security and Privacy Workshops, pp. 151–158 (2015). https://doi.org/10.1109/SPW.2015.22
19. Pattakou, A., Mavroeidi, A.G., Diamantopoulou, V., Kalloniatis, C., Gritzalis, S.: Towards the design of usable privacy by design methodologies. In: 2018 IEEE 5th International Workshop on Evolving Security Privacy Requirements Engineering (ESPRE), pp. 1–8 (2018). https://doi.org/10.1109/ESPRE.2018.00007
20. Pooch, U.W.: Translation of decision tables. ACM Comput. Surv. **6**(2), 125–151 (1974). https://doi.org/10.1145/356628.356630
21. Rindell, K., Ruohonen, J., Holvitie, J., Hyrynsalmi, S., Leppänen, V.: Security in agile software development: a practitioner survey. Inf. Softw. Technol. **131**, 106488 (2021). https://doi.org/10.1016/j.infsof.2020.106488
22. Teresa Baldassarre, M., Santa Barletta, V., Caivano, D., Piccinno, A.: Integrating security and privacy in HCD-Scrum. In: CHItaly 2021: 14th Biannual Conference of the Italian SIGCHI Chapter. CHItaly 2021. Association for Computing Machinery, New York (2021). https://doi.org/10.1145/3464385.3464746
23. Van Blarkom, G., Borking, J., Olk, J.: Handbook of Privacy and Privacy-Enhancing Technologies. The Case of Intelligent Software Agents (2003)

# bRIGHT – A Framework for Capturing and Adapting to Context for User-Centered Design

Rukman Senanayake and Grit Denker(✉)

SRI International, 333 Ravenswood Avenue, Menlo Park, CA 94025, USA
{rukman.senanayake,grit.denker}@sri.com

**Abstract.** The ability to create and maintain a highly accurate model of an end user's context is an extremely useful feature. Achieving this ability poses many challenges, especially since a great degree of partial information and uncertainty is involved in capturing the user's context. The bRIGHT human-computer interaction (HCI) framework and workstation address these challenges by creating a highly accurate context model of a user engaging with a computer system. In this paper we discuss the architectural design of bRIGHT, which addresses performance and scalability to build accurate user context models, and the benefits we expect from this improved version. We also discuss technological advances in other related fields that influenced our decision-making.

**Keywords:** User context modeling · Run-time adaptation and automation · User assistance · Context-aware automation · Context-aware filtering · Context-aware prediction · Cognitive autofill · User-centered design architecture · User-centered system

## 1 Introduction

The term context-awareness was coined with the rise of ubiquitous computing [1] and quickly became an important topic in human computer interaction (HCI) [2]. Context of use is fundamentally important in providing meaningful, efficient, effective, and adaptive user experiences (UX). Understanding the user and her context is the key enabling factor in tailoring to current needs and making user experiences relevant, and it also opens the path to dynamically adaptive system designs.

The word context covers a broad set of meanings in the UX and conventional HCI arenas. For the purpose of this paper, and with respect to the bRIGHT system (Fig. 1) and its current capabilities, we are focused on the aspects of the user's context that can be observed and recorded in terms of interactions with a computer system. There are many other aspects to a user's context [3–5]: location; physical vs. logical, societal relationships and impacts (e.g., a pandemic changing how a user works); environmental impacts; and interface interactions with a computer or a machine. We are focused on modeling the subset of the user's context that can be directly observed in terms of their engagement with the system. The research questions we are investigating are:


Published by Springer Nature Switzerland AG 2022
C. Ardito et al. (Eds.): INTERACT 2021, LNCS 13198, pp. 158–173, 2022.
https://doi.org/10.1007/978-3-030-98388-8_15

- Can an accurate and detailed user context model positively and ongoingly enhance UX during system operation?
- What degree of accuracy is required in a context model for achieving transformational gains in UX?

In particular, bRIGHT does **not** aim to improve by adapting the user interface (UI) itself; rather, it works with given UIs and improves the UX of the users in those UIs (cf. Sect. 2). Currently, bRIGHT does not include technology to detect and integrate events in external, environmental objects, but the framework allows for such extensions that we plan for the future.

bRIGHT is a sensing, modeling, and analysis framework that allows accurate modeling and adaptation to a user's context. The *bRIGHT context models* store each user action in a machine-processable and meaningful way that can be queried and used in algorithms to determine user interest and provide predictions and assistance to the user. bRIGHT allows rich and meaningful context and contains information at an abstraction level to permit semantically equivalent statements such as, "After the company's West coast network security administrator read an email from her East coast colleague about an ongoing attack on the company's network, she proactively redirected identified traffic through the company's honeynets." Observational approaches use less-rich context data such as keystrokes, heat maps, or gaze patterns.

bRIGHT is beneficial for human-centered software engineering (HCSE) in two ways. In the short term, user-centered design processes can make use of bRIGHT's user context (and future cognitive) models to design systems that can adapt to new requirements or changes in use. It is common for user modeling and context to be used in the design and implementation of interfaces and interface components. But approaches in which the user's context is tracked and modeled in real time and then used to adapt the entire user experience are still rare. bRIGHT was designed and developed to model a user's context, maintain the context model as accurately as possible, and evolve the UX by offering proactive assistance to the user. The scope of our work covers the development of a research framework that captures the user's context and allows formal modeling of mechanisms and techniques to update the model accurately. We also include the ability to reason about the dynamics in the context model, and to investigate software and hardware designs that would enable adaptive UX and properly harness the synergy of these features. In addition, bRIGHT's user context models do not forget; they represent a time-machine-like record of all observed user actions. As such, these models are useful in the short- and long term because they provide a basis for context of use and evolutionary trends.

Section 2 provides some related work and Sect. 3 gives an overview of the bRIGHT system. A use case is presented in Sect. 4. Details of the approach and status of development are provided in Sect. 5. Section 6 summarizes the next steps for bRIGHT development and application and contains our conclusions.

## 2 Related Work

With increasing regularity, humans are interacting with autonomous systems and also with systems powered by artificial intelligence (AI). In such interactions, the systems' ability to observe, model, and leverage the user's context becomes vital in improving system effectiveness and efficacy. The context is pivotal to the decision-making process of the user; decision-making does not happen in a vacuum and is almost always grounded in user context. If autonomous systems or AI-based systems are capable of tracking and reasoning about the user's context, then they can also play a role in providing the right kind of assistance at the right time and place.

To characterize bRIGHT with respect to other context-aware systems, and following the nomenclature in [4], bRIGHT is a context-server based approach, and in particular a context-aware framework, because it allows extension to specific context. bRIGHT uses a semantic type system to model context that is similar to ontological approaches, but does not use the full power of ontological relationships. bRIGHT's type system records for each contextual model instance the context type and value, time stamp, and the (sensor) source and confidence of the contextual instance. Context processing is done in bRIGHT in various ways: We use rules for interest modeling as well as context interpretation (e.g., knowledge about domain-specific classes like Internet Protocol (IP) address, types of attacks, and so on in the security domain). bRIGHT is not currently handling security and privacy yet, but in a separate project we have implemented an ontology-based policy reasoner for privacy and security that could easily be integrated with bRIGHT. Historical context data is by default integrated into bRIGHT, since bRIGHT's context model does not forget and keeps the entire user context history.

It is common for user modeling and their context to be used in the design and implementation of interfaces and interface components. For example, (contextual) personas [6] are an approach to enrich the communication between designer and developer, and contextual personas [7] include aspects of the digital work environment. Value-Based Requirements Engineering (VBRE) [8] makes users' values explicit through analysis with a reference taxonomy. The taxonomy contains concepts such as values, motivations, and emotional reactions, all of which are important in decision making. VBRE can be used in requirements engineering to support user-centric design (UCD) (e.g., as done in [9] for a health decision support system). These approaches are used in the requirements or design phase of systems. bRIGHT's approach is different in that it is used during system operation. bRIGHT observes the user, builds a contextual model of the user's interest, and uses that model to dynamically adopt the UX at runtime. This use of bRIGHT is in line with work that aims to improve processes through integration of machine learning (ML) [10] and benefits user experiences in Web Internet of Things (IoT) applications [11]. bRIGHT's implementation is intentionally generic so that it can serve as a basis for many possible applications.

Currently, bRIGHT's focus is on modeling user interactions with a set of computer applications to create an accurate user context model during operation. bRIGHT uses its context model for a variety of adaptation techniques such as "right information at the right time" or "workflow/task automation" or "contextual auto-fill from context model." Section 4 provides examples of those adaptation techniques.

Other approaches aim to improve usability through adaptive behavior of the UI. For example, [12] provides users with a minimal feature-set and an optimal layout based on the context of use. They are using Role-Based UI Simplification (RBUIS) based on a-priori statically defined user roles and tasks. Role-based UI models support feature-set minimization by assigning roles to task models and layout optimization through workflows that represent adaptive UI behavior visually and through code. The main difference to our approach is that the roles and corresponding adaptations are determined a-priori, whereas our approach models the user at runtime and determines adaptations very specifically to what the user is and has been looking at and what actions the user has done so far. The adaptations are thus very tuned to the current user's context. As such, bRIGHT's approach could be used in conjunction with RBUIS or similar UI adaptation frameworks.

Another line of research focuses on enabling end users to easily and autonomously personalize the behavior of their applications. For example, [5] presents an approach that allows end users without programming experience to customize the context-dependent behavior of their IoT applications through the specification of trigger-action rules. The goal is to support the dynamic creation and execution of personalized application versions that are more suitable for users' needs in specific contexts of use. bRIGHT's context model is accessible through programming interfaces and could be used for end user development activities as described in [4], but we have not investigated this avenue of research.

bRIGHT also does not attempt to automate UI generation adapted to a person's devices, tasks, preferences, or abilities, like SUPPLE [13], which formally defines interface generation as an optimization problem that is feasible for a particular class of cost functions. The notions of cost functions for adaptations as used in SUPPLE would be interesting to investigate in the future for bRIGHT as a quantitative measure of value added by automations provided by bRIGHT. For example, one of the cost functions in [13] models a person's ability to control the pointer and allows SUPPLE to generate user interfaces adapted to unusual interaction techniques or abilities, such as an input jittery eye tracker or a user's limited range of motion due to a motor impairment. bRIGHT's automation techniques could be beneficial in some of these circumstances (e.g., avoiding the need to control the pointer by providing pre-filled choices that users can confirm through other means (voice, return key).

In the future, it would also be interesting to integrate the foundational context language ContextML presented in [14] with bRIGHT's context model. This would enable the use of the bRIGHT's context model as part of the Model-Driven UI Development framework of [14] (assuming appropriate framework APIs). bRIGHT's context model is rich with domain-specific context and could be beneficial to more user- and context-specific adaptations.

The context model built by bRIGHT is similar in many ways to context models defined using ontological approaches such as [15–17]. Using ontologies allows us to use general concepts to build a basic context model that has the necessary extensibility to support domain-specific concepts. The user-profiling ontology developed by Skillen [15] and COBRA-ONT developed by Chen et al. [16] are extensive, and we will consider them for integration into future bRIGHT developments.

## 3 Overview of bRIGHT

We are using bRIGHT (Fig. 1) to focus on understanding what type of hardware and software design can lead to systems that accurately model user context and use the model and its dynamics to capture user's needs and interests. This information can be used to help the user in a more efficient and effective way. In addition, our approach supports the study of context of use, long-term evolutionary trends, and their impact on the user.

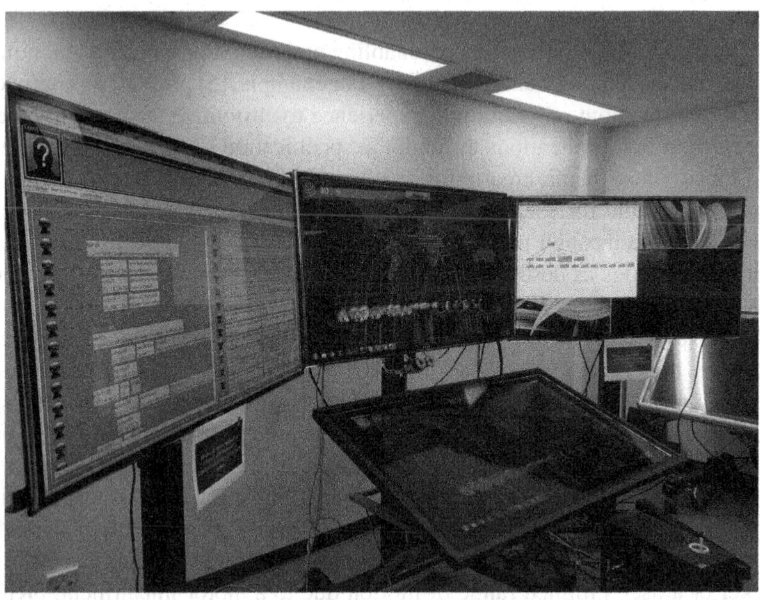

**Fig. 1.** A bRIGHT workstation consisting of a touch table with proximity detection for positioning controls under the hands of users. The center monitor has a gaze tracking system mounted on the bottom that records what the user is looking at. The user is working with a cybersecurity application that is rendered on the center monitor. The left monitor visualizes the recorded raw data regarding the user's interactions with the application (what the user did) and the user's gaze (what the user looked at). The right monitor visualizes the generated user context model that represents the user's interest at any given time.

We have used bRIGHT as an HCI research framework and as the backbone technology for future human-centered, resilient, and adaptive system designs. In a military application, we used bRIGHT as an HCI framework to study opportunities to integrate AI into counter unmanned aerial systems in simulated environments. We instrumented the simulation software to record user activities and conducted human subject research (HSR) using complementary measures such as video recording of user behaviors and screens, physiological measurements of pulse waveforms, annotations of recordings, task performance measures, interviews, and self-assessment. Analysis of the data collected by bRIGHT helped identify possible optimizations for the counter unmanned aerial simulation system via contextual filtering and cognitive autofill; these made user interface interactions easier by auto-filling relevant data from short-term memory.

We also used bRIGHT as a backbone technology framework in cybersecurity applications and demonstrated user context models dynamically adapting and enabling context-based filtering and task automation [18, 19] as shown in the next section.

## 4 bRIGHT Runtime Adaptation – A Use Case

We are illustrating bRIGHT's automation adaptations at runtime with a use case from the cybersecurity background. SRI has developed several cybersecurity analysis tools that were instrumented with bRIGHT: BotHunter[1] is a malware detection and analysis tool and Infected America is a tool to visualize IP reputation data. Typically, a network operator or security specialist would use these and other tools to help in the analysis of network status and investigate potential security threats. Since these tools are bRIGHT-enabled, user interactions with these tools are observed and recorded in a user context model. We will show in a step-by-step use case how a context model is used to provide automation on the fly and improve the UX.

Figure 2, 3, 4, 5, and 6 show a sequence of actions performed by the user in the BotHunter malware detection and analysis tool. Figure 2 shows the main Bothunter interface that provides several analytical dashboard options. Users have the option to see forensic graphs that summarize infection status per IP address. Other dashboard panels summarize infection patterns or show the infection profiles in a table format with detailed meta-information per infection. Finally, a table of external interactions for each IP is available. For the use case, the network operator will use the "Forensic Confidence Composition Graph" to understand how different IP addresses in his network have been attacked and the "External Interactions" table to understand with what external IPs his infected devices have communicated.

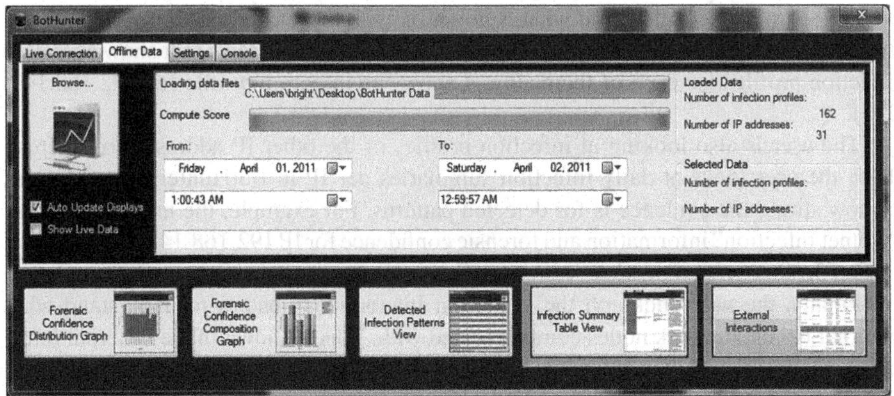


**Fig. 2.** BotHunter main UI with several analytical dashboard options. The cybersecurity application BotHunter is bRIGHT-instrumented. As the user interacts with BotHunter (and other applications), bRIGHT creates the user context model.

[1] https://en.wikipedia.org/wiki/BotHunter and http://www.bothunter.net/about.html.

Opening up the "Forensic Confidence Composition Graph" results in Fig. 3. For each IP in the operator's network, it shows a color-coded summary of the different types of evidence classes over IP addresses, such as scores for RBN (Russian Business Network), RepeatScanner and DNSCheckIn among others.

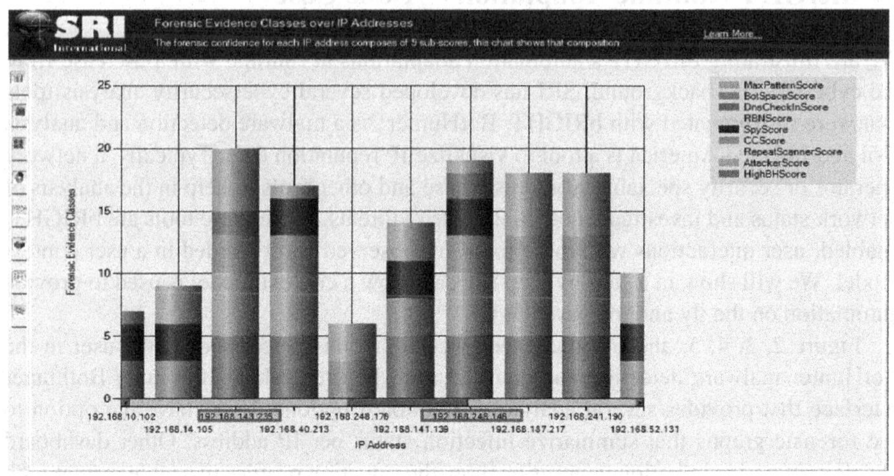


**Fig. 3.** The Forensic Evidence Classes graph shows for each IP and summary of the kinds of evidence that was collected. The graph is zoomable and clickable so that more details of evidence can be explored by the user.

The network operator is interested in two of the IPs, namely 192.168.143.235 and 192.168.248.146 each of which represents internal IP addresses (PCs or servers) and would like to better understand what is going on with these assets. Double clicking the bar graphs of these two IP addresses opens up new dialog windows that show so-called infection profiles for each of them (Fig. 4 shows an infection profile for 192.168.143.235).

The user is also looking at infection profiles of the other IP addresses of interest. Then the user looks at daily infection summaries per IP in BotHunter to get an idea of how strong the evidence is for detected patterns. For example, the user looks at the "Botnet Infection" information and forensic confidence for IP 192.168.143.235 as shown in Fig. 5.

Finally, the user clicks on the "External Interactions" button to understand what external IPs his network nodes communicated with. This is shown in the External Interactions Table (Fig. 6). The information about communications with external IPs is useful for another cybersecurity application in which the user can get more information about those external IPs and whether they are known to be malicious. All this helps the user to get a complete picture of the situation and decide what actions are necessary to counter a potential attack.

The user's interactions with BotHunter have been recorded in a contextual model that is illustrated in Fig. 7.

**Fig. 4.** Infection Profile View for one of the chosen IP addresses that are of interest to the user. Each infection profile view may have several infection profiles, each consisting of a list of icons that symbolize the various evidence classes (e.g., inbound attack, egg download, connection to malicious Command and Control (C&C) Server, connection to Russian Business Network (RBN), or outgoing attack)). Infection Profiles provides a quick overview for the operator what has been going on with the network asset in question and where the attack stands. This will enable the user to quickly decide where to put his attention and act on isolating network nodes to limit the damage and contain the exposure.

The user next launches the Infected America application (shown in Fig. 8) to determine the IP reputation data of one of the external IP addresses to which the system associated with IP 192.168.143.235 is connected. At this point, a set of external IP addresses in the user's context model can be used for pre-populating this field. bRIGHT's context model then sends this list of IP addresses to the Infected America application to provide the user contextual auto-fill entries that match both the type (IP address) and the fact that they need to be external addresses and not internal ones (e.g., 192.168.248.146 and 192.168.143.235), since Infected America is used for obtaining information about external IP addresses and their historical behavior, not internal ones.

Infection summary for each IP address with dynamic level of detail

| | IP Address | Forensic Confidence | Detected Patterns | Pattern Description |
|---|---|---|---|---|
| | 192.168.1.102 | 11 | Malware Coordination | This system has been observed conducting communications that appear related to malware command and control. |
| | 192.168.10.102 | 7 | Malware Coordination | This system has been observed conducting communications that appear related to malware command and control. |
| | 192.168.14.105 | 9 | Malware Download | This system has downloaded potentially malicious software from an external untrusted location. |
| | 192.168.141.139 | 14 | Spyware | This system is interacting with external hosts using known spyware dialog patterns. |
| ▶ | 192.168.143.235 | 20 | Botnet Infection | This system has been successfully infected via a remote attack. It has uploaded malicious software, has coordinated with its control server, and is now spreading malware across the Internet. |
| | 192.168.15.15 | 4 | Malware Coordination | This system has been observed conducting communications that appear related to malware command and control. |
| | 192.168.162.142 | 10 | Sasser | This system has been successfully infected with a Sasser-like malware application. |

**Fig. 5.** Detected Infection Patterns View shows for each IP the kind of detected patterns such as malware coordination, spyware and malicious download and how much forensic evidence was collected for each pattern along with other meta data

External Interactions Table

Map

Infection summary for each IP address with dynamic level of detail

| IP Address of Victim | External Interactions | External IP Category | ISP | Domain | Country | City |
|---|---|---|---|---|---|---|
| | 98.172.183.8 | -Uncategorized- | COX COMMUNICATIONS | COX.NET | UNITED STATES | OKLAHOMA CITY |
| | 60.190.223.75 | Malware Propagator | SHAOXING TELECOM BUREAU | YZTRADECN.COM | CHINA | BEIJING |
| | 122.224.6.164 | Malicious Site, Mail Abuser, Malware Controller | SHAOXING TELECOM BUREAU | YZTRADECN.COM | CHINA | BEIJING |
| 192.168.143.235 | 195.88.191.59 | Malware Propagator | BIGNESS GROUP LTD. NETWORK | PTRZONEZ.COM | RUSSIAN FEDERATION | - |
| | 70.166.97.88 | -Uncategorized- | COX COMMUNICATIONS | COX.NET | UNITED STATES | PHOENIX |
| | 60.190.223.75 | Malware Propagator | SHAOXING TELECOM BUREAU | YZTRADECN.COM | CHINA | BEIJING |
| | 122.224.6.164 | Malicious Site, Mail Abuser, Malware Controller | SHAOXING TELECOM BUREAU | YZTRADECN.COM | CHINA | BEIJING |
| 192.168.248.146 | 61.147.99.179 | Malware Propagator | CHINANET JIANGSU PROVINCE NETWORK | 163DATA.COM.CN | CHINA | BEIJING |
| | 174.123.157.154 | Malicious Site, Mail Abuser, Malware Controller | THEPLANET.COM INTERNET SERVICES INC | THEPLANET.COM | UNITED STATES | DALLAS |
| | 64.38.232.180 | Malicious Site, Mail Abuser, Malware Controller | DOMAIN DEVELOPMENT | - | UNITED STATES | CALABASAS |
| | 83.133.119.197 | Malicious Site, Mail Abuser, Malware Controller | LNCDE-GREATNET-NEWMEDIA | GREATNET.DE | GERMANY | - |

**Fig. 6.** External Interactions Table shows for each local IP to which external IPs is has connected. This information is useful as it allows the user to now broaden the analysis outside of his own network and further investigate attacking nodes from the wider internet and decide mitigation strategies (such as taking the local IP off the network and rerouting traffic to that node to a honey net to further understand attackers).

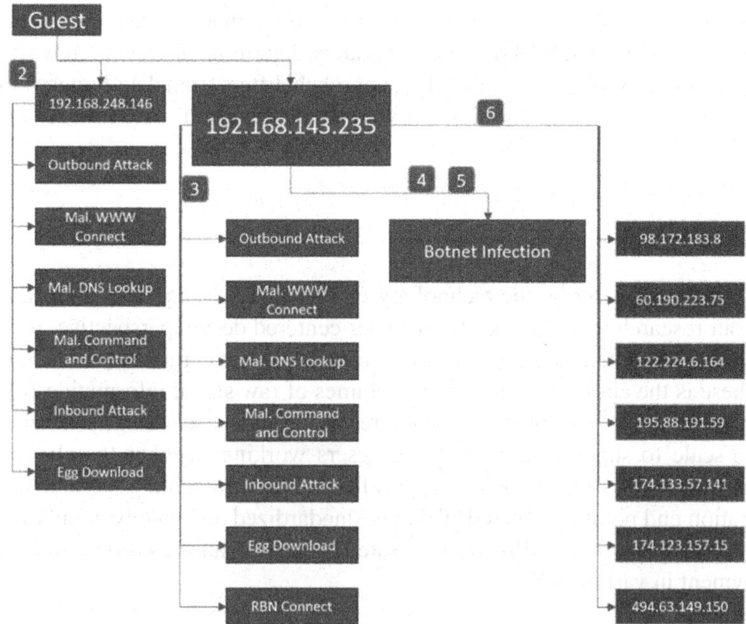


**Fig. 7.** Context model of a user interacting with BotHunter.

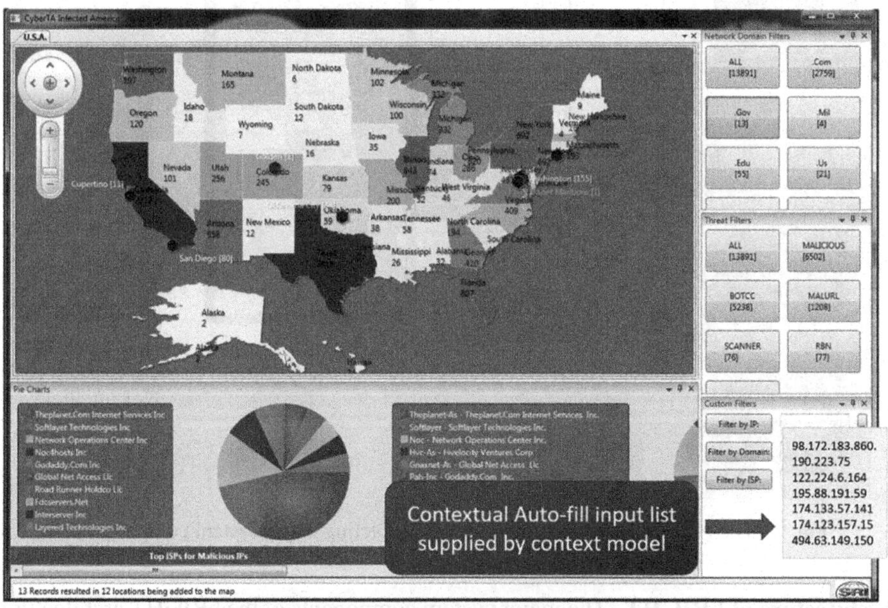


**Fig. 8.** Infected America, another bRIGHT-instrumented cybersecurity application.

bRIGHT's context model is a result of only a few minutes of user interaction with bRIGHT. This means that bRIGHT can accurately determine interest even with limited user data. In this way, bRIGHT's modeling approach differs from data-hungry modeling approaches such as machine learning to dynamically determine user interest with high accuracy.

## 5 Approach

In this section, we describe the technology of bRIGHT's design and illustrate how it impacts our research methodology from a user-centered design perspective.

The bRIGHT system is designed and developed to meet certain requirements. Chief among these is the ability to handle high volumes of raw signal information from gaze tracking, multi-touch, and biometric (face recognition, iris scanning) sensors and the ability to scale to support large groups of users working together to solve complex problems. bRIGHT's framework has support for the Kafka streaming server to introduce an integration end point into bRIGHT that is standardized and widely popular.

The use of open-source APIs was motivated by performance considerations and ease of deployment in various labs.

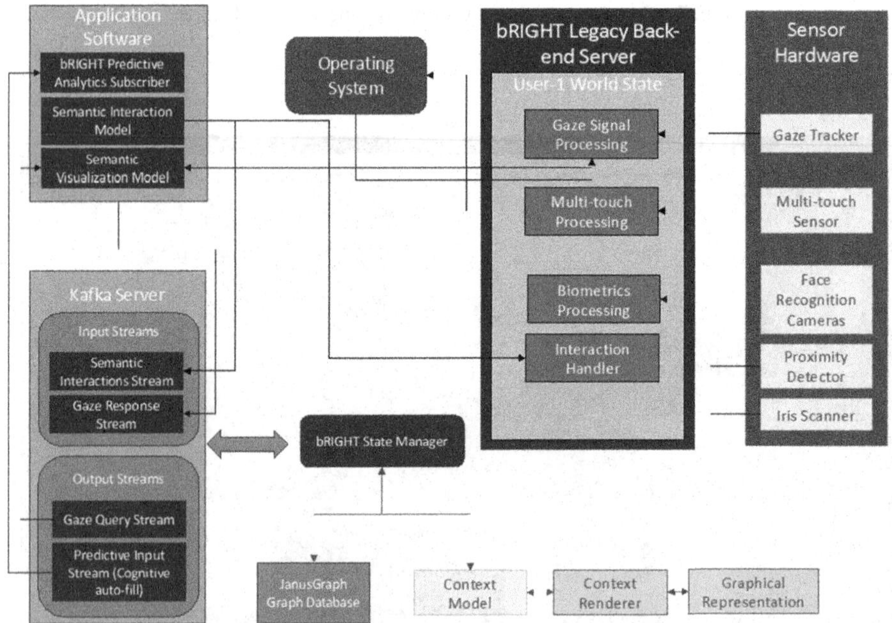


**Fig. 9.** The bRIGHT architectural overview depicting major system components.

**Architecture of bRIGHT.** The major system components of the bRIGHT architecture are shown in Fig. 9. In the following sections we describe the roles of components and how they integrate as a cohesive HCI framework that facilitates our research. This is a technical viewpoint of context modeling that facilitates our user-centered research. Our methodological viewpoint will be described in a future publication.

**Extending the Application Model.** The bRIGHT system is designed as a research framework and concept design for a future workstation. It allows us to investigate application paradigms such as object-oriented programming, which supports capture of accurate user context. bRIGHT has extensions to a typical application's business logic that include the bRIGHT analytics subscriber module (BASM), semantic interaction model (SIM), and the semantic visualization model (SVM) for each application. Further information about the application modeling enhancements in bRIGHT can be found in [19, 20]. The BASM is a component that connects to the bRIGHT analytical reasoner via the Kafka output stream from the bRIGHT state manager. The main purpose of BASM is to update the application's state with input from the bRIGHT analytics module. Such input could provide predictive data when an analytics module determines the user will need to match a required entry in a field in the application interface.

**Knowledge Representation.** The persistent data storage model for bRIGHT's state management uses a distributed, open-source, massively scalable graph database technology called JanusGraph. The scenarios in which graph databases outperform traditional relational databases are well documented. Given the nature of bRIGHT's knowledge representation, a graph representation is used as the primary form over which the analysis modules execute their reasoning. We use JanusGraph (part of the Apache TinkerPop[2] graph computing framework) and Gremlin[3] as the graph traversal machine and language for implementation of the connected component representing bRIGHT's world state.

The bRIGHT state manager (BSM) is the component responsible for connecting to the JanusGraph database back-end and populating the initial world state when the bRIGHT system powers up (see Fig. 9 above). In addition, the BSM subscribes to all of the input and output streams from the Kafka server, and based on the data flow on these streams, builds and manages the context model. The bRIGHT analytics module connects to the BSM and uses updates from the BSM to run various run-time analyses of the graph representation to enable predictive input and task automation, etc. The results are sent back to the BSM as state updates and passed along to the corresponding components of the system via the Kafka output streams. The bRIGHT analytics module also uses graph analytics techniques to identify regions of the graph or relationships that may be of interest in studies related to long-term evolution of context. These features are experimental and in advanced prototype stages.

**Context Model.** The BSM creates the context model based on various graph queries that execute due to triggers received from the Kafka input streams. This could be a user-action-associated semantic interaction model instance (i.e., pressing the "Send Mail" button in a mail client creates a SIM instance associated with being streamed into the BSM via the Kafka input stream), or it could be a gaze context response from the application for a query generated by the bRIGHT back-end server. This might happen because the user's gaze fell on a part of the screen being tracked for this application. The

[2] https://tinkerpop.apache.org/.

[3] https://tinkerpop.apache.org/gremlin.html.

graph queries utilize a system that is built on open domain knowledge and encapsulates some common concepts required for state management. Example domain knowledge could be the format of an IP address and its relationship to the network mask. Common concepts useful in such a case could be that IP addresses are often associated with geolocations, which contain properties such as "Country", "State", and "Zip Code".

Since the entire system is engineered end-to-end with the ability to stream signals such as gaze and also interprets the operational semantics of such signals at the user level—i.e., instead of updating the context model with gaze at point $P(X_i, Y_j)$, we update it with higher-level concepts such as: The user looked at the "Subject line of an unopened email containing ..."—in real-time speed. As such, there is no loss of information in terms of what interactions the user took in engaging the system, and the context model reflects almost all the information and concepts the user is currently interested in. It is not an exaggeration to claim that all the major design decisions in the bRIGHT system were made to maintain high accuracy of the context model.

The BSM maintains a journal of all updates applied to the context model; therefore, the evolution of the context model can be played forward and back in time when experiments are conducted. The Kafka stream data are also available, and we can fully replay any specific experiment or scenario, recreating the results from the signal streams upward. This allows us to run various graph analysis algorithms over the evolution of the context model and develop insights into long-term effects and patterns.

In cybersecurity demonstrations and experiments, we have seen the context models grow to contain thousands of entries and fairly complex connected components within the span of a few hours. Most of the content is from the gaze-tracking input, since cyber operators consume a lot of information both in terms of transaction rate and volume. It is not surprising that the context model of a cyber operator grows rapidly as a consequence of workflow. Cyber operators are constantly monitoring complex intrusion detection and malware detection software as well as routinely communicating with multiple team members to effectively collaborate. This complex and detailed context model also highlights why it is extremely difficult to track operator interests and anticipate their needs without such a rich and complex representation.

**Kafka Streaming Server.** The 3rd-generation bRIGHT system generates approximately 6 gigabits of sensor data every second. In addition, it creates intermediate sensor processing results such as blob detection output from the multi-touch surface, proximity detectors, face recognition status sensors, and so forth. bRIGHT needs to handle all of these streams of high sustained transfer-rate-oriented signals while performing complex context-oriented reasoning. As such, we chose to improve the scalability of our signal streaming capacity by integrating the Apache Foundation's Kafka streaming server into the bRIGHT framework[4].

The Kafka server has bRIGHT-friendly input streams (see Fig. 9, application status data and sensor data) and output streams (gaze queries being sent to applications, task automation, or predictive input results from the analytics module). Any future experiments conducted using this platform will be done by integrating software relevant to the

[4] https://kafka.apache.org.

experiment and connecting to a new Kafka input stream and output stream specific to that experiment context.

One of bRIGHT's core abilities is tracking the user's interest and responding to queries in the user's context model to execute application functionality in the near future. This "predictive input" is an extremely accurate form of autofill. When certain applications are fully integrated with bRIGHT, input parameters can be populated for an application feature and will auto-execute if there is enough evidence in the context model to suggest the user may do this in the near future. Task automation and predictive input are some of the outputs from the bRIGHT analytics module that are streamed to the application software using the Kafka output. Accurately tracking the context of the user allows proactive engagement that supports the user with needed information for input and task automation.

## 6 Future Work and Conclusions

A major focus for future work is to evaluate bRIGHT in user studies. While we have applied bRIGHT internally to various projects to experiment with task automation and cognitive autofill as means to adapt to user context, we have yet to conduct large and formal user studies.

Given the revolutionary gains in performance of AI-based systems and the rapid increase in deployment of autonomous systems in defense and disaster recovery, every aspect of human-machine interaction (HMI) is transforming rapidly. Understanding the user's context and leveraging it has always been significant in HMI, but this is now becoming one of the key areas for research and development because a much broader and more accurate definition of context will be needed in the future. We can expand our ability to capture user context by integrating better sensor systems, as evidenced in autonomous driving systems; however, to achieve truly transformational gains, we need advances in fundamental computing principals such as application modeling paradigms. These must be updated from vastly outdated models such as object-oriented programming, etc. As we have shown in our previous work [19, 20], expanding modeling so the application can respond to contextual queries about rendering context on screen and user interactions is important. We must provide a rich operational semantics level to create highly accurate context models of the user.

By improving the knowledge representation scheme in bRIGHT and adding support to embed high-level decision theory constructs such as "value maximization", "semantic framing", "attribute framing", "loss aversion", and "temporal discounting" among others, we will support identification and tracking of human decision-making based on context.

At present, the entire bRIGHT framework is built upon a very narrow definition of the user's context. Adding support for high-level concepts such as societal and environmental characteristics will increase the broader impact of this technology.

Our work in the last 8 years has allowed us to capture information and adapt the bRIGHT platform to the user's context in the short term. The ability to track long-term evolution of human experiences, interests, and values is useful. Indeed, rapid advances in AI and the predominance of autonomous systems will change the future.

We have demonstrated a need to extend basic computing principles such as application modeling paradigms to better support understanding the user's context. We extended existing applications by adding semantic interaction models and semantic visualization models that better describe the user-level operational semantics of the interactions and on-screen content. When the user engages with the system, we are able to identify, track, and adapt their context so that a response to change happens in near-real-time fashion. As such, we designed the entire bRIGHT framework end-to-end with these requirements in mind. To make revolutionary gains in capturing a broad swath of the user context (including societal and environmental aspects), user-centered design processes must follow a holistic approach that accounts for advances in sensor systems, software architectures, and application modeling. Consideration of short-term trends and long-term evolutionary patterns will also be important.

## References

1. Schilit, B., Adams, N., Want, R.: Context-aware computing applications. In: First Workshop on Mobile Computing Systems and Applications, pp. 85–90. IEEE (1994)
2. Moran, T.P. (ed.): Special issue on context in design. Hum.-Comput. Interact. **9**, 1–149 (1994)
3. Calvary, G., Coutaz, J., Thevenin, D., Limbourg, Q., Bouillon, L., Vanderdonckt, J.: A unifying reference framework for multi-target user interfaces. Interact. Comput. **15**(3), 289–308 (2003)
4. Baldauf, M., Dustdar, S., Rosenberg, F.: A survey on context-aware systems. Int. J. Ad Hoc Ubiquitous Comput. **2**(4), 263–277 (2007)
5. Ghiani, G., Manca, M., Paternò, F., Santoro, C.: Personalization of context-dependent applications through trigger-action rules. ACM Trans. Comput.-Hum. Interact. **24**(2), 1–33 (2017)
6. Matthews, T., Whittaker, S., Moran, T., Yuen, S.: Collaboration personas: a new approach to designing workplace collaboration tools. In: Proceedings of the SIGCHI Conference on Human Factors in Computing Systems, pp. 2247–2256 (2011)
7. Wang, R., Larusdottir, M., Cajander, Å.: Describing digital work environment through contextual personas. IFIG WG 13.2 Workhop at INTERACT 2021 (2021)
8. Thew, S., Sutcliffe, A.: Value-based requirements engineering: method and experience. Require. Eng. **23**(4), 443–464 (2017). https://doi.org/10.1007/s00766-017-0273-y
9. Sutcliffe, A.: Conflicting requirements and design trade-offs. In: IFIP WG 13.2 + 13.5 Workshop on Dealing with Conflicting User Interface Properties in User-Centered Development Processes. Mumbai (2017)
10. Johansen, P.S., Jacobsen, R.M., Bysted, L.B.L., Skov, M.B., Papachristos, E.: Designing a machine learning-based system to augment the work processes of medical secretaries. In: Loizides, F., Winckler, M., Chatterjee, U., Abdelnour-Nocera, J., Parmaxi, A. (eds.) Human Computer Interaction and Emerging Technologies: Adjunct Proceedings from the INTERACT 2019 Workshops, pp. 191–196. Cardiff University Press, Cardiff (2020)
11. Perera, C., Zaslavsky, A., Christen, P., Georgakopoulos, D.: Context aware computing for the internet of things: a survey. IEEE Commun. Surv. Tutor. **16**(1), 414–454 (2013)
12. Akiki, P.A., Bandara, A.K., Yu, Y.: RBUIS: simplifying enterprise application user interfaces through engineering role-based adaptive behavior. In: Proceedings of the 5th ACM SIGCHI Symposium on Engineering Interactive Computing Systems. pp. 3–12 (2013)
13. Gajos, K., Weld, D.S.: SUPPLE: automatically generating user interfaces. In: Proceedings of the 9th International Conference on Intelligent User Interfaces, pp. 93–100 (2004)

14. Yigitbas, E., Jovanovikj, I., Biermeier, K., Sauer, S., Engels, G.: Integrated model-driven development of self-adaptive user interfaces. Softw. Syst. Model. **19**(5), 1057–1081 (2020). https://doi.org/10.1007/s10270-020-00777-7
15. Skillen, K.-L., Chen, L., Nugent, C.D., Donnelly, M.P., Burns, W., Solheim, I.: Ontological user profile modeling for context-aware application personalization. In: Bravo, J., López-de-Ipiña, D., Moya, F. (eds.) UCAmI 2012. LNCS, vol. 7656, pp. 261–268. Springer, Heidelberg (2012). https://doi.org/10.1007/978-3-642-35377-2_36
16. Chen, H., Finin, T.: An ontology for a context aware pervasive computing environment. In: IJCAI Workshop on Ontologies and Distributed Systems, Acapulco (2005)
17. Wang, X.H., Zhang, D.Q., Gu, T., Pung, H.K.: Ontology based context modeling and reasoning using OWL. In: IEEE Annual Conference on Pervasive Computing and Communications Workshops, Proceedings of the Second, pp. 18–22. IEEE (2004)
18. Porras, P.A., Senanayake, R., Kaehler, J.: Revolutionizing the visual design of capture the flag (CTF) competitions. In: Proceedings of the 21st International Conference on Human-Computer Interaction HCI'19. Orlando, Florida, USA 26–31 July 2019
19. Senanayake, R., Denker, G., Lincoln, P.: bRIGHT – workstations of the future and leveraging contextual models. In: Yamamoto, S., Mori, H. (eds.) HIMI 2018. LNCS, vol. 10904, pp. 346–357. Springer, Cham (2018). https://doi.org/10.1007/978-3-319-92043-6_29
20. Senanayake, R., Denker, G.: Workstations of the future for transformational gains in solving complex problems. In: Kurosu, M. (ed.) HCII 2019. LNCS, vol. 11568, pp. 476–488. Springer, Cham (2019). https://doi.org/10.1007/978-3-030-22636-7_36

# Affordance-Derived Declarative Interaction Models for Context Adaptation

Cristian Bogdan(✉)

KTH Royal Institute of Technology, Stockholm, Sweden
cristi@kth.se

**Abstract.** Automatically adapting an interactive application to its use context is highly dependent on the existence of a declarative model. The Model-Based User Interface Development research made important progress in fully declarative specifications on interactive applications. However, the Abstract User Interface declarative models, such as task-based or communication-based models, are unfamiliar to designers and developers. This paper presents early explorations into a research program aimed at achieving fully declarative interactive applications: outlining a static concrete user interface and deriving the interaction from its affordances. The basic assumption is that for a well-designed user interface, the UI *function* can be derived from its *form* through affordance mechanisms. As the static aspects like the UI initial form are already being described declaratively in industrial practice, fully declarative interactive applications would result from the new research program.

**Keywords:** Affordance · Affordance-derivation · Declarative interaction · Context of use · Adaptation

## 1 Introduction

A large proportion of the digital systems source code deals with user interface [1,25] and the prominent area driving the quest to reduce user interface development time and costs is Model Based User Interface Development (MBUID), which is about to complete its fourth decade of research [23]. They have achieved fully declarative user interface representations with important advantages, many related to contextual adaptation: transferring an interactive system between devices [26], across modalities [13], ability to analyze the interactive system e.g. to assess safety [28], etc.

MBUID proposes representing interaction at two major levels. *Abstract User Interfaces* (AUI) are independent of the interaction modality (e.g. speech, gesture, graphical interface) and are represented either as Task models [8,30], or Dialog models [12,18,33]. *Concrete User Interfaces* are then derived from AUI, through *model transformations*, i.e., a top-down approach.


Published by Springer Nature Switzerland AG 2022
C. Ardito et al. (Eds.): INTERACT 2021, LNCS 13198, pp. 174–182, 2022.
https://doi.org/10.1007/978-3-030-98388-8_16

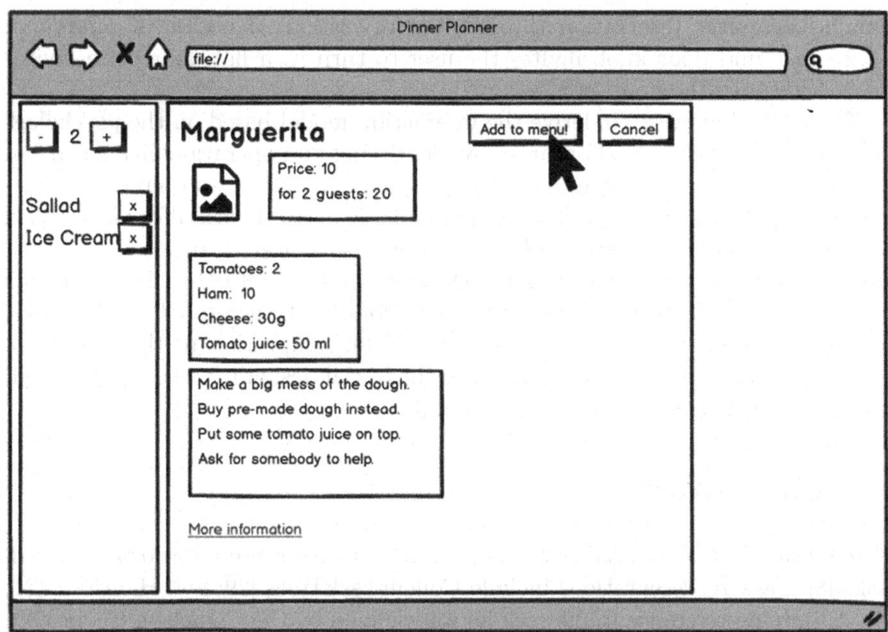


**Fig. 1.** Example user interface. The basic assumption outlined in the paper is that users understand or find out that pressing "Add to Menu" will add to the dish list on the left. Pressing "X" buttons on the left will remove from the list. Pressing the + and − buttons will adjust the price and ingredient information accordingly. Can we instruct computers to do the same?

While research in MBUID is still going on by e.g. unifying various approaches [11], such abstract declarative representations are not used in industrial practice as already pointed out in 2000 [24] and re-confirmed in 2011 [23]. One important issue is that interaction designers and users prefer to work at the *concrete* user interface level, and while they may be able to engage with the abstract user interfaces, they feel that they loose control over the automatically generated concrete UI.

The approach proposed in this paper for achieving a declarative description of interaction starts from the observation that, faced with a sufficiently well designed concrete user interface (e.g. Fig. 1), a user will be able to determine how to use it. For example, thousands of *apps* are downloaded and used directly nowadays without any user manual. In other words, the human will be able to anticipate the consequences of interacting with various controls that are part of the interface. *Can we teach computers to do the same?* Our preliminary results indicate that this is possible, and a few leads for how this can be achieved are described below.

The basic hypothesis of the proposed research program is that for well-designed (usable) user interfaces, the interaction stems from the interface. This 'inviting' relationship between the artifact *form* and its *function* [37], i.e. the anticipation of dynamic behavior from the static appearance is known in

Human-Computer Interaction through the psychological notion of *affordance* [14,27]: a round door knob invites the user to turn it, a flat door plate invites the user to push the door, etc.

Therefore, I suggest to derive the interaction model based on the psychological perception theory of affordance, by identifying and operationalizing some of the mechanisms that come into effect when humans understand interfaces. Furthermore, once a declarative interaction model is derived with affordance-based techniques, a *bottom-up* approach to modeling is suggested. Instead of moving top-down from an Abstract User Interface to the Concrete User Interface, the aim is to derive an Abstract User Interfaces from the Concrete UI . From there, automatic transformations can be made, e.g. for adaptation to the context of use, using approaches like [38]. Also once the initial design has been established, alternative designs can be explored using [36].

## 2 Related Work

*MBUID based on Task Models* draws from declarative representations of human tasks [8]. Task representations include ConcurTaskTrees [29] and Hamsters [21, 28]. A unifying reference framework [6] was defined by the Cameleon EU project and even standardized at the World Wide Web consortium (W3C).

The weak applicability in industrial practice is illustrated by a large German automotive industry project [22] that aimed to create automotive user interfaces using the Cameleon reference framework. The project used the usual top-down approach, from Abstract to Concrete User Interface, but "especially designers have problems with the more abstract layers (task/AUI)". To address this, designers from automaker Porsche had to devise a plug-in for the Balsamiq (concrete) user interface prototyping tool, for designers to be able to adjust the generated user interfaces.

*MBUID based on Discourse Models* [2,18] draw from theories of human communication like Rhetorical Structure Theory [15] and Conversation Analysis [12,33]. Like the task-based approach, a tool set exists for modeling at the abstract level and moving on to the concrete levels, but the abstract level is similarly difficult for interaction designers and other practitioners.

*Formal methods* for representing and analysing user interfaces (e.g. [5]) are relevant because they are declarative. They are, however, equally hard to engage with by practitioners, yet they can be of use in the proposed approach.

*Adaptive user interfaces* [13] lately use machine learning techniques that can be relevant during this research. For example, [36] aims to anticipate what would be beneficial changes to the user interface and tries to avoid making changes with no benefits.

At the same time as the MBUID research, *industrial user interface engineering practice* has recently taken important steps towards declarative representations at the Concrete User Interface levels. Rendering the user interface has long used declarative formats (e.g. XAML, XML, HTML), but nowadays programmers do not need to write imperative code for user interface *update* either.

Instead, the user interface is re-rendered in memory, resulting in a new UI hierarchy, represented as a tree, and then a tree comparison heuristic [10,31] is used to update the existing user interface tree with a minimal number of operations. This *declarative update* technique introduced around 2015 by the Facebook's React.js UI development framework [9] is now in wide use in multiple frameworks and UI platforms and toolkits.

Rendering and updating application data are thus declarative in current practice. What is left to achieve a fully declarative representation is to model the ways in which *user interactions* like e.g. user event listeners are modifying the application data. This concern is still currently addressed with imperative code in most cases.

## 3 Approach: Affordance-Derived Interaction Model

Deriving interaction from UI form by emulating the human ways of doing so is a specific form of Artificial Intelligence, and several AI techniques will be used such as pattern matching through supervised machine learning, and natural language processing. To practically derive interaction from computationally-detected concrete user interface affordance, the research aims to detect *affordance cues*, i.e., signs found within the concrete user interface that suggest a certain interaction. Such cues range from *graphical hierarchy* which has semantic implications, to *language cues*, i.e., the wording used in the user interface and its relationship to other notions in the application domain, and *exploration cues*, i.e., the user tries out different low-risk parts of the interface, to figure out their function by examining their effects. This is sometimes termed *exploring affordances.*

For example in Fig. 1 *graphical hierarchy* suggests a sidebar and a "main content" presenting application data in different ways. *Language cues* include the food terminology such as "menu", as well as names of dishes from the example data (Sallad, Ice Cream, Marguerita), but more importantly actions such as "Add to menu" when on the left we have a list of dishes, which is a synonym to "menu". Also "X" buttons in the context of a list suggest removal. The *graphical hierarchy*, more specifically the proximity (cf the Gestalt proximity law, see also w [32]) of the "+" and "−" buttons in relation to the number of dinner guests (2) are cues to a relationship between them: "+" adds to the number, "−" subtracts from the number.

There are also *machine-level cues* which are not based directly on user perception, but more on designer intent. Users do not have access to such cues but designers and developers do. A user interface design will often be described using a declarative tree-oriented language such as XML, XAML or HTML, and the hierarchy in that tree is our *hierarchy cue* and usually has semantic implications that can corroborate the user-level *graphical cue.* Designers often populate user interfaces with example data, and this gives our *data cues.* Such cues can help detect the application domain (food in Fig. 1) or data entity structures and relationships. Figure 2 shows data annotations in blue that are needed to achieve the non-interactive form of the Concrete UI, populated with data from a data

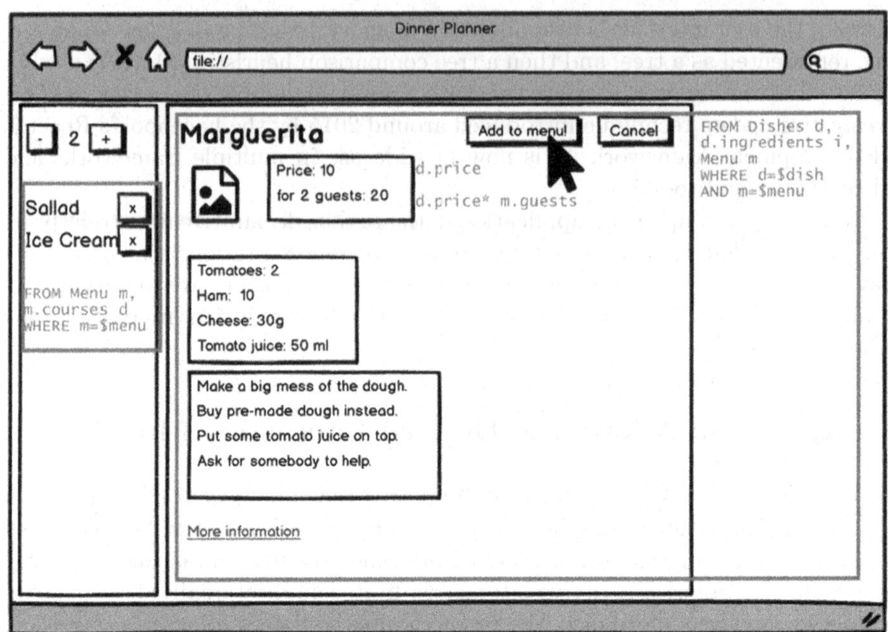


**Fig. 2.** Example machine-level data cues. By adding data annotation better specify the concrete UI form, more can be derived automatically about its function. In addition to the language cues, the data annotations now make it clear that the sub-interfaces on the left and center show data of the same type, and that the "Add" button should fulfill the conditions for "Marguerita" to be included in the list at the left

source. These data annotations are *data cues* that can help an interaction engine figure out the concrete effect of the "Add" button at the data processing level i.e., ensure that the dish will be added to the list at the left by adding the dish to the `m.dishes` collection.

The data source or application back-end will sometimes be specified, then this specification can be used to automatically interface the generated behavior with the respective back-end, so a complete interactive application results. Designers of graphical user interfaces also often produce declarative navigation charts describing how "screens" follow each other depending on user interaction. This is a *navigation cue* as it can be used to derive further interactive behavior. The list of cues is preliminary and will be extended and corrected during further research.

## 4 Preliminary Results

The author has been active in the area of fully declarative interactive application representations [18] and, in the research framework suggested here, has worked with *data cues* [2,4,16,17,19], exemplified also in Fig. 2. An implementation of the data cues approach [3] was used in real life for two decades in a student organization constructing and maintaining a large intranet and automated public web site (the scale is towards 1000 concrete user interfaces). At the time of the tool creation, only form-based Web 1.0 interaction was available, but further experimentation was conducted with direct manipulation interfaces with advanced interaction patterns such as drag and drop [16].

Furthermore, a few of the other cue types are being researched in the prestudy illustrated in Figs. 1 and 2. It was found that user level *visual cues* can be detected using recent work on "computational layout" [20] based on four Gestalt laws of visual perception [32]: Proximity, Similarity, Common region and Element Connectedness. This is an encouraging early result in interpreting visual affordance cues.

A few example application with no imperative code and fully generated interaction from declarative notations have been implemented.

- a task planner [16] using *data cues* to implement direct manipulation.
- the meal planner (Fig. 1) uses *language cues* to produce interaction (button action listener) that adds item to a list. Through natural language processing we determined that "Add to menu" needs to add to a list of dishes (i.e., synonym to a menu) which was found in the user interface via the *data cue* by three types of inferences: (1) the example data showed food terminology, (2) the type of the data element shown is the same as the data type of the individual list elements (Fig. 2) and (3) the type names/ontology used in the food dish description.
- a lab student queue system where a newly created object (representing the student waiting in a course queue) is added to the nearest list based on the *visual cue* and *hierarchy cue* that detected the Gestalt principle of Proximity.

## 5 Discussion and Conclusions

Automatically adapting an interactive application to its use context is highly dependent on the existence of a declarative model for that application. This paper described an approach for deriving the interaction model (*feel*) of the interactive application from its static appearance (*look*) as sketched by an interaction designer (cf [7,34]), by using various forms of artificial intelligence and heuristics. A few examples have been prototyped at the early stage but much more needs to be done. Once a completely declarative representation of the application exists, adapting it to various contexts of use will be done in future research through declarative transformations.

Deriving a user interface from its static affordance cues has significant potential in interactive computing. Not only will we be able to program interfaces by specifying how they look, but we will arrive to a completely declarative specification of a user interface, with both the form (Concrete User Interface) and the function (interaction) specified in a declarative notation, i.e., a completely declarative model that, unlike current models [24], is completely under the control of interaction designers.

Starting from such a model, one can determine an Abstract User Interface, and then enjoy all the advantages expected from [23,28] such as abstract model transformations towards cross-modality applications, assessing safety etc.

A further important step is that we are applying techniques like *natural language processing* and *pattern matching* to derive interaction, and such techniques can be refined to detect e.g. *genres* of applications, additional knowledge from the application domain (detected by pattern matching) etc. Pattern matching can also be used to identify and re-enforce user interface design patterns [35] or even design styles. We may for example be able in the future to help a designer apply their interaction design style, which we machine-learn through affordance-derivation, to a new product.

## References


1. Beaudouin-Lafon, M., Mackay, M.: Prototyping Tools and Techniques, pp. 1006–1031. Lawrence Erlbaum Associates Inc., USA (2002)
2. Bogdan, C., et al.: Generating an abstract user interface from a discourse model inspired by human communication. In: Proceedings of the 41st Annual Hawaii International Conference on System Sciences (HICSS 2008), p. 36 (2008)
3. Bogdan, C.: IT Design for Amateur Communities. Ph.D. thesis, KTH, Numerical Analysis and Computer Science, NADA (2003). (qC 20100420 NR 20140805)
4. Bogdan, C., Mayer, R.: Makumba: The role of the technology for the sustainability of amateur programming practice and community. In: Proceedings of the Fourth International Conference on Communities and Technologies. pp. 205–214. Association for Computing Machinery, New York, NY, USA (2009)
5. Bowen, J., Reeves, S.: Generating obligations, assertions and tests from UI models. In: Proceedings of ACM Human-Computer Interaction 1 (EICS), June 2017. https://doi.org/10.1145/3095807
6. Calvary, G., Coutaz, J., Thevenin, D., Limbourg, Q., Bouillon, L., Vanderdonckt, J.: A unifying reference framework for multi-target user interfaces. Interact. Comput. **15**(3), 289–308 (2003). Computer-Aided Design of User Interface
7. Coyette, A., Vanderdonckt, J.: A sketching tool for designing Anyuser, Anyplatform, anywhere user interfaces. In: Costabile, M.F., Paternò, F. (eds.) INTERACT 2005. LNCS, vol. 3585, pp. 550–564. Springer, Heidelberg (2005). https://doi.org/10.1007/11555261_45
8. Crandall, B., Klein, G.A., Hoffman, R.R.: Working Minds: A Practitioner's Guide to Cognitive Task Analysis. The MIT Press, Cambridge (2006)
9. Facebook: React reconciliation (2021). https://reactjs.org/docs/reconciliation.html. Accessed 9 Apr 2021
10. Finis, J.P., Raiber, M., Augsten, N., Brunel, R., Kemper, A., Färber, F.: RWS-diff: flexible and efficient change detection in hierarchical data. In: Proceedings of the 22nd ACM International Conference on Information and Knowledge Management, pp. 339–348. CIKM 2013, Association for Computing Machinery, New York, NY, USA (2013)
11. Forbrig, P., Dittmar, A., Kühn, M.: A textual domain specific language for task models: generating code for coTAL, CTTE, and HAMSTERS. In: Proceedings of the ACM SIGCHI Symposium on Engineering Interactive Computing Systems. EICS 2018, Association for Computing Machinery, New York, NY, USA (2018)

12. Garfinkel, H.: Studies in Ethnomethodology. Prentice-Hall, Englewood Cliffs (1967)
13. Ghiani, G., Manca, M., Paternò, F., Rett, J., Vaibhav, A.: Adaptive multimodal web user interfaces for smart work environments. J. Amb. Intell. Smart. Environ. **7**(6), 701–717 (2015)
14. Gibson, J.J.: The Ecological Approach to Visual Perception. Houghton Mifflin, Boston (1979)
15. Hou, S., Zhang, S., Fei, C.: Rhetorical structure theory: a comprehensive review of theory, parsing methods and applications. Expert Syst. App. **157**, 113421 (2020)
16. Kis, F., Bogdan, C.: Lightweight low-level query-centric user interface modeling. In: 2013 46th Hawaii International Conference on System Sciences, pp. 440–449 (2013)
17. Kis, F., Bogdan, C.: Declarative setup-free web application prototyping combining local and cloud datastores. In: 2016 IEEE Symposium on Visual Languages and Human-Centric Computing (VL/HCC), pp. 115–123 (2016)
18. Kis, F., Bogdan, C., Kaindl, H., Falb, J.: Towards fully declarative high-level interaction models: an approach facilitating automated GUI generation. In: 2014 47th Hawaii International Conference on System Sciences, pp. 412–421 (2014)
19. Kis, F., Bogdan, C.: Generating interactive prototypes from query annotated discourse models. i-com **14**(3), 205–219 (2015)
20. Koch, J., Oulasvirta, A.: Computational layout perception using gestalt laws. In: Proceedings of the 2016 CHI Conference Extended Abstracts on Human Factors in Computing Systems, pp. 1423–1429. CHI EA 2016, Association for Computing Machinery, New York, NY, USA (2016)
21. Martinie, C., Palanque, P.: Task models based engineering of interactive systems. In: Companion Proceedings of the 12th ACM SIGCHI Symposium on Engineering Interactive Computing Systems. EICS 2020 Companion, Association for Computing Machinery, New York, NY, USA (2020)
22. Meixner, G., Orfgen, M., Kümmerling, M.: Evaluation of user interface description languages for model-based user interface development in the German automotive industry. In: Kurosu, M. (ed.) HCI 2013. LNCS, vol. 8004, pp. 411–420. Springer, Heidelberg (2013). https://doi.org/10.1007/978-3-642-39232-0_45
23. Meixner, G., Paternò, F., Vanderdonckt, J.: Past, present, and future of model-based user interface development. i-com **10**(3), 2–11 (2011)
24. Myers, B., Hudson, S.E., Pausch, R.: Past, present, and future of user interface software tools. ACM Trans. Comput. Hum. Interact. **7**(1), 3–28 (2000)
25. Myers, B.A., Rosson, M.B.: Survey on user interface programming. In: Proceedings of the SIGCHI Conference on Human Factors in Computing Systems, pp. 195–202. CHI 1992, Association for Computing Machinery, New York, NY, USA (1992)
26. Nebeling, M., Paternò, F., Maurer, F., Nichols, J.: Systems and tools for cross-device user interfaces. In: Proceedings of the 7th ACM SIGCHI Symposium on Engineering Interactive Computing Systems, pp. 300–301. EICS 2015, Association for Computing Machinery, New York, NY, USA (2015)
27. Norman, D.A.: The Design of Everyday Things. Basic Books, New York (2002)
28. Palanque, P., Martinie, C., Winckler, M.: Designing and assessing interactive systems using task models. In: Bernhaupt, R., et al. (eds.) INTERACT 2017. LNCS, vol. 10516, pp. 383–386. Springer, Cham (2017). https://doi.org/10.1007/978-3-319-68059-0_35
29. Paterno, F., Mancini, C., Meniconi, S.: ConcurTaskTrees: A Diagrammatic Notation for Specifying Task Models, pp. 362–369. Springer, Boston (1997). https://doi.org/10.1007/978-0-387-35175-9_58

30. Paternò, F., Santoro, C., Spano, L.D.: MARIA: a universal, declarative, multiple abstraction-level language for service-oriented applications in ubiquitous environments. ACM Trans. Comput. Hum. Interact. **16**(4), 1–30 (2009)
31. Pawlik, M., Augsten, N.: Tree edit distance: robust and memory-efficient. Inf. Syst. **56**, 157–173 (2016)
32. Rock, I., Palmer, S.: The legacy of gestalt psychology. Sci. Am. **263**(6), 84–90 (1990)
33. Schegloff, E.A., Sacks, H.: Opening up closings. Semiotica **8**(4), 289–327 (1973)
34. Sermuga Pandian, V.P., Suleri, S., Jarke, P.D.M.: UISketch: a large-scale dataset of UI element sketches. In: Association for Computing Machinery, New York, NY, USA (2021). https://doi.org/10.1145/3411764.3445784
35. Silva-Rodríguez, V., Nava-Muñoz, S.E., Martínez-Pérez, F.E., Pérez-González, H.G.: How to select the appropriate pattern of human-computer interaction?: a case study with junior programmers. In: 2018 6th International Conference in Software Engineering Research and Innovation (CONISOFT), pp. 66–71 (2018)
36. Todi, K., Bailly, G., Leiva, L.A., Oulasvirta, A.: Adapting user interfaces with model-based reinforcement learning. In: CHI Conference on Human Factors in Computing Systems (CHI 2021), Yokohama, Japan, May 2021. https://hal.sorbonne-universite.fr/hal-03160272
37. Westerlund, B.: Form is function. In: Proceedings of the 4th Conference on Designing Interactive Systems: Processes, Practices, Methods, and Techniques. pp. 117–124. DIS 2002, Association for Computing Machinery, New York, NY, USA (2002)
38. Yigitbas, E., Grün, S., Sauer, S., Engels, G.: Model-driven context management for self-adaptive user interfaces. In: Ochoa, S.F., Singh, P., Bravo, J. (eds.) UCAmI 2017. LNCS, vol. 10586, pp. 624–635. Springer, Cham (2017). https://doi.org/10.1007/978-3-319-67585-5_61

# Ensuring User Interface Adaptation Consistency Through Triple Graph Grammars

Kai Biermeier(✉), Enes Yigitbas, Nils Weidmann, and Gregor Engels

Paderborn University, Paderborn, Germany
{kai.biermeier,enes.yigitbas,nils.weidmann,engels}@upb.de

**Abstract.** As modern User Interfaces (UIs) are used in varying context-of-use situations, sophisticated mechanisms to control UI adaptations are needed. UI adaptations describe the process of manipulating the initial UI to fit the current context-of-use. Typically, the UI and context-of-use are formalized by models. If these adaptations are not well-defined or checked properly, undesirable application of multiple adaptations may threaten consistency. To prevent conflicting UI adaptations and ease the specification of UI adaptation rules, we introduce a notion of adaptation consistency based on Triple Graph Grammars (TGGs) augmented with a 0–1 priority system. We choose TGGs because it is a formalism for consistency maintenance in model-driven engineering. We extend the TGG semantics with a 0–1 priority system to assess for consistency regarding application order. Based on this solution idea, we present the implementation of a prototypical TGG interpreter to suggest a design- and run-time solution for ensuring consistency of UI adaptations.

**Keywords:** Adaptive User Interface · Consistency · Triple Graph Grammars

## 1 Introduction

Adaptive User Interfaces (UIs) were proposed to cope with the arising amount of different contexts-of-use. A UI adaptation system should transform a UI into another one that is suitable for the current context of use. As for model-based and model-driven adaptive UIs, adaptations are typically defined as independent rules. They can interact in non-deterministic and therefore potentially undesired ways. For illustration, we assume that a user runs a calendar application with UI adaptation capabilities on a smartphone. The user is on the way to his car. After some time, a context change happens as the user enters the car. By this means, he changes the context property: location. As he switched from the smartphone to the infotainment system of the car, he also changes the context property: target device. Based on the new location, it might be a good idea to change from a graphical to a vocal UI (adaptation rule 1). In this way, the user, as the driver, can better watch the traffic. An infotainment system has more screen space than


Published by Springer Nature Switzerland AG 2022
C. Ardito et al. (Eds.): INTERACT 2021, LNCS 13198, pp. 183–192, 2022.
https://doi.org/10.1007/978-3-030-98388-8_17

a smartphone. Therefore, based on the target device switch, the system shows more elements on the screen (adaptation rule 2). Therefore, adaptation rules 1 and 2 conflict with each other by the way they would change the set of graphical UI elements. Applying adaptation rule 1 would imply switching to the vocal UI while adaptation rule 2 would imply showing more graphical elements. They are also triggered at the same time which hardens the conflict. To overcome such scenarios and prevent conflicting UI adaptations, we propose a consistency management framework for UI adaptations based on TGGs [10].

First, we briefly introduce TGGs to provide some background information on their basic concepts (Sect. 2). After that, we present our consistency management framework and describe how conflict-free UI adaptations can be ensured at design- and run-time (Sect. 3). Then, we briefly summarize and discuss related work (Sect. 4). Finally, we conclude the paper and give an outlook for future work (Sect. 5).

## 2 Triple Graph Grammars

TGGs are a declarative, rule-based approach allowing bidirectional model transformations [10]. They are most often used for synchronization problems between two models represented as graphs. To model the consistency relation between two models, a third *correspondence* model is introduced, connecting source and target.

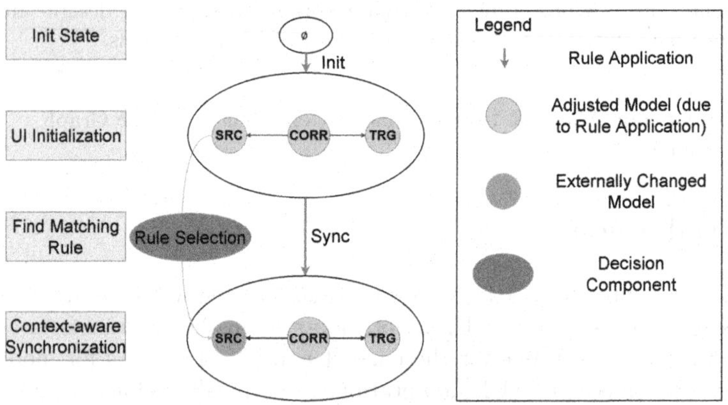


**Fig. 1.** TGG synchronization procedure

TGGs evolve out of Pair Grammars which do not achieve complete context sensitivity regarding language expressiveness. This is the reason why TGGs introduce a third model (Correspondence) to consider the creation history and not only link the source (SRC) and target (TRG) models directly as it is the case with Pair Grammars. From the perspective of a TGG, a model triple is consistent if the TGG language can generate it. Therefore, a TGG consists of multiple

production rules like context-sensitive string grammars. Since the language is context-sensitive, one can define model elements that are needed to apply a production rule and model elements that will be created when applying this rule. This holds for all three models formally named as the source, target, and correspondence. The circumstance that the underlying grammar synchronously creates both models can be utilized as a synchronization mechanism.
The synchronization procedure is illustrated in Fig. 1. By these means, the TGG can be used to derive triples of a source and target (and correspondence) models such that the partial source model matches a given source model. In consequence, the target model is the one synchronized to the source model. At this point, we have defined a synchronization from a source model to the target domain if a target model does not exist already. If a target model was already defined and was previously synchronized to a prior version of the source model, we delete all rule orders that do not start with a rule order that creates the priorly synchronized target model. Only if this set is empty, we also consider the previously deleted application orders. Finding rule orders is often done by backtracking. The interested reader may refer to [1] to get detailed information about TGGs.

## 3 Consistency Management Framework

As most of the existing UI adaptation approaches rely on the technique of model-based or model-driven development, the translation system of context-of-use and the user interface is the core of every adaptive UI (e.g. [15]). It manages the consistency between the context-of-use and the UI. Consistency is critical because it preserves the context-awareness of the UI. It is also complex, because of conflicts that might occur while applying UI adaptation rules. To manage and formalize consistency, we have decided to use TGGs as a bidirectional model transformation language as suggested in [3]. Reddy presented some techniques to gain consistency for UI adaptation systems at design-time [9]. First of all, a specification should be formal to assess for flaws. Additionally, the formal specification should be transformed through a code generator into a decision component to select UI adaptations. Deriving the code from a formal model with a generator ensures that quality properties that hold at design time most likely also hold at run-time. Assessing a generator for flaws is typically more efficient than checking every new adaptive UI. The AdaptUI approach [14] uses such a generator.

### 3.1 Consistency at Design-Time

We suggest a generative approach to apps with adaptation capabilities because these are often faster than interpretative solutions. Additionally, a generative approach can preserve properties from design-time models. TGGs serve well for adaptation conception at design time because of their graphical style, intuitive relation-like notion, and semantics. The formal development process for adaptive UIs using our consistency management framework based on TGGs is illustrated

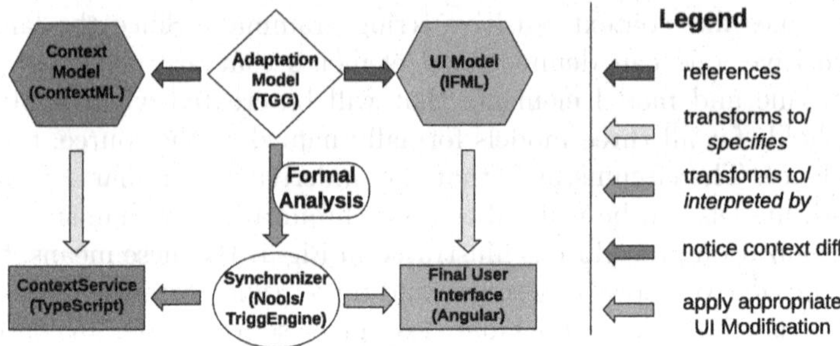


**Fig. 2.** Consistency management framework for UI adaptations (at design and at run-time)

in Fig. 2. The first step in formalizing adaptation rules as TGG rules is to think of explicit relations between the context-of-use and UI. Because in our approach we make use of ContextML [12] for describing the context-of-use and IFML[1] [5] for the UI, the user has to describe the items of the relation in terms of these languages. The relation is then specified via the correspondence model. The TGG-formalized adaptation model can be seen as a refinement of simple UI adaptation rules which are usually specified based on the event-condition-action (ECA) paradigm. As an example, a TGG adaptation rule specification described as a triple could be: the context property daytime with *value* attribute set to night, a link object, and the color schema dark background with bright text. Depending on the approach, one has to also specify rules that have no context dependency. These rules formalize the initial construction of the UI that does not rely on a special context property. TGGs as a model synchronization formalism are well studied to formally check quality aspects (e.g. [8]). Moreover, several important properties, such as termination, are well-researched [2]. With such a suitable formalism, one could for example use a state-space analysis to see whether conflicting states can occur. One could then further reason about their real-world impact. There exist conflicts that are not critical, hence, if we have two options that can be weighted both reasonable, but not important, it is of less importance which to apply. However, there are real-world scenarios where you want to be sure that one adaptation will be preferred over the others. On the one hand, the rule can be refined for a more specific (application) context. On the other hand, one could attach a priority system for adaptation reasoning at run-time. Nevertheless, more interesting for design-time is the formal analysis. In the case of UI adaptations, especially backward transformations seem to be suitable as starting point. A backward transformation means transforming the target model into the source domain. In our case, the target model domain is the UI and the source model domain is the context-of-use. The purpose of those backward transformations is to check whether the correct context can be derived from a concrete UI model. The intuition behind this analysis approach is that

[1] https://www.ifml.org/.

people typically see the relation of context and UI directed from the context to the UI. Therefore, most adaptation rules will be defined targeting this direction. To have a complete specification, it is needed to be precise and complete in both directions. Therefore, a backward transformation can reveal under-specification, conflicts, or the producibility of badly structured final UIs.

**Implementation.** To implement the design-time solution idea, we make use of eMoflon[2] as a Java-based TGG tool. eMoflon is a toolkit for model-driven software development with a concrete syntax for defining and executing TGGs on EMF models. This toolkit was developed as a plug-in for Eclipse such that it integrates very well with other EMF tools. The UI developer can therefore remain using his known tools. He only has to specify the adaptation system in a TGG specification. Following the visual syntax used in eMoflon, a TGG-based UI adaptation rule could be visualized like in Fig. 3. This TGG rule describes adaptation rule 2 from the motivating example. Green elements are considered to be created by the rule. Black elements need to exist before rule application. The correspondence relation is visualized as dashed arrows.

**Example.** Consider the conflict presented in the introduction section. The goal of the design-time approach is to analyze the state space and find that conflict. Because we are using TGGs, the state space is completely computable. Therefore, we would recognize the described conflict, i.e. we would find no state where the environment is a car and the platform is an infotainment system. Another option is trying to backward transform a UI model with annotations for a vocal user interface and with an overview table. This should be impossible when our TGG specification is complete. Nevertheless, if we forgot to forbid the existence of graphical UI elements when we have changed the modality to vocal, it is possible to gain such a UI. When creating a synchronized triple, the TGG tool would also log their creation history by application order. In this way, the developer can analyze the conflict and can refine the application conditions (positive and negative) for the adaptation [6]. In the example case, one could use a negative application condition (modality != vocal) for adaptation rule 2 such that adaptation rule 1 will be preferred. This behavior is induced by the TGG semantics. Nevertheless, the other and easier option at design-time is to implement a priority mechanism that explicitly prefers adaptation rule 1. We favor this option to prevent important adaptations from being skipped, but in the general case, the semantics should define the application order.

### 3.2 Consistency and Conflict Resolution at Run-Time

As we already considered consistency at design-time, one could ask why further consider consistency at run-time. The reason is that often not every conflict can

[2] https://emoflon.org/.

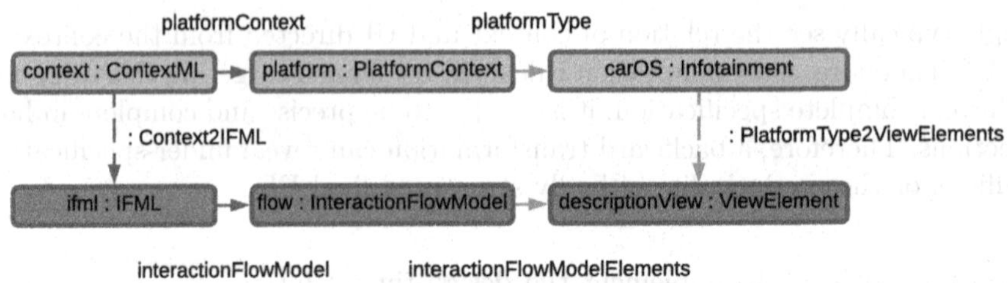


**Fig. 3.** eMoflon: example TGG adaptation rule (Color figure online)

be solved appropriately at design-time. For example, one wants to allow potentially conflicting rules, i.e., they would make incompatible changes on the UI. Let us consider that these conflicts will in practice arise not very frequently or we do not want to specify the system completely in advance. Therefore, it could be suitable that we allow potential conflicts to remain in the specification and address them if they arise. For this purpose, we have implemented the TriggEngine[3] which allows domain experts to specify UI adaptation rules with priorities. Prioritizing one rule means consider it first when transforming a source model to the target domain or the reverse. A priority system in a TGG interpreter will, therefore, not change its semantics. Only if there exist multiple options to transform one model to the other domain, the result may differ. If there is no synchronization solution found with the preferred adaptations, also the not preferred adaptations will be considered to find a triple that can be generated by the TGG and can therefore be considered as consistent. Rule application in the TGG formalism can be viewed similarly to context-sensitive grammars. The TriggEngine's basic synchronization process is visualized in Fig. 2. The TriggEngine synchronizes in our proposed framework typescript data structures that conform to the EMF metamodels of the context-of-use and the UI. Since Angular is written in TypeScript, an Angular template is a special case of a TypeScript data structure. The 0–1 priority system is a very simple priority system and therefore easy to use. The application order of the same rule set is similar because a 0–1 priority system does not completely determine the order of application. In this way, we get flexibility in applying adaptations while also preserving crucial consistency in rule application order. If a conflict arises at run-time based on the priority, the system decides which adaptation to prefer. If both adaptations have the same priority, the activation time serves as a tie-breaker. Therefore, the adaptation that arises first will be applied (or stay applied) as long as there does not arise an adaptation with higher priority. Preferring the firstly raised adaptation that occurs is based on the idea of UI stability. If we cannot decide which adaptation is more important, then we do not want to change the UI more than necessary [4]. Instability in the UI would result in a worse user experience because it increases the cognitive load needed to handle a task. Another benefit of using the TGG specification at run-time is the dependency loss to a model-to-text

[3] https://github.com/caiusnol/TriGG.js.

transformation for application generation. So, that artifact has not to be checked for its correctness. One could argue that we now have to ensure that the newly implemented TGG interpreter has to be evaluated for correctness and this component is much more complex than a simple model-to-text transformation. Nevertheless, we have tools like eMoflon and other good reference implementations where we could check the implementation against. Since the metamodels proposed by Yigitbas et al. in [13] are based on EMF, we could check the interpreter's output against any TGG tool that uses or can import EMF models. Since EMF is one of the most commonly used modeling standards, many tools implement support for those models.

**Implementation.** The TriggEngine is a proof of concept implementation of our consistency management framework for UI adaptations which focuses on the run-time perspective. It allows us to forward synchronize two models, in our case synchronizing from context to UI models. The special feature of this engine in comparison with the fully-fledged TGG tool eMoflon is its support for 0–1 priorities. The lower priority is called cold while the higher priority is called hot. The naming convention is inspired by the Modal profile for UML Sequence Diagrams [7]. To guarantee consistency at run-time, the engine prefers hot rules and overwrites cold ones if necessary. This behavior is not implemented in the original TGG approach. If both rules are marked as hot or cold, the first adaptation will be considered as of higher importance. This enhances stability because the UI will not undergo unnecessary changes. The schema and idea behind hot and cold UI adaptation rules are depicted as an overview in Fig. 4.

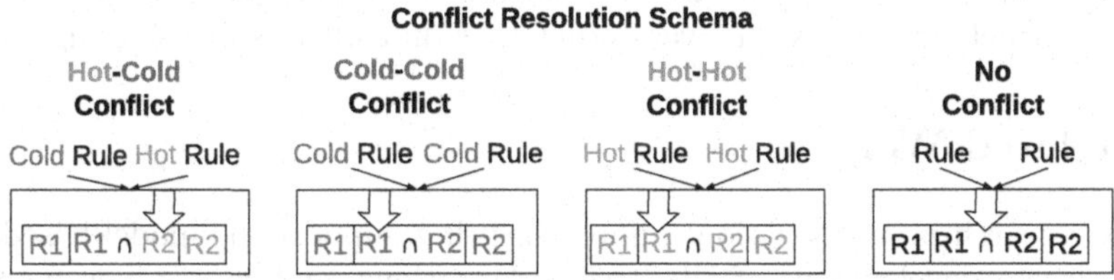


**Fig. 4.** TriggEngine conflict resolution schema

**Example.** An example UI adaptation rule that was written for the TriggEngine is visualized in Fig. 5. As mentioned before, this rule defines in each case the structural adaptation of the UI model and not just an annotation. For simplicity reasons, Fig. 5 only contains a trivial UI adaptation rule. This rule describes the following operation: Already having a *Context* entity, if a *PlatformContext* will be created, there should also a *CorrespondenceLink* and an *InteractionFlowModel* be generated additionally. The *InteractionFlowModel* should have the *modality* attribute set to vocal. The rule is marked as *hot*. That means that it is an important rule and will be preferred if possible. A real rule would be

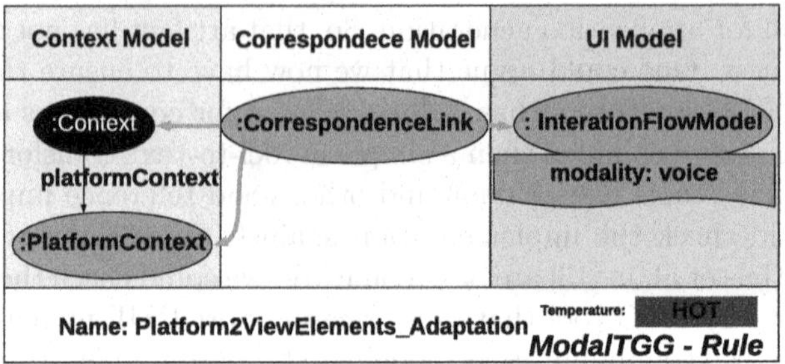


**Fig. 5.** Example TGG rule for TriggEngine

much larger and more complex. For implementing adaptation rule 1, for example, one would have to define in detail how the overview table would look like. If we annotate a higher priority to adaptation rule 1, we can ensure that in neither case adaptation rule 2 would block the application of adaptation rule 1. Since the vocal UI mode is more safety-critical than adding a UI element, this sounds reasonable. Using 0–1 priority augmented TGGs at run-time instead of only a simple priority system in a rule engine is beneficial because it allows the interpreter to stay flexible in adaptation application while still preferring the most important rules. Additionally, the developer cannot introduce as much complexity in the rule choice procedure. This can also be a disadvantage, but in this way, we also force the developer to address as many conflicts as possible with the design-time solution, which will enhance the performance at run-time. We force the developer in such terms that he cannot address each conflict at run-time with our priority system. By these means he should only solve conflicts at run-time which are impossible, very crucial, or difficult to solve at design-time.

## 4 Related Work

Recent research provides various approaches that support the model-based and model-driven development of UIs, their adaptations, and consistency management. In the following we briefly describe the main approaches that are dealing with UI adaptations with a special focus on the consistency of adaptations. The AdaptUI approach [13] serves as an integrated solution for building adaptive UIs. This approach uses Angular as a UI framework and, based on it, supports the generation of adaptive UIs. For this purpose, it uses three different domain-specific languages (DSLs). These DSLs are ContextML, IFML (see Footnote 1) and AdaptML. The three DSLs are used to describe the context-of-use, the abstract UI, and the UI transformations needed if the context changes. Its adaptation specification is not supporting formal consistency analysis of UI adaptations as proposed in this paper. Nevertheless, this approach founds the basis of the presented approach. Furthermore, Trollman describes in [11] a formal framework for considering adaptation conflicts at run-time. It is well situated with proofs utilizing category theory, but remains very abstract and rather usable as a meta-framework than an actual out-of-the-box usable approach. Anjorin et al. [3] introduce a smart definition of consistency for run-time UI adaptations. They also name challenges to address when using bidirectional model transformation languages to model UI adaptations. These are: conformance to the system layer, compatibility of the initial structure of the UI and adaptation logic, checking for desirable properties of the adaptation logic. While this work mainly focuses on the discussion of the above-mentioned challenges, we have shown a practical framework to cope with the latter two of them. The strengths of our approach lie in its applicability in a ready-to-use solution contrary to the approach in [11]. Anjorin et al. discuss in [4] some challenges and solution ideas to consistency between the context-of-use and UI on different abstraction layers. They do this through initial modification to only one layer. The changes done on one layer must potentially be propagated to other abstraction layers to ensure that all models still describe the same UI. We only focus on the concrete and final UI layer in this work. Moreover, they discuss consistency between different models on the concrete layer. The idea is that multiple (adapted) concrete UI models should still show the same things. This is closer to the challenge that we address in this paper, but we do not aim for complete consistency of all potentially concrete UIs. We focus in this paper on preserving similarity by grounding on the same initial UI and prioritizing important adaptations. So, if we start at the very same concrete UI and do the same adaptations in the nearly same order (based on 0–1 priorities), we will get at least similar results.

## 5 Conclusion

Adaptive UIs have been promoted as a solution for context variability due to their ability to automatically adapt to the context-of-use at run-time. Engineering such adaptive UIs, ensuring consistency of UI adaptations, is a challenging task. On the one hand, the specification of UI adaptation rules at design time gets complex with increasing adaptation logic. On the other hand, due to unforeseen events, conflicting UI adaptations may happen at run-time. To prevent such inconsistencies owing to conflicting and incorrect UI adaptation rules, we present a consistency management framework for UI adaptations. Our framework is based on TGGs and supports a formal specification and analysis of UI adaptation rules. For the presented consistency management framework for UI adaptations, we have implemented a proof-of-concept implementation that supports ensuring consistency at design- and run-time. In future work we aim to analyze the efficiency and effectiveness of our consistency management framework. As the described tool-chain is still in development, we plan to extend its validation capabilities for further consistency properties (e.g. conformance to system layer, consistency between abstraction layer ...) besides conflict-free UI adaptation rules.

## References


1. Anjorin, A., Leblebici, E., Kluge, R., Schürr, A., Stevens, P.: A systematic approach and guidelines to developing a triple graph grammar. In: Bx@ STAF, pp. 81–95 (2015)
2. Anjorin, A., Leblebici, E., Schürr, A.: 20 years of triple graph grammars: a roadmap for future research. Electron. Commun. EASST. **73**, 1–20 (2016)
3. Anjorin, A., Yigitbas, E., Kaindl, H.: Consistent runtime adaptation of user interfaces. In: Bx@ PLW, pp. 61–65 (2019)
4. Anjorin, A., Yigitbas, E., Kaindl, H., Popp, R.: On the development of consistent user interfaces. In: Conference Companion of the 2nd International Conference on Art, Science, and Engineering of Programming, pp. 18–20 (2018)
5. Brambilla, M., et al.: The interaction flow modeling language (IFML). Technical report. version 1.0. Object Management Group (OMG) (2014)
6. Golas, U., Ehrig, H., Herrmann, F.: Formal specification of model transformations by triple graph grammars with application conditions. Electron. Commun. EASST. **39**, 1–27 (2011)
7. Greenyer, J., et al.: Scenario tools-a tool suite for the scenario-based modeling and analysis of reactive systems. Sci. Comput. Program. **149**, 15–27 (2017)
8. Hermann, F., Ehrig, H., Golas, U., Orejas, F.: Efficient analysis and execution of correct and complete model transformations based on triple graph grammars. In: Proceedings of the First International Workshop on Model-Driven Interoperability, pp. 22–31 (2010)
9. Reddy, S.: Quality Assurance of Adaptive User Interfaces. Master's thesis, Paderborn University, July 2018
10. Schürr, A.: Specification of graph translators with triple graph grammars. In: Mayr, E.W., Schmidt, G., Tinhofer, G. (eds.) WG 1994. LNCS, vol. 903, pp. 151–163. Springer, Heidelberg (1995). https://doi.org/10.1007/3-540-59071-4_45
11. Trollmann, F.: Detecting adaptation conflicts at run time using models@run.time. Doctoral thesis, Technische Universität Berlin, Fakultät IV - Elektrotechnik und Informatik, Berlin (2015). http://dx.doi.org/10.14279/depositonce-4327
12. Yigitbas, E., Grün, S., Sauer, S., Engels, G.: Model-driven context management for self-adaptive user interfaces. In: Ochoa, S.F., Singh, P., Bravo, J. (eds.) UCAmI 2017. LNCS, vol. 10586, pp. 624–635. Springer, Cham (2017). https://doi.org/10.1007/978-3-319-67585-5_61
13. Yigitbas, E., Jovanovikj, I., Biermeier, K., Sauer, S., Engels, G.: Integrated model-driven development of self-adaptive user interfaces. Softw. Syst. Model. **19**(5), 1057–1081 (2020). https://doi.org/10.1007/s10270-020-00777-7
14. Yigitbas, E., Sauer, S., Engels, G.: Adapt-ui: an ide supporting model-driven development of self-adaptive UIS. In: Proceedings of the ACM SIGCHI Symposium on Engineering Interactive Computing Systems, pp. 99–104 (2017)
15. Yigitbas, E., Stahl, H., Sauer, S., Engels, G.: Self-adaptive UIs: integrated model-driven development of UIs and their adaptations. In: Anjorin, A., Espinoza, H. (eds.) ECMFA 2017. LNCS, vol. 10376, pp. 126–141. Springer, Cham (2017). https://doi.org/10.1007/978-3-319-61482-3_8

# HCI-E^2: HCI Engineering Education - for Developers, Designers and More

# Teaching HCI Engineering: Four Case Studies

Sybille Caffiau[1], José C. Campos[2], Célia Martinie[3], Laurence Nigay[1], Philippe Palanque[3], and Lucio Davide Spano[4(✉)]

[1] Univ. Grenoble Alpes, CNRS, Grenoble INP, LIG, 38000 Grenoble, France
{Sybille.Caffiau,Laurence.Nigay}@univ-grenoble-alpes.fr

[2] University of Minho and HASLab/INESC TEC, Braga, Portugal
jose.campos@di.uminho.pt

[3] Université Paul Sabatier-Toulouse III, IRIT, Toulouse, France
{martinie,palanque}@irit.fr

[4] Department of Mathematics and Computer Science, University of Cagliari, Via Ospedale 72, 09124 Cagliari, Italy
davide.spano@unica.it

**Abstract.** The paper presents the work carried out at the HCI Engineering Education workshop, organised by IFIP working groups 2.7/13.4 and 13.1. It describes four case studies of projects and exercises used in Human-Computer Interaction Engineering courses. We propose a common framework for presenting the case studies and describe the four case studies in detail. We then draw conclusions on the differences between the presented case studies that highlight the diversity and multidisciplinary aspects to be taught in a Human-Computer Interaction Engineering course. As future work, we plan to create a repository of case studies as a resource for teachers.

**Keywords:** Teaching HCI engineering · User-Centered Design · Software engineering

## 1 Introduction

Engineering interactive systems is a multidisciplinary activity positioned at the intersection of Human-Computer Interaction (HCI), software engineering, usability engineering, interaction design, visual design and other disciplines. The field of Human-Computer Interaction Engineering (HCI-E) is concerned with providing methods, techniques and tools for the systematic and effective analysis, design, development, testing, evaluation and deployment of interactive systems in a wide range of application domains. This field, thus, requires an understanding of both HCI and Software Engineering topics as highlighted by the ACM/IEEE-CS Software Engineering [11] and ACM SIGCHI Human-Computer Interaction [5] curricula.

There are many challenges in teaching HCI [7]: keeping up to date courses and curricula because technologies and methods evolve fast, ensuring the involvement


Published by Springer Nature Switzerland AG 2022
C. Ardito et al. (Eds.): INTERACT 2021, LNCS 13198, pp. 195–210, 2022.
https://doi.org/10.1007/978-3-030-98388-8_18

of students with users because computer science students are familiar with various interactive technologies and may not grasp the fact that other types of users may struggle with interactive systems. Whereas these challenges do not target teaching HCI-E specifically, they also fully concern HCI-E and a curricula in HCI-E should contain pedagogical materials that help to take them into account. Beyond these field related challenges, Aberg [1] highlighted potential problems of existing curricula in HCI for computer science students and pointed out the need to propose to students pedagogical activities which make them "*create something that works*", "*focus on technology and issues that they feel related to*", and which provide them with "*a sense of realism, with projects or assignments connected to real and ongoing projects*".

In this paper, we discuss the teaching of HCI Engineering. More specifically, we present four case studies of student projects and exercises used as part of courses on teaching HCI-E. The case studies satisfy different pedagogical goals, including designing or developing interactive systems. We first present the common framework for presenting the case studies, then each of the four case studies, and at last, we discuss how they address the main challenges and needs of teaching HCI-E.

## 2 Presentation Framework

To present the case studies, we propose a framework made of five categories:

- An overall description as an identity card of the case study including title, type of case study, the studied type of interaction, the available resources, and a brief description of the case study;
- A description of the students and their pre-requisite levels in the disciplines involved in HCI-E, including HCI and Software Engineering (SE);
- A description of the pedagogical objectives of the case study;
- A description of the pedagogical management of the case study, including the tools used and the initial materials provided;
- A description of the expected outcomes and their evaluation.

## 3 Case Study 1: Kart Racing Game

### 3.1 Identity Card

- **Title:** Kart Racing Game
- **Type:** Project
- **Application domain:** Game
- **Interaction techniques:** WIMP and post-WIMP
- **Brief description:** The case study is based on an existing open-source kart racing game SuperTuxKart (https://supertuxkart.net/). The goal is to design input controllers to drive the kart in the kart racing game. The set of input commands includes: turn right, turn left, slow down, speed up, backtrack, back view and standard view. By starting with an existing game and a set of input commands, the goal is to focus only on the input interface and not on the other parts of the interactive system, including the game engine and the output interface.

### 3.2 Targeted Students and Pre-requisites

The Kart Racing Game case study is used in a Master course in Computer Science. But this case study could be used for teaching HCI to UX designers or ergonomists. The pre-requisite in HCI for this case study includes knowledge on how to design the software of an interactive system in particular event-based principles and automata. There is no pre-requisite in Software Engineering since it is not required to develop an interactive system.

### 3.3 Objectives

The main objective is to apply a User-Centered Design (UCD) approach. To guide students, several methods, concepts and tools that support the UCD steps are taught in the course related to this case study. The case study is a practical application of the fundamental HCI methods and concepts to follow the UCD principle, that are necessary to any practitioner involved in the design of useful and usable interactive systems.

### 3.4 Pedagogical Steps/Monitoring, Initial Materials and Tools

In order to help students to focus on UCD principles, 1) the functional core is provided, and the focus is only on the input user interface 2) the provided elements to start the UCD process are realistic representations of starting points of industrial projects.

During a 6-week period, groups of 4/5 students design and sketch/develop the game controller of SuperTuxKart karting races[1]. The set of commands and the output device (a screen) are fixed. As starting materials, we also provide realistic answers of three potential users to the question "Do you ever play video games such as kart racing?" (Fig. 1). These answers are fictive ones but allow students to define persona and realistic contexts of use. They are defined to present contexts of use with characteristics (Table 1). Such starting materials are unusual for the students (in computer science).

Based on these initial materials, the pedagogical steps that are discussed each week with the teacher include:

- Analysis of the answers to define persona. A canvas for describing persona is provided (Fig. 2). This canvas is adapted from a framework of the Marketing domain to define buyer-persona. From this analysis, student groups choose to target one or two user profiles.
- Analysis of the answers to define different contexts of use and the requirements they imply.
- Iterative design of different mock-ups or functional prototypes (for instance wire-frame prototypes using Balsamiq https://balsamiq.com/). The various solutions are discussed with a simple notation as QOC (Questions, Options, and Criteria) [8] for analysing the designed solutions in relation to the context requirements. Figure 3 presents examples of designed solutions.

[1] https://ihm2019.afihm.org/#challenge.html.

| | |
|---|---|
| A1 | Yes, but not often. I started because one of my granddaughters, Laura, came to our house during a recent holiday with her video game console. Usually when she comes, we go to the park but this time she was a little sick so we opted to stay inside most of the time. So, she spent a lot of time playing with her console. Of course, when I was a kid, I didn't have that, so I wanted to see how it works and what she is doing with it. I am curious. My granddaughter wanted to try but I didn't understand the game she was playing. They're heroes now, you see ... I don't know them. But Laura had a kart game and she said to me "OK grandpa, you know how to drive, so you have no excuse" and I couldn't say no: my granddaughter challenged me. I played and... I lost. I lost because this thing is not the same as driving. But now when Laura comes, she always takes her console to play with me. She is happy because for once she is teaching me something so she is proud. |
| A2 | Yes, very often. I've always played on consoles or on the phone. About the car races... we mostly do it with my roommates because it is quick and everyone likes it. And in fact, we use it to plan household tasks. The apartment quickly gets dirty if we don't clean the house but nobody wants to do it so we take turns but hey ... sometimes it doesn't work. So we use the kart racing game to challenge ourselves and the one who loses has a pledge. It can be something other than cleaning, but often that's it. We even defined rules. The pledge must be known beforehand, the person who is challenged has the right to refuse the race but if s/he accepts it, s/he is the one who chooses the race and the vehicles... It's more fun than bickering all the time. |
| A3 | Yes, but not often. Me, I like it but Mom, she doesn't like that I play too long so she doesn't let me play often. I am not allowed when there is school... and I am not allowed to play in my room, I have to be in the living room. The other day, my big brother looked after me and since I didn't bother him, he let me play, but we cannot tell Mom. When I have the right, Mom tells me how long on the clock and I have to stop when it's time. I do it because otherwise I have no right to play at all. |

**Fig. 1.** Answers of fictive users, used as the starting point for designing the controller of the karting race game.

**Table 1.** Characteristics of the contexts that are used by the teacher to define the fictive answers.

| | User profile | Motivation/Goal | Playing mode | Enviornment |
|---|---|---|---|---|
| A1 | Grandfather (novice, adult, 65 y.o) Granddaughter (regular player, child, 9 y.o) | Challenge the other, to spend time together | 2 players | Living room, No dedicated space, isolated from other inhabitants |
| A2 | Young roommate (expert player, young adult, 20 y.o) | Plan household tasks | >2 players (several) | Shared living room |
| A3 | Son (novice player, child, 7 y.o) | Pleasure, reward | 1 player | Shared living room (with parental time control) |

- Evaluation based on heuristics that are specific for games [9] are applied to the designed solutions (at least one of the designed solutions).
- The last required step is to perform a simplified usability study. The pedagogical objective is to learn that the evaluation of an interactive system implies to perform a user study. They need 1) to identify a usability question to evaluate (e.g., user satisfaction, efficiency), 2) to define the data to be collected in order to answer the usability question (such as number of errors while performing a task, questionnaires e.g., SUS [2], AttrakDiff [6]), and 3) to define the instructions for the participants. From these specifications, they perform the test with at least three users, and they try to conclude on the usability of their designed solution.

| | PERSONA 1 |
|---|---|
| SOCIOLOGICAL PROFIL | |
| FIRST NAME | |
| AGE | |
| SEX | |
| LANGUAGE | |
| CULTURE | |
| HOBBIES | |
| CURRICULUM | |
| | |
| EXPERIENCE (ACTIVITY) | |
| ROLE | |
| RESPONSABILITIES | |
| LEVEL OF EXPERTISE | |
| FREQUENCY | |
| | |
| | |
| NEEDS | |
| MOTIVATIONS | |
| POINTS TO TECHNOLOGY HELPS | |
| | |
| | |
| TECHNOLOGY KNOWLEDGE | |
| LEVEL OF EXPERTISE | |
| DIFFICULTIES | |
| PREFERENCES | |

FIRST NAME
AGE
FAMILY
SITUATION
PERSONALITY
CURRICULUM
OBJECTIVES & CHALLENGES
FEARS
HABITS

**Fig. 2.** Canvas to help students define persona.

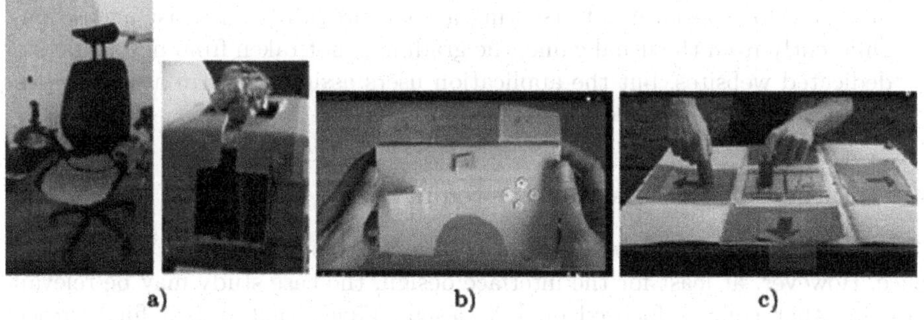


**Fig. 3.** Examples of designed solutions a) for a novice grandfather, b) for an expert roommate student, c) for a 7-year-old child.

### 3.5 Expected Outputs and Evaluation

The expected output is the design of a game controller of SuperTuxKart kart racing game that matches the requirements extracted from at least one of the three initial answers. The most important results of the project are the justifications provided to show that the designed controllers match the initial responses, the users' profiles and the contexts for using the game. The evaluation grid is set to focus on the presentation and argumentation of the designed solution. Intermediate productions are not evaluated. Students provide a video and possibly a text document to present their game controller and explain their design choices.

The 10-point evaluation grid includes:

- 5 points for the presentation of the interactive solution
  - 3 points for the presentation of the solution in its context of use
  - 1 point for the presentation of the interaction (dynamic specification)
  - 1 point for the presentation of the elements of controls, their positions and their shapes
- 5 points for explanation of design choices
  - 4 points to explain the choices made according to the context of use
  - 1 point to explain the limitations of the currently designed solution.

## 4 Case Study 2: Fantasy Soccer

- **Title:** Fantasy Soccer
- **Type:** Project
- **Application domain:** Sport, Leisure, Game
- **Interaction techniques:** WIMP (mobile)
- **Brief description:** The Fantasy Soccer application is a peer-to-peer variant of the usual game with top-league soccer players. The idea is to replicate such a game for lower leagues: the players create their fantasy team, including players from real teams. For each league turn, they will get points according to the grade (0 to 10) obtained by each player they put in the field, with some modifiers for special events (scoring a goal, providing an assist and so on). Differently from the usual game, the grading is not taken from newspapers or dedicated websites, but the application users assign scores in a peer-to-peer manner, attending the league games.

### 4.1 Targeted Students and Pre-requisites

The Fantasy Soccer app project is used in a Bachelor Course in Computer Science. However, at least for the interface design, the case study may be relevant also in other courses focused on UX design. Given that it is a final project assignment for assessing an introductory HCI course, the pre-requisites include both a basic knowledge of the HCI design principles and, for implementing the app, proficiency in Object-Oriented and event-based Graphical User Interface programming.

### 4.2 Objectives

The main objective is to practice the HCI principles discussed in the introductory course and apply a UCD approach. In particular, the students will go into the prototyping phase at different levels of fidelity (low and high). They will also perform a small user study to assess the overall usability of the proposed solution. Since it is a group project, the objective is also to develop the students' team-working skills, including the management of possible conflicting ideas in the design and implementation process.

### 4.3 Pedagogical Steps/Monitoring, Initial Materials and Tools

The students should focus on applying the UCD process and implementing the prototypes. Therefore, the other aspects of the applications should be only drafted. For instance, they can avoid implementing a proper account subsystem or include method stubs returning hard-coded values for avoiding using databases. Since these are techniques we often use in the prototyping phase, but they require some experience for avoiding getting stuck into less relevant details, we provide the students with:

- Templates for the delivery of all the assessed material.
- Sample projects developed by the teachers, including all the required deliverables, with explanations regarding the implementation.
- Mentoring throughout the entire course and during the implementation of the high-fidelity prototype.

The steps for completing the project are the following:

- During the first half of the course, the students know each other during class and lab lessons. We ask them to define groups of 2 to 4 students. After the process finishes, we create random groups of the same size for those people that did not express any preference.
- During the lab lessons in the second part of the course, they must complete design exercises in the lab. This includes familiarising with design and prototyping techniques (scenarios, personas, sketching etc.). Students can work together and discuss ideas and problems with teachers. This leads to an iterative design of the application interface.
- The last lab lesson includes a discussion of the main principles for designing the evaluation. The students are provided with samples evaluation design and collected data from different types of applications. They learn how to define an evaluation goal, prioritise and select the correct metrics and/or questionnaires for collecting meaningful data (e.g., SUS [2]). Their task is to define the goal, the material, the questionnaire, and the metrics for evaluating the Fantasy Soccer application.
- At the end of the course, they must send an intermediate deliverable that the teachers will assess. It includes the specification of the requirements, the personas and scenarios, the discussion of a low fidelity prototype for the application. They receive feedback on such deliverable, which they must consider for the final implementation of the application.

- After that, they start with the implementation of a high-fidelity prototype. They must focus on the interface-related development aspects. The application back-end should include only stubs. Students are free to request a meeting with the teachers whenever they would like to.
- When the implementation is completed, the students must conduct a small usability study, including one or two metrics and about 10 people. They must identify which changes or improvements would be possible in the next iteration.
- Finally, at the end of the development, they must present the implementation results to the teachers. The discussion includes an introductory PowerPoint presentation, a demo of the high-fidelity prototype, the presentation of the evaluation results, and a question-and-answer session.

### 4.4 Expected Outputs and Evaluation

The expected output is the design and implementation of a mobile application supporting the team management and the players in the peer-to-peer grading for each game. The expected outcomes are basically two: an intermediate deliverable including the low-fidelity prototype and a final deliverable including the high-fidelity prototype. The evaluation focuses on the application of basic HCI design principles and on the ability of the group to justify the design choices.

The evaluation grid for the project assigns 19 points out of the 30 available for the entire course, distributed as follows:

- 8 points for the low-fidelity prototype deliverable
  - 1 point for the identification of the requirements
  - 3 points for the identification of the scenarios and personas
  - 4 points for the development of the low fidelity prototype
- 11 points for the high-fidelity prototype
  - 5 points of the explanation of the design choices
  - 4 points for the high-fidelity prototype interface
  - 2 points for the usability evaluation

## 5 Case Study 3: Home Finder

### 5.1 Identity Card

- **Title:** Home finder
- **Type:** Exercise
- **Application domain:** databases
- **Interaction technique:** WIMP
- **Brief description:** The Home Finder is an interactive application allowing the editing and the visualisation of a real estate database. It is composed of two main windows. The first one enables the user to edit the database. The second one enables the user to filter real estate according to different criteria (surface area, distance from the workplace, etc.) and to view the details of a selected real estate (Fig. 6).

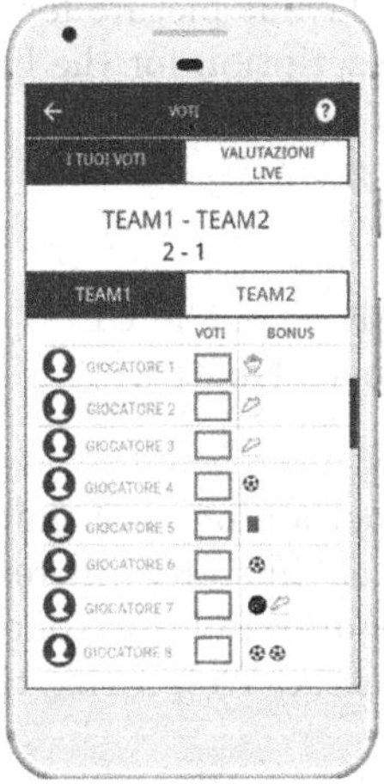


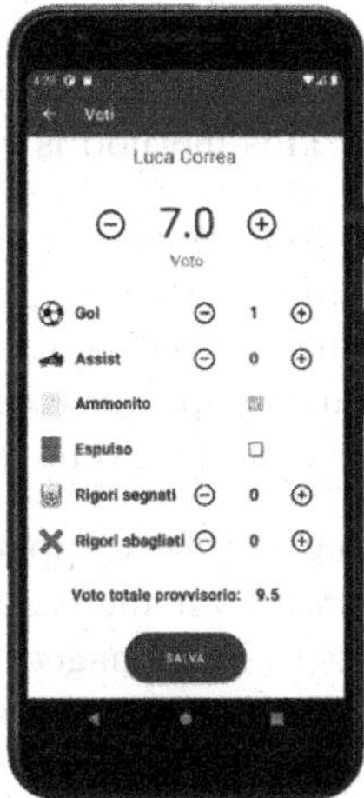


**Fig. 4.** A sample low-fidelity prototype for the live scoring interface (by Eligio Cabras) and the high fidelity prototype for the same interface (by the group Urlo del sIUM: Alessandro Pruner, Alessio Piriottu, Eligio Cabras and Marco Mulas).

### 5.2 Targeted Students and Prerequisites

The main target type of student is a person enrolled in a Master in Computer Science which has been tuned to address interactive critical system aspects [4], and following the learning unit named "Interactive Systems Software Engineering". The main prerequisite is to have basic knowledge about databases, as well as about the Java Swing graphical toolkit for the programming of user interfaces.

### 5.3 Objectives

The main objective is to make the students understand that most of the code is dedicated to UI and that to program functions for users to add/modify/remove data is complicated. In addition, this exercise also aims to highlight that:

- the design of the UI can be relatively independent from the functional core users' tasks have to be identified,
- multiple interfaces are possible for a given task,
- some design solutions are more usable than others.

### 5.4 Pedagogical Steps/Monitoring, Initial Materials and Tools

This exercise is the last exercise in the pedagogical progression of the learning unit "Interactive Systems Software Engineering" and tackles the programming of a user interface from a behavioral specification of a UI. The students have previously learned to read and to build a behavioral specification of interactive systems behavior. They also have previously learned a method to program a user interface from a specification composed of a layout picture for the presentation part of the user interface and of a textual description for the behavioral part of the user interface. This method is composed of 5 steps:

1. Identify all possible events
2. Identify all possible actions
3. Build the automaton to describe the behavior of the UI
4. From the automaton, produce the state/event matrix
5. Program source code for event handlers

The students have already applied this method on very simple exercises and then on exercises with an increasing level of difficulty (increasing number of states and of events to be managed). For this exercise, the students have already produced the automaton and state/event matrix. We provide the students with the following statement:

"*You will conceive an interactive application allowing the editing and the visualization of the real estate database. The entries from the database can be manipulated via the editing interface of* (Fig. 5) *which behaves as specified in the automaton produced and validated during supervised work session 3 (at a previous stage of the learning unit). This interface allows adding, modifying or deleting entries in the database. This information can be visualized via the visualization interface in* Fig. 6 *which behaves as specified in the automaton produced and validated during supervised work session 3 (at a previous stage of the learning unit). This interface allows you to filter real estate according to different criteria (surface area, distance from the workplace, etc.) and to view the details of a selected real estate (Visual Information Seeking Mantra by Shneiderman* [10]*: Overview first, zoom and filter, then details-on-demand).*"

The students have to focus on implementing the user interfaces to be compliant with the specifications and on organizing the software using the Seeheim software architecture.

They have to use the Java Swing graphical toolkit and the NetBeans Integrated Development Environment.

## 5.5 Expected Output and Evaluation

The expected output is a software archive containing the code source of the program of the Home Finder user interface, as well as an executable version of the Home Finder. The evaluation focuses on the consistency between the specification automaton and the program, as well as on the consistency between the software architecture and the Seeheim architecture. The evaluation grid for the exercise is as follows:

- Programming method
  - Compliance with the automaton and state/event matrix: 5 points
  - Software project preparation in the NetBeans IDE: 1 point
  - Compliance of the UI layout with the specification: 1 point

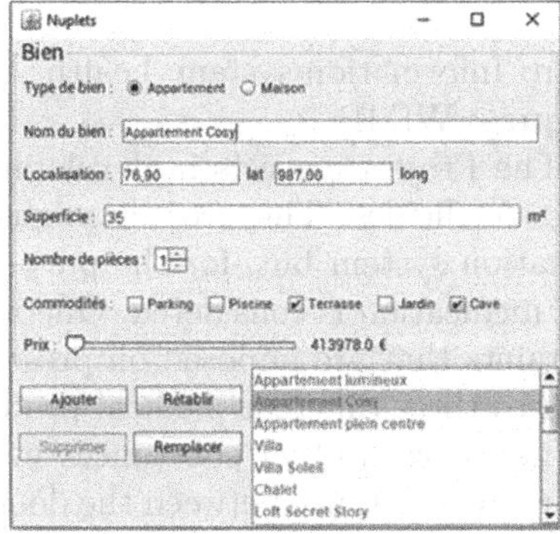


**Fig. 5.** Database editing user interface of the Home Finder

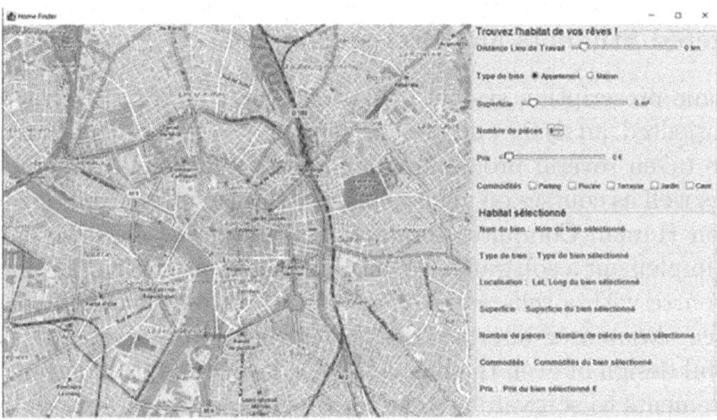


**Fig. 6.** Visualisation user interface of the Home Finder

  - One to one mapping between a UI component and an event handler: 1 point
  - One to one mapping between a column of the state/event matrix and the event handlers in the code: 1 point
- Coding rules
  - Java coding rules followed: 2 points
  - Legibility (explicit naming of variables, methods and functions...) and correct usage of the IDE refactoring commands: 2 points
  - Software architecture compliant with the Seeheim architecture: 2 points
- Functioning
  - The UI runs as specified: 5 points

## 6 Case Study 4: Electronic Prescription System

### 6.1 Identity Card

- **Title:** Electronic prescription system

- **Type:** Project
- **Application domain:** Information system, health
- **Interaction techniques:** WIMP
- **Brief description:** The Project consists in developing a system to support doctors in prescribing medicines. The project might be seen as part of a larger medical information system but, for the purpose of the project, only the act of prescribing medication is considered. One interesting aspect of the project are the constraints that are imposed on prescriptions: each prescription can only have up to three different medical products, and psychotropic medicines cannot be mixed with other substances in the same prescription. This can potentially create a distance between the doctor's goal of prescribing a treatment, and how the medical products needed for that treatment must be organized into prescriptions.

### 6.2 Targeted Students and Prerequisites

The electronic prescription system project was first used in a third-year course on object-oriented analysis and design (OOAD). The students attending the course have taken several programming courses (functional, imperative, object oriented), as well as courses on algorithms, program synthesis, among others, but no course on Human-Computer Interaction. During the course, students must design and implement a software system. Experience shows that a) most students reach the course with a self-centered view of software development, and b) lack of knowledge about user interface design and development creates barriers for the successful design of even the business logic layer (and it undermines the step from requirements to software architecture). The electronic prescription system project has shown to be useful in raising students' awareness of user-centered concerns in the engineering of interactive computing systems.

The pre-requisite for the project is proficiency in object-oriented programming (although the project can also be framed in the context of web programming). The project runs in parallel with the course, in which students learn OOAD (resorting to UML [3]). Basic notions of HCI and user interface prototyping (for example, the MVC pattern) are also introduced (4 h).

### 6.3 Objectives

As stated above, from an HCI Engineering perspective, one objective of the project is to raise students' awareness of user-centered concerns. From that perspective, the focus is on taking into consideration user requirements and designing a user interface that addresses those requirements. Students will capture functional requirements in a use case model and later prototype a user interface to answer those requirements.

Use cases are analyzed in terms of how well they support the users in achieving their goals. Ideally, students will realize that the burden of organizing a list of medical products into valid prescriptions can be moved from the doctor to the system. Whether doctors will feel comfortable with that loss of control, however, needs to be validated.

At a later stage in the project, the students must design and implement a system that answers the identified requirements. This is done by first defining the API needed at the business logic layer (starting from the use case descriptions and user interface prototype), and then designing an appropriate architecture and implementing it. One goal, here, is to realize the impact that different user interface designs will have on the architecture of the system. For example, depending on the strategy used to validate/generate prescriptions, different APIs and supporting architectures will make sense at the business logic layer.

### 6.4 Pedagogical Steps/Monitoring, Initial Materials and Tools

The students self-organize in groups of 3 to 5 to carry out the project. The project is executed during the semester as the topics are worked on in class. Given its length the project is divided into three main steps: requirements, design, and implementation. Each stage is awarded a weight in the final grade (typically 30/30/40).

At the start of the project, students are provided with a copy of the Portuguese electronic medical prescription decree law, access to a database containing information about human medicines[2], and a set of scenarios describing how doctors prescribe medicines. Working from those scenarios, functional requirements are captured in a use case model. A user interface prototype is then produced to address usability concerns. The Pencil tool[3] is introduced, but students are free to choose the prototyping tool of their choice.

During the design phase, students define the control logic for the user interface, the architecture of the system and behavioral models for the business logic. Modelling is done using UML diagrams. Students are encouraged to start by using pen and paper and later, once stable models are reached, a modelling tool (currently Visual Paradigm). In the final phase the system is implemented.

Mentoring is provided throughout the semester on students' request. One aspect that requires attention is managing the complexity of the proposed solution. The goal is to present the project as something realistic, that they could be developing professionally. Typically, students will propose systems that they are not able to fully implement in the timespan of the project. Managing and prioritizing requirements is also a skill the project aims to promote. This is challenging for students and guidance must be provided. One approach that has been attempted is to reduce the set of requirements to consider from phase to phase. However, this creates problems when the proposed solutions diverge on how requirements are handled. Additionally, it can cause frustration as students feel that they are not being allowed to pursue their initial idea for the system. An alternative approach is to define a minimum set of scenarios that the system should support.

[2] Infomed - Infarmed's medicinal products database. http://extranet.infarmed.pt/INFOMED-fo/index.xhtml (accessed on 20/10/2021).

[3] https://pencil.evolus.vn/ (accessed on 20/10/2021).

After each stage, students must hand in a report describing what they have achieved. General feedback on the first two reports is given in class, commenting on the main positives and negatives of the submitted materials, as a whole. The final delivery must be defended by each group at the last week of the semester, and individual feedback is then provided. The defense includes a discussion of the final report and a demonstration of the system.

### 6.5 Expected Outputs and Evaluation

The expected outputs are the models mentioned above and the corresponding system implementation. More specifically, students should hand in: a use case model and a user interface prototype, from the first phase of the project; UML architectural and behavioural models for the system to be implemented; and the actual implementation and related deployment models. The project contributes 9 points out of 20 to the final grade of the course. The other 11 points are distributed by a final exam (9 points) and a continuous evaluation component (2 points). Projects are graded based on an evaluation of the quality of requirements analysis, system design and system implementation:

- 2.7 points for the requirements analysis
- 2.7 points for the system's design
- 2.6 points for the implementation
- 1.0 point for report

Final project marks, however, are attributed on a per student basis. Each student's contribution to the project is evaluated using a peer assessment approach. Three times during the length of the project, students distribute a fixed number of points between the members of their group (themselves included) in a number of criteria that are discussed and agreed upon at the start of the project. For each criteria, the points to be distributed are a multiple of the group size so, in an ideal situation, all members of the group receive the same number of points. Each student's final mark in the project is the result of combining the project and peer assessment marks. Peer assessment is supported by the TeamMates tool[4].

## 7 Discussion

The four case studies illustrate the diversity of types of projects and goals that reflect the multidisciplinary (i.e., Human-Computer Interaction, Software Engineering) aspects to be taught in a Human-Computer Interaction Engineering course.

Except for Case Study 3 on the Home Finder, which is used as a common framework for a set of exercises, the other case studies define projects made by groups of students during several months as part of a project-based learning strategy. Group work promotes discussion and the development of analysis capabilities. One potential issue is guaranteeing that all students contribute to the

[4] https://teammatesv4.appspot.com/ (accessed 10/11/2021).

project in a balanced manner. Case study 4 addresses this through peer assessment within the groups. This both promotes responsibility and self-assessment during the running of the project and helps discriminate the students and award fairer grades.

The four case studies are integral parts of courses taught in Computer Science curricula in different Universities in Europe. The targeted students are computer scientists. The first case study, which does not require the software development of the designed solution, could be taught to non-computer scientists, for instance user experience (UX) designers.

To compare the four case studies, we position them according to the steps of the design and development of a software system: analysis, UI design, software specification, development, verification and validation.

- Case study 1 on the Kart Racing Game focuses on analysis and UI design.
- Case study 3 on the Home Finder is dedicated to software development and compliance with software specification (UI behaviour).
- Case study 2 on Fantasy Soccer and Case study 4 on Electronic Prescription System cover all the steps. Nevertheless, for Case Study 4, the project starts by considering the entire system to be designed and then focuses on a subpart for its development due to time constraints.

These differences in the coverage of the design and development steps of a software system are also reflected in the depth of the concepts and methods applied for each step. While Case studies 1 and 3 go deeper for a subset of steps with the corresponding assessment methods, Case studies 2 and 4 cover all the steps without going into detail on each step. Additionally, while Case study 2 aims for students to practice the HCI principles and UCD approach approach taught in an HCI course, Case study 4 is framed in the context of a OOAD course, and its goal is to raise students awareness to UCD, even if the approach is not fully explored in the course.

When we compare the case studies against main identified HCI-E teaching challenges and needs:

- **Fast evolution of technologies and methods:** all of the case studies focus on teaching main HCI principles and targets learners who are new to the domain, then the issue of the evolution of methods does not impact them much. Case study 1 and 2 rely on recent technologies (innovative interaction techniques with gaming consoles, smartphones) whereas case studies 3 and 4 target legacy systems (desktop computers, medical devices). From an engineering point of view, both are interesting and important as future professionals have also to be able to develop interactive applications for legacy interactive systems.
- **Students' involvement with users:** all of the case studies clearly highlight the importance of the users to the students, especially by providing them with a set of the potential issues in not taking into account user needs and in not applying user centered design principles. They then all may foster the students' involvement with users.

- **Create something that works:** case studies 2, 3, and 4 include software programming activities and enable students to concretely run their produced user interface, whereas case study 1 stops once medium fidelity prototypes are produced.
- **Use tech they feel related to:** case study 1 and 2 may foster more motivation amongst students as they concern technologies they were born with and certainly use daily for most of them.
- **Real life systems:** all of the case studies deal with real life systems.

As future work, we plan to create a repository of case studies as an educational resource for teachers. In particular the repository can be enriched by case studies provided by the members of the IFIP WG2.7/13.4 (http://ui-engineering.org/) on "User Interface Engineering". Such a repository could support teachers to leverage resources and to address the main challenges in teaching HCI-E.

## References


1. Aberg, J.: Challenges with teaching HCI early to computer students. In: Proceedings of ITiCSE 2010, pp. 3–7. ACM, New York, NY, USA (2010)
2. Brooke, J.: SUS: a "quick and dirty" usability scale. In: Jordan, P., Thomas, B., Weerdmeester, B., McClelland, I. (eds.) Usability Evaluation in Industry, pp. 189–194. Taylor & Francis, London (1996)
3. Fowler, M.: UML Distilled: A Brief Guide to the Standard Object Modeling Language, 3rd edn. Addison-Wesley Professional, Boston (2004)
4. Galindo, M., Martinie, C., Palanque, P., Winckler, M., Forbrig, P.: Tuning an HCI curriculum for master students to address interactive critical systems aspects. In: Kurosu, M. (ed.) HCI 2013. LNCS, vol. 8004, pp. 51–60. Springer, Heidelberg (2013). https://doi.org/10.1007/978-3-642-39232-0_6
5. Hewett, T.T., et al.: ACM SIGCHI curricula for human-computer interaction. ACM, Technical report (1992)
6. Lallemand, C., Koenig, V., Gronier, G., Martin, R.: Création et validation d'une version française du questionnaire attrakdiff pour l'évaluation de l'expérience utilisateur des systèmes interactifs. Eur. Rev. Appl. Psychol. **65**(5), 239–252 (2015)
7. Lazar, J., Preece, J., Gasen, J., Winograd, T.: New issues in teaching HCI: pinning a tail on a moving donkey. In: CHI 2002 Extended Abstracts, pp. 696–697. ACM, New York, NY, USA (2002)
8. MacLean, A., Young, R.M., Bellotti, V.M., Moran, T.P.: Questions, options, and criteria: elements of design space analysis. Hum. Comput. Interact. **6**(3–4), 201–250 (1991)
9. Schaffer, N.: Heuristics for usability in games (white paper), April 2007. https://gamesqa.files.wordpress.com/2008/03/heuristics_noahschafferwhitepaper.pdf. Accessed 11 Dec 2021
10. Shneiderman, B.: The eyes have it: a task by data type taxonomy for information visualizations. In: The Craft of Information Visualization, pp. 364–371. Elsevier (2003)
11. The Joint Task Force on Computing Curricula: Software Engineering 2014: Curriculum guidelines for undergraduate degree programs in software engineering. Technical report, ACM and IEEE-Computer Society, New York, NY, USA (2015)

# The Curriculum for Education in Engineering Interactive Systems at the Master in HCI of the University Toulouse III - Paul Sabatier

Philippe Palanque(✉) and Célia Martinie

ICS-IRIT, Université Toulouse III - Paul Sabatier, Toulouse, France
{palanque,martinie}@irit.fr

**Abstract.** The master in HCI of the University Toulouse III Paul Sabatier is a degree in Computer Science that aims to educate specialists in HCI that are able to develop interactive systems that match user needs. A particularity of the this master in HCI compared to other ones in France or in the world is that it implements a large set of courses dedicated to the engineering of interactive systems. This set of courses belongs to a curriculum in engineering interactive systems and distributes amongst the 2 years of the degree following a progression in level of knowledge and skills. This paper presents this curriculum in engineering interactive systems, its motivations, and the pedagogical approach implemented for the curriculum.

**Keywords:** Interactive systems engineering · Education

## 1 Introduction

The master in HCI of the University Toulouse III Paul Sabatier is a degree in Computer Science that aims to educate specialists in HCI that are able to develop interactive systems that match user needs. In particular, the educational path aims to make them be able: implementing user centered design approaches to design interactive systems, leading an engineering process for the development of interactive systems. The master in HCI target to graduate students who know how to exploit knowledge in human factors and psychology to design interactive systems that match user needs, characteristics and tasks. It also target to graduate students who know how to apply design and development techniques for legacy interactive systems as well as for recent types of interactive systems (multimodal interaction techniques, mobile, AR/VR…), and who know how to evaluate performance of interactive systems in both quantitative and qualitative ways. Thanks to the multidisciplinary aspect of the knowledge acquired during the two years of the master's program, graduates are able to join design and development teams with a wide variety of profiles, such as graphic designers, ergonomists, interaction designers, web developers, or developers of critical interactive systems. A particularity of the this master in HCI compared to other ones in France or in the world is that it implements a large set of courses dedicated to the engineering of interactive systems. This set of courses belongs to a curriculum in engineering interactive systems and distributes among the 2 years of the degree following a progression in level of knowledge and skills. This


Published by Springer Nature Switzerland AG 2022
C. Ardito et al. (Eds.): INTERACT 2021, LNCS 13198, pp. 211–220, 2022.
https://doi.org/10.1007/978-3-030-98388-8_19

paper presents this curriculum in engineering interactive systems, its motivations, and the pedagogical approach implemented for the curriculum. The structure of the paper is as follow. Section 2 presents an overview of the master. Section 3 explains the main motivations for integrating a curriculum in engineering interactive systems throughout the 2 years of the master in HCI. Section 4 presents the main themes covered by the curriculum. Section 5 provides an example of course topic and of an associated practical work. Section 6 concludes the paper.

## 2 Overview of the Master in HCI

The Master in HCI of the University Toulouse III Paul Sabatier is a degree in Computer Science and contains courses in HCI that aim to provide in-depth knowledge in the field of software engineering, complementary to what has been acquired by students during a computer science bachelor's degree (which is a prerequisite for access to the training). Beyond this knowledge, the objective of the HCI Master's degree is to train high-level professionals specializing in the design and development of interactive applications, mastering techniques specific to computer science and those from the field of human factors.

In the first year of the master's degree, students will acquire general skills (linked to the computer science basics and more particularly to the knowledge acquired with the software engineering courses):

- Master the methods and tools of a software engineer job;
- Master the processes of software development from the analysis of user needs to the deployment of the system in its socio-technical context;
- Master object-based design and programming as well as model-based design of computer systems;
- Master the methods, techniques and tools for the validation and verification of computer systems.
- Know how to manage a computer project
- Design and plan one's own work and that of one's teams
- Organize, coordinate and manage work within a team

In the second year of this master, a high level of theoretical and technological education is offered to students, allowing them to access the many opportunities in the industry and technological training is offered to the students, allowing them to access the numerous openings in the industry but also to continue their studies in doctorate. The educational offer is centered on the following thematic areas:

- Human factors and psychology,
- Interactive systems engineering as a set of concepts, methods and development tools,
- Technology and techniques for interactive system development,
- Scientific research in HCI,
- Design and prototyping of interactive systems,
- Interaction techniques and application domains.

In addition to courses and practical work, students have demonstrate they are able to apply their knowledge and skills by taking an internship, of at least 3 months during the 1st year of the master and of at least 4 months during the second year of the master.

## 3 Motivations for the Curriculum in Engineering Interactive Systems

The master in HCI responds to a strong demand on the job market at the engineering level, in the field of interactive software development. Nowadays, all application domains require interactive software developers and graduated students get hired in small regional to large international companies whatever the application domain. Moreover, around 50% of the internships performed during the 2nd year of Master as well as employment after graduation belong to the space and aviation application domains (Thales, Airbus, CNES, Amadeus, Rockwell Collins…). This is mostly due to the local industrial context of the Toulouse region as explained in [16]. This is however stable over a long period of time as this information is similar to the former study of 2013 reported in [10].

Such employers require graduated students to have specific skills related to the design and development of interactive critical systems. Such systems require different methods than mass-market products. While HCI and discount software engineering approaches promote iterative processes producing rapidly modifiable artifacts, interactive critical systems call for systematic verifiable methods, processes and tools to provide means of assessing the resilience of the systems [3, 17]. New phases within the development process appear with prominent places such as traceability (as required in standards such as DO178B [9] and ESARR 6 [8]), training [20], barrier identifications and incident/accident analysis [1] and support for certification [9]. Moreover, contributions have proposed complex processes trying to bridge this, at first glance, unbridgeable gaps [14].

## 4 Main Themes Covered by the Curriculum and Their Implementation

The main themes covered by the curriculum in engineering interactive systems distributes on the 2 years of the master in HCI. A prerequisite to enter the master is to have a graduation of Bachelor's degree in Computer Science. Figure 1 presents the main themes covered by the curriculum in engineering interactive systems. Each year target to highlight a specific property of interactive systems. The courses and practical work aim to teach methods that will enable future professionals to deal with such properties. When starting the master, students are supposed to know usability and to know how to apply UCD methods and techniques to reach usability of interactive systems. Moreover, they are already familiar with programming with a graphical toolkit as they are supposed to have learned it during the bachelor's degree courses. During the bachelor's degree they learn to use Java Swing, a simple graphical toolkit, to program a user interface, while having a WYSIWYG support for the building of the user interface layout in the Netbeans IDE. Once they master the basics of graphical toolkits and event programming, they learn to use more complicated and demanded recent technologies (e.g. Javascript and vue.js) during the Masters' degree.

During the first year of the master (M1), the students start to learn event programming and Finite State Machine models based programming of WIMP interactive systems in order to be able to develop reliable and modifiable interactive software. The students also learn the design pattern MVC as well as the main development processes that applies in the industry.

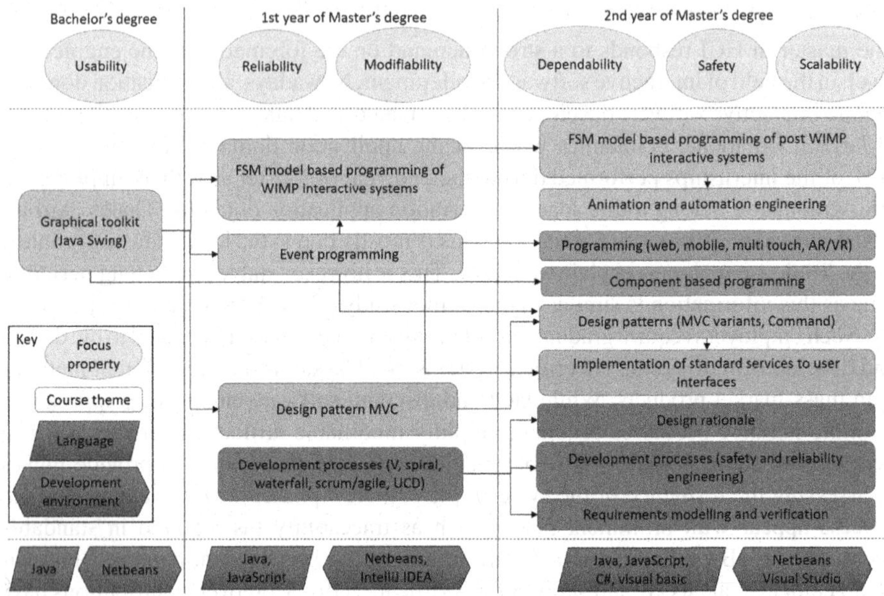


**Fig. 1.** Overview of the implementation of the curriculum

The second year of the master (M2) focuses on the dependability, safety and scalability properties. Each main theme is thus deepen to provide future professionals with methods and techniques that target critical systems important properties and that cover a wider range of type of interactive systems.

## 5 A Typical Example

To demonstrate the specificities of this curriculum on interactive systems engineering, we present an exercise done by the students both at M1 and M2 levels. While M1 level focusses on the modeling and the modeling transformation to event-driven code, the M2 course focusses on properties verification over FSM models and modifiability of code. This process follows the modelling and transformation model presented in [18] but uses FSMs instead of Petri nets.

Our case study is an application simulating a traffic light. This application, displayed in Fig. 2, is made up of three light bulbs (the top one is red (see Fig. 2b), the middle one is orange (see Fig. 2c) and the bottom one is green (see Fig. 2d)). The traffic light exhibits three different modes of operation: i) when it is stopped, ii) when it is working and iii) when it is faulty. In the stopped mode, all the light bulb are switched off (see Fig. 2a). In the faulty mode, the orange light bulb is blinking (it is switched off during 400 ms and switched on during 600 ms). Finally, the working mode is different following the countries in which it is deployed. We will further details this working mode in the following section for four difference traffic lights: French, British and the Austrian traffic light (for which two different alternatives will be provided).

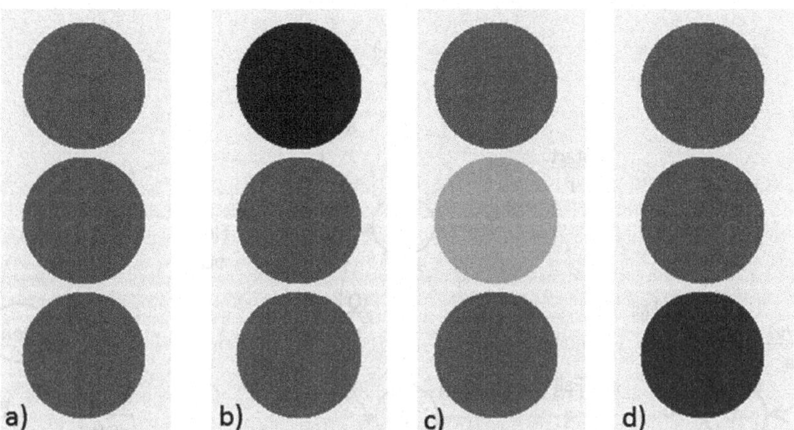


**Fig. 2.** Screenshots of the traffic light application: a) when it is stopped, b) when the red light bulb is switched on, c) when the orange light bulb is switched on and d) when the green light bulb is switched on. (Color figure online)

The French traffic light is the simpler one and the other ones are more complex and precise behavior of the French one. When entering the working mode, the traffic light starts with only the red light on, after 1000 ms the red lightbulb is switched off and the green lightbulb is switched on. This bulb remains on for 2000 ms before being switched off while the orange light is switched on for 500 ms. When this delay is elapsed, the traffic light comes back to the initial state with only the red light on (Fig. 3).

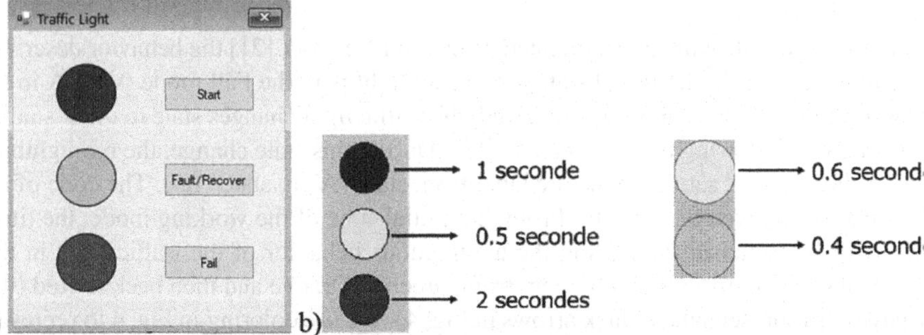


**Fig. 3.** a) The user interface of the traffic light - command and control buttons on the right-hand side. b) Temporal aspects of displays

At any time, a fault event may occur that will set the traffic light to the faulty mode. When entering this mode whatever light which is on is switched off and the orange light is switched on for 600 ms (as explained in the informal presentation of the case study above). At any time, a recover event may be triggered setting the traffic light to the initial state of the working mode (i.e. only the red light switched on). A fail event may also occur. When this occurs, whatever state the traffic light is in, it is set to the Fail mode (represented by the state A in Fig. 4).

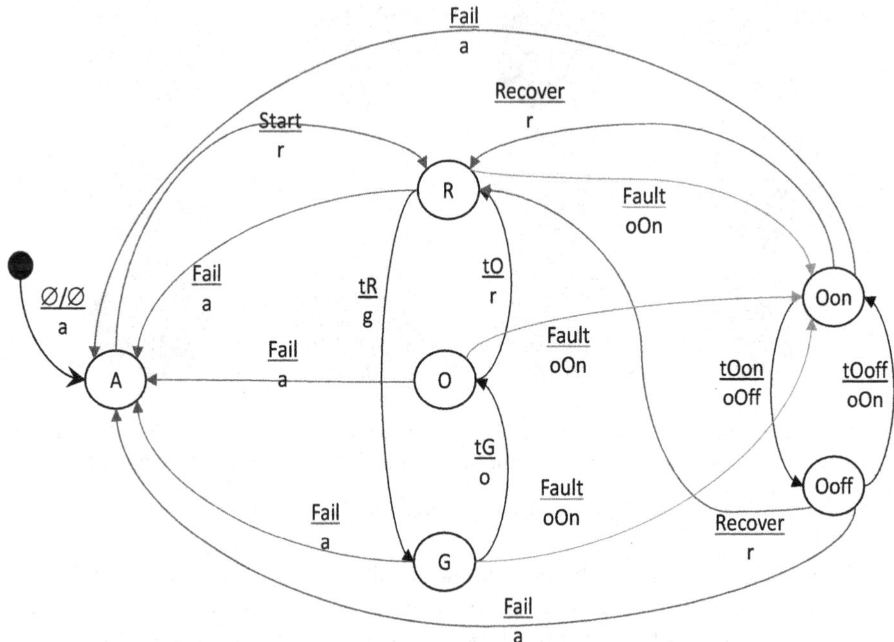


**Fig. 4.** Automaton of the French traffic light with three different modes: stopped (state A), nominal functioning (states R, G and O) and failure mode (states Oon and Ooff)

*Behavioral Model*

Figure 4 represents with an Augmented Transition Network [21] the behavior described informally above. In the initial state, the traffic light is in the Fail mode (state A in the diagram). When an event Start is received, the traffic light changes state to the R state in the diagram (following the arc labeled $\frac{\underline{Start}}{r}$). During this state change, the red lightbulb is switched on ("r" action on the arc label from state "A" to state "R"). The code of the "r" function is given on Fig. 7b). From that initial state of the working mode, the timer "tR" will be switched on starting the autonomous behavior of the traffic light in this mode, alternating from Red to Green, from Green to Orange and then back to Red (this behavior is represented by black arrows in Fig. 4). We use coloring in Fig. 4 to represent the three main mode of the traffic light:

- In black the nominal functional behavior (alternating from Red to Green to Orange to Red to Green …)
- In orange the transitions related to faults and failures ending up in the degraded functioning (alternating from Orange to Black to Orange to Black …)
- In red the transitions stopping the traffic light (the three lights turned to black) (Figs. 5 and 6)

| **Action Name on the automaton** | **Corresponding Actions on the lights** | **Visual Basic code** |
|---|---|---|
| a | Red light OFF<br>Orange light OFF<br>Green light OFF | OvalRed.fillstyle=1<br>OvalOrange.fillstyle=1<br>OvalGreen.fillstyle=1 |
| r | Red light ON<br>Orange light OFF<br>Green light OFF | OvalRed.fillstyle=0<br>OvalOrange.fillstyle=1<br>OvalGreen.fillstyle=1 |
| O | Red light OFF<br>Orange light ON<br>Green light OFF | OvalRed.fillstyle=1<br>OvalOrange.fillstyle=0<br>OvalGreen.fillstyle=1 |
| g | Red light OFF<br>Orange light OFF<br>Green light ON | OvalRed.fillstyle=1<br>OvalOrange.fillstyle=1<br>OvalGreen.fillstyle=0 |
| oOn | Red light OFF<br>Orange light ON<br>Green light OFF | OvalRed.fillstyle=1<br>OvalOrange.fillstyle=0<br>OvalGreen.fillstyle=1 |
| oOff | Red light OFF<br>Orange light OFF<br>Green light OFF | OvalRed.fillstyle=1<br>OvalOrange.fillstyle=1<br>OvalGreen.fillstyle=1 |

**Fig. 5.** Code for the graphical rendering (Color figure online)

| | **Start** | **Fault/Recover** | **Faill** | **tR** | **tG** | **tO** | **tOon** | **tOoff** |
|---|---|---|---|---|---|---|---|---|
| **A** | S=R r | Impossible | Impossible | Impossible | Impossible | Impossible | Impossible | Impossible |
| **R** | Impossible | S=Oon o | S=A a | S=G g | Impossible | Impossible | Impossible | Impossible |
| **O** | Impossible | S=Oon o | S=A a | Impossible | Impossible | S=R r | Impossible | Impossible |
| **G** | Impossible | S=Oon o | S=A a | Impossible | S=O o | Impossible | Impossible | Impossible |
| **Oon** | Impossible | S=R r | S=A a | Impossible | Impossible | Impossible | Impossible | S=Ooff oOff |
| **Ooff** | Impossible | S=R r | S=A a | Impossible | Impossible | Impossible | S=Oon oOn | Impossible |

**Fig. 6.** State/Event matrix

We need an enum variable called S with possible values for the set of states of the automaton: A, R, O, G, Oon, Ooff.

a)
```
Private Sub BStart_Click(sender As Object, e As EventArgs) Handles BStart.Click
    Select Case s
        Case "A"
            s = "R"
            r()
            BStart.Enabled = False
            BFault.Enabled = True
            BFail.Enabled = True
            tR.Enabled = True
            tG.Enabled = False
            t_O.Enabled = False
            tOon.Enabled = False
            tOoff.Enabled = False
        Case "R"
            'impossible
        Case "O"
            'impossible
        Case "G"
            'impossible
        Case "Oon"
            'impossible
        Case "Ooff"
            'impossible
    End Select
End Sub
```

b)
```
Private Sub r()
    OvalRed.FillStyle = 0
    OvalOrange.FillStyle = 1
    OvalGreen.FillStyle = 1
End Sub
```

**Fig. 7.** Event-driven code from the State/Event matrix. a) the even handler code is structured according to the state/event matrix. b) the code of the graphical rendering (colors of the traffic lights). The backcolor of the oval shape components are set to the color of the traffic light (OvalRed to Red, OvalOrange to Orange and OvalGreen to Green) (Color figure online)

Property 1

Never BStart and BFail available at the same time

si |= [AG (BStart.enabled ∧ not BFail.enabled) ∨ (not BStart.enabled ∧ not BFail .enabled)]

Property 2

Always one light is switched off

si |= [AG (OvalR.Fillstyle=1 ∧ OvalO.Fillstyle=1 ∧ OvalG.Fillstyle=1)]

**Fig. 8.** Two properties expected for the traffic light

The properties given in Fig. 8 are demonstrated on the Augmented Transition Network presented in Fig. 4. This is done by proving temporal logic properties over an automata as presented in [19].

Until today, the curriculum focuses on the application of the Augmented Transition Network notation rather than more expressive notations such as Statecharts [12] and Petri nets [2], because the students do not have prior knowledge about formal methods. The learning of more expressive notations would require to have more time than the amount that is currently allocated to the curriculum or to cut other parts of the curriculum. In this HCI engineering module we favor the understanding of the process, the importance of modelling, the possibility to go from models to application code and that properties verification is easier than testing (even though testing interactive systems can also be supported by such a modeling process as demonstrated in [4]). In addition, the authors in [6] have demonstrated the need for a more powerful notation that automata to support testing of interactive applications offering post-WIMP interactions. Similarly, if the interactive application requires dynamic instantiation of widgets (like in a drawing application for instance), the notation must be more powerful [5]. This is even more salient if we go for more recent interactions such as multi-touch ones [] where dynamicity is also at the input device level (e.g. each finger added or removed from the touchscreen corresponds to an addition or a removal of an input device).

It is important to note too that such approaches can be supported by tools. A comparison of three formal tools is proposed in [7]. However, in this teaching module we decided to teach the manual transformation from models to code as this skill involves a deeper understanding by the students of the mechanics that the simple use of a tool.

## 6 Conclusion

There a strong demand on the job market at the engineering level, in the field of interactive software development. Nowadays, all application domains require interactive software developers and the variety of types of technologies requires that graduated students have a solid conceptual background as well as practical skills for implementing dependable, safe and scalable interactive systems. The ACM Curriculum Guidelines for Undergraduate Degree Programs in Computer Engineering highlights the important of usability, reliability, dependability, and safety properties [1] and embed teaching unit that aim to consider these properties. The master in HCI curriculum in engineering interactive systems builds on top of the knowledge and skills that students acquire during an ACM Computing Engineering Curriculum compliant bachelors' degree. Although the educational team of the master in HCI curriculum in engineering interactive systems takes care that the curriculum complies with the ACM curriculum, the major drivers remain the adequacy of the courses with the state of the art in engineering interactive systems and the adequacy of the graduated students' skills and knowledge with the industrial needs. These major drivers also apply to select the particular aspects of the courses. For example, the programming course unit (in the second year of the master's degree) aims to provide students with knowledge and skills about recent programming languages that correspond to a demand on the job market. These major drivers then imply that the curriculum is regularly updated.

## References


1. ACM. Computer Engineering Curricula 2016, CE 2016, Curriculum Guidelines for Undergraduate Degree Programs in Computer Engineering, December 15th. ACM (2016)
2. Bastide, R., Palanque, P.: A Petri net based environment for the design of event-driven interfaces. In: De Michelis, G., Diaz, M. (eds.) ICATPN 1995. LNCS, vol. 935, pp. 66–83. Springer, Heidelberg (1995). https://doi.org/10.1007/3-540-60029-9_34
3. Bouzekri, E., et al.: Engineering issues related to the development of a recommender system in a critical context: application to interactive cockpits. Int. J. Hum. Comput. Stud. **121**, 122–141 (2019)
4. Canny, A., Martinie, C., Navarre, D., Palanque, P., Barboni, E., Gris, C.: Engineering model-based software testing of WIMP interactive applications: a process based on formal models and the SQUAMATA tool. Proc. ACM on Hum.-Comput. Interact. **5**(EICS), 1–30 (2021). https://doi.org/10.1145/3461729

5. Canny A., Palanque P., Navarre D.: Model-based testing of GUI applications featuring dynamic instantiation of widgets. In: 2020 IEEE International Conference on Software Testing, Verification and Validation Workshops (ICSTW), pp. 95–104 (2020). https://doi.org/10.1109/ICSTW50294.2020.00029
6. Canny, A., Navarre, D., Campos, J.C., Palanque, P.: Model-based testing of post-WIMP interactions using object oriented petri-nets. In: Sekerinski, E., et al. (eds.) FM 2019. LNCS, vol. 12232, pp. 486–502. Springer, Cham (2020). https://doi.org/10.1007/978-3-030-54994-7_35
7. Campos, J.C., Fayollas, C., Harrison, M.D., Martinie, C., Masci, P., Palanque, P.: Supporting the analysis of safety critical user interfaces: an exploration of three formal tools. ACM Trans. Comput.-Hum. Interact. **27**(5), 1–48 (2020). https://doi.org/10.1145/3404199
8. ESARR 6. EUROCONTROL Safety Regulatory Requirement. Software in ATM Systems. Edition 1.0 (2003). http://www.eurocontrol.int/src/public/standard_page/esarr6.html
9. European Organisation for Civil Aviation Equipment. DO-178B, Software Consideration in Airborne Systems and Equipment Certification. EUROCAE (1992)
10. Galindo, M., Martinie, C., Palanque, P., Winckler, M., Forbrig, P.: Tuning an HCI curriculum for master students to address interactive critical systems aspects. In: Kurosu, M. (ed.) HCI 2013. LNCS, vol. 8004, pp. 51–60. Springer, Heidelberg (2013). https://doi.org/10.1007/978-3-642-39232-0_6
11. Hamon, A., Palanque, P., Silva, J-L., Deleris, Y., Barboni, E.: Formal description of multi-touch interactions. In: Proceedings of the 5th ACM SIGCHI Symposium on Engineering Interactive Computing Systems (EICS '13). Association for Computing Machinery, New York, NY, USA, 207–216 (2013).https://doi.org/10.1145/2494603.2480311
12. Harel, D.: Statecharts: a visual formalism for complex systems. Sci. Comput. Program. **8**, 231–274 (1987)
13. Hollnagel, E.: Barriers and Accident Prevention. Ashgate, Aldershot, UK (2004)
14. Manna, Z., Pnueli, A.: A hierarchy of temporal properties. ACM Symposium on Principles of Distributed Computing 1990, pp. 377–410 (1990)
15. Martinie, C., Palanque, P., Navarre, D., Barboni, E.: A development process for usable large scale interactive critical systems: application to satellite ground segments. In: Winckler, M., Forbrig, P., Bernhaupt, R. (eds.) HCSE 2012. LNCS, vol. 7623, pp. 72–93. Springer, Heidelberg (2012). https://doi.org/10.1007/978-3-642-34347-6_5
16. Master in HCI of Université Toulouse III Paul Sabatier, history of internships. https://masterihm.fr/promotions-m2/stages. Accessed on May 2021
17. Palanque, P., Barboni, E., Martinie, C., Navarre, D., Winckler, M.: A model-based approach for supporting engineering usability evaluation of interaction techniques. In: Proceedings of the 3rd ACM SIGCHI Symposium on Engineering Interactive Computing Systems (EICS 2011), pp. 21–30. Association for Computing Machinery, New York, NY, USA (2011)
18. Palanque, P.A., Bastide, R., Dourte, L., Sibertin-Blanc, C.: Design of user-driven interfaces using Petri nets and objects. In: Rolland, C., Bodart, F., Cauvet, C. (eds.) CAiSE 1993. LNCS, vol. 685, pp. 569–585. Springer, Heidelberg (1993). https://doi.org/10.1007/3-540-56777-1_30
19. Pnueli, A.: Applications of temporal logic to the specification and verification of reactive systems: a survey of current trends. In: de Bakker, J.W., de Roever, W.-P., Rozenberg, G. (eds.) Current Trends in Concurrency, pp. 510–584. Springer Berlin Heidelberg, Berlin, Heidelberg (1986). https://doi.org/10.1007/BFb0027047
20. Salas, E., Cannon-Bowers, J.A.: The science of training: a decade of progress. Ann. Rev. Psychol. **52**(1), 471–499 (2001). https://doi.org/10.1146/annurev.psych.52.1.471
21. Wood, W.A.: Transition network grammars for natural language analysis. Commun. ACM **13**(10), 591–606 (1970)

# Interface Engineering for UX Professionals

Alan Dix[(✉)]

The Computational Foundry, Swansea University, Wales, UK
alan@hcibook.com
https://alandix.com/academic/papers/IE4UX2021

**Abstract.** This paper describes a small unit for teaching interface implementation to user experience (UX) designers. Where human–computer interaction (HCI) textbooks and courses include aspects of user interface engineering, they are usually focused towards computer science students. The unit described here is part of a larger online HCI course where the majority of learners are UX professionals, who found it hard to understand why they needed to learn about implementation. The paper explains why the author felt it important to include aspects that help the UX designer understand the behavioural and practical implications of 'low level' coding, and also the elements included in the unit. The resulting unit includes many concrete examples linking user behaviour to internal structure and having produced the material, it seems that this may also be a good way to introduce the topic to more technical students before digging into lower level details.

**Keywords:** User experience · Implementation · Events · Networks · Seeheim · MVC

## 1 Introduction

I have taught HCI for many years and even co-authored one of the major textbooks in the area [6]. However, the vast majority of my general HCI teaching has been to computing students, both undergraduate and postgraduate. For these students the HCI educator's main task is usually to encourage the students to think more about the people who will eventually use the systems they build. We offer them tools and techniques, and in general seek to enculture them into user-centred thought patterns.

Part of this has included implementation issues including software architectures for UI, such as Seeheim and MVC, toolkits and lower-level features such as event models. Teaching practice has included Java projects in labs and also live coding lectures – there is no better way for students to learn than seeing their lecturer make mistakes!

Recently however I was faced with a new challenge, teaching implementation issues to UX professionals. For this I needed to ask hard questions: first whether it was even desirable to try, and second, if it was worth doing, what should be taught.


Published by Springer Nature Switzerland AG 2022
C. Ardito et al. (Eds.): INTERACT 2021, LNCS 13198, pp. 221–235, 2022.
https://doi.org/10.1007/978-3-030-98388-8_20

My personal answer to the first question is a definitive "Yes", just as developers need to understand the human user, UX designers need to understand aspects of how a system is constructed. The second is harder to answer.

This paper describes the circumstances leading to this need, the reasoning behind my answer to the first question, and my first steps at answering the second. Several aspects of this are a personal journey, so the paper will freely use "I" where appropriate. Furthermore, this is a work in progress.

The paper presents a curriculum for teaching critical aspects of interface implementation and software architecture to UX professionals, and it will form a key part of the Interaction Design Foundation course "Human–Computer Interaction" for some years to come. However, it is not the only or definitive answer, and undoubtedly, in some years' time, if there is another iteration of the course, this is an area that will be updated further.

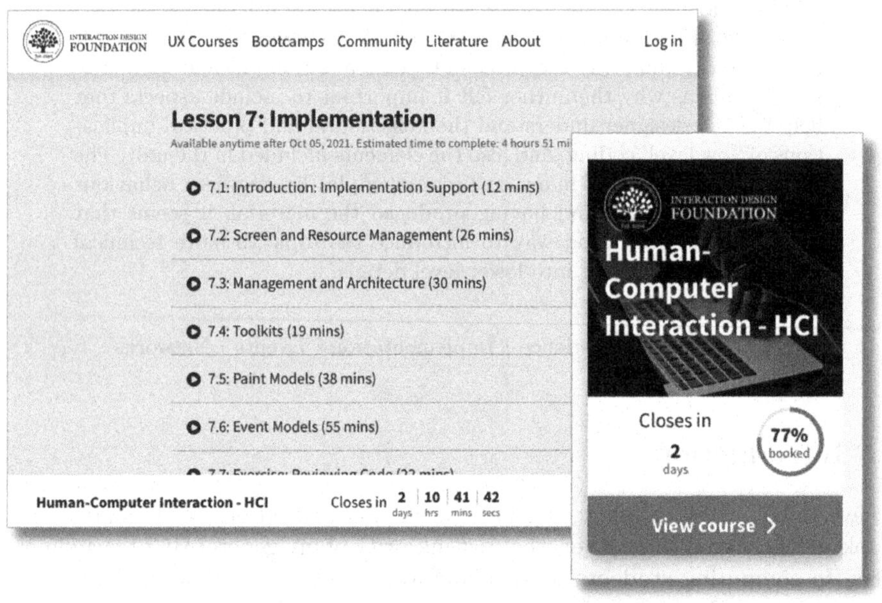


Fig. 1. Implementation lecture as part of original IxDF course on Human–Computer Interaction.

## 2 Why Implementation for UX Professionals?

### 2.1 Background

In 2012 I produced a short HCI MOOC that was delivered between late 2012 and early 2013. I have described some of the lessons from doing this in previous work [3,4]. Subsequently the video material was used as the basis for an Interaction Design Foundation course on Human Computer Interaction [5], that has proved popular over the intervening years.

Interaction Design Foundation (IxDF) is a non-profit foundation dedicated to providing high-quality UX learning materials as freely as possible to everyone. It began its life as a free online encyclopaedia of interaction created by its founders Mads Soegaard and Rikke Friis Dam. As this became more popular, they invited guest contributors, and the encyclopaedia entries often became definitive essays in their respective topics, Later still the site became a full open education platform and is now used daily by thousands of UX professionals over more than 100 countries.

In 2020, IxDF approached me to update the HCI course and refilm the material using higher quality recording equipment. Some the updating was simply a matter of using new examples, but the implementation unit (see Fig. 1), required far more detailed examination.

### 2.2 Do We Need Implementation for UX?

As noted my personal background had been in teaching HCI to CS students. For many topics such as fundamentals of human perception and cognition or evaluation techniques, there is little difference in what one would teach to a CS undergraduate, a psychology student or a UX professional. Their backgrounds may differ so some topics may be slightly repetitive or more novel, but the range of material is similar.

However, for implementation this is not the case. It is easy to use terms that are unrecognizable to someone with a design background, and furthermore many of the UX professionals taking the course could not see the relevance of the unit to their practice. The options were:

1. Drop the unit from the course
2. Update it radically

The first would have been the easiest option, but I believe the wrong one.

Anyone working on HCI within a computing background will have heard phrases such as "just slap a user interface on it", or describing HCI as "adding the pretty bits". We rightly either roundly condemn or possibly benignly spot the opportunity to educate the simplistic software engineer into the nuances of human-centred design. Sad to say, these attitudes, while less common, can still be found.

For those of us versed in HCI/UX disciplines it is clear that while it is not necessary for a software developer to understand the user-focused design issues in the same depth and detail as a UX expert, they should still appreciate the necessity and complexity of designing a system that is actually fit for purpose amongst real users. That is, they should understand enough that they know that they *need to* work alongside a knowledgeable UX designer and have *sufficient common language* for that collaboration.

However, equally over the years I've heard first interaction designers and then UX designers say "just code it". Sometimes the plasticity of coding as a creative medium makes all things appear equally possible and equally easy. The sweat and tears of debugging, refactoring, and pizza-fuelled all-nighters are hidden beneath the pixels of the resulting system.

In reality, those who understand code know that the 'bits leak out', the underlying architectural decisions 'under the hood' have a habit of impacting the user in terms of unexpected edge behaviours, robustness, maintainability or ease of change.

One example of this used in the course is of an Excel spreadsheet that had been generated as an output report from enterprise software. The spreadsheet was quite small in terms of content, but had an enormous footprint on the disk and was very slow to load and sluggish to scroll. It turned out that this was due to large numbers of empty cells as an accident of the way it had been coded. This made no difference to the visual appearance of the spreadsheet (hence escaped review and handover) but had a major impact on responsiveness and hence user experience.

In general, features that sound trivial may be all but impossible, and those that seem like science fiction may turn out to be trivial. The idea that you can design from the outside and then leave it to the developer to make it happen is as facile in HCI as it is in F1 design.

It is clear that while it is not necessary for a UX designer to understand the software design issues in the same depth and detail as a developer, they should still appreciate the necessity and complexity of designing a system that is tractable to code and robust to run in a real computing environment. That is, they should understand enough that they know that they *need to* work alongside a knowledgeable developer and have *sufficient common language* for that collaboration.

### 2.3 Motivating Examples - The Code-Aware Designer

The course begins with some motivating examples so that the learner understands why they are being asked to study aspects of software architecture and implementation. These are also concrete examples of the arguments above.

One high-level example is the way that internal representations of arrays and pixelmaps in most programming languages favour rectangular structures with zero-based coordinate systems. While this is (debatably) acceptable on many rectangular screens, there are situations where it is more problematic including smart-watch faces, phones where the front-facing camera intrudes on the display, and special shaped displays such as car dashboards. While there is no intrinsic limitation to rectangular objects, they may be easier to create and hence become the default. As a counter example to this, the course describes the Firefly intelligent lighting system. This starts with arbitrarily placed light sources, which are retrospectively located in 3D using image analysis, enabling a voxel-based display paradigm. In particular, in Firefly, text at an angle is not 'special'; all angles of view are equal [2].

Two more concrete examples are (i) the way some web forms keep scrolling the page to the top whenever an entry is made, which is likely to be due to the developer forgetting to cancel the default event behaviour for hyperlink, or possibly redraw errors; and (ii) the example described above where apparently small spreadsheets are very big on disk because empty cells may take up memory.

### 2.4 What Does a UX Developer Need to Know About Implementation?

The follow on question to "*do UX professionals need to know about implementation?*" is "*what do they need to know?*". The next section outlines the main elements of the implementation unit and this is expanded in more detail in Appendix A. However there are a number of general themes that thread through the unit.

First although as instructor I might be convinced that it is important for a designer to have an appreciation of underlying implementation/engineering concerns, it is important that the learner also has the understanding. The introduction of the unit has quite a strong "*hearts and minds*" feel, motivating why a designer should be interested, but this is reiterated continually throughout the other parts of the units.

Second is the content itself, which includes issues such as event models, where state is stored, network-based systems and overall layering and architecture of systems. In each part the internal details are related to the external behaviours that they engender, for example inconsistencies due to race conditions. In addition, where appropriate, this leads to lessons in terms of design features that may need to be considered to avert potential problems, for example, building 'action lists' rather than halting awaiting user interaction during long-running processes.

Finally, these are constantly applied in mini-case studies and examples of particular interface elements. This is for two reasons. *Pedagogically*, this makes the somewhat abstract discussions of architecture or event propagation concrete, in parallel explaining the observable behaviour and giving life to the abstractions. As important, *rhetorically*, this serves to emphasise that it is important to have some understanding of these issues.

Note that the course does not suggest that the UX designer should be able to code themselves, only that they should be aware of the implications of coding. That said, there may be value for the designer being able to do some level of coding in order to prototype ideas. Happily, there are tools that allow elements of prototyping using no-code or low-code techniques.

## 3 Course Content

The implementation unit is one part of a larger course at IxDF. The material for this unit corresponds roughly to the material one might present in a few hours lectures in a week of a face-to-face course.

### 3.1 Outline

The content is structured over five parts as follows, each of these is described in more detail in Appendix A.

1. ***Introduction*** – This part is about orienting and motivating the learner as to why they should have some understanding of underlying implementation details.
2. ***Understanding states and events*** – The idea of system states and events transforming them are fundamental to both implementing and understanding any interactive system.
3. ***Network-based interaction*** – This topic could be a whole course in itself! Nearly every application now-a-days involves some sort of network. This part covers a few of the ways this affects user interaction and experience.
4. ***Digging below the application*** – The original implementation unit included material on windowing systems which was both quite low level and also rather desktop oriented. The replacement is a relatively small part that introduces the job of operating systems, and the various layers between it and the actual application.
5. ***Architecture*** – Software architectural design is a major influence on many aspects of systems, some are immediately obvious in the interface behaviour, but others, possibly more critical, only become apparent once a system has been deployed including reliability and ease of maintenance.

### 3.2 An Example – Mute Wars

To give a flavour of the course material, we'll look at 'Mute Wars' an example used in the "Network-based interaction" part of the course. This was chosen as a 'deep dive' because it is an issue that most participants will have encountered. In their own day-to-day interactions with video-conferencing software such as Zoom or Microsoft Teams.

The example is introduced after a short section describing different aspects of networks: bandwidth, latency, jitter, and intermittent glitches and the way that buffering can be used for streaming media, but not for interactive content as it creates additional delays. The "Mute Wars" example illustrates these issues and in particular the potential for race condition. The presentation starts by describing the problem:

- You start to speak and the chair says "you're on mute" ... we have all been there!
- You try to click your unmute button, but it doesn't seem to work.
- You try again, and again, maybe sometimes you see it flick momentarily to 'unmute' state, but then back to muted.
- Eventually, apparently randomly, it works and you can speak

The reason for this problem is that both you and the meeting chair are trying to unmute you at the same time. This could be a problem even if everything were working instantaneously, and arguably the visual and dynamic interaction design should take this into account. However, due to network latency and race conditions, the period for potential overlapping actions is increased. This process is described using a simple network timeline diagram (Fig. 2).

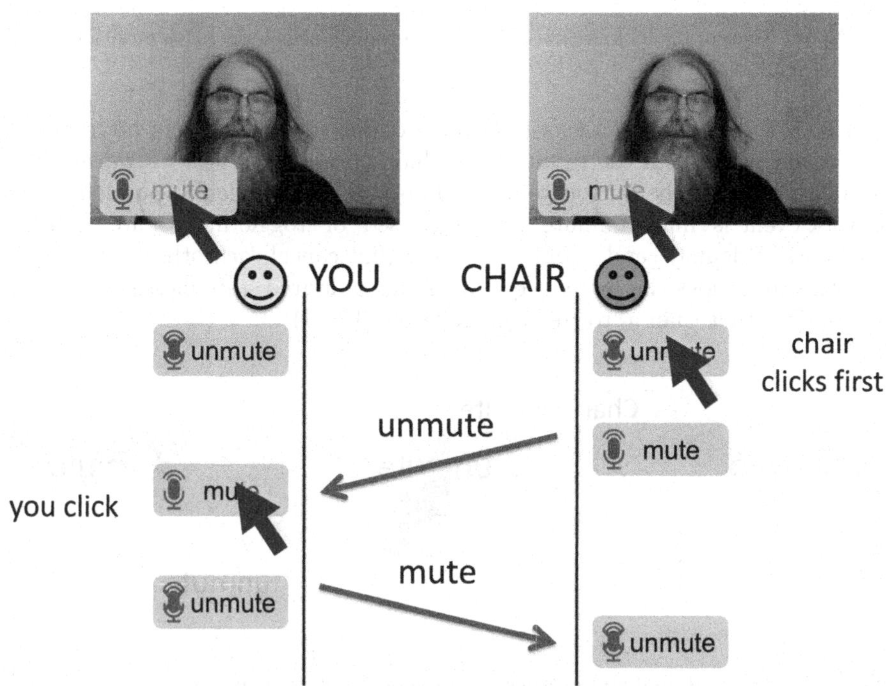


**Fig. 2.** Mute Wars - timeline of events.

This description of the problem is used to emphasise how one sometimes needs an understanding of how underlying implementation mechanisms, in this case network delays, may have an impact on user experience. To reinforce this message, the internal description of problem is used to suggest potential design solutions.

The first solution is focused on the potential for user-level 'race conditions' even when there are no network delays, that is when both you and the chair near simultaneously press the unmute button. The problem here is that the button will have changed between 'muted' and 'unmuted' visual states, but there is no time for the user to notice if they are in the process of clicking the button. When it is possible that the target of a click or other user action is changing while they are in the process of acting, it is general good practice (but rarely observed) to temporarily freeze/lock the button or other action object for a few moments during the transition to prevent accidental actions (Fig. 3).

**Fig. 3.** Temporary lock/freeze of button to reduce user-level race conditions.

This prevents nearly all user-level race conditions, but may not address network race conditions if the result of the chair's 'unmute' is still in transit when you reach to press the button yourself. This can be a particular problem if the network event is 'mute/unmute button pressed' or 'toggle mute state'. In such cases both ends may send 'toggle' messages that cancel each other out. In general, race conditions can be reduced by sending a desired state message "become unmuted" rather than a 'toggle' change event (Fig. 4).

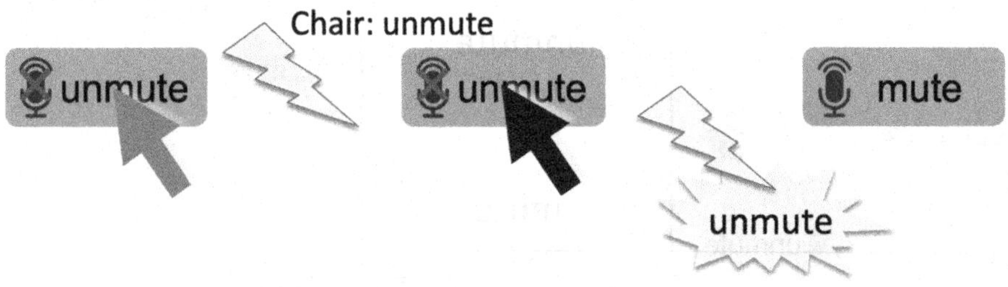


**Fig. 4.** Send desired final state rather than toggle event to reduce network race conditions.

The aim of this example is not to teach the particular race-condition problem and solutions, but to illustrate the more general importance of understanding the properties of networks at a non-technical level and being able to discuss both interface-level and underlying implementation-level interventions to improve user experience.

## 4 Discussion

While I am confident that the material covered is good for the UX designer to know, I am certain there are gaps. To some extent this is inevitable, there are so many issues, especially if one start to look towards more specific areas, for example digital interfaces for physical products. Perhaps the more crucial questions are (i) whether this is the most critical content and (ii) whether it is presented in the best manner for the audience. This said, the most important lesson from this, indeed in many courses, is if the learner has obtained a broad appreciation of the nature of the topic and in a position to learn more, ideally as part of active collaboration with developers, when the need arises.

Having repackaged this material for UX designers, many of the alterations in foci or means of motivating or describing issues look as though they would also be better ways of presenting this form of material to technical computing students. Those coming with software development skills would need additional details. However, the focus on examples that connect external behaviour and internal structure, while formulated to help designers appreciate the coding complexity and importance, may well also help the coder understand the human complexity and importance.

# A Appendix: Unit Content – Implementation for UX

This material is just a single unit of the IxDF HCI course, which corresponds roughly to the material one might present in a few hours lectures in a week of a face-to-face course.

## A.1 Introduction

This part is about orienting and motivating the learner as to why they should have some understanding of underlying implementation details.

***Human roles in delivering systems to users*** – The unit starts by looking widely at the various human roles in the design and delivery of a computer system. This includes designers, implementors, sales, maintainers and of course the users themselves. It also discusses how these human roles interact at different stages from project management and requirements gathering through design, deployment, maintenance and support. The aim is to give a wide angle view beyond the design and development stages that are often the focus for UX and also to reinforce the value of each of the human roles (Fig. 5).

***Three use words*** – This wide angle view is reiterated using the three use words for a system that had been introduced at the beginning of the whole HCI course: useful, usable and used. This leads into a discussion of the way a product has to meet user needs, be able to be delivered technically and also have a route to market. If any fails, they all fail, but the precise order might vary from project to project.

***Do I need to know how it's put together?*** – Hopefully by this stage the learner accepts that the process of creating and delivering a product is a multi-faceted where the UX design is critical, but only one part. This last part of the introduction seeks to demonstrate that the implementation of the system is not only important, but also important to understand – it cannot be dismissed as mere 'implementation details'.

This includes describing how the final system must be possible to deliver given current technology and the time available, how the tools chosen may influence the kinds of systems created and how 'the bits leak out', the underlying architecture, toolkits and coding methods will have an impact on user experience.

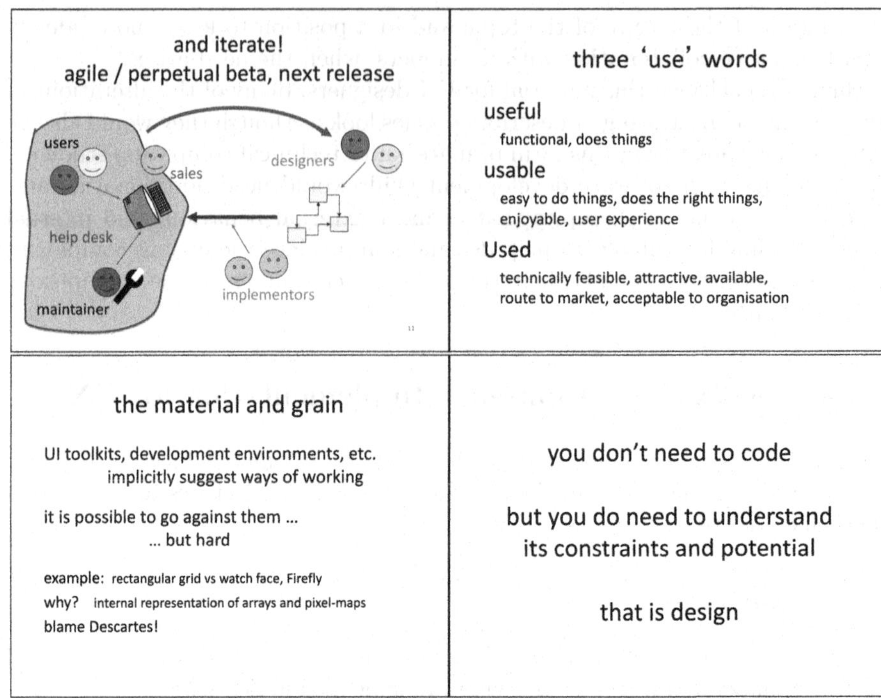


**Fig. 5.** Sample slides from "Introduction".

The final message is "you don't need to code, but you do need to understand its constraints and potential" – and indeed that creating given this understanding is the essence of good design.

### A.2 Understanding States and Events

The idea of system states and events transforming them are fundamental to both implementing and understanding any interactive system.

***Continuity*** – This part start by using Zeno's hare and tortoise to discuss continuity: how the physical world is largely continuous, but the digital world is discrete operating usually in time steps, albeit often so fast that the distinction may be hard to observe. In particular, the learner is introduced to status-status mappings such as the relation between a finger position on a touchscreen and an object being dragged. The user sees continuous motion, the computer a series of discrete changes, but the designer needs to be aware of both.

***Events*** – The focus then moves into more detail about events including the way there may be events at different levels of abstraction from raw touch/mouse events, through widget events such as 'button pressed' and higher-level compound events such as 'file saved'.

Buxton's three state model [1] is used to explore the way different device might have hover states for tooltips, whilst others do not. The learner is also introduced to the fact that event orders may differ between platforms and that there are many kinds of system and network-initiated events as well as user-initiated ones leading to the potential for race conditions.

***State*** – State is introduced as the holder of memory from the past for the future. Inspiration is drawn from different forms of state in the physical human world including memory, books and physical arrangements. The various forms of computer memory are then discussed including where it resides in the system: local device, web browser, server, or cloud and how this affects properties such as longevity, access speed, availability and reliability.

Building on the earlier discussion of status-status mappings issues of consistency are discussed including synchronisation issues between multiple devices and constraint maintenance within the interface (Fig. 6).

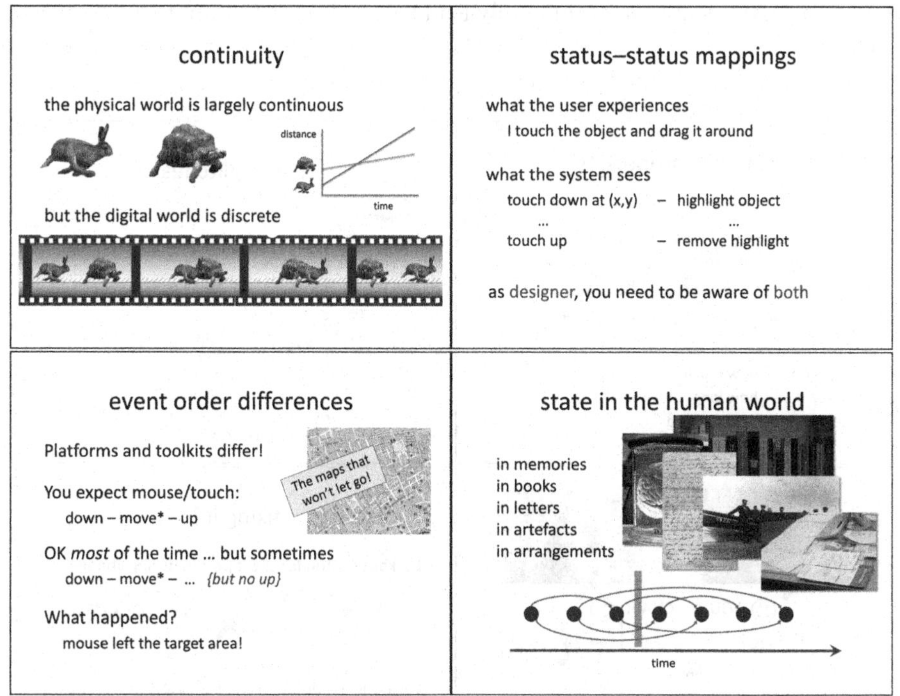


**Fig. 6.** Sample slides from "Understanding states and events"

## A.3 Network-Based Interaction

This topic could be a whole course in itself! Nearly every application now-a-days involves some sort of network. This part covers a few of the ways this affects user interaction and experience.

***Network properties and issues*** – Critical network properties and metrics are introduced: bandwidth, latency and jitter. These are discussed initially in relation to media delivery including the way buffering can reduce jitter at the cost of additional latency. This leads to the problem of 'glitches', short breaks in connectivity, that are longer than can be regarded as jitter, but shorter than full periods of disconnection. This in turn is used to motivate 'network aware' design, interactions that are resilient to different forms of network effects.

***Case study: race conditions in mute-wars*** – A practical case study is to reinforce the messages in this part. One assumes that the memory of long days full of Zoom/Teams meetings will not be forgotten quickly. The case study explains the race conditions that give rise to 'mute wars', the way meetings chair and participants can accidentally lead to simultaneous unmute/mute events (Fig. 7).

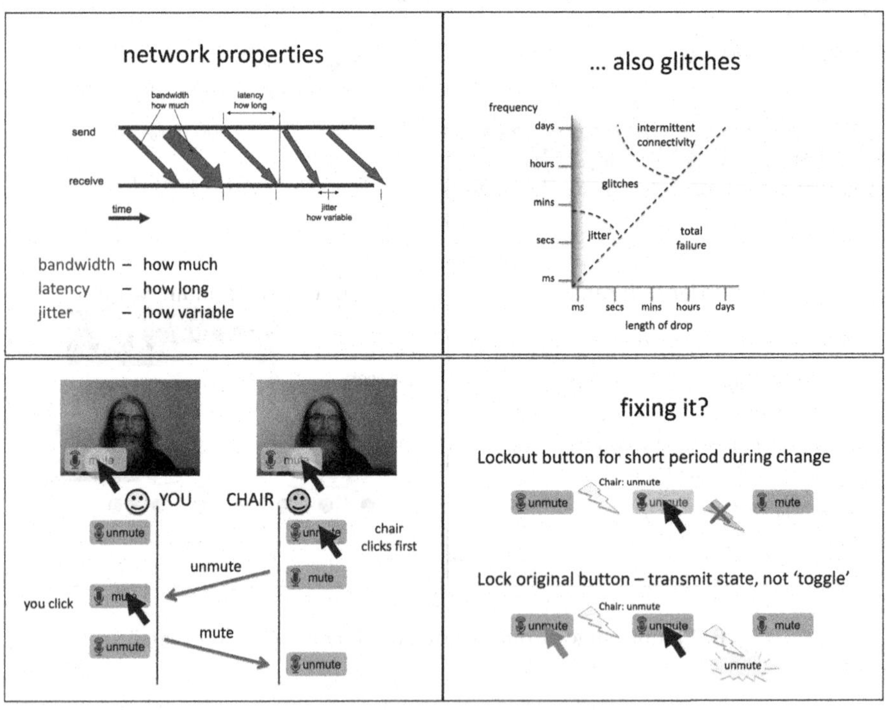


**Fig. 7.** Sample slides from "Network-based interaction"

## A.4 Digging Below the Application

The original implementation unit included material on windowing systems which was both quite low level and also rather desktop oriented. This short part starts with the way that operating systems and windowing systems abstract away from details of particular devices and effectively share the fixed physical resources (screen, keyboard, etc.) between multiple applications. Examples are given of different ways to share screen real-estate such as scrollable vertical tiled layouts such in side bars, and overlapping windows on the desktop. This part also briefly discusses non-screen resources such as power and network access, and inter-application management issues including consistency, the clipboard and changing the active app (Fig. 8).

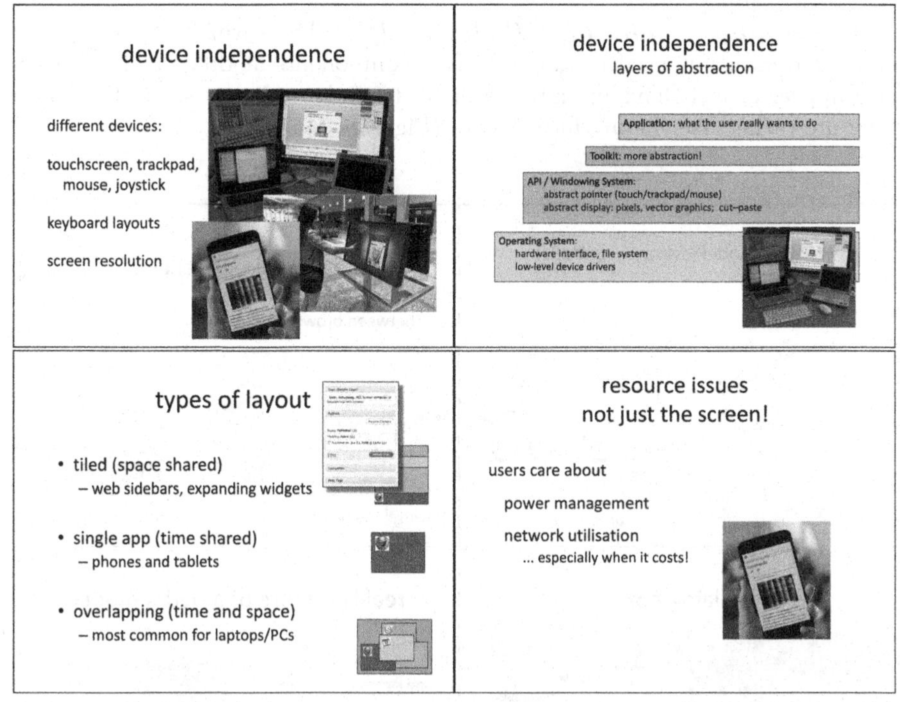


**Fig. 8.** Sample slides from "Digging below the application"

## A.5 Architecture

Software architectural design is a major influence on many aspects of systems, some are immediately obvious in the interface behaviour, but others, possibly more critical, only become apparent once a system has been deployed including reliability and ease of maintenance.

***Overview*** – This introduces the idea of software architecture. It uses the analogy of cities and buildings: the way they have structure at different levels, and flows of vehicles and people between them.

***Seeheim*** – The Seeheim model is described first in terms of its historic role, but also in the way that it gives a language to think both of the internal construction of a user interface, but also the structure of the interface itself. A save/delete dialog box is used to illustrate the levels of presentation, dialog and functionality.

***Model–View–Controller*** – The MVC model is presented both in relation to the Seeheim model and in terms of its strengths in separation of concerns, reuse, and offering multiple views for the same underlying state. The original 'pure' MVC is described first followed by an explanation of how many systems that describe themselves as 'MVC' actually amalgamate the view and controller as a single component.

***The Reality – more of a Hydra model*** – The save/delete dialog box introduced earlier is used to illustrate how components at different levels each have appearance, behaviour, interaction state and persistent state, forming a structure rather like the mythical Hydra (Fig. 9).

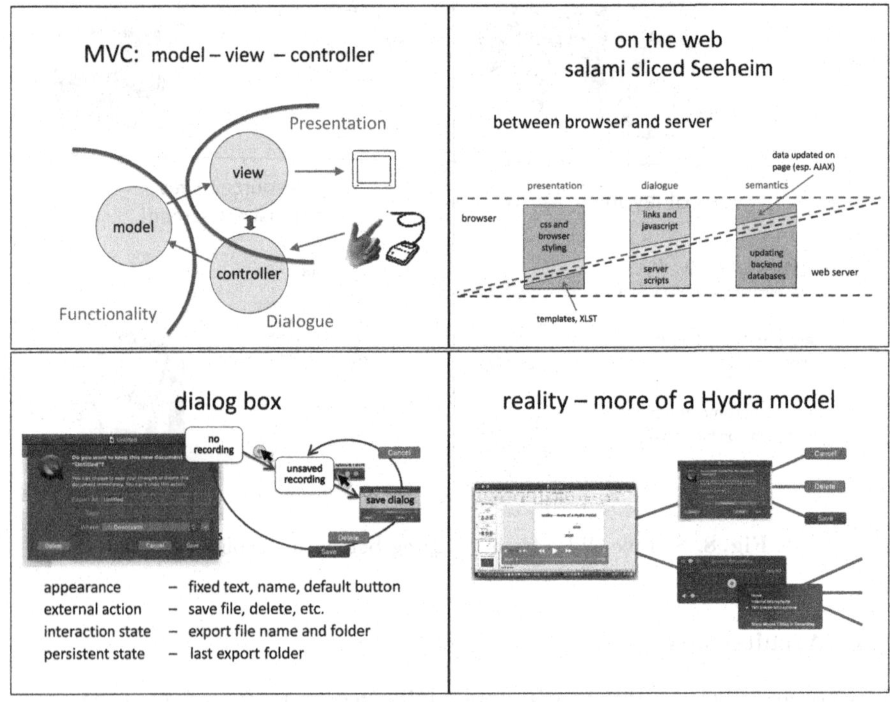


**Fig. 9.** Sample slides from "Architecture"

## References

1. Buxton, W.: A three-state model of graphical input. In: Proceedings of the IFIP TC13 Third Interational Conference on Human-Computer Interaction, pp. 449–456. INTERACT 1990, North-Holland Publishing Co., NLD (1990)
2. Chandler, A., Finney, J., Lewis, C., Dix, A.: Toward emergent technology for blended public displays. In: Proceedings of the 11th International Conference on Ubiquitous Computing, pp. 101–104. UbiComp 2009, Association for Computing Machinery, New York, NY, USA (2009). https://doi.org/10.1145/1620545.1620562
3. Dix, A.: Reuse of moocs: bringing online content back to the classroom. In: Proceedings of Alt-C 2015 (2015). https://www.alandix.com/academic/papers/altc2015-reuse-of-moocs/
4. Dix, A.: More than one way to flip a class: learning analytics for mixed models of learning. Compass: J. Learn. Teach. **8**(12) (2016). https://doi.org/10.21100/compass.v8i12.275, https://journals.gre.ac.uk/index.php/compass/article/view/275
5. Dix, A.: Human-Computer Interaction (online course). Interaction Design Foundation (2021). https://www.interaction-design.org/courses/human-computer-interaction Accessed 10 Dec 2021
6. Dix, A., Finlay, J., Abowd, G.D., Beale, R.: Human Computer Interaction, 3 edn. Prentice Hall, Harlow, England (2004)

# Adult Students Become Professionals Teaching or Learning – What's in a Name?

Gerrit van der Veer[1(✉)] and Teresa Consiglio[2]

[1] Vrije Universiteit Amsterdam, Amsterdam, The Netherlands
gerrit@acm.org

[2] Open Universiteit Nederland, Heerlen, The Netherlands

**Abstract.** We provide our experience-based vision on teaching Interaction Design-related courses in multiple cultures. We explain how students should be treated as adults with their own learning goals and their own competence of assessing the level of professionalism reached. We analyse our approach in relation to the ACM-IEEE CC2020 Curriculum Guidelines. Finally, we provide an example of our teaching approach during lock-down.

**Keywords:** Interaction design · Education · Adult learning · Blended learning

## 1 Experience-Based Vision on Professional Learning on Usability and Experience Design

The authors worked with generations of students. The first author was responsible for adult education for many decades, teaching in domains that evolved in parallel to the technical developments in ICT and educational technics: from paper "teaching machines" and TV broadcasted lectures to web-based learning environments and blended learning. Based on our growing understanding of adult learning in the domain of interactive systems design, the authors developed a vision on how to systematically provide learning support. Our insights are based on experience in many different educational cultures, in many different curricula, and in a variety of contextual opportunities and restrictions of interaction between students, and of interaction between students and domain experts [1–4].

We always considered our students to be adult learners. Our definition: students that bring their own motivation for the knowledge domain, for the skills, and for the dispositions they consider relevant [5]. Among our students, we count University students (Bachelor, masters, and post masters) in faculties like Cognitive Psychology, Computing, AI, Medicine and Health Care, and Architecture and Design. Another type of adults we met when providing courses for teacher trainers, for professionals in the design domain that aimed for additional and state of the art novel insights and practice, and professional artists and cultural heritage curators.


Published by Springer Nature Switzerland AG 2022
C. Ardito et al. (Eds.): INTERACT 2021, LNCS 13198, pp. 236–247, 2022.
https://doi.org/10.1007/978-3-030-98388-8_21

The authors experienced the challenges to provide appropriate learning support, as well as the opportunities for an equivalent solution, in rather different cultures of education. We have been involved with developing and teaching HCI related Bachelor and MSc. education of interaction design in many different educational cultures: (multiple universities in each of the countries Italy, Spain, Romania, Netherlands, and China), and in a broad range of departmental curricula (Cognitive Psychology, Software engineering, Cognitive Ergonomics, Artificial Intelligence, Human-Media Interaction, Multimedia and Culture, Usability engineering, Architecture and Design, Human-Computer Interaction, etc.). The language of working with our students (communicating, resources) has always been English, which was a second language for all.

In the next sections we provide our conceptual view of the domain of human centered interaction design, and we show how our understanding has been applied in providing actual learning support in various cultures of academic learning.

## 2 A Model for the Knowledge Domain

The first author contributed to the ACM-IEEE Curricula Recommendations: in Computer Science, 2013 [6], one of our courses was described as an example for the domain HCI, and one of the authors acted as a Steering Committee member for Information Technology 2017 [7], and the Computing Curricula Overview report CC2020 [8]. Our view on a model of knowledge for adult learning in the domain of Interaction Design is equivalent to what CC2020 labels "Competency based Computing Education: Competency = Knowledge + Skills + Dispositions… *in Context*", see Fig. 1, where *Knowledge* is the "know-what" dimension, *Skills* introduce the capability of applying knowledge to actively accomplish a task, and *Dispositions* frame the "know-why" dimension of competency and prescribe a temperament of quality of character in task performance.

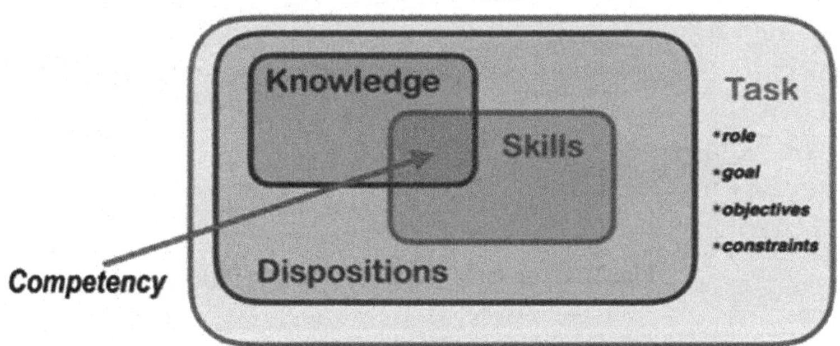


**Fig. 1.** Conceptual structure of the CC2020 competency model [8]

### 2.1 Knowledge

CC2020 lists 6 knowledge categories: Users and Users and Organizations; Systems Modeling; Systems Architecture and Infrastructure; Software Development; Software

Fundamentals; and Hardware. These categories are filled with knowledge areas, among which we identify the core areas of Interaction Design like: User experience design; Requirements Analysis and Specification; Verification and Validation; and Graphics and Visualization, and to which we add specific HCI Knowledge areas like Human Information Processing, and Task domains like Service Design and Design for Cultural and Arts. For a more elaborated view see Fig. 2.

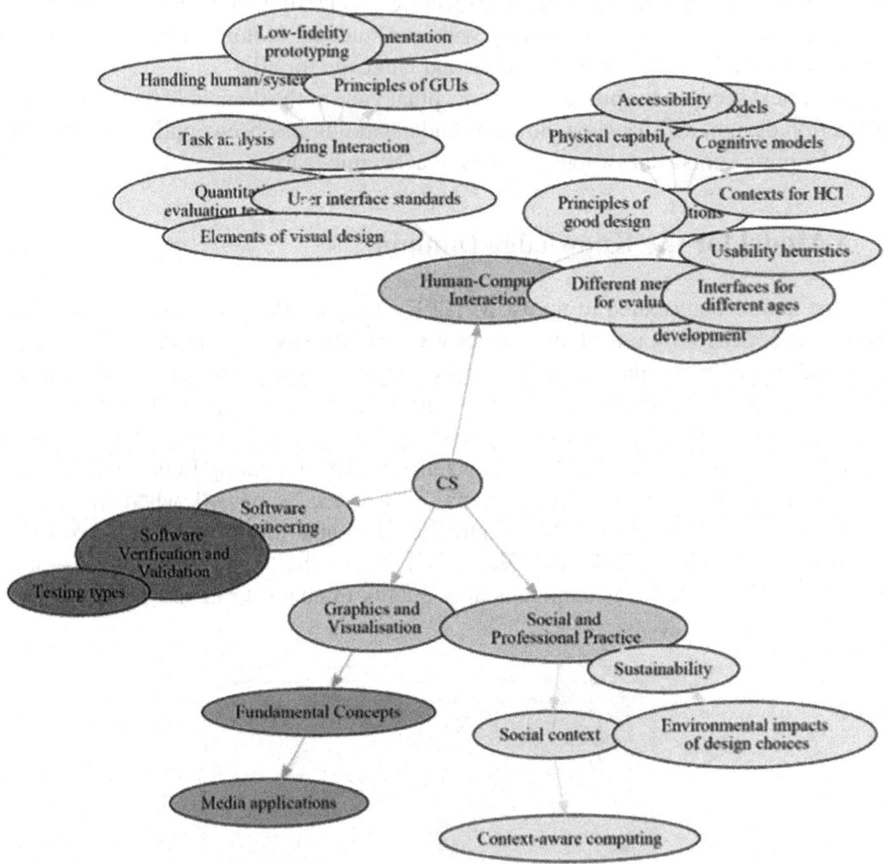


**Fig. 2.** Close-up of the HCI part (from [8]).

## 2.2 Skills

CC2020 considers knowledge in each area at 6 levels of cognitive skills: Remembering; Understanding; Applying; Analyzing; Evaluating; and Creating, where each level presupposes skills at the previous level.

### 2.3 Dispositions

Dispositions define the third dimension of competency. According to CC2020, every competent computing graduate is required to be: Adaptable; Collaborative; Inventive; Meticulous; Passionate; Proactive; Professional; Purpose-driven; Responsible; Responsive; and Self-driven.

## 3 Interaction Design - A Wide Landscape

The courses that we develop and teach are all part of what we consider the domain of interaction design. In many cases the first course is an introduction to the domain, chosen by the University as a try-out of a new curriculum or major, or chosen by us with a plan for subsequent courses in mind. The name might vary in relation to the context and the intended audience. E.g., in Amsterdam we started a course that was labeled "Introduction to Cognitive Ergonomics" for Psychology students, but "Introduction to HCI" for Computer Science students. Both groups were in the same room at the same time, and, subsequently, worked in mixed teams on the exercises.

We often teach a course on Interactive Systems Design in general, followed by a special course on Human Information Processing, a course on User Research Methods, and course on Task Analysis. In another University, we provided a series starting with Visual Design, followed by a course on Research Methods for Usability and Experience Engineering, ending in a course on Service Design.

In another context, when our students (or their University Curriculum) express a specific application focus, we teach a course on Computers in Education, or on Design for Cultural heritage, or on Web/Internet Culture.

All our courses cover a different part of the knowledge domain, but our approach in developing the course, working with the students, and supporting their learning are similar.

## 4 Learning in the Real World

Our students live in many different countries. Even in a single course, we sometimes work with students living in 3 different countries, spread out in Europe and Middle America. Our students need to collaborate in teams in each course and they want to. Working in design teams, they often work for a read client, located in a place far away from part of the team. We are mostly only part time able to meet the students face-to-face. Courses may be co-located, but often they are at least partly supported by internet tools to provide access to all resources as well as to the history traces of a course. All our meetings are video recorded. The video shots are kept to a maximum of 15 min, which seems enough for discussing one concept, showing one example, pointing to one extra resource, providing an experience of one interaction event, etc. And our students tell us "we watch your lecture while riding the train, but 10 min is long enough". Meeting between far-away time zones requires strict scheduling. And to support the majority of all concerned, the teacher often will be available at nightly hours, to allow students to keep their local food breaks. Depending on local traditions of Institute hours, holidays, and semester durations, courses may be very compact full time periods, or course meetings may be spread out during several months, restricting face-to-face availability of a teacher.

In all our courses, the language for all aspects of the course is English as a second language. In some situations, there is a need for language support (either an interpreter when a design client outside of the institute was participating in a session, or a tutor to help students when needed, to prepare their presentations or documents), e.g., in some Universities in Italy or Spain, though in other institutes in the same countries there was no need for this.

Even if the students in our courses do most of the presentations, and in fact, of the teaching, we found that there is a restriction of the number of students a teacher can support single-handed. In courses of up to 25 students, we never needed support. In courses with a larger number of participants, we always used support (about 1 person for 25 students): paid student assistants who had taken an equivalent course before, or a PhD student from the domain of interactive systems design. These met with the teacher just before each plenary meeting, discussed the work done by "their" students, the intended new work after the session to come, and resources that might be useful in case of student requests of needs.

# 5 Structuring a Course

Before we start detail design of the course, we approach some of the students (mostly identified by their institute on our request) and discuss our ideas about the content in relation to their actual needs and. We ask students to propose a time schedule for plenary meetings and hours of student hours. Student hours in fact always are scheduled for teamwork. Courses may have variable time span and duration, sometimes running for 7 consecutive days of 9 h a day (in China), sometimes for 2 full days each fortnight for 4 months.

In addition, we ask the students to propose case studies that are available to them to feature in the practical part of the course.

Examples:

- Safety control at the entrance of the new Dalian Metro system
- Safety and payment of an unmanned petrol station in Alghero
- An expanding collection of historic pictures on Bilboa in the 60's
- A need for collaboration between hotels and tourist attractions in Sassari

## 5.1 Learning Goals

Adult students arrive with their own learning goals. These may be derived from the state of the art of their (intended) discipline, required by their industry or profession, or dictated by their educational institute or by curriculum recommendations. The goals are certainly dependent on a student's background and previous learning, and on their current learning plans and opportunities.

### 5.2 Knowledge Content

At the first plenary meeting (whether co-located or through the internet), we provided an overview of the subdomain, and we related the content to the intended practical examples chosen for the course. The domain overview is provided as a graphic representation, to be explored and available during the course as an interactive roadmap, see Fig. 3 and Fig. 4. The various labels in these representations indicate in fact the main concepts, tools, techniques, and patterns that form the knowledge area of a course. Discussing the meaning of these elements, the actual knowledge that the students consider already available to them, or most needed in their current situation, we reached agreement.

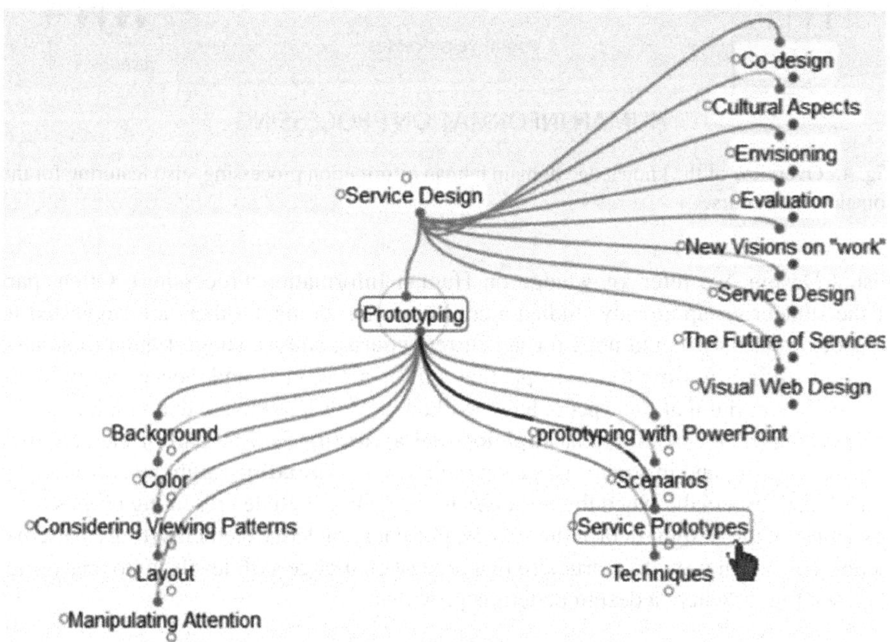


**Fig. 3.** Interactive overview of the knowledge domain service design.

Most of the time the result was close to what we planned, though surprises at our side tended to result in a quick adaptation of our plans. E.g., when, during a course on Service Design, the teacher suggested that a certain tool would not make sense for the chosen practice case. A student disagreed, and she accepted to volunteer trying out and reporting about this.

### 5.3 Skill Levels

In our recent courses, we introduce the CC2020 concept of skill levels. In some courses, part of the knowledge domain may have been considered before (e.g., In courses on

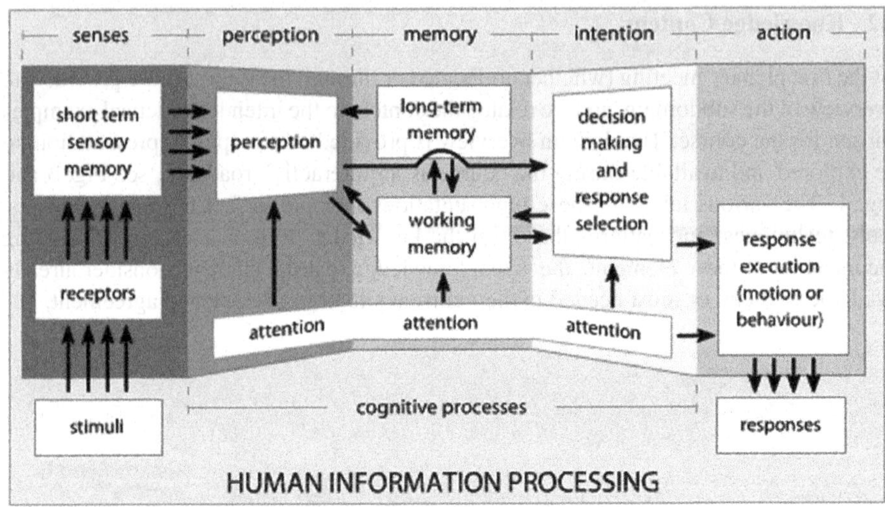


**Fig. 4.** Overview of the knowledge domain human information processing, also featuring for the domain of the course

Visual Design, we refer knowledge on Human Information Processing). Often, part of the student group already studied a course on that domain, others are suggested to consider what they would need for the current course, and we suggest them to at least consider **understanding** the concepts that will be mentioned, and, hence, use pointers to course material that their peers have worked on. For knowledge that features in the current course, we mention that **applying** and **analyzing** will be part of the activities that we propose, and in some cases even the level of **evaluating** might be considered a course goal, especially when the exercises in the course include presenting proposals to customers of the design. In fact, the way we present knowledge elements (tools, patterns, techniques) often provide a structure that at least challenge skill levels up to analyzing. E.g., see Fig. 5, where a design pattern is provided.

## 5.4 Dispositions

When talking to computing professionals in practice, whether in industry or in research, qualifications like the CC2020 identified dispositions are often the first requirements mentioned for selecting apprentices, colleagues, or employees, even if recruiting officers seem to categories these as "soft skills". Some academic education authorities seem to expect students will acquire their dispositions during internships and by participating in group work.

We have learned to create a learning ecosystem, and structured our learning context on purpose, to support development by creating a natural environment:

- Students explicitly co-develop learning goals at the start of a course.
- Students find examples to design or to exercise their skills, including clients that are available as audience for the presentation of the learning results.

**Horizontal Menu**

Basics | Examples | Forces | How | When_why

**Problem**

Users need the means to move and navigate from one page on the website to the other

**Solution**

Place an always visible menu at a fixed position on the page. Support this main menu with additional navigation tools.

**Fig. 5.** An element from a collection of visual design patterns.

- Students are asked at the start of the course to compose teams of about 3 peers (when we have students from different backgrounds, like computer science students and psychology students, or computing students and museum professionals, these teams should be mixed). Teams prepare for each next meeting but for the final meeting, "exam", which is an individual contribution.
- After meeting day 1, the teacher suggests which concepts (definition, example), tools, techniques, pointers, patterns could be relevant to be studied and presented. student teams are asked to collaborate between teams, and each choose one knowledge element to present at the next meeting.
- After day 1, the teacher mainly provides observations after each student presentation, when needed pointing to alternative interpretations or to issues that need further exploration, at the same time pointing to dispositions that have been exercised, or, alternatively, could help to improve learning results.
- Requested by students, we now always ask teams to upload their presentation 2 h before the next meeting, allow them to read and comment on each other's work, and await teacher comments before the actual presentation. In practice, sometimes a student accidentally is unable to deliver at the location or the time agreed for the next meeting. Our students turn out to be responsible enough to provide as soon as possible a video of their presentation to teacher and peers.
- Students are asked to keep a personal individual diary from day 1 of the course, and to upload their diary page each day there has been a class meeting (whether the meeting is co-located or through the Internet) 2 h after the meeting. Their diary entry

is suggested to contain what they learned, and from what sources they learned each knowledge element:

- team preparation of presentation,
- presenting themselves based the teamwork,
- teacher presentation,
- teacher provided resources,
- own/team discovered resources,
- presentations by other teams,
- videos from each teacher presentation on a single knowledge element. These are mostly about 5–10 min, and standard publicly available on Youku or YouTube.
- Video recordings from student presentation, which are always available with password protection.

We expect, and observe, that in this way many of the dispositions are challenged and exercised: collaboration, passion, being inventive, proactivity, responsibility, etc.

### 5.5 Assessment

Academic institutes often expect teachers to grade students' performance after a course. Wherever we are teaching, we explained our view: Our students are adults aiming at being a professional. At the end of a course, they should have acquired metacognition on the course domain: they should be able to understand what they learned, how they reached their level of professionality, and how they intend in future to keep up with their developing domain of professional computing [9].

Our "exam" consists of each student that feels ready, to develop for the final meeting a document describing all that has been learned, in such a way that it could be part of a portfolio to be used by applying for a job or a next educational level like a PhD. The document should show what has been performed in a team, what has been learned from other resources (see Sect. 5.4), how in future new knowledge and skills may be acquired. Next to this document, each student will provide a presentation and will receive the video of the presentation to keep with the portfolio document.

There is no mark, but a document stating the student finished the course. In fact, we experience on average 10–20% of students withdraw before the exam session, mostly telling us they lack sufficient time and will try next year.

## 6 Tools in Practice

In parallel with our teaching, we and our students designed and implemented electronic learning environments. These environments are mainly of 3 types:

a. Stand-alone stable websites that provide an interactive structure of knowledge for a certain subdomain of interactive systems design, explaining the general domain (e.g., see Figs. 3, 4 and 5), providing basic knowledge and examples, pointers to alternative electronically available resources, and providing experiments to experience first-hand the meaning of concepts.

b. Websites that provide a wizard to allow interactive exploration of the collet ion of tools, patterns, etc., allowing students and beginning professionals to analyze and search the design space.
c. Living electronic learning environment, dedicated to a single course, with access only by the students and teachers, where most of the learning activities mentioned in Sect. 5 are in fact being performed and stored. This type of learning environment, we build for each course separately in a Moodle environments. It includes opportunities for the teacher as well as the students to upload presentations and additional relevant material, to use a forum for discussions, and to upload diary entries for each student (See Fig. 6).

These working environments are discussed in [2–4]. Below, we will report of a recent case of one of our courses during a strict Covid lockdown, where none of the participants could physically meet any other.

### 6.1 A Challenging Example: Learning in Lock-Down in China

The first author is responsible for teaching 4 courses on interaction design topics in an MSc program in China. One of his recent courses was scheduled in the depth of a Chinese Lockdown. All students were spread over the country in their parents' home, the teacher was stuck in Europe, 7 time zones behind. Students worked in teams using WeChat, daily course meetings took place in Zoom.

For this course, on tools and techniques for experience design, the main content structure was of type a, as illustrated in Fig. 3. The students were pointed to several resources of the type b, allowing Design Space Analyses, in fact one on task analysis that was used before, designed by the authors, and an interactive resource for service design tools [10] by Roberta Tassi.

The electronic classroom was specifically furnished for this instance of the course in Moodle. Since there were no natural opportunities for chats during breaks and for walks through the lab, the learning community made extensive use of the diary forum. Figure 6 shows a part of a student-teacher discussion triggered by the student's diary.

The actual meetings between Teacher and students were all in Zoom, the students collaborated in their own (3 person) teams through WeChat. The Zoom meetings were recorded, in sections of about 10 min that each contained one knowledge domain element (a model, a concept, a definition, a tool, an example) if the element was presented by a student (as was the case for most of these after the first meeting) it was always concluded by a brief remark from the teacher, intended to provoke metacognitive reflections regarding the knowledge element, the skill level, and/or relevant dispositions. Each short recording was immediately after the meeting labeled, indicating the domain element, and made online available for all students.

In this course, 7 consecutive days of 9 h of student work including 3 h of plenary meetings, all participants did reach their goal, including a portfolio documenting what they learned and how they will keep up with the knowledge state of the art in future. After the course, a Chinese colleague teacher let us know:

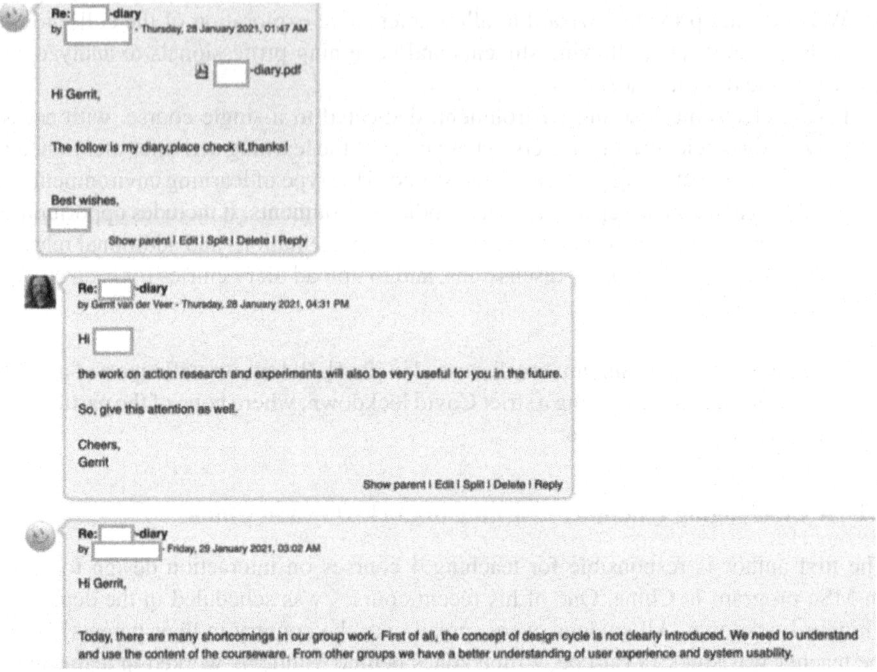


**Fig. 6.** Student diary entry with subsequent discussion by teacher (student name removed).

*"The feedback I received from the students are quite good. They especially appreciate a few things they think quite helpful:*

(1) *online delivering made them now focus attention more on the slides that helps them understand better, as for them textual is better than oral communication;*
(2) *more online resources than before were provided on the website that is helpful*
(3) *your feedback in text in real time on their deliverables is more helpful than in oral before.*

*So, we did learn something."*

## 6.2 Learning is Never Finished

The previous section is just an example, special because of the unexpected conditions, and surprising because it showed a new way to organizing adult learning and trigger metacognition in situations where blended learning is anyhow a sensible solution. We would like to show the value of our approach and the relation with the CC2020 vision, and to share our understanding and the methods and tools that we developed, including the learning environment and content that we provide to our students.

## References

1. Van der Veer, G.C., Consiglio, T., Benvenuti, L.: Service design - a structure for learning before teaching. In: Marti, P., Soro, A., Gamberini, L., Bagnara, S., (eds) Facing Complexity - Adjunct Proceedings CHItaly 2011, pp. 144–147. ACM Digital Library (2011)
2. Consiglio, T., van der Veer, G.C.: Designing an interactive learning environment for a worldwide distance adult learning community. In: Dittmar, A., Forbrig, P., (eds) Designing Collaborative Activities - Proceedings of ECCE 2011, pp. 225–228. ACM Digital Library (2011)
3. Consiglio, T., van der Veer, G.C.: Design for free learning: a case study on supporting a service design course. In: WikiSym 2012: Proceedings of the Eighth Annual International Symposium on Wikis and Open Collaboration (2012)
4. Consiglio, T., van der Veer, G.C.: ICT support for collaborative learning - a tale of two cities. In: Sampson, D.G., Spector, J.M., Ifenthaler, D., Isaias, P. (eds) IADIS International Conference on Cognition and Exploratory Learning in Digital Age (CELDA 2013), pp. 125–132 (2013)
5. Rogier, E., Uras, S., van der Veer, G.C.: What learners teach us: e-learning patterns for adult ICT education. In: ECCE 2013, Proceedings of the 31st European Conference on Cognitive Ergonomics. Article No. 8. ACM New York, NY, USA (2013)
6. https://dl.acm.org/doi/book/10.1145/2534860
7. https://dl.acm.org/doi/book/10.1145/3173161
8. https://www.acm.org/binaries/content/assets/education/curricula-recommendations/cc2020.pdf
9. Blanco, M.M., van der Veer, G.C., Benvenuti, L., Kirschner, P.A.: Design guidelines for self-assessment support for adult academic distance learning. In: Hai-Jew, S. (ed.) Constructing Self-Discovery Learning Spaces Online: Scaffolding and Decision Making Technologies, pp. 169–198. Hershey, PA (2012)
10. https://servicedesigntools.org/

# Addressing Interactive Computing Systems' Concerns in Software Engineering Degrees

José Creissac Campos(✉) and António Nestor Ribeiro

Department of Informatics, University of Minho & HASLab/INESC TEC
Campus de Gualtar, 4710-057 Braga, Portugal
{jose.campos,anr}@di.uminho.pt

**Abstract.** This paper arises from experience by the authors in teaching software engineering courses. It discusses the need for adequate coverage of Human-Computer Interaction topics in these courses and the challenges faced when addressing them. Three courses, at both *licentiate* and master's levels, are used as triggers for the discussion.

The paper argues that the lack of relevant Human-Computer Interaction concepts creates challenges when teaching and learning requirements analysis, design, and implementation of software systems. The approaches adopted to address these challenges are described.

**Keywords:** Human-Computer Interaction · Software engineering · Education

## 1 Introduction

As pointed out by John et al. [4], Software Engineering and Human-Centred Development (HCD) [3] processes have different concerns. Typically, the former will be more concerned with the quality of systems from a technical perspective, while the latter will be more concerned with the human aspects of such quality. Computer Science and Software Engineering degrees should provide students with a balanced perspective of both types of concerns. This is not always the case, and sometimes the degrees can be biased towards one area or the other.

This paper arises from experience by the authors in teaching software engineering courses on an integrated master's degree[1] on Informatics Engineering at the University of Minho. It discusses the need for adequate coverage of Human-Computer Interaction (CHI) topics, and the challenges faced when addressing them in the particular context of the degree in question.

The paper focuses, in particular, on three courses. One at the end of the *licentiate* level (Software Systems development – Semester 5). Two others at the master's level (Applications Architectures and Interactive Systems – both on

[1] A five years degree awarding a *licentiate* at the end of 3 years and a master's on completion.


Published by Springer Nature Switzerland AG 2022
C. Ardito et al. (Eds.): INTERACT 2021, LNCS 13198, pp. 248–256, 2022.
https://doi.org/10.1007/978-3-030-98388-8_22

Semester 8). Together these courses cover from model-based software development to Web-based applications development.

Human-Computer Interaction topics appear only at the master's level, in the Interactive Systems course, and this creates a number of challenges that are discussed herein. The paper outlines the approaches adopted to address these challenges and describes recent changes to the degree.

The paper is structured as follows: Sect. 2 provides context on the Informatics Engineering degree and on the three courses; Sect. 3 discusses human-centred concerns in relation to the courses; finally, Sect. 4 presents some concluding remarks.

## 2 The Degree and the Courses

In this section we briefly describe the integrated master's on Informatics Engineering and the three courses mentioned in the previous section.

### 2.1 The Informatics Engineering Degree

The degree is a combination of a *licentiate* and a master's degree in Informatics Engineering (see Fig. 1). It aims to prepare computer engineers, capable of intervening in all phases of the development of computer solutions, from analysis to installation, through design and implementation. The degree lasts ten academic semesters, from which six semesters are for the *licentiate*, and four for the master's course. It awards a total of 300 ECTS[2] [2] credits.

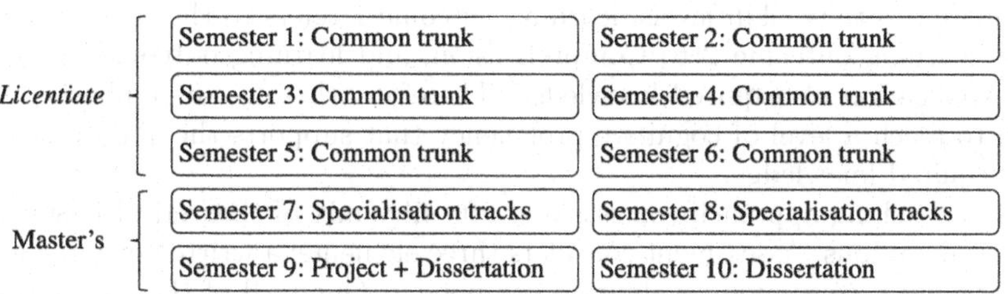


**Fig. 1.** The integrated master's structure

The *licentiate* part correspond to a general training in Informatics Engineering, constituting a common core in which the study plan is essentially composed of mandatory courses. At the master's level, students must choose two specialisation tracks in the fourth year, and carry out a project and dissertation in the fifth. All courses are 5 ECTS, except for the fifth year project (15 ECTS) and the dissertation (45 ECTS).

The Applications Architectures and Interactive Systems courses are part of a specialisation track on Web applications engineering.

[2] European Credit Transfer and Accumulation System.

## 2.2 The Software Systems Development Course

This is a course at *licentiate* level, appearing in the fifth semester of the degree. The course follows on from an introductory Object Oriented Programming course, and aims to provide students with object-oriented modelling skills (in UML [1]) in order to enable them to design and develop applications of a larger scale and complexity.

In terms of the learning outcomes that are intended to be achieved, students should be able to:

1. Characterise the different phases of the Unified Process [6] and related activities;
2. Interpret the different types of UML diagrams;
3. Assess which diagram is the most appropriate according to the different modelling needs;
4. Critically evaluate models (requirements/structural/behavioural) described in UML;
5. Design software systems using UML;
6. Implement software systems based on UML models.

The ACM/IEEE-CS curricula on Software Engineering [8] defines three cognitive skill levels:

- Knowledge: the ability to remember previously learned information
- Comprehension: the ability to understand the information
- Application: the ability to use learned information

Compared to these skill levels, learning outcome 1 refers to the level of Knowledge, learning outcome 2 to Comprehension, and learning outcomes 3 to 6 to the Application of acquired knowledge. Therefore, there is an emphasis on the need to reach a level of cognitive proficiency that supports the ability to apply the acquired knowledge.

The teaching approach consists of a fifty-fifty mix of theoretical lessons and practical sessions. Assessment considers three elements: a written exam, a group project and a continuous evaluation component. One goal of the course is that students develop an application according to the three tier architecture, covering the data, business and user interface layers. While a databases course is being taught in parallel, covering the aspects related to the construction of the data layer, students have no previous exposure to HCI topics.

## 2.3 The Web Applications Engineering Track

As mentioned above, the master's component of the degree is organised into specialisation tracks, each composed of four courses on the track's topic. The Web applications engineering track consists of courses covering from database infrastructures to user interfaces development. Two courses are relevant here: the Applications Architectures (AA) course, which covers the business layer of Web applications (e.g. applications servers, components, services), and the Interactive Systems (SI) course, which covers the user interface layer of Web applications.

In terms of learning outcomes, after the **Interactive Systems course**, students should be able to:

1. design user interfaces with consideration for usability aspects
2. apply model-based approaches to design user interfaces
3. select and apply the most appropriate interface assessment techniques for a given context
4. apply appropriate user interface development techniques
5. develop the user interface layer of applications with support for controlled and independent evolution of the logic and data layers

Students in the **Applications Architectures course** should be able to:

1. know the main structural and behavioural patterns used for software system development
2. know how to design parametrisable software architectures
3. identify the main characteristics of the most commonly used application servers
4. design computational layers that allow controlled and independent evolution of presentation and data layers

The teaching approach consists mainly on practical sessions. In both cases, the emphasis is on developing the capabilities to perform independent work and acquire relevant knowledge independently (the Comprehension and Application skills). Assessment includes a written exam, a group project, shared between both courses, and a continuous evaluation mark, reflecting the students performance during the sessions.

## 3 Human-Centred Concerns

As already mentioned, during the period under analysis the degree lacked a course on Human-Computer Interaction. This had several implications in the courses described above. They are discussed in this section.

### 3.1 Implications in the Software Systems Development Course

Originally, the course was very much focused on modelling and developing the business layer of applications. The success of the course notwithstanding, this created a number of challenges at several levels, namely:

- At the requirements analysis level
- At the design level
- At the implementation level

Additionally, the students' motivation must also be considered.

**Requirements Analysis.** Students faced challenges in focusing on the problem, instead of the solution. Indeed, when discussing requirements, it was easy to quickly get caught on the technical details of an idealised solution, without paying proper attention to the problem under analysis, which typically involved considering the users of the (to be developed) system and their needs.

Additionally, students had difficulties in establishing a clear separation between functional requirements and user interface specifications, which proved to be a very strong constraint. Indeed, given the lack of a user interface design step, it was all too common for students to express user interface related concerns, such as dialogue control, in the use case specifications thus creating too complex and unfocused specifications.

The above points to the need of having a basic knowledge of Human-Computer Interaction, in particular, Human-Centred Development processes. Exploring the links between requirements engineering and HCI techniques will help highlight the role and impact of users in the definition of system requirements. Including an explicit user interface design step, will help separate requirements from the design of a system that satisfies them.

**Design.** Students faced challenges in deriving an architecture for the business logic layer from requirements models. The first step in the approach that was taught was to derive an application programming interface (API) for the business logic layer, starting from the use case specifications. This API needs to adequately support a user interface satisfying the requirements expressed in the use cases. However, without a model of the user interface control logic and an understanding of the specific nature of the user interface layer programming model (e.g. its event-based nature), students faced difficulties deriving this API.

Attempts to use a unified modelling approach to support the process, covering from use cases to business logic, were faced with problems. On the one hand, the step from functional requirements to business logic API, without any intermediating model for the user interface, required making assumptions about how functionalities would be provided to users, since that would have an impact on which operations would be needed at the business logic (e.g. "will undo support be needed?"). On the other hand, since different modelling approaches are better suited for each layer (cf. state machines for expressing dialogue control in the user interface vs. sequence diagrams for expressing cooperation between objects at the business logic layer), expressiveness problems were felt when trying to use a single notation.

The above points to the need to introduce user interface design and, in particular, prototyping, as a means to bridge from functional requirements to the business logic. The goal is to support a process where the business logic API is driven by the needs of the user interface needed to satisfy the identified requirements. This will surely create a smoother process in what concerns the elicitation of the required API, and the correct identification of where the relevant handlers are in the user interface.

**Implementation.** At the level of the implementation, the lack of knowledge of user interface development technologies proved a difficulty when attempting to develop the three tiered implementation that was sought. Although relevant architectural patterns for the user interface layer (e.g. the Model-View Controller pattern [5]) were in fact covered in previous courses, user interface programming models, toolkits and frameworks had no formal coverage. Hence, there was a need to address basic knowledge of user interface programming, from layout management to event-based programming. In this case, Java technologies were used.

**Managing Students' Motivation.** Given the profile of the degree, students attending the course tended to be mainly focused on the technical aspects of software development. This was coupled with limited experience in developing complex software systems, which the course was designed to address. Hence, not only had the students be shown the potential benefits of using a model-based approach in the development of complex software systems. They had also be made aware of the relevance of considering the users during the design and development of such systems.

The group project can play a major role in addressing these challenges. The project presented an opportunity to challenge the students to develop a reasonable complex system in the course of the semester. Additionally, by choosing appropriate themes for the project, it can be used to stress the need to consider user concerns. The goal is to propose topics where user tasks have a reasonable level of complexity, so that students are prompted to consider how best to support them.

A typical example is a system to support electronic prescriptions, since they have to obey a number of rules on how medication can be combined that do not necessarily match the goal of the doctor to prescribe a treatment. One issue, then, is to know who the responsibility of creating valid prescriptions will be shared between user and system.

### 3.2 Implications in the Applications Engineering Track

Although basic knowledge of user interface development (e.g. the notion of usability and notions of rapid prototyping) started being addressed in the Software Systems Development course, the Interactive Systems course of the Applications Engineering track was the first truly HCI course in the degree. This had several implications to that course and the track.

A first tension emerged when defining the syllabus, between covering Human-Centred Development topics vs. covering the technical aspects of (Web-based) user interface programming. On the one hand, technical skills are, of course, needed in order to allow for the project to be carried out, and to support the integration with the other courses in the track. Indeed, as mentioned above, students are already mainly focused on the technical aspects of software development. That said, a confounding factor is the current diversity, and rate of change, of frameworks supporting the development of Web-based user interfaces. They present a challenge, not only because the choice of a specific framework is a decision whose merits might change from year to year, but also because of the continued evolution of any specific framework, which means they are in fact a moving target. This, coupled with a diverse range of previous competences at the technical level by the students, raised further difficulties, making it harder to identify the best approach to cover the technical aspects.

On the other hand, students mostly lacked the Human-Centred Design competences to design and develop quality user interfaces, making it a necessity to cover those topics. Through a number of iterations of the course, the option became to give prominence to Human-Centred Design, with a roughly two-thirds/one-third split. The goal being to make students aware of the need to consider users during the design and development of interactive computing systems, and provide them with the fundamental skills to do so.

Two complementary approaches were used to put the above into practice. More guided lectures on the HCD part, focusing on HCI fundamentals, task analysis, prototyping and expert inspection methods. Tutorial based lectures, allowing students to progress at their own pace, on the programming technologies related part. Additionally, students were free to use their Web technology of choice in the group project, with concrete frameworks being introduced as examples in the tutorials (e.g., Bootstrap[3] and Vue.js[4]). A tutorials based approach has the additional advantage of making it easier to adapt to new technologies or the evolution of the ones used.

With regard to the Applications Architectures course, we attempted to make up for this lack of knowledge about HCI processes and principles by resorting to the construction of low-fidelity prototypes, focusing particularly on the identification of the call points to the business layer API.

## 4 Concluding Remarks

We have illustrated the relevance of an HCI perspective on a software engineering degree. Decisions regarding the design of the user interface can have serious implications on the implementation of the whole system, not just the user interface implementation. Even in the case of non-interactive systems, input from the HCI body of knowledge can help in understanding the impact of the system in the overall context, when this context involves humans.

In practice, however, reconciling the two views on development becomes difficult. This can be attributed to a number of factors. We highlight the following two:

- different views on where the development focus lies – Software Engineering is mainly interested in solving the technical difficulties faced when implementing a given functionality; HCI is mainly about solving the problem of which

[3] https://getbootstrap.com, last visited November 15, 2021.
[4] https://vuejs.org, last visited November 15, 2021.

functionality should be provided, and how to optimise the way in which it is provided to users;
- communication difficulties – not always the same terms are used to describe the same concepts in the two communities, this hinders communication; at best it can slow it down, and at worst it can be misleading, with the two parties thinking that they are talking about the same thing when in fact they are not. This is particularly relevant in a teaching context, since concepts need to be presented in a clear and non confusing way.

Partly as a result of the experience with these courses, the decision was made to create a new *licentiate*-level course on Human-Computer Interaction. This new course will free up the master's level course to address more advanced topics, but means the tension between HCD methodology and programming technology will now be transferred to a course were students have less background.

In order to balance them, it is relevant to understand how the current approach fairs. Through informal interviews and questionnaires it was possible to clearly identify two groups of students. Those with some previous knowledge of Web programming technologies, tended to feel that the lectures were too guided and would like more room for exploration. Those without that previous knowledge, tended to prefer a more guided approach. These results point to two very different perspectives. Considering the profile of the students in the new course, a more guided approach seems favourable. The issue remains of how to establish a balance between HCD and user interface programming.

A pilot study was also carried out, applying the Usability Experience Questionnaire (UEQ) [7] to asses the tutorials, in the latest edition of the course. While, preliminary results pointed to a somewhat neutral to positive evaluation of the experience of using the tutorials, the number of responses (37) was too small to allow confidence in the results. One relevant question is whether this is the best approach to evaluate the students' experience with the tutorials and their value as a learning tool. There were indications of relevant inconsistencies in some the answers that raise questions at this level.

Overall, the expectation is to have a split between HCD and user interface programming topics that will be closer to fifty-fifty. The rationale is that students will need more guidance in the programming part. It should be possible to achieve this balance with minimal impact on the HCD topics, since *licentiate* courses have 33% more contact hours when compared to master's courses, which reply more heavily on independent work by the students. At the master's level, the goal is now to address more advanced topics in the engineering of interfaces, in particular related to the development of safety critical interactive systems.

## References

1. Arlow, J., Neustadt, I.: UML 2.0 and The Unified Process: Practical Object-Oriented Analysis and Design, 2nd edn. Addison-Wesley Professional, Boston (2005)
2. Directorate General for Education, Youth, Sport and Culture: ECTS users' guide 2015. European Commission (2015)

3. ISO: ISO 9241-210:2019 Ergonomics of human-system interaction - part 210: human-centred design for interactive systems. International Organization for Standardization
4. John, B., Bass, L., Adams, R.J.: Communication across the HCI/SE divide: ISO 13407 and the Rational Unified Process. In: Stephanidis, C. (ed.) Proceedings of the Tenth International Conference on Human-Computer Interaction, pp. 484–488 (2003)
5. Krasner, G., Pope, S.: A description of the model-view-controller user interface paradigm in the smalltalk-80 system. J. Object Oriented Program. **1**(3), 26–49 (1988)
6. Kruchten, P.: The Rational Unified Process, 3rd edn. Addison-Wesley Professional, Boston (2004)
7. Schrepp, M.: User experience questionnaire handbook (2019). https://www.ueq-online.org/Material/Handbook.pdf
8. The Joint Task Force on Computing Curricula: Software Engineering 2014: curriculum guidelines for undergraduate degree programs in software engineering. Technical report, ACM & IEEE-Computer Society, New York, NY, USA (2015)

# Teaching End-User Development in the Time of IoT and AI

Fabio Paternò[✉]

HIIS Laboratory, CNR-ISTI, Via Moruzzi 1, 56124 Pisa, Italy
fabio.paterno@isti.cnr.it

**Abstract.** The combination of the Internet of Things (IoT) and Artificial Intelligence (AI) has made it possible to introduce numerous automations in our daily environments. Many new interesting possibilities and opportunities have been enabled, but there are also risks and problems. Often these problems originated from approaches that have not been able to consider the users' viewpoint sufficiently. We need to empower people in order to actually understand the automations in their surroundings environments, modify them, and create new ones, even if they have no programming knowledge. It is thus important that the curricula of programs in several disciplines (artificial intelligence, computer science, human-computer interaction, psychology, design, …) discuss these problems and some possible solutions able to provide people with the possibility to control and create their daily automations. In this paper I propose a possible way to organise and structure teaching of the concepts, methods and tools for this purpose, and which can be adopted in the relevant curricula.

**Keywords:** Internet of things · End-user development · Tailoring environments · Trigger-action programming

## 1 Introduction

The main technological trends of recent years have been the Internet of Things and Artificial Intelligence. Their combination has made it possible to introduce numerous automations that can manifest themselves in different ways in our daily environments. Many new possibilities and opportunities have been created, but also risks and problems. Often these problems originated from approaches that have not been able to consider the human point of view sufficiently. In particular, the user has often been considered as a passive element with respect to the new possibilities instead of being the central subject. People in their lives often have dynamic needs, which sometimes stem from episodes, even unpredictable ones. The most effective automations are often the ones that can be dynamically customized and created to meet these changing and different needs that only the users know completely. Thus, we need to empower people in order to actually understand the automations active in their surrounding environments, modify them, and create new ones, even if they have no particular programming knowledge [13].


Published by Springer Nature Switzerland AG 2022
C. Ardito et al. (Eds.): INTERACT 2021, LNCS 13198, pp. 257–269, 2022.
https://doi.org/10.1007/978-3-030-98388-8_23

For such reasons it is of paramount importance that designers and developers be aware of such issues and of some possible solutions to provide people with the ability to control and create their daily automations. Thus, it is important that they are trained in courses aiming to allow attendees to gain knowledge and skills in addressing problems and solutions involved in end-user creation, control, monitoring, debugging automations that can be deployed in daily environments (such as home, office, shops, industries, …). Such courses should provide a discussion of the possible solutions in terms of concepts, techniques, and tools, with particular attention to those supporting the trigger-action paradigm. The courses should discuss how to enable people who are not professional developers to indicate the various dynamic events and conditions that can occur in their contexts of use (considering aspects related to user, technology, environment), and the possible associated actions.

These types of topics are interesting for courses in several areas: computer science, engineering, digital humanities, human-computer interaction. In general, such topics are to be aimed at those who want to understand the issues involved in introducing automations in daily environments, and the corresponding possible solutions that can empower end users in controlling, modifying and creating new ones. In case of research students, they allow participants to understand the relevant state of art in order to think about novel solutions in this area. Thus, there should not be any particular prerequisites for attending such courses. Some basic knowledge of Internet of Things technologies would make them easier to follow, but all the relevant concepts should be introduced in such a way to be understandable also to those who are not familiar with them.

The next sections present a description of the recommended content for such courses that is based on my personal experience in teaching them at the Digital Humanities degree of University of Pisa, and in tutorials at mayor HCI international conferences, as well as in the research work carried out for several years in relevant areas in national and international projects.

## 2 Content

The content for this type of course can be structured into four main parts: introduction, trigger-action programming, tailoring tools, intelligent services. The initial one should provide some background information and explain the motivations for addressing such topics. Thus, it should introduce the main current technological trends (internet of things and artificial intelligence) with their potentialities and risks, and end-user development, and explain why it can be useful to mitigate such risks. The next part should be dedicated to trigger-action programming, which is the programming paradigm that seems most relevant when considering contexts of use characterised by the presence of numerous connected objects and devices, with the need of tailoring the automations involving them according to the dynamic events that can occur. The various possible compositional styles to create the trigger-action rules need to be introduced with example of tools for each of them. Thus, the various compositional styles are described: visual data flow, wizard-like, block-based, and conversational. The forth part can be dedicated to introducing additional support that can increase the possibilities of the tailoring environments. Thus, in this part it is possible to introduce the role of intelligent recommendations in this context, for example while people are creating trigger-action rules. Another important relevant topic is how to provide explanations that allow end users to understand why or why not a certain rule can be executed in a given context of use. One further aspect that is important to consider is also issues and possibilities that are available when deploying in real world platforms for executing such rules, and how to monitor their behaviour. Table 1 provides a summary of the course content.

**Table 1.** Possible course structure

| Subject |
|---|
| Introduction course |
| The technological trends (IoT + AI) |
| The dark side of intelligent automations |
| Trigger-action programming |
| Automation specification exercise |
| Environments for end user creation of automations |
| Real world deployment, execution, monitoring |
| Exercise with tool for end user automation creation |
| Intelligent automation recommendations |
| Explainable automations |
| Augmented reality support for serendipitous creation |
| Final discussion |

## 2.1 Introduction

This type of course should start with an introduction to the main current technological trends (internet of things and artificial intelligence). For this purpose, it can be useful to report current forecasts[1] that indicate how in the next years we expect that the number of connected objects populating our homes, cars, working environments will be continuously increasing while the number of devices (smartphones, laptops, PCs) will only increase slightly. Artificial intelligence will be exploited more and more in this context in order to create automations based on the data that can be collected. However, the following will include a discussion of the problems end users encounter when their viewpoint is not considered (see for example the study reported in [18]), such as the learning system fails to understand user intent or the system's behaviour is hard to understand. Thus, one of the main challenges in the coming years is how to obtain tools that allow users to control and configure smart environments consisting of hundreds of interconnected devices, objects, and appliances, tools that allow people to obtain "*humanations*": automations that users can understand, monitor, and modify.

[1] https://www.statista.com/statistics/1101442/iot-number-of-connected-devices-worldwide/.

At this point there should be a brief introduction to end-user development, its importance to empower people to customize their applications, the main approaches in terms of metaphors and programming styles that have been considered, and the aspects that have to be addressed in order to provide effective solutions. Various generations of contributions based on main technological trends (graphical desktop, Web, Mobile, …) have been put forward in this area over time. The last generation aims to empower users to exploit ecosystems of smart things characterised by the presence of various types of sensors and actuators.

## 2.2 Trigger-Action Programming

The trigger-action programming paradigm [1, 3, 7, 8] is suitable for end-user development because of its compact and intuitive structure, and it is relevant for the Internet of Things characterised by the presences of a multitude of sensors and actuators, since it connects the dynamic events and/or conditions with the expected reactions. It is relevant also because it does not require the use of complex programming structures or particular algorithmic abilities. This approach has been used in several domains, such as home [17], ambient assisted living [102], robots [9], finance [5]. In particular, it should be explained that triggers represent situations/events that are relevant to the users and may relate to their emotional or physical state, or the surrounding environment or available devices or applications. Trigger information is derived from various sensors (for example, movement, proximity, light, noise, breathing, heartbeat, …) and applications and services. Actions represent what the objects, device, applications available are able to do. For example, they can control objects (such as turning on/off lights, opening/closing doors, activating TV/radio), or activate reminders, alarms, user interface changes. The triggers can be composed of events and/or conditions. In this discussion it should also be introduced the aspects that sometimes are unclear for end users [1, 8] when they have to approach automations in internet of things scenarios. For example, sometimes it is not immediate to distinguish between events and conditions. Failure to understand the distinction between events and conditions can cause unwanted behaviours (e.g. opening a door at the wrong time or turning on the heater when it is not needed). For example, these two rules have different effects (and in one case it can be rather annoying):

- When I get home the bell rings
- If I'm at home the bell rings

Thus, it is useful to explain that an event happens in a point in time: when user enters a room, when it starts to rain, when kitchen temperature exceeds 30°, at 8 o'clock. While a condition is a state that lasts for a longer period of time: while user is inside a room, as long as it's raining, if kitchen temperature is over 30°, between 8:00 and 11:30. When writing the rules, the use of different keywords helps to differentiate them. Thus, often "WHEN" is used for events, and "IF" or "WHILE" are used for indicating conditions. Other useful trigger operators can be introduced for specific cases. There are rules that are triggered if an event does not occur in a specific interval of time (e.g. when medicine has not been taken between 10 a.m. and 11 a.m.). In other cases, there are rules that are triggered when a specific ordered sequence of events occurs (e.g. "When the user enters a room and then he exits"; or "When the temperature becomes more than 20 degrees and then the humidity level becomes more than 50%") or when an event occurs a specified number of times (event iteration), e.g. "When the user goes to the bathroom 5 times during the night".

It is possible to compose events and conditions through logical or temporal operators (although it may not be immediate to understand the result) [8]. In particular, the composition of an event and a condition is an event that should occur when the condition is verified. The composition of two events is still an event but is an event with a very low probability, since it is unlikely that two events can happen at the same time. The composition of two conditions is something more frequent since it indicates the intersection of the times when the two conditions are verified.

The actions too have a temporal dimension [8], which can be classified in instantaneous (e.g. send email), extended (e.g. brew coffee), and sustained (e.g. turn the light on). In some cases, the temporal aspects of both triggers and actions can generate some ambiguity. For example, if we consider the rule.

*IF I am at home DO send email to John.*

We have a condition as a trigger, which means something that is verified for some time, and an instantaneous action. This can be interpreted in two ways: one is that the action should be performed multiple times as long as the condition is true, the other one, more realistic in this case, is that the action should be performed once. One further potential ambiguity can occur when combining a condition and a sustained action. For example:

*IF time is between 8 and 11:30 pm, DO turn on the living room light.*

What should happen after 11.30? If users express interest for a similar rule, probably they expect that the light should be on in the indicated period of time but then it should be switched off.

When writing automations in trigger-action format, which can be considered personalization rules, there can be different styles [4]: device-centric, a personalization whose subject is the physical medium with which it is executed (e.g. "when the motion sensor in the kitchen becomes active"); information-centric, a personalization whose subject is the underlying information, regardless of the physical medium with which it is manipulated; people-centric, a personalization where users, their actions, and/or feelings are at the center of the interaction, independently of any physical and virtual medium (e.g. "when I enter the bedroom").

At this point, the participants should be asked to actually write some examples of automations with different complexity in natural language in pairs (one trigger and one action, two triggers and one actions, two triggers and two actions …). During this exercise it should be discussed together the rules created, and how well they specify the desired behaviour in order to allow participants to better understand possible ambiguities and problems in their execution.

### 2.3 Environments for End-User Creation of Automations

Once the basic concepts have been introduced, it is possible to present the possible approaches for supporting the composition of automation rules, and then examples of specific tools. Tailoring environments can guide the rule development process through different approaches:

- Data flow (focused on how information goes through the various parts)
- Wizards (aiming to drive users by limiting their possible selections)
- Visual blocks (Using visual cues to suggest possible compositions)
- Conversational (exploiting natural language and AI support)

Node RED[2] is an example of the data flow approach; it supports the creation of nodes and flows for connecting together objects and online services. It includes many pre-defined nodes. The user will have to define some behaviours, which requires writing some JavaScript code.

Probably, the best-known example of the wizard approach is IFTTT[3]. It is a Web and mobile environment that allows users to create and share rules, called «applets», in the form if trigger then action. Triggers and actions can be chosen from existing services (for example, Facebook, Evernote, Weather, Dropbox, etc.). In 2017 it was estimated that 320,000 applets involving 400 service providers were installed more than 20 million times. Services are peripherals, hubs, wearable devices, devices in the car, online services, social networks, messaging,... IFTTT developers have recently changed their business model. Now, there is a limited version for free that can be used to create at most three applets, and then there is an IFTTT Pro version, which can be used by paying a subscription fee, which supports multiple features (multi-step, conditional logic, queries, filter code, multi-action). In general, IFTTT suffers from some limitations. It does not distinguish between events and conditions, it is not easy to extend the list of the connected applications, and it shows long lists of potential channels to compose where it is easy to get lost.

Another example of wizard-like tool is TARE (the Trigger-Action Rule Editor)[4], which is part of a more general platform for supporting creation, execution, and monitoring of personalization rules (TAREME [11]). In order to help users to find the relevant triggers and actions, they are organised in a hierarchical structure with the main categories at the top level, and then more specific elements are detailed. The triggers are classified according to three main contextual aspects (see Fig. 1): users (for example associated with physiological or emotional aspects or their activities), environments (for aspects such as noise, light, temperature), and technology (associated with the available devices and appliances). The actions can be reminders, alarms, or effects on appliances or devices and their functionalities. On the left side there is also an interactive sidebar that indicates what has been done and what should be done to complete the creation of the rule, while on the top part there is a natural language description of the rule being edited.

---

[2] https://nodered.org/.

[3] https://ifttt.com/create.

[4] https://tare.isti.cnr.it/RuleEditor/login.

When selecting the triggers, users are explicitly asked to indicate whether it should be an event or a condition in order to make them more aware of the difference.

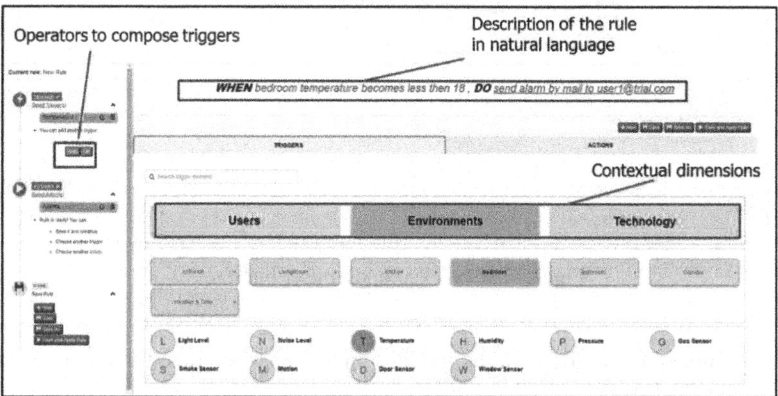


**Fig. 1.** The TARE user interface.

The block-based approach aims to apply the puzzle metaphor in the composition process of the automations. This type of metaphor has been long considered in the end-user development area starting from the Scratch[5] project first, and then the App Inventor[6] environment for developing mobile apps. Potentially, it can stimulate more creative, easy, satisfying, engaging experiences. It is used in several domains, such as education, IoT, industrial robotics. There are libraries, such as Google Blockly, that facilitate its implementation in specific tools. In this area, the puzzle elements should be designed in such a way that their shapes drive the process of creating rules structured in terms of triggers and actions. An example contribution in this area is BlockComposer[7] [14]. The user interface of this tool has three main parts (see Fig. 2).

On the left side there is the list of elements available for creating the rules, in the central part there is the main working area where the puzzle associated to the rule should be composed, and in the right side there is an area where recommendations of possible useful and relevant elements are presented. Thus, the rule block has two separate sections, one for inserting trigger blocks, one for action blocks. The "trigger" blocks are blue, and the "action" ones are green. The same colour is used for the part of the "rule" block indicating where triggers and actions can be inserted. Blocks that define the composition and the behaviours of triggers and actions (such as and/or/not operators, group and parallel) use the same colour with a different saturation level. To make clear the distinction between events and conditions, a modal window is shown every time a user selects a trigger type block. In both cases, an appropriate icon, a description of the temporality it models, and two possible cases are shown. The different representations

[5] http://scratch.mit.edu.
[6] http://appinventor.mit.edu/explore/.
[7] https://giove.isti.cnr.it/demo/pat/.

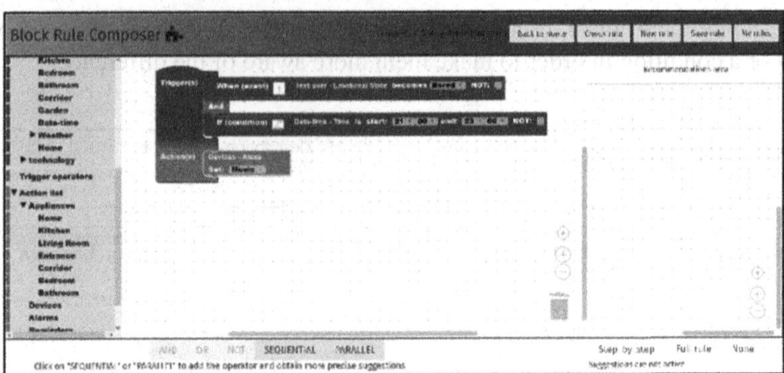

**Fig. 2.** The blockcomposer user interface

used for events and conditions in the modal window are then maintained on the trigger blocks in the workspace.

The conversational approach seems relevant and interesting to support the specification of flexible automations in trigger-action format since it allows people to indicate the desired automation through natural language. However, the conversation should be able to remove possible ambiguities and allow the users to indicate precisely the desired effects. RuleBot[8] [6] is an example of conversational agent dedicated to supporting the end user in creating automations in environments populated by sensors and smart objects, with the ability to manage multiple triggers and actions, and clearly distinguish between events and conditions, which was not supported by previous solutions. It has been implemented with DialogFlow, and is able to perform a conversation with the user thanks to the use of machine learning and natural language processing techniques, and can manage the creation of personalization rules even starting from complex inputs. Figure 3 shows an example of conversation in Italian, where the chatbot asks the user for input, the answer is that if at 9 he has not taken the medicine then a message should be sent him to remember it. At this point the chatbot asks the user for the text that should be used in the remainder.

Some initial studies [6] aiming at comparing the usability of the different compositional styles found that with the wizard style, where the user is guided in performing the relevant interactions, it is easy and fast to create simple rules, but creating more complex and elaborate rules may become long and tedious. Moreover, the chatbot requires first sometime before users get used to how the tool expects them to indicate the automations, in particular the types of natural language expressions that it is able to elaborate immediately, and then it becomes direct and efficient in understanding and activating the requested rules. In general, the performance of a chatbot depends on how the associated intents have been modelled, and the level of training received.

**Real World Deployment.** In order to make the discussion more concrete and interesting, examples of deployments of these types of tools in real world should be provided. In

8 https://africa.isti.cnr.it/.

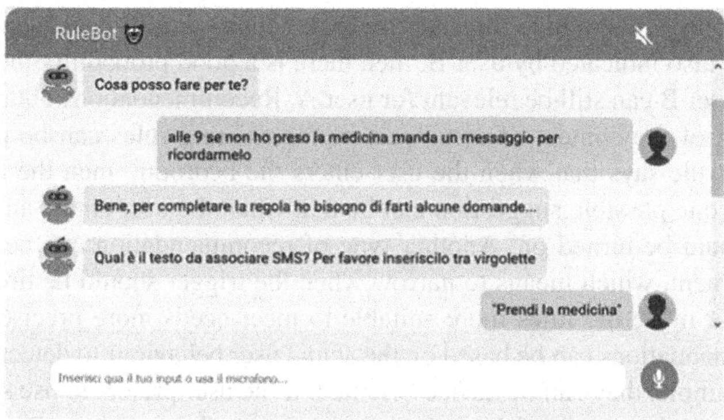


**Fig. 3.** The rulebot user interface

this way it is possible to better understand the possible issues and advantages in deploying this approach in real cases studies. For example, some real experiences have been carried out in the PETAL European project, which aims to support remote older adults assistance through personalisation rules specified by caregivers or the older adults themselves. A number of trials have been carried out for some months with a personalization platform deployed in the homes of older adults with mild cognitive impairments, and some tools have been proposed to monitor when the rules have been created, activated and executed [11]. Another experience was carried out with a students' home, which was equipped with a number of sensors and appliances, and it showed some possible conflicts that can occur amongst rules created by different inhabitants of the same apartment [2]. Further experiences with small families have been recently reported [15]. Results and issues in such experiences can provide useful insights to understand how to deploy and use tools for personalising automations in general. In this context, it can also be useful to review the various social needs that such automations can help users to address (such as security, safety, well-being, health, energy saving, sociality) by providing specific examples.

Then, course participants should be asked to specify some automations in the form event/condition/action, with at least two rules including at least two triggers, and each rule should refer to different contextual aspects, by using two different visual tools publicly available on the Web (e.g. IFTTT and TAREME). In this way, they can take direct experience on these types of tools, and discuss possible advantages and disadvantages.

## 2.4 Intelligent Support

Intelligent support can be introduced in several ways in the process of creating automations. One is the use of recommendations. Rule editing is a process comprised of multiple steps, where appropriate suggestions should consider what has already been inserted. Beginners can benefit from being guided to discover the tailoring environment being used by seeing the structure of the rules and the possible next steps to take in order to complete the editing process. Advanced users can discover new possibilities on their own. There are various possible types of recommendations relevant in trigger-action programming. In collaborative filtering the basic idea is that if user A has specified a rule, which is also indicated by user B, then there is a good probability that other rules specified by user B can still be relevant for user A. Recommendations obtained through generalization of the content of some part of the existing rules can be possible. For example: if a rule says that when the user enters the bedroom, then the lights should be turned on, one possible suggestion can be that when the user enters any room, then the lights should be turned on. Another type of recommendation can be obtained by trigger refinement, which means to narrow when the trigger should be fired by adding conditions that make the rules more suitable to meet needs more precisely specified. Other recommendations can be based on the actual user behaviour to detect their preferences. For example, they can be device-oriented: if the user prefers to use some specific device, then it can be meaningful to suggest rules that exploit it, for example for sending alarms. One further aspect is to have location-dependent recommendations, which aim to provide suggestions when the users are in a specific area that they seem to prefer. There are also time-oriented recommendations, which are rules with triggers associated with specific periods of the day, when the user is more inclined to receive information (e.g. reminders).

BlockComposer supports two policies in recommendations while users create rules: step-by-step in which the tool provides suggestions for the next element to include in the rule under editing; or full rule, in which complete rules are suggested. It exploits a data set of rules publicly available[9], and the generation of the recommendations is based on the use of compact prediction trees. RuleSelector [16] follows an approach where a set of rules are proposed based on the user behaviour detected through the smartphone sensors, from which the user can select the most relevant. The rules are proposed based on some metrics, for example, by applying confidence measures of the likelihood of the user performing action a when the context descriptors in the pre-condition frequent context itemset are true. Trace2TAP [19] is a different solution aiming to combine trigger-action programming and automated learning. For this purpose, it takes as input traces of user behaviour, and automatically generates rules that could automate a good portion of the observed instances of human actions. It clusters rules based on the similarity of their actuations, and ranks both clusters and the rules within each cluster based on a number of relevant characteristics.

At this point it can be useful to propose an exercise with the students concerning the various criteria to consider for determining the rules to recommend, how to present such recommendations, and the effectiveness of the different modalities for presenting such recommendations.

Another aspect where the intelligent support can be useful is in helping users to understand whether the rules created actually perform the desired behaviour. For example, when multiple rules are created for a given context of use it can happen that there are conflicts, which means that different rules at the same time indicate to perform in different ways a certain object. For this purpose, previous work [12] has proposed to provide visual representations of the state of the relevant contextual aspects, and automatically generate explanations of why or why not a given rule can be performed in that context. In this context the XAI question bank proposed for explainable AI [10] seems relevant

[9] https://github.com/andrematt/trigger_action_rules.

since it provides a set of important questions that indicate many aspects that users often need to understand when looking at some automatic intelligent system.

Lastly, intelligent support can be useful to provide serendipitous support in creating, monitoring, and modifying automations in daily environments. In this perspective, smartphone-based augmented reality can play an important role. Indeed, it would avoid using special devices that many do not have and provide the possibility of direct interaction with the object of interest, monitoring nearby automations while moving, and the ability to select a real object directly and know the automations that involve it, add new automations, or modify existing automations. For this purpose, it can be useful to exploit object detection, which is a computer vision technique that has undergone significant improvement over the last years with the development of Convolutional Neural Networks (CNN) for the estimation of the position and class of the various objects that are present in an image.

The last part of the course can be dedicated to discussing with the participants the various concepts and tools presented, and also to analyse together whether other design aspects should be considered, and it can be concluded with a short discussion of a research agenda for this area.

## 3 Practical Work

It is important to highlight that practical work is important in order to acquire and consolidate the proposed concepts. There can be at least two types of interactive exercises, and a final discussion session. In the first exercise participants in pairs write for example five examples of automations in natural language, with different complexity and structure:

- Elementary trigger + elementary action
- Elementary trigger (including the NOT operator) + composed action
- Composed trigger (event + condition) + elementary action
- Composed trigger (conditon + condition) + composed action
- Composed Trigger (event + condition) + composed action

During this exercise participants can discuss together the rules specified and how well they specify the desired behaviour in order to allow participants to better understand possible ambiguities and problems in their execution.

Once the tools for creating rules have been introduced, participants should be asked to specify four automations in the form event/condition/action, with at least two rules including at least two triggers, and each rule should refer to different contextual aspects, by using two different visual tools publicly available on the Web (e.g. IFTTT and TAREME). In this way they can take direct experience on this type of tools and discuss possible advantages and disadvantages.

A third exercise can be focused on the possible criteria to automatically recommend possible relevant automations. Thus, the students should think about and discuss what data should be used for this purpose, and which criteria should be applied to select the most relevant automations to recommend. They should also discuss and indicate possible effective ways of presenting such recommendations.

The final discussion should aim to summarise the main relevant concepts and receive feedback from the participants on to what extent they are able to apply them in designing automations for the contexts that are interesting for them.

## 4 Conclusions

In modern training of designers, engineers, AI specialists, it is fundamental to assimilate a number of concepts, methods, and tools that can be useful to empower people to control the many connected objects and devices that they can encounter at home, work, and while moving.

In this paper I indicate a set of concepts, methods and exercises that can be useful for this purpose. They have been derived from my teaching experience and research work. There are also indications of examples of publicly available tools that can be useful in the teaching activities.

**Acknowledgments.** This work is partially supported by the Italian Ministry of University and Research (MUR) under grant PRIN 2017 "EMPATHY: EMpowering People in deAling with internet of THings ecosYstems".

## References

1. Brackenbury, W., et al.: How users interpret bugs in trigger-action programming. In: CHI, p. 552 (2019)
2. Corcella, L., Manca, M., Paternò, F.: Personalizing a student home behaviour. In: Barbosa, S., Markopoulos, P., Paternò, F., Stumpf, S., Valtolina, S. (eds.) IS-EUD 2017. LNCS, vol. 10303, pp. 18–33. Springer, Cham (2017). https://doi.org/10.1007/978-3-319-58735-6_2
3. Corno, F., De Russis, L., Monge Roffarello, A.: Empowering end users in debugging trigger-action rules. In: CHI 388 (2019)
4. Corno, F., De Russis, L., Monge Roffarello, A.: Devices, information, and people: abstracting the internet of things for end-user personalization. In: Fogli, D., Tetteroo, D., Barricelli, B.R., Borsci, S., Markopoulos, P., Papadopoulos, G.A. (eds.) IS-EUD 2021. LNCS, vol. 12724, pp. 71–86. Springer, Cham (2021). https://doi.org/10.1007/978-3-030-79840-6_5
5. Elsden, C., Feltwell, T., Lawson, S., Vines, J.: Vines: recipes for programmable money. In: CHI, p. 251 (2019)
6. Gallo, S., Manca, M., Mattioli, A., Paternò, F., Santoro, C.: Comparative analysis of composition paradigms for personalization rules in iot settings. In: Fogli, D., Tetteroo, D., Barricelli, B.R., Borsci, S., Markopoulos, P., Papadopoulos, G.A. (eds.) IS-EUD 2021. LNCS, vol. 12724, pp. 53–70. Springer, Cham (2021). https://doi.org/10.1007/978-3-030-79840-6_4
7. Ghiani, G., Manca, M., Paternò, F., Santoro, C.: Personalization of context-dependent applications through trigger-action rules. ACM Trans. Comput. Hum. Interact. **24**(2), 1–33 (2017)
8. Huang, H., Cakmak, M.: Supporting mental model accuracy in trigger-action programming. In: Proceedings of the 2015 ACM International Joint Conference on Pervasive and Ubiquitous Computing (UbiComp 2015), pp. 215–225 (2015)
9. Leonardi, N., Manca, M., Paternò, F., Santoro, C.: Trigger-action programming for personalising humanoid robot behaviour. In: ACM Conference on Human Factors in Computing Systems (CHI 2019), Glasgow, p. 445 (2019)

10. Liao, Q.V., Gruen, D., Miller, S.: Questioning the AI: informing design practices for explainable AI user experiences. In: CHI (2020)
11. Manca, M., Paternò, F., Santoro, C.: Remote monitoring of end-user created automations in field trials. J. Ambient Intell. Humaniz. Comput. (2021). https://doi.org/10.1007/s12652-021-03239-0
12. Manca, M., Paternò, F., Santoro, C., Corcella, L.: Supporting end-user debugging of trigger-action rules for IoT applications. Int. J. Hum. Comput. Stud. **123**, 56–69 (2019)
13. Markopoulos, P., Nichols, J., Paternò, F., Pipek, V.: End-user development for the internet of things. ACM Trans. Comput. Hum. Interact. (TOCHI) **24**(2), 1–3 (2017)
14. Mattioli, A., Paternò, F.: A visual environment for end-user creation of IoT customization rules with recommendation support. In: International Conference on Advanced Visual Interfaces (AVI 2020) (2020). https://doi.org/10.1145/3399715.3399833
15. Salovaara, A., Bellucci, A., Vianello, A., Jacucci, G.: Programmable smart home toolkits should better address households' social needs. In: CHI Conference on Human Factors in Computing Systems (CHI 2021), May 8–13, Yokohama, Japan, p. 14. ACM, New York, NY, USA (2021)
16. Srinivasan, V., Koehler, C., Jin, H.: Ruleselector: selecting conditional action rules from user behavior patterns. Proc. ACM Interact. Mob. Wearable Ubiquitous Technol. **2**(1), 1–34 (2018)
17. Ur, B., McManus, E., Ho, M.P.Y., Littman, M.L.: Practical trigger-action programming in the smart home. CHI **2014**, 803–812 (2014)
18. Yang, R., Newman, M.W.: Learning from a learning thermostat: lessons for intelligent systems for the home. In: 2013 ACM international joint conference on Pervasive and ubiquitous computing, pp. 93–102 (2013)
19. Zhang, L., et al.: Trace2TAP: synthesizing trigger-action programs from traces of behavior. Proc. ACM Interact. Mob. Wearable Ubiquitous Technol. **4**(3), 1–26 (2020). https://doi.org/10.1145/3411838

# Teaching Human-Computer Interaction in the Software Engineering Master's Degree Program of the University Grenoble Alpes

Sybille Caffiau(✉) and Laurence Nigay

Univ. Grenoble Alpes, CNRS, Grenoble INP, LIG, 38000 Grenoble, France
{Sybille.Caffiau,Laurence.Nigay}@univ-grenoble-alpes.fr

**Abstract.** The training of the Master's degree in software engineering of the University Grenoble Alpes covers foundational courseware in computer science (programming, complexity, database, networks, interactive systems) during the first year and more advanced engineering courses (in terms of cloud computing, large-scale data management, architecture, program testing and verification) during the second year. This paper focuses on two HCI courses as part of this curriculum in software engineering, and describes the content and the pedagogical approach we implemented for teaching HCI to computer science students. The paper explains why the authors adopt a tool-based approach for the first-year course on engineering HCI and a project-based approach with experimental evaluation for the second-year course on advanced interaction including multimodality.

**Keywords:** Software engineering · Human-Computer Interaction · User-centered design · Multimodality · Augmented reality · Education

## 1 Introduction

The Master's degree in software engineering at the University of Grenoble Alpes welcomes students with a Bachelor's Degree (three years) in either Computer Science or Computer Engineering with courses in computing and practice in programming. This Master's degree responds to a very strong demand in the job market (including the numerous software firms in the Grenoble region – ATOS, CAPGEMINI, KELKOO, etc.) on software development and management. Nearly all the students (>95%) obtained permanent employment as developers, architects, analysts and project managers (after few years) before the final defense of their 24-week internship of the second year. Very few students (less than one per year) are starting a PhD after receiving this Master's diploma.

In this context, as teachers in Human-Computer Interaction (HCI) within a software engineering program, our goal is to train the students to have specific skills related to the design and development of interactive software systems.


Published by Springer Nature Switzerland AG 2022
C. Ardito et al. (Eds.): INTERACT 2021, LNCS 13198, pp. 270–278, 2022.
https://doi.org/10.1007/978-3-030-98388-8_24

During the last year (before the 24-week internship), such HCI skills are put into practice as part of a unifying multidisciplinary large project managed by a group of teachers including an HCI teacher. The goal of the project made by groups of students is to design, develop and evaluate a commercial website. The pedagogical goal is to apply taught concepts, methods and tools of three domains: Agile Software Engineering, Distributed Systems and Human-Computer Interaction (HCI).

The HCI skills are taught through three dedicated courses. One course is on programming interactive systems, including event-based programming, automata, design patterns and toolkits. Because this course focuses on software design and development, it is more easily well perceived by the future software engineers than the two other courses. The paper focuses on these two other HCI courses of the Master's program that are given after the course on programming interactive systems (Fig. 1). One course is given during the first year and focuses on user-centered design and development of interactive systems. The second one is given after the previous one during the second year of the Master's program: the course focuses on advanced interaction techniques beyond standard graphical user interfaces (WIMP). The identified difficulty for these two courses is to motivate the students to understand the users, their tasks and contexts when using the system that they designed and developed. Based on the teaching experience of the authors, the paper outlines the approaches to overcome this difficulty.

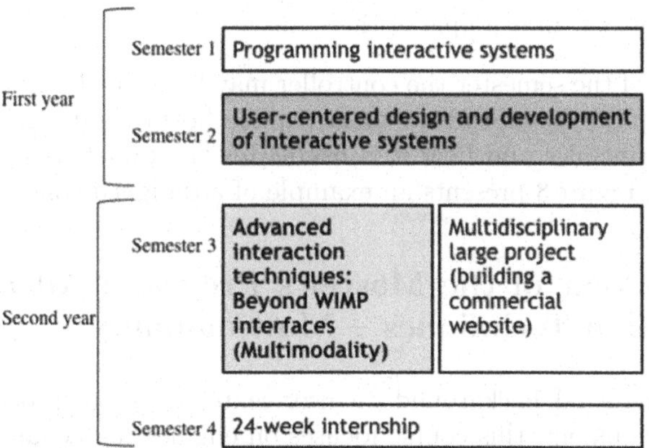


**Fig. 1.** The HCI courses within the Master's program in software engineering of the University of Grenoble Alpes.

The paper is structured as follows: Sect. 2 describes the approach for the first year Master's course on user-centered design and development of interactive systems and Sect. 3 presents the approach for the course during the second year on advanced interaction techniques beyond WIMP interfaces. Finally, we present concluding remarks on the smooth articulation of these two courses within the Master's program on software engineering.

## 2 First Year of the Master's Program: User-Centered Design and Development

The course is organized along the steps of a user-centered design approach. The goal of this course is to understand the conceptual foundations, models and notations in HCI that are necessary to any practitioner involved in the design, implementation and evaluation of useful and usable interactive systems (Table 1).

For each design step, exercises are performed using software tools when available. For instance, for task modeling, the tool K-MADe is used to produce task models [2], for evaluation, the students use usability testing tools (such as https://www.optimalworkshop.com or https://interfacemetrics.aalto.fi).

In addition to the exercises to illustrate each part of the course, a project is conducted. 5-student groups have to design a controller to drive a kart in a kart racing game. To design this controller, teachers provide:

- the functional core of a game: a kart racing game. The students must design and develop the controller of SuperTuxKart kart racing game. The set of commands and the output device (a screen) are fixed. The game and its commands are described at https://ihm2019.afihm.org/#challenge.html;
- Three answers of three potential users (a grandfather, a 7-year-old child and a roommate student) to the question D̈o you ever play video games such as kart racing? ẗo start the user-centered design process. These answers are fictive ones but allow students to define persona and realistic contexts of use. Figure 2 provides an example of these answers.

At the end of the semester the controller may be in the form of a mock-up or a (functional) prototype. Students must explain how they designed it according to the UCD principles and how it is usable for the target user and the target context of use. Figure 3 presents an example of a designed controller.

## 3 Second Year of the Master's Program: Advanced Interaction Techniques – Multimodality

Building on the solid background on user-centered design processes and user interfaces development, this course focuses on engineering advanced interaction techniques, beyond WIMP interfaces. The goal of this course is that the students acquire insight into the ergonomic and software design of multimodal user interfaces. The objectives of the course include:

**Table 1.** Topics of the first-year course of the master's program.

| | |
|---|---|
| 1 Introduction | |
| | Domain - History - Definitions - Challenges |
| 2 User-centered Design and the user needs | |
| | User-centered design |
| | Activity Analysis |
| | Persona |
| | Design scenarios |
| | Collection methods (interviews and observation) |
| 3 Design models and their integration within software engineering life cycles | |
| | Task modeling: formalisms and notations |
| | Low and high-fidelity mock-ups |
| | Dialog models |
| 4 UI Presentation | |
| | Exploration and creativity tools |
| | Flat design, skeuomorphism design, responsive design |
| | Psychology and ergonomics guidelines (Gestalt's laws, Nielsen's heuristics) |
| 5 Evaluation methods of interactive systems | |
| | Evaluation dimensions |
| | Evaluation by experts (Hick's and Fitt's laws, KLM-GOMS methods |
| | User tests |

Yes, but not often. I started because one of my granddaughters, Laura, came to our house during a recent holiday with her video game console. Usually when she comes, I went with her to the park but this time she was a little sick so we opted to stay inside most of the time. So, she spent a lot of time playing with her console. Of course, when I was a kid, I didn't have that, so I wanted to see how it works and what she is doing with it. I am curious. My granddaughter wanted to try but I didn't understand the game she was playing. They're heroes now, you see ... I don't know them. But Laura had a kart racing game and she said to me "OK grandpa, you know how to drive, so you have no excuse" and I couldn't say no: my granddaughter challenged me. I played and …I lost. I lost because this thing is not the same as driving. But now when Laura comes, she always takes her console to play with me. She is happy because for once she is teaching me something so she is proud.

**Fig. 2.** Example of an answer of a fictive user, used as the starting point for designing the controller of the kart racing game.

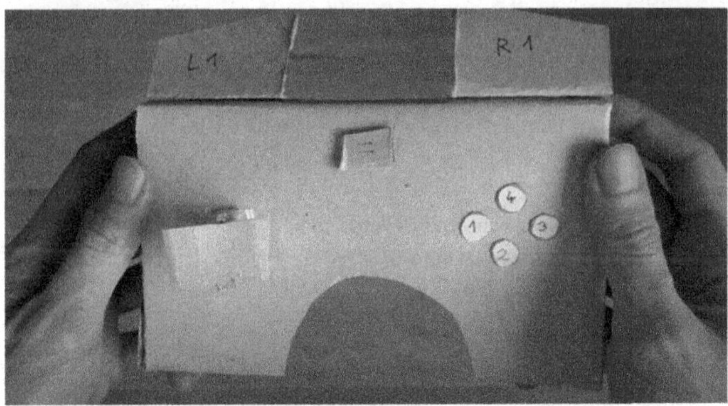


**Fig. 3.** Example of a designed controller of the kart racing game.

- Introduction of the key principles and examples of multimodal interaction (including multimodal interaction techniques on mobile devices and augmented reality)
- Presentation of the ergonomic design space of multimodal interaction
- Introduction of the main issues in software design for multimodal interaction.

The course consists of lectures and a group-work project on designing and developing a multimodal interactive system (Table 2).

The topics of Table 2 are only introduced during lectures with supporting documents. Concepts and methods are then applied during a group-work project. To guarantee a user-centered design approach instead of a technology-driven approach, the project is made of two parts. The first part is to design a multimodal interactive system with no development. The second part is to develop and experimentally test a sub-part of the designed system.

The project starts after the first lecture on definitions and on multimodal application examples. For the project, the students identify an application domain and a potential interaction problem that could require advanced interaction techniques. The identified problem is the motivation of the project and must be based on activity analysis including interviews with users as well as observations. The identified problem is presented by means of activity scenarios from which requirements are identified. By applying a user-centered design approach taught the year before that is enriched by the new design elements on interaction modalities and multimodality, the students design an "ideal project" with projected scenarios as a representation of future activities (Fig. 4-a). In addition to scenarios, the steps include a task model, as well as the rationale for the choice of interaction modalities and of their combinations based on CARE diagrams. The "ideal project" is designed independently of the difficulty of developing it.

The second step is to select a specific part of the designed "ideal project" to be implemented and experimentally evaluated with users. Since some modalities may be difficult to implement (hardware and software) and fusion mechanisms difficult to implement, only a subpart of the "ideal project" is implemented

**Table 2.** Topics of the second-year course of the master's program.

| | |
|---|---|
| 1 Introduction | |
| | Domain - Definitions - Challenges |
| 2 Multimodal applications | |
| | Examples - Application domains illustrated by videos |
| 3 Elements on human perception and action | |
| | Why study human perception/action |
| | Human modalities |
| | Multisensory perception |
| | ICS: Interactive Cognitive Sub-systems |
| 4 Ergonomic Design | |
| | Underlying concepts |
| | MSM |
| | Pipe-Line [6] |
| | Definition of a modality |
| | Design Space |
| | Selection of one or several modalities: Actors & Criteria |
| | Characterization of a modality |
| | Composition of modalities - CARE properties [3,6] |
| 5 Usage | |
| | Empirical results |
| | Ten myths of multimodal interaction [7] |
| 6 Software Design | |
| | Fusion mechanism |
| | Several approach |
| | Fusion criteria [4] |
| | Software architecture [5,6] |
| | Tools |
| | Prototyping tools - Wizard of Oz [9] |
| | Component-based approach (ICARE [1], OpenInterface [8] |

within the time limit of the course (14 weeks). Figures 4 and 5 present two examples of developed projects. Moreover, the developed project can include simulated modalities applying the taught wizard of Oz approach. This wizard of Oz approach has been often used to simulate speech recognition.

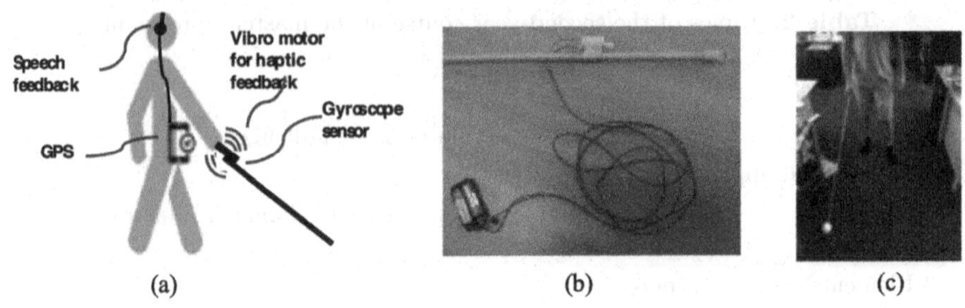


**Fig. 4.** Example of a project: (a) "Ideal project" (b) Developed prototype with haptic feedback (c) tested by users.

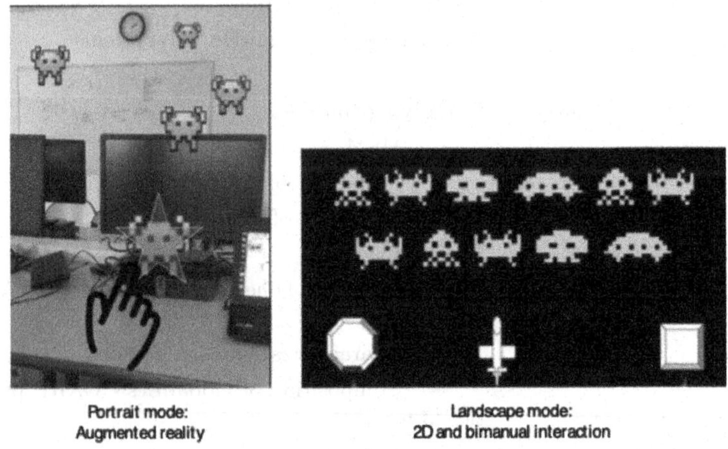


**Fig. 5.** Example of a developed project on mobile phone: the game has been tested with 11 players on a mobile phone.

## 4 Conclusion

In this paper we described our approach for raising students' awareness of the importance of the users, the contexts and tasks in the design, development and evaluation of interactive systems. Two courses are proposed to the Master's degree students.

The first one aims at acquiring fundamental HCI methods and concepts to follow the user-centered design principle. Students have to apply them in a project to design an input interface adapted to specific users and contexts of use to control a kart in a racing game. The specificities of the project are 1) that the functional core is provided and the focus is only on the input user interface 2) that the provided elements to start the user-centered design process are realistic representations of starting points of industrial projects.

Based on this first course, the second course on advanced interaction techniques adopt a complementary approach that is based on the experience gained during the first course. We adopt a project-based learning strategy:

- The starting point of the project is a problem chosen by the students including users' capabilities, context of use for which advanced interaction techniques may be required. So, the students start from the requirement analysis that motivates the project.
- The project follows a user-centered design approach as taught during the first course and enriched with new design elements for multimodality, augmented reality and mobile interaction. The project is fully designed without considering the technical issues of implementing it. It is the first part of the project entitled the "ideal project".
- Because the project involves advanced interaction techniques that are complex to develop and tune, the students develop only a selected part of the "ideal project" that must be experimentally evaluated with representative users. Wizard of Oz techniques are used to enable the experimental study with users when an interaction modality is not available.

The topics of these two HCI courses are not specific to software engineering students. Persona, scenarios, design models, testing methods are taught in other Master's degrees but we have adapted the manner to teach them:

- We use many different application examples to facilitate the generalization/specification of concepts (well-understood process for computer scientists).
- We systematically use software tools to apply the HCI concepts.
- We drive students to question the usability of the interactive systems that they designed during group-work project by adopting the user's point of view.

This overall approach relying on two courses (for a total of 120 h including 60 h with the students and 60 h of personal work) enables us to motivate the students who are future software engineers in industry to learn HCI. One comment from a second-year student "After this course, the way I perceive user interfaces and systems in general is changed".

As HCI teachers, our goal is to train the students to obtain specific skills related to the design and development of interactive software systems as part of an HCI teaching curriculum for software engineers. We believe that it is important to acquire such HCI skills since these software engineers will develop the future interactive systems of our everyday life.

## References

1. Bouchet, J., Nigay, L., Ganille, T.: ICARE software components for rapidly developing multimodal interfaces. In: Proceedings of the 6th international conference on Multimodal interfaces, pp. 251–258 (2004)

2. Caffiau, S., Scapin, D., Girard, P., Baron, M., Jambon, F.: Increasing the expressive power of task analysis: systematic comparison and empirical assessment of tool-supported task models. Interact. Comput. **22**(6), 569–593 (2010)
3. Coutaz, J., Nigay, L., Salber, D., Blandford, A., May, J., Young, R.M.: Four easy pieces for assessing the usability of multimodal interaction: the care properties. In: Human—Computer Interaction. IAICT, pp. 115–120. Springer, Boston (1995). https://doi.org/10.1007/978-1-5041-2896-4_19
4. Lalanne, D., Nigay, L., Palanque, P., Robinson, P., Vanderdonckt, J., Ladry, J.F.: Fusion engines for multimodal input: a survey. In: Proceedings of the 2009 International Conference on Multimodal Interfaces, pp. 153–160 (2009)
5. Nigay, L., Coutaz, J.: A generic platform for addressing the multimodal challenge. In: Proceedings of the SIGCHI Conference on Human Factors in Computing Systems, pp. 98–105 (1995)
6. Nigay, L., Coutaz, J.: Multifeature systems: The care properties and their impact on software design. Intelligence and multimodality in multimedia interfaces (1997)
7. Oviatt, S.: Ten myths of multimodal interaction. Commun. ACM **42**(11), 74–81 (1999)
8. Serrano, M., Juras, D., Nigay, L.: A three-dimensional characterization space of software components for rapidly developing multimodal interfaces. In: Proceedings of the 10th International Conference on Multimodal Interfaces, pp. 149–156 (2008)
9. Serrano, M., Nigay, L.: Temporal aspects of care-based multimodal fusion: from a fusion mechanism to composition components and WoZ components. In: Proceedings of the 2009 International Conference on Multimodal Interfaces, pp. 177–184 (2009)

# Control Rooms in Safety Critical Contexts: Design, Engineering and Evaluation Issues

# Control Rooms from a Human-Computer Interaction Perspective

Tilo Mentler[1], Philippe Palanque[2(✉)], Michael D. Harrison[3], Kristof Van Laerhoven[4], and Paolo Masci[5]

[1] Trier University of Applied Sciences, 54293 Schneidershof, Trier, Germany
T.Mentler@inf.hochschule-trier.de
[2] ICS-IRIT, University of Toulouse, Toulouse, France
palanque@irit.fr
[3] School of Computing, Newcastle University, Urban Sciences Building, Newcastle upon Tyne, UK
michael.harrison@ncl.ac.uk
[4] Ubiquitous Computing, University of Siegen, 57076 Siegen, Germany
kvl@eti.uni-siegen.de
[5] National Institute of Aerospace, 100 Exploration Way, Hampton, VA 23666, USA
paolo.masci@nianet.org

## 1 Introduction

As defined in *Paper 2* presented at the workshop, whose presentations and discussions are introduced in this paper, "control rooms are work spaces that serve the purpose of managing and operating physically dispersed systems, services and staff".

Control rooms are a central element of critical infrastructures and safety-critical contexts (e.g. aviation, emergency services, healthcare). Research relating to these environments is challenging for various reasons (e.g. limited access, limited prototyping and obstacles to evaluation). Cross-domain knowledge transfer is an important stimulus for research and the development of future control rooms enabling an overall socio-technical understanding. However, transfer of knowledge must be carried out carefully, as control rooms in different areas sometimes differ greatly from one another. Some might not even be considered or named as control rooms in the first place. These issues were illustrated in the papers that were presented in the CRiSCC (Control Rooms in Safety Critical Contexts) as recorded in this book. The papers include examples and overview summaries of research in air traffic control, emergency services, healthcare, plant operations, space operations, suppliers and traffic management. In order to bring some coherence to these various examples a taxonomy is introduced in this paper that can be used to characterise control rooms in terms of socio-technical aspects (for example, proximity between operators and critical process elements) and to identify domain-specific features more easily. This taxonomy is discussed in Sect. 2.

Traditionally the focus of studies of control rooms have been concerned with physical spaces where the control of processes (plants, aircraft, trains) are located. Studies reported at the workshop therefore focused on the complexity


C. Ardito et al. (Eds.): INTERACT 2021, LNCS 13198, pp. 281–289, 2022.
https://doi.org/10.1007/978-3-030-98388-8_25

of displays and other output media and associated controls. Previous considerations in relation to the "usability" of these systems have been concerned with issues such as moding of these displays, and other characteristics of the relation between action and display that affect the ease with which controllers can understand and manage such systems. These studies address concerns about workload, distribution of work among operators, situation awareness and allocation of function as well as the management of the display and the control configurations as physical elements that require control as they are added to or removed from the controlled system.

The notion of "control room" has evolved as control has become more distributed and this extending of the notion is reflected in the collection. These papers provide a snapshot of the current preoccupations of the control room community and as such deal with the following issues:

*Paper 2* entitled "A Generic Framework for Structuring Configuration Management for Socio-Technical System: Application to Control Rooms" is concerned with the *configuration* of a control system, involving, for example, the systems, space and people involved in the control room.

*Paper 3* entitled "Improving resilience by communicating predicted disruptions in control rooms" focuses on *resilience* of the system considering visualisations to indicate upcoming disruptions. The paper discusses the interface design of such information and focuses on the problem of managing cognitive biases (both personal biases and organisational biases).

*Paper 4* entitled "Proving Display Conformance and Action Consistency: the Example of an Integrated Clinical Environment" explores "control rooms" as they might be understood in healthcare specifically intensive care. This paper is concerned with demonstrating that the distributed network of healthcare devices and their control systems provide information consistently. A model is briefly described and proofs that the various layers of the device are consistent are summarised.

*Paper 5* entitled "Towards Control Rooms as Human-Centered Pervasive Computing Environments" describes the control room as a distributed system of output devices (such as shared public screens), work stations, multi-modal alarm systems and recognises the usability and user experience issues that are peculiar to such configurations as well as the opportunities provided to support more flexible models of working. The paper includes a short systematic review and illustrates some design concepts introduced to improve user experience. These concepts are presented in a questionnaire in order to evaluate the role that such concepts might play in such systems.

*Paper 6* entitled "LstSim-Extended: Towards Monitoring Interaction and beyond in Web-Based Control Room Simulations" uses an existing and community-driven web-based simulator to explore operator behaviour in an emergency dispatch centre. The paper describes a method to elicit realistic control room scenarios and to measure the user's interactions and vital signs through wrist worn devices. A plug-in is developed that logs user interactions (for example delays between actions) and a smart watch is connected wirelessly to provide physiological data during the simulation. A short evaluation is described to indicate what data are collected.

*Paper 7* entitled "UX for Some and Usability for Others: Issues of Blending Multi-user and Multi-properties in Control Centers" is concerned with the precise criteria that relate to usability and user experience in safety critical systems in general and control rooms in particular. An example is used to explore these ideas, namely the Jupiter 2 Control Centre. An interesting feature of this control room is that three "types" of user are involved, namely operators, as well as external audience and press who are involved during launch. The analysis is based on a study of documentation and reports by experts. Particular criteria that describe usability and user experience are introduced. In the process of considering these criteria conflicts are identified.

As stated above, key problems in understanding configurations are traditionally *workload* [13], *situation awareness* [9] and *allocation of function* [28]. Function allocation is a key problem that permeates all aspects of the design of control rooms from a human computer interaction perspective. Designing this allocation is a well known problem that requires a deep understanding of the users, their work environment and their context [7]. The concern is when to automate different aspects of the system without affecting situation awareness negatively while at the same time enabling a manageable workload. Important themes in these chapters which have an important bearing on balancing these different preoccupations are:

- the link between user experience and usability in the context of a potentially complex working environment with multiple stakeholders;
- how to support and analyse issues relating to safety. This is described in terms of visualisations that indicate potential disruptions and the analysis of the relationship between multiple representations of the same physical devices;
- the analysis of operator and other stakeholder behaviour.

## 2 A Brief HCI Taxonomy of Control Rooms

There are key differences in control rooms that are critical from an HCI perspective. To clarify these differences a brief taxonomy of control rooms based on two dimensions is proposed:

- *location of the control room:* is it fixed or does it change?
- *degree of operator involvement:* concerning the level of automation with particular reference to the level of engagement by operators in the event of accidents (directly or indirectly).

While control rooms of power plants or rescue forces are examples of fixed locations with respect to the first dimension, ship bridges and aircraft cockpits are examples of control rooms "on the move". This aspect is of particular importance in two ways: on the one hand, control rooms of the latter category are exposed to changing environmental influences (e.g. light and weather conditions); while on the other hand, operators "on board" such control rooms can often perceive these environmental influences directly and take them into account in their decision-making.

With respect to the second dimension (*degree of operator involvement*), a distinction must be made between control rooms in which operators are most likely to be directly and immediately endangered in the event of damage, and control rooms in which negative consequences are essentially indirect. Pilots on board an aircraft or operators in a nuclear power plant are examples of the first group, operators in control centres of network operators (electricity, gas, water) or surgeons are examples of the second group.

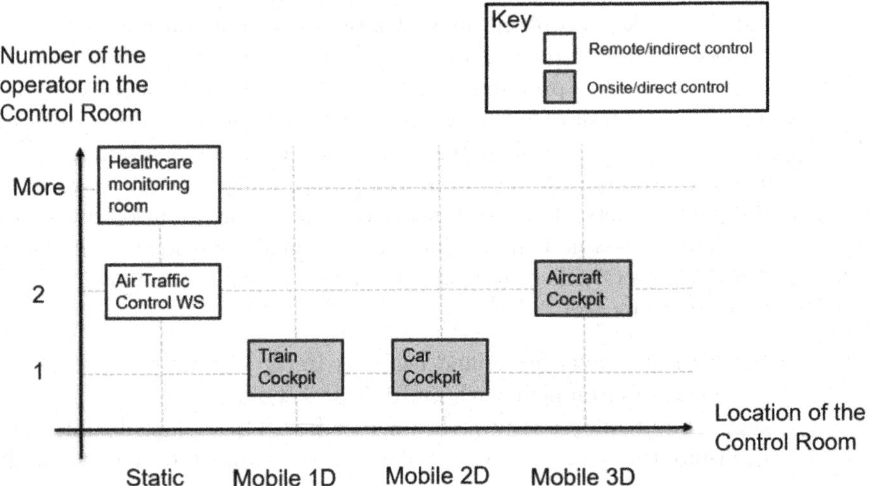


**Fig. 1.** Types of control rooms according to their location and their number of users

Figure 1 presents on a single diagram these dimensions and examples of control rooms positioned with respect to these dimensions. In addition the vertical axis represents number of operators in the control room. For instance, rocket launching control rooms would involve many operators all located in the same room operating remotely the launchpad and the rocket. In the case of aircraft cockpits, the control room is evolving in a three dimensional space and control directly the aircraft and moves together with the aircraft.

## 3 User Experience and Usability

An important distinction in the understanding of control room design and the communities that use them relate to user experience and usability. Control rooms may be configured to provide resource for different communities and for this purpose user experience may be a key issue. The example in *Paper 7* involves controllers and spectators for which there are quite different user experience requirements. Likewise issues of usability will differ depending on the user and their particular expertise. These are important issues that require further understanding. *Paper 3* introduces the important issue of "cognitive bias" that must be understood in relation to the design of an interface.

## 4 Safety in Design and Safety in Action

Two important focuses in the design of control rooms are (1) that the software used to control the system is safe and (2) that the software itself predicts and reminds the operator of environment circumstances that are unsafe. There is much relevant work in both categories. In the case of safety, major works such as [17] are relevant but also specifically in relation to the Integrated Clinical Environment discussed in *Paper 4*, specific requirements are described in [18] which have a particular focus on the safety in terms of usability of these systems. Many examples of predictive systems have been developed, for example there are many examples of collision avoidance systems [19].

The papers touch on both these issues. For example, *Paper 4* is concerned with the consistency of actions across different representations of the same state of the configuration. This formal methods based approach to the analysis of a control room has potential in providing part of the argument for the safety of the configuration (see for example [12] for a simple example). In the case of paper 4 the consistency requirement provides an example of a safety requirement that is user-centred. *Paper 3* discusses the issue of "upcoming disruptions" and deals with issues associated with predicting potential problems. Here allocation of function is important in deciding what automation is appropriate.

## 5 Control Rooms and Interaction Techniques

While Human Factors approaches [4] and User-Centered Design [30] have been used to design and evaluate control rooms for a considerable time, the interaction technologies they offer are usually several steps behind what can be found in areas such as home entertainment or gaming where, for example, safety and security are less significant. Control rooms are deployed in very different domains such as crisis management, emergency medical services, intensive care units, fire services, power supply, maritime navigation, and traffic management.

More recent work has been focusing on the use of new technologies in the context of control rooms exploiting new interaction techniques and new interaction technologies introduced in research contributions from the Human-Computer Interaction area. Speech was considered early as an input modality [1] while the issues raised by its deployment were matters of concern, see for example [15]. Auditory information was used as an alerting system in addition to the traditional display of information in [23] though studies have shown [8] that the human brain filters out information when there is high workload or stress. Tactile feedback has been introduced in cockpits more recently [21] (in these cases feedback is used in combination with information displays) and tangible interactions have been introduced as a means to bring interactions closer to traditional mechanisms, such as levers and knobs [20]. Multi-touch interactions have also been studied recently both in control rooms [27] and interactive cockpits [6]. These design opportunities have raised many significant issues relating to usability and safety in control room contexts. Ambient displays [5] and head mounted displays [29] have been used to add a digital layer of information on top of control room elements to support situation awareness and attention in safety critical environments. This introduction of what were within the control room community non-standard modalities, led to multi-modal interactions (both in terms of input and output) that were still considered a challenge in 2016 [14] while the early work from Bolt in that domain was introduced more than 25 years earlier [3]. Multi-modality as input was however introduced successfully in industrial control rooms [10] or military aircraft cockpits [2] while multi-modal output was largely used for alerting flight crews [26].

Beyond interaction technologies, the typically centralised nature of control rooms was questioned [16] and mobile solutions were proposed to support control and monitoring activities on the move. However, the introduction of these technologies in critical systems raised the issue of their dependability and their security as soon as the environment loses its closeness nature.

While state of the art in deployed control rooms is still characterised by stationary workstations with several smaller screens and large wall-mounted displays, introducing mobile and wearable devices, as well as IoT solutions distributed in the environment could enable more flexible and cooperative ways of working. However, turning control rooms into pervasive computing environments can be expected to raise user-related challenges such as usability and user experience, system-related ones such as reliability and dependability and more global ones such as safety and security [22]. However, it is clear that control rooms must evolve and integrate advanced interaction technologies [24] so that operations can be improved.

## 6 Conclusion

This workshop promoted the sharing of experiences in designing, implementing, and evaluating interactive systems in control rooms in safety critical contexts. It gathered work from various application domains (including healthcare, aviation, and emergency dispatch) and provided theories, methods and tools to support designers and analysts. Even though the design of control rooms has received little recent attention from researchers in the field of Human-Computer Interaction, their involvement in safety-critical systems deserves more. Indeed, research contributions in that area should support both usability and user experience and thus contribute ultimately to safety. Some recent contributions such as the survey in [25] and workshops in several conferences such as [11] have demonstrated a new interest in exploring new organisations of work (focusing on user experience properties), new interaction techniques and systematic explorations of success stories from different domains. We hope that the results of the current workshop will add to this thread and attract more contributions.

## References


1. Baber, C., Usher, D., Stammers, R., Taylor, R.: Feedback requirements for automatic speech recognition in the process control room. Int. J. Man-Mach. Stud. **37**(6), 703–719 (1992). https://doi.org/10.1016/0020-7373(92)90064-R, https://www.sciencedirect.com/science/article/pii/002073739290064R
2. Barbé, J., Spaggiari, L., Clay, A., Bérard, P., Aissani, A., Mollard, R.: Why and how to study multimodal interaction in cockpit design. In: Proceedings of the 15th Ergo "IA" Ergonomie Et Informatique Avancée Conference, pp. 1–8 (2016)
3. Bolt, R.A.: "Put-that-there": voice and gesture at the graphics interface. In: Proceedings of the 7th Annual Conference on Computer Graphics and Interactive Techniques, SIGGRAPH 1980, pp. 262–270. Association for Computing Machinery, New York (1980). https://doi.org/10.1145/800250.807503
4. Carvalho, P.V., dos Santos, I.L., Gomes, J.O., Borges, M.R., Guerlain, S.: Human factors approach for evaluation and redesign of human-system interfaces of a nuclear power plant simulator. Displays **29**(3), 273–284 (2008). https://doi.org/10.1016/j.displa.2007.08.010, https://www.sciencedirect.com/science/article/pii/S0141938207000820
5. Cobus, V., Heuten, W., Boll, S.: Multimodal head-mounted display for multimodal alarms in intensive care units. In: Proceedings of the 6th ACM International Symposium on Pervasive Displays, PerDis 2017. Association for Computing Machinery, New York (2017). https://doi.org/10.1145/3078810.3084349
6. Cockburn, A., et al.: Turbulent touch: touchscreen input for cockpit flight displays. In: Proceedings of the 2017 CHI Conference on Human Factors in Computing Systems, CHI 2017, pp. 6742–6753. Association for Computing Machinery, New York (2017). https://doi.org/10.1145/3025453.3025584
7. Dearden, A., Harrison, M.D., Wright, P.: Allocation of function: scenarios, context and the economics of effort. Int. J. Hum. Comput. Stud. **52**(2), 289–318 (2000). https://doi.org/10.1006/ijhc.1999.0290, https://www.sciencedirect.com/science/article/pii/S1071581999902902
8. Dehais, F., Causse, M., Vachon, F., Régis, N., Menant, E., Tremblay, S.: Failure to detect critical auditory alerts in the cockpit: evidence for inattentional deafness. Hum. Factors **56**(4), 631–644 (2014). https://doi.org/10.1177/0018720813510735, PMID: 25029890
9. Endsley, M.R., Bolte, B., Jones, D.G.: Designing for Situation Awareness: An Approach to User-Centered Design. CRC Press, Boca Raton (2003)
10. Fagerlönn, J., Hammarberg, K., Lindberg, S., Sirkka, A., Larsson, S.: Designing a multimodal warning display for an industrial control room. In: Proceedings of the 12th International Audio Mostly Conference on Augmented and Participatory Sound and Music Experiences. AM 2017. Association for Computing Machinery, New York (2017). https://doi.org/10.1145/3123514.3123516

11. Fröhlich, P., et al.: Automation experience across domains: designing for intelligibility, interventions, interplay and integrity. In: Extended Abstracts of the 2020 CHI Conference on Human Factors in Computing Systems, CHI EA 2020, pp. 1–8. Association for Computing Machinery, New York (2020). https://doi.org/10.1145/3334480.3375178
12. Harrison, M.D., et al.: Formal techniques in the safety analysis of software components of a new dialysis machine. Sci. Comput. Program. **175**, 17–34 (2019)
13. Hart, S.G., Wickens, C.D.: Workload assessment and prediction. In: Booher, H.R. (ed.) Manprint, pp. 257–296. Springer, Dordrecht (1990). https://doi.org/10.1007/978-94-009-0437-8_9
14. Heimonen, T., Hakulinen, J., Sharma, S., Turunen, M., Lehtikunnas, L., Paunonen, H.: Multimodal interaction in process control rooms: are we there yet? In: Proceedings of the 5th ACM International Symposium on Pervasive Displays, PerDis 2016, pp. 20–32. Association for Computing Machinery, New York (2016). https://doi.org/10.1145/2914920.2915024
15. Huber, K.: Does speech technology have a place in the control room? In: IEEE Power Engineering Society General Meeting, 2005, vol. 3, pp. 2702–2703 (2005). https://doi.org/10.1109/PES.2005.1489558
16. Juhlin, O., Weilenmann, A.: Decentralizing the control room: mobile work and institutional order. In: Proceedings of the Seventh Conference on European Conference on Computer Supported Cooperative Work, ECSCW 2001, pp. 379–397. Kluwer Academic Publishers, Norwell (2001)
17. Leveson, N.G.: Engineering a Safer World: Systems Thinking Applied to Safety (Engineering Systems). MIT Press, Cambridge (2011)
18. Masci, P., Weininger, S.: Usability engineering recommendations for next-gen integrated interoperable medical devices. Biomed. Instrum. Technol. **55**(4), 132–142 (2021). https://doi.org/10.2345/0890-8205-55.4.132
19. Mukhtar, A., Xia, L., Tang, T.B.: Vehicle detection techniques for collision avoidance systems: a review. IEEE Trans. Intell. Transp. Syst. **16**(5), 2318–2338 (2015)
20. Müller, J., Schwarz, T., Butscher, S., Reiterer, H.: Back to tangibility: a post-wimp perspective on control room design. In: Proceedings of the 2014 International Working Conference on Advanced Visual Interfaces, AVI 2014, pp. 57–64. Association for Computing Machinery, New York (2014). https://doi.org/10.1145/2598153.2598161
21. Nojima, T., Funabiki, K.: Cockpit display using tactile sensation. In: First Joint Eurohaptics Conference and Symposium on Haptic Interfaces for Virtual Environment and Teleoperator Systems. World Haptics Conference, pp. 501–502 (2005). https://doi.org/10.1109/WHC.2005.27
22. Palanque, P., Basnyat, S., Bernhaupt, R., Boring, R., Johnson, C., Johnson, P.: Beyond usability for safety critical systems: how to be sure (safe, usable, reliable, and evolvable)? In: CHI 2007 Extended Abstracts on Human Factors in Computing Systems, CHI EA 2007, pp. 2133–2136. Association for Computing Machinery, New York (2007). https://doi.org/10.1145/1240866.1240966
23. Patterson, R.D., Mayfield, T.F.: Auditory warning sounds in the work environment [and discussion]. Philos. Trans. R. Soc. Lond. Ser. B Biol. Sci. **327**(1241), 485–492 (1990). http://www.jstor.org/stable/55320
24. Roth, E., O'Hara, J.: Integrating digital and conventional human-system interfaces: lessons learned from a control room modernization program. Division of Systems Analysis and Regulatory Effectiveness Office of Nuclear Regulatory Research U.S. Nuclear Regulatory Commission Washington, DC 20555–0001 (2002). https://www.nrc.gov/reading-rm/doc-collections/nuregs/contract/cr6749/index.html

25. Roto, V., Palanque, P., Karvonen, H.: Engaging automation at work – a literature review. In: Barricelli, B.R., Roto, V., Clemmensen, T., Campos, P., Lopes, A., Gonçalves, F., Abdelnour-Nocera, J. (eds.) HWID 2018. IAICT, vol. 544, pp. 158–172. Springer, Cham (2019). https://doi.org/10.1007/978-3-030-05297-3_11
26. Selcon, S.J., Taylor, R.M., Shadrake, R.A.: Multi-modal cockpit warnings: Pictures, words. or both? Proc. Hum. Factors Soc. Ann. Meet. **36**(1), 57–61 (1992). https://doi.org/10.1177/154193129203600115
27. Selim, E., Maurer, F.: EGrid: supporting the control room operation of a utility company with multi-touch tables. In: ACM International Conference on Interactive Tabletops and Surfaces, ITS 2010, pp. 289–290. Association for Computing Machinery, New York (2010). https://doi.org/10.1145/1936652.1936720
28. Sheridan, T.B.: Adaptive automation, level of automation, allocation authority, supervisory control, and adaptive control: distinctions and modes of adaptation. IEEE Trans. Syst. Man Cybern. Part A Syst. Hum. **41**(4), 662–667 (2011)
29. Stratmann, T.C., Kempa, F., Boll, S.: Lame: Light-controlled attention guidance for multi-monitor environments. In: Proceedings of the 8th ACM International Symposium on Pervasive Displays. PerDis 2019, Association for Computing Machinery, New York, NY, USA (2019). https://doi.org/10.1145/3321335.3324935
30. Ulrich, T.A., Boring, R.L.: Example user centered design process for a digital control system in a nuclear power plant. Proceedings of the Human Factors and Ergonomics Society Annual Meeting **57**(1), 1727–1731 (2013) https://doi.org/10.1177/1541931213571385

# A Generic Framework for Structuring Configuration Management for Socio-technical System: Application to Control Rooms

Célia Martinie[1], Philippe Palanque[1](✉), Sandra Steere[2], David Navarre[1], and Eric Barboni[1]

[1] ICS-IRIT, Université Toulouse III Paul Sabatier, Toulouse, France
{martinie,palanque}@irit.fr

[2] Centre Spatial Guyanais (CSG), Centre National d'Etudes Spatiales (CNES), Paris, France

**Abstract.** Control rooms are workspaces that serve the purpose of managing and operating physically dispersed systems, services and staff. They embed multiple types of systems and software, which may themselves have several characteristics. Configuration management consists in processes and techniques to systematically identify and manage the characteristics of these systems and software, as well as their changes, in order to ensure the reliability of the operations. However, systems and software are not the only elements for which several characteristics are to be managed in order to ensure the reliability of the operations in a control room. The following elements are also important: procedures, organizational processes, team structures and crewmembers. In addition, the characteristics of these elements may also vary over time. Operational procedures may change, as well as processes, team structure and crewmembers skills' level and knowledge level. In this paper, we propose a conceptual framework to address in a systematic and integrated way, and from a socio-technical point of view, the configuration management of all of the elements of a control room. These elements are systems and software, crewmembers that are in charge of the operations, operational procedures the crewmembers apply, as well as processes and standards released by organizations that are responsible for the operations.

**Keywords:** Control rooms · Configuration management · Reliability

## 1 Introduction

Many types of industries require the use of control rooms, to lead missions, to centralize information on on-going operations, as well as to take appropriate actions. For example, railway stations have control rooms to manage train tracks allocation, to monitor traffic and to adapt schedules. Control rooms are large central workspaces that support the management of physically dispersed systems, services and staff. They embed multiple types of systems (e.g. central processing units, display units, phones, servers…) and software (e.g. operating systems, telemetry retrieval applications, summary graphs,


Published by Springer Nature Switzerland AG 2022
C. Ardito et al. (Eds.): INTERACT 2021, LNCS 13198, pp. 290–301, 2022.
https://doi.org/10.1007/978-3-030-98388-8_26

logbook...), which may have several characteristics (e.g. version identifier, memory footprint...). Configuration management consists of processes and techniques to systematically identify and manage the characteristics of these systems and software, as well as their changes, between or during operations, in order to ensure the reliability of the operations. However, systems and software are not the only elements that have characteristics in a control room. Operational procedures, organizational processes, team structures and crewmembers are elements that have their own characteristics, which may affect the operations. In addition, the characteristics of these elements may also vary over time. Operational procedures may change, as well as processes, team structure and crewmembers' levels of skills and knowledge.

In several disciplines and application domains, configuration management for software and system applies using standards [5, 9, 19] to ensure the reliability of operations. However, issues in management of human skills and knowledge (e.g. inconsistent training programs), or in management of operational procedures or organizational processes (e.g. selecting an outdated version of an operational procedure or organizational process) can also cause problems during operations.

In this paper, we propose to address in a systematic and integrated way, from a socio-technical point of view, configuration management of all of the elements of a control room: systems and software, crew members that are in charge of the operations, operational procedures they apply, as well as processes and standards released by organizations that are responsible for the operations. The paper structure is as follows. Section 2 presents the main aspects of change management in command and control applications as well as the POISE (People Organization Interactive Systems and Environment) conceptual framework. Section 3 presents the related work on configuration management in command and control rooms. Section 4 presents an illustrated argument for structuring configuration management according to the POISE conceptual framework.

## 2 Change Management in Command and Control Rooms

A control room is a workspace, which serves the purpose of managing and operating physically dispersed systems, services and staff for a plant, a factory, a service or a particular event. It contains furniture, computing systems, screens, devices and user interfaces. Such control rooms can be found in space centers [1, 25] and power plants (nuclear, electric...) [13]. Figure 1 presents a picture of a control room at the French National Space Study Center (CNES) Guiana Space Center.

Command and control rooms may gather large sets of various types of interactive systems and of people with different roles and tasks within organizations. In that sense, they can be referred to as Socio-technical Systems (STS). We use the POISE conceptual framework in order to explicitly take into account the specificities of control rooms. POISE decomposes into four different inter-connected type of elements [22]: People, Organization, Interactive Systems and Environment, hence its acronym POISE. Figure 2 represents these four aspects, three of them at a corner of the triangle (People, Organization and Interactive Systems) to which the grey circle adds the fourth one, which is the environment in which the socio-technical system evolves. The content of the triangle highlights the main aspects to take into account for configuration management of the control room.

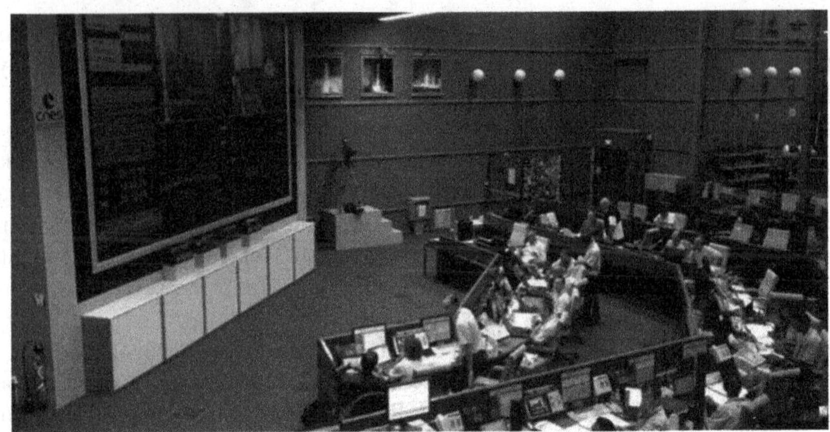

**Fig. 1.** Control room at the Guiana space center (CNES)

### 2.1 Diversity and Multiplicity People, Organizations and Interactive Systems in a Command and Control Room

The pentagon represents the main connections between the three apexes of the triangle. POISE is a refinement of the early work from Meshkati [16], claiming that the resilience of socio-technical systems requires addressing Human Organization and Technology in the same single framework. Such need to address these three aspects together and for having a global perspective on technical, human and organizational aspects for system design and generic frameworks dealing with all of these aspects have been proposed, such as the socio-technical view on work [8].

**People: Many Roles, Many Tasks.** Several people are usually involved in command and control of physically dispersed systems, services and staff [7]. Each of them is in charge of a specific role and performing specific tasks for this role. For example, in the Flight Control Team who run the operations of the ATV Jules Verne mission to ISS, five members of the Toulouse Control Center were in charge during the active phases of the mission [7]. They were a leader who coordinated the team, a "commander" who configured and sent telecommands to ATV, a "support" member who managed maneuvers and consumables, a "monit1" member who managed ground alarms, and a "monit2" member who monitored ATV subsystems.

**Organizations: Many Processes, Many Procedures.** Control rooms may involve interactive systems and staff that belong to several different organizations (e.g. national organizations, industrial partners). For example, several national and international agencies in the world manage and supervise the ISS operations [14], and industrial partners may be in charge of the operations' tasks [14]. Processes documents define and describe the operations in the control centers [13, 14]. The operations in control rooms are performed applying procedures [13, 18]. As defined in ECSS-E-ST-70C [4], a procedure is "*an elementary component of the mission operations plan that defines the actions to achieve a specific operational objective. The complete set of operational procedures*

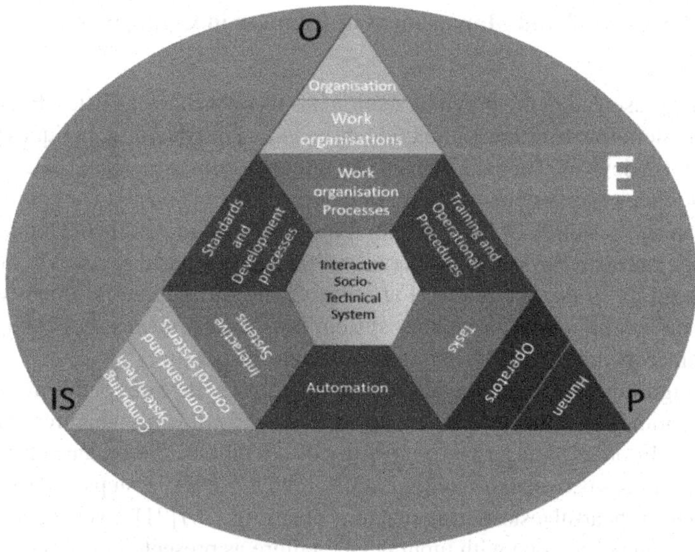


**Fig. 2.** Socio-technical view of interactive systems from [22]

*covers all planned operations for the space and ground segments. An operations procedure is a "building block" used in the construction of the actual operations to be performed in a given mission phase. An operations procedure may be called up by a mission timeline, an automatically executing schedule, another procedure or it can be initiated manually*". Procedures are central artefacts for the operations as they define the team members' tasks, the systems' functions and services' functions, as well as the interleaving between all of them [18]. An organization produces and validates its own procedures, in accordance with the regulation of its application domain. Regulation authorities (e.g. European Space Agency, International Standard Agency, International Electro technical Commission…) release standards for the systems and the operations in control rooms [12, 13].

**Interactive Systems: Many Systems and Software, Many Technologies.** Control rooms may gather different types of interactive systems, e.g. workstations, displays, large screens, that aim to present information about the systems and services that are being monitored. All of these interactive systems may rely on different technologies for their hardware, electrical, electronics, and software components [13]. Software components may be refined in type as follows: software for human computer interfaces, software for automation and control, and software for services systems. These interactive systems and technologies, which are highlighted in the previous sentence may contain automation, aiming to support crewmembers to perform their tasks and to support the stakeholder organizations objectives. The MIODMIT architecture [3] brings together the software and hardware parts of the interactive system in a single integrated framework. The connection with the human operator and this architecture is detailed in [2].

### 2.2 Need for Control and Management of Changes in Configuration of Control Rooms

Each artefact presented in the previous section has its own characteristics. For example, interactive systems provide a set of functionalities and of interaction techniques that use a set of interactive devices. They run with an Operating System, which interfaces with local or remote services and systems. This set of characteristics is named configuration. The identification and selection of the configurations that fulfill requirements for each of the control room interactive systems and for each of the systems and services is mandatory before proceeding to the operations. Furthermore, the configuration of a system may depend on the configuration of another system [26], which means that configurations have to be interoperable, controlled and selected altogether.

The configurations of systems and software may change between or during operations in a control room [21] because of: defect corrections, incoming new features, deprecated technology… In order to ensure the reliability of operations, the organizations have to trace the differences between the configuration deployed at all the steps of the operations (e.g. during the rehearsal tests, during real time operations…) [21]. Even the interactions may be reconfigured to cope with input device failure as presented in [20].

Changes in configuration of systems and software is not the only type of change that may occur. Operational procedures may change between or during operations [17]. Crewmembers may also change between [7] or during operations [23]. Even crewmembers' characteristics may vary between operations [21] (e.g. acquired new skills and knowledge as a result of training, or forgotten or lost knowledge and skills by not following a rehearsal) or during operations (e.g. fatigue, boredom, complacency…). At last, organization processes may change between or during operations.

All of these changes may affect the operations and may lead to potential issues. System configuration errors can be a major cause of service-level failures [26]. In 2003, the IAEA (International Atomic Energy Agency) reported that 25% of nuclear power plant recorded incidents were caused by configuration errors. Representing carefully and exhaustively the potential operators' errors in relationship with their tasks (as proposed in [6]).

## 3 Related Work on Configuration Management

In the discipline of Software and System Engineering, Configuration Management is defined as [1]: "*A discipline applying technical and administrative direction and surveillance to: identify and document the functional and physical characteristics of a configuration item, control changes to those characteristics, record and report change processing and implementation status, and verify compliance with specified requirements*".. The handbook on configuration management guidance MIL-HDBK-61B [19] defines configuration as "*A collection of an item's descriptive and governing characteristics that can be expressed in functional terms (i.e., what performance the item is expected to achieve) and in physical terms (i.e., what the item should look like and consist of when it is built)*". Whereas configuration management is standardized and systematically applied for systems and software in many application domains, we did not find in the literature such detailed and systematic standards for configuration management of people, teams, organizations, processes and procedures. Section 3.1 provides an overview of existing standards that cover the "IS" branch of the triangle of the POISE framework. Section 3.2 provides an overview of existing standards that cover the "P" and "O" branches of the triangle of the POISE framework.

### 3.1 Software and System Configuration Management (SCM) Processes

Standards, processes and tools aim to support the configuration management of software and systems, whatever the application domain [5, 9, 19]. These standards precisely specify activities for configuration management of software and systems. Figure 3 presents the process from the MIL-HDBK-61B handbook that summarizes the main functions of configuration management. These functions provide support for ensuring that changes to released configuration documentation are: properly identified, documented, evaluated for impact, approved by an appropriate level of authority, incorporated, and verified. Such process aims to: "*...control modifications and releases of the products, record and report the status of the products and modification requests, ensure the completeness, consistency and correctness of the product...*" (page 23) [5].

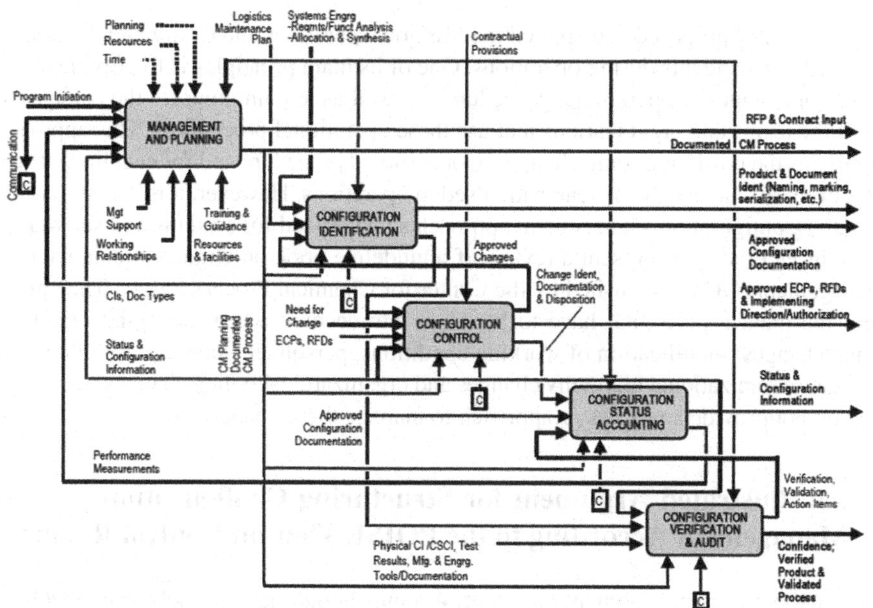


**Fig. 3.** Top-level configuration management process from [19]

The function "Management and planning" (depicted at the top left in Fig. 3) is the set of activities that aim to start the configuration management program, to ensure communication between all of the configuration management functions, and to select information and performance measurement for the configuration management. This function is in charge of releasing a configuration management process.

The function "Configuration identification" (second block from left to right and from top to bottom in Fig. 3) is the set of activities that aim to produce configuration documentation (identifiers, nomenclature, numbering) as well as the list of approved characteristics to be traced for systems and software.

The function "Configuration control" (third block from left to right and from top to bottom in Fig. 3) is the set of activities that process changes to system and software characteristics according to the configuration documentation and to the configuration management process.

The function "Configuration status accounting" (fourth block from left to right and from top to bottom in Fig. 3) is the set of activities that aim to track and maintain, using a database, the history of each change that has been performed.

The function "Configuration verification and audit" (depicted at the bottom right in Fig. 3) is the set of activities that aim to check that the current version of systems and software match requirements, and to check that they have been accurately documented in the configuration documentation.

### 3.2 Processes for Change Management of Human and Organizational Aspects in Control Rooms

Welz et al. [24] proposed and applied the Mission Operations and Command Assurance approach for incidents during operations. One of its main principles is to provide traceability of changes in operational procedures, as well as to communicate the changes to all of the teams and organizations that use these operational procedures. This approach highlights the need for tracing changes in operational procedure and for enabling awareness of these changes by the teams involved in operations. However, it is less structured than the Configuration Management approach standardized for systems and software.

Wincek et al. [25] present a review of a guideline book on Organizational Change Management (OCM) published by the Center for Chemical Process Safety. They highlight the main aspects that have to be taken into account when managing organizational changes: modification of working conditions, personnel changes, task allocation changes, organizational hierarchy changes and organizational policy changes. However, they do not provide a process or approach to manage these changes.

## 4 An Illustrated Argument for Structuring Configuration Management According to the POISE View on Control Rooms

The configuration management of a control room should manage each type of POISE element of the control room as systematically and exhaustively as the standards on configuration management of system and software propose (e.g. identification, listing and documentation). If one of these elements change, the process should enable the analysis, authorization, performance and tracking of this change.

In this section, we focus on the application of the approach for a particular example of control room in the space application domain: a control room in a satellite ground segment. This section aims at arguing for the extension of system and software configuration management to support the assessment of the impact of a system or software change on elements of all types in the POISE conceptual framework. Moreover, it also aims at arguing that all the types of elements in the POISE framework require that their possible changes are treated as changes in system and software configuration management practices.

### 4.1 Overview of the Space Application Domain

The space application domain is split into two parts (depicted in Fig. 4): the on-board part (the upper one including the spacecraft and called the space segment) and the ground part (made up of antennas for communication plus the mission control system) called the ground segment. The command and control system in charge of operations are represented at the bottom of Fig. 4. This command and control system is in charge of maintaining the spacecraft in operation and is thus heavily dependent of the spacecraft software and hardware infrastructure.

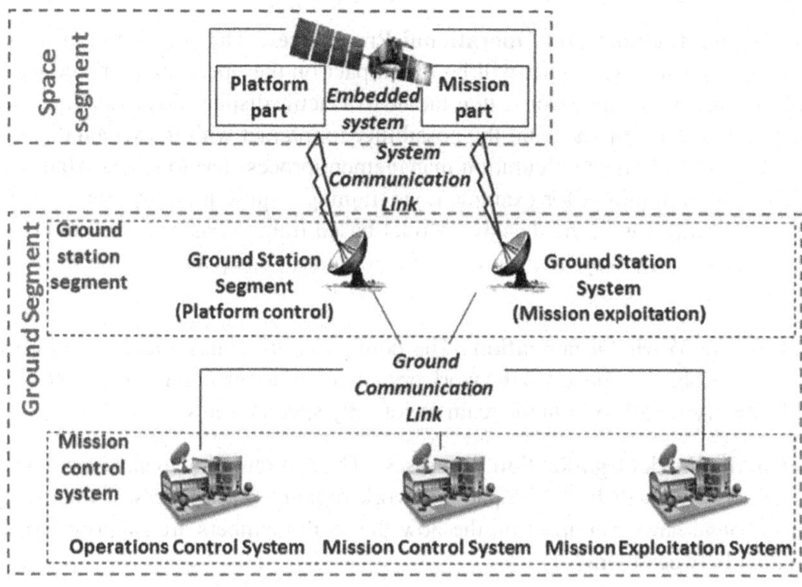


**Fig. 4.** Overview of the satellite application domain

The following sub-sections present examples of changes that may occur in a control room in a satellite ground segment. Such changes would justify the application of the proposed approach, according to the type of POISE elements.

### 4.2 Implications of a Change of an Element Belonging to the Type "Interactive Systems" Using the POISE Approach

Workstations, input/output devices (e.g. mice, keyboards, and displays…), servers, are the main elements belonging to the type of element Interactive Systems. A display is an element part of the command and control systems. The operations may require a change of display in favor of another type of display, for example because of a malfunctioning problem or because of its obsolescence. The new display may differ from the previous one on several characteristics. For example, its size and resolution may be higher or lower, it may be tactile instead of non-tactile or the opposite. We argue to assess this change in terms of impact on each of the POISE elements.

**Impact on the Operator.** The configuration management process must assess what will be the impact on the operators using this display, for example will the operator have the ability to see the displayed colors? Will the display resolution be adequate given the operators' abilities? In case of a change from a non-tactile to a tactile display, which operators are familiar with this technology?

**Impact on the Task.** The configuration management process has to assess what will be the impact on the task, for example will the information display in the same way than with the previous display?

**Impact on the Training and Operational Procedures.** The configuration management process has to assess what will be the impact on the operational procedures, for example, in case of a change from a non-tactile to a tactile display, do procedures require modifications to take into account the possibility to interact with the screen directly to trigger a command? The configuration management process has to assess what will be the impact on the training, for example does training require modifications to explain the new possibilities with the display? Model-based training, as proposed in [15] and [18] is one of the only ways to ensure that the training is adequate with the work of the operator.

**Impact on the Work Organization.** The configuration management process has to assess what will be the impact on the work organization, for example, should the change of display apply for all roles in the team or for only specific roles?

**Impact on the Work Organization Processes.** The configuration management process has to assess what will be the impact on work organization processes, for example, will this change have an impact on the how the team members are supposed to share information between them?

**Impact on the Standards and Development Processes.** The configuration management process has to assess what will be the impact on standards and development processes, for example, what will there specific characteristics be required for the new display to be compliant with standards and development processes? Alternatively, if this new display is crucial for operations, are there changes to perform in the development process to integrate it?

**Impact on the Command and Control Systems.** The configuration management process has to assess what will be the impact on other command and control systems, for example, will the installation of new drivers be required to enable the integration of this new display in the control room? Will the input/output devices need to be changed/updated to run in adequacy with the new display?

**Impact on the on Automation.** The configuration management process has to assess what will be the impact on automation, for example, in case of a change from a non-tactile to a tactile display, which consequences will the touch interaction technique have on the selection and trigger of commands in the software applications? Will some tasks previously performed by the operator be allocated to the command and control application of the interactive system? A touch could trigger the selection plus sending of a command (automation of selection) while previously the user made the selection by clicking and then triggered the command in a second step.

## 5 Conclusion and Perspectives

This position paper argues for the extension of software and system configuration management to support the assessment of the impact of a change overall the socio-technical system, as well as on the application of configuration management on all the types of elements that make a socio-technical system. As illustrated in previous sections, the introduction of a new technology in a control room may affect several types of elements of a socio-technical system: operators, tasks, training and operational procedures, work organization, work organization processes, standards and development processes, command and control systems, as well as automation. Moreover, depending on the application domain, there may be differences between short-term (emergency) configuration changes and long-term management issues. Once we acknowledge these problems, we have to study whether existing advanced processes and techniques for configuration management of software and systems do apply for other types of elements of a socio-technical system (e.g. tasks, training, operational procedures, work organization…). We also have to study whether new techniques and processes could be required to support the configuration management of a control room from a socio-technical system perspective. Furthermore, the POISE conceptual framework explicitly takes into account the environment in which the socio-technical system runs, thus we also have to study how to assess the possible impact of change in the environment on the configuration of the socio-technical system.

## References


1. Beck, T., Schmidhuber, M., Scharringhausen, J.: Automation of complex operational scenarios - providing 24/7 inter-satellite links with EDRS. In: AIAA 2016–2417, SpaceOps 2016 Conferences, Daejeon, Korea, 16–20 May 2016
2. Canny, A., Bouzekri, E., Martinie, C., Palanque, P.: Rationalizing the need of architecture-driven testing of interactive systems. In: Bogdan, C., Kuusinen, K., Lárusdóttir, M.K., Palanque, P., Winckler, M. (eds.) HCSE 2018. LNCS, vol. 11262, pp. 164–186. Springer, Cham (2019). https://doi.org/10.1007/978-3-030-05909-5_10
3. Cronel, M., Dumas, B., Palanque, P., Canny, A.: MIODMIT: a generic architecture for dynamic multimodal interactive systems. In: Bogdan, C., Kuusinen, K., Lárusdóttir, M.K., Palanque, P., Winckler, M. (eds.) HCSE 2018. LNCS, vol. 11262, pp. 109–129. Springer, Cham (2019). https://doi.org/10.1007/978-3-030-05909-5_7

4. ECSS Secretariat. ESA-ESTEC, Requirements & Standards Division: Space engineering: Ground systems and operations, ECSS-E-ST-70C, Noordwijk, The Netherlands, 31st July 2008
5. ESA Board for Software Standardisation and Control (BSSC). ESA Ground Segment Software Engineering and Management Guide, Part B Management. Issue 1 (2002)
6. Fahssi, R., Martinie, C., Palanque, P.: Enhanced task modelling for systematic identification and explicit representation of human errors. In: Abascal, J., Barbosa, S., Fetter, M., Gross, T., Palanque, P., Winckler, M. (eds.) INTERACT 2015. LNCS, vol. 9299, pp. 192–212. Springer, Cham (2015). https://doi.org/10.1007/978-3-319-22723-8_16
7. Frard, V., Francillout, L., Galet, G., Michel, S.: ATV-CC vehicle team staffing from Jules Verne to Johannes Kepler mission. In: SpaceOps 2010 Confernce, Huntsville, Alabama (2010). https://doi.org/10.2514/6.2010-2165
8. Hollnagel, E.: Cognitive ergonomics: it's all in the mind. Ergonomics **40**(10), 1170–1182 (1997)
9. IEEE 828–2012 - IEEE Standard for configuration management in systems and software engineering. In: IEEE (2012)
10. International Atomic Energy Agency.. "Configuration management in nuclear power plants", IAEA-TECDOC-1335, Vienna (2003)
11. ISO/IEC/IEEE 24765:2010 Systems and Software Engineering—Vocabulary, ISO/IEC/IEEE (2010)
12. Jones, M., Merri, M., Diekmann, M., Valera, S., Parkes, A.: Evolution of the ECSS-E-70 ground segment and operations standards. In: Space Ops 2008 Conference (2008)
13. Kitamura, M., Fujita, Y., Yoshikawa, H.: Review of international standards related to the design for control rooms on nuclear power plants. J. Nuclear Sci. Technol. **42**(4), 406–417 (2005). https://doi.org/10.1080/18811248.2005.972640
14. Kuch, T., Sabath, D.: The Columbus-CC—operating the european laboratory at ISS. Acta Astronaut. **63**(4), 204–212 (2008). https://doi.org/10.1016/j.actaastro.2007.12.041
15. Lallai, G., Loi, Z.G., Martinie, C., Palanque, P., Pisano, M., Spano, L.D.: Engineering task-based augmented reality guidance: application to the training of aircraft flight procedures. Interact. Comput. **33**(1), 17–39 (2021). https://doi.org/10.1093/iwcomp/iwab007
16. Meshkati, N.: Technology transfer to developing countries: a tripartite micro- and macro ergonomic analysis of human-organization-technology interfaces. Int. J. Ind. Ergon. **4**, 101–115 (1989)
17. Martinie, C., Navarre, D., Palanque, P.: A multi-formalism approach for model-based dynamic distribution of user interfaces of critical interactive systems. Int. J. Hum. Comput. Stud. **72**(1), 77–99 (2014). https://doi.org/10.1016/j.ijhcs.2013.08.013
18. Martinie, C., Palanque, P., Navarre, D., Winckler, M. A., Poupart, E.: Model-based training: an approach supporting operability of critical interactive systems: application to satellite ground segment. In: ACM SIGCHI Conference Engineering Interactive Computing Systems (EICS 2011), Pise, Italie, 13/06/11–16/06/11 (pp. 589–609)
19. MIL-HDBK-61B. Department of Defense Handbook: Configuration Management Guidance, 07-Apr-2020
20. Navarre, D., Palanque, P., Basnyat, S.: A formal approach for user interaction reconfiguration of safety critical interactive systems. In: Harrison, M.D., Sujan, M.-A. (eds.) SAFECOMP 2008. LNCS, vol. 5219, pp. 373–386. Springer, Heidelberg (2008). https://doi.org/10.1007/978-3-540-87698-4_31
21. Paine, S., et al.: Satellite mission operations best practices. In: AIAA Space Operations and Support Technical Committee, April 20$^{th}$ (2001)
22. Palanque, P.: POISE: a framework for designing perfect interactive systems with and for imperfect people. In: Ardito, C., et al. (eds.) INTERACT 2021. LNCS, vol. 12932, pp. 39–59. Springer, Cham (2021). https://doi.org/10.1007/978-3-030-85623-6_5

23. Siegel, A.W., Schraagen, J.M.C.: Beyond procedures: team reflection in a rail control centre to enhance resilience. Saf. Sci. **91**, 181–191 (2017). https://doi.org/10.1016/j.ssci.2016.08.013
24. Welz, L.L., Bruno, K.J., Kazz, S.L., Potts, S.S., Witkowski, M.M.: Mission Operations and Command Assurance: Flight Operations Quality Improvements. NASA JPL Technical Report Server, 1993–08–03 https://trs.jpl.nasa.gov/handle/2014/35654
25. Wincek, J., Sousa, L.S., Myers, M.R., Ozog, H.: Organizational change management for process safety. Proc. Safety Prog. **34**, 89–93 (2015). https://doi.org/10.1002/prs.11688
26. Xu, T., Zhou, Y.: Systems approaches to tackling configuration errors: a survey. ACM Comput. Surv. **47**(4), 1–47 (2015). https://doi.org/10.1145/2791577

# Improving Resilience by Communicating Predicted Disruptions in Control Rooms

Suvodip Chakraborty[1,2(✉)], Peter Kiefer[2], and Martin Raubal[2]

[1] ETH Zurich, Future Resilient Systems, Singapore-ETH Centre, 1 CREATE Way #06-01 CREATE Tower, Singapore 138602, Singapore
schakraborth@ethz.ch

[2] ETH Zurich, Institute of Cartography and Geoinformation, Stefano-Franscini-Platz 5, 8093 Zurich, Switzerland
{pekiefer,mraubal}@ethz.ch
http://gis.ethz.ch

**Abstract.** Control rooms are essential for the functioning of critical infrastructure, and thus for the economy and society as a whole. Since disruptions in control rooms can have severe cascading effects, it is of utmost importance that control rooms are designed in a way that contributes to the resilience of the cyber-physical system they are monitoring. Even though the importance of resilience for control rooms is generally acknowledged, cognitive resilience is often not taken into account properly during control room design. This vision paper aims at improving the cognitive resilience in control rooms through advancements in three key research areas: 1) automated detection of upcoming disruptions, 2) visualization of spatio-temporal uncertainty, 3) cognition-aware interaction design. The paper then discusses challenges related to our vision and the crucial advancements required to overcome these challenges.

**Keywords:** Resilience · Uncertainty visualization · Control rooms · Cognition awareness

## 1 Introduction

Control rooms are used to surveil, control and manage complex systems, providing real-time data and meaningful insights that are used by decision-makers [1]. Modern control rooms are complex socio-technical systems with a target to maintain high safety despite the pressure. Here, we consider the design of control rooms with a particular focus on resilience. Resilience has been defined as the ability of a system to recognize, adapt and absorb disturbances while retaining critical functionality [2]. The concept of resilience has been used to gain insights from research into the failures of complex systems, which can be used to manage risk proactively [3]. Studies have demonstrated the effectiveness of using resilience metrics to facilitate and manage road recovery activities in post-disaster scenarios [4]. Similar systems have been developed for coping with


C. Ardito et al. (Eds.): INTERACT 2021, LNCS 13198, pp. 302–315, 2022.
https://doi.org/10.1007/978-3-030-98388-8_27

natural disasters such as floods, where up to 50% reduction in damage could be achieved [5]. Researchers have demonstrated the possibility of a reduction in travel time, vehicle operating cost, and increase of safety by incorporating suitable resilience measures into transportation systems [6]. In the context of control room design, resilience plays a role in two ways: on the one hand, the control room infrastructure itself must be resilient against disturbances, such as power outages. On the other hand – and this is our focus here – well-designed control rooms can contribute to the resilience of the monitored system. We suggest that resilience improvement for complex systems, such as urban traffic, can be achieved by considering automated detection, better visualization and cognition-aware HCI in the design of the control rooms used for monitoring these systems.

A plethora of advancements have taken place in control rooms. The current state-of-the-art control rooms have a real-time feed and enjoy seamless communication amongst stakeholders, such as operators and decision-makers. However, the cognitive states and biases of the stakeholders are still neglected while communicating important information and events [7,8]. In addition to this, the spatio-temporal implications and effects are often unclear to the stakeholders. For example, Cisco (San Jose, California), could not comprehend the effect of the Colorado wildfire in 2012 on its infrastructure [9]. Spatio-temporal uncertainty visualizations of the wildfire would have created an awareness among the stakeholders by communicating the possibility of a potential disruption. Additional information, such as a spatio-temporal representation of the prediction model uncertainty and the reasoning behind the prediction, could also be communicated to the stakeholders. This will result in an efficient and informed decision-making process and work towards reducing the cognitive bias of the decision-makers.

The decision-makers in a control room require real-time information, a high degree of situation awareness, and alertness in order to make decisions effectively and efficiently [10]. They are frequently subjected to high-stress scenarios. The ability of the personnel to overcome the stress and maintain a high degree of cognitive function can be attributed to cognitive resilience [11]. Therefore, apart from high organizational resilience, control rooms should also consider monitoring cognitive states of their operators as a measure of cognitive performance and operators' resilience to stress [11].

In this paper, the interface design and data visualization technology for state-of-the-art control rooms are briefly reviewed in Sect. 2. Then, a vision of future control rooms is developed in Sect. 3. The discussion compares the vision with the present technology and identifies the key research areas that must be addressed to facilitate the vision in the future control rooms. Potential challenges that may occur before our vision becomes a reality are discussed in Sect. 4. The paper concludes with an outlook on the immediate next steps in Sect. 5.

## 2 Interface Design and Data Visualization in State-of-the-Art Control Rooms

The current trend throughout the world is to design the control rooms ecologically, taking the infrastructure and demands from different agencies into consideration [1,12]. One of the most critical aspects in supporting decision makers is data visualization.

Visualizations are used to depict a large amount of complex data from multiple sources (cameras, vehicle counters, speed, etc.) to the stakeholders. Previously, control room personnel had to manually monitor the feeds. Such data-intensive practices require a lot of cognitive effort; currently, infographics are used to convey the data [12]. The sheer amount of data (structured and unstructured) makes it impossible for the stakeholders to manually monitor the data feeds. This has brought forward a need for advanced data visualization techniques [1,12]. Advancements in data visualization, such as map-based visualization, can be used to operationalize resilience in control rooms [13]. Map-based visualizations can be used to help decision-makers by depicting multiple attributes spatially and providing adequate means of map interaction [14]. Combining the principles of map-based visualization with ubiquitous computing has been proven to be effective in aiding decision-makers in control rooms [1]. Researchers have shown the effectiveness of such approaches in different scenarios ranging from nuclear releases to floods and cyclones [15–17]. For example, the spatial decision support system developed by Heinzlef *et al.* demonstrates the feasibility of map-based visualizations in increasing a city's resilience in case of floods [16]. Their work overcomes theoretical obstacles in realizing resilience by designing indicators capable of assessing resilience both at a micro and a macro scale. They demonstrated the potential for improving resilience through mapping tools as a medium for making the stakeholders aware of the concept and helping them integrate resilience into their risk management strategies. Their proposed integration of visualizations with the expertise of stakeholders makes the decision-making process more resilient [16].

Recently, automation reliability has given rise to a situation where the predictions from the system can be uncertain (owing to both the performance of the system as well as the environment). The stakeholders, who are in charge of primary decision-making, i.e., acceptance or rejection of the recommendation from the automation, often operate without suitable information about the uncertainty of the prediction [12]. A survey by Hullman *et al.* has reported that only 3% of studies have represented uncertainty to the viewers [18]. In addition to this, most of the time, the organizations have limited tolerance to ambiguity. This often results in new data being force-fitted into existing mental models or scenarios [19]. As the development of an alternate hypothesis is a cognitively intense procedure, the stakeholders choose to adopt a single view even if it is not necessarily the right one [18]. Several studies have indicated that depicting uncertainty can help in the development of outcome monitoring, which is a key component of cognitive control [20,21]. However, visualizing uncertainty can have adverse effects on the control room's performance if the usability of such a proposed framework is not studied in detail.

Human-computer interaction (HCI) research has studied how to design, evaluate and improve such frameworks [22–24]. The usual user interface design process involves a human designer mapping one particular problem to propose a solution [22]. Researchers have designed UIs using genetic programming to automate the critical parts of the UI design process for control rooms [23]. The approach involves defining essential content elements, which are automatically designed by the algorithm and modified using the user's eye-tracking and mouse movement data [23]. The resulting user interfaces were generalizable, following clearly defined guidelines for designing user interfaces. The effectiveness of such approaches of UI design has been illustrated through empirical evidence using subjective measures such as NASA-TLX and eye-tracking measures such as fixation duration, fixation count, and dwell time in nuclear control room interfaces [24].

Eye-tracking is often used to study the mental effort of a person while working on a task [25,26]. Eye-tracking parameters, such as pupil diameter [26] and intrinsic variations of it [25] have been used by researchers as a measure of cognitive load. Cognitive load and working memory are closely knitted subjects. An increase in cognitive load is often accompanied by loss of information from the short-term working memory, thereby decreasing the performance, which can have disastrous consequences in control rooms [27]. Researchers have used eye-tracking to gain insights into the cognitive states of the participants [28]. For example, Li *et al.* demonstrated the feasibility and effectiveness of monitoring vigilance levels of operators in the control room based on eye-tracking and contextual factors [29]. Their study highlighted the correlation between eye-tracking metrics and fatigue. Eye-tracking has also been used in control rooms to study human information processing using individual differences in eye movements [30]. It was found that the scan patterns of individuals demonstrated significant variations when viewing different modalities and performing different tasks, with a strong coupling between eye and head movement. To sum it up, we believe that eye-tracking can also be a very powerful tool in studying the cognitive states of control room operators, and it can be used as a medium of interaction [8,15].

## 3 Vision for Next Generation Control Rooms

The previous section has argued why current control rooms are not capable of supporting decision-makers to the fullest, thus reducing resilience. Now we take a look at cognitive biases that plague decision-making and how we plan to address them. Schoemaker *et al.* reports that both stakeholders and organizations are susceptible to cognitive biases as represented in Fig. 1 [19].

We argue that personal biases, such as incomplete information and selective perception, can be subdued to some extent by visualizing spatio-temporal uncertainty. Organizational biases like stress-induced group thinking and poor information sharing can be addressed by monitoring cognitive states and using HCI methods for information sharing. Research efforts are needed to make the future control rooms devoid of such shortcomings. To implement this vision, critical technologies need to be developed and deployed.

The purpose of this vision paper is to present a unique vision for modern control rooms. We begun this paper by discussing the UI and visualizations

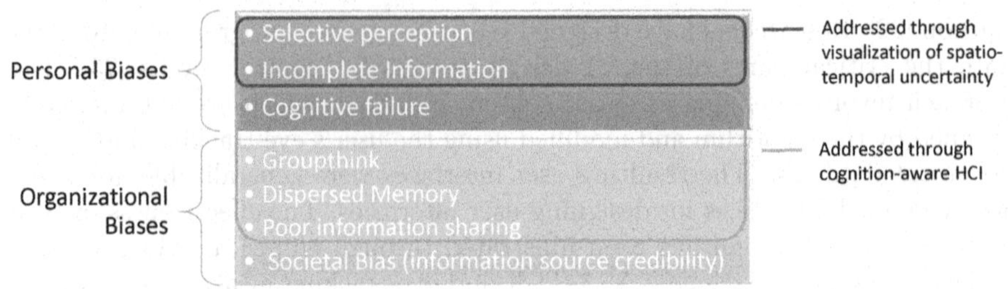


**Fig. 1.** Personal and organizational biases in decision making [19]

employed in state-of-the-art control rooms and the technological gaps. As main gaps, we have identified the ad-hoc visualization and interaction requirements in future control rooms based on conclusions drawn from a literature review. Based on these results, we propose key research areas in three domains to support decision-makers. Figure 2 illustrates the three key research areas in which advancements are required for the implementation of our vision:

- Automated detection of upcoming disruptions
- Visualization of spatio-temporal uncertainty
- Cognition-aware HCI

### 3.1 Automated Detection of Upcoming Disruptions

Control rooms currently operate in a reactive approach (wait for the disruption and then find the cause). Several data sources (mobility, social media, meteorological, and geographical information) can be used to monitor the infrastructure [31]. In many instances seemingly benign problems have resulted in catastrophic consequences [3,9,19,32]. Such problems can stem from improper data analysis, cognitive failure of decision-makers, and missed weak signals [3]. Modern control rooms are still heavily dependent on the abilities, experience, and intuitions of human operators for assimilating data from multiple tools into decision-making without offering the operators much context. Advancements in Artificial intelligence (AI) and Machine learning (ML) have been primarily used to support decision-makers. Data fusion algorithms can incorporate data from multiple sources viz. mobility, meteorological, social media, geographical and historical data, and predict changes or issue warnings of potential disruptions [33,34]. Often during emergencies and disruptions, human operators control the system manually.

Proactive detection of disruptive events in control rooms (e.g. traffic, railways, power grids etc.) is one of the leading research issues [14,35,36]. ML approaches such as support vector machine (SVM) have been used in the prediction of disruptions [37,38]. Recently researchers have used deep learning for the detection of upcoming disruptions [39]. However, detection can be a double-edged sword. An oversensitive system can cause false alarms leading to distrust

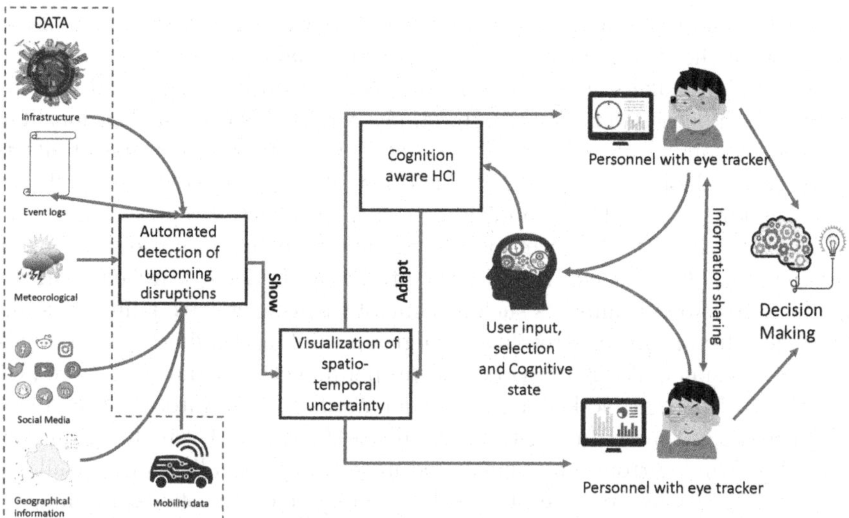


**Fig. 2.** Vision for next generation control rooms. Multiple data sources are combined for the automatic detection of upcoming disruptions. Results are visualized with their spatio-temporal uncertainty. The interface adapts using cognition-aware HCI, based on control room operators' user inputs and cognitive states. The eye trackers will also enable the users to share information amongst each other, thereby making the decision-making process collaborative.

among stakeholders. On the other hand, under-sensitive systems can miss critical events resulting in damage that would have been avoidable [9]. One of the most important steps towards mitigating the impacts of disruption is early detection. Early detection of upcoming or ongoing disruptions can help decision-makers in better preparing and in some cases avoiding disruptions [9]. Proactive detection of disruptions will enhance the resilience by contributing to increased resistance and faster recovery [40]. We propose the integration of algorithms capable of generating pre-emptive alerts based on the fusion of multi-modal data both from natural phenomena (meteorological data) and human activities (e.g. mobility, and social media data) with spatio-temporal uncertainty visualizations. Our vision is to relieve the operators of cognitive load by offloading event detection. The forecast will be available to the stakeholders in the form of a map-based spatio-temporal visualization.

### 3.2 Visualization of Spatio-Temporal Uncertainty

One of the predominant factors to human error is the incomplete use or incorrect interpretation of visual information; it is one of the major cognitive biases for decision-makers. Automation results are often presented without the associated uncertainty in prediction and contextual information [41,42].

Resilience of an organization is enhanced when there are constructive discussions amongst the stakeholders [43]. Map-based visualizations have been used to support decision-makers in risk assessment, resilience improvement, and studying their effects on decision making [13,16,44,45]. Although such visualizations have been used to communicate disruptive events and their spatio-temporal effects, very few works look at how the visualizations affect the stakeholders and their decision-making [44,46,47]. In addition to this, the effect of representing uncertainty and the contextual information (e.g., meteorological conditions, change in governmental policies, social media data, etc.) is an under-researched topic.

In high-stress environments such as control rooms, cognitive failure of stakeholders can often result in stress-induced group thinking leading to catastrophic failures of decision making [19]. However, proper depiction of uncertainty reduces the number of mental models a stakeholder needs to take into account during decision making, thus reducing the mental workload [18]. Even though a large body of literature surrounding map-based uncertainty visualization is available, empirical evaluations are rare [48]. A large number of options (e.g., choice of color, texture, glyphs) are offered for representing uncertainty in geographic maps [48]. All these visualization strategies have the common goal of supporting decision making, therefore it becomes imperative to understand the effect of such representations on the process of decision making. Through eye-tracking, we intend to gain insights into the process of data retrieval, comprehension, and analysis in such complex visualizations. In a nutshell, we will like to explore the possibility of making suitable changes to lessen the cognitive load on the stakeholders.

### 3.3 Cognition-Aware HCI

Visualization of large amounts of data is a crucial aspect of control rooms. Generally, a shared display with multiple personalized displays is employed for visualization. Researchers have tried using an integrated approach into real-time dashboards to facilitate the information retrieval for stakeholders [1,12]. Eye movements play a vital role in visual information processing and can also be used to gain insight into the cognition, decision-making process, and alertness levels of the stakeholders [10,49–55]. One of the most common problems with such frameworks is the negative impact of undue and interruptive notifications on users' productivity [56,57]. Additionally, the operators are forced to interact with the system through legacy devices which results in much slower interactions and does not allow for natural interaction [58]. Researchers have tried to address this using intent recognition through eye-tracking [59,60]. However, real-time application and accuracy of such algorithms are still an ongoing research topic [59].

Advancements in eye-tracking can facilitate the decision-makers by aiding in the process of information retrieval [61]. Recent studies on control room operators have inferred that changes in cognitive states are reflected in the actions of the operator and therefore can be tracked using the actions taken by the operator [62]. Recently, Sturman *et al.* have used cerebral oxygenation as a measure to study cognitive resource consumption and cognitive load in control room operators [63]. This study also incorporated the cognitive states of perceiving, remembering, and knowing through a series of test batteries designed by Wiggins *et al.* [64]. Eye movements can be used as a medium for interaction on large screens as well as shared displays [15,65,66]. A large body of research has identified the viability of employing eye-tracking for sharing important and relevant information within teams [66,67]. Such a setup can facilitate the control room personnel in sharing information on the common display, which can replace the current need for physical movements to interact with the big screens [68–70].

Our vision for the future is to take the cognitive state (such as visual search, selective attention, and visual working memory) of the operators into account while presenting data visualizations and notifications. This will negate the negative impacts of current interfaces on the stakeholders. Moreover, information of cognitive states can be used to provide proper support (e.g. highlighting critical elements, and modifications to notification presentation) to be rendered in real-time to the operators. The effects of integrating uncertainty information on decision-making and cognitive states are yet to be explored. The development of real-time cognitive state algorithms is crucial for this stage. We believe such new and upcoming innovations can result in better interface design. Such interfaces can promote high situational awareness and, in turn, can make the decision-making process more versatile and adaptive without adding to the mental load of the users.

## 4 Challenges

Seamless inclusion of new technologies in an existing ecosystem has always been a challenging task. Automatic detection of upcoming disruptions, on the one hand, can reduce the cognitive load of an operator; on the other hand, it can result in over-reliance of decision-makers on automation, and it may introduce boredom. Boredom is already a prevalent problem in control rooms where the vigilance level of the control room operators is affected [29]. Special efforts should be put into the explainability of the automation to promote a sense of trust and introduce resilience through distributed cognition [9].

Moreover, the explainability of automation systems can help build knowledge models for extreme and unknown scenarios or black swan events [71]. Black swan events, by their definition, are rare and highly uncertain. Current automation fundamentally works towards promoting a sense of certainty to decision-makers.

Representation of uncertainty to decision-makers seems to be an obvious choice for dealing with uncertainty [18]. However, historically visualizations have been designed to promote a sense of certainty to decision-makers [18]. Control room operators will need to adapt to the new visualizations portraying uncertainty. The visualizations themselves will have to be designed to represent the underlying uncertainty without obstructing the signal [18]. Such visualizations will need to be tested holistically with the operators in control rooms where safety is of paramount importance.

Control room UIs often run on several screens, and it becomes challenging for the operators to gather information from all the separate screens. A well-functioning UI will improve operator performance and efficiency while reducing errors and mental and physical workload. User experience studies can help consolidate these interfaces and present alerts and notifications while optimizing the workload. The impact of uncertainty representations can be assessed through HCI techniques such as eye-tracking [23]. In control rooms, as opposed to ideal laboratory conditions, the lighting conditions might vary, which could affect the parameters computed through eye-tracking. Many operators use infrared reflective coating on their glasses, and this might cause interference in eye-tracking data. As eye trackers are still primarily used by researchers, proper setup, maintenance, and debugging problems in eye trackers will need specialized support. Operators spend a significant part of their working time in front of screens; eye trackers can be regarded as potentially intrusive to their privacy. Eye-tracking can also serve as a medium for interactions in control rooms. However, this can result in unintentional or accidental interactions with the user interface, also known as the "Midas touch problem" [72]. Midas touch could cause the control room operators to lose faith in the cognition-aware HCI.

## 5 Conclusion and Next Steps

In this paper, we have presented our vision for the next generation of control rooms. We began the paper by discussing the necessity of cognitive resilience in control rooms. Then we reviewed the interface design and data visualization in state-of-the-art control rooms. Based on the conclusions drawn from the review we have identified the technological gaps and proposed advancements in three key research areas which are vital for the development of next-generation of control rooms.

Innovations in automated detection of upcoming disruptions will make sure that the automation will be able to predict future disruptions. While the detection task will have been offloaded to the AI, the stakeholders will be able to holistically focus on decision-making. Modern control rooms still rely on decision-makers in case of emergencies. At a glance, introducing automation in control rooms might appear to improve efficiency and decrease workload, but while facing black swan events, the automation itself might fail. In addition to this, when too many functions are automated, operators become dependent on the automation, causing a decrease in the ability and knowledge of manual performance. Therefore we should work towards introducing explainability in automated systems and communicate the uncertainties through proper visualizations.

Our vision to develop visualization of spatio-temporal uncertainty has stemm-ed from the gaps in modern map-based decision support systems. We aim to provide enhanced support to operators through interactive map-based visualization incorporating uncertainty and prediction reasoning. Control room operators operate under a lot of stress. Decision-makers under stress can exhibit various behaviors, including seeking certainty, being less tolerant of ambiguity, and looking for fast choices. Proper uncertainty visualizations should be designed and tested to ensure decision-makers are properly supported.

Although decision-making is a complicated process that can potentially be influenced by many different factors, cognitive states are perhaps the most critical ones. Considering that faulty decision-making can lead to a sub-optimal outcome, monitoring cognitive states is one of the essential aspects in next-generation control rooms. The developments needed in cognition-aware HCI have been derived from the conclusions and insights from shortcomings in visualization and interaction in control rooms. Based on these considerations, we have highlighted the importance of unifying information about cognitive-state information with decision support systems. Although the effects of time pressure on decision-making in general have been explored to a certain degree, the particular case of control rooms remained under-explored. As the control room operators frequently face intense time pressure and cognitive load, proper assessment of the combined effects of time pressure and cognitive load is crucial. Assessing operator performance can be beneficial for both the operator and supervisor. The supervisor can be kept in the loop through cognition-aware information sharing while the operator can receive real-time support from the UI. Although not exhaustive, HCI techniques can also be used to identify fatigue and stress and facilitate much more natural interaction with the interfaces. New visualization techniques should be tested using both objective and subjective evaluations. The developed visualizations will aid the decision-makers in better understanding the situation and thereby improve the control room's resilience as a whole. A diligent framework capable of assisting decision-makers will improve the quality of interaction. Implementing HCI in control rooms opens possibilities for promoting collaboration with experts from multiple domains. This will make the collaboration between domain experts even easier, thereby reducing the risk, improving safety, and reducing recovery times. User experience studies of such a framework can later be used as a reference and basis for user interfaces in control rooms.

**Acknowledgement.** This work is an outcome of the Future Resilient Systems project at the Singapore-ETH Centre (SEC) supported by the National Research Foundation, Prime Minister's Office, Singapore under its Campus for Research Excellence and Technological Enterprise (CREATE) programme.

## References

1. Kostakos, V., Ojala, T., Juntunen, T.: Traffic in the smart city: exploring city-wide sensing for traffic control center augmentation. IEEE Internet Comput. **17**(6), 22–29 (2013)
2. Back, J., Furniss, D., Hildebrandt, M., Blandford, A.: Resilience markers for safer systems and organisations. In: Harrison, M.D., Sujan, M.-A. (eds.) SAFECOMP 2008. LNCS, vol. 5219, pp. 99–112. Springer, Heidelberg (2008). https://doi.org/10.1007/978-3-540-87698-4_11
3. Woods, D.D.: Creating foresight: how resilience engineering can transform NASA's approach to risky decision making. Work **4**(2), 137–144 (2003)

4. Caunhye, A.M., Aydin, N.Y., Duzgun, H.S.: Robust post-disaster route restoration. OR Spectr. **42**(4), 1055–1087 (2020). https://doi.org/10.1007/s00291-020-00601-0
5. Schinke, R., Kaidel, A., Golz, S., Naumann, T., López-Gutiérrez, J.S., Garvin, S.: Analysing the effects of flood-resilience technologies in urban areas using a synthetic model approach. ISPRS Int. J. Geo Inf. **5**(11), 202 (2016)
6. Chacon-Hurtado, D., Losada-Rojas, L.L., David, Yu., Gkritza, K., Fricker, J.D.: A proposed framework for the incorporation of economic resilience into transportation decision making. J. Manag. Eng. **36**(6), 04020084 (2020)
7. Hodgetts, H.M., Vachon, F., Chamberland, C., Tremblay, S.: See no evil: cognitive challenges of security surveillance and monitoring. J. Appl. Res. Mem. Cogn. **6**(3), 230–243 (2017)
8. Domova, V., Ralph, M., Vartiainen, E., Muñoz, A.A., Henriksson, A., Timsjö, S.: Re-introducing physical user interfaces into industrial control rooms. In: ACM International Conference Proceeding Series, Part F1311, pp. 162–168 (2017)
9. Sheffi, Y.: Preparing for disruptions through early detection. MIT Sloan Manag. Rev. **57**(1), 31 (2015)
10. Li, F., Chen, C.H., Xu, G., Khoo, L.P.: Hierarchical eye-tracking data analytics for human fatigue detection at a traffic control center. IEEE Trans. Hum. Mach. Syst. **50**(5), 465–474 (2020)
11. Staal, M.A., Bolton, A.E., Yaroush, R.A., Bourne, L.E., Jr.: Cognitive performance and resilience to stress. In: Biobehavioral Resilience to Stress, pp. 259–299 (2008)
12. Baber, C., Morar, N.S., McCabe, F.: Ecological interface design, the proximity compatibility principle, and automation reliability in road traffic management. IEEE Trans. Hum.-Mach. Syst. **49**(3), 241–249 (2019)
13. Frazier, T.G., Thompson, C.M., Dezzani, R.J., Butsick, D.: Spatial and temporal quantification of resilience at the community scale. Appl. Geogr. **42**, 95–107 (2013)
14. Kalamaras, I., et al.: An interactive visual analytics platform for smart intelligent transportation systems management. IEEE Trans. Intell. Transp. Syst. **19**(2), 487–496 (2017)
15. Savioja, P., Norros, L.: Systems usability framework for evaluating tools in safety-critical work. Cogn. Technol. Work **15**(3), 255–275 (2013)
16. Heinzlef, C., Becue, V., Serre, D.: A spatial decision support system for enhancing resilience to floods: Bridging resilience modelling and geovisualization techniques. Nat. Hazard. **20**(4), 1049–1068 (2020)
17. Liu, L., Padilla, L., Creem-Regehr, S.H., House, D.H.: Visualizing uncertain tropical cyclone predictions using representative samples from ensembles of forecast tracks. IEEE Trans. Visual Comput. Graphics **25**(1), 882–891 (2018)
18. Hullman, J.: Why authors don't visualize uncertainty. IEEE Trans. Visual Comput. Graphics **26**(1), 130–139 (2019)
19. Schoemaker, P.J., Day, G.S.: How to make sense of weak signals. In: Leading Organizations: Perspectives for a New Era, p. 37 (2009)
20. Mushtaq, F., Bland, A.R., Schaefer, A.: Uncertainty and cognitive control. Front. Psychol. **2**, 249 (2011)
21. Yoshida, W., Ishii, S.: Resolution of uncertainty in prefrontal cortex. Neuron **50**(5), 781–789 (2006)
22. Salem, P.: User interface optimization using genetic programming with an application to landing pages. In: Proceedings of the ACM on Human-Computer Interaction, vol. 1(EICS) (2017)
23. Diego-Mas, J.A., Garzon-Leal, D., Poveda-Bautista, R., Alcaide-Marzal, J.: User-interfaces layout optimization using eye-tracking, mouse movements and genetic algorithms. Appl. Ergon. **78**, 197–209 (2019)

24. Fernandes, A., Renganayagalu, S.K., Eitrheim, M.H.R.: Using eye tracking to explore design features in nuclear control room interfaces. In: Human Factors and Ergonomics Society Europe Chapter, vol. 4959, pp. 267–278 (2016)
25. Duchowski, A.T., et al.: The index of pupillary activity: measuring cognitive load vis-à-vis task difficulty with pupil oscillation. In: Proceedings of the 2018 CHI Conference on Human Factors in Computing Systems, pp. 1–13 (2018)
26. Kiefer, P., Giannopoulos, I., Duchowski, A., Raubal, M.: Measuring cognitive load for map tasks through pupil diameter. In: Miller, J.A., O'Sullivan, D., Wiegand, N. (eds.) GIScience 2016. LNCS, vol. 9927, pp. 323–337. Springer, Cham (2016). https://doi.org/10.1007/978-3-319-45738-3_21
27. Barrouillet, P., Bernardin, S., Portrat, S., Vergauwe, E., Camos, V.: Time and cognitive load in working memory. J. Exp. Psychol. Learn. Mem. Cogn. **33**(3), 570 (2007)
28. Marshall, S.P.: Identifying cognitive state from eye metrics. Aviat. Space Environ. Med. **78**(5), B165–B175 (2007)
29. Li, F., Chen, C.H., Xu, G., Khoo, L.P., Liu, Y.: Proactive mental fatigue detection of traffic control operators using bagged trees and gaze-bin analysis. Adv. Eng. Inform. **42**, 100987 (2019)
30. Starke, S.D., Baber, C., Cooke, N.J., Howes, A.: Workflows and individual differences during visually guided routine tasks in a road traffic management control room. Appl. Ergon. **61**, 79–89 (2017)
31. Jin, X., Zhang, Z., Gan, A.: Traffic Management Centers: Challenges, Best Practices, and Future Plans, August 2014
32. Kuwata, Y., Ishikawa, Y., Ohtani, H.: An architecture for command and control in disaster response systems. In: 2000 26th Annual Conference of the IEEE Industrial Electronics Society, IECON 2000, 2000 IEEE International Conference on Industrial Electronics, Control and Instrumentation. 21st Century Technologies, vol. 1, pp. 120–125. IEEE (2000)
33. Lau, B.P.L., et al.: A survey of data fusion in smart city applications. Inf. Fusion **52**, 357–374 (2019)
34. Madhavi, K.S.L., et al.: Advanced electricity load forecasting combining electricity and transportation network. In: 2017 North American Power Symposium (NAPS), pp. 1–6. IEEE (2017)
35. Cadarso, L., Maróti, G., Marín, Á.: Smooth and controlled recovery planning of disruptions in rapid transit networks. IEEE Trans. Intell. Transp. Syst. **16**(4), 2192–2202 (2015)
36. Pavlov, A., Ivanov, D., Werner, F., Dolgui, A., Sokolov, B.: Integrated detection of disruption scenarios, the ripple effect dispersal and recovery paths in supply chains. Ann. Oper. Res., 1–23 (2019)
37. Xiao, J.: SVM and KNN ensemble learning for traffic incident detection. Phys. A **517**, 29–35 (2019)
38. Cannas, B., et al.: Support vector machines for disruption prediction and novelty detection at jet. Fusion Eng. Des. **82**(5–14), 1124–1130 (2007)
39. Doriguzzi-Corin, R., Millar, S., Scott-Hayward, S., Martinez-del Rincon, J., Siracusa, D.: LUCID: a practical, lightweight deep learning solution for DDoS attack detection. IEEE Trans. Netw. Serv. Manage. **17**(2), 876–889 (2020)
40. Grafton, R.Q., et al.: Realizing resilience for decision-making. Nature Sustain. **2**(10), 907–913 (2019)
41. Schwarz, T., Butscher, S., Mueller, J., Reiterer, H.: Content-aware navigation for large displays in context of traffic control rooms. In: Proceedings of the Workshop on Advanced Visual Interfaces AVI, pp. 249–252 (2012)

42. Zeng, W., Fu, C.W., Arisona, S.M., Erath, A., Qu, H.: Visualizing mobility of public transportation system. IEEE Trans. Visual Comput. Graphics **20**(12), 1833–1842 (2014)
43. Radhakrishnan, M., Pathirana, A., Ashley, R., Zevenbergen, C.: Structuring climate adaptation through multiple perspectives: framework and case study on flood risk management. Water **9**(2), 129 (2017)
44. Kübler, I., Richter, K.F., Fabrikant, S.I.: Against all odds: multicriteria decision making with hazard prediction maps depicting uncertainty. Ann. Am. Assoc. Geogr. **110**(3), 661–683 (2020)
45. Barroca, B., Serre, D.: Risks revealed by cartography-cartography renewed by the geovisualization of risks. Int. J. Cartogr. **4**(1), 1–3 (2018)
46. Hope, S., Hunter, G.J.: Testing the effects of positional uncertainty on spatial decision-making. Int. J. Geogr. Inf. Sci. **21**(6), 645–665 (2007)
47. Cheong, L., Bleisch, S., Kealy, A., Tolhurst, K., Wilkening, T., Duckham, M.: Evaluating the impact of visualization of wildfire hazard upon decision-making under uncertainty. Int. J. Geogr. Inf. Sci. **30**(7), 1377–1404 (2016)
48. MacEachren, A.M., et al.: Visualizing geospatial information uncertainty: what we know and what we need to know. Cartogr. Geogr. Inf. Sci. **32**(3), 139–160 (2005)
49. Göbel, F., Giannopoulos, I., Raubal, M.: The importance of visual attention for adaptive interfaces. In: Proceedings of the 18th International Conference on Human-Computer Interaction with Mobile Devices and Services Adjunct, MobileHCI 2016, pp. 930–935, September 2016
50. Bochynska, A., Laeng, B.: Tracking down the path of memory: eye scanpaths facilitate retrieval of visuospatial information. Cogn. Process. **16**(1), 159–163 (2015). https://doi.org/10.1007/s10339-015-0690-0
51. Schulte-mecklenbeck, M., Renkewitz, F., Scherbaum, S.: Forward inference in risky choice: mapping gaze and decision processes running head: FORWARD INFERENCE IN RISKY CHOICE Forward Inference in Risky Choice: Mapping Gaze and Decision Processes Technische Universität Dresden University of Bern Max Planck I, January 2019
52. Rashid, U., Nacenta, M.A., Quigley, A.: Factors influencing visual attention switch in multi-display user interfaces: a survey. In: ACM International Conference Proceeding Series (2012)
53. Wallace, J.R., Scott, S.D., Stutz, T., Enns, T., Inkpen, K.: Investigating teamwork and taskwork in single- and multi-display groupware systems. Pers. Ubiquit. Comput. **13**(8), 569–581 (2009)
54. Wallace, J.R., Scott, S.D., Lai, E., Jajalla, D.: Investigating the role of a large, shared display in multi-display environments. Comput. Support. Coop. Work **20**(6), 529–561 (2011)
55. Bulling, A., Zander, T.O.: Cognition-aware computing. IEEE Pervasive Comput. **13**(3), 80–83 (2014)
56. Okoshi, T., Nozaki, H., Nakazawa, J., Tokuda, H., Ramos, J., Dey, A.K.: Towards attention-aware adaptive notification on smart phones. Pervasive Mob. Comput. **26**, 17–34 (2016)
57. Iqbal, S.T., Bailey, B.P.: Oasis: a framework for linking notification delivery to the perceptual structure of goal-directed tasks. ACM Trans. Comput.-Hum. Interact. **17**(4), 1–28 (2010)
58. Zhang, X., Liu, X., Yuan, S.M., Lin, S.F.: Eye tracking based control system for natural human-computer interaction. Comput. Intell. Neurosci. **2017** (2017)

59. Slanzi, G., Balazs, J.A., Velásquez, J.D.: Combining eye tracking, pupil dilation and EEG analysis for predicting web users click intention. Inf. Fusion **35**, 51–57 (2017)
60. Huang, C.-M., Andrist, S., Sauppé, A., Mutlu, B.: Using gaze patterns to predict task intent in collaboration. Front. Psychol. **6**, 1–12 (2015)
61. Bednarik, R., Eivazi, S., Vrzakova, H.: A computational approach for prediction of problem-solving behavior using support vector machines and eye-tracking data. In: Nakano, Y., Conati, C., Bader, T. (eds.) Eye Gaze in Intelligent User Interfaces, pp. 111–134. Springer, London (2013). https://doi.org/10.1007/978-1-4471-4784-8_7
62. Das, L., Iqbal, M.U., Bhavsar, P., Srinivasan, B., Srinivasan, R.: Toward preventing accidents in process industries by inferring the cognitive state of control room operators through eye tracking. ACS Sustain. Chem. Eng. **6**(2), 2517–2528 (2018)
63. Sturman, D., et al.: Control room operators' cue utilization predicts cognitive resource consumption during regular operational tasks. Front. Psychol. **10**, 1967 (2019)
64. Loveday, T., Wiggins, M.W., Auton, J.C.: Expert Intensive Skills Evaluation (Expertise) Test. Macquarie University, Sydney (2015)
65. Christian, L., Sven, G., Antonio, K., Boring, S., Bulling, A.: GazeProjector: location-independent gaze interaction on and across multiple displays, September (2015)
66. Prouzeau, A., Bezerianos, A., Chapuis, O.: Awareness techniques to aid transitions between personal and shared workspaces in multi-display environments. In: ISS 2018 - Proceedings of the 2018 ACM International Conference on Interactive Surfaces and Spaces, pp. 291–304 (2018)
67. O'Hara, K., Kjeldskov, J., Paay, J.: Blended interaction spaces for distributed team collaboration. ACM Trans. Comput.-Hum. Interact. **18**(1), 1–28 (2011)
68. Kern, D., Marshall, P., Schmidt, A.: Gazemarks: gaze-based visual placeholders to ease attention switching. In: Conference on Human Factors in Computing Systems - Proceedings, May 2014, vol. 3, pp. 2093–2102 (2010)
69. Ball, R., North, C., Bowman, D.A.: Move to improve: promoting physical navigation to increase user performance with large displays. In: Conference on Human Factors in Computing Systems - Proceedings, Figure 1, pp. 191–200 (2007)
70. Shivakumar, A., Bositty, A., Peters, N.S., Pei, Y.: Real-time interruption management system for efficient distributed collaboration in multi-tasking environments. Proc. ACM Hum.-Comput. Interact. **4**(CSCW1), 1–23 (2020)
71. Taleb, N.N.: The Black Swan: The Impact of the Highly Improbable, vol. 2. Random House, New York (2007)
72. Mohan, P., Goh, W.B., Fu, C.-W., Yeung, S.-K.: DualGaze: addressing the Midas touch problem in gaze mediated VR interaction. In: 2018 IEEE International Symposium on Mixed and Augmented Reality Adjunct (ISMAR-Adjunct), pp. 79–84. IEEE (2018)

# Proving Display Conformance and Action Consistency: The Example of an Integrated Clinical Environment

Michael D. Harrison[1(✉)] and Paolo Masci[2]

[1] School of Computing, Newcastle University, Urban Sciences Building, Newcastle upon Tyne, UK
michael.harrison@ncl.ac.uk

[2] National Institute of Aerospace, 100 Exploration Way, Hampton, VA 23666, USA
paolo.masci@nianet.org

**Abstract.** Medical systems are currently being developed that integrate the multiple devices that are often connected to patients, for example in intensive care or where there are multiple patients in medical wards managed by limited numbers of clinicians. This position paper considers a model of such integrated devices, and the human factors engineering challenges that are important considerations in their development. The model is used as a basis for proof that specific use-centred safety requirements hold of a design that satisfies the model. The paper describes how a model may be used to prove two classes of use-related properties. The first concerns the consistency of multiple displays of the same information while the second proves that actions relating to the same device and patient invoked in different work stations have equivalent effect.

## 1 Introduction

This paper explores the analysis of use-related requirements for *integrated clinical environments* (they will be referred to as ICE), a new kind of healthcare systems that allow simultaneous and coordinated monitoring and control of multiple medical devices. The advantage of ICE is that interventions that are clinically necessary may be expedited, automated or alerted through the "co-operation" of devices. Particular examples are discussed in [9] and include chemotherapy, where an infusion may be paused or the infusion rate modified as a result of changes in the patient's vital signs, and radiotherapy where the position of a patient on a bed may be modified automatically so that the precision of the therapy beam may be enhanced. Such systems may be considered to be control rooms in the sense that a control room is a shared room used by operators as a central hub for monitoring and control. In the ICE system, the nurse station is clearly a control room in the traditional sense of the term. Patient stations could also be interpreted as control rooms because a team of clinicians can use them to monitor and control a set of integrated medical devices delivering a therapy to a patient.


Published by Springer Nature Switzerland AG 2022
C. Ardito et al. (Eds.): INTERACT 2021, LNCS 13198, pp. 316–328, 2022.
https://doi.org/10.1007/978-3-030-98388-8_28

ICE systems are part of a new generation of healthcare information technologies [14] that will provide functionalities for seamless integration of medical devices and other IT systems through standard communication networks. In this vision, medical devices are no longer considered stand-alone elements, but rather *interoperable components* of an integrated ecosystem. Clinicians will be able to assemble new advanced medical systems simply by composing existing devices [3]. An interoperable component can be, for example, a medical device equipped with a network interface, a health information system, or a mobile medical app executed on a device connected to the hospital network.

A common characteristic of interoperable components is their ability to exchange commands and/or data with other interoperable components. They may provide one or multiple operator interfaces that allow clinicians to interact with the device itself, with connected devices, or with the whole integrated system. As Arney et al. [2] comment, medical device interoperability has the promise to improve patient treatment by aligning in novel and life-saving ways information that was previously compartmentalised. For example, clinicians will be able to enhance existing medical devices with safety interlocks, smart alarms, and clinical decision support system tailored to the specific clinical needs of a patient.

The scale of the problem with use-related safety issues is already significant in stand-alone medical devices (see, e.g., [8]). Use-related safety issues will be more problematic in ICE and other integrated medical systems [9]. A key concern is whether the integrated system as a whole can be operated safely by clinicians. When assessing these and other aspects, it should be recognised that the system will be operated by clinicians under time pressure and frequent interruptions. While each interoperable device may be certified safe by their vendors, new issues may arise from their integration as new interaction pathways will be enabled that are simply not possible when the device is used as a stand-alone system.

This paper focuses on two general use-related requirements (that extend those described in [1,11] and [5,7]) capturing the notions of *conformance* and *consistency* as they relate to the design, engineering and evaluation of user interfaces in ICE systems. The focus is on a formal (i.e., mathematical) representation of these requirements, and how the formal representation facilitates the analysis of the extent to which a proposed system design would satisfy these requirements.

The *contribution* of this position paper therefore is the formal modelling of two key use-centred safety requirements, and a demonstration of how a formal analysis of the requirements can inform the design of a realistic ICE system prototype.

## 2 A Proposed ICE System Design

The ICE system design considered in this paper is in the process of development and it aims to be extensible. It revolves around the concept of multiple connected "user stations" that can be used by clinicians to monitor and control the ICE system. Displays on the user stations should be consistent with those of the actual devices that they display. At the same time, actions that are permitted in a particular user station should have consistent effects that map to the actions supported by the devices connected to that user station. The ASTM-F2761-09:2013 standard [4] introduces high-level requirements and architectural considerations for the ICE system. The AAMI/UL-2800-1:2019 standard on medical device interoperability [3] presents usability engineering recommendations for ICE and other integrated medical systems. The recommendations address design aspects related to the dependencies between user interface functionalities provided by different components (medical devices, apps, user stations) of the integrated system. Example design aspects include, e.g., consistency between controls provided on the front panel of a device and those provided on the user stations linked to the device; complexity of feedback for frequent or important events that involve multiple integrated devices.

User stations should therefore satisfy *use-centred safety requirements* that help prevent user actions that could have disastrous consequences. Two types of requirement are considered in this paper: (1) *conformance:* all visualisations of the distributed state should be maintained consistently and should reflect the current state of the system; (2) *consistency:* where the same action can be taken at different locations in the environments then the action should be *available* and have consistent effect wherever it takes place. Conformance of displays and consistency of actions can be interpreted as an instantiation for the ICE system of the AAMI/UL-2800-1:2019 [3] guidelines on consistency and complexity of control and feedback.

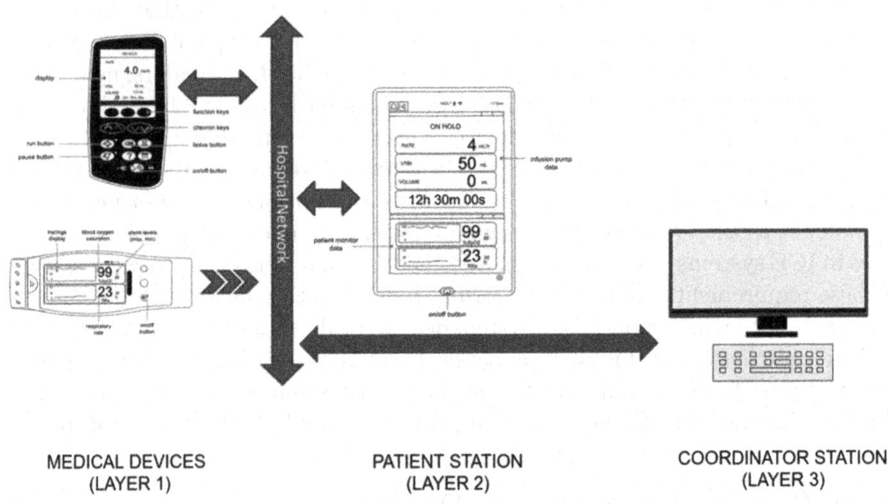


**Fig. 1.** ICE system example.

To explore these two types of requirement in more detail, a specific instance of the ICE system is considered here that can ground the discussion on concrete design aspects. The considered ICE system is simple but realistic. It includes two medical devices: an infusion pump similar to that described in [6], and a vital signs monitor. The design of such an ICE system builds on three conceptual layers (see Fig. 1). These layers are as follows.

1. The first layer includes a multiplicity of devices that are connected to patients in the integrated environment. While the design assumes a plug-in approach including a possible range of devices, just two types of device are assumed (an infusion pump and a vital signs monitor) as they are sufficient for the illustrative purpose of this paper. It is intended that user interfaces at this first layer will be the multiplicity of manufacturer interfaces that allow the clinician to interact with the individual devices, just as they would today in most hospital environments.
2. The second layer consists of a set of "patient stations". These stations support the control of the individual devices for the patient. The display of a patient station provides an overview of key parameters relating to the connected devices and key actions that can be taken. These parameters and actions are set up in the patient station. A top level display element indicates which device has been selected. When a device is selected, all the parameters and actions for that device (other than physical actions such as opening and closing doors) are visible and accessible to be activated. The patient station also enables a definition of the parameters and actions that are available in the coordinator. An edit mode allows the clinician to set up the patient view as it is seen in the coordinator. Finally a further mode allows constraints to be defined. For example the clinician may want to pause an infusion and set off an alarm if blood pressure reaches a particular value. Rules can be set up in the patient station to achieve these constraints.
3. The third layer includes a "coordinator station", which may well be sited centrally (for example the nurses' station in an intensive care ward) and enable clinicians an overview of the situation. The coordinator station provides information and actions at three levels. A top level display element provides an overview of key parameters relating to all patients that are currently connected, and devices within patients are displayed. This top level display element is always visible. A middle display element shows data and actions that were defined as key at the patient level, and can be seen when a patient is selected. At this level, not only parameters are displayed but also actions that are available. These actions and parameters relate to all devices connected to the patient. They are key elements for the patient that can be readily accessed. The lowest level shows a selected device, and provides a richer interface to interact with the device. All these display levels are configured in the patient station.

More details relating to the displays will be discussed in the following Sect. 3. From a human factors engineering point of view, two classes of use requirements are important: safety-related, and security-related. The first class (safety-related requirements) will be considered in more detail in this paper.

# 3 Developing a Formal Specification of the ICE System

Formal specifications and theorems described in this paper use the "Prototype Verification System" (PVS [13]). PVS combines an expressive specification language based on higher-order logic with a theorem proving assistant. It has been used extensively in several application domains and has been used in related work, see for example [7].

A formal specification in PVS is expressed as a collection of *theories*, which consist of declarations of names for types and constants, and expressions in terms of these names. Types supported in the PVS language include the basic types (Booleans, integers, reals, etc.), as well as complex data types such as records, tuples, and lists. Theories and types can be parametrized with types and constants, and can use definitions created in other PVS theories. Properties of a PVS specification are expressed as named formulas declared using the keyword `THEOREM`. More details on the PVS syntax will be provided in the following as needed, while presenting the formal specification of the ICE system.

In order to model and analyse the *conformance* and *consistency* requirements discussed in the introduction, a notion of equivalence is required. To do this, the formal model needs to specify relevant information about the functionalities of the ICE system that are available to the user, and how the various ICE system components are synchronised and exchange commands.

## 3.1 Modelling the Functionalities of the ICE System

A convenient way to model the functionalities of the ICE system in PVS is to represent the overall system as a state machine. The state machine captures the state of devices in the system, as well as the information exchanged between devices. Transition rules define how the system state changes following user actions or automated events.

A PVS record type can be used to specify the system state, where each record field captures relevant information about the system under analysis with the most appropriate data type. Some elements of the system state are used as global elements that capture information exchanged between ICE system components. Functions transforming the current system state into the next system state specify the transition rules of the state machine.

An example system state suitable to model the considered ICE system is in Listing 1.1. A field `nde_state` defines the state of the message passing environment. It represents a function mapping elements of state `node` to buffers that contain messages waiting to be processed. Two fields `p_nodes` and `d_nodes` are global elements describing the mapping between patients and devices and the nodes that are used by them in the message passing system. The set of patient names that are currently connected to the coordinator are defined by `ps`. The patient states are represented by two elements `patient_menus` and `pdb`. Each element is a function mapping patient names to the current patient menu and the current patient state respectively. The patient state includes information that is specific to the patient station as well as a mapping from devices to device states.

Similarly, coord_menu and coord_st specify the current coordinator menu as well as state details of the coordinator station.

```
state: TYPE = [#
  nde_state: n_state,
  p_nodes: node_to_patient,
  d_nodes: node_to_pd,
  ps: patients_type,
  patient_menus: patient_mn_type,
  pdb: patient_db_type,
  coord_st: i_state,
  coord_menu: coord_menu.menu_type
#]
```

**Listing 1.1.** The ICE system state

### 3.2 Keeping Displays up to Date

Update of user station displays is achieved in the considered design by periodic "ticking" functions that trigger the exchange of messages between three ICE system elements: integrated medical devices, linked patient stations, and the coordinator station. These ticking functions are specified in PVS using expressions that transform the current system state (st of type state) into a new system state where relevant device panels in the patient and coordinator stations have been synchronised. Additional arguments can be used in the functions to specify information that is specific to certain ticking functions. For example, function tick_pan_device represents a ticking action passing messages between a specific device and patient (see first declaration in Listing 1.2) while tick_pan_coordinator represents a similar ticking action between all connected patients and coordinator.

```
tick_pan_device(d: device, p: patient, st: state): state
tick_pan_patient(p: patient, st: state): state
tick_pan_coordinator(st: state): state
```

**Listing 1.2.** Ticking functions for updating device panels

Messages exchanged when updating device panels take the following form:

```
pan_message_type: TYPE = [#
  pat_nd: node,
  msg_nd: node,
  mhdr: msg_hdr_type,
  pan: panel
#]
```

**Listing 1.3.** Messages exchanged when updating device panels

Two integer record fields pat_nd and msg_nd specify the identifier of the nodes that connect the devices to the patients and to the coordinator. A field mhdr of the enumerated type msg_hdr_type indicates the message kind. Field pan of type panel captures the characteristics and functionalities of the manufacturer's user interfaces.

An example PVS record type that can be used to specify a generic device panel is in Listing 1.4. It includes information on what device parameters can be set by the user (field pars), what actions are available to the user in the current device mode (field cmds), and what information can be displayed on the panel (fields num_disp and enum_disp).

```
panel: TYPE = [#
  pars: parset,
  enum_disp: enum_parameter,
  num_disp: num_parameter,
  cmds: action_ids
#]
```

**Listing 1.4.** Device panel

The field num_disp captures information on continuous numeric values used by the device, such as physiological measurements obtained through sensors (e.g., heart rate) or physical quantities representing therapy parameters (e.g., volume to be infused). The field enum_disp captures information on operating modes of the device.

### 3.3 Communicating Actions

In addition to the ticking functions that are used to update device panels, there are also ticking functions that transmit actions to selected devices. These ticking functions are also assumed to be activated periodically.

```
tick_act_device(d: device, p: patient, st: state): state
tick_act_patient(p: patient, st: state): state
```

**Listing 1.5.** Ticking function for communicating actions

The message type in this case is as follows:

```
act_message_type: TYPE = [#
  pat_nd: node,
  msg_nd: node,
  mhdr: msg_hdr_type,
  act: action_id
#]
```

**Listing 1.6.** Action message structure

When a patient station receives an action message from the coordinator, the patient station relays the message to the relevant device. When the message is received by the device, a corresponding action is triggered in that device. The functions described in Listing 1.7 describe the mechanism for invoking a command in the coordinator (a similar function is used to invoke a command in the patient station). The full specification of the function is shown here to give the reader an idea of the language constructs that can be used in the PVS language. A concise explanation of the specification is given in the following, which is sufficient for the purpose of this paper.

The function coord_act_mono assumes that the selected action has already been entered through a defined function that enables entry of the action into the coordinator's (is is the coordinator state) entry window (is`entry_window). The function assigns this action to be selected_action in either the patient display or device display depending on the display focus (`is`disp_focus`). The function `c_act_mono` is invoked with this modified state. This function invokes `execute_patient_device` with arguments action, patient name, device name obtained from the coordinator state and depending on the display focus. This function compiles a message that is sent to the selected patient station. The coordinator station menu is changed to enable the user of the coordinator to continue their activities.

```
c_act_mono(st: state): state =
  LET is = st`coord_st,
    p = (is`disp_patient)`current_patient,
    d = IF (is`disp_focus = patient_focus)
      THEN (is`disp_patient)`selected_device
      ELSE (is`disp_device)`current_device ENDIF,
    a = IF (is`disp_focus = patient_focus)
      THEN (is`disp_patient)`selected_action
      ELSE (is`disp_device)`selected_action ENDIF,
    st1 = st WITH [
      coord_st :=
        IF is`disp_focus = patient_focus
        THEN is WITH [ disp_patient := is`disp_patient WITH [
          selected_device := nil_device,
          selected_action := nil_action ]]
        ELSE is WITH [ disp_device := is`disp_device WITH [
          selected_action := nil_action ]]
        ENDIF
      ] IN execute_patient_device(a, p, d, st1)

coord_act_mono(st: state): state =
   LET is = st`coord_st,
      st1 = IF is`disp_focus = patient_focus
          THEN st WITH [
            coord_st := is WITH [
            disp_patient := is`disp_patient WITH [
            selected_action := (is`entry_window)`ent_action ]]]
          ELSE st WITH [
            coord_st := is WITH [
            disp_device := is`disp_device WITH [
            selected_action := (is`entry_window)`ent_action ]]]
          ENDIF,
    st1 = c_act_mono(st1)
   IN st1 WITH [ coord_st := change_is_menu(top_menu, st1`coord_st) ]
```

**Listing 1.7.** Coordinator action invocation

### 3.4 Filtering Relevant Information

Each patient station enables filtering of parameters and actions so that salient information (as required) can be displayed on the coordinator station. The state of the patient station therefore includes elements that describe the various filters. For example, filters can be used to indicate which parameters and actions are displayed when a device display for a particular patient is selected in the coordinator station. In the same way, the patient station provides a patient display that filters all the device panels. This filtered information is also displayed at the patient station when in an appropriate mode. The same information is also displayed at the coordinator station when the patient is selected. The patient station contains a "top" display that indicates which parameters are always displayed in the coordinator. In the coordinator station, this top display combines information from multiple devices and multiple patients. From the coordinator station, it is therefore necessary to select a patient if a command is to be issued for a device that is connected to the patient.

## 4 Conformance and Consistency

Previous work used templates [7] to express and prove properties capturing use-centred safety requirements associated with single devices, in particular the example used was a model of an infusion pump. The description of the present paper only offers a flavour of the full description of the ICE system model. The main focus of this paper is to explore the relationship between the displays and actions supported in the devices.

Conformance and consistency are critical to the safety of the ICE system, they are concerned with the issue of "unsafe control loop" described in [11]. There are three conceptual challenges that need to be addressed in specifying and proving these two properties. The first is to specify what property needs to be proved (*the property*). The second is to specify what system states should be checked against the property (*the filter*). Finally, the third is to specify the specific modes and conditions in the user stations that must hold for the property to be true (*the guard*). These three terms are used in the discussion of verification templates in [7]. They are illustrated in the following for the specific case of connected infusion pumps. Similar properties have been proved of combinations of infusion pumps and vital signs devices.

### 4.1 Conformance

Conformance requires that (subject to the most recent tick) the displays relating device, patient and coordinator should be conformant. The simplest version of this property requires that the data used in the coordinator when a patient or device is selected are consistent with the data that are provided by the device and the patient. A proof is developed to gain confidence that, whenever a message has been transmitted by a device that contains the current state of the device panel `d` connected to patient `p`, then the patient station and the coordinator will show the same parameters and actions shown on the device display.

The two states that are of interest are the result of the sequence of ticking functions that update both the patient station and the coordinator. This sequence is represented in Listing 1.8, where `ps3` is the updated state of the patient station, and `is3` is the updated state of the coordinator. The sequential execution of the functions is specified in PVS with a `LET-IN` construct, where a series of local bindings (`st1`, `st2`, etc.) are used to store partial results. Each local binding can be used in the expressions that follow the local binding.

The core elements of the property to be proved (*the property*) are specified using Boolean expressions. The expression checks that relevant elements of the device displays of the user stations (*the filter*) are identical after they have received the new message and the parameter values and actions of the device are as displayed (see Listing 1.9). The filter focuses on the parameters that are visible as well as the actions that are available. In this case the patient state that is currently visible is defined in ps3`p_disp_device and those aspects of the coordinator station state that are visible are defined in is3`disp_device.

```
LET st1 = tick_pan_device(d, p, st),
    st2 = tick_pan_patient(p, st1),
    st3 = tick_pan_coordinator(st2),
    ps3 = st3`pdb(p),
    is3 = st3`coord_st IN ...
```

**Listing 1.8.** Setting up the relation

The property is that enumerated and numerated parameters and commands are equal (see Listing 1.9).

```
(is3`disp_device)`e_disp = (ps3`p_disp_device)`enum_disp
AND (is3`disp_device)`n_disp = (ps3`p_disp_device)`num_disp
AND (is3`disp_device)`av_c_disp = (ps3`p_disp_device)`cmds
```

**Listing 1.9.** Simple conformance

To prove this property, hypotheses must be formulated about the state of the device, the patient and the coordinator (*the guard*). These include (see Listing 1.10):

- the device should not be switched off (line 1 in Listing 1.10).
- the patient station is in filtering mode dc_mode, device d is selected, and the device is known to the patient station (lines 2–4).
- the coordinator station is in d_mode (Line 6: the device is displayed)
- the patient and device are known to the coordinator (lines 7 and 9)
- the current patient in the coordinator is p (line 8)
- the current device in the coordinator is d (line 10)

With these hypotheses, the theorem can be proved automatically in PVS by splitting cases and repeatedly expanding definitions. It is important to note that many of these hypotheses are *not obvious* and were not clearly understood at the time when the proof was initially developed. They were discovered gradually, while performing the proof in PVS, through counter-examples produced by the theorem prover during different proof attempts. Recognising these assumptions is important in understanding the integrity of the design of the system.

```
1  (ps`ip_state(d))`m /= off
2  AND ps`pmode = dc_mode
3  AND (ps`p_disp_top)`sel_device=(#dv:=d,dt:=infusion_pump#)
4  AND (ps`p_disp_top)`devs(d) = infusion_pump
5    ...
6  AND (is`mode = d_mode)
7  AND ((is`disp_top)`patients)(p)
8  AND ((is`disp_patient)`current_patient = p)
9  AND ((is`disp_patient)`devices(d) = infusion_pump)
10 AND ((is`disp_device)`current_device = d)
11   ...
```

**Listing 1.10.** Assumptions

### 4.2 Consistency

Consistency requires that, given the same patient and device, if the same action is performed on the patient station and the coordinator station, then the same effect is obtained on the ICE system.

This property builds on two chains of `tick_act` functions (see Listing 1.11). The two functions `coord_act_mono` (the activation function in the coordinator) and `patient_act_mono` (the activation function in the patient station) both start the chain by sending an action message to the patient station and device, respectively.

```
LET st1 = coord_act_mono(st),
    st2 = tick_act_patient(p, st1),
    st3 = tick_act_device(d, p, st2)
    ...
    sta = patient_act_mono(p, st),
    stb = tick_act_device(d, p, sta) IN ...
```

**Listing 1.11.** Setting up the consistency relation

The property to be proved is that the two device states (*the filter*) produced as a result of these two sequences are equal (Listing 1.12). The state for each device that is connected to a patient is contained in the patient state, that is `st3`pdb(p)` and `stb`pdb(p)` respectively.

```
    st3`pdb(p)`ip_state(d) = stb`pdb(p)`ip_state(d)
```

**Listing 1.12.** Setting up the relation

A number of hypotheses must be made (*the guard*) for this equation to be proved. These include the list in Listing 1.13. The property assumes either that the invocation is using the device display in patient station and coordinator (see Lines 2 and 12–15) or the patient display (Lines 3 and 14–19).

```
1  ps`pmode = d_mode
2  OR ps`pmode = p_mode
3    AND ps`p_disp_main`p_actions(d))(a)
4    AND ps`emode = edit_none
5    AND ((ps`p_disp_top)`sel_device)`dv = d
6    AND ((ps`p_disp_top)`sel_device)`dt = infusion_pump
7    AND (ps`p_entry_window)`ent_act = a
8    AND (is`disp_top)`patients)(p)
9    AND (is`entry_window)`ent_action = a
10   AND is`disp_patient`current_patient = p
11   AND
12   ((is`disp_focus = device_focus
13        AND is`mode = d_mode
14        AND (is`disp_device)`av_c_disp(a)
15        AND (is`disp_device)`current_device = d)
16     OR
17     (is`disp_focus = patient_focus
18        AND is`mode = p_mode
19        AND (is`disp_patient)`av_main_act(d))(a)))
20   AND is`disp_patient`selected_device = d
```

**Listing 1.13.** Setting up the relation

As in the case of the conformance property, under the hypotheses shown in Listing 1.13, the consistency be proved automatically in PVS by splitting cases and repeatedly expanding definitions.

## 5 Conclusions

The analysis discussed in this work is intended to indicate the significance of notions such as conformance and consistency in the design of networks of user stations designed to control safety critical processes. There are two other roles that analysis of this kind can play. In the case described the development of the model was part of a design process. Although it is detailed for a specific example, it captures important human factors engineering properties that are of general applicability to interactive systems with integrated interoperable devices. It makes limited assumptions about the message passing system with the aim of enabling further generalisation.

Regarding the presented example, several aspects of the considered design have been specified and made explicit, e.g., the menu structure of the user stations. However, there are many additional details that need to be further developed. Under this perspective, an area for future research would be to create an interactive simulation based on the developed specification. This can be done, e.g., using PVSio-Web [10], which is a rapid prototyping toolkit based on PVS. PVSio-Web is part of the standard distribution of vscode-pvs, the new PVS front-end [12]. The approach would produce a reference simulation that is verified against use-centred requirements and upon which a full implementation can be based. A second possibility is to analyse a software implementation retrospectively, by creating a formal model that captures the behaviour of the software and then verifying the formal model against use-centred design requirements. This approach was taken in [5] in relation to medical devices and use-centred safety requirements discussed in draft documentation by the FDA.

## References


1. Arney, D., et al.: Generic infusion pump hazard analysis and safety requirements. Technical report. MS-CIS-08-31, University of Pennsylvania, February 2009
2. Arney, D., Plourde, J., Goldman, J.: OpenICE: an open, interoperable platform for medical cyber-physical systems. In: ACM/IEEE International Conference on Cyberphysical Systems (ICCPS), April 2014. https://doi.org/10.1109/ICCPS.2014.6843734
3. Association for the Advancement of Medical Instrumentation (AAMI): Medical device interoperability: Standard for safety. Technical report. ANSI/UL 2800–1, February 2019
4. ASTM: ASTM F2761 Medical Devices and Medical Systems – Essential safety requirements for equipment comprising the patient-centric integrated clinical environment (ICE) - Annex B: Clinical Scenarios (2009)
5. Harrison, M.D., Masci, P., Campos, J.C., Curzon, P.: Verification of user interface software: the example of use-related safety requirements and programmable medical devices. ACM Trans. Hum. Mach. Syst. **47**(6), 834–846 (2017). https://doi.org/10.1109/THMS.2017.2717910
6. Harrison, M., Campos, J., Ruksenas, R., Curzon, P.: Modelling information resources and their salience in medical device design. In: EICS 2016 Proceedings of the 8th ACM SIGCHI Symposium on Engineering Interactive Computing Systems, pp. 194–203. ACM Press (2016)

7. Harrison, M., Masci, P., Campos, J.: Verification templates for the analysis of user interface software design. IEEE Trans. Software Eng. **45**(8), 802–822 (2019)
8. James, J.T.: A new, evidence-based estimate of patient harms associated with hospital care. J. Patient Saf. **9**(3), 122–128 (2013)
9. Lee, I., Sokolsky, O.: Medical cyber physical systems. In: IEEE Design Automation Conference, pp. 743–748. IEEE Press, June 2010
10. Masci, P., Mallozzi, P., Luca, F., Angelis, D., Di Marzo, G., Curzon, P.: Using PVSio-web and SAPERE for rapid prototyping of user interfaces in integrated clinical environments. In: 3rd Workshop on Verification and Assurance (Verisure 2015), at CAV-2015, San Francisco, CA, USA (2015)
11. Masci, P., Weininger, S.: Usability engineering recommendations for next-gen integrated interoperable medical devices. Biomed. Instrum. Technol. **55**(4), 132–142 (2021). https://doi.org/10.2345/0890-8205-55.4.132
12. Masci, P., Muñoz, C.A.: An integrated development environment for the prototype verification system. Electron. Proc. Theoret. Comput. Sci. **310**, 35–49 (2019). https://doi.org/10.4204/eptcs.310.5. https://doi.org/10.4204/EPTCS.310.5
13. Shankar, N., Owre, S., Rushby, J.M., Stringer-Calvert, D.: PVS System Guide, PVS Language Reference, PVS Prover Guide, PVS Prelude Library, Abstract Datatypes in PVS, and Theory Interpretations in PVS. Computer Science Laboratory, SRI International, Menlo Park, CA (1999). http://pvs.csl.sri.com/documentation.shtml
14. Sutherland, J., Minear, M.: Informatics-a catalyst for operating room transformation. In: Operating Room of the Future, p. 22. No. 21702–5012. U.S. Army Medical Research and Materiel Command, Fort Detrick, Maryland (2003)

# Towards Control Rooms as Human-Centered Pervasive Computing Environments

Nadine Flegel[1(✉)], Jonas Poehler[2], Kristof Van Laerhoven[2], and Tilo Mentler[1]

[1] Trier University of Applied Sciences, Schneidershof, 54293 Trier, Germany
N.Flegel@hochschule-trier.de

[2] University of Siegen, Adolf-Reichwein-Straße 2a, 57076 Siegen, Germany

**Abstract.** State-of-the-art control rooms are equipped with a variety of input and output devices in terms of single-user workstations, shared public screens, and multimodal alarm systems. However, operators are bound to and sitting at their respective workstations for the most part of their shifts. Therefore, cooperation efforts are hampered, and physical activity is limited for several hours. Incorporating mobile devices, wearables and sensor technologies could improve on the current mode of operation but must be considered a paradigm shift from control rooms as a collection of technically networked but stationary workstations to control rooms as pervasive computing environments being aware of people and processes. However, based on the reviewed literature, systematic approaches to this paradigm shift taking usability and user experience into account are rare. In this work, we describe a root concept for control rooms as human-centered pervasive computing environments and introduce a framework for developing a wearable assistant as one of the central and novel components. Furthermore, we describe design challenges from a socio-technical perspective based on 9 expert interviews important for further research on pervasive computing environments in safety-critical domains.

**Keywords:** Control room · Pervasive computing environment · Wearable assistant · Scalable interaction design · Usability · User experience

## 1 Introduction

Whether an ambulance is necessary, (air) traffic needs to be managed, a ship must be commanded, or uninterrupted supply of power must be ensured, control rooms, as "location[s] designed for an entity to be in control of a process" [1], are of particular importance for security and well-being of humans in various circumstances of life [2–5]. Operators bear major responsibility within these critical infrastructures.

While control rooms have changed considerably with respect to information and communication technologies within the last 30 years, operators' work is still characterized by sitting in front of a certain workstation with several screens (private spaces) [4]. While larger wall-mounted screens (public spaces) and central alarm systems facilitate information sharing and group awareness to a certain degree, cooperation efforts are


Published by Springer Nature Switzerland AG 2022
C. Ardito et al. (Eds.): INTERACT 2021, LNCS 13198, pp. 329–344, 2022.
https://doi.org/10.1007/978-3-030-98388-8_29

still hampered because operators need to sit at their workstations for major parts of their shifts to access information. Furthermore, their physical activity is limited for several hours resulting in fatigue and health issues like musculoskeletal symptoms [6].

Incorporating mobile devices, wearables and sensor technologies could improve on the current mode of operation by enabling more flexible ways of working, e.g., while making decisions in consultation with other control room operators at their workstations or while standing/moving in the control room.

While there are technical issues to solve, e.g., secure wireless connections, this approach must not be seen as a technical challenge of introducing novel hardware and infrastructure only. Rather, it must be considered a paradigm shift from control rooms as a collection of technically networked but stationary workstations to control rooms as pervasive computing environments where people and devices can be mobile and access services in their vicinity with the aid of wireless networking technologies [7, 8]. They should complement the existing structures.

To prevent mobility and dynamics from adding complexity to already complex control room environments [9, 10], it is important that both people in terms of activities, cognitive loads, and affective states, as well as processes in terms of workflows and modes of operation (routine, emergency) are adequately represented. Therefore, interaction design, usability, and user experience (UX) [11] will be major issues to consider.

After summarizing related work in Sect. 2, we describe a root concept for control rooms as human-centered pervasive computing environments and introduce a framework for a wearable assistant as one of its central and novel components. Part of the framework is a pattern language for scalable interaction design in control rooms (see Sect. 3). Subsequently, method and results of 9 interviews with control room experts regarding our approach are described (see Sect. 4 and 5). Finally, research and development challenges are discussed from a socio-technical perspective (see Sect. 6). These findings can support designers of pervasive computing environments in other safety-critical domains, e.g., intensive care units, operating rooms, or cockpits.

## 2 Background and Related Work

Human-computer interaction (HCI) and computer-supported cooperative work (CSCW) in control room have been subjects of research for over 30 years [12–15]. Approaches included workplace studies (e.g., [13, 16]), evaluation of human-centered design activities (e.g. [12, 17]) as well as user interface and interaction design in terms of visualizations [18] or multimodal interaction (touch, gesture, voice) for future workstations [15, 19].

In this regard, blended interaction, a conceptual framework for Post-WIMP interaction design [20], has framed research on "holistic control room design" [21]. By considering four design domains (personal interaction, physical environment, social interaction, and communication/workflow), novel visualization and interaction concepts (e.g., foldable interactive maps) have been elaborated.

Despite the previously mentioned research, a search for "control room[s]" as "pervasive computing environment[s]" showed no results in ACM Digital Library, IEEE Xplore and ScienceDirect (as of May 2021). Search on SpringerLink showed 7 results.

Because pervasive computing environments are referred to as smart environments by some [22], "smart control room" was used as a keyword as well (see Table 1).

**Table 1.** Search results for "smart control room[s]" and "controls room[s]" in connection with "pervasive computing environments[s]" in different digital libraries

| Library | Keywords | Results (total) |
|---|---|---|
| ACM Digital Library | "control room" AND "pervasive computing environment" "smart control room" | 4 |
| IEEE Xplore | "control room" AND "pervasive computing environment" "smart control room" | 1 |
| ScienceDirect | "control room" AND "pervasive computing environment" "smart control room" | 3 |
| SpringerLink | "control room" AND "pervasive computing environment" "smart control room" | 14 |

Search results were checked for relevance regarding human-centeredness mentioned in the introduction by means of their abstracts. If there were direct references to usability, user experience, user interface or interaction design, the contribution was reviewed in full. Results are summarized in Table 2.

**Table 2.** Summary of research on "smart control room[s]" and "control room[s]" in connection with "pervasive computing environment[s]"

| Category | Exemplary research topics |
|---|---|
| No or only an indirect connection to control rooms as human-centered pervasive computing environments | Agent-based Peer-to-Peer Systems [23]<br>Automatic Configuration of Camera Systems [24]<br>Control Systems for Smart Meter [25]<br>Economic Modelling [26]<br>E-learning and Training [27]<br>Governance and Ethics of AI Machines [28]<br>Project Classes with Multi-disciplinary Teams [29]<br>Real-Time GPU-Based Voxel Carving [30]<br>Sensor networks in Ubiquitous Healthcare [31]<br>Small Modular Reactors [32] |
| User interface and interaction design with respect to specific aspects of control rooms as human-centered pervasive computing environments | Gaze-supported Mouse Interaction [33]<br>Multi-display Human-Machine-Interaction [34]<br>Multi-touch Sensitive Displays [35]<br>Open Source, Modularity and Styleguides [4]<br>Quality of UX in Ubiquitous Systems [36]<br>Situation Aware Interaction [37]<br>Smart Collaborative Interface (affordance table) [38] |
| Systemic or holistic approaches to control rooms as human-centered pervasive computing environments | Human-in-the-Loop Model Predictive Control [39]<br>Tangible Control and Desktop Interaction [40] |

In addition, standards like ISO 11064-4:2013 [41] which has been reviewed and confirmed in 2019, describe ergonomic design of control rooms in detail but are "applicable primarily to seated, visual-display-based workstations, although control workstations at which operators stand are also addressed". It can be concluded that further research on usability of novel control room systems and user experience of operators is required in order to take account of the growing demands on control room activities on the one hand and technical developments on the other.

## 3 Control Rooms as Human-Centered Pervasive Computing Environments

The following sections describe our root concept for control rooms as human-centered pervasive computing environments (see Sect. 3.1) and explain the wearable framework approach consisting of two parts: a pattern language for scalable interaction design in control rooms (see Sect. 3.2) and a wearable assistant (see Sect. 3.3). The wearable framework takes individual needs and resources of a control room operator into account by modelling cognitive load and affective state.

### 3.1 Root Concept

According to Rosson and Carroll [42], a root concept represents a "shared understanding of the project's high-level goals". More specifically, it contains a vision and rationale, groups of people who will be interested or affected and a list of starting assumptions that might have an impact. Table 3 summarizes these aspects regarding the idea of control rooms as human-centered pervasive computing environments.

**Table 3.** Root concept of controls rooms as human-centered pervasive computing environments

| Component | Description |
|---|---|
| High-level vision | Control rooms are human-centered pervasive computing environments being aware of operators' activities, cognitive load, and affective state as well as workflows and modes of operation |
| Basic rationale | More flexible ways of working are beneficial both for operators' health/well-being and safe operations in daily routine and in extraordinary situations |
| Stakeholder groups | - Control room operators<br>- Domain experts from different areas related to control rooms, e.g., HCI, information security, process control<br>- Developers of control room systems & applications, e.g., Supervisory Control and Data Acquisition (SCADA) |
| Starting assumptions | - Operators' cognitive load and affective states are assessable<br>- Activities and workflows can be modeled and identified |

One of the main challenges in translating this vision into research prototypes and practical solutions is how to deal with the starting assumptions mentioned before. As will be described in the following two sections, wearable technology, and a pattern language for scalable interaction design in control rooms are key elements to handling them within a human-centered design process.

### 3.2 Pattern Language for Scalable Interaction in Control Rooms

Adding mobile devices, wearables, and sensor technologies to control rooms already filled with (stationary) interactive systems could, at worst, make the work of operators more difficult if this were done in the sense of simply offering more opportunities for interaction. Therefore, this challenge can be described as a scalability issue with respect to user interface and interaction design.

We approach this challenge by focusing on the (rather) strict environment of a control room, in which tasks and processes tend to be rigidly set, and represent modes of operation (routine, emergency). Design patterns will be derived within a human-centered design process involving the stakeholders mentioned in Table 3.

In this regard, it is worth mentioning that the term design patterns here stand in summary for interaction design patterns as "general repeatable solution[s] to [...] commonly-occurring usability problem in interface design or interaction" [43] as well as environmental or behavioral patterns, e.g., cooperative problem-solving [44].

To illustrate this with an example: A reoccurring problem in state-of-the-art control rooms is, that information is provided to many control room operators in different ways at the same time ignoring their individual current workload or affective state. A solution, according to the "load and state balancer"[1] pattern (see Fig. 1), could be that the control room operators' cognitive load and affective state (stress in particular) are modelled on an operator-worn computer (see the following section). A dispatcher determines which operator will handle the request based on different policies (e.g., forwarding requests after a short period of time without acknowledgment).

Another conceivable scenario concerns more situation-specific information processing: if an operator is not sitting in front of his/her primary workstation, short-term important messages could be displayed or projected in other formats (e.g., audio signal) or on screens/walls the operator is looking at.

A collection of single design patterns needs to be organized as a pattern language in terms of relationships, purposes, scopes, levels or even contradictions to be an efficient aid for designers. For example, "load and state balancing" might contradict with necessary handling of interrelated sequences of tasks by one operator. A worst-case scenario would be increased coordination efforts or tasks being left undone if assignments were made solely based on individual states. Therefore, operation modes, levels of automation, degree of individual or cooperative work, workflows and available input/output modalities will serve as structural elements for the pattern language.

[1] The basic idea is derived from a software engineering design pattern of the same name for scalable systems.

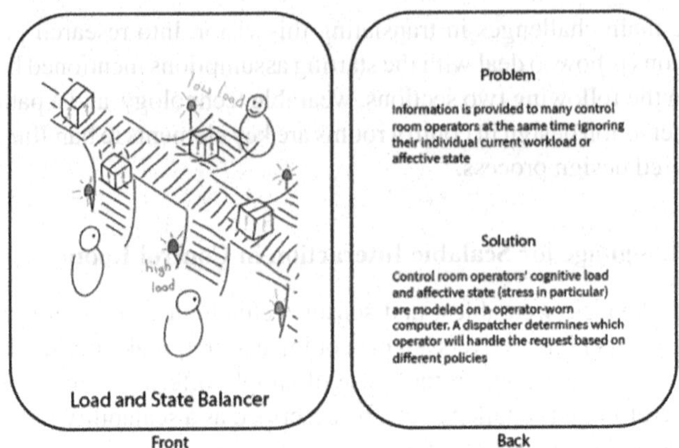


**Fig. 1.** Draft of a pattern card for the "load and state balancer" pattern

### 3.3 Wearable Control Room Assistant

Within a wearable framework (see Fig. 2), control room operators' cognitive load and affective state will be modelled on a user-worn computer and used to influence information flow to the operator. The concept of micro-interactions [45] is ideally suited for designing representation and interaction with operators through the wearables, by including the human operator's cognitive load, stress levels, and current tasks as important resources.

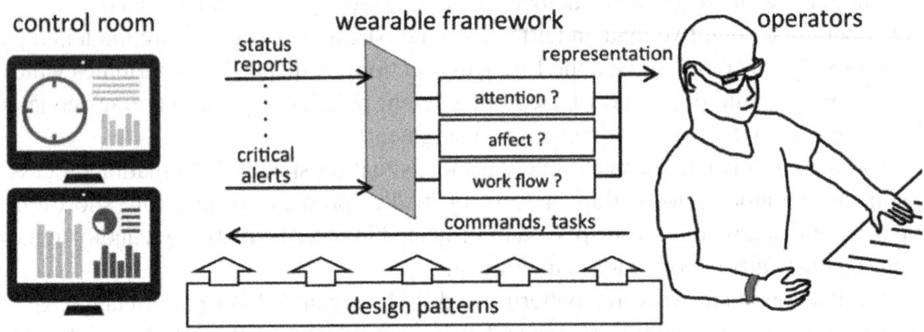


**Fig. 2.** Overview of the wearable framework, and the way the design patterns affect and influence the selection of an operator, representation of information, and the choice of (micro-)interaction with the help of the individual models.

On the one hand, the framework maintains models for the estimation of the wearer's attention, affective states (especially stress), and gestures or interaction steps in a workflow, and on the other hand implements the design patterns (see Sect. 3.2) that can be implemented in a wearable system.

Having the attentive and affect models for each of the human operators in place and combined with the model for the tasks at hand, the wearable assistant can respond in a more informed manner to events according to the most crucial information features in the control room, by presenting situation-tailored feedback, e.g., alarms and other control room events, appropriately. The workflow model, however, is relevant to logging tasks as detected by the operator's wearable setup.

A wearable feedback effort follows the model designs, in which the wearable framework can be integrated into the control room functionalities to display appropriate, situation-dependent information and alerts as guided by the design patterns.

## 4 Methods

In the following, details of semi-structured interviews with 9 control room operators and researchers on HCI/human factors (HF) in safety-critical systems from different countries[2] are described (see Table 4).

They were selected and solicited based on relevant publications, appropriate public appearances (talks, interviews), or leadership positions in professional bodies. Participants (3 female, 6 male) were interviewed to discuss potentials and challenges on future control rooms (30–40 min; recorded videoconference sessions). They were asked about the state-of-the-art of digitalization in control rooms, digital assistance systems in control rooms and their opinion about control rooms as human-centered pervasive computing environments.

**Table 4.** Overview of participants' working areas and years of experience.

| ID | Area (research/industry) | Years of experience regarding control rooms |
|---|---|---|
| 1 | Research on maritime safety-critical systems – HCI/HF, with work experience on ship bridges as a captain | 20 |
| 2 | Research in technical ship navigation with work experience on ship bridges as a captain | 40 |
| 3 | Work experience on ship bridges as a captain | 18 |
| 4 | Head of fire and rescue control center | 10 |
| 5 | Research on safety-critical systems – HCI/HF | >30 |
| 6 | Research on safety-critical systems – HCI/HF | 20 |
| 7 | Research on maritime safety-critical systems – HCI/HF | 10 |
| 8 | Operator in control room of fire and rescue forces | 12 |
| 9 | Research on safety-critical systems - HCI/HF | >22 |

[2] For reasons of anonymity, a more precise assignment is omitted because identification of participations would be possible easily in some cases by combining work area, years of experience, gender, and location/nationality.

Interviews were structured in 5 categories (see Table 5) involving questions asked to both groups and questions asked to one of the groups only, e.g., practitioners about work experience in control rooms. Two participants (ID 1 & 2) belong to both groups, because they have professional practical experience as well as research experience.that cameras are always

**Table 5.** Semi-structured interview guide for researchers (R)/control room operators (O)

| Category | Example questions |
|---|---|
| Both: Work experience | How many years have you been working in the domain of [control rooms I HCI/HF/safety-critical systems]? |
| R: Research on safety-critical systems<br>O: Work/Tasks in Control Rooms | Are you aware of any training activities or performance indicators of professionals on the job (observable by technology)?<br>Are you aware of any health-/well-being related activities (e.g., relaxation exercises) that are carried out on the job? |
| R: User Experience & Usability of digital systems in safety-critical domains<br>O: Digitalization in Control Rooms | How do you assess the state of digitalization in [control rooms I safety-critical domains]?<br>Where is the most "digitalization potential"?<br>What role has UX in safety-critical systems? |
| Both: Digital Assistance Systems in safety-critical domains – State-of-the-Art | Are you aware of any mobile or wearable devices or sensor technologies?<br>What would be your expectations of a body-worn computer system to be used in everyday professional life in the control center? |
| R: User-Centered Pervasive Computing Environments<br>O: Future of digital assistance systems in control rooms | Are there situations/scenarios (experience from related projects/approaches) in which you could imagine meaningful support through such and other technical solutions<br>Scenario 1: Distribution of tasks according to individually measured workload?<br>Scenario 2: Support of closer cooperation through appropriate processing of messages/alerts? |

Participants received a short introduction to the topic of pervasive computing (environments). The 2 previously mentioned scenarios (see Sect. 3.3) served as illustrations. The scenarios were briefly described to the participants in 1–2 sentences and further explained if needed. At the end of the interview, participants could provide comments and open questions. Recorded interviews were transcribed and analyzed by themes/topics. Results are summarized in the following section.

The semi-structured interviews were conducted as a starting point of our research, which will be followed up by workshops with experts and field observations in the further part.

## 5 Results

From the point of view of the experts interviewed there are potentials but also challenges and concerns with respect to our vision of control rooms as human-centered pervasive computing environments. To structure the feedback, the concept of human, technology, and organization (HTO) served as a template. Complemented by societal and cultural aspects (environment in a more general sense), it offers a framework for understanding working environments as socio-technical systems [46, 47].

The following sections describe results according to workflows and user experience ("human"); wearables, mobile devices, and sensor technologies ("technology"); performance and health ("organization"); and social and cultural aspects ("environment").

### 5.1 Workflows and User Experience ("Human")

In this section, feedback on the 2 scenarios ("load and state balancing", more appropriate processing of messages/alerts) and user experience of control rooms as human-centered pervasive computing environments in general is summarized.

First, all participants stated that considering user experience going beyond usability in terms of actions, beliefs, emotions, preferences, and perceptions occurring from before to after usage [11] is advisable but has been rarely done in safety-critical domains yet. One expert stated that "You get the most out of people, you get the best performance out of people" (ID 5), if you pay attention to user experience. And not just in the control system design and how you interact with it, but in the whole working environment. Lighting, windows, colors, etc., a "calming environment" are important.

One expert (ID 4) sees high potential in the "load and state balancing" scenario because practical experience showed that operators often do not even notice that they need help and are in state of cognitive overload: "We do this human factor training, I already said that, and the idea behind it is that you notice I'm overworked, and I raise my hand and say I need help. That doesn't work because the employees don't understand [...] they don't notice [...] and the manager behind them doesn't notice either."

For the second scenario of more appropriate processing of messages/alerts, feedback was diverse. On the one hand, potential to increase flexibility of workflows has been assessed. An operator (ID 3) with 18 years of experience in different control rooms pointed out, as an example, that although there are redundancies in the displays on large ships, e.g., 4 monitors on the ship's bridge showing the same values, in some situations, such as the ship docking in port, some data is not available because you are not located near these screens during this process. "When a ship docks and you are in one side of the ship, [...] and there you are really like in a small room, in order to have an overview of the entire length of the ship [...] then a kind of visualization would suffice that perhaps shows the distances or a water stream or the wind sensors again or a speed through the water, so that I have simply shown certain data again, which until now have been integrated in a complicated way in a monitor."

However, some experts also pointed out that this scenario would only work under certain conditions. The system must have a carefully designed, context-aware, alarm management, so that only the important information is displayed and there is no flood of alarms and information massages, which is still a problem in many domains.

The way and form how the technology is provided could play a major role in the acceptance by control room operators. Experts were asked about their opinion about a "clearly visible vs. unobtrusive" way of integrating cameras and sensor technologies into a control room. Most of the experts said, that a camera, that looks like an ordinary security camera, wouldn't be good, because cameras are associated with supervision in control room settings and that would reflect on getting the information to human resources department, so it shouldn't look like an ordinary camera was the most frequently mentioned answer on that question: "I would say that cameras are always negative. Well, because you always feel like you are being observed, and you always know them from our environment as supervision cameras and stuff like that. If it disappears into a buttonhole and is not perceptible, then maybe the way we deal with it is completely different." (ID 4).

However, operators need to be informed where cameras are located and what area they cover in the control room and what happens with the data: "This is always a very sensitive topic when it comes to supervision. Where perhaps there would also be strong concerns. People say I'm being permanently monitored here, so I think you have to sell that very well to the people and also accompany them and tell them exactly what is being done with the data, because otherwise I think there are very big concerns." (ID 8). This expert said that it would be better to have clearly visible cameras.

## 5.2 Wearables, Mobile Devices and Sensors ("Technology")

In this section the results of state-of-the-art of wearables, mobile devices and sensor technologies in control rooms are summarized and challenges with respect to the technical view are described.

Experts were asked, if they were aware of any wearables, mobile devices or sensors technologies used in state-of-the-art control rooms. Up to their knowledge, there are hardly any of these devices used in control rooms. One exception was a tablet called Portable Pilot Unit (ID 7) used by operators on ship bridges in Germany to communicate with each other and to have synchronized information between themselves and their station.

The experts were also asked if they are aware of any sensor technology that detects presence and health conditions of operators in the control room. In many domains, there is a requirement that control rooms must always be manned by at least one or two people. Sensors could measure whether the control room is really manned and whether there is a medical emergency. However, the experts stated there are no known sensor that measure things like that.

On the one hand, experts see potential to make workflows more flexible with mobiles and wearables and to use sensors for the safety of the overall process (see Sect. 5.1). On the other hand, a reoccurring pattern in the interviews was concerns about security risks. Representatives of both groups expressed concerns about devices and sensors that are highly connected and work wirelessly. One expert belonging to both groups (ID 1) stated that "the more you connect stuff the more you open up yourself to cyber risks. [...] nothing on board is protected for that. Everything is very vulnerable and open to attacks and then even systems that we don't have on board, but we sort of use sensors there everything can be hacked and spoofed, so that's probably a lot of risk.".

Obviously, security is an important factor that must always be considered when developing for safety-critical systems: "There is no safety without security" (ID 9). Otherwise, these developments will not be able to be used in the real environment, as an expert on HCI in safety-critical domains pointed out. It is important to investigate what could support peoples' activities with respect to new technologies and new ways of interacting, but the solution must be stable, functioning and fulfill and pass security requirements before it can be integrated into a safety-critical system.

### 5.3 Performance, Mental and Physical Health ("Organization")

The results addressing the awareness of accessibility or inclusive-/ability-based design or health- or well-being related activities (e.g., relaxation exercises) that are carried out by professionals (on the job) show, that there is hardly anything known, except shorter shifts, more breaks, opportunities for movement to support the health of the operators. But that is, according to a head of a fire and rescue control center (ID 4) something which a lot of thought is being given and solutions sought: "Well, that's really astonishing. I have not observed anything that they do. So, this is also a topic that we have on the agenda again and again. […] They are simply overloaded. […] Unfortunately, there is nothing good, or we haven't found anything yet, to prepare the staff for something like that".

Another question was, if the experts are aware of any training activities or performance indicators of professionals on the job (observed by the control room system itself), because these measurements would be interesting, to investigate how the control room as a human-centered pervasive computing environment could distinguish certain events or behaviors to support operators. Experts said that such things would only exist in predefined training scenarios in control room simulators but not during real operations.

Experts were also asked, if they are aware of accessibility or inclusive-/ability-based design in safety-critical domains, like individual focus on the operator, so that in the control room setting the application somehow vary depending on the individual per-son. Taking a strong focus on what the single operator as a person is good at or not good up to physical activities but also mental (very good in problem-solving vs. very good in decision-making). But there is also little known.

One of the experts (ID 8) pointed out a major potential advantage of the first scenario: "Because in the end it is always an important factor for the argumentation when one says, I need more staff. That concerns the superiors. Of course, they ask for reliable data. […] Why do you need a fourth man or woman? What did the three of them do? Were they all working at full capacity all the time? If you can back that up with hard facts, […] say here, the people who are all present at the same time, they all already had a certain stress level with certain tasks. Maybe not just once a day, but on a regular basis. Then I think that is the best argument to make to the decision-makers. This can only be said in the public sector via the political track, and we have a need for personnel because otherwise we are simply endangering the health of our employees."

### 5.4 Social and Cultural Aspects ("Environment")

According to an expert (ID 3) who has worked on passenger ships with international crews, there are major cultural differences in the assessment of cameras and surveillance and how to deal with them: "For a part of the person, maybe even in America, it's normal. There are cameras everywhere, but for the Germans it was really a huge thing at first [...] - this feeling of always being under control and so on. On the other hand, if you say: Yes, and it serves safety, if something happens, you can understand that."

The role of user experience, if aspects like aesthetics and positive emotions, being proud on your workstation contribute to the safety and dependability of the overall system, might differ in control room domains. There is a difference in control rooms which are physically separated from the system, being controlled (e.g., fire and rescue services, energy control rooms) and control rooms which are physically integrated in the system (e.g., aircraft cockpit, ship bridge). In the latter, it is a requirement, to record conversations. One expert (ID 2) said that some shipping companies forbid private conversations on the ship bridge, which does not work, because the ship crew usually live together on the ship for several weeks to months, and the ship bridge is not only the control center but also the first meeting place for the team, during breaks to drink coffee, chat, etc., which is important for the crew on board. The expert said that some shipping companies only see the people's role as professionals and forgot that they are human beings, therefore these UX issues sometimes get minor attention.

## 6 Discussion

The results of the expert interviews show that the vision of control rooms as human-centered pervasive computing environments is promising but associated with numerous challenges of a socio-technical nature. They involve human, technical, organizational, and environmental aspects.

Interactions between control room operators, mobile and stationary technology, control operations and the wider environment must be carefully considered. For example, the development of a wearable assistant is not just a matter of data models and algorithms but equally a question of user interface and interaction design within certain professional cultures (e.g., "camera look equals surveillance"). This also shows that user-related considerations must not be restricted to the usability factor but must be holistic in the sense of user experience. Enabling operators to move within in the control room without losing connection to their work could be beneficial in various ways from health management to cooperation efforts. In total, this could improve process control from the point of view of the operators. However, questions and conflicts arise beyond the user perspective, for example, about the security and reliability/dependability of wireless network connections that would accompany such mobile components. In the context of safety-critical systems, these different perspectives and competencies must be brought together, and contradictions must be dealt with. Not everything that would be accepted and usable well contributes to overall safety. Not everything that would contribute to safety would be accepted and used as intended.

### 6.1 Limitations

Our literature review should not be considered exhaustive. Related search terms (e.g., "ubiquitous computing") can return further results. The same applies to control room-like contexts, which are comparable in their characteristic properties.

Even though the participants have years to decades of experience with relation to control room environments, results must be evaluated cautiously because it is not a systematically representative survey and due to the small sample and different work domains. Challenges described before should not be understood as a conclusive list. However, they can serve as a starting point for further research and development on safety-critical pervasive computing environments.

The views of the other stakeholder groups described in Sect. 3.1 have also not (yet) been considered to a sufficient extent at this point. In further exchanges with control room operators and developers of control room systems/applications, possible additions and contradictions will have to be incorporated.

In addition, a root concept was introduced, the concrete realization of which is still pending. However, it has already been started and builds on established research findings in the areas of HCI and pervasive computing.

### 6.2 Conclusions

In this paper, we have presented a root concept for control rooms as human-centered pervasive computing environments. We have introduced the concept of a wearable assistant as one of the central components of such environments and proposed work-related design patterns as a solution to the scalable interaction design challenge resulting from the integration of wearables, mobile devices, and sensor technologies. Interviews with 9 control room experts from research and practice showed that there are several challenges related to humans (operators), technology, organization and (social) environment to solve.

To involve one of the stakeholder groups which have not been considered so far, a questionnaire on digitalization and workflows in control rooms as well as the vision of control rooms as human-centered pervasive computing environments has been created. By the beginning of May 2021, more than 120 control room operators have already participated – many of them open for follow-up interviews. In this regard, user experience research will be based on the question: Do control room operators perceive a portable assistant based on design patterns as paternalism (in terms of autonomy and expertise) or support (in terms of safety)?

Development of the interaction design patterns as a comprehensive collection of single design patterns will follows a human-centered design approach with feedback by control room experts passing different states (e.g., applied pattern, approved pattern). Pattern candidates have already been derived from a literature review on software engineering patterns for scalability in terms of performance and technical reliability.

**Acknowledgements.** This project is funded by the Deutsche Forschungsgemeinschaft (DFG, German Research Foundation) – 425868829 and is part of Priority Program SPP2199 Scalable Interaction Paradigms for Pervasive Computing Environments.

## References

1. Hollnagel, E., Woods, D.D.: Joint Cognitive Systems: Foundations of Cognitive Systems Engineering. Taylor & Francis, Boca Raton (2005)
2. Filippi, G., Theureau, J.: Analyzing cooperative work in an urban traffic control room for the design of a coordination support system. In: de Michelis, G., Simone, C., Schmidt, K. (eds.) Proceedings of the Third European Conference on Computer-Supported Cooperative Work. ECSCW 1993, pp. 171–186. Springer, Dordrecht (1993). https://doi.org/10.1007/978-94-011-2094-4_12
3. Garg, A.B., Govil, K.K.: Empirical evaluation of complex system interfaces for power plant control room using human work interaction design framework. In: Campos, P., Clemmensen, T., Nocera, J.A., Katre, D., Lopes, A., Ørngreen, R. (eds.) HWID 2012. IAICT, vol. 407, pp. 90–97. Springer, Heidelberg (2013). https://doi.org/10.1007/978-3-642-41145-8_8
4. Mentler, T., Rasim, T., Müßiggang, M., Herczeg, M.: Ensuring usability of future smart energy control room systems. Energy Inform. **1**(1), 167–182 (2018). https://doi.org/10.1186/s42162-018-0029-z
5. Wulvik, A.S., Dybvik, H., Steinert, M.: Investigating the relationship between mental state (workload and affect) and physiology in a control room setting (ship bridge simulator). Cogn. Technol. Work **22**(1), 95–108 (2019). https://doi.org/10.1007/s10111-019-00553-8
6. Bazazan, A., Dianat, I., Feizollahi, N., Mombeini, Z., Shirazi, A.M., Castellucci, H.I.: Effect of a posture correction–based intervention on musculoskeletal symptoms and fatigue among control room operators. Appl. Ergon. **76**, 12–19 (2019)
7. Mezgár, I., Grabner-Kräuter, S.: Role of privacy and trust in mobile business social networks. In: Cruz-Cunha, M.M., Gonçalves, P., Lopes, N., Miranda, E.M., Putnik, G.D. (eds.) Handbook of Research on Business Social Networking: Organizational, Managerial, and Technological Dimensions, pp. 287–313. IGI Global (2012)
8. Lyytinen, K., Yoo, Y.: Issues and challenges in ubiquitous computing. Commun. ACM **45**(12), 62–65 (2002)
9. Woods, D., Patterson, E., Roth, E.: Can we ever escape from data overload? A cognitive systems diagnosis. Cogn. Technol. Work **4**, 22–36 (2002). https://doi.org/10.1007/s10111 0200002
10. Kluge, A.: Controlling complex technical systems: the control room operator's tasks in process industries. In: Kluge, A. (ed.) The Acquisition of Knowledge and Skills for Taskwork and Teamwork to Control Complex Technical Systems, pp. 11–47. Springer, Dordrecht (2014). https://doi.org/10.1007/978-94-007-5049-4_2
11. ISO 9241-11:2018. Ergonomics of human-system interaction – part 11: usability: definitions and concepts
12. Petersen, R.J., Banks, W.W., Gertman, D.I.: Performance-based evaluation of graphic displays for nuclear power plant control rooms. In: Nichols, J.A., Schneider, M.L. (eds.) Proceedings of the 1982 Conference on Human Factors in Computing Systems - CHI 1982, pp. 182–189. ACM Press, New York (1982)
13. Heath, C., Luff, P.: Collaborative activity and technological design: task coordination in London underground control rooms. In: Bannon, L., Robinson, M., Schmidt, K. (eds.) Proceedings of the Second European Conference on Computer-Supported Cooperative Work, ECSCW 1991, pp. 65–80. Springer, Dordrecht (1991). https://doi.org/10.1007/978-94-011-3506-1_5
14. Griem, U., Oberquelle, H.: Die Gestaltung der Benutzungsschnittstelle von Prozeßleitsystemen nach der Leitstandsmetapher. In: Liskowsky, R., Velichkovsky, B.M., Wünschmann, W. (eds.) Software-Ergonomie 1997: Usability Engineering: Integration von Mensch-Computer-Interaktion und Software-Entwicklung, pp. 167–177. B.G.Teubner, Stuttgart (1997)

15. Heimonen, T., Hakulinen, J., Sharma, S., Turunen, M., Lehtikunnas, L., Paunonen, H.: Multimodal interaction in process control rooms. In: Müller, J., Memarovic, N., Ojala, T., Kostakos, V. (eds.) Proceedings of the 5th ACM International Symposium on Pervasive Displays - PerDis 2016, pp. 20–32. ACM Press, New York (2016)
16. Wozniak, P.W., et al.: Understanding work in public transport management control rooms. In: Lee, C.P., Poltrock, S., Barkhuus, L., Borges, M., Kellogg, W. (eds.) Companion of the 2017 ACM Conference on Computer Supported Cooperative Work and Social Computing - CSCW 2017 Companion, pp. 339–342. ACM Press, New York (2017)
17. Savioja, P., Aaltonen, I., Karvonen, H., Koskinen, H., Laarni, J., Liinasuo, M.: Systems usability concerns in hybrid control rooms. In: Proceedings of the 8th International Topical Meeting on Nuclear Plant Instrumentation and Control and Human-Machine Interface Technologies. American Nuclear Society, San Diego (2012)
18. Ntoa, S., Birliraki, C., Drossis, G., Margetis, G., Adami, I., Stephanidis, C.: UX design of a big data visualization application supporting gesture-based interaction with a large display. In: Yamamoto, S. (ed.) HIMI 2017. LNCS, vol. 10273, pp. 248–265. Springer, Cham (2017). https://doi.org/10.1007/978-3-319-58521-5_20
19. Nebe, K., Klompmaker, F., Jung, H., Fischer, H.: Exploiting new interaction techniques for disaster control management using multitouch-, tangible- and pen-based-interaction. In: Jacko, J.A. (ed.) HCI 2011. LNCS, vol. 6762, pp. 100–109. Springer, Heidelberg (2011). https://doi.org/10.1007/978-3-642-21605-3_11
20. Jetter, H.-C., Reiterer, H., Geyer, F.: Blended Interaction: understanding natural human–computer interaction in post-WIMP interactive spaces. Pers. Ubiquit. Comput. **18**(5), 1139–1158 (2013). https://doi.org/10.1007/s00779-013-0725-4
21. Butscher, S., Müller, J., Schwarz, T., Reiterer, H.: Blended interaction as an approach for holistic control room design. workshop "blended interaction: envisioning future collaborative interactive spaces". In: CHI 2013 - 2013 ACM SIGCHI Conference on Human Factors in Computing Systems, Paris, 27 April–2 May 2013 (2013)
22. Al-Muhtadi, J., Saleem, K., Al-Rabiaah, S., Imran, M., Gawanmeh, A., Rodrigues, J.J.P.C.: A lightweight cyber security framework with context-awareness for pervasive computing environments. Sustain. Cities Soc. **66**, 102610 (2021)
23. Helin, H., Syreeni, A.: Intelligent agent-based peer-to-peer systems (IP2P). In: Schumacher, M., Schuldt, H., Helin, H. (eds.) CASCOM: Intelligent Service Coordination in the Semantic Web. Whitestein Series in Software Agent Technologies and Autonomic Computing, pp. 11–29. Birkhäuser, Basel (2008)
24. Münch, D., Grosselfinger, A.-K., Hübner, W., Arens, M.: Automatic unconstrained online configuration of a master-slave camera system. In: Chen, M., Leibe, B., Neumann, B. (eds.) ICVS 2013. LNCS, vol. 7963, pp. 1–10. Springer, Heidelberg (2013). https://doi.org/10.1007/978-3-642-39402-7_1
25. Wang, J., Qi, C.: The design of control system for smart meter. In: Proceedings of the 2012 International Conference on Computer Science and Service System (CSSS 2012), pp. 1961–1964. IEEE Computer Society (2012)
26. Putilov, A.V., Timokhin, D.V., Bugaenko, M.V.: The use of the economic cross method in IT modeling of industrial development (using the example of two-component nuclear energy). In: Samsonovich, A.V., Gudwin, R.R., Simões, Ad.S. (eds.) BICA 2020. AISC, vol. 1310, pp. 391–399. Springer, Cham (2021). https://doi.org/10.1007/978-3-030-65596-9_47
27. Arnold, S., Fujima, J.: The potentials of meme media technology for web-based training at the emergency situation map. In: Arnold, O., Spickermann, W., Spyratos, N., Tanaka, Y. (eds.) WWS 2013. CCIS, vol. 372, pp. 155–165. Springer, Heidelberg (2013). https://doi.org/10.1007/978-3-642-38836-1_13
28. Marwala, T.: Human vs machine ethics. In: Marwala, T. (ed.) Rational Machines and Artificial Intelligence, pp. 211–222. Elsevier (2021)

29. Siewiorek, D., Smailagic, A., Siewiorek, D., Smailagic, A.: A QUARTER CENTURY of user-centered design engineering project classes with multi-disciplinary teams. GetMobile: Mob. Comput. Commun. **20**(1), 5–9 (2016)
30. Schick, A., Stiefelhagen, R.: Real-time GPU-based voxel carving with systematic occlusion handling. In: Denzler, J., Notni, G., Süße, H. (eds.) DAGM 2009. LNCS, vol. 5748, pp. 372–381. Springer, Heidelberg (2009). https://doi.org/10.1007/978-3-642-03798-6_38
31. Kim, Y.B., Yoo, S.K., Kim, D.: Ubiquitous healthcare: technology and service. In: Ichalkaranje, N., Ichalkaranje, A., Jain, L. (eds.) Intelligent Paradigms for Assistive and Preventive Healthcare Studies in Computational Intelligence. SCI, vol. 19, pp. 1–35. Springer, Heidelberg (2006). https://doi.org/10.1007/11418337_1
32. Choi, S.: Small modular reactors (SMRs). In: Ingersoll, D.T., Carelli, M.D. (eds.) Handbook of Small Modular Nuclear Reactors, 2nd edn, pp. 425–465. Woodhead Publishing (2021)
33. Flegel, N., Pick, C., Mentler, T.: A gaze-supported mouse interaction design concept for state-of-the-art control rooms. In: Ahram, T., Taiar, R., Groff, F. (eds.) IHIET-AI 2021. AISC, vol. 1378, pp. 208–216. Springer, Cham (2021). https://doi.org/10.1007/978-3-030-74009-2_26
34. van de Camp, F., Stiefelhagen, R.: GlueTK: a framework for multi-modal, multi-display human-machine-interaction. In: Proceedings of the 2013 International Conference on Intelligent User Interfaces, pp. 329–338 (2013)
35. Koskinen, H.M.K., Laarni, J.O., Honkamaa, P.M.: Hands-on the process control: users preferences and associations on hand movements. In: CHI 2008 Extended Abstracts on Human Factors in Computing Systems, pp. 3063–3068 (2008)
36. da Silva Junior, D.P., de Souza, P.C., Maciel, C.: Establishing guidelines for user quality of experience in ubiquitous systems. In: Streitz, N., Markopoulos, P. (eds.) DAPI 2016. LNCS, vol. 9749, pp. 46–57. Springer, Cham (2016). https://doi.org/10.1007/978-3-319-39862-4_5
37. Aehnelt, M., Bader, S., Ruscher, G., Krüger, F., Urban, B., Kirste, T.: Situation aware interaction with multi-modal business applications in smart environments. In: Yamamoto, S. (ed.) HIMI 2013. LNCS, vol. 8018, pp. 413–422. Springer, Heidelberg (2013). https://doi.org/10.1007/978-3-642-39226-9_45
38. Laarni, J., Norros, L., Koskinen, H.: Affordance table - a collaborative smart interface for process control. In: Jacko, J.A. (ed.) HCI 2007. LNCS, vol. 4553, pp. 611–619. Springer, Heidelberg (2007). https://doi.org/10.1007/978-3-540-73111-5_69
39. Ghosh, S., Bequette, B.W.: Framework for the control room of the future: human-in-the-loop MPC. IFAC-PapersOnLine **51**(34), 252–257 (2019)
40. Müller, J., Schwarz, T., Butscher, S., Reiterer, H.: Back to tangibility: a post-WIMP perspective on control room design. In: Proceedings of the 2014 International Working Conference on Advanced Visual Interfaces, pp. 57–64 (2014)
41. ISO 11064-4:2013. Ergonomic design of control centres—part 4: layout and dimensions of workstations
42. Rosson, M.B., Carroll, J.M.: Usability Engineering: Scenario-Based Development of Human Computer Interaction. Morgan Kaufmann, San Francisco (2009)
43. Folmer, E.: Interaction design patterns. In: Papantoniou, B., et al. (eds.) The Glossary of Human Computer Interaction. The Interaction Design Foundation (2015)
44. Tidwell, J.: Designing Interfaces: Patterns for Effective Interaction Design. O'Reilly & Associates, Sebastopol (2005)
45. Ashbrook, D.L.: Enabling mobile microinteractions. Ph.D. dissertation, Georgia Institute of Technology, Atlanta, GA, USA (2010). Advisor(s) Thad E. Starner. AAI3414437
46. Karltun, J., Karltun, A., Berglund, M.: Activity – the core of human-technology-organization. In: Black, N.L., Patrick Neumann, W., Noy, I. (eds.) IEA 2021. LNNS, vol. 219, pp. 704–711. Springer, Cham (2021). https://doi.org/10.1007/978-3-030-74602-5_96
47. Ulich, E.: Arbeitssysteme als soziotechnische Systeme–eine Erinnerung. J. Psychol. des Alltagshandelns **6**(1), 4–12 (2013)

# LstSim-Extended: Towards Monitoring Interaction and Beyond in Web-Based Control Room Simulations

Jonas Poehler[1(✉)], Nadine Flegel[2], Tilo Mentler[2], and Kristof Van Laerhoven[1]

[1] University of Siegen, 57076 Siegen, Germany
jonas.poehler@uni-siegen.de
[2] Trier University of Applied Sciences, 54293 Trier, Germany
https://ubicomp.eti.uni-siegen.de

**Abstract.** Control room operators rely on a range of technologies to communicate crucial information and dependably coordinate a disparate collection of tasks and procedures. Tools that are capable to design, to implement, and to evaluate interactive systems that can assist the tasks of control room operators in these environments therefore play an important role. This paper offers a framework that facilitates the early research steps into evaluating work flows, interfaces, and wearable sensors in the context of an emergency dispatch center. It entails a primarily web-based, quick-to-deploy, and scalable method that specifically targets preliminary studies in which large-scale and situated deployments are not feasible. By using open-source and affordable wrist-worn sensors, it furthermore enables investigating any relationships between interaction design in control rooms and operators' physiological data. Our evaluation on a preliminary study with 5 participants shows that basic scenarios are able to induce differences which can be measured by reaction times in the interactions as well as in the data from the smartwatch.

**Keywords:** Usable safety and security · Control rooms · Web-based simulations · Interfaces and cognitive load · Emergency dispatch

## 1 Introduction

Control rooms are among the more critical human-computer interaction systems, as they play a crucial role in safeguarding the security and well-being of humans in a range of situations. Whether an emergency requires an ambulance to be dispatched, crucial traffic flows need to be managed, or to guarantee an uninterrupted supply of utilities such as power, gas or water, control rooms represent critical infrastructures and their operators bear substantial responsibilities.

This project is funded by the Deutsche Forschungsgemeinschaft (DFG, German Research Foundation) – 425868829 and is part of Priority Program SPP2199 Scalable Interaction Paradigms for Pervasive Computing Environments.


C. Ardito et al. (Eds.): INTERACT 2021, LNCS 13198, pp. 345–356, 2022.
https://doi.org/10.1007/978-3-030-98388-8_30

While control rooms have changed considerably with respect to available information and communication technologies, human-machine task allocation and levels of automation within the last decades, user interfaces and interaction design in this area are still characterized by the windows, icons, menus, pointers (WIMP) paradigm, using established software available at stationary devices with displays of various sizes.

We propose in this paper an evaluation framework that aims at researching human-computer interaction aspects for emergency dispatch situations in a simplified but scalable manner. The contributions are threefold:

1. We extend a community-driven and web-based emergency dispatch simulator with a browser plugin and a web-based Bluetooth LE connection to a smartwatch. This allows us to monitor both user interactions and user vital signs during simulations.
2. We demonstrate that the browser plugin reflects the users' workflows and response times during the emergency simulations.
3. Users' realtime feedback can be measured by the user's smartwatch simultaneously. An evaluation on this data illustrates that certain features reflect significant changes between low-stress and high-stress scenarios.

The remainder of this paper is structured as follows: After Sect. 2 is dedicated to related research in this area, we introduce the workings of LstSim in Sect. 3. Our framework is then presented in Sect. 4, detailing how we intend to monitor user interactions and user's smartwatch data during emergency dispatch simulations. Section 5 describes our first evaluations and experiences with deploying our framework. The results are then reported on and discussed in Sect. 6, before we conclude our paper in Sect. 7.

## 2 Related Work

Control rooms have been defined as "location[s] designed for an entity to be in control of a process" by [7]. Ethnographically-inspired workplace studies and contexts of use analyses (e.g. [5]; Wozniak et al., 2017) have provided insights into the complex socio-technical nature of control rooms and the challenges that their operators face. Apart from maintenance, two basic operating modes can be distinguished as identified by (Herczeg, 2014): first, *routine operations* are characterized by control room operators handling well-known and predefined tasks based on standard operating procedures and experience. Routine operations should not be confused with undemanding work, as they are mentally and physically challenging due to sedentary occupation, shift duty, lowered vigilance, alarm fatigue, and overall information overload [3]. Second, *emergency operations* to respond to incidents and accidents are characterized by control room operators trying to limit damages and bring the system state under time-critical circumstances back to a normal operation. Emergency operating procedures and contingency procedures might in this case be available to a certain degree.

Control room modernization has led to predominantly virtual interaction and control elements that are operated via desktop computers. Studies have meanwhile confirmed that although such interactions tend to be faster to execute, control actions could be recalled significantly better using tangible interface elements [9].

Previous research has explored user-centered design processes to analyze how processes of management in critical environments such as control rooms can be optimized. Through interviews and site visits, prototypes using novel interaction techniques such as multi-touch, tangible and pen-based interactions were devised as demonstrators, to then gather feedback from operators [10]. Research exploring the potential of employing multi-modal interactive displays to support work and collaboration in control rooms indicates that it supports the feeling of control and safety during interactions, enables efficient access to information from a distance, and offers flexibility of use anywhere in the room [6].

Simulations to evaluate human-system interactions are a well-established method, with several studies investigating specific scenarios such as power plants [1] or police control rooms [4]). Simulations provide the opportunity to study control room procedures in a controlled environment. It is possible to play through certain scenarios and train defined situations. In contrast to observation in day-to-day operation, the observer has more parameters available to control what happens. On the one hand, it enables safe observation without interfering with daily business as well as the generation and observation of rare events.

System that are aware of a user's experienced cognitive load may help improve performance in complex, time-critical situations such as control rooms. Since measuring a user's cognitive load in a robust fashion and in real-time is not a trivial task, research has explored using different, non-intrusive features such as linguistic features [8].

This paper proposes to complement the above to provide a method to elicit realistic control room scenarios and being able to measure the users' interactions and vital signs through wrist-worn devices, simultaneously. This would provide us with insight how these interactions affect the physiological states of the operator. Our framework is easy to roll out, as it can be started from any study participants' browser and assumes only the presence of a low-cost smartwatch. This thus allows more in-depth research into interfaces and the effects of operators' vital signs at an early stage, without requiring potentially intrusive, on-site visits.

## 3 LstSim

The control room simulator LstSim, which is a shortened form from the German word for control room simulator ("Leitstellensimulator"), offers the opportunity to slip into the role of a dispatcher at a rescue control center through a browser-based game. The game interface is a simplified replica of processes and software used in control rooms for the scheduling of emergency operations and patient transports. For an example screenshot of LstSim, see Fig. 1. The window is divided into five areas, which will be presented below.

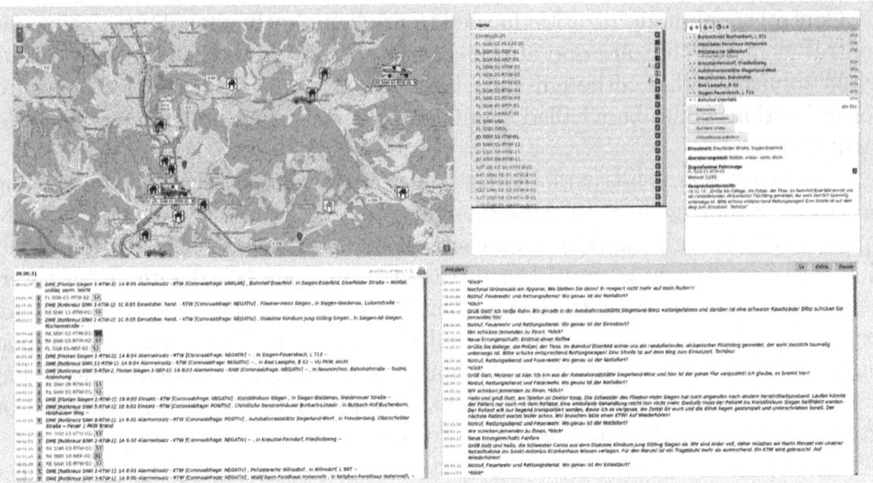

**Fig. 1.** LstSim is a control room simulator that can be played without registration online on https://lstsim.de/. Its interface incorporates elements from an emergency dispatch center into a single browser window, such as displays and controls through an overview map (top-left), lists of available units (top-centre) and current emergency phone calls (bottom-right). (Color figure online)

The map is one of the main elements. It is shown in the upper left of the window. It is used for geographical orientation and overview of the current area of operation. It shows not only the entire road network, important places such as landmarks, or city districts, but also the vehicles that are currently in operation and the corresponding locations. In addition, the available rescue stations and hospitals are displayed on the map. In the Fig. 1 a rescue station is visible (green symbol with house). For the different rescue stations there are seven different symbols, which represent different types and different staffing. This increases the complexity, but also ensures a consistent representation. For example, there are symbols to indicate whether a rescue station is staffed with emergency ambulances, or with ambulances, or with patient transport vehicles, or with no vehicle at all. The map thus primarily provides a geographical overview of the entire deployment.

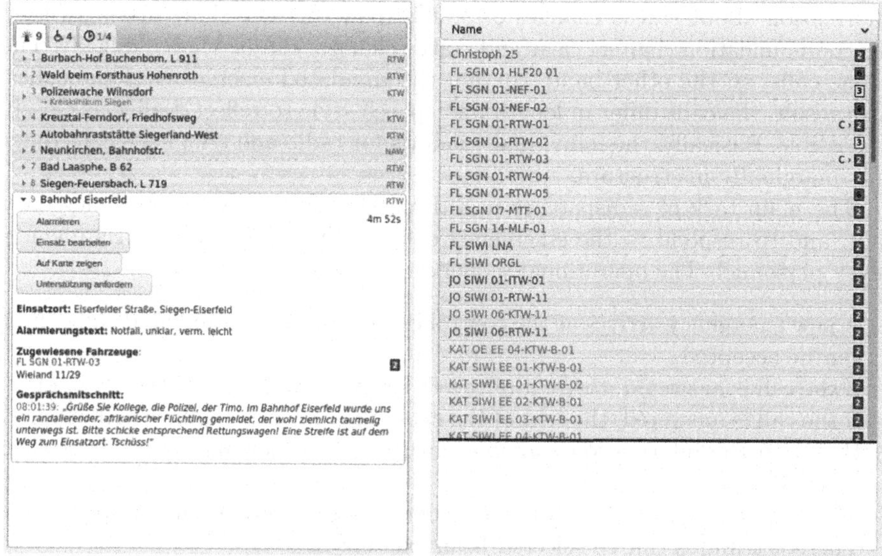


**Fig. 2.** LstSim mission module

**Fig. 3.** LstSim FMS module

In the Operations Overview module (see Fig. 2), shown in the upper right corner, current and upcoming operations are listed. The list contains important information about each operation, such as location, assigned vehicles or alert text. There are three different categories of operations. First of all, there are missions with a special urgency. Furthermore, missions with a low priority are also displayed. These include ambulance transports and emergencies that are less urgent. Finally, there is also an overview of planned patient transports that will only be carried out in the future. A deployment can be edited, or displayed on the map. By editing a deployment, additional vehicles can be assigned, or the deployment can be terminated.

The radio reporting system ("Funkmeldesystem"/FMS) tableau, shown in the upper center to the right (see Fig. 3), of the control center simulator is used for the vehicle overview. At a glance you can see which vehicles are available for an operation and which vehicles are currently in operation. There are also further options in the FMS tableau. For example, it is possible to request the status of an emergency vehicle or to alert a vehicle. Similar to the map, the user also needs explicit knowledge for this window, such as knowledge of the individual FMS statuses, or which vehicles or vehicle types are behind the abbreviations. However, this provides the user with as real a simulation as possible.

The radio calls are essential to communicate with the currently deployed emergency forces, while the communication with requesting persons (citizens, care services, etc.) is done via telephone calls. Both channels are displayed in separate windows in the simulator. The radio calls in the lower left and the telephone calls in the lower right. The radio conversations contain only short information about status changes or status requests. The short messages keep the communication channel clear and status changes can be viewed quickly. The phone calls, on the other hand, contain the simulated emergency of the caller. As a result, the calls differ in length and speech style to reflect reality as closely as possible. Basically, the individual windows for radio and telephone calls differ only marginally in structure.

The main task of a dispatcher in a dispatch center is to receive emergency calls, and to respond to the emergency calls by dispatching appropriate emergency personnel. The operational sequence is as follows:

- A new emergency arrives at the control center through a simulated call, which can be accepted.
- If the call is answered, the text of the caller appears in the phone call window.
- If the call is answered, the text of the caller appears in the phone call window.
- Based on the information contained in the call, a new operation must then be created.
- This requires the specification of an operation keyword and a transport type. These attributes can be selected from existing lists.
- Finally, at least one vehicle must be assigned to the operation. When these entries have been made, the operation can be created and the vehicles can be alerted at the same time.

Once the operation has been created and the vehicles have been alerted, they are displayed on the map with their current location. During an ongoing operation, it can be edited at any time. When the operation is finished, the FMS status of the emergency forces changes automatically, so that they are ready for action again.

Also for the creation of an operation - especially for the specification of the operation keyword - the user needs a certain amount of expert knowledge in order to draw the right conclusions from the information of the telephone call.

Although the active development of LstSim has ceased in 2017 and no new updates are supplied, the scenarios which are available are quite realistic and retain a large and active user base. LstSim therefore remains an attractive browser-based (and thus low-fidelity) simulation environment for control rooms.

## 4 Our Framework

This paper proposes to build upon the rich community contributions that were implemented in the LstSim simulator, by adding (1) a browser plugin that captures all user interactions within it, as well as adding (2) a web-based Bluetooth connection to a low-cost, open-source smartwatch to get physiological data from the user during the simulations.

### 4.1 Browser Telemetry Plugin

The user's interaction with LstSim is recorded by a browser plugin. This hooks into the games engine and records various parameters of the game that allow a subsequent evaluation of the player's success. One parameter is the length of time until the player reacts to an incoming phone call as well as the time needed to process this call. The content of the phone call is also stored. This makes it possible to subsequently find the emergency in the database of all possible emergencies and to compare the user's solution with the correct solution. Furthermore, the rescue equipment selected by the user for the mission is stored. Another parameter stored is the time needed by the user to respond to incoming requests in the window for communication with the deployed rescue resources. Finally, the number of open missions divided into high priority missions, low priority missions and planned ambulance transports is stored. This gives an overview of how many simultaneous operations the user has to process.

The data is sent by the browser plugin to a back-end server and stored in a database for subsequent processing.

### 4.2 Browser-Controlled Wristwatch

**Fig. 4.** The open-source Bangle.js smartwatch acquires a user's physiological data while an LstSim simulation is in progress.

The Bangle.js smartwatch was used to record the physiological data. In addition to acceleration sensors, this also provides a photoplethysmography (PPG) sensor. The data from this sensor was primarily used for this work. The built-in sensor is a BD 1668 optical analog pulse sensor. It measures the reflection of the emitted light signal and thus determines the pulse rate. The Bangle.js allows to read this sensor directly, so that a PPG raw signal is available. The sensor is queried at a rate of 100 Hz. The smartwatch always aggregates 10 measurements to a data packet which is transmitted to the user's computer every 100 ms. Here, the data packet is received via a browser-based Bluetooth Low Energy (WebBLE) interface and the measured values are displayed (Fig. 4). The browser-based interface can be seen in Fig. 5. After a completed experiment, the data can be downloaded as a CSV file for later analysis.

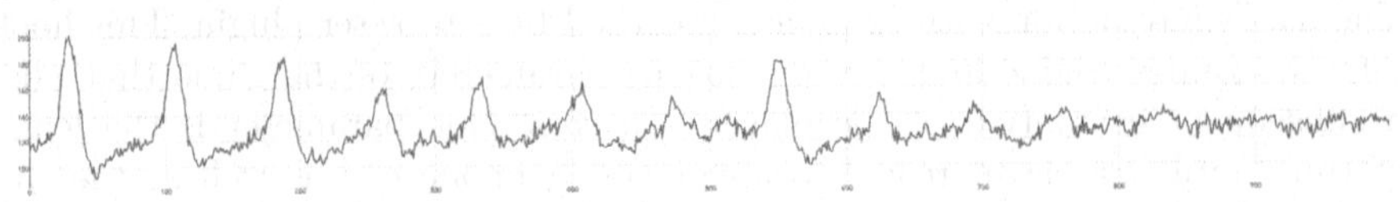


**Fig. 5.** A web based framework is used to control the BangleJS wristwatch and to capture physiological data from the test participants while they go through the emergency dispatch center scenarios. The above plot shows photoplethysmography (PPG) data with the user's heartbeats visible as peaks.

## 5 Evaluation

We recruited 5 participants (3 female, 2 male). The mean age was 27.6 years (SD = 3.07, min = 22 years, max = 31 years). 1 participant was left-handed. These participants were briefed by the author. All participants had no prior knowledge of LstSim and no prior in depth knowledge about rescue operations and emergency responses.

Two scenarios were followed for a feasibility evaluation of our framework. The study participants played each scenario for 10 min at a time on a provided laptop with a single screen. The first run was performed with the standard (relatively low) probabilities for the occurrence of an emergency. In the second run, the probabilities were increased by a factor of 40 instead. This provides an average of 0.8 calls per minute in the first run and 3.8 calls per minute in the second run. The increase in average emergency calls should provide a measurably higher cognitive load.

**Table 1.** Metrics used for evaluation and corresponding hypothesis about the reaction to cognitive load

| Name | Function | Hypothesis |
|---|---|---|
| Mean RR | Mean of RR | ↓ |
| IBI | Interbeat interval | |
| SDRR | Standard deviation of RR intervals | ↓ |
| SDSD | Standard deviation of successive differences | |
| RMSSD | Root mean square of successive differences | ↓ |
| pNN20 | Proportion of successive differences above 20 ms | |
| pNN50 | Proportion of successive differences above 50 ms | ↓ |
| MAD | Median absolute deviation of RR intervals | |
| Breathingrate | The breathing rate of the subject | |
| LF | Low-frequency, frequency spectrum between 0.05–0.15 Hz | ↑ |
| HF | High-frequency, frequency spectrum between 0.15–0.5 Hz | ↓ |
| HF/LF | The ratio high frequency/low frequency | ↑ |

During the game, the PPG signal is recorded via Bangle.js wristwatch. For evaluation, the events in the game are used to determine metrics such as the call lead time, which indicates how long a call has to wait to be processed by the control room operator. On the other hand, vital signs metrics are calculated via the PPG signal: Table 1 shows these calculated metrics. For seven of these metrics we can hypothesize how they will react to the stress scenario [2]. This is also marked in the table. A downward pointing arrow means that this metric should decrease under stress, an upward pointing arrow means that this metric should increase under stress. To calculate the metrics, the PPG signal is first filtered. A bandpass filter with the frequency spectrum [0.75, 3.5] Hz is used. Then each metric is calculated on a window of 30 s length with an overlap of 0.25. Results for the PPG metrics are reported in Table 2.

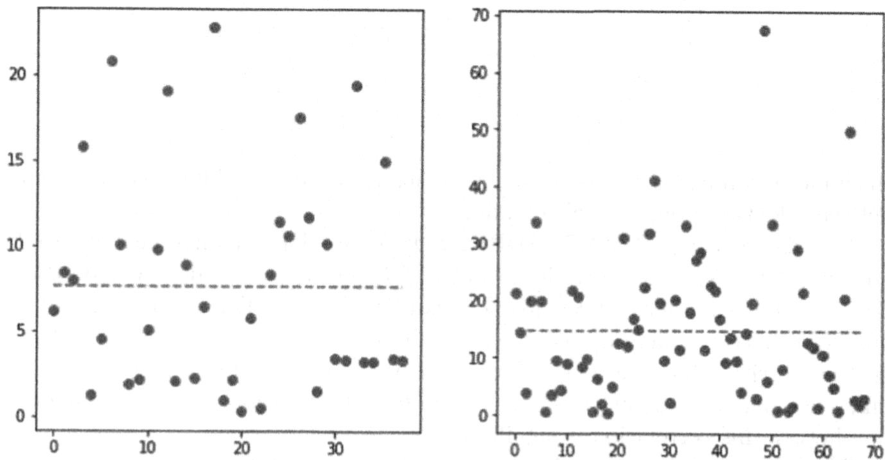

**Fig. 6.** Call lead time in seconds for low stress (left) and high stress scenario (right). The dotted line represents the mean value.

The call lead time increases from 6.81 s for the low stress scenario to 13.38 s for the high stress scenario as reported in Fig. 6. This indicates that the volume of calls make it more difficult for the operator to adequately categorise and dispatch each call as well as that the time needed to handle a call leads to a pileup of follow up calls.

## 6 Discussion

The results of the preliminary study, even though they originated from a small amount of participants, contain several points of interest. It can be seen that the increase in call volume leads to a significantly higher workload for the participants. This is evident in the increased time to start processing a call. For the PPG metrics, only a few show up with a significant effect size. Only breathing rate and pnn20

**Table 2.** Results of the PPG metrics

| Name | Development | Cohen's d | p-Value |
|---|---|---|---|
| Mean RR | ↑ | 0.2481 | 0.3364 |
| IBI | ↓ | 0.2917 | 0.2592 |
| SDRR | ↑ | 0.4720 | 0.0703 |
| SDSD | ↑ | 0.4536 | 0.0816 |
| RMSSD | ↑ | 0.5075 | 0.0521 |
| pNN20 | ↑ | 0.6516 | **0.0135** |
| pNN50 | ↑ | 0.4208 | 0.1056 |
| MAD | ↑ | 0.1419 | 0.5815 |
| Breathingrate | ↓ | 0.7044 | **0.0078** |
| LF | ↑ | 0.3663 | 0.1578 |
| HF | ↑ | 0.4889 | 0.0611 |
| HF/LF | ↑ | 0.0368 | 0.8859 |

show more significant effects. Here, statistically significant differences ($p < 0.05$) between the two groups are also found.

For the features RMSSD, SDRR, SDSD and HF, smaller effects can be observed but no statistically significant differences between the two groups can be found. For all other metrics no effect can be detected. The development of the observed metrics differs clearly from the hypothesis. Only for LF and HF/LF do the metrics follow the hypothesis. However, since no statistically significant difference between the metrics can be found here, no statement can be made as to whether this correlation is significant.

The difference between the observed metrics and the hypothesis can be explained by the small size of the study. A larger follow-up study should be conducted to further investigate the effects.

## Limitations

The preliminary study described in this paper, with its small number and heterogeneity of study participants, makes it hard to establish statements about the size and impact of the observed effects on cognitive load. Likewise, a statistically valid statement about the direction of the observed effects in the selected metrics is not possible. The lacking knowledge about emergency dispatch operations also could amount to an unwanted bias. A study with experienced dispatch operators would be logical next step to explore their reactions in this simulated environment. Nevertheless, we argue that these results are encouraging and that the ease of which these results were obtained do show the promise of the presented methodology. We therefore are currently planning a larger study with expert users to delve deeper into studying how reliable we can characterize cognitive load in these settings.

**Application Scenarios**

There are several potential use cases in which our proposed framework can be deployed. The existing control room software is today rather challenging to use. An interesting study focus would therefore be to explore whether a detected potentially higher cognitive load can be attributed (1) to the user interface itself, (2) to the time pressure; or (3) whether this relates to the experience of the operator or the concrete situation in dispatching ambulances for critical or non critical emergencies. All of this research questions can be explored from within our framework before an actual in-situ study needs to be developed and performed.

## 7 Conclusions

In this paper, we have presented a web-based framework for the monitoring of interactions between control room systems and their operators. Building up from a popular and web-based simulator for dispatchers at a rescue control centre, we have added a telemetry browser plugin and a WebBLE-based wearable framework that monitors physiological data, such as the heart rate, from the operator's wrist.

A preliminary study with five participants has shown that this system is able to capture data from interactions and smartwatch simultaneously. The evaluation on a basic scenario shows that different phases show notable differences in reaction times. Features from the wearable photoplethysmography (PPG) sensor has furthermore illustrated that certain features display significant differences between low-stress and high-stress situations, across participants.

We currently plan a larger follow-up study, which is necessary to determine the significance of the observed effects, but the deployments – held during the COVID-19 pandemic – already show the ease and scalability of this approach.

## References

1. Carvalho, P.V., dos Santos, I.L., Gomes, J.O., Borges, M.R., Guerlain, S.: Human factors approach for evaluation and redesign of human-system interfaces of a nuclear power plant simulator. Displays **29**(3), 273–284 (2008). https://doi.org/10.1016/j.displa.2007.08.010
2. Castaldo, R., Melillo, P., Bracale, U., Caserta, M., Triassi, M., Pecchia, L.: Acute mental stress assessment via short term HRV analysis in healthy adults: a systematic review with meta-analysis. Biomed. Sig. Process. Control **18**, 370–377 (2015). https://doi.org/10.1016/j.bspc.2015.02.012
3. Ghalenoei, M., Mortazavi, S.B., Mazloumi, A., Pakpour, A.H.: Impact of workload on cognitive performance of control room operators. Cogn. Technol. Work (2021). https://doi.org/10.1007/s10111-021-00679-8
4. Günal, M.M., Onggo, S., Pidd, M.: Improving police control rooms using simulation. J. Oper. Res. Soc. **59**(2), 171–181 (2008). https://doi.org/10.1057/palgrave.jors.2602517

5. Heath, C., Luff, P.: Collaborative activity and technological design: task coordination in London underground control rooms. In: Bannon, L., Robinson, M., Schmidt, K. (eds.) ECSCW 1991, pp. 65–80. Springer, Dordrecht (1991). https://doi.org/10.1007/978-94-011-3506-1_5
6. Heimonen, T., Hakulinen, J., Sharma, S., Turunen, M., Lehtikunnas, L., Paunonen, H.: Multimodal interaction in process control rooms: are we there yet? In: Proceedings of the 5th ACM International Symposium on Pervasive Displays, PerDis 2016, pp. 20–32. Association for Computing Machinery, New York (2016). https://doi.org/10.1145/2914920.2915024
7. Hollnagel, E., Woods, D.D.: Joint Cognitive Systems: Foundations of Cognitive Systems Engineering. CRC Press/Taylor and Francis, Boca Raton (2005)
8. Khawaja, M.A., Chen, F., Marcus, N.: Measuring cognitive load using linguistic features: implications for usability evaluation and adaptive interaction design. Int. J. Hum. Comput. Interact. **30**(5), 343–368 (2014). https://doi.org/10.1080/10447318.2013.860579
9. Müller, J., Schwarz, T., Butscher, S., Reiterer, H.: Back to tangibility: a post-wimp perspective on control room design. In: Proceedings of the 2014 International Working Conference on Advanced Visual Interfaces, AVI 2014, pp. 57–64. Association for Computing Machinery, New York (2014). https://doi.org/10.1145/2598153.2598161
10. Nebe, K., Klompmaker, F., Jung, H., Fischer, H.: Exploiting new interaction techniques for disaster control management using multitouch-, tangible- and pen-based-interaction. In: Jacko, J.A. (ed.) HCI 2011. LNCS, vol. 6762, pp. 100–109. Springer, Heidelberg (2011). https://doi.org/10.1007/978-3-642-21605-3_11

# UX for Some and Usability for Others: Issues of Blending Multi-user and Multi-property in Control Centers

Elodie Bouzekri[1](✉), Célia Martinie[1], Philippe Palanque[1], Erwann Poupart[2], and Sandra Steere[2]

[1] University of Toulouse, Toulouse, France
elodie.bouzekri@irit.fr, {celia.martinie, philippe.palanque}@cnes.fr

[2] Centre National d'Etudes Spatiales (CNES), Paris, France
{erwann.poupart,sandra.steere}@cnes.fr

**Abstract.** When designing an interactive system, considering usability is important in order to ensure that users can perform their tasks with the interactive system and that each information or function they need to perform their tasks is available at most relevant time. Consideration of the user experience is also important in order to take into account how users feel about using the interactive system. In case where users belong to different user profiles, design of the interactive system may have to consider conflicts between target usability and user experience. From study of the documentation and users' knowledge, we present a multi-user and multi-property control center: Jupiter 2 Control Center at Guiana Space Center of French space studies center (CNES). As public audience and press are allowed to assist to launch in the Jupiter 2 Control Center, they can see operators' work and information displayed in the control center. Then, specificity of this control center compared to others is that different user profiles with different goals use it at the same time. Some users use it to perform their work, whereas others use it to enjoy the launch. We use the Jupiter 2 Control Center as an example to find potential design issues for a future control center with similar characteristics. Conflicts between the different users' goals and the related properties are discussed in this paper.

**Keywords:** User Centered Design · Usability · User experience · Multi-user control centers

## 1 Introduction

Application of a User-Centered Design (UCD) process to build an interactive system or a user interface requires to identify and to analyze users and their needs [9]. The UCD process and its most common associated techniques (e.g., prototyping, user testing…) aim to ensure a target level of usability and user experience (UX) for the target users. Considering usability is important in order to ensure that the users can perform their tasks


Published by Springer Nature Switzerland AG 2022
C. Ardito et al. (Eds.): INTERACT 2021, LNCS 13198, pp. 357–367, 2022.
https://doi.org/10.1007/978-3-030-98388-8_31

with the interactive system and that each information or function they need to perform their tasks is available at most relevant time. Considering UX is important to consider the users' feelings when they use the interactive system. However, as Mentler and Herczeg [13] point out, there is a lack of consensus for precise UX criteria and dedicated measures making UX difficult to assess for safety-critical systems. They highlight as well that UX focus more on well-being than on performance leading to a potential disregard of goal achievement [13]. However, UX can be a motivating factor for operators and a property that operators expect [13]. Beyond these considerations concerning safety-critical systems operators, UX and usability need to be considered jointly if different user profiles with different goals are involved (e.g., operators and general public). Then, analysis and design process of the interactive system must manage the conflicts between the target usability and the target UX.

We selected the example of the Jupiter 2 Control Center at the Guiana Space Center of French space studies center "*Centre National d'Etudes Spatiales*" (CNES) because of its characteristic of allowing both operators and external audience during launches. From this example, we envisioned potential design issues for the design of a future control center as different user profiles use it at the same time. This analysis is based on study of CNES documentation and knowledge from experts who are co-signers of this paper (person in charge of managing the measures and operations quality expert of the CNES). The studied documentation describes operators' procedures during practice and effective launch. For example, during both practices and the effective launch, information displayed in the control center must support operators' tasks in order to be usable. The information displayed has also to be aesthetic, to be stimulating and to convey significant meaning and value to the external audience. The aim of these potential requirements is to make the external audience live a positive UX when they attend the launch event. Conflicts between usability and UX arise because operators' tasks require information that are necessary to ensure usability but that will decrease UX. For example, the display of very precise and technical information decreases the experience of the external audience (e.g., audience may be drowned and bored to look at logging information incoming from an electronic card in a server belonging to a radio station).

In this paper, we present envisioned design issues emerging from the study of Jupiter 2 Control Center: a multi-user and multi-property control center. Section 2 presents definitions of usability and user experience as well as relationships between these two properties. Section 3 presents the Jupiter 2 Control Center. Section 4 presents the different user profiles, their tasks, and the properties to consider for each of them. Section 5 presents the potential impacts of the different user profiles' goals and properties to be supported on the control center design. Section 6 concludes the paper.

## 2 Definitions of Usability and User Experience (UX)

This section presents the definitions we use for identification of potential design issues emerging from the study of a multi-user and multi-property control center.

### 2.1 Usability

Usability is the "extent to which a system, product or service can be used by specified users to achieve specified goals with **effectiveness**, **efficiency** and **satisfaction** in a specified context of use" [9]. Efficiency and effectiveness are two contributing factors to usability that can be measured objectively. Efficiency addresses performance and errors (as cost of recovering from errors) while effectiveness addresses the number of operator tasks that are supported by the interactive system. Satisfaction is a contributing factor to usability that is more subjective as it depends on user and that it corresponds to "physical, cognitive and emotional responses that result from the use of" the interactive system [9].

### 2.2 User Experience (UX)

User experience is related to the way user feels when using an interactive system. According to ISO 9241 standard, UX is "a person's perceptions and responses that result from the use and/or anticipated use of a product, system or service". This definition is quite generic, and we identified additional definitions to be able to map the contributing factors of properties with specific elements of design that support user tasks.

Hekkert and Desmet [8] define UX as "the entire set of affects that is elicited by the interaction between a user and a product including the degree to which all our senses are gratified (aesthetic experience), the meanings we attach to the product (experience of meaning), and the feelings and emotions that are elicited (emotional experience)". This definition brings precise contributing factors that are aesthetics, meaning and emotions. Winckler et al. [17] identified additional contributing factors. In the rest of the paper, we will use this consolidated set of contributing factors for UX that are:

- **Aesthetics**: the extent to which the interactive system's delights one or more of the user sensory modalities
- **Emotion**: the extent to which the interactive system makes the user have feelings such as happiness, boredom, sadness, or anger.
- **Meaning and value**: the extent to which the interactive system reflects the personal or symbolic significance that users give to the interactive system. Value refers to the extent to which it reflects or represents values that are important to the user.
- **Stimulation**: the extent to which the interactive system can support the human need for innovative and interesting functions, interactions, and contents.
- **Identification**: the extent to which the interactive system enables the user to communicate information to peers that the user finds relevant
- **Social connectedness**: the extent to which the interactive system facilitates communication with peers as well as contributes to socio pleasure.

### 2.3 Usability and User Experience Relationship

Sauer et al. [15] pointed out that similarities and discrepancies between usability and user experience vary accordingly to the definition considered to define these properties. In the present paper, we consider ISO definitions of usability and user experience. In addition, we consider aesthetics, emotion, meaning and values, stimulation, identification, and social connectedness as contributing factors to user experience to complete the ISO definition in accordance with Hekkert and Desmet definition [8].

Then, as they are both subjective, we can wonder if the satisfaction contributing factor to usability overlap with contributing factors to UX. Satisfaction is linked to success in using a system to achieve user goals related to user expectations, whereas pleasure enables to go beyond these considerations [7]. According to [15], the definition of UX we chose focuses on users' emotions and make usability and user experience separated properties. The authors acknowledge some degree of overlap between satisfaction and UX contributing factors. However, they consider them sufficiently different to justify treating usability and user experience separately when the definitions we chose are considered. UX encompasses all subjective affective dimensions that result to the usage of the system whereas our conception of satisfaction focuses more on users' beliefs about the usage of the system. This is in accordance with [17] that considers usability and UX as separated concerns as the two properties can evolve separately.

In addition, these two properties can conflict with each other in cases where affective dimensions are more important than the ease of use. A positive usability does not lead necessarily to a positive UX and vice-versa. Authors of [17] use the example of games: a very easy game is not necessarily enjoyable. In the present paper, we will focus on the fulfillment of usability property for the users who must work in control center and on UX for the users who must enjoy their venue to the control center. This choice is done in accordance with [13] that highlights that the usability property is more important to support for operators in critical context. However, like [13] we acknowledge that considering hedonic dimensions can beneficiate to the design solutions offered to these users. Following sections detail users' profiles, goals, and context of use. In addition, we discuss how conflicts between usability and UX and the context of use impact design choices for an envisioned design. In [1] and [2] the authors have extended the task modeling notation HAMSTERS [11] and user centered processes to include user research into those models bringing experience and usability together. This notation offers also the opportunity to address use errors [5] which is usually overlooked by user experience research.

## 3 Informal Description of the CNES Guiana Space Center Jupiter 2 Control Center

The Jupiter 2 control center, located at the CNES Guiana Space Center, is a large auditorium. This control center centralizes the tasks performed by operators to monitor the launch of a satellite or a space rocket of different launch centers: Ariane 5, Soyuz, and Vega. The operators must follow a precise chronology of tasks following the countdown displayed in the control center. This chronology defines a specific start time to perform the operators' tasks. The Jupiter 2 control center is composed of two main parts separated by a large glass bay (presented in Fig. 1). Both parts stand in front of a large screen: the MIO (which stands for "*Mur d'Images Opérationnel*" in French, meaning Display Wall for Operations). The part that is the closest to the MIO (front rows presented in Fig. 1a.) hosts the operational teams and the part that is behind the glass bay (presented

**Fig. 1.** Pictures of the Jupiter 2 control center from [1] (Color figure online)

in Fig. 1b) hosts the external audience and the press. Information displayed on the MIO is visible to everyone and is thus public.

The MIO displays launch images and the states of each parameter of the launch: telecommunication, weather, telemetry, etc. The background of the display areas of the parameters is different depending on the state of the systems. The background is green in normal situation. In case of abnormal situations, the background is red.

## 4 Users of Jupiter 2 Control Center

The MIO is visible to three user profiles of the control center: **operational operators**, **audience,** and **press** (depicted in Fig. 2).

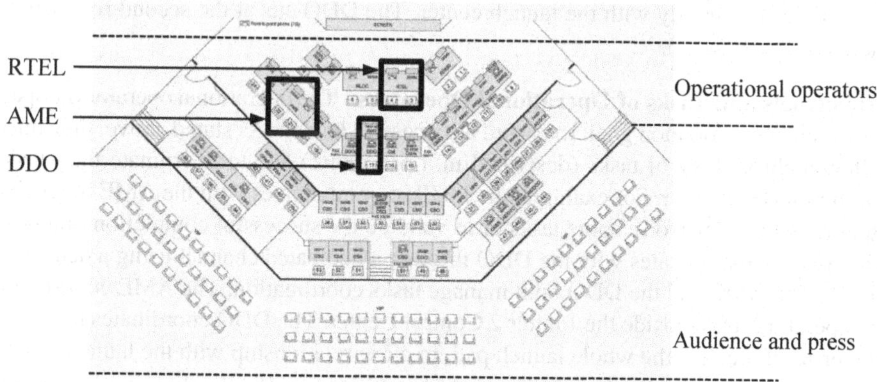


**Fig. 2.** Positioning of operational operators, audience and press in Jupiter 2 Control Center

Figure 3 presents a summary of the data flows between the different user profiles and roles presented below. Each user profile can read information on the MIO. However, only operational operators can update the information displayed on the MIO (double arrow on Fig. 3).

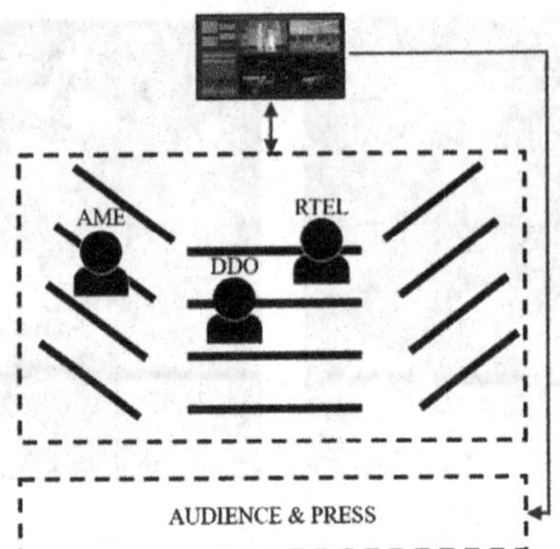


**Fig. 3.** Summary of the information data flows between the different user profiles and roles

### 4.1 Operational Operators

**Description of Roles.** In front rows of Jupiter 2 Control Center (see Fig. 1a. and Fig. 2), the operational operators manage and supervise the space launch. The operators have their backs to their immediate superiors. Each operational operator has a specific role and sits on the corresponding desk. For example, the "*Responsable TELécommunication*" in French (RTEL) is an operator in charge of managing telecommunications. The RTEL sits in front of the MIO (see Fig. 2). The "*Adjoint MEsure*" in French (AME) is an operator in charge of managing the measures and logs incoming from all the ground and space systems. The AME coordinates and allows (or not) the tasks of other roles including the RTEL. The AME sits at the second row (see Fig. 2). The "*Directeur D'Opération*" in French (DDO) is the director of operations. The DDO orchestrates the launch and communicates directly with the launch center. The DDO sits at the second row behind the RTEL (see Fig. 2).

**Main Goals and Tasks of Operational Operators.** The operational operators cooperate to achieve a common goal: to ensure a successful launch. As stated above, they must follow a chronology of tasks (described in a procedure) and to coordinate their tasks by phoning each other. For example, the RTEL communicates with the AME to receive authorizations to perform some tasks or to validate the successful completion of a task. The AME communicates with the DDO through a dedicated channel using a dedicated phone. The AME and the DDO both manage tasks coordination. The AME coordinates the operators' tasks inside the Jupiter 2 Control Center. The DDO coordinates tasks at a higher-level, i.e., for the whole launch pad, in close relationship with the launch center. In addition, as depicted in Fig. 3, operational operators control the display of the states of the parameters they manage on the MIO. For example, the RTEL can modify the displayed state of telecommunication parameter on the MIO. All operational operators see the MIO. Interactive systems of the control center must enable operators to perform the procedures. Thus, these systems must support operators to perform specific tasks at the specified time. This is directly related to the effectiveness contributing factor of usability. Furthermore, the operators have also to perform specific tasks at a specific pace for the chronology of operations, which means that the interactive systems must enable operators to perform their tasks in a limited time frame. This is directly related to the efficiency contributing factor of usability. Finally, the systems should enable the operators to meet their own expectations in terms of achieving their tasks. This is directly related to the satisfaction contributing factor of usability. As exposed in Sect. 2.3, usability is the target property to support for these users, but affective aspects convey by control center systems can impact users' mood or engagement. All contributing factors to UX are potentially involved but we provide examples on a subset of these factors. Concerning the Emotion contributing factor, to not be able to achieve their tasks may make the operators feel negative emotions. Low workload may make them feel bored. Concerning the Meaning and value contributing factor, being in charge of a mission aligned with their personal values.

### 4.2 External Audience

**Description of Roles.** The external audience is mainly composed of clients (who come to see the launch of their satellites) and institutional collaborators. Public can also assist to the launch if there is sufficient seating.

**Main Goals and Tasks of External Audience.** External audience wants to enjoy the launch like a show and to see the operations in real time. Thus, UX property is important to support for these users. Earphones are available and enables to listen commentaries translated in several languages. In addition, as depicted in Fig. 3, they see the MIO which displays information about the launch and launch images. As they cannot interact with the MIO, they only see the states of operational parameters those operational operators decide to display. They cannot be in direct contact with the operational team. We propose how a future control center configuration may support each dimension of this property for these users:

- **Aesthetics**: the control center may display on the MIO high-quality real-time videos of the launch and present clean representation of parameters states without information overload for the audience
- **Emotion**: the control center may make feel positive emotions to the audience such as joy and pride by highlighting the successful phases of the launch
- **Meaning and value**: the control center may reflect scientific excellence, seriousness, and value for money to the audience as most of them are the clients
- **Stimulation**: the control center may avoid repetitive long breaks between the different launch phases and show that the tasks performed in the control center are part of one of the most advanced scientific innovations of humankind (sending objects into space) and possible future opportunities. The control center may make the audience feel more involved in the launch by offering to see the takeoff on the panoramic terrace as proposed in the current control center.
- **Identification**: the control center may make the audience close to the operations and make them part of the launch by displaying the images of satellite of clients in the audience
- **Social connectedness**: the control center may allow the audience to share their experience with other people through social media for example.

### 4.3 Press

**Description of Roles.** Above the audience, there is a dedicated space to the written and audiovisual press.

**Main Goals and Tasks of the Press.** The press people observe the event, comment the launch, and take notes to later work on writing articles about the events that occurred during the launch. As depicted in Fig. 3 and like the audience, they can see but not interact with the MIO. Interac-tive systems of the control center must enable the press people to perform their tasks during the launch. This is directly related to **effectiveness** dimension of usability. In addition, they must cover the events following the chronology of operations and a limited time. This is directly related to **efficiency** dimension of usability. Finally, the interactive systems of the control center must enable the press people to meet their own expectations in achieving their tasks. This is directly related to **satisfaction** con-tributing factor of usability. Similarly, to the audience, the press wants to assist to an enjoyable launch to cover. Then, UX property is important to support for these users. We propose how a future control center configuration may support each dimension of UX property for these users:

- **Aesthetics**: control center may display high-quality real time videos of the launch and clean representation of parameters states that can be photograph or film by the press
- **Emotion**: the control center may make feel positive emotions to the press such as joy, pride or making them inspired by highlighting the successful phases of the launch
- **Meaning and value**: the control center may reflect scientific excellence and seriousness to the press
- **Stimulation**: the control center may show that the tasks performed in the control center are part of one of the most advanced scientific innovations to motivate commentaries
- **Identification**: we believed this dimension is not relevant for these users
- **Social connectedness**: control center may enable communication with the audience, between members of the press and with the outside world to share the coverage of the events

## 5 Impact on Design Issues

The control center configuration, the different goals, and properties to be supported for the different users may impact control center design issues.

### 5.1 Control Center Configuration and People Positioning Impact on Usability

Because operators turn their backs on some other operators, the use of non-verbal communication is cumbersome. Solutions like [4] enabling non-verbal communication on graphical interfaces can be considered.

In addition, the operators do not see their superiors behind them, but superiors can see the operators' work in front of them. This may cause additional or less stress depending on the context. Then, the time critical nature of the launch may impair operators' performance.

Because the operators communicate only relevant information to their superiors, each operator filters some information about the systems they manage. In case of abnormal situation, this distribution of information may make difficult the global understanding of the current situation. To help operators to carry out procedures in time critical situation, Johnson et al. [10] propose mixed reality to provide real-time guidance integrating information and visual cues in user's environment in health domain (cardiopulmonary resuscitation). Solutions like this proposition may be studied.

### 5.2 Conflict Between Efficacy, Efficiency, and UX

The MIO is a common display but used for different goals by the different user profiles. The MIO is visible to everyone in Jupiter 2 control center providing a global awareness about the status of the important systems for the launch. The operators need the MIO to coordinate their tasks and to perform their tasks effectively and efficiently. Operators can control and filter some of the released status information so that every parameter does not displays to the other operators and to external audience… This is because not all status information is relevant for operators and external audience. For example, the AME operator, in order to perform her tasks in an efficient way, may have to be aware of the status of telemetry communication link but not of the radio frequency used to transfer the telemetry (which), and thus the RTEL operator will filter out the radio frequency. External audience have a different goal as they want to enjoy the launch like a show and to see the operations in real time. Therefore, the MIO displays a couple of camera views on the rocket, whereas these views are not needed for all the operators' tasks. In consequence, the MIO must support UX property even though this can conflict with the usability property. For an envisioned future design, different interfaces could be considered. For example, to split the MIO in two interfaces: an interface supporting the goal of operators and another one supporting the goal of the audience. However, this solution may negatively impact UX as the audience could feel more distant from operators' work. Another possibility could be to consider augmented reality to display additional relevant information for their enjoyment.

### 5.3 Noise Impact on Users' Awareness and Goal Completion

The vocal communication has the advantage of being easily recordable for future analysis. However, its exclusive usage may cause some limitations. Indeed, because of the Lombard effect, people spontaneously increase their vocal intensity when talking in noisy environment [14]. Operational operators perform different tasks concurrently. This concurrency generates different discussions at the same time causing noises. This noisy environment may impact tasks requiring focused attention [16] which may impair the understanding of the current situation in control center. A possible solution is to provide a visual feedback of the operators' vocal intensity when speaking to make them control it [14]. In addition, using system aiding to support the communication and cooperation between operators may be considered. Yun et al. [18] investigate the use of speech recognition in NASA's launch control center to make vocal information analyzable by systems.

### 5.4 Attacks Prevention Impact on Social Connectedness

Privacy of some operational information is needed in order to ensure security in the control center. Some operational information is not publicly exchanged, and a large glass bay separates physically operators from audience and press. However, as the audience want to be as closely as possible to the operations, they can see the operators' work in real time. Thus, a particular attention must be paid to audience taking pictures or videos to share their experience with others. Indeed, it is possible that the information captured impaired security if shared.

## 6 Conclusion

Because of the three different user profiles of the Jupiter 2 control center, we found different user goals needing different properties to consider. Operational operators must ensure a successful launch. They need usable systems to perform this time critical goal. Audience is in the control center to enjoy the launch like a show. User experience property can be considered for these users. Based on the example of the Jupiter 2 control center, we discussed possible impacts on future control center design that the conflicting properties to be supported raise. Although usability is a necessary property for safety-critical systems, UX property may be considered as irrelevant for such systems [13]. However, we highlighted the relationships between UX and operators' tasks of such safety-critical systems. In addition, the multiple target user profiles for specific types of safety-critical systems (e.g., the MIO) require UX consideration. In such cases, there is a need for considering hedonics dimensions and users' emotions to propose design solutions that support the different users' goals. This paper mainly focuses on usability and UX, but several other properties are involved. Previous section presented examples for the privacy property, but dependability and situation awareness are also important target properties for such control centers. The design of interactive systems for control centers that involve multi-user and multi-property thus requires to deal with several potentially conflicting design solutions. As User Centered Design approaches are iterative and produce several design solutions, and this for each user profile, the conflicts between properties may be difficult to track and to manage. This type of issue also arises in the case of conflicting design guidelines [12]. Future work will investigate how such conflicts between properties could be managed at design time. A possibility could be to use a notation to track relationships between properties and to identify and represent to what extent a design solution supports a property [6].

## References

1. Bernhaupt, R., Palanque, P., Drouet, D., Martinie, C.: Enriching task models with usability and user experience evaluation data. In: Bogdan, C., Kuusinen, K., Lárusdóttir, M.K., Palanque, P., Winckler, M. (eds.) HCSE 2018. LNCS, vol. 11262, pp. 146–163. Springer, Cham (2019). https://doi.org/10.1007/978-3-030-05909-5_9
2. Bernhaupt, R., Palanque, P., Manciet, F., Martinie, C.: User-test results injection into task-based design process for the assessment and improvement of both usability and user experience. In: Bogdan, C., et al. (eds.) HCSE/HESSD -2016. LNCS, vol. 9856, pp. 56–72. Springer, Cham (2016). https://doi.org/10.1007/978-3-319-44902-9_5

3. CNES. La Salle de Contrôle Jupiter. https://centrespatialguyanais.cnes.fr/fr/centre-de-controle. Accessed June 2021
4. Conversy, S., Gaspard-Boulinc, H., Chatty, S., Valès, S., Dupré, C., Ollagnon, C.: Supporting air traffic control collaboration with a TableTop system. In: Proceedings of the ACM 2011 Conference on Computer Supported Cooperative Work, pp. 425–434. Association for Computing Machinery, New York (2011). https://doi.org/10.1145/1958824.1958891
5. Fahssi, R., Martinie, C., Palanque, P.: Enhanced task modelling for systematic identification and explicit representation of human errors. In: Abascal, J., Barbosa, S., Fetter, M., Gross, T., Palanque, P., Winckler, M. (eds.) INTERACT 2015. LNCS, vol. 9299, pp. 192–212. Springer, Cham (2015). https://doi.org/10.1007/978-3-319-22723-8_16
6. Clemmensen, T., Rajamanickam, V., Dannenmann, P., Petrie, H., Winckler, M. (eds.): INTERACT 2017. LNCS, vol. 10774. Springer, Cham (2018). https://doi.org/10.1007/978-3-319-92081-8
7. Hassenzahl, M.: The thing and I: understanding the relationship between user and product. In: Blythe, M., Overbeeke, K., Monk, A., Wright, P. (eds.) Funology: From Usability to Enjoyment, pp. 31–42. Kluwer Academic Publishers, Dordrecht (2005)
8. Hekkert, P., Desmet, P.M.A.: Framework of product experience. Int. J. Des. **1**, 57–66 (2007)
9. International Organization for Standardization. Ergonomics of human-system interaction—Part 11: Usability: Definitions and concepts, ISO 9241–11:2018(E), ISO (2018)
10. Johnson, J.G., Rodrigues, D.G., Gubbala, M., Weibel, N.: HoloCPR: designing and evaluating a mixed reality interface for time-critical emergencies. In: Proceedings of the 12th EAI International Conference on Pervasive Computing Technologies for Healthcare, pp. 67–76. Association for Computing Machinery, New York (2018). https://doi.org/10.1145/3240925.3240984
11. Martinie, C., Palanque, P., Bouzekri, E., Cockburn, A., Canny, A., Barboni, E.: Analysing and demonstrating tool-supported customizable task notations. In: Proceedings of the ACM Human-Computer Interaction, EICS, vol. 3, p. 26, Article 12, June 2019. https://doi.org/10.1145/3331154
12. Masip, L., Martinie, C., Winckler, M., Palanque, P., Granollers, T., Oliva, M.: A design process for exhibiting design choices and trade-offs in (potentially) conflicting user interface guidelines. In: Winckler, M., Forbrig, P., Bernhaupt, R. (eds.) HCSE 2012. LNCS, vol. 7623, pp. 53–71. Springer, Heidelberg (2012). https://doi.org/10.1007/978-3-642-34347-6_4
13. Mentler, T., Herczeg, M.: On the Role of User Experience in Mission- or Safety-Critical Systems (2016). https://doi.org/10.18420/muc2016-ws01-0001
14. Pick, H.L., Siegel, G.M., Fox, P.W., Garber, S.R., Kearney, J.K.: Inhibiting the Lombard effect. J. Acoust. Soc. Am. **85**, 894–900 (1989). https://doi.org/10.1121/1.397561
15. Sauer, J., Sonderegger, A., Schmutz, S.: Usability, user experience and accessibility: towards an integrative model. Ergonomics **63**(10), 1207–1220 (2020)
16. Smith, A.P.: Noise and aspects of attention. Br. J. Psychol. **82**, 313–324 (1991). https://doi.org/10.1111/j.2044-8295.1991.tb02402.x
17. Winckler, M., Bernhaupt, R., Bach, C.: Identification of UX dimensions for incident reporting systems with mobile applications in urban contexts: a longitudinal study. Cogn. Technol. Work **18**(4), 673–694 (2016). https://doi.org/10.1007/s10111-016-0383-1
18. Yun, K., Osborne, J., Lee, M., Lu, T., Chow, E.: Automatic speech recognition for launch control center communication using recurrent neural networks with data augmentation and custom language model. arXiv:1804.09552 [cs] (2018)

# Pilot Implementation: Testing Human-Work Interaction Designs

# A Summary of the Workshop on Pilot Implementation for Testing Human-Work Interaction Designs

Morten Hertzum(✉)

University of Copenhagen, Karen Blixens Plads 8, 2300 Copenhagen, Denmark
hertzum@hum.ku.dk

**Abstract.** Pilot implementations are field tests of properly engineered, yet unfinished, systems. By exposing systems to their intended environment, pilot implementations emphasize realism and collect real-use feedback for system finalization. While practitioners recognize pilot implementations as a means of testing the fit between a system and its use environment, pilot implementations have received less attention from researchers in human-computer interaction. The workshop on pilot implementation for testing human-work interaction designs aimed to create research interest in pilot implementation and to provide a forum for discussing and maturing such research. The seven workshop papers included in this post-proceedings volume span a variety of angles on pilot implementation. They contribute valuable insights but also leave open questions. Collectively, they provide illustrative case studies and inspiration for further research.

**Keywords:** Pilot implementation · Field test · Human work interaction design

## 1 Introduction

The workshop on pilot implementation for testing human-work interaction designs was organized by Working Group 6 – Human Work Interaction Design – under IFIP TC13. Working Group 6 contends that the integration of work analysis and interaction design is pivotal to the successful development and implementation of workplace systems [1]. Pilot implementations contribute to this integration by being an in situ method for working to ensure the usefulness and adoption of systems.

The aim and focus of the workshop were laid out in the workshop description [8]. In brief, the aim was to help make pilot implementation a more mature method by collecting case studies of pilot implementations and by analyzing the strengths, weaknesses, opportunities, threats, and open questions related to pilot implementation. This summary of the workshop provides a framing for the case studies presented at the workshop. The workshop papers report from the individual case studies. The analysis of strengths, weaknesses, opportunities, threats, and open questions will be reported in a separate paper authored jointly by workshop participants.


Published by Springer Nature Switzerland AG 2022
C. Ardito et al. (Eds.): INTERACT 2021, LNCS 13198, pp. 371–375, 2022.
https://doi.org/10.1007/978-3-030-98388-8_32

## 2 Pilot Implementation

A pilot implementation is "*a field test of a properly engineered, yet unfinished system in its intended environment, using real data, and aiming – through real-use experience – to explore the value of the system, improve or assess its design, and reduce implementation risk*" [7]. Four points may serve to unpack this definition:

- Pilot systems are, by definition, not fully developed. While properly engineered, they are unfinished. Contrary to mock-ups and prototypes, a pilot system is sufficiently complete to be tested in the field rather than the lab. Contrary to full-scale implementation, a pilot implementation is conducted to get feedback for the finalization of the system.
- By being tests, pilot implementations are limited in scope and time. The site of the pilot implementation will involve only some of the intended users of the system, and they will stop using the pilot system at a pre-specified date. The pre-specified end date creates a decision point: What should happen after the pilot implementation?
- Pilot implementations are conducted in the intended use environment. This characteristic of pilot implementations sets them apart from usability tests, which are normally conducted in the lab. Compared to usability tests in the lab, pilot implementations emphasize realism and allow for evaluating organizational usability [3].
- Pilot implementations are conducted to learn about the fit between the system and its use environment. This characteristic sets pilot implementation apart from full-scale implementation. While full-scale implementations are conducted to realize benefit from the new system through continued use, pilot implementations are conducted to learn through temporary use.

By recognizing the technical as well as the social, organizational, and contextual qualities of systems, pilot implementations are a means of bridging the gap between technical development and organizational implementation. They are conducted in the final stages of technical development [16] or in the preparations for organizational implementation [6]. While pilot implementations are not restricted to information systems, a literature on pilot implementation as a method for developing and implementing information systems is emerging [e.g., 7, 9, 10, 12, 13, 16, 19].

## 3 Contributed Papers

Of the eleven papers presented at the workshop, seven are included in this post-proceedings volume. All papers have been revised and extended after they were presented and discussed at the workshop.

Two papers analyze pilot implementations that have been completed and now provide the involved organizations with a basis for deciding whether to proceed with full-scale implementation. These pilot implementations have gone through planning, technical configuration, organizational adaptation, pilot use, and learning [7]. The papers focus on what has been learned and show that important learning may result from the period of pilot use as well as from the preparations leading up to it. In addition, some of the learning may already become apparent during the pilot implementation and influence how it proceeds. The two papers in this group are:

- Pereira et al. [14], who have pilot implemented a social media campaign to enlist more students in a university master program. The campaign ran for two consecutive years and involved creating two blogs and regularly posting on these blogs and on social media. Key learnings from the pilot implementation are that social media posts have a much larger audience than blog posts and that the campaign probably contributed to a substantial increase in new students.
- Herbæk et al. [5], who analyze how a company pilot implemented a self-service system directed at the company itself and its customers. The main contribution of the pilot implementation is to cause organizational alignment and, thereby, smoothen the transition into using the system. As part of this alignment, the company revised its incentive structures. A mismatch between the system and the incentive structures could have been a severe adoption barrier.

A group of four of the papers presented at the workshop studies the pilot implementation of systems developed for a market, rather than a specific customer organization [4]. These pilot implementations focus on testing a technological system in an operational setting to evaluate whether it delivers accurate and useful outputs. Organizational issues are not considered. With this focus, these papers investigate pilot implementations that have many similarities with usability tests. A couple of the papers appear to use the terms pilot implementation and usability test interchangeably, thereby blurring a distinction that warrants attention. It may be argued that a test of the social, organizational, and contextual issues associated with using the systems will also be needed before a decision about their full-scale implementation can be made. Three papers from this group are included in this post-proceedings volume:

- Mathesul et al. [11], who investigate a system that generates images from textual descriptions. Eleven users participated individually in the pilot implementation and provided their feedback. On the basis of the feedback, the development team plans to improve the resolution of the images and to provide better options for choosing among the generated images.
- Pradhan et al. [15], who have tested a web application for detecting hateful content in social media posts. Twelve users provided real-world input to the application and rated their user experience and the accuracy of the classifications made by the application. The test shows that the accuracy needs to be improved before the application is ready for operational use.
- Wawage and Deshpande [18], who have pilot implemented an app for improving traffic safety. The app classifies driver behavior on the basis of smartphone sensor data. A single driver used the app for seven days. The app achieved high classification accuracy, but the paper does not explain how the app will contribute to the inherently sociotechnical challenge of improving traffic safety.

A group of three of the papers presented at the workshop studies pilot implementation in relation to systems that are in the process of being designed in a specific organizational context. These papers focus on understanding the needs of users and organizations and on matching these needs with system functionality. This focus has a lot in common with the analysis phase in systems development. In contrast, the papers largely bypass technical issues. The role of the pilot implementation varies in this group of papers, but all three papers are mainly situated in the preparation phase of a pilot implementation, that is, before the period of pilot use. The preparation phase is far from trivial and may generate important learning before the pilot system enters the period of pilot use [12]. This post-proceedings volume includes one paper from this group:

- Saadati et al. [17], who have conducted co-design workshops at an airport as a precursor to future pilot implementations of autonomous technologies. The airport has experience with pilot implementations (trials, in their terminology) but considers them a suboptimal method. The co-design workshops serve to elicit workplace needs and clarify which technologies to select for further consideration and pilot implementation.

Finally, two of the papers presented at the workshop approach pilot implementation from a conceptual point of view, rather than through a case study. One of these papers is included in this post-proceedings volume:

- Clemmensen [2], who starts from the premise that pilot implementations entail a move from the technical toward the social and discusses the components of this move. Pilot implementations are theorized as adaptive sociotechnical interventions. These interventions interject change in the relations between work practices and information systems. At the same time, the interventions should themselves be changeable to allow for adapting the use of the pilot system to local circumstances.

## 4 Conclusion

Pilot implementations are recognized among practitioners as a means of testing the fit between a system and its use environment. However, they have received less interest from researchers in human-computer interaction than, for example, usability tests. The papers from the workshop on pilot implementation for testing human-work interaction designs provide illustrative case studies and inspiration for further research.

**Acknowledgments.** The organizers of the workshop were Barbara Rita Barricelli, Ganesh Bhutkar, Pedro F. Campos, Torkil Clemmensen, Frederica Gonçalves, Morten Hertzum, Arminda Guerra Lopes, and José Abdelnour Nocera.

## References

1. Clemmensen, T.: Human Work Interaction Design: A Platform for Theory and Action. Springer, Cham (2021). https://doi.org/10.1007/978-3-030-71796-4
2. Clemmensen, T.: Dropping a bomb or providing a gentle loving touch? Towards a relation artefact theory of pilot implementation. In: Ardito, C., et al. (eds.) INTERACT 2021. LNCS, vol. 13198, pp. 429–439 (2022)
3. Elliott, M., Kling, R.: Organizational usability of digital libraries: case study of legal research in civil and criminal courts. J. Am. Soc. Inform. Sci. **48**(11), 1023–1035 (1997). https://doi.org/10.1002/(SICI)1097-4571(199711)48:11%3c1023::AID-ASI5%3e3.0.CO;2-Y

4. Grudin, J.: Interactive systems: bridging the gaps between developers and users. IEEE Comput. **24**(4), 59–69 (1991). https://doi.org/10.1109/2.76263
5. Herbæk, L.K., Hansen, C.E.D., Clemmensen, T.: Pilot implementation: Organizational alignment when implementing an IT-system. In: Ardito, C., et al. (eds.) INTERACT 2021. LNCS, vol. 13198, pp. 391–396 (2022)
6. Hertzum, M.: Organizational Implementation: The Design in Use of Information Systems. Morgan and Claypool. San Rafael, CA (2021). https://doi.org/10.2200/S01081ED1V01Y202103HCI049
7. Hertzum, M., Bansler, J.P., Havn, E., Simonsen, J.: Pilot implementation: learning from field tests in IS development. Commun. Assoc. Inform. Syst. **30**(1), 313–328 (2012). https://doi.org/10.17705/1CAIS.03020
8. Hertzum, M., et al.: Pilot implementation: testing human-work interaction designs. In: Ardito, C., et al. (eds.) INTERACT 2021. LNCS, vol. 12936, pp. 570–574. Springer, Cham (2021). https://doi.org/10.1007/978-3-030-85607-6_79
9. Hertzum, M., Manikas, M.I., Torkilsheyggi, A.: Grappling with the future: the messiness of pilot implementation in information systems design. Health Inform. J. **25**(2), 372–388 (2019). https://doi.org/10.1177/1460458217712058
10. Korn, M., Bødker, S.: Looking ahead - how field trials can work in iterative and exploratory design of ubicomp systems. In: Proceedings of the UbiComp2012 Conference on Ubiquitous Computing, pp. 21–30. ACM Press, New York (2012). https://doi.org/10.1145/2370216.2370221
11. Mathesul, S., Bhutkar, G., Rambhad, A.: AttnGAN: realistic text-to-image synthesis with attentional generative adversarial networks. In: Ardito, C., et al. (eds.) INTERACT 2021. LNCS, vol. 13198, pp. 397–403 (2022)
12. Mønsted, T., Hertzum, M., Søndergaard, J.: A socio-temporal perspective on pilot implementation: bootstrapping preventive care. Comput. Supp. Cooper. Work (CSCW) **29**(4), 419–449 (2019). https://doi.org/10.1007/s10606-019-09369-6
13. Pal, R., Sengupta, A., Bose, I.: Role of pilot study in assessing viability of new technology projects: the case of RFID in parking operations. Commun. Assoc. Inform. Syst. **23**, 257–276, article 15 (2008). https://doi.org/10.17705/1CAIS.02315
14. Pereira, M.C., Ferreira, J.C., Moro, S., Gonçalves, F.: University digital engagement of students. In: Ardito, C., et al. (eds.) INTERACT 2021. LNCS, vol. 13198, pp. 376–390 (2022)
15. Pradhan, T., Bhutkar, G., Pangaonkar, A.: Prototype design of a multi-modal AI-based web application for hateful content detection in social media posts. In: Ardito, C., et al. (eds.) INTERACT 2021. LNCS, vol. 13198, pp. 404–411 (2022)
16. Rzevski, G.: Prototypes versus pilot systems: Strategies for evolutionary information system development. In: Budde, R., Kuhlenkamp, K., Mathiassen, L., Zullighoven, L. (eds.) Approaches to Prototyping: Proceedings of the Working Conference on Prototyping, pp. 356–367. Springer, Heidelberg (1984). https://doi.org/10.1007/978-3-642-69796-8_30
17. Saadati, P., Abdelnour-Nocera, J., Clemmensen, T.: Co-design workshops as a step towards pilot implementation for complex workplaces: case study of London-based airport future workplace. In: Ardito, C., et al. (eds.) INTERACT 2021. LNCS, vol. 13198, pp. 421–428 (2022)
18. Wawage, P., Deshpande, Y.: Pilot implementation for driver behaviour classification using smartphone sensor data for driver-vehicle interaction analysis. In: Ardito, C., et al. (eds.) INTERACT 2021. LNCS, vol. 13198, pp. 412–420 (2022)
19. Winthereik, B.R.: The project multiple: enactments of systems development. Scandinavian J. Inform. Syst. **22**(2), 49–64 (2010). https://aisel.aisnet.org/sjis/vol22/iss2/3

# University Digital Engagement of Students

Maria C. Pereira[1,2(✉)], João C. Ferreira[1,2(✉)], Sérgio Moro[1(✉)], and Frederica Gonçalves[3(✉)]

[1] Instituto Universitário de Lisboa (ISCTE-IUL), ISTAR, Lisbon, Portugal
{maria_c_pereira,Joao.Carlos.Ferreira,Sergio.Moro}@iscte-iul.pt
[2] INOV – Instituto de Engenharia de Sistemas e Computadores, Inovação, 1000-029 Lisbon, Portugal
[3] ITI/LARSyS, Universidade da Madeira - Escola Superior de Tecnologias e Gestão, Funchal, Portugal
frederica.goncalves@iti.larsys.pt

**Abstract.** Most of the prospective university students, especially from abroad, search on the online social networks what other students, present and former, are saying about the universities and the programs. Students express their sentiments regarding universities, programs, and courses they attended, or they are attending, in informal conversations on online social networks. We aim to understand how universities' and programs' enrolment numbers, relate to students' sentiments expressed on online social networks, and how this electronic word of mouth relates to the dissemination of information about the universities and the programs on online social networks. The research goal of this study is to test an approach to engage with students on online social networks and measure the impact of this interaction by analyzing the feedback from former and present students, and the enrolment numbers of new students.

**Keywords:** Universities · Social media · Sentiment analysis

## 1 Introduction

With the growing number of universities in the last decades and the decrease of public funding, universities must compete to get students, and international students are particularly important because they pay higher tuition fees [1]. Internationalization in higher education (HE) is simultaneously a consequence and a force towards globalization [2–4]. Higher education and research benefit from cooperation, diversity, multiculturalism [5–7], and the funds from international students' tuition fees. In the databases we queried, Scopus and Web of Science, we found 104 articles between 2008 and 2020, highlighting the importance of the use of online social networks (OSN) to internationalize universities [1, 8]. We also found studies pointing to the dissemination of programs and universities on OSN as an efficient and very affordable mean to attract new students [9–12]. We did other queries in the same databases to have an idea of the numbers of studies done, involving online social networks, advertise, sentiment analysis and universities or other business:


C. Ardito et al. (Eds.): INTERACT 2021, LNCS 13198, pp. 376–390, 2022.
https://doi.org/10.1007/978-3-030-98388-8_33

- Querying by "advertising on online social networks" we had 12,082 hits and querying by "university or program advertising on online social networks" we had only 25 hits.
- Querying by "reputation with sentiment analysis on electronic word of mouth eWoM" we had 315 hits and querying by "reputation with sentiment analysis on electronic word of mouth eWoM about universities" we had only 7 hits.
- Querying by "customer sentiment on electronic word of mouth eWoM we had 74 hits and querying by "students' sentiment on electronic word of mouth eWoM and universities" we had only 2 hits.

From the above-described findings, we perceive the lack of studies that relate eWoM, students' sentiments, universities, and programs advertising on OSN.

One of the most recent studies we found, concerning the use of OSN by universities to recruit foreign students, analyzes the use of Chinese OSN Weibo and WeChat, by UK universities to advertise and to interact with Chinese students in Mandarin [13]. This study has limited data because it was manually collected, but even so, it was possible to detect a positive association between the UK universities' reputation showed on Chinese OSN and the number of Chinese students enrolling in those universities. This study also identifies some effective strategies to gain followers and consequently more attention and dissemination on OSN.

Now, everyone is carrying smartphones, tablets, PCs, and intensively use the Internet and OSN [8, 14]. All the texts, photos and videos published, constitutes social media (SM) data, and have a story to tell [15], that is embedded in lots of words from informal conversations [16]. Student's comments on their scholar life creates eWoM that allow to infer about their perceptions on the quality of the universities [17]. On the universities' official SM pages, publications may influence future student's choices and have feedback from past and present students [1] about implemented policies, organized events or the global impression retained from the institution [8]. Data from such unsupervised environments can provide valuable knowledge, however, analyzing such big data (BD), is a challenging task that requires automatic data analysis with human interpretation, about the complexity of personal experiences described on OSN [18]. The intensive use of OSN generates massive unstructured data, that need to be properly collected, cleaned, structured, analyzed, and interpreted to produce knowledge [15].

There are various studies addressing the issue of university students' satisfaction, based on various approaches: rankings, surveys, education data, and some, based on small universes of SM data. We found a study [19] whose authors propose to implement sentiment analysis on texts written in Serbian, obtained from an online platform used to rate professors (a Serbian platform such as "Rate my Professor"). The stated goal of their research, is to propose a fully automated process to constant monitoring of students' sentiments and satisfaction, expressed on texts written in Serbian on OSN, and integrate the results in the universities' management systems to contribute to the improvement of students' recruitment. For now, they are collecting and manually annotating texts to construct the corpus for HE in Serbian language, to future use in automatic sentiment classification. We are developing a wider investigation where the goal is quite related to the previous research except that we will extract texts written in Portuguese and English, from OSN, about Portuguese universities. We aim to create a prototype of a decision support system, based on information extracted from online social networks and data collected in the universities' information systems, to assist universities' managers in the decision-making process concerning internationalization. The present study, which is testing an approach to engage with students on OSN, is part of that wider investigation.

Other researchers are interested in the information search behavior of the prospective university students on OSN, to reveal what are the more important factors in the decision-making process, of choosing a degree program to attend, or a master's degree or a PhD program and/or a university. That is the case of a study [20] we found, which collected data in Quora from prospective university students in Australia. In that research the authors performed qualitative and quantitative analysis on the questions about programs and universities and confirmed that prospective people (students, family, friends), expect answers from who has experience about what they want to know, including when they search for information that they could find in the universities' websites. This finding may indicate that they rely more in eWoM than in official information, or that they see the search in OSN simpler than in universities websites. Another relevant finding is that the reputation of programs and universities is a common question from prospective people.

Both approaches, university students' satisfaction analysis and the prospective university students' queries behavior, have the same objective: acquire knowledge to improve universities success. In the search for what is being done using sentiment analysis to relate eWoM on OSN to university rankings, universities and programs dissemination, and university enrolment numbers, one of the most interesting and somehow related to our proposed goal, in the wider research work, is the study by S. Gunduz et al. [21], which makes sentiment analysis of publications and comments, in Turkish language on Twitter, and tries to relate those sentiments with Turkish universities academic success on Turkish university ranking trying to understand if prospecting students are influenced by the rankings.

In our research work, we extract students' sentiments from OSN and promote a digital process to obtain new students. We are investigating universities' reputation, performing sentiment analysis on data collected on OSN, to understand if eWoM is an important source of candidates' recruitment. We aim to find if there is a relationship between universities and programs reputation in eWoM and, the enrollment numbers in that programs and universities, in the same period. Besides, we want to compare the results of the sentiment analysis obtained from SM data to the results of the universities' periodic surveys to their students, to find out how they relate. We want also to investigate the impact of university dissemination in OSN into the enrollment numbers of new students and, to have measurable data, we conducted a pilot implementation disseminating a master's degree program from ISCTE-IUL - Portugal, Mestrado em Sistemas Integrados de Apoio à Decisão (MSIAD), starting in July 2020. In the years before 2020, MSIAD received a very low number of new students what eases the study of the effect of the dissemination.

**Objectives for the pilot implementation**:

- 1st improve the number of new students enrolling in MSIAD.
- 2nd understand which platforms and which type of contents achieve more interactions.
- 3rd promote the dialogue with present and former students of MSIAD to have their feedback about the masters' program and the professors.

Our pilot implementation was developed in two phases:

- The first phase ran from July to August 2020 and the dissemination was made by two persons.
- The second phase ran from January to August 2021 and the dissemination was made by one person.

In the next sections we describe the methodology we followed in our pilot implementation.

## 2 Proposal Concept – Action Planning and Action Tacking

In the pilot implementation we followed an action research methodology (ARM) [22], depicted in Fig. 1. The activities we developed in the steps Action Planning, Action Tacking, and Evaluate of the ARM are quite like the activities proposed for a pilot implementation by Hertzum et al. [23]. After the definition of the objectives, which we already done in the previous section, we define the strategies to follow and the products to be created. Following the plan, we did the technical configuration. We created online platforms to disseminate MSIAD: blogs, profiles on OSN in name of MSIAD-ISCTE, contents about MSIAD to disseminate online, and we implemented the dissemination making publications and sharing those publications on OSN. After tacking actions, we need to evaluate the effects on MSIAD, considering the numbers of new students' applying and enrolling, the interactions on OSN, and the feedback received from former and present students of MSIAD. This is done in the Evaluation, in next section. Except for the first step, Objectives, the remaining steps must be iterated to improve the Action Planning and Action Tacking with the feedback obtained from the Evaluation and the scientific community.

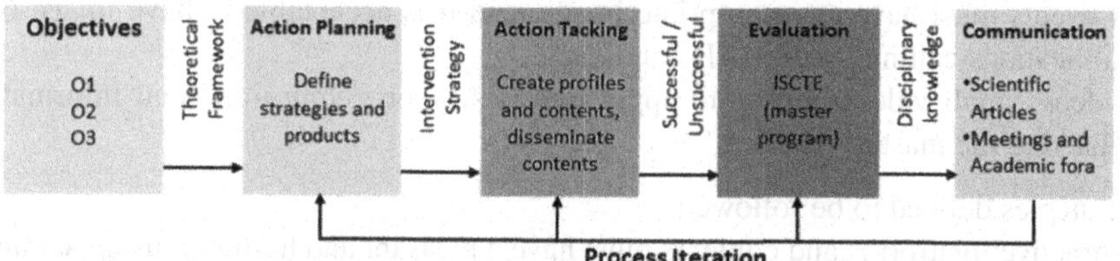


**Fig. 1.** Action research methodology: objectives, action planning, action taking, evaluation, communication. The last four steps must be iterated to improve the results with the learnings and the feedback received

## 2.1 Planning and Design

In planning and design of the pilot implementation we developed the activities included in Action Planning of the ARM, where we define the products to be created and the strategies to follow.

Global plan to disseminate MSIAD:

- 1st create online platforms and profiles.
- 2nd create and publish, and/or disseminate contents (texts, images, videos).

Strategies defined to the contents:

- 1st must be attractive.
- 2nd must be informative and/or formative.

Products planned to be created:

- Platforms: blog written in Portuguese (PT) to disseminate information about the masters' degree, since it is taught in Portuguese; blog written in English (EN) to disseminate thesis and scientific publications, written in English and authored by MSIAD students; Facebook page to reach a broad range of public, even who doesn't have a Facebook account; Facebook group to aggregate students (former, present, future) and improve the exchange of experiences; LinkedIn to capture attention of professionals that want to enrich they education with a master degree; Twitter, Instagram, YouTube, Quora and Reddit, all of them to enlarge the dissemination and capture a broader range of public.
- Texts: information about the master's degree program (MSIAD); information about events related to MSIAD, or the subjects studied in the master's degree; thesis and the scientific publications authored by MSIAD students.
- Images: all the publications must have an image. Thesis and scientific publications from MSIAD students must have at least one image as illustration, announcements of events must have an appropriate image, and it is acceptable to have image-only publications calling for MSIAD candidacy.
- Videos: small videos calling to apply to MSIAD, or giving important information related to the master's degree.

Strategies defined to be followed:

- Attractive: platforms and contents must have a pleasant and harmonious appearance.
- Informative: create and publish informative contents about MSIAD and the subjects studied in the master program.
- Formative: publish formative contents related to the subjects studied in the master program.

In Fig. 2 we depict and characterize the planned activities.

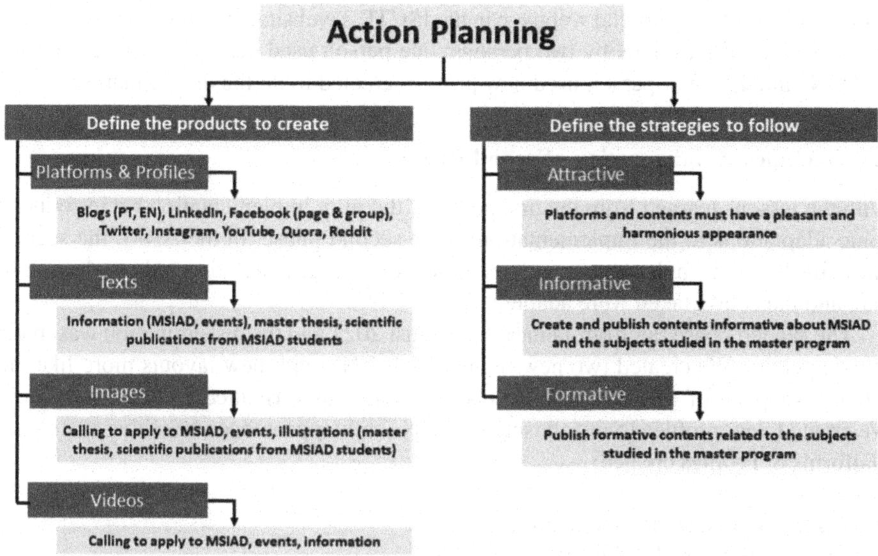


**Fig. 2.** Action Planning: define products (platforms & profiles, texts, images, videos) to create and strategies (attractive, informative, and formative) to follow

## 2.2 Technical Configuration - First Phase

Technical configuration activities of the pilot implementation have a close match with the activities we developed in action tacking of the ARM.

The first phase was very short, only two months from July to August 2020, so we decided to implement only a subset of the planned products and strategies. First were created two blogs (PT & EN), Facebook groups and page, and new profiles on Twitter and Instagram. Platforms & Profiles created:

- https://msiad2020.blogspot.com
- https://mibis-2020.blogspot.com
- https://www.facebook.com/groups/highereducationinternationalization
- https://www.facebook.com/groups/sistemasintegradosdeapoiodecisao
- https://www.facebook.com/HigherEducationInternationalization
- https://www.instagram.com/universityinternationalization
- https://twitter.com/hei_smartedu

After the creation of the online platforms and profiles we created and published the contents. New publications, with text and one image, was done in each blog in alternate days and after that, the blogs' posts were shared on online social networks. Statistics from Google Analytics and the number of new students enrolled in MSIAD, were collected during the period of the dissemination. We also collected feedback from former students in a small questionnaire that was shared online.

The layouts for the two blogs (PT & EN), in the first phase of the pilot implementation, were selected to cause visual impact. All the posts have an invitation to apply for MSIAD, following a link to the official webpage in the ISCTE's website. Dissemination on online social networks[1] was done by two persons: one person used her own personal profiles on OSN, and the other person used new profiles created to do the dissemination.

### 2.3 Technical Configuration - Second Phase

With the lessons learned from the first phase of the pilot implementation we introduced some adaptations to the implementation in the second phase. In the ARM, the second phase of the pilot implementation corresponds to a process iteration, where the action plan and the action taken were adapted.

The second phase ran from January to August 2021 and the dissemination was made by one person. We created two new blogs (PT & EN), with new layouts more like the official webpage of MSIAD. The Facebook group was formatted to has a new look. We created new profiles to msiad.iscte on OSN, with appearances matching the blogs. Platforms & Profiles created:

- https://msiad-iscte.blogspot.com
- https://mibis-iscte.blogspot.com
- https://www.facebook.com/iscte.msiad
- https://www.facebook.com/groups/msiad.iscte
- https://www.facebook.com/msiad.iscte
- https://www.instagram.com/msiad.iscte
- https://twitter.com/IscteMsiad
- https://www.linkedin.com/in/msiad-iscte
- https://www.reddit.com/user/MSIAD-ISCTE
- https://pt.quora.com/q/msiadiscte
- https://www.youtube.com/channel/UCWR6cHPHdH3cHPuzc3Rhmxw/videos

In the blogs were published, occasionally, new posts consisting primarily of thesis and papers produced by students of MSIAD and after, the publications were shared on OSN. On OSN profiles of msiad.iscte were posted other contents[2], consisting primarily of images and small videos calling, directly or indirectly to apply on MSIAD. Those posts were shared on other personal profiles, from followers. We collected statistics from Facebook Business suite (Facebook page and Instagram), from Facebook group, from Twitter, from LinkedIn, from Quora, from YouTube, and from Google Analytics (MSIAD blogs, and ISCTEs' official webpage of MSIAD). We received spontaneous feedback from present students in messages received on Facebook. We also collected the number of new students enrolled in MSIAD, during the period of the dissemination.

### 2.4 Use

All platforms and profiles created on OSN to disseminate MSIAD functioned as extensions of the official MSIAD page on the ISCTE website. The information about MSIAD

[1] Facebook, LinkedIn, Twitter, Instagram, Pinterest, Tumbir.

[2] https://drive.google.com/drive/folders/1ntADiiO-BcCvmiJW4eVVVh0_S1JPymsV?usp=sharing.

disseminated, is alike what is on the official webpage, but we experimented diverse looks and *media* (texts, images, videos) to present the information about MSIAD, trying to attract more attention and more new students.

**In the first phase** of the pilot implementation: the PT blog was primarily used to inform about MSIAD, replicating part of the information on the official webpages of the ISCTE's website. The PT blog was used also to share posts of MSIAD's former students about the subjects studied in the master's degree. The EN blog was used, primarily to disseminate scientific articles authored by students of MSIAD and to inform about the master's degree.

**In the second phase** of the pilot implementation: the PT blog was primarily used to disseminate thesis authored by students of MSIAD with high scores, and to inform about events and about MSIAD, using various appearances, such as images and a flipbook. The use of the EN blog was not changed from the first to the second phase of the pilot implementation. In Fig. 3 we summarize the activities, concerning platforms and contents, developed in the action tacking step from the ARM, with texts, images and videos following what was planned.

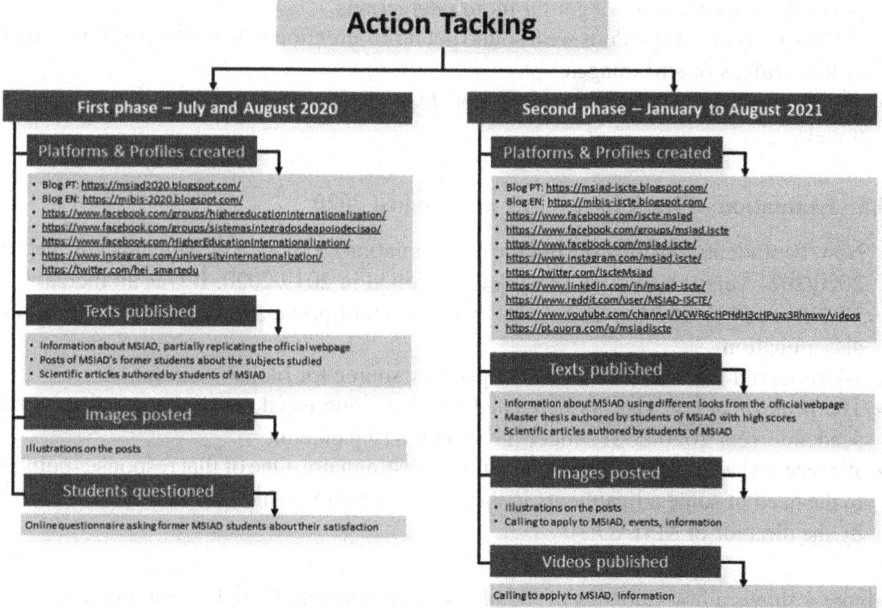


**Fig. 3.** Action Tacking: first phase (created blogs and OSN profiles, disseminated texts and images, questioned MSIAD students), second phase (created new blogs and OSN profiles, created and disseminated texts, images and videos)

## 3 Evaluation - Results from the Pilot Implementation Applied to a PT Master's Degree

In the evaluation step of the ARM, we analyze what we learned with our pilot implementation and the results versus the proposed objectives: improve the enrollment number of new students in MSIAD and understand what strategies, platforms, and contents gets more interaction on OSN. These activities are the same witch must be developed in the step Learning from a pilot implementation.

### 3.1 Learning

In our pilot implementation, disseminating a master's degree program in online social networks, we can summarize our learnings in four lessons:

- 1st lesson: daily sharing external links on Facebook, leads to being classified as a spammer by Facebook. If the posts are created directly on Facebook, they can be shared as many times as we want and everywhere (pages, groups, profiles) on Facebook.
- 2nd lesson: blogs are important by the extension and diversity of contents they permit, but online social networks get far more interactions.
- 3rd lesson: very short videos with sound get more attention than videos without sound, or long videos or still images.
- 4th lesson: images with embedded short texts get more interactions than texts with images.

### 3.2 Evaluation - First Phase - July and August 2020

- New 10 students enrolled during the dissemination. A total of 27 students enrolled in 2020/2021 versus a total of 18 students enrolled in 2019/2020. It was an increase of 50% from 2019/2020 to 2020/2021 but we cannot prove that it was because of our dissemination.
- We observed that Facebook was the primary source for blogs' visitors.
- The peak of blogs' visitors happened when we published about the opening of the academic year 2020/2021, under the COVID-19 pandemic.
- We received a few responses on the online questionnaire. One of that responses pointed to the need of some adjustments in the master program, what was tacked into account by the director of MSIAD.

Figure 4 shows a few statistics of the blogs compiled from Google Analytics where we can observe that the number of visualizations of the blogs' publications is close to the number of the visitors that came to the blogs, starting from links on Facebook.

### 3.3 Evaluation - Second Phase - February to August 2021

- A total of 50 new students applied to MSIAD and 35 were enrolled, thus exhausting the 35 available places for the 2021/2022 academic year. Never before the places were exhausted in MSIAD. In the previous academic year, 2020/2021, 27 new students were enrolled.

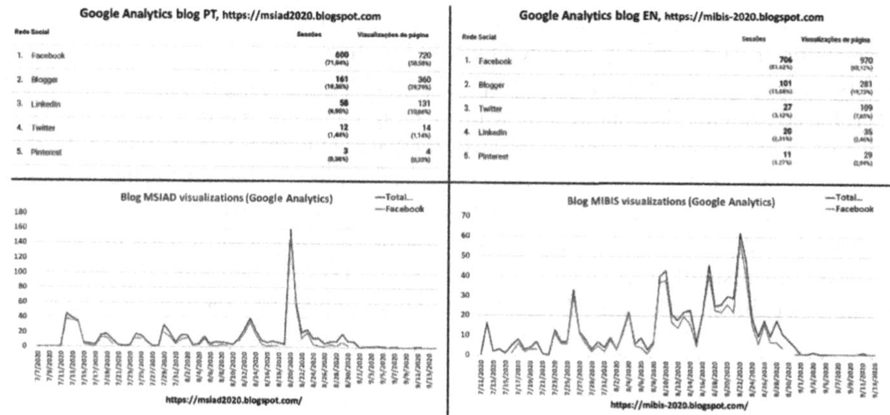


**Fig. 4.** Statistics of the blogs compiled from Google analytics, regarding July and August 2020

- We received private messages on Facebook, from one present student expressing the unsatisfaction of a group of colleagues, including himself, with the behavior of a teacher. The director of MSIAD did what he could to address the issues and improve the students' satisfaction.
- We applied a small questionnaire to the 35 new students, asking them to choose from the various platforms "*Where I saw MSIAD when I thought about applying for a master's degree*". We received a response from 74% of them (26 of the 35 students). In the responses obtained, 23% (6 of the 26), report having seen the information about MSIAD on some of the platforms we used in this pilot implementation: 33% (2 of the 6), saw information on more than one platform; the most viewed platforms were the blogs followed by LinkedIn and Facebook.
  In Fig. 5 we can see summaries of the responses organized in two ways. In the table on the left are the answers from each student that reported have seen our dissemination. Student A saw our dissemination on LinkedIn and in the Facebook group, student C saw on blogs, Instagram, and YouTube, and the remaining reported have seen only one of all platforms, we used to disseminate MSIAD. In the graphic on the right is the distribution, in percentage per platform viewed. Blogs are the platforms most viewed with 34% of the reported visualizations, followed by LinkedIn with 22% of reported visualizations and Facebook page, 11%, plus Facebook group, 11%, which sums to 22% of the reported visualizations.
- The small video with more interactions is a presentation of information about MSIAD. On the left of Fig. 6 we show a snip of this small video, and on the right is the image with more interactions. This image alerts to MSIAD candidates with reservation tax not yet paid.
- Based on the responses to the questionnaire, the blogs were the most viewed platforms. Based on the blogs statistics the most popular publications are those shown in Fig. 7. On the PT blog, the most saw post is a master thesis, from an MSIAD student, which got the maximum grade. This master thesis originated two scientific articles, [24, 25], published in high quality journals. On the EN blog, there are two posts with equal

number of visualizations, that are the most popular posts. Both are dissemination of scientific articles, [26, 27], authored by MSIAD students.

- Disseminating on a broader range of platforms allowed us to get a better idea of the preferred contents. The publication with the largest absolute reach, of all platforms, is a post on Facebook page announcing an event that is a Summer School with ECTS that can be equivalent to an optional MSIAD course. See Fig. 8 on the left. On the responses to the questionnaire, LinkedIn was reported as one of the most seen platforms. The most viewed post on LinkedIn is an interview to the director of MSIAD in which he speaks about smart cities, Internet of Things, and ISCTE's projects. This post has a link to a publication on the PT blog to read the full interview. See Fig. 8 on the right.

**Platforms seen by each of the 6 students**

| Students | Linkedin | Facebook Group | Facebook Page | Blogs | Instagram | YouTube |
|---|---|---|---|---|---|---|
| A | X | X | | | | |
| B | | | | X | | |
| C | | | | X | X | X |
| D | | | X | | | |
| E | | | | X | | |
| F | X | | | | | |

**23% of new students saw MSIAD on these platforms**

YouTube 11%
Instagram 11%
Facebook Page 11%

Fig. 5. Summary of the answers of the new students to the questionnaire. On the left are the answers from each student and on the right is the distribution per platform

Fig. 6. Snip of the short video with more interactions, on the left: presentation of information about MSIAD. On the right is the image with more interactions which is an alert to MSIAD candidates with reservation tax not yet paid.

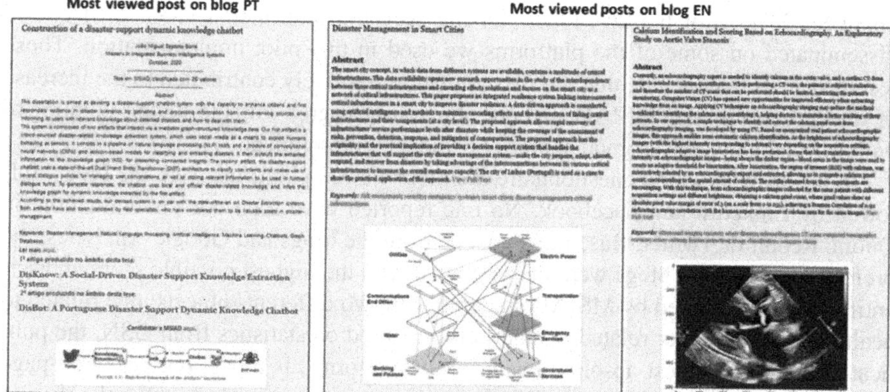


**Fig. 7.** The most popular posts on the blogs. On the left is the most saw post on PT blog It is the Abstract of a thesis, from a student of MSIAD, graded with the highest possible score. This master thesis originated two scientific articles [24, 25]. On the right are the two posts with equal number of visualizations, that are the most popular posts on EN blog. Both are Abstracts of scientific articles [26, 27], authored by MSIAD students

**Fig. 8.** Preferred contents on OSN. On the left is the post with largest absolute reach in all platforms: a post on Facebook page announcing an event. On the right is the post most viewed on LinkedIn: an interview to the director of MSIAD.

## 4 Conclusions and Future Work

The first objective of this pilot implementation was to increase the number of new students enrolling on MSIAD. That objective was fully accomplished considering the exhaustion of the places to new students in the academic year 2021/2022. The exhaustion of the places was never accomplished before. The questionnaire we applied to the new 35 students received response from 74% of them (26 of the 35 students). In the responses obtained, 23% (6 of the 26), report having seen the information about MSIAD we disseminated on some of the platforms we used in this pilot implementation. Those results lead us to conclude that our dissemination positively contributed to the increase of students enrolling in MSIAD, and our observations agree with the studies pointing to online social networks as good sources of students' recruitment.

In the answers to the questionnaire the most viewed platforms were the blogs, followed by LinkedIn and Facebook. No one reported have seen our dissemination on Quora, Reddit or Twitter. Based in statistics from the blogs and Google Analytics, the preferred contents on blogs were thesis graded with the highest possible score and scientific articles authored by MSIAD students with two different subjects: one related to health exams and other related to smart cities. Based on statistics from OSN, the publication with the largest absolute reach, of all platforms, is a post on Facebook page announcing an event. The posts with more interactions, were also on Facebook, and were a small video presenting information about MSIAD, like the information in the official webpage of MSIAD, and an image alerting to MSIAD candidates with reservation tax not yet paid. Those observations agree with our findings, in investigations of other researchers, that related prospective people searching on OSN for information that could be found in the official website of the universities. On the responses to the questionnaire, LinkedIn was reported as one of the most seen platforms. The most viewed post in LinkedIn is an interview to the director of MSIAD. These observations permit us say that the second objective to this pilot implementation, understand which platforms and which type of contents achieve more interactions, was also satisfied.

The third objective of our pilot implementation was: promote the dialogue with present and former students of MSIAD to have their feedback about the masters' degree program and the professors. The questionnaire to the satisfaction of MSIAD students applied online, and the spontaneous feedback received from MSIAD students on OSN, permitted identify some issues and implement improvements in the masters' degree.

We are collecting more data and implementing other types of analysis, *e.g.*, sentiment analysis, to understand the universities and programs' reputation in eWoM and relate to enrollment numbers. Online social networks are indicators of universities and programs reputations. We observed that some platforms, like Quora, Reddit and Twitter, had very low number of interactions. Probably the types of publications in those platforms need adjustments. We also observed that the most of interactions was passive: people saw the posts, but they do not comment. It could be tested, in the future, create different types of publications, calling directly for action.

We are enthusiastic about the results of our pilot implementation and recommend the replication, adaptation and new implementations in other programs, universities, and countries.

**Acknowledgement.** This work was supported by EEA Grants Blue Growth Programme (Call #5). Project PT-INNOVATION-0045 – Fish2Fork.

## References

1. Choudaha, R.: Social media in international student recruitment. Association of International Education Administrators (AIEA) Issue Brief (2013)

2. Knight, J.: Education hubs: a Fad, a Brand, an innovation? J. Stud. Int. Educ. **15**(3), 221–240 (2011). https://doi.org/10.1177/1028315311398046
3. Knight, J.: Updated definition of internationalization. Int. High. Educ. **33**, 2–3 (2015). https://doi.org/10.6017/ihe.2003.33.7391
4. Hudzik, J.K.: Changing paradigm and practice for higher education internationalisation (2013)
5. Altbach, P.G., Knight, J.: The internationalization of higher education: motivations and realities. J. Stud. Int. Educ. **11**(3–4), 290–305 (2007). https://doi.org/10.1177/1028315307303542
6. Knight, J.: Internationalization remodeled: definition, approaches, and rationales. J. Stud. Int. Educ. **8**(1), 5–31 (2004). https://doi.org/10.1177/1028315303260832
7. Hawawini, G.: The internationalization of higher education institutions: a critical review and a radical proposal. SSRN Electron. J. (2012). https://doi.org/10.2139/ssrn.1954697
8. Asderaki, F, Maragos, D.: The internationalization of higher education: the added value of the European portals and social media pages for the national and the institutional internationalization strategies. In: International Conference on Information Communication Technologies in Education, pp. 498–510 (2012). http://www.academia.edu/download/30213190/Internationalization_HE_EU_portals.pdf
9. Oliveira, L.G.: A framework for the development of social media content strategies for higher education institutions. Estudos em Comunicacao **30**, 21–48 (2020). https://doi.org/10.25768/20.04.03.30.02
10. Constantinides, E., Stagno, M.C.Z.: Potential of the social media as instruments of higher education marketing: a segmentation study. J. Mark. High. Educ. **21**(1), 7–24 (2011). https://doi.org/10.1080/08841241.2011.573593
11. Thornton, K.K.: Understanding the role of social media on a student's college choice process and the implications on a university's enrollment and marketing strategies. ProQuest Dissertations and Theses, p. 234 (2017). https://search.proquest.com/docview/1931958050?accountid=17242
12. Oliveira, L., Figueira, Á.: Improving the benchmarking of social media content strategies using clustering and KPI. Procedia Comput. Sci. **121**, 826–834 (2017). https://doi.org/10.1016/j.procs.2017.11.107
13. Zhu, Y.: Social media engagement and Chinese international student recruitment: understanding how UK HEIs use Weibo and WeChat. J. Mark. High. Educ. **29**(2), 173–190 (2019). https://doi.org/10.1080/08841241.2019.1633003
14. Keith, K., van Belle, J. P.: The use of a social networking site in the facilitation of internationalization in higher education: a case study using the actor network theory perspective. In: Proceedings - 4th IEEE International Conference on Big Data and Cloud Computing, BDCloud 2014 with the 7th IEEE International Conference on Social Computing and Networking, SocialCom 2014 and the 4th International Conference on Sustainable Computing and C, pp. 516–523 (2014). https://doi.org/10.1109/BDCloud.2014.72
15. Ghareh, F., Saniee, M.: A survey of data mining techniques for steganalysis. Recent Adv. Steganography (2012). https://doi.org/10.5772/53989
16. Talawar, M.B., Kundur, N.C.: Analyzing social media data in educational sectors using data mining techniques. Int. J. Comput. Sci. Inf. Technol. **7**(4), 2125–2129 (2016)
17. Zhou, R.: Education web information retrieval and classification with big data analysis. Creat. Educ. **07**(18), 2868–2875 (2016). https://doi.org/10.4236/ce.2016.718265
18. Chen, X., Vorvoreanu, M., Madhavan, K.P.C.: Mining social media data for understanding students' learning experiences. IEEE Trans. Learn. Technol. **7**(3), 246–259 (2014). https://doi.org/10.1109/TLT.2013.2296520
19. Grljević, O., Bošnjak, Z., Kovačević, A.: Opinion mining in higher education: a corpus-based approach. Enterp. Inf. Syst. **00**(00), 1–26 (2020). https://doi.org/10.1080/17517575.2020.1773542

20. Le, T.D., Dobele, A.R., Robinson, L.J.: Information sought by prospective students from social media electronic word-of-mouth during the university choice process. J. High. Educ. Policy Manag. **41**(1), 18–34 (2019). https://doi.org/10.1080/1360080X.2018.1538595
21. Gunduz, S., Demirhan, F., Sagiroglu, S.: Investigating sentimental relation between social media presence and academic success of Turkish universities. In: Proceedings - 2014 13th International Conference on Machine Learning and Applications, ICMLA 2014, pp. 574–579 (2014). https://doi.org/10.1109/ICMLA.2014.95
22. Baskerville, R.L.: Investigating information systems with action research. In: Communications of the Association for Information Systems, vol. 2, October 1999. https://doi.org/10.17705/1CAIS.00219
23. Hertzum, M., Bansler, J.P., Havn, E.C., Simonsen, J.: Pilot implementation: learning from field tests in IS development. Commun. Assoc. Inf. Syst. **30**(2012), 313–328 (2012). https://doi.org/10.17705/1cais.03020
24. Boné, J., Dias, M., Ferreira, J.C., Ribeiro, R.: DisKnow: a social-driven disaster support knowledge extraction system. Appl. Sci. **10**(17) (2020). https://doi.org/10.3390/app10176083
25. Boné, J., Ferreira, J.C., Ribeiro, R., Cadete, G.: DisBot: a Portuguese disaster support dynamic knowledge chatbot. Appl. Sci. **10**(24), 1–20 (2020). https://doi.org/10.3390/app10249082
26. Elvas, L.B., Mataloto, B.M., Martins, A.L., Ferreira, J.C.: Disaster management in smart cities. Smart Cities **4**(2), 819–839 (2021). https://doi.org/10.3390/smartcities4020042
27. Elvas, L.B., Almeida, A.G., Rosario, L., Dias, M.S., Ferreira, J.C.: Calcium identification and scoring based on echocardiography. An exploratory study on aortic valve stenosis. J. Pers. Med. **11**(7) (2021). https://doi.org/10.3390/jpm11070598

# Pilot Implementation: Organizational Alignment When Implementing an IT-System

Linnea Krista Herbæk, Carl Emil Derby Hansen, and Torkil Clemmensen(✉)

Copenhagen Business School, Howitzvej 60, 2000 Frederiksberg, Denmark
{Lihe18ad,Caha18aj}@student.cbs.dk, tc.digi@cbs.dk

**Abstract.** Pilot implementation can be seen as a socio-technical design approach. This paper presents a design case that focused on the optimal implementation and organizational change process when a new IT system is to be implemented in an organization. The case was a pilot implementation of a new self-service-oriented IT system for both customers and employees in a Danish SME 'proptech' company. 'Proptech' denotes companies dealing with property and technology. The underlying epistemic view of the design case was that of functional pragmatism, and the collection and interpretation of data were aimed at analyzing how the case company managed to implement a new IT system from technical, organizational, and economical perspectives. The analysis revealed that though the case company management did not do what the current theory in the area prescribes, the company still thrived with the pilot implementation. Our position is thus that organizational alignment is an important aspect of pilot implementation, and that it can be analyzed by analyzing various management practices related to the pilot implementation.

**Keywords:** Pilot implementation · Organizational alignment · Organizational structure

## 1 Introduction

Organizational alignment is the process of aligning the organizational structure, culture, and resources with the individuals in the organization. In connection with pilot implementation, it is the process of giving the team behind the pilot implementation the best environment and resources that complement the development, feedback loop and implementation of the new IT system. This paper argues for the importance of organizational alignment for a pilot implementation to thrive when implementing an IT system. The current theory about pilot implementation presents it as a temporary opportunity to let a part of the target users (employees) experience how the new system will be like to work with [1–3], see also [4–7]. This paper adds to the current theory about pilot implementation by focusing on the organizational alignment that is necessary for pilot implementation.


Published by Springer Nature Switzerland AG 2022
C. Ardito et al. (Eds.): INTERACT 2021, LNCS 13198, pp. 391–396, 2022.
https://doi.org/10.1007/978-3-030-98388-8_34

This paper builds on prior research done by Herbæk and Hansen [8]. They did a case study in a small company that implemented a new IT system through pilot implementation. The findings from the case study support this paper's points, and the case study highlights strengths and limitations in the studied company's organizational structure and how it affected their implementation process. Herbæk and Hansen's [8] design case focused on the optimal implementation and change process when a new IT system is to be implemented in an organization. The case was the pilot implementation of new self-service-oriented IT system for both customers and employees in a Danish SME 'proptech' company. 'Proptech' denote companies dealing with property and technology. The underlying epistemic view of the design case was that of functional pragmatism, and the collection and interpretation of data were aimed at analyzing how the case company managed to implement a new IT system from technical, organizational, and economical perspectives. The analysis revealed that though the case company did not do what current theory in the area prescribes, they still succeeded with their pilot implementation through drawing on ideas from a combination of multiple theories, which complemented each other. This combination of several theories meant that they did not have to follow any specific theory to the letter. This study is focusing on the management's role in pilot implementation of IT systems. Below we unfold the findings and the argument from the case.

## 2 Objectives

There are three main objectives for this paper:

- To emphasize the importance of ensuring alignment between the technical side and organizational side of a pilot implementation.
- To contribute to the design of the optimal pilot implementation framework/process/model.
- To contribute with the findings of a conducted case study on pilot implementation.

## 3 Organizational Alignment

### 3.1 Why is Organizational Alignment Crucial for Conducting Pilot Implementation?

Pilot implementation is defined as "a field test of a properly engineered, yet unfinished system in its intended environment, using real data, and aiming – through real-use experience – to explore the value of the system, improve or assess its design, and reduce implementation risk" [2]. With the introduction of an unfinished system comes certain obstacles which the management must focus on to make the development and implementation process thrive.

We use the notion of organizational alignment to describe interventions that ensure that the pilot implementation and the current and the long-term business goals of the organization are aligned. It is well established that one of the key factors for successful organizations is the close linkage of its IT strategy and business strategy [9], and this is also true for socio-technical design and business strategy. Different conceptualizations of organizational strategies exist, and we follow the idea of strategy as practice [10] where the study object is how management practices are used to put strategy into practice. Thus, the practices of managers should be aligned with the practices of designers to achieve successful pilot implementation.

However, if the organization is not aligned with the pilot implementation it could lead to stagnation of the implementation process, and to inefficiency in the work, test, and development flow [8]. Herbæk and Hansen analyzed organizational alignment initiatives based on the theory of the three legged stool of organizational architecture [11], which focuses on 1. decision-making rights, 2. performance evaluation, and 3. reward systems. They supported their analysis with Kotter's 8 steps for organizational change [12, 13] and the principles for lean startups of companies [14, 15]. The three-legged stool stipulates that decision-making rights, performance evaluation, and reward systems must be in balance and aligned to the company's current situation to create success in what is desired to be accomplished. A finding from the analysis of these three areas was that the initiatives of the case company management affected the pilot implementation in both positive and negative ways, and that though the case company did not do what the current theory in the area prescribes, they still succeeded with their pilot implementation [8].

### 3.2 The Importance of Data Management in Pilot Implementation

In the case of the company studied by Hansen and Herbæk [8], the company desired to develop and implement a new IT system through pilot implementation. In theory, pilot implementation requires iterative testing and flowing communication between the developers and employees participating in the testing of the new unfinished system [2]. The developers require the decision rights to develop and test anything they find valuable for the new system, if it is based on the feedback generated by the end-users of the new system [14]. It is important to minimize the bureaucracy and allow developers to test as this generates feedback about the system in development which is crucial in pilot implementation. For the feedback loop to generate sufficient and valid feedback about the system in development, good communication tools and data management for developers are required. These are also needed for the test participants, the end-users who are involved in the pilot implementation. Testing a system during pilot implementation will influence the productivity of the test participants' daily work. Therefore the test participants must have the decision rights to switch back and forth between using the new system under development and the old already established system. This decision right or mindset is crucial to incorporate in the pilot implementation, because if the test participants feel forced to test the system in development the incentives for them taking part in the development fails [8]. Furthermore, when utilizing a system in development in real work assignments it is common for the system to have limitations and/or flaws that will impact productivity. Forcing test participants to keep working in a system in development will therefore have a negative impact on that worker's productivity [8].

However, while our design case revealed a significant amount of freedom in the communication and reporting of feedback between the developers and employees, it also revealed a lack of structured data management when multiple employees reported

**Fig. 1.** Feedback without data management.

feedback about the system in development to the developers. The lack of structured data management led to confusion among the developers, as the feedback data got unmanageable as there was a lack of overview [8]. The case study finding was thus that pilot implementation required a more refined data management structure to get the most out of the feedback generated from the employees. Without data management, there is no structure of the feedback. With no structure of the feedback, developers will have a tough time knowing what attribute of the system in development the feedback is concerning. If developers want to build something, they need a plan. Each feedback the developers get is like a brick in a Lego set. Without data management as the blueprint and plan of what the developers need the brick for, the feedback will end up looking like a random pile of Lego, Fig. 1. A pile of Lego without a plan causes more confusion than utility, as the developers do not know what each part is to be used for. Likewise, we saw in the case study that that pile of feedback created more confusion than benefit for the developers due to the unmanageability [8].

### 3.3 Alignment of Organizational Reward Systems to Design Practices

The use of an unfinished system in real-use experience tends to be accompanied by lower efficiency in the workflow in which the system is used. This can lead to employees choosing to not utilize the new system in full, as it does not generate the same outcome as the already established system. This resistance needs to be addressed by the management. If the organizational performance evaluation is not aligned with the need for testing the new system, developers will have a harder time getting the necessary feedback which they use to further develop the new system.

In the case of the company studied by Hansen and Herbæk [8], the management lowered their performance evaluation goals as a mean to empower the employees' engagement in testing the new system. The lowering of the organization's performance evaluation goals furthered the development of the new system through organizational alignment and ensured that the employees' individual needs and the organization's vision and strategy were aligned [8].

*"For my job it has been important to align expectations with those who sat and tested. [...] So if they did not get to answer the 30 emails, and if they did not onboard the 10 customers, then that was okay as the priority should be that they should test. I could feel that if we had not had that expectation alignment, then I'm quite sure that it had created a lot of frustration, because it's clear that all of a sudden they had to spend several hours, let say 4 h on testing, because they had to write feedback, etc."* [8].

As the quote illustrates, the engagement of the employees used for testing as well as the developers was crucial for the pilot implementation in our case. Thus, the allocated decision rights and the freedom that follows these decision rights must support to sustain the level of engagement. This can be done through financial incentives. In our case, the case of the company studied by Hansen and Herbæk [8], the organization allowed for the full time workers to obtain warrants that represented an equity in the firm, as part of their salary. The inclusion of warrants generated a sense of ownership in the employees and further boosted their engagement in the pilot implementation. They became aware that whatever obstacles they faced would be worth overcoming since doing that would benefit both the organization and them as individuals. The organizational alignment of organizational reward systems to design practices therefore benefitted the development, testing, and implementation process of a pilot implementation [8].

## 4 Discussion and Conclusion

This paper asks what management can do to support a successful pilot implementation and answers the question by pointing to organizational alignment. The major insight from the design case was that though the case company management did not do exactly what current theory in the area prescribes, their initiatives were still important to the pilot implementation. Thus, the practices of managers were aligned with the practices of designers and users to achieve successful pilot implementation. This contrasts somewhat current theory that does not mention management except as project management [2] or as a stop/go decision maker for pilot implementation [1]. Our position is that organizational alignment is an important aspect of pilot implementation, and that it can be analyzed as Herbæk and Hansen [8] did it by analyzing various management practices related to the pilot implementation. Future research on pilot implementation may analyze management not as external stakeholders but as co-designers.

We provide two starting points for further research on organizational alignment in pilot implementation. First, the management of feedback data should be studied by looking at how the feedback data management systems need to align with the feedback requested and tests that are being conducted. Furthermore, innovative accounting practices should be studied with an eye on measuring progress using test and quantitative data derived from the tests conducted to supplement the qualitative descriptions of the progress that the development team would do. Second, the design of reward structures and performance evaluations related to the individuals participating in the pilot implementations should be studied with a focus on generating motivation to participate in generating feedback, as the individuals participating in the are likely to not utilize the system in development as much as needed for pilot implementation if it affects their performance bonuses.

## References

1. Mønsted, T., Hertzum, M., Søndergaard, J.: A socio-temporal perspective on pilot implementation: bootstrapping preventive care. Comput. Support. Coop. Work **29**, 419–449 (2019)
2. Hertzum, M., Bansler, J.P., Havn, E.C., Simonsen, J.: Pilot implementation: learning from field tests in IS development. Commun. Assoc. Inf. Syst. **30**, 20 (2012)
3. Hertzum, M.: Organizational implementation: the design in use of information systems. Synth. Lect. Hum.-Centered Inform. **14**, i–109 (2021)
4. Bansler, J.P., Havn, E.: Pilot implementation of health information systems: issues and challenges. Int. J. Med. Inform. **79**, 637–648 (2010)
5. Hertzum, M., Simonsen, J.: Effects-driven IT development: an instrument for supporting sustained participatory design. In: Proceedings of the 11th Biennial Participatory Design Conference, pp. 61–70 (2010)
6. Hertzum, M., Manikas, M.I., á Torkilsheyggi, A.: Grappling with the future: the messiness of pilot implementation in information systems design. Health Inform. J. **25**, 372–388 (2019)
7. á Torkilsheyggi, A., Hertzum, M.: User participation in pilot implementation: porters and nurses coordinating patient transports. In: Proceedings of the 26th Australian Computer-Human Interaction Conference on Designing Futures: The Future of Design, pp. 290–299 (2014)
8. Hansen, C.E.D., Herbæk, L.K.: Proper - a study of a change and implementation process (unpublished bachelor thesis) (2021)
9. Baets, W.: Aligning information systems with business strategy. J. Strateg. Inf. Syst. **1**, 205–213 (1992)
10. Jarzabkowski, P.: Strategy as practice: recursiveness, adaptation, and practices-in-use. Organ. Stud. **25**, 529–560 (2004)
11. Brickley, J., Smith, C., Zimmerman, J.: Managerial Economics and Organizational Architecture. McGraw-Hill Education, New York (2015)
12. Kotter, J.P.: Leading change. Harv. Bus. Rev. **2**, 1–10 (1995)
13. Appelbaum, S.H., Habashy, S., Malo, J., Shafiq, H.: Back to the future: revisiting Kotter's 1996 change model. J. Manag. Dev. (2012). https://doi.org/10.1108/02621711211253231
14. Ries, E.: The Lean Startup: How Today's Entrepreneurs Use Continuous Innovation to Create Radically Successful Businesses. Crown Business, New York (2011)
15. Eisenmann, T.R., Ries, E., Dillard, S.: Hypothesis-driven entrepreneurship: the lean startup, Harvard Business School Entrepreneurial Management Case (2012)

# AttnGAN: Realistic Text-to-Image Synthesis with Attentional Generative Adversarial Networks

Shubham Mathesul(✉), Ganesh Bhutkar, and Ayush Rambhad

Vishwakarma Institute of Technology, Pune, India
shubham.mathesul19@vit.edu

**Abstract.** In this paper, we propose a prototype design for manifold refinement to fine grained text-to-image generation by using Attentional Generative Adversarial Network (AttnGAN) We concentrate on creating realistic images from text descriptions. We have used a collection of Attentional Generative Adversarial Network layers that are able to correctly select the modal meaning at the word-level and sentence-level. Generative Adversarial Networks (GANs) prove to be fundamental structure for many design applications from Game design, Art, Science and Modelling applications. We use GANs for contrastive learning and as a information maximisation approach, and we do extensive research to find the further advancements in image generation. Our prototype is easy to implement and practical; choosing the most relevant word vectors and using those vectors to generate related image sub-regions. The prototype in its current state generates image designs only for the bird species to satisfy the claim for its image generation ability. With due consideration to findings of usability testing, the develpment team in future iterations of the application, hopes to improve the generated image resolution. They plan to provide a choice for created variety of images with further improvements to the image generation algorithm.

**Keywords:** GAN · Text-to-image synthesis · Artificial intelligence · Artificial neural networks · DAMSM · Attentional Generative Adversarial Networks

## 1 Introduction

GANs are generative modelling approaches that use deep learning methods such as convolutional neural networks. Since the introduction of Generative Adversarial Networks (GAN), the area of generative modelling has seen tremendous progress. The objective of the research work was to use Generative Adversarial Networks (GAN) to create photorealistic images based on text descriptions provided by the user. Understanding the relationship between visual information and natural languages is a critical first step toward Artificial Intelligence. Although GAN has had impressive results over the years, it still lacks the ability to intelligently select the modal meaning at the word-level and sentence-level [3]. To solve this issue, we propose the use of Attentional Generative Adversarial Networks (AttnGAN), which provide a manifold refinement to fine


Published by Springer Nature Switzerland AG 2022
C. Ardito et al. (Eds.): INTERACT 2021, LNCS 13198, pp. 397–403, 2022.
https://doi.org/10.1007/978-3-030-98388-8_35

grained text-to-image generation process. Each generated image has elements that are not included in the text captions provided by the user, demonstrating that this artificial intelligence model has an artificial imagination.

Automatic generation of image designs based on natural language descriptions is a primary task in many domains, including art generation, design industry and computer-aided design. It also propels research in multimodal learning and inference through vision and language, which has been one of the most active research fields in recent years [3]. The use of AttnGAN for automatic generation of images will help image designers to instantly create highly compelling image designs as per their preference ranging from music album covers, room interior designs, game posters and will solve their distress of designing an image by hand or using Computer-Aided Designing (CAD) software, which usually consumes quite a few productive hours out of their day and many times the users are not always fully satisfied with their image design.

## 2 Literature Review

In the literature review, following interesting papers were studied to get useful insights into the domain.

In the first paper, Xu et al. built a attentional generative network for the AttnGAN to use in a multi-stage cycle to produce high-quality images [3]. Their AttnGAN outperformed many previous GAN models, increasing the highest observed inception performance on the Caltech-University of California San Diego (UCSD) Birds dataset by 14.14%. Their attention-driven image-text matching score helped them to assess the similarity of an image-sentence pair based on an attention model between the image and the text.

In another paper, Zhu et al. proposed a dynamic memory module to optimise the fuzzy image contents, where the initial images are not well generated [4]. Their technique involved choosing the important text information based on the initial image material allowed their application to produce images accurately from the text definition.

In the next paper, Lee et al. proposed a framework to solve two fundamental concerns in GANs - catastrophic forgetting of the discriminator and mode collapse of the generator [5]. The team achieved this by using GANs for contrastive learning and information maximization approach to understand the source for improvements. Using this framework, the team was able to improve the stability while training the GAN and improving GAN performance over the test dataset.

## 3 Research Methodology

### 3.1 Application Design

Our proposed implementation methodology is to train a Convolutional Neural Network (CNN) trained on text features encoded by a text-encoder which provides sentence-level and individual word-level features. More specifically, each word in the sentence is encoded into a word vector in addition to the natural language description being encoded into a global sentence vector. Both the generator network G and the discriminator network D perform feed-forward inference training on the text features provided by the text-encoder and output a photo-realistic image as output of the network. In the first stage, the generative network uses the global sentence vector to generate a low-resolution image. It then makes use of the word vector to subsequently improve the quality of the image generated in the next stages. Despite the amazing progress made by these multi-stage techniques, two issues persist. First, the quality of the initial pictures has a significant impact on the subsequent generating output. If the initial generated image is of poor quality, then the image generator cannot make impactful improvement in subsequent design of images. Second, each word in an input sentence has a distinct amount of information about the image's content. The refining procedure aids in the encoding of information from the text description and the addition of missing features based on the text description and picture content. The picture information should be used when determining the significance of each word for refining. The proposed Attentional Generative Adversarial Network (AttnGAN) constitues of two neoteric units: the attentional generative network and the deep attentional multimodal similarity model. When producing pictures from caption-like text descriptions, this system is trained to pay special attention to specific word and sentence formations. To understand the details of the text-to-image generation process, the application architecture of AttnGAN is shown in the Fig. 1 below.

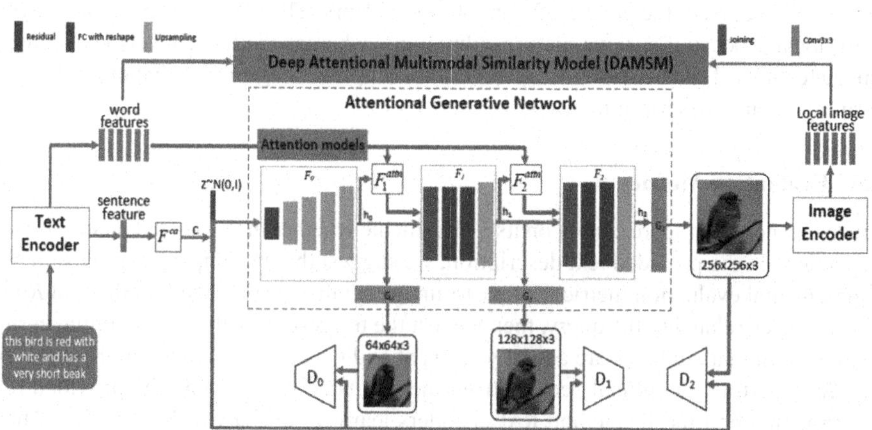


**Fig. 1.** AttnGAN application architecture [3]

## 3.2 Attentional Generative Network

Current GAN-based models for text-to-image generation usually encode the entire sentence-text definition into a single vector as the condition for image generation, but lack fine-grained word-level detail [3]. We propose to draw all the different image sub-regions, based on keywords that are most important to each suchsub-regions. With reference to Fig. 1. above, the proposed attentional generative network has *m* generators (*G0*, *G1*, ..., *Gm* − *1*), which take the hidden states (*h0*, *h1*, ..., *hm* − *1*) as input and generate images of small-to-large resolutions (*^x0, ^x1, …, ^xm − 1)*. Here, $z$ is often a noise vector taken from a normal standard distribution. $\bar{e}$ is a vector of a global sentence, $e$ is the module of vectors of words. The attention model is given the word features and image features as an input from the preceding hidden layer and then we compute a word-context vector for each image sub-region depending on its hidden features. To determine the model's diverse image generation capabilities and the variability between the generated images, we produce numerous pictures using the same text description while changing the noise vectors allowing the model to generate a different image in every iteration. To get the final realistic image design after multiple iterations, the final function of attentional generative network generates a balance of two expressions: Firstly, GAN loss where the unconditional loss decides whether the image is realistic or fake and the conditional loss determines whether or not the image and the text description fit. Second, the Deep Attentional Multimodal Similarity Model (DAMSM) computed image-text matching loss, which will be detailed in the following section.

### 3.3 Deep Attentional Multimodal Similarity Model

The DAMSM employs artificial neural networks that map image sub-regions with word features in the sentence to a shared space, which helps in measuring text-image similarity at the individual word-level to compute the loss for image generation. The text encoder generates connotation vectors from the text description. The image encoder maps the generated images to the generated connotation vectors. The CNN's intermediate layers learn local aspects of various picture subregions, whereas the latter levels learn global image features. The DAMSM loss matches the complete image with a sequence of words forming the text description.

### 3.4 Evaluation Metrics

Since the inception score cannot on its own indicate whether the produced picture is well dependent on the provided text description, we suggest that we employ R-precision as a supplemental evaluation metric for text-to-image synthesization. We find the first $R$ relevant images related to the query, then we test the top results of the relevant images and then we find that $r$ images are actually relevant and hence we calculate the R-precision as $r/R$. To extract the global vectors from the produced pictures and the provided text descriptions, first the image and text encoders learnt in our DAMSM are used. Then, similarities between global vectors of images and global text vectors are calculated. Finally, for each picture, we classify candidate text descriptions with decreasing similarity and find the top r descriptions of R-precision calculations. Our technique is capable of improving understanding of the logic of the text captions and presenting a more clear structure using the visuals.

## 4 Usability Testing

Usability testing is performed to capture the user experience of the AttnGAN-the developed application prototype with its users and to get the suggestions for effective application design of next version. Due to pandemic situation in India, the development team created a questionnaire to collect the user's quantitative responses using the Likert scale [8]. Different types of users including game designers, art designers, Computer Aided Design (CAD) designers, albumcover designers and interior designers were provided with the online application and were asked their response/feedback about the quality, quantity of the generated image, their opinion on using artificial intelligence for image designing along with their suggestions for further improvement in the designed prototype. About 11 users including 8 male and 3 female users were involved in this pilot testing [7].

The responses received in this pilot testing showed that the respondent users were satisfied with the image generated from the AttnGAN project. About 80% of the respondents were keen on using the application in future to assist their domains and would also recommend it to their peers. Although many of the respondents were happy with the quality of the generated image, they implored that an improvement in the quality/resolution of images would help them even more with their designs. There were mixed opinions with the variety of images that the application provided as each image provided a distinct design which some users preferred while the others deferred. They appealed for the option to choose between the generated variety of images. As the prototype aims to cover varied domains like CAD image generation, music album cover generation, the users felt the necessity for the prototype to be explored more with other domains other than bird images to satisfy their need for this prototype. Almost everyone agreed on the fact that artificially generated images acted as a satisfactory base for designers to further build their design upon (Fig. 2).

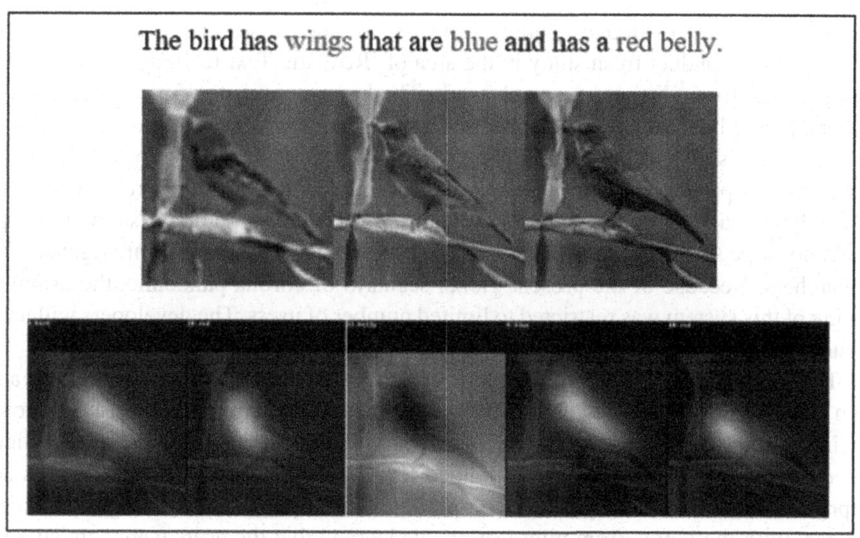


**Fig. 2.** Results of trained AttnGAN model (Color figur online)

## 5 Results and Conclusion

We have compared the prototype AttnGAN's findings with its previous generated images to help explain what it has learned. The reported scores are mentioned in Table. 1. below which measures the quality and the variance in the generated image designs. The model perfectly captures the primary scene based on the most significant subject and logically arranges the rest of the descriptive elements, improving the overall structure of the image.

**Table. 1.** Performance of inception score and R-precision evaluation metrics on AttnGAN.

| Dataset | Metric | Accuracy | Model |
|---|---|---|---|
| Caltech-University of California San Diego Birds (CUB) | Inception score | 12.80% | AttnGAN |
| Caltech-University of California San Diego Birds (CUB) | R-precision | 72.88% | AttnGAN |

## 6 SWOT (Strengths, Weakness, Opportunities and Threats) Analysis

As the topic of Text-to-Image creation is under-researched, researchers can come up with novel ways to conduct fresh study in the area of 'Realistic Text-to-Image Synthesis'. It has provided strength to the research work. The key prerequisite of picture creation is that the model be trained using appropriate image datasets; however, the availability of such datasets is restricted to certain areas (e.g. birds domain in our project). It can be considered as project weakness. Due to the fact that this topic is under-researched, this research topic and its implementation have the potential to be the first system of its type as a innovative system. It can be looked as an opportunity for Artificial Intelligence (AI) researchers. Because of the present global scenario of corona pandemic, the usability testing of this system was restricted to limited number of users. The developers will need to thoroughly evaluate and enhance the system in future versions.

The initial phase of prototype emphasizes on the shape and the color of the object and then allocates the attention to the key features of the text descriptions. In most situations, the initial stage creates a fuzzy image with rough form and colour, which is then fine-tuned to be more realistic with fine-grained textures, while the subsequent images are improved further on the input text and provides more photo-realistic high resolution images. With the inputs from pilot testing, we learned that the users were content with the generated image and stated that they would use it as a base to their designs if given the option to choose between the generated images and, if the prototype is further improved on other image domains as the prototype currently generates only bird design images. In this paper, we proposed the prototype AttnGAN for photo realistic text-to-image synthesis. We introduced a deep attentional multimodal similarity model to compute the text-image matching loss for training the generator of the AttnGAN. Experimental results clearly depicts the importance of the proposed model for text-to-image generation in ever-growing fields of science, art and design.

During the experiment, we observed that when the size of training group was increased, training outcomes improved up to a certain amount with the help of increased data which significantly improves the image generation algorithm. However, due to Central Processing Unit (CPU) and Graphics Processing Unit (GPU) limitations the current system consisted of only 3 hidden layers and trained on around 1204 images from the dataset and the resolution set to 256 × 256 in resolution. In future, the developer team plans to work on the learning from the user experience of pilot testing to improve resolution of generated image from the prototype in order to assist the designers with higher quality images and to scale the images to a higher resolution. This team also plans to add an option for the users to choose between the varied image designs generated from the application over multiple domains.

**Acknowledgement.** We thank all the users/participants of pilot testing of AttnGAN, in Pune, India, for their cooperation and support.

## References

1. Campo, M.: Architecture, language and AI - language, attentional generative adversarial networks (AttnGAN) and architecture design. In: Proceedings of the 26th CAADRIA Conference, vol 1, Hong Kong, pp. 211–220 (2021)
2. Hashemiet, A., Mozaffari, S.: Secure deep neural networks using adversarial image generation and training with noise-GAN. Comput. Secur. **86**, 372–387 (2019)
3. Tao, X., et al.: AttnGAN: fine-grained text to image generation with attentional generative adversarial networks. In: IEEE/CVF Conference on Computer Vision and Pattern Recognition, pp. 1316–1324 (2018)
4. Minfeng, Z., Pingbo, P., Wei, C., Yi, Y.: DM-GAN: dynamic memory generative adversarial networks for text-to-image synthesis. In: IEEE/CVF Conference on Computer Vision and Pattern Recognition (CVPR), pp. 5795–5803 (2019)
5. Hajar, E., Majid, M., Ming, D., Chinnam, R.: SPA-GAN: spatial attention GAN for image-to-image translation. IEEE Trans. Multimed. **23**, 391–401 (2020)
6. Lee, K., Ngoc-Trung, T., Ngai-Man, C.: InfoMax-GAN: improved adversarial image generation via information maximization and contrastive learning. In: NeurIPS Workshop on Information Theory and Machine Learning, pp. 3941–3951 (2021)
7. Hertzum, M., Bansler, J.P., Havn, E., Simonsen, J.: Pilot implementation: learning from field tests in IS development. Commun. Assoc. Inf. Syst. **30**(1), 313–328 (2012)
8. Bhutkar, G., Mehetre, A., Sagale, U., Kendre, A., Bhole, D., Jathar, N.: Heuristic evaluation of an eye-free android application. In: Proceedings of the 6th International Conference on M4D Mobile Communication Technology for Development, Kampala, Uganda, Karlstad University Studies, pp. 206–215 (2019)
9. California Institute of Technology. Caltech-UCSD Birds 200. CNS-TR-2010-001 (2010). http://www.vision.caltech.edu/visipedia/CUB-200.html. Accessed 29 July 2021

# Prototype Design of a Multi-modal AI-Based Web Application for Hateful Content Detection in Social Media Posts

Tejas Pradhan(✉), Ganesh Bhutkar, and Aditya Pangaonkar

Department of Computer Engineering, Vishwakarma Institute of Technology, Pune, India
tejas.pradhan18@vit.edu

**Abstract.** Hate-Speech Detection and filtering of hateful content is an important aspect of any social media post. The ever increasing amount of content posted daily on social media has led to an excessive amount of digital hate being spread in the form of posts, images and comments. The proposed system is developed in order to act as a tool for determining if a particular social media post is hateful and is aimed to aid any benign social media user who has been affected by hate speech and wants to report it. The proposed system uses a multimodal artificial intelligence based approach by classifying different formats of posts, i.e., images and comments or captions separately. An ensemble convolutional neural network architecture is used for this classification, thus, proving to be a strong tool for finding evidence of any prevalent hate speech. This system is tested using the Likert scale for its user interface, accuracy and utility. Based on the result this paper proposes a prototype design of a web application which can be used for hateful content detection.

**Keywords:** Hate speech · Classification · Convolutional neural networks · Ensemble · Multimodal · Interface

## 1 Introduction

Social media is an extremely fast mechanism to spread information. With the increasing amount of social media usage, millions of users are sharing photos, posts and reviews every day. While social media is a really effective tool, it has also become a channel for quick and aggressive spread of hatred among different communities. Hate speech is a term coined for those kinds of messages or comments which directly or indirectly hurt the sentiment of a particular community or an individual. However, hateful content is not only limited to text, but also images and audio files which can be potential instruments of spreading hateful content. This use of social media to spread hateful content encourages discrimination, prejudice and abuse, which makes it a dangerous and unsafe environment. Hateful content is almost always misinformation as well. Hence, mitigation of hate-speech and how effective it will be are important questions. However, there is no standardized legal jurisdiction for the same as of now [1]. A majority of the young


C. Ardito et al. (Eds.): INTERACT 2021, LNCS 13198, pp. 404–411, 2022.
https://doi.org/10.1007/978-3-030-98388-8_36

population is affected by offensive content online which mainly includes teenagers. Potential threats to teenagers and adolescents include exposure to inappropriate content, online abuse and cyberbullying [2]. Managing and curbing the spread of hateful content through social media is the need of the hour in this digital world. However, detecting hateful content is not deterministic in nature. The main reason behind this is that hateful content is extremely subjective. It is dependent on the context and community being addressed at hand.

The subjective nature of offensive content on social media has made it very difficult for autonomous intelligent systems to detect it [3]. Many existing content filtering algorithms and systems use post tagging and sentiment analysis based approaches to detect hate speech. As discussed above, hateful content is not just in the form of text, but also images and text embedded in images (memes). The proposed system aims to incorporate all of these aspects of spreading social media hate into developing an algorithm to correctly identify offensive content and report it. The system will be deployed as a web application so that users from anywhere in the world would be able to verify if a particular message or image is offensive or not and report it to the concerned authorities. It uses a hateful content detection engine which is trained on multiple hate speech tagged comments and other textual format using data from Twitter and Facebook. The engine also includes a model trained on violent images to detect any image, which is potentially offensive or inappropriate. An important feature of this system is its multimodal nature, which can accept inputs in more than one form and still produce binary outputs.

The focus of the proposed web application is to provide utility to users who want to report hateful content and need evidence for the same. The target user group for this system includes:

1. Victims of social media hatred.
2. Respondents, i.e., users who have been provoked by or responded aggressively to hateful content.
3. Blog or small social media forum owners.

The victims of social media hatred often find it difficult to report hateful content. Social media aggression due to online hate is another important issue at hand which needs to be restrained. Blog owners, too, need to rely on third party content filtering mechanisms. The application will be tested for its accuracy and utility value taking the above user group into consideration. Thus, the robustness of the system will also be tested. Since the target user group involves a wide variety of users, feedback will be taken on the design using the Likert Scale [9] and suggested improvements will be incorporated into the final prototype.

## 2 Related Work

When dealing with the detection and classification of hate speech a lot of problems would arise, that is if the speech is universally accepted hateful or not, handling bias, or dealing with unbalanced data [1]. To classify hate speech, language and words are necessary. Researchers have deployed a wide range of more sophisticated feature representations, including word n-grams, syntactic features, and distributional semantics [3]. This article within the journal considers the uncertainty, lastly that the most effective understanding of Waldron's argument in his book is that hate speech tends to cause damage - a weak sort of the consequentialist case for its proscription. His argument isn't advanced by his apparent reliance on speech-act theory [4].

In the paper, HaterNet, an intelligent system that is presently getting used by the Spanish National workplace Against Hate Crimes of the Spanish State Secretariat for Security is conferred that identifies and monitors the evolution of hate speech in Twitter. The contributions of this analysis include many interesting aspects. It introduces the primary intelligent system that monitors and visualizes, mistreatment social network analysis techniques, hate speech in Social Media and conjointly it introduces a completely unique public dataset on hate speech in Spanish consisting of 6000 expert-labeled tweets [5]. This article within the journal aims to critique and augment posts associated with cyber hate. This would be achieved by emphasizing a particular feature of the content in contrast to alternative options, like simple access, size of audience, and namelessness, which are usually overlooked [6].

## 3 System Architecture

The hateful content detection system is deployed as a web application and is intended to be a detection tool for checking if a particular image or comment falls into the category of hateful content. This will be specifically useful for people who have been affected by hate speech and want evidence to report it. The block diagram or system architecture of the proposed system is shown in Fig. 1.

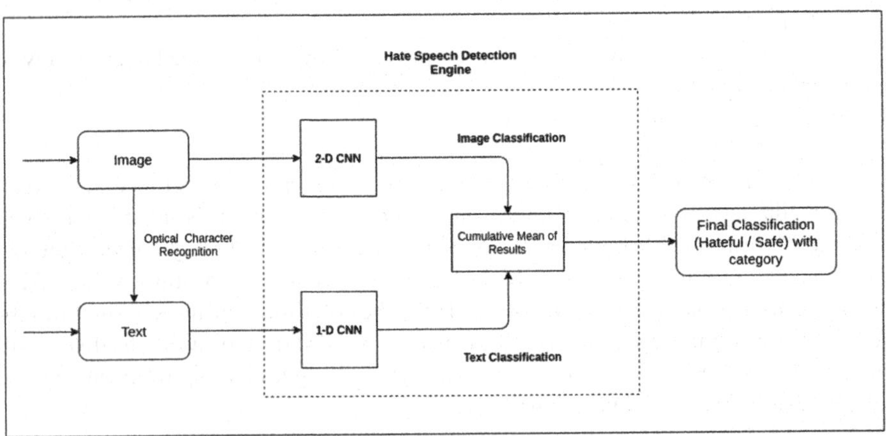


**Fig. 1.** Block diagram of hateful content detection system

### 3.1 Input to the System

Since the nature of the proposed system is multimodal, input to the application can be given in three ways:

1. Text (Comments or Posts on Social Media)
2. Image (Photos from Social Media)
3. Image with Embedded Text (Memes)

Based on the type of given input, the system either uses pure image classification mechanisms, pure text classification mechanisms or both, i.e., multimodal classification mechanisms. Prior to classification, text needs to be extracted from the image. This is done using optical character recognition. This is done using a module called tesseract OCR, which uses an adaptive classification mechanism to automatically find lines and textual features in images. It then chops off the sentences found into words based on pitch detection techniques which is followed by word recognition [11]. The extracted text is first cleaned to remove any non-alphanumeric characters and words which will not be used for offensive content detection. This includes links, email ids, phone numbers etc. This cleaned text is then preprocessed to bring it into readable and interpretable format in order to vectorize it and pass it as an input to the hateful content detection engine. This cleaned and preprocessed text is converted into word embeddings by the embedding layer in the neural network for text classification. Figure 2 shows the extraction of text from images using OCR.

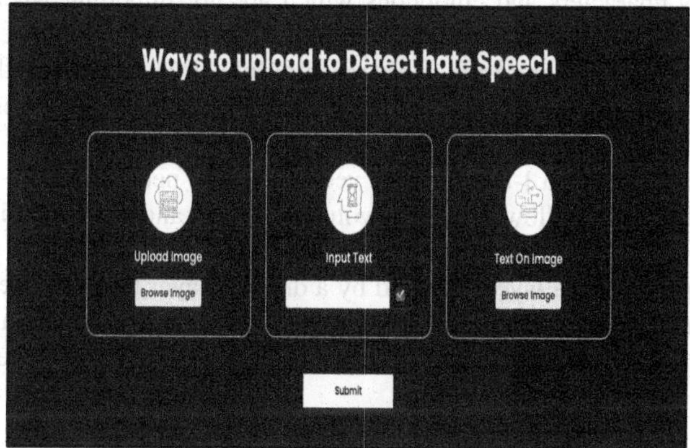


**Fig. 2.** Design of the web application

## 3.2 Detecting Hateful Content Using Classification Algorithms

The classification technique follows a multi-modal/ensemble approach. In the first stage, images and text are classified separately. We have used deep neural networks for classifying text and images since they have shown to perform better than most statistical machine learning approaches for hate speech detection [4]. For image classification, the system uses a 2-D convolutional neural network. The network consists of two convolution layers of kernel size $3 \times 3$ followed by a 2D Max Pooling layer respectively. This is followed by flattening the intermediate output and passing it to a dense layer for further feature extraction. The output layer of the network uses a softmax activation function,

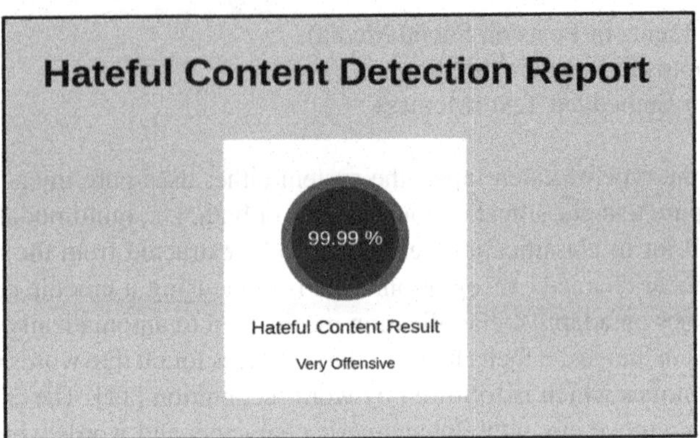


**Fig. 3.** Hateful content detection report

since this is a multi-class classification problem. Figure 4 shows the architecture of the image classification neural network (Fig. 3).

For detecting hate speech from text, each comment is first cleaned, preprocessed and tokenized to make it suitable for classification. Social media data contains a lot of unnecessary characters and emoticons which are not important when it comes to classification. Text preprocessing includes removing these characters, removing stop-words (a, an, the etc.) and preserving only meaningful words. This text is then converted into word vectors using the count vectorization approach before finally sending it to the hate speech classifier. Text classification uses a 1-D convolutional Neural Network with each word represented as a 1-dimensional vector [7]. The neural network consists of an initial embedding layer followed by a convolutional layer and a max pooling layer. This is followed by another convolutional layer followed by a global 1D max pooling layer. The next layer is a Dense layer followed by a dropout layer to avoid overfitting of the model. The final layer is a Dense layer with softmax activation function consisting of three neurons. Figure 5 shows the architecture of the text classification neural network.

### 3.3 Output of the System

A mean of the individual classification probabilities is calculated and used for detection of hateful content. There are 3 categories for classification.

1. Not Offensive
2. Mildly Offensive
3. Very Offensive

This probability is then converted into percentage and the output is given as a report to the user. The report contains the percentage of the given input to be hate-speech along with the category. The current implementation of our application can categorize violence and offensive speech.

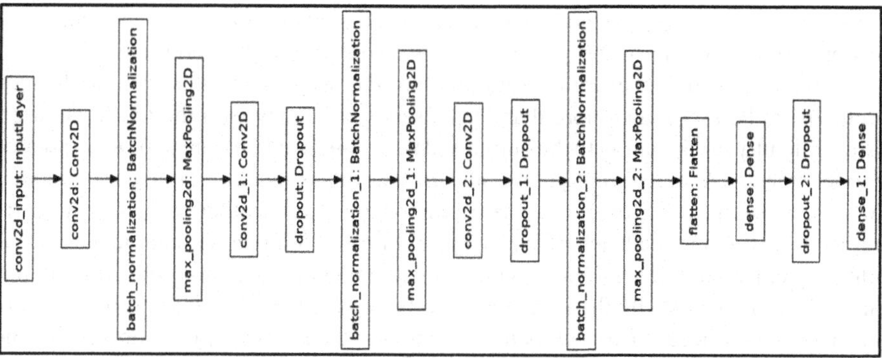


**Fig. 4.** Architecture of the image classification neural network

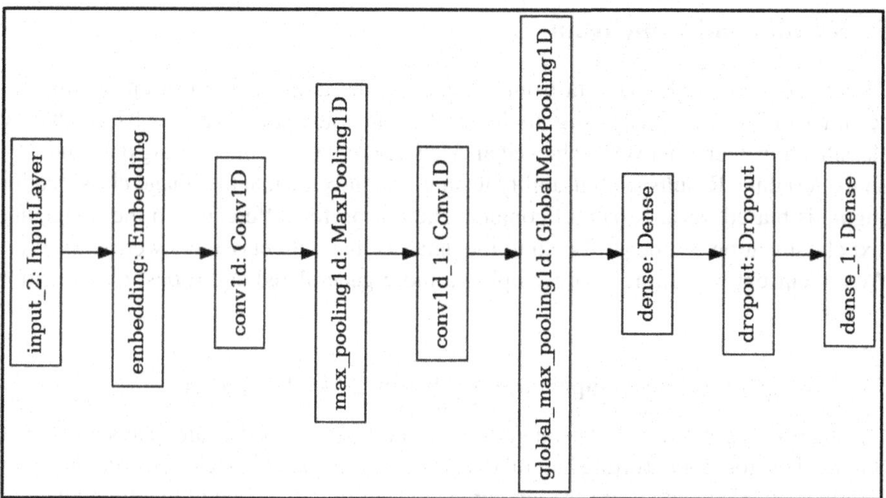


**Fig. 5.** Architecture of the text classification network

## 4 Pilot Testing

Since hateful content is extremely subjective in nature, pilot testing is the best strategy to test such a system. Testing the system with diverse groups of users will give a good idea of the performance of the model on different types of hateful content. Hence, the proposed system is tested in two phases. In the first phase, users testing the system are asked to give different forms of input to the system and test its robustness. A diverse group of users - including victims or witnesses of hateful content and cyber-bullying have been asked to test the system by feeding in different images, posts and sentences of hate speech which they had previously encountered. This group includes 8 males and 4 females. The average age range is 17–22 with 2 users above the age of 45 years. They are asked to fill a detailed questionnaire [11] which highlights different aspects of the system including design, accuracy of classification and overall user experience. The feedback of a preliminary group of 12 users is recorded using 'Likert scale' [9].

Current data from the testing suggests that the users found this web application prototype to be useful and more than 90% users were happy with the UI. Some users faced difficulty in navigating to the output and these improvements are to be incorporated into the system. Another point highlighted after testing is that the classification models are susceptible to a high false negative rate. These classification models will be re-trained based on the feedback given by users. In the second phase, final testing of the pilot implementation [8] will be completed before deploying it into production. In this phase the ratings given by the users will also be discussed with them in order to better understand their needs. This will help in improving the user experience drastically and also help in finding exact points of failure. In this way, a feedback loop will be created to train the model as well as improve the user experience using pilot testing.

## 5 Results and Conclusion

On testing with validation data from the dataset, the image classification obtained an accuracy of 75.8%, which is slightly lesser than the training accuracy of 87%. The text classification neural network achieved an accuracy of 95% on the training data and 92% on the test data. Results from usability testing also indicate that the image classification engine is biased towards hateful content. The reason for differences in the image and text classification can be attributed to the datasets that both classifiers were trained on. We are currently working on developing a more generalized and robust classification system.

### 5.1 Strength Weakness Opportunities Threats (SWOT) Analysis

The main strength of the proposed system is that it can be used as an open sourced and standardized tool for reporting hateful content. Installing such systems and making them readily available to end users can encourage the curbing of spread of hateful content on social media. It can be an active measure to keep people who spread offensive content and misinformation at bay, thereby helping in creating a safer digital environment for everyone. The subjective nature of offensive content is a major weakness of the system as it is very hard to standardize content that is hateful for everyone. This weakness can be overcome to a great extent by incorporating data from diverse sources into training of the models and creating a robust classification system. Social media has become increasingly popular and people are using it for everything right from entertainment to business. The increasing number of users on social media can be seen as a good opportunity for systems similar to the one proposed in this paper. However, increased restrictions on social media usage and companies trying to filter content on their own backend can make external reporting systems obsolete and this is a big threat.

### 5.2 Conclusion

The testing results also show that users prefer the design of such apps to be concise and simple with minimum amount of navigation to be needed. Color coding of results with percentage of hate speech has also been an effective means of displaying the report as tested by the users. The input sections for the app can be completely isolated from each other and their respective reports can be displayed on a separate page specifically for results. This will reduce the number of clicks and make the user experience better in the later versions of this application.

We are currently working on developing a more generalized and robust classification system. Collecting data from users of different nationalities and regions can make this system extremely diverse and can enhance its capabilities to generalize outputs. The user interface of web applications can also be enhanced in the later versions to include audio signals as well, which can be then parsed into text inputs and fed to the same model. The later versions can also feature a more detailed classification report with in-depth analysis of the given input. Such a report would tell the user exactly which words or features in the image were considered in order to classify something as potentially offensive or safe. This would increase the explainability of the model, making it more interpretable and understandable.

## References


1. Kovács, G., Alonso, P., Saini, R.: Challenges of hate speech detection in social media. SN Comput. Sci. **2**, 95 (2021). https://doi.org/10.1007/s42979-021-00457-3
2. Social Media and Teens, American Academy of Child and Adolescent Psychiatry. https://www.aacap.org/AACAP/Families_and_Youth/Facts_for_Families/FFF-Guide/Social-Media-and-Teens-100.aspx
3. Salminen, J., Hopf, M., Chowdhury, S.A., et al.: Developing an online hate classifier for multiple social media platforms. Hum. Cent. Comput. Inf. Sci. **10**, 1 (2020). https://doi.org/10.1186/s13673-019-0205-6
4. Barendt, E.: What is the harm of hate speech? Ethic Theory Moral Prac. **22**, 539–553 (2019). https://doi.org/10.1007/s10677-019-10002-0
5. Pereira-Kohatsu, J.C., Quijano-Sánchez, L., Liberatore, F., Camacho-Collados, M.: Detecting and monitoring hate speech in Twitter. Sensors **19**(21), 4654 (2019). https://doi.org/10.3390/s19214654
6. Brown, A.: What is so special about online (as compared to offline) hate speech? Ethnicities **18**(3), 297–326 (2018). https://doi.org/10.1177/1468796817709846
7. Kiranyaz, S., Avci, O., Abdeljaber, O., Ince, T., Gabbouj, M., Inman, D.J.: 1D Convolutional Neural Networks and Applications – A Survey. https://arxiv.org/abs/1905.03554
8. Hertzum, M., Bansler, J.P., Havn, E., Simonsen, J.: Pilot implementation: learning from field tests in IS development. Commun. Assoc. Inf. Syst. **30**(1), 313–328 (2012). https://citeseerx.ist.psu.edu/viewdoc/download?doi=10.1.1.1064.4529&rep=rep1&type=pdf
9. Bhutkar, G., Mehetre, A., Sagale, U., Kendre, A., Bhole, D., Jathar, N.: Heuristic evaluation of an eye-free android application. In: 6th International Conference on M4D Mobile Communication Technology for Development, pp. 206–215 (2018). https://doi.org/10.1007/978-981-10-4980-4_36
10. Simth, R.: An Overview of the Tesseract OCR Engine. Google Inc. https://static.googleusercontent.com/media/research.google.com/en//pubs/archive/33418.pdf
11. Bhutkar, G., Raghvani, V., Juikar, S.: User survey about exposure of hate speech among Instagram users in India. Int. J. Comput. Appl. **183**(19), 24–29 (2021). https://www.ijcaonline.org/archives/volume183/number19/32033-2021921536

# Pilot Implementation for Driver Behaviour Classification Using Smartphone Sensor Data for Driver-Vehicle Interaction Analysis

Pawan Wawage(✉) and Yogesh Deshpande(✉)

Vishwakarma University, Pune, India
{pawan.wawage-026,yogesh.deshpande}@vupune.ac.in

**Abstract.** Driving is considered one of the most difficult tasks because the driver is responsible for a variety of other responsibilities in addition to driving. The primary responsibility of a driver should be to properly operate a vehicle while concentrating solely on driving. However, he/she must also complete various secondary jobs at the same time. For example, operating the steering wheel and the controls situated on the dashboard and steering wheel, operating the brake, accelerator, and clutch pedals while shifting gears as needed, and so forth. Modeling realistic driving behaviour proved tough for researchers and scientists. In this work, we examine the necessity for driver behaviour analysis as well as a method for visualising and estimating driver behaviour patterns utilising smart phone sensor data.

**Keywords:** Driving behaviour · Fuel efficiency · Control Area Network (CAN) · On-Board Diagnostics (OBD) · ADAS · SVM · MLA

## 1 Introduction

Many research projects have focused on modelling driver behaviour, whether for studying driving patterns or raising awareness for safe driving. The purpose of these studies is to use a computer model to determine the effect of driving patterns and other factors that influence driving behaviour. Given that driving is a complicated undertaking involving a wide range of internal and external variables, it has been established that the majority of road accidents are caused by human errors such as traffic law violations, distraction, inattention, drowsiness, exhaustion, and so on. It is now possible to investigate this field, thanks to advancements in the data analysis domain throughout time. The advancement of these methods improved the quality of driving pattern and driver behaviour analysis while also opening up new application areas [5].

However, we discovered that no standard model has been proposed in the literature and that there is a lack of a cohesive framework for assessing driver behaviour. We tried to capture a set of quantitative and qualitative elements that are important in analyzing driver behaviour. These elements are either related to the driver, the driving events that were performed, or traffic circumstances. These elements are the result of a study and


Published by Springer Nature Switzerland AG 2022
C. Ardito et al. (Eds.): INTERACT 2021, LNCS 13198, pp. 412–420, 2022.
https://doi.org/10.1007/978-3-030-98388-8_37

literature review that combines the study's goal with multiple models, derives the data used, and considers various factors related to driver behaviour.

We will offer a literature overview, the need for driver behaviour analysis, the methods used for analysis, and the critical inner and outside aspects influencing driver behaviour in this work. The rest of this paper is organized as follows: first, we'll go over the study strategy we used, then we'll show you how to classify driver behaviour using smart phone sensor data. After that, we'll go over the experimental setup and the findings of our research.

## 2 Literature Survey

Driving behaviour provides an examination of how he or she is driving, including aggressive driving such as over-speeding, quick braking, abrupt lane changes, and sharp turning. Monitoring driving is crucial and required since it improves driver performance, efficiency, and safety while consuming less fuel and requiring less maintenance. It leads to safer driving and fewer traffic accidents.

According to a survey published by the Ministry of Petrol and Natural Gas, the transportation sector alone consumes 70% of diesel and 99.6% of petrol. Cars, utility vehicles, and three-wheelers account for the majority of overall diesel sales [13].

Since 2016, according to data from the Open Government Data Platform India (data.gov.in), there has been a frightening spike in accidental deaths caused by cars on Indian roadways. According to [7], deaths and injuries on highways due to driver inattention or unplanned moves have increased by 5% in the last ten years.

[9] Discusses how driver behaviour analysis is driving up demand for smart infrastructure solutions like as Connected Vehicle Technology (CVT), Vehicle to Infrastructure connection (V2I), and allowing apps with real-time traffic data, as well as forward collision warning. The connected vehicle technology will keep drivers informed of traffic conditions while on the road, resulting in safer driving.

According to the findings of the survey, aggressive driving behaviour and road rage incidents such as speeding in heavy traffic, lane cutting, and rapid braking of drivers during short-term and long-term driving should be addressed [1]. The efforts to identify the risk posed by aggressive driving by taking into account a driver's behavioural and emotional aspects would result in fewer road accidents and insurance claims. The findings of this study will aid motor insurance companies in more correctly assessing driving risk and proposing a solution for calculating individualized premiums based on driving behaviour with a focus on risk prevention.

According to the findings, the distribution of road fatalities and injuries in India differs by age, gender, vehicle type, and time of day. The distribution of causes of road accidents in India is depicted in Fig. 1. It can be shown that the fault of the driver is regarded as the most important component in road accidents. With 79% of total incidents caused by driver error, drivers are the most at fault. Accidents caused by over speeding, aggressive driving, and rapid turning made for a large share of the category of driver fault [8].

Table 1 gives a summary of research done on driver behaviour classification, the purpose of the research, the data used for the analysis, and the algorithm used for analysis.

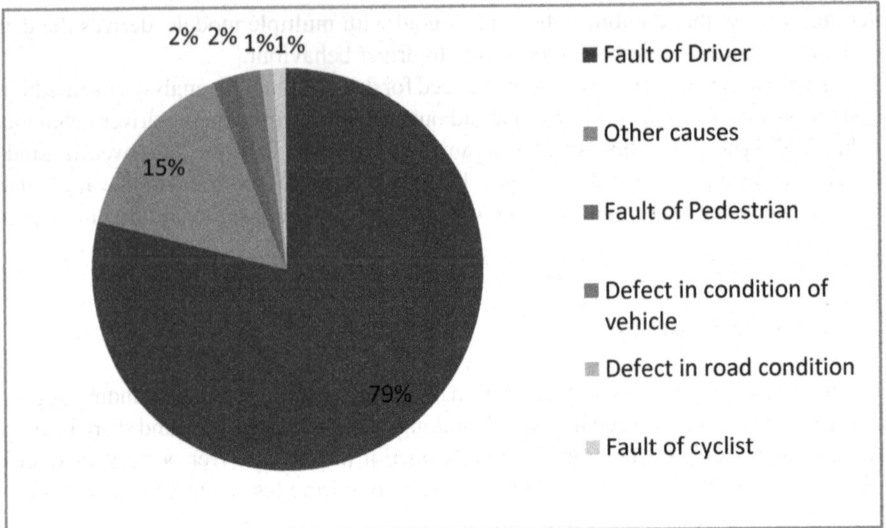


**Fig. 1.** Causes of road accidents

**Table 1.** Classification of research done on diver behaviour

| Purpose | Data | Algorithm |
|---|---|---|
| Driver behaviour recognition | Smartphone sensors | AI and ML |
| Intelligent driving style analysis systems | Accelerometer, Gyroscope, Magnetometer, and GPS sensor data | Classification algorithm |
| Driver behaviour profiling | Telematics boxes | Fuzzy logic |
| Modeling driver distraction | Monitoring cameras | Hidden Markov model |
| Recommendation systems to prevent accidents | OBD-II parameters, weather data, Traffic data | Support vector machines |
| Saving fuel consumption | OBD-II parameters | Dynamic time wrapping |
| Usage-based insurance | OBD-II parameters, smart phone sensor data | Artificial neural networks |

## 3 Methodology

Many studies have been published on various approaches of driver behaviour analysis, with an emphasis on driver-oriented applications, which are divided into three categories: accident prevention, driving pattern evaluation, and driver behaviour prediction [6]. The methods are classified according to the goal, which might be one of the sub-applications listed above, and their input components are taken into account during the analysis phase. Quantitative or qualitative parameters can be used. We took into account both quantitative (driving data, sensor parameters, etc.) and qualitative (road condition, weather condition, etc.) elements in our research, including smart phone sensor data and drivers inner and outer factors.

The first stage in analyzing driver behaviour is to collect driving data while the driver is doing the driving activities. But, before we collect data, we need to choose a model driver (persona) who will carry out these actions in a realistic setting. As a result, we first construct a driver persona to better understand the future model vehicle drivers.

## 3.1 Creating Driver Persona

Personas are fictional, all-encompassing depictions of your model vehicle drivers. They assist you in better understanding your potential drivers and make it easier to tailor material to the needs, behaviours, and concerns of various groups. Personas can be formed by gathering information from the target audience through research, polls, and interviews. We looked at how people actually drove, including aspects like phone usage, honking, infotainment system use, and more, rather than utilizing hypothetical variables like gender, age, driving experience, and educational background to create personas to assess drivers' behaviour.

With the use of a driver survey form, the participants were asked to answer a few questions. Participants were asked to fill in the following information:

- Personal history (Name, Age, Gender, Qualification),
- What kind of driver is he/she? (Lessons in driving, experience, skills, daily distance, hours spent, average speed)
- What are the Influences on Driving Behavior? (Driving event time, use of air conditioning, traffic, road, honking, lane cutting, environmental conditions, in-car stereo system, distraction)
- Is he/she aware of any available in-car driving assistance (awareness, usefulness, navigation system used)?
- In addition to all of the features (safety, infotainment, ADAS, and so on) offered in the vehicle, what else is required/suggested for safe driving.

We were able to choose one person to portray the model vehicle driver based on the responses we received. The next section is a brief description of the persona.

## 3.2 Driver Persona

Persona Name: Mr. Jivan Thakare.

Demographics: Male, 35 years.

Background:

He's a doctor by trade, and he's dedicated to his work and to taking care of his entire family. He has professional and personal expertise as a car driver. With over 5 years of driving experience, he is a confident driver. Others regard him as a good human being, a sensible and self-assured authoritative figure. He hails from the Maharashtra state of India's Amravati district. He graduated with a Bachelor of Ayurvedic Medicine and Surgery (BAMS) degree and has been practicing since 2012. He has two adorable children, Aarav and Arnav. His wife works as a doctor as well. His family consists of eight members, including himself. His mother is a housewife, while his father is a retired bank manager. His elder brother is working in a Finance Company as a Manager at Nagpur, Maharashtra, India.

Mr. Jivan used to go around 20 km to his clinic and back to his house as part of his daily routine. He spends the full day at the clinic and returns on the same National Highway between 4 and 5 p.m.

## 4 Pilot Implementation

### 4.1 Objective

To record the smart phone sensor data while the driver executed particular driving events in a naturalistic traffic.

### 4.2 Experimental Setup

The next step is to create the experiment and the experimental conditions once the model driver (persona) has been finalized. We ran the experiment for seven days, with the driver making two journeys each day. Each one-way trip was around 17.2 km long and took an average of 25 min. We utilized an Android application to record data from smart phone sensors (accelerometer, gyroscope) in this experiment. While the driver was conducting the driving activities, the smart phone was horizontally fixed on the car's utility box. The experimental setup is detailed in Table 2.

**Table 2.** Experiment setup

| Setup | Description |
|---|---|
| Android application used for recording smartphone sensor data | Sensor record (ver. 2.3.0) |
| Smartphone sensor | Accelerometer, gyroscope |
| Vehicle type | LMV |
| Vehicle model | New Maruti Suzuki Swift VXI |
| Smartphone used for recording sensor data | Redmi 4 with Android version 7.1.2 |
| Smartphone location and position | Horizontally fixed in the car's utility box |
| Sampling rate | 50 Hz default |
| Driving experience | 5+ years |
| Weather condition | Sunny |

### 4.3 Inner Variables

To comprehend the driver's behaviour, we must investigate the other aspects that influence his or her driving performance. One of the factors that must be examined for driver behaviour classification is internal variables, or the in-car environment. In our scenario, inner variables such as driving setting, secondary tasks undertaken, phone usage, emotional status, and so on are taken into account as a factor influencing driver behaviour when executing driving events.

1. Driver context (passengers, infotainment system, in-car environment etc.)
   a. Driver Alone, No co-passenger.
   b. Radio ON.
2. Driver secondary tasks (phone conversation, chat with co-passenger, eating/drinking, etc.)
   a. Rare phone conversation (mostly patient issues).
3. Driver objective/s (safety, on time, comfort, enjoyment etc.)
   a. Reaching Clinic safely with comfortable drive.
4. Driver status (stress, fatigue, drowsiness, experience, self-confident etc.)
   a. At-ease
   b. A self-confident regular drive.
5. Driver primary goal (momentary)
   a. Keep consistent speed, maintain safe distance to vehicles in front and stay inside lane.

### 4.4 Outer Variables

When assessing driver behaviour, external variables like as traffic conditions, road situations, ambient conditions, and so on must also be taken into account. We took care of these variables in our experiment when recording sensor data.

1. Traffic condition (nearby vehicles, rush hour, traffic- jam, etc.)
   a. Moderate traffic.
2. Road situation (highway, rural, urban)
   a. National Highway.

3. Road environment (wet surface, daylight, sun, darkness, fog etc.)

   a. Good weather conditions,
   b. Summer, mostly sunny,
   c. Dry road surface,
   d. Early morning start and afternoon return journey.

4. Main task (overall)

   a. Highway driving.

### 4.5 Results

The trial lasted for seven days. Every day for two trips, the driver completed the driving events. Data from Smartphone sensors such as the accelerometer and gyroscope was recorded in a CSV file with time stamps and used for driver profile analysis.

Driver behaviour is a major contributor to traffic safety, fuel/energy consumption, and pollution. Driver behaviour profiling aims to learn how a driver performs behind the wheel and how driving behaviour (normal, rash, etc.) influences other variables. Typical driver behaviour profiling activities entail automated data collection, calibration, and application of computer models to provide a classification that describes the driver's driving profile. The process of driver behaviour profiling entails:

- Automated collection of the driving data (e.g., speed, acceleration, breaking, steering, and location) and applying a Computational Model to them.
- Input sensor (Accelerometer, Gyroscope) data (CSV file).
- Data collecting phase, driving a car, and gathering data from several different sensors (accelerometer, gyroscope, magnetometer, GPS, etc.).
- Pre-processing.
- Events mainly detected by calculating mean of successive accelerometer readings on certain axes and comparing them to empirical fixed/dynamic thresholds.
- Calculating Mean of certain axes.
- Applying MLA (SVM and Logistic Regression) for classification of driver behaviour (Normal/Aggressive).
- Comparing values with threshold and applying SVM algorithm.
- Comparing values with threshold and applying Logistic Regression algorithm.
- Driver Behaviour Classification (Normal/Aggressive)

## 5 Conclusion and Future Scope

Using data acquired from Android smart phone sensors, we presented our method for driving behaviour classification and evaluated the performance of two MLAs (Support Vector Machine and Logistic Regression) (accelerometer and gyroscope). For seven days, we collected samples of these event kinds in the actual world, with a driver performing the driving events.

Our findings show that:

(i) Smart phone sensors can be used to classify driver behaviour; (ii) the accelerometer and gyroscope are the best sensors for detecting driving events; (iii) MLA such as SVM and Logistic Regression can be used to classify driver behaviour; and (v) the behaviour classification accuracy with available dataset for SVM is 99.98% and for Logistic Regression is 99.81%.

In the future, we plan to gather a larger number of driving event samples with different vehicles, on various roads, and in varied weather and temperature situations. We also plan to run the experiment with a larger group of drivers. Finally, we plan to create an Android application that can identify driving events in real time and calculate a driver behaviour score.

## References


1. Eftekhari, H.R., Ghatee, M.: A similarity-based neuro-fuzzy modeling for driving behaviour recognition applying fusion of smartphone sensors. J. Intell. Transp. Syst. **23**, 72–83 (2019)
2. Baheti, B., Gajre, S., Talbar, S.: Detection of distracted driver using convolutional neural network. In: IEEE/CVF Conference on Computer Vision and Pattern Recognition Workshops (2018)
3. Eftekhari, H.R., Ghatee, M.: Hybrid of discrete wavelet transform and adaptive neuro fuzzy inference system for overall driving behaviour recognition. Transp. Res. Part. F. **58**, 782–796 (2018)
4. Lu, D.-N., Nguyen, D.-N., Nguyen, T.-H., Nguyen, H.-N.: Vehicle mode and driving activity detection based on analyzing sensor data of smartphones. Sensors **18**, 1036 (2018)
5. Zinebi, K., Souissi, N., Tikito, K.: Driver behaviour analysis methods: applications oriented study. In: The 3rd International Conference on Big Data, Cloud and Applications – BDCA 2018, Morocco (2018)
6. Ferreira, J.Jr., et al.: Driver behaviour profiling: an investigation with different smartphone sensors and machine learning. PLOS ONE. **12**, e0174959 (2017). https://doi.org/10.1371/journal.pone.0174959
7. Singh, S.K.: Road traffic accidents in India: issues and challenges. Transp. Res. Proc. **25**, 4708–4719 (2017)
8. Ahuja, V.K.A.: Traffic and road safety management in India. Int. J. Res. Educ. Sci. Methods (IJARESM). **4**(3), (2016). ISSN: 2455–6211
9. Munigety, C.R., Mathew, T.V.: Towards behavioral modeling of drivers in mixed traffic conditions. Transp. Dev. Econ. **2**(1), 1–20 (2016). https://doi.org/10.1007/s40890-016-0012-y
10. Wu, M., Zhang, S., Dong, Y.: A novel model-based driving behaviour recognition system using motion sensors. Sensors. **16**, 1746 (2016)
11. Liu, Z., Wu, M., Zhu, K., Zhang, L.: SenSafe: A Smartphone-Based Traffic Safety Framework by Sensing Vehicle and Pedestrian Behaviours. Hindawi Publishing Corporation Mobile Information Systems Volume (2016)
12. Meiring, G.A.M., Myburgh, H.C.: A review of intelligent driving style analysis systems and related artificial intelligence algorithms. Sensors. **15**, 30653–30682 (2015)
13. Press Information Bureau: Government of India, Ministry of Petroleum and Natural Gas. https://pib.gov.in/newsite/printrelease.aspx?relid=102799
14. Paefgen, J., Kehr, F., Zhai, Y., Michahelles, F.: Driving Behaviour Analysis with Smartphones: Insights from a Controlled Field Study. ACM (2012)

15. Eren, H., Makinist, S., Akin, E., Yilmaz, A.: Estimating driving behaviour by a smartphone. In: Intelligent Vehicles Symposium (2012)
16. Amdahl, P., Chaikiat, P.: Personas as drivers: an alternative approach for creating scenarios for ADAS evaluation. Master thesis in Cognitive Science, Linköping University, Sweden (2007)

# Co-design Workshops as a Step Towards Pilot Implementation for Complex Workplaces

## A Case Study of London-Based Airport Future Workplace

Parisa Saadati[1(✉)], José Abdelnour-Nocera[1,2], and Torkil Clemmensen[3]

[1] University of West London, London, UK
{parisa.saadati,abdejos}@uwl.ac.uk
[2] ITI/Larsys Portugal, Funchal, Portugal
[3] Copenhagen Business School, Frederiksberg, Denmark
tc.digi@cbs.dk

**Abstract.** This study has investigated how a complex multi-level organisation like a London-based airport can benefit from participatory design workshops using ecological interface design tools (i.e., Abstraction Hierarchy) for selecting or designing better future systems. Many complex organisations are using trials (pilot in our context) for selecting future autonomous technologies. This case is driven by a member of the innovation department of the airport and UX researchers. Our main objective was to employ participatory design and work domain analysis (WDA) as part of a framework to co-design and plan trials for future automated systems for smart work in airport terminal operations. The term automation in this paper also covers some of the so-called AI or more sophisticated automation. Over two weeks in two workshops in a London-based airport, we ran co-design workshops to help the decision-makers understand workplace needs and employee welfare while selecting future automated systems. We also explored potential issues in the work domain that the traditional user-centred design (UCD) methods could not systematically assess (e.g., information exchange or contextual effects). We conclude that WDA as part of co-design workshops prior to selecting the trials could be considered part of the pilot implementation for selection and design systems in complex workplaces, but it has complications.

**Keywords:** HCI · Participatory design · Automation · Personas · Interaction design · Abstraction hierarchy · Trials · Pilot implementation

## 1 Introduction

Automation and the introduction of Industry 4.0 interactive technologies in industrial work systems have brought new ambiguities in the challenges and burdens on interactive systems designers [15]. Socio-technical system design has identified and addressed several problems in understanding and developing complex autonomous systems [1, 3, 7, 9]. Therefore, service design and co-design processes are utilised to facilitate collaboration in new ways [18]. Designing future technologies needs more cross-organisational


Published by Springer Nature Switzerland AG 2022
C. Ardito et al. (Eds.): INTERACT 2021, LNCS 13198, pp. 421–428, 2022.
https://doi.org/10.1007/978-3-030-98388-8_38

collaborations to produce innovative and creative outcomes. Many organisations prefer to select future systems by running trials and customising the existing systems instead of in-house designing. In such cases planning for a better selection of the trials is crucial and can bring more on-time competitive advantages. Trials can be defined as pilot implementation, and therefore their main objective is to learn. Hertzum et al. [13] defined pilot implementations as "an information-system development technique that aims to feed experiences from real use back into development by having users try out a system on a restricted scale before the design of the system is finalised". The pilot implementation can help organisations understand how to improve the system, adapt the organisation, and capture the benefits of introducing the system [13]. They can also help understand the less visible socio-technical issues and (hopefully) improve them in the subsequent intervention. As pilot implementations considered field tests, using the intended environment with real data, they can learn how a system may support its users in their work. Therefore, one of the potential improvements from the pilot is changes in UX. On the other hand, more studies on UX and innovation are needed in light of advances in Artificial Intelligence (AI) and the growing use of more sophisticated automation technologies [9]. Thus, using pilot implementation for these systems is beneficial in determining the value of the system and its design while reducing the implementation risks [13].

Simultaneously, there is a need for cooperation and better communication in human teams and individuals and AI systems to achieve better UX goals for future automation scenarios, namely AI/UX goals [1, 17]. Hence, future autonomous systems need to be carefully co-designed and tested in the field before or during the design. This should be properly engineered and bring some lessons learned to improve the system. In this paper, we report on a case study that employs participatory design and work domain analysis (WDA) [5] as a means for planning, co-design, and selecting trials for future automated systems considering AI/UX goals in the context of airport terminal operations.

This paper describes the process of a team of researchers and operational decision-makers of an airport in co-design two scenarios supporting smart work in the airport's terminals. Workshop sessions resulted in two future work scenarios leading to their rough prototyping using a WDA tool known as Abstraction Hierarchy (AH) [4]. The objective is to explore and illustrate how a London-based airport uses participatory design, interaction design, and WDA methods to decide on future autonomous systems trials based on the users' needs. The paper concludes with lessons we learned using such workshops prior to or as an initial stage to the pilot implementation phase.

## 2 Participatory Design and Work Domain Analysis

Approaches that have emerged to promote user engagement in system development have been implemented in different industries, such as aviation [19, 21, 22]. In addition, the participatory design approach has gained interest in the development of commercial and business applications [8]. The participatory design process emphasises mutual learning, as none of the participants, either 'designer' or 'user' knows everything.

WDA is a framework that supports and structures the analysis needed when designing a flexible and adaptive system [23]. Using WDA has two distinct advantages. First, WDA is a multi-dimensional analysis that incorporates the physical and the social environment to provide a detailed description. Secondly, WDA can be paired with interface design [12] to generate new system designs.

From the WDA toolset, we decided to use AHs since they provide a discreet and complete description of a work domain at different abstraction and concrete levels. Furthermore, AHs are suitable to use by stakeholders from different backgrounds with little or no experience of WDA [2, 4]. AHs are used for human-machine systems design in empirical studies of operators' fault-finding strategies. AH determine what kinds of information should be displayed on the system interface and how the information should be arranged [12]. The main focus of AHs is to assess socio-technical relations, which allows the identification of contextual aspects otherwise only visible in pilot implementations, referred to as trials in our context.

## 3 Case Study Questions

This study followed a user-centric design approach for understanding domain experts necessities who are directly and indirectly working towards selecting the new technologies, their usability and UX goals. We offered a guideline to follow in the form of a co-design workshop based on our empirical for future systems. We co-created scenarios, personas, and AH as design methods to answer several questions: can co-design workshops lead to optimal design/selection of future autonomous systems? Can this be acceptable as part of the pilot implementation?

### 3.1 Workshop's Settings

We noticed that multi-levelled large organisations (i.e., our airport) mainly select their future technologies by running trials and observing how they proceed. However, customer and employee satisfaction and UX in the trials were not easily assessed and articulated or, in many cases, neglected. Our observations on the trials and the shortfalls seen regarding the use, usability, and UX of these tested technologies helped us suggest the airport user-centred design tools and methods for introducing new automated systems.

A success factor in any organisation is aligning the IT and business strategies, which is also true for socio-technical approaches. Thus, the strategy makers (managers) should be aligned with the system designers for successful implementation, including any pilot implementation. Otherwise, it will result in inefficiency in work, development and testing of the system, and failure in the pilot implementation. In our observations, we have noticed that one of the main factors neglected in selecting or running a trial is the primary users' (employees and end-users) need and requirement, which should assess technically and socially in the bigger organisational picture. Before selecting the future systems and replacing the new system with employees' day-to-day practices, strategy-makers should consider the culture, reward systems, employees' wellbeing and more socio-technical factors.

Considering these factors, we suggested that implementing co-design workshops with their domain expert (employees) before selecting future trials is beneficial for both the strategy makers and the end-users. These types of selected trials are expected to have better user engagement and interaction than the others.

This suggestion triggered two co-design workshops with 14 participants, including researchers, industry decision-makers, and employees from different departments. Two researchers acted as facilitators in the workshops and used various topics and techniques to engage participants in prototyping system concepts. This system could be an autonomous system that is required in their departments. All participants had enough experience with autonomous technologies and leading Industry 4.0 implementation. In pair, they have discussed their proposed systems for short and concrete experiences in the future.

After a short cognitive walkthrough and group discussion for each system, the participants ranked the systems based on their value proposition and benefits for the airport. From a list of suggested scenarios (automated helpers, autonomous tugs, context-aware guest invites system, baggage tracing, and smart asset management.), participants selected two; Autonomous Tug and Pushback Taxi (ATPT) and Automated Asset Management and Maintenance (AAMM).

In workshop 2 we used Customer Job Canvas (part of value proposition canvas), persona's template, AI/UX goals [17] and AI guidelines [1], sketching, and AH [6] to prototype the short-listed future scenarios selected in the workshop 1. Researchers fulfilled facilitator roles supporting unfamiliar participants with the design tools while engaged as active designers in other tasks. Participants found it easier to work with the tools where they could have a role played in them, such as an employee or the end-user. Therefore, their engagement was high in customer job canvas, persona, sketching and testing AI/UX goals, compared to the difficulties faced while working on AH layers for the proposed systems. Thus, facilitators had to provide more tangible examples to shape the AH five layers; physical form, physical function, generalised function, abstract function and functional purpose. In developing AHs participants both analysed their work domain (e.g. airport service) and work tasks (e.g., checking people in).

In the last stage of workshop 2, each group walked through their concept [25] using their low fidelity prototypes and received feedback from other colleagues and decision-makers on how likely the idea was feasible. Finally, group members evaluated their design with UX goal templates [1, 17]. The quick result of this workshop was rejecting one of the trials due to functional viability and employees' welfare.

### 3.2 Data Collection and Analysis Methods

Data were gathered during the workshops via various sources. All group walkthroughs and final discussions were audio-recorded and transcribed verbatim. The data collected are audio recordings of the group work sessions during the workshop and written documents delivered during the workshop, such as personas, sketches, and observation notes. All in all, we analysed two scenarios' walkthroughs followed by the discussion and feedback from other teams lasting app 40 min, and we report the findings partially in this paper. Similarly to Friess [10], we analysed the conversational turns, but we left out single words and irrelevant conversations. The analysis started with open coding to provide a solid interpretive pattern and foundation for the thematic units [11]. For this paper, we only used some of the themes related to the pilot (trial) selection and implementation and the benefits the decision-makers mentioned about the workshop, such as "UX goals", "employees' welfare", "financial viabilities", and "Risks of sharing responsibilities between the machine and human".

## 4 What We Learned - Pros and Cons of Such Workshops

We have learned that combining external academics and company employees can bring more efficiency to company workshops by providing recommendations viable on the industry that can be academically backed up. We also learned that employees are the best consultants for analysing the functions allocations for an optimal distribution of both functions and tasks between a partly autonomous system and the user [3]. Also, we observed that in complex jobs (e.g., terminal asset manager) in which employees deal with a high volume of data, there is more desire to share the work with a machine (e.g., robots and AI systems) rather than in low-skilled jobs (e.g., receptionist). This is specifically the case for tasks with a range of unpleasant, repetitive, too exhausting, or unsafe nature [16, 24]. We also learned that trust and safety considerations are more important in aviation than in other sectors as aviation insurance policies associate AI technologies with risks and uncertainty as these technologies take a degree of control of humans. We looked into the possibility of using such workshops as the initial stage of pilot implementation, for which we add the pros and cons here.

### 4.1 Pros and Cons of Co-design Workshops Prior to the Trials

One of the main strengths of this method was discovering the users' pains and gains in an early stage before selecting the system or trials using value proposition canvas. This helped the decision-maker understand the current situation better and realise the future gains or requirements well. Such practices provide temporary opportunities for the stakeholders to quickly assess how the proposed future system can fail in the organisation's environment and culture. In addition, understanding of the work domain and employees can shape into a shared vocabulary of technical and social requirements between the developers and decision-makers. Users can help in prototyping the technical configuration of the future systems using Abstraction Hierarchy.

Participatory workshops can bring more user engagement and empowerment (e.g., employees) by involving them in the design process. There is also an opportunity of changing the design requirements before the actual pilot implementation based on testing the usability goals. Therefore, we argued that such workshops should be an initial stage to the pilot implementation or the feasibility study for the pilot implementation.

One of the main cons for these workshops is the involvement of academics as facilitators to provide knowledge to the participants before the co-design workshop and during using AH to determine the technical configurations. This may not be accepted in some industries. Also, strong participants can influence the group decisions in such workshops and make them bias. Participatory workshops with WDA may not be accepted as pilot studies; in many cases they should rather be labelled and treated as feasibility studies.

### 4.2 Co-design Workshop Settings

All participants confirmed that using trials and writing lengthy reports is not optimal for planning and designing future scenarios. They found the workshop a quicker way to assess if the system works in the airport domain or not. However, on the other hand, bringing all these decision-makers to a co-design workshop for a couple of hours was not an easy practice. For a better result in the ideation process, providing a context, scenario, and better facilitation is required. Previous studies cover how the ideation process can be more comfortable and quicker for the participants [14, 20]. We observed that selecting the right design tool can better reflect the participants' knowledge. For example, participants found AH complicated to use without the design researchers' help. Adding more tangible elements [20], such as pre-structured cards and easy-to-use collaborative tools, can always be beneficial.

Moreover, there is a need to use data-driven design tools for the co-design workshops for future scenarios. Preparing the environment to ideate is another important factor; participants should understand the scenario, products, and the future system's domain and environment. The process provided the participants with an exemplary scenario to generate and manage their ideas. Otherwise, we must provide sufficient (internal/external) data for the context and persona creation. In line with the environment preparation and facilitator's instructions, planning for a scenario in advance for every co-design workshop for future systems is essential. This can help the participant access context and a road map to look forward and share more relevant information.

By the end of workshop 2, most participants understood how a future automation prototype could better fit their work environment through increased awareness of the work domain. Furthermore, they have agreed that there is a relation between modes of discovery, design improvements, interaction, and socio-spatial aspects. At the end of the session, one senior manager praised co-design and WDA methods to select and design new trials of future automation use cases and prototypes for the airport.

## 5 Conclusion

This case study's main contribution is about helping the airport co-design automation scenarios to incorporate workers' UX and work. During the design process in the workshops, we used WDA to contextualise the systems and assessed employees' acceptance of these systems. The presented case study's main aim is to explore and illustrate how a London-based airport uses participatory design, interaction design, and WDA methods to make decisions on trials for future autonomous systems that incorporate workers' experiences. We show how these co-design workshops and WDA design tools can yield early contextual socio-technical insights typically only found during pilot implementations. We empirically assessed our hypothesis on the proposed systems ATPT and AAMM scenarios in an airport domain based on customer profiles, personas, scenarios, AH, and a rough prototype to achieve this goal. We observed that this method could help designers or decision-makers foresee factors that may not be systematically assessed with other traditional UCD methods during the design process (e.g., information exchange or contextual effects). Producing the five layers for AH more efficiently with the help of academics and providing more tangible examples was one of the main motivations in producing the final designs. After the workshop, it was highlighted in the senior participants' responses that using this method helps them better understand workers and the aviation sector's needs and perspectives for selecting the new autonomous systems, which was not part of their practices.

All in all, before conducting pilots in such large organisations, WDA in the form of co-design workshops can be used to select the available trials and their pilot implementation. The result can be used as an improvement in the intervention and design. WDA methods will be more effective when the key domain workers and stakeholders participate.

## References

1. Amershi, S., et al.: Guidelines for human-AI interaction. In: Proceedings of the 2019 CHI Conference on Human Factors in Computing Systems. pp. 1–13. Association for Computing Machinery, New York, NY, USA (2019). https://doi.org/10.1145/3290605.3300233
2. Barcellini, F., et al.: Designers' and users' roles in participatory design: what is actually co-designed by participants? Appl. Ergon. **50**, 31–40 (2015). https://doi.org/10.1016/j.apergo.2015.02.005
3. Barricelli, B.R., et al.: Human work interaction design. In: Designing Engaging Automation: 5th IFIP WG 13.6 Working Conference, HWID 2018. Espoo, Finland, 20–21 August 2018, Revised Selected Papers. Springer, Cham (2019). https://doi.org/10.1007/978-3-030-05297-3
4. Bodin, I., et al.: Work domain analysis of an intensive care unit: an abstraction hierarchy based on a bed-side approach. In: Proceedings of the Human Factors and Ergonomics Society Europe Annual Conference, pp. 109–118 (2016)
5. Burns, C.: Cognitive work analysis: new dimensions. In: Campos, P., Clemmensen, T., Nocera, J.A., Katre, D., Lopes, A., Ørngreen, R. (eds.) HWID 2012. IAICT, vol. 407, pp. 1–11. Springer, Heidelberg (2013). https://doi.org/10.1007/978-3-642-41145-8_1
6. Burns, C.M., et al.: Evaluation of ecological interface design for nuclear process control: situation awareness effects. Hum Factors. **50**(4), 663–679 (2008). https://doi.org/10.1518/001872008X312305
7. Cabrero, D.G., et al.: A hermeneutic inquiry into user-created personas in different Namibian locales. In: Proceedings of the 14th Participatory Design Conference: Full papers-Volume 1, pp. 101–110. ACM (2016)
8. Chin, G., Rosson, M.: A case study in the participatory design of a collaborative science-based learning environment. Presented at the (2004)
9. Dikmen, M., Burns, C.: Trust in autonomous vehicles: the case of Tesla Autopilot and Summon. In: 2017 IEEE International Conference on Systems, Man, and Cybernetics (SMC), pp. 1093–1098 (2017). https://doi.org/10.1109/SMC.2017.8122757
10. Friess, E.: Personas and decision making in the design process: an ethnographic case study. In: Proceedings of the SIGCHI Conference on Human Factors in Computing Systems. pp. 1209–1218. Association for Computing Machinery, New York, NY, USA (2012). https://doi.org/10.1145/2207676.2208572
11. Guba, E.G., Lincoln, Y.S.: Competing paradigms in qualitative research. Handbook Qual. Res. **2**(163–194), 105 (1994)
12. Hajdukiewicz, J., Burns, C.: Strategies for bridging the gap between analysis and design for ecological interface design. Proc. Hum. Fact. Ergon. Soc. Ann. Meet. **48**(3), 479–483 (2004). https://doi.org/10.1177/154193120404800344
13. Hertzum, M. et al.: Pilot Implementation: Learning from Field Tests in IS Development. Communications of the Association for Information Systems, vol. 30 (2012). https://doi.org/10.17705/1CAIS.03020

14. Inie, N., Dalsgaard, P.: How interaction designers use tools to manage ideas. ACM Trans. Comput.-Hum. Interact. **27**, 2, 7:1–7:26 (2020). https://doi.org/10.1145/3365104
15. Kadir, B.A., Broberg, O.: Human-centered design of work systems in the transition to industry 4.0. Appl. Ergon. **92**, 103334 (2021). https://doi.org/10.1016/j.apergo.2020.103334
16. Kirk, A.K., Brown, D.F.: Employee assistance programs: a review of the management of stress and wellbeing through workplace counselling and consulting. Aust. Psychol. **38**(2), 138–143 (2003). https://doi.org/10.1080/00050060310001707137
17. Kymalainen, T., et al.: Evaluating future automation work in process plants with an experience-driven science fiction prototype. In: 2016 12th International Conference on Intelligent Environments (IE), pp. 54–61. IEEE, London, United Kingdom (2016). https://doi.org/10.1109/IE.2016.17
18. Mugglestone, M., et al.: Accelerating the improvement process. Clin. Govern.: An Intl J. **13**(1), 19–25 (2008). https://doi.org/10.1108/14777270810850599
19. Oostveen, A.-M., Lehtonen, P.: The requirement of accessibility: european automated border control systems for persons with disabilities. Technol. Soc. **52**, 60–69 (2018). https://doi.org/10.1016/j.techsoc.2017.07.009
20. Rygh, K., Clatworthy, S.: The use of tangible tools as a means to support co-design during service design innovation projects in healthcare. In: Pfannstiel, M.A., Rasche, C. (eds.) Service Design and Service Thinking in Healthcare and Hospital Management, pp. 93–115. Springer, Cham (2019). https://doi.org/10.1007/978-3-030-00749-2_7
21. Simonsen, J., Robertson, T.: Routledge International Handbook of Participatory Design. Routledge (2012). https://doi.org/10.4324/9780203108543
22. Tan, W., Boy, G.A.: Tablet-based information system for commercial aircraft: onboard context-sensitive information system (OCSIS). In: Harris, D. (ed.) EPCE 2018. LNCS (LNAI), vol. 10906, pp. 701–712. Springer, Cham (2018). https://doi.org/10.1007/978-3-319-91122-9_55
23. Vicente, K.J.: Cognitive Work Analysis: Toward Safe, Productive, and Healthy Computer-Based Work. CRC Press (1999)
24. Yerkes, R.M., Dodson, J.D.: The relation of strength of stimulus to rapidity of habit-formation. Punishment: Issues and experiments. pp. 27–41 (1908)
25. Tools|Service Design Tools. https://servicedesigntools.org/tools.html. Accessed on 27Jan 2021

# Dropping a Bomb or Providing a Gentle Loving Touch? Towards a Relation Artefact Theory of Pilot Implementation

Torkil Clemmensen(✉)

Copenhagen Business School, Howitzvej 60, 2000 Frederiksberg, Denmark
tc.digi@cbs.dk

**Abstract.** This position paper is about socio-technical interventions in pilot implementation contexts. It argues that human work interaction design provides massive push towards such interventions. It does so through theorizing the continuous relation-building between empirical work analysis and interaction design activities that creates new local solutions for the stakeholders involved. It raises the question of how hard of soft that this push should be. The discussion provides clarity as to what is implemented in the Relation Artefact theory of pilot implementation and gives examples that may help to judge how hard or soft the push should be.

**Keywords:** Socio-technical user experiences · Organizational alignment · Digital work legacy · Interaction design interoperability · Human work interaction design

## 1 Introduction

This paper is about pilot implementation understood as socio-technical interventions in organizational and wider contexts. Pilot implementation is a notion that stems from IT health research [1] and thus alludes to a medical science epistemology of 'effect'-driven intervention [2]. Today, it is however a broader concept that captures the moment in design when the wider organizational and beyond context is involved in the design [3–6]. It has recently been established as (part of) 'organizational implementation' that aims at organizational change [7].

This paper argues that the human work interaction design (HWID) approach provides a massive push towards such interventions, through the continuous relation-building between empirical work analysis and interaction design activities that creates new local solutions for the stakeholders involved. How hard should this push be: should pilot implementation be as dropping a bomb or as providing a gentle loving touch?


C. Ardito et al. (Eds.): INTERACT 2021, LNCS 13198, pp. 429–439, 2022.
https://doi.org/10.1007/978-3-030-98388-8_39

## 2 Pilot Implementation as a Movement from the Technical Towards the Social

Socio-technical HCI design approaches can be used for different directions of socio-technical interventions. Sometimes technology is assumed to lead to social changes, (e.g., [8]), sometimes social changes are assumed to change technology, (e.g., [9]). For example, the practice based computing approach [10] is mostly interested in the empirical effects of new technology such as ongoing work interaction design for learning and development. In contrast, the experience design approach [11] builds on theoretical knowledge about human psychology to come up with novel interaction designs. The HWID platform supports any of the directions for socio-technical interventions. However, the HWID platform has a strong focus on the socio-technical relations themselves.

Socio-technical approaches to human-automation collaboration in general aim to take participatory and co-design approaches seriously across a variety of HCI, CSCW, IS, UI engineering, and technical psychology topics, and all the way through the lifecycle of an IT artefact. A requirement to being able to do that is to have an open mind about how to link the social and the technical also when it comes to pilot implementation.

## 3 HWID Relation Artefact Pilot Implementation

HWID Relation Artefact pilot implementation is a design move from the technical to the social that fills the gap between these with Relation Artefacts. HWID Relation Artefacts are socio-technical IT artefacts that relate empirical work analysis and interaction design [12, 13]. They are different from 'relational artefacts', that is, social robots [14] and other anthropomorphic interfaces, which are things that people relate to. HWID Relation Artefacts may impose a certain order in time and space of the design. In this paper, the Relation Artefacts are: interaction design interoperability checkups, digital legacy interventions, and organizational strategy alignments, Fig. 1. They present a move from the technical to the social as shown by the arrow in Fig. 1. The design move for pilot implementation interventions begins with the technical, that is, the interaction designs and move towards organizational and social interventions, that is, the strategy alignments.

**Interaction Design Interoperability Checkups.** Interaction design interoperability checkups are important concerns in pilot implementations because novel interaction designs should be able to co-exist with interaction designs of other systems in use in the organization. Interaction interoperability checkups are Relation Artefacts that aim to increase the UX related to interoperability of interaction designs. The interoperability of interaction designs has been studied as continuity in multi-device interactions where interactions move, or transition, from one device to another. A first checkup on the interoperability of novel interaction designs may focus on UX of sequential multi-device use [15]. Second, interoperability has been studied as socio-technical interoperability of HCI in work domains with multiple workers and multiple devices collaborating. Kwon et al. [16] suggested that socio-technical interoperability of HCI in work domains concerns (1) sharedness, (2) readiness, (3) awareness, (4) adaptiveness, and (5) coupledness of the multiple workers and multiple devices collaborating. To assess these dimensions would

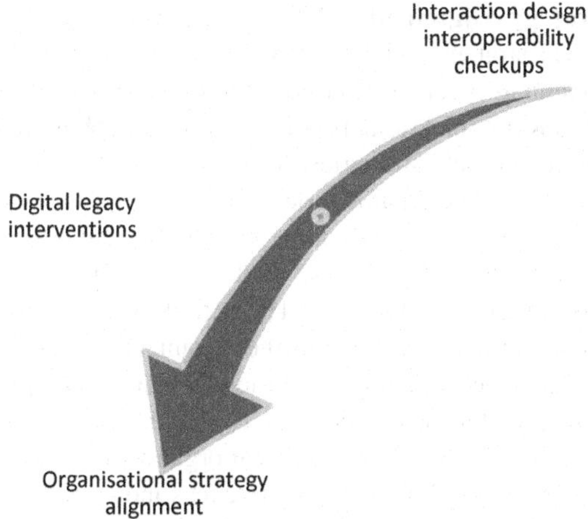


**Fig. 1.** Relation Artefacts for socio-technical interventions

be a second checkup. Third, cross-validations of the proposed solution's interoperability could be done by evaluating it in the lab, the field, and the gallery [17], which all may contribute to increases in novel knowledge and confidence in the interoperability checks of the novel interaction designs. When doing interaction interoperability checkups and other design interventions no single of the three evaluation approaches are the correct one, hence all should probably be used in a triangulation manner.

**Digital Legacy Interventions.** Digital legacy interventions are important concerns in pilot implementations because today workers are often creative 'co-designers' of the new design and they leave traces in terms of hacks and improvements across the new and old system. Digital legacy interventions are socio-technical interventions that in some way change (improve, hopefully) the new interaction designs' relation to the organization's legacy systems. To do this requires reconceptualizing what we mean by organizational legacy systems and what are interaction designs for digital legacy. It raises questions such as how employees' experience their organization's business-critical but obsolete systems, and what can employees do about their own digital legacy in their organization. The socio-technical view of UX of legacy systems is then that they are socio-technical systems that are technically and/or socially obsolete, old, and need lots of maintenance, but solve problems for organizations and meet individual employees' needs [18]. Creating new relations between work/organization analysis and interaction design is what solves legacy issues, not simply software modernization. Furthermore, employees' digital legacy is from a HWID perspective central for digital legacy interventions. Users' digital legacy can be defined as "the meaningful and complex way in which information, values, and possessions are passed on to others" [19]. Employees could benefit from organization-owned add-ons, plugins, and data scrapers. These could support employees' legitimate extracting their legacy from organizational storage and other places where employees generate and collect personal digital data, and also support employees in transferring their digital legacy to private storage or to their next employers' storages.

**Organizational Strategy Alignments.** A factor that makes organizations successful is a close linkage of the IT strategy and the business strategy [20]. Strategy as practice [21] tells that it is management practices that put strategy into practice. Pilot implementation thus should entail Relation Artefacts that are about morphing interaction design for human work into organizational strategies, for example by aligning the organizational UX culture with business and organizational goals. The activities that IT managers engage in to ensure that they are in the room, when important business decisions about product direction and business strategy are made, have been identified by UX leaders from industry and by researchers [22, 23]. The activities include broader questions of developing and managing a UX culture in the organization. UX leaders see the UX strategy at the corporate level as being about the UX teams' alignment with the overall goals and objectives of the business. They aim to shape the strategic plans, operational needs, and interdependencies between their own organization and the rest of the company, and thereby increase the UX teams' effectiveness and synergies with other business functions. They see UX strategy at the level of a business unit as being about plans for delivering products, systems, or services that offers a high value to customers, and differentiates the company's brand. However, this requires multiple parts of the organizations to be involved [23]. Thus, UX strategy alignment is done with a UX organizational culture that can support the strategy and make it realistic and ensure it has an impact on company outcomes [22].

## 4 Dropping a Bomb or Providing a Gentle Loving Touch?

First-stage intervention = {relation artefact type intervention a}
IF evaluation = {nonresponse}
THEN second-stage intervention = {intensify relation artefact type intervention a}
ELSE IF evaluation = {response}
THEN at second stage = {continue with relation artefact type intervention b}

**Fig. 2.** Decision rules in adaptive interventions in socio-technical design. The sequence shown in the figure is continued with Relation Artefacts type intervention c, and repeated as long as it takes to reach closure with type intervention c. Adapted from [24].

In HWID, like in most HCI design, evaluations are most of the time formative evaluation with the purpose of improving the design. This implies that there is a systematic and sequential overlap between construction and evaluation/ intervention activities. In HWID pilot implementations the sequence of artefact designs and actions and evaluations thereof can perhaps be conceptualized as an 'adaptive intervention'. Adaptive intervention is a method proposed in psychology to allow greater individualization and adaptation of intervention options (i.e., intervention type and/or strength) over time [24]. Adaptive interventions in socio-technical design are thus a string of different Relation

Artefacts evaluated to adapt to workers' and organizations' characteristics and changing needs over time, with the general aim to optimize the long-term effectiveness of the overall socio-technical intervention. Figure 2 shows how decision rules can be used to operationalize adaptive interventions with three types of Relation Artefacts (e.g., those three types discussed in Sect. 3).

## 5 Discussion

In this paper, a design move from the technical to the social with HWID Relation Artefacts is proposed as a theory of pilot implementation. The proposed Relation Artefacts types are interoperability, digital legacy, and organisational alignment. In addition, the notion of 'adaptive interventions' help explain how the design move is made. Our proposed theory of pilot implementation conceptualizes the moment(s) in design when a broader set of stakeholders are invited as co-designers. Below we discuss what it is that is pilot implemented, seen from the perspective of a HWID Relation Artefact theory of pilot implementation.

### 5.1 What Is 'Pilot Implemented' with HWID Relation Artefacts?

It is a choice to start with either the technical or the social in pilot implementation. Most often pilot implementation is thought of as beginning with the technical and either neglects or is vague about the social. Bansler and Havn [1] appear to argue that pilot implementation is only about correcting technical design shortcomings, while the Relation Artefact approach proposed here obviously invites to see the pilot implementation as including design of the social. It is however unclear in many design cases with what the pilot implementation begins. For example, in a study of the design of a Digital Twins pilot implementation, Barricelli [25] states that pilot implementation is to "satisfy needs and requirements that cannot be fully anticipated at prototyping time". These needs and requirements beyond the prototype can thus in principle be either social needs or technical needs or both.

The prototype could be what is pilot implemented, but it is often not clear that or how (much) the 'prototype' is social or technical. In the practice-based computing approach [10] pilot implementation can be said to begin the moment when there is a mature technical prototype that workers can use in daily work. It is then their social appropriation of the mature prototype that is studied as pilot implementation. In the experience design approach [11] the theoretical knowledge about human psychology helps define basic user needs to the fulfilled. The pilot implementation can then be studied as the novel technical interaction design in a product prototype.

In the Relation Artefact approach, the prototype is however a type of Relation Artefacts, which can for example be organizational action hypothesis, work experience prototypes, and UX-at-work goals [12]. A Relation Artefact pilot implementation such as the one proposed here is therefore not really an implementation of any 'thing' or any 'process', or at least not of a single object, such as a software prototype or a set of basic human needs. It is rather a design move to fill a gap between the social and the technical with intervention and evaluation artefacts. If there is any 'history' or connection back to earlier designs it will be in the form of feedback loops configured to provide feedback to Relation Artefacts in other design moves.

### 5.2 'Interoperability' Examples

The idea of the Relation Artefact 'interoperability' in pilot implementation is to focus on the interoperability of the technical system on the level of usability and UX. That is, the focus is on the fit between the interaction designed and other interaction patterns in the organisation.

For example, in a study of road safety, Salve and Bhutkar [26] pilot implemented a mobile app that deals with potholes in the roads. Yearly up to 5000 accidents happens in India alone, and the numbers may be comparable in other countries. They did a SUS scale usability test of the app with 10 participants and reached a rating of 74 out of 100, which is considered good. As a 'interoperability' relation artefact, a SUS usability test is a minimum version, which in a quick and dirty way indicates if a convenience sample of a target user population finds its interaction design to have a usability at the level of other interaction designs that they are familiar with.

A second example is a study by Pereira et al. [27] of how to engage prospective students in a dialogue with the client university. Pereira et al. [27] observed that common interaction design patterns among students were social media postings and dialogues, where they expressed their sentiments about universities, programs, and courses they attended. This observation led them to conceptualize the interaction design patterns often used in the organisation – as electronic Word of Mouth – and the realization that a prototype of a decision support system for managers should be interoperational with the students' online social networks. They concluded that their study shows that the dissemination of programs in social networks deserves more attention from the universities' managers. This can be interpreted as a feedback loop setup in pilot implementation with an UX interoperability artefact to inform the technical outcome of a previous prototyping design move.

A third example of interoperability Relation Artefacts is from França et al.'s [28] study of rehabilitation from physical sports injuries using an extended reality setting. They found that introducing an immersive environment in such a large and diverse organization such as a Premier league football club is not trivial in terms of organizational adaptation. Many different people with many different backgrounds intervene in the pilot implementation in one way or another, while at the same time there is a continuous, almost real time pressure for results. This is a situation not so different from the studies of socio-technical interoperability of HCI in safety-critical work domains with multiple workers and multiple devices collaborating by Kwon et al. [16]. The Relation Artefact interoperability in França et al.'s [28] study concerned for example the challenge of calibration due to different users' body sizes, arms' length, etc., which made it necessary to configure the parts of the extended reality system to fit the pilot site and the interaction patters with the users'other systems.

### 5.3 'Digital Legacy' Examples

The digital legacy Relation Artefact in pilot implementation is meant to capture issues of threats to privacy but also positive and wanted personal digital heritage and legacy issues.

For example, Lopes and Cerejo [29] did a study of solutions to promote active aging in a village setting in an European country. Specifically, they studied application design to stimulate development of different activities: cognitive, physical, entertainment and social interaction. During use, the users were for example stimulated to improve their thinking by having to answer questions about music, mathematics, Portuguese language, history of Portugal, and geography. The application also supported novel ways for participants to experience their family photo gallery. The organisational setting for the pilot implementation was a nursery home. The application acted as a digital legacy Relation Artefact since it had functions that gave the participants some control over how they experienced and what happened with the personal answers and family photos that they delivered to the organisational system.

A second example of digital legacy Relation Artefact is from a study by Barricelli [25] of a Digital Twins pilot implementation in manufacturing. They applied an end user programming perspective which they defined as "the set of methods, techniques, tools, and socio-technical environments that allow end users to act as professionals in those ICT-related domains in which they are not professionals, by creating, modifying, extending and testing digital artifacts without requiring knowledge in traditional software engineering techniques". Obviously, this casts the users in the role of creators beyond the 'normal' work that they are hired to do. Such in many ways positive perspective however also raise questions of IPR and informal ownership practices, see e.g., [30], which should be designed explicitly as part of the pilot implementation. In this case of Digital Twin implementation, even if the role of workers' end user programming was limited to changing the way information were viewed, adding new features or asking for them, and discussing among them about the features that are already in place, workers were creators of digital legacy. Therefore, the pilot implementation may be an example of designing digital legacy Relation Artefacts.

### 5.4 'Organisational Strategy Alignment' Examples

The organisational strategy alignment Relation Artefact in pilot implementation is the one(s) that express the alignment between the organisation's long-term goals and the goals of the design project. This can be interpreted as alignment of managers' practices with designers' (developers, end user programmers, UX managers, etc.) practices.

For example, Herbæk et al. [31] presented a design case that focused on the optimal implementation and organizational change process in a pilot implementation of a new self-service-oriented IT system for both customers and employees in a SME 'proptech' company (companies dealing with property and technology). They analysed how the company managed to implement a new IT system from technical, organizational, and economical perspectives, and how this resulted in that the company thrived with their pilot implementation. Thus, Herbæk et al. found that organizational alignment is an important aspect of pilot implementation, and that it can be analysed by analysing various management strategic practices related to the pilot implementation. Managers are not to be treated as external stakeholders but as co-designers. Besides the example with management practices, other examples of organisational alignment Relation Artefacts that may be interpreted from Herbæk et al.'s study include design of the management of feedback data, design of innovative accounting practices for test results, and design of incentive structures for employees motivation to participate.

A second example is from a study by Saadati et al. [32] who employed participatory design and work domain analysis (WDA) in a pilot implementation of a set of future automated systems design ideas with focus on AI UX goals in the context of airport terminal operations. Their aim was to do trial planning of the future automated systems by designing AI use scenarios that could help the airport organization to understand the less visible socio-technical factors. The organizational alignment Relation Artefact interpretation can help to point out that in this study the usage scenarios covered both management and employee perspectives. The scenarios were created on basis of abstraction hierarchies that was used as a design tool because they allowed a description of a work domain at different abstraction and concrete levels in a co-design workshop with researchers, employees, and industry decisionmakers from different departments. These participants were then asked to use sharing and voting sessions to discuss and converge on the most appealing alternative future scenarios. The management participants responses were that using this method helped them to better align the workers' and the aviation sector's needs and perspectives when selecting the new autonomous systems.

### 5.5 Adaptive Interventions in Design

In this paper, we suggest that adaptive interventions from psychology [24] is a method that should be used in socio-technical design. Further developments in the health sciences of the notion of adaptive interventions, see e.g., [33, 34], have begun to spill over into healthcare UX and HCI [34]. However, what we do in this paper is to suggest that adaptive interventions [24] may be an important aspect of not only in the health IT domain, but in all kinds of pilot implementations in HCI and IS. Thus a 'Relation Artefacts' intervention should be repeated as long time as it takes to reach closure among stakeholders, before the next Relation Artefact in the design move are applied and evaluated. The aim is to adapt dynamically to workers' and organizations' characteristics and changing needs over time in a pilot implementation period.

The use of adaptive interventions in pilot implementations is different from the idea of iterative design, we suggest. Rather than being a tool for designers in iterative design cycles, adaptive interventions aims to catch individuals' human work interaction designs over time, (for HCI over time, see [35]). In the papers discussed in the above examples [25–29, 31, 32], doing several iterations of design would aim to improve the design for user groups that are represented by static personas in design. However, adaptive interventions are about using knowledge and data about individual participants to provide interventions tailored to the individual's needs and context. This can be for example be done by using persona definitions that are less static and more dynamic than traditional personas [34], which could help design gentle, individual-context oriented, and dynamic pilot implementations.

## 6 Conclusion

In conclusion, this paper's answer to the title question is to do pilot implementation with adaptive interventions, which is perhaps closer to the gentle loving touch than to dropping a bomb. Furthermore, the paper proposes the following as possible elements towards a theory of pilot implementation as Relation Artefacts: (1) HWID Relation Artefacts of three types, (2) a movement from the technical to the social, and (3) the notion of adaptive interventions. The proposal for a theory leads to a brief discussion of 'what' is 'pilot implemented', i.e., if the designs in pilot implementation are things and/or actions. This paper also discusses examples of HWID Relation Artefacts for pilot implementation that should help to see how HWID pushes massively, but gently, towards socio-technical pilot implementation.

## References


1. Bansler, J.P., Havn, E.: Pilot implementation of health information systems: issues and challenges. Int. J. Med. Inform. **79**, 637–648 (2010)
2. Hertzum, M., Simonsen, J.: Effects-driven IT development: an instrument for supporting sustained participatory design. In: Proceedings of the 11th Biennial Participatory Design Conference, pp. 61–70 (2010)
3. Hertzum, M., Bansler, J.P., Havn, E.C., Simonsen, J.: Pilot implementation: learning from field tests in IS development. Commun. Assoc. Inf. Syst. **30**, 20 (2012)
4. Hertzum, M., Manikas, M.I., á Torkilsheyggi, A.: Grappling with the future: the messiness of pilot implementation in information systems design. Health Inform. J. **25**, 372–388 (2019)
5. Torkilsheyggi, A.Á., Hertzum, M.: User participation in pilot implementation: porters and nurses coordinating patient transports. In: Proceedings of the 26th Australian Computer-Human Interaction Conference on Designing Futures: the Future of Design, pp. 290–299 (2014)
6. Mønsted, T., Hertzum, M., Søndergaard, J.: A socio-temporal perspective on pilot implementation: bootstrapping preventive care. Comput. Supp. Cooper. Work **29**(4), 419–449 (2019). https://doi.org/10.1007/s10606-019-09369-6
7. Hertzum, M.: Organizational implementation: the design in use of information systems. Synth. Lect. Hum.-Center. Inform. **14**, i–109 (2021)
8. Kling, R.: Learning about information technologies and social change: the contribution of social informatics. Inf. Soc. **16**, 217–232 (2000)
9. Seaver, N.: What should an anthropology of algorithms do? Cult. Anthropol. **33**, 375–385 (2018)
10. Wulf, V., Müller, C., Pipek, V., Randall, D., Rohde, M., Stevens, G.: Practice-based computing: empirically grounded conceptualizations derived from design case studies. In: Wulf, V., Schmidt, K., Randall, D. (eds.) Designing Socially Embedded Technologies in the Real-World. CSCW, pp. 111–150. Springer, London (2015). https://doi.org/10.1007/978-1-4471-6720-4_7
11. Hassenzahl, M.: Experience design: technology for all the right reasons. Synth. Lect. Hum.-Center. Inform. **3**, 1–95 (2010)
12. Clemmensen, T.: Human Work Interaction Design: A Platform for Theory and Action. Springer Nature (2021). https://doi.org/10.1007/978-3-030-71796-4
13. Goldkuhl, G.: The IT artefact: an ensemble of the social and the technical?–a rejoinder. Syst. Signs Actions. **7**, 90–99 (2013)

14. Turkle, S., Taggart, W., Kidd, C.D., Dasté, O.: Relational artifacts with children and elders: the complexities of cybercompanionship. Conn. Sci. **18**, 347–361 (2006)
15. Raptis, D., Kjeldskov, J., Skov, M.B.: Continuity in multi-device interaction. In: Proceedings of the 9th Nordic Conference on Human-Computer Interaction - NordiCHI '16 (2016). https://doi.org/10.1145/2971485.2971533
16. Kwon, G.H., Smith-Jackson, T.L., Bostian, C.W.: Socio-cognitive aspects of interoperability: understanding communication task environments among different organizations. ACM Trans. Comput. Interact. **18**, 1–21 (2011)
17. Koskinen, I., Binder, F.T., Redström, J.: Lab, field, gallery, and beyond. Artifact J. Des. Pract. **2**, 46–57 (2008)
18. Khadka, R., Batlajery, B. V., Saeidi, A.M., Jansen, S., Hage, J.: How do professionals perceive legacy systems and software modernization? In: Proceedings of the 36th International Conference on Software Engineering - ICSE 2014, pp. 36–47 (2014). https://doi.org/10.1145/2568225.2568318
19. Gulotta, R., Odom, W., Forlizzi, J., Faste, H.: Digital artifacts as legacy: exploring the lifespan and value of digital data. In: CHI '13 (2013). https://doi.org/10.1145/2470654.2466240
20. Baets, W.: Aligning information systems with business strategy. J. Strateg. Inf. Syst. **1**, 205–213 (1992)
21. Jarzabkowski, P.: Strategy as practice: recursiveness, adaptation, and practices-in-use. Organ. Stud. **25**, 529–560 (2004)
22. Friedland, L.: Culture eats UX strategy for breakfast. Interactions **26**, 78–81 (2019)
23. Lachner, F., Naegelein, P., Kowalski, R., Spann, M., Butz, A.: Quantified UX: towards a common organizational understanding of user experience. In: Proceedings 9th Nordic Conference on Human-Computer Interaction - NordMedia '16, vol. 56, pp. 1–56:10 (2016). https://doi.org/10.1145/2971485.2971501
24. Nahum-Shani, I., et al.: Experimental design and primary data analysis methods for comparing adaptive interventions. Psychol. Methods. **17**, 457–477 (2012)
25. Barricelli, B.R.: Socio-technical and collaborative design of pilot implementations of digital twins. In: Hertzum, M., et al. (eds.) Implementation for Testing Human-Work Interaction Designs. Unpublished pre-proceedings from a workshop at IFIP INTERACT2021, Bari, Italy
26. Salve, S., Bhutkar, G.: Usability evaluation of mobile app to support road safety. In: Hertzum, M., et al. (eds.) Implementation for Testing Human-Work Interaction Designs. Unpublished pre-proceedings from a workshop at IFIP INTERACT2021, Bari, Italy
27. Pereira, M.C., Ferreira, J.C., Moro, S., Gonçalves, F.: University digital engagement of students. In: Hertzum, M., et al. (eds.) Implementation for Testing Human-Work Interaction Designs. Unpublished pre-proceedings from a workshop at IFIP INTERACT2021, Bari, Italy
28. França, C., Sousa, M., Gonçalves, F., Gouveia, É.R., Gouveia, B., Campos, P.: Pilot implementation in virtual reality: pitfalls, tensions and organizational issues. In: Hertzum, M., et al. (eds.) Implementation for Testing Human-Work Interaction Designs. Unpublished pre-proceedings from a workshop at IFIP INTERACT2021, Bari, Italy
29. Lopes, A.G., Cerejo, I.: Mental happiness - a pilot implementation for elderly people. In: Hertzum, M., et al. (eds.) Implementation for Testing Human-Work Interaction Designs. Unpublished pre-proceedings from a workshop at IFIP INTERACT2021, Bari, Italy
30. Miric, M., Boudreau, K.J., Jeppesen, L.B.: Protecting their digital assets: The use of formal and informal appropriability strategies by App developers. Res. Policy. **48**, 103738 (2019)
31. Herbæk, L.K., Hansen, C.E.D., Clemmensen, T.: Pilot implementation: organizational alignment when implementing an IT-system. In: Hertzum, M., et al. (eds.) Implementation for Testing Human-Work Interaction Designs. Unpublished pre-proceedings from a workshop at IFIP INTERACT2021, Bari, Italy

32. Saadati, P., Abdelnour-Nocera, J., Clemmensen, T.: Co-designing workshop as pilot implementation for complex workplaces. In: Hertzum, M., et al. (eds.) Implementation for Testing Human-Work Interaction Designs. Unpublished pre-proceedings from a workshop at IFIP INTERACT2021, Bari, Italy
33. Cheverst, K., Davies, N., Mitchell, K., Friday, A., Efstratiou, C.: Developing a context-aware electronic tourist guide: some issues and experiences. In: Proceedings of the SIGCHI Conference on Human Factors in Computing Systems, pp. 17–24. ACM, New York, NY, USA (2000). https://doi.org/10.1145/332040.332047
34. Trujillo, A., Senette, C., Buzzi, M.C.: Persona design for just-in-time adaptive and persuasive interfaces in menopause self-care. In: Marcus, A., Wang, W. (eds.) DUXU 2018. LNCS, vol. 10920, pp. 94–109. Springer, Cham (2018). https://doi.org/10.1007/978-3-319-91806-8_8
35. Wiberg, M., Stolterman, E.: Time and temporality in HCI research. Interact. Comput. **33**, 250–270 (2021). https://doi.org/10.1093/iwc/iwab025

# Wearables, Humans, and Things – Addressing Problems in Education

# Towards Advanced Evaluation of Collaborative XR Spaces

Vera Marie Memmesheimer(✉) and Achim Ebert

Human Computer Interaction Lab, Technische Universität Kaiserslautern, 67663 Kaiserslautern, Germany

{memmesheimer,ebert}@cs.uni-kl.de

**Abstract.** Extended Reality (XR) technologies such as head-mounted displays are deemed beneficial for the collaboration of co-located as well as distributed people. As such, XR technologies appear particularly promising for supporting distant and hybrid teaching which became highly relevant during the Covid-19 pandemic. Despite the potential awarded to such technologies, practical applications are still very rare. In order to investigate the impediments to the practical adoption of XR technologies, the respective systems should be evaluated in real-world settings. Existing evaluation tools are, however, not suited for this purpose. In this paper, we explain why today's evaluation tools such as questionnaires, observation, and performance measurements are not sufficient for evaluating long-time, exploratory, and collaborative tasks that are typical in educational settings. To address this gap, we follow a top-down approach: Based on an existing model of user acceptance, we specify the variables that are to be optimized by HCI research and outline the potential of wearable-based measuring instruments to quantitatively assess these parameters. Eventually, we point out related research gaps that should be addressed by future research.

**Keywords:** Wearable-based evaluation · Extended Reality (XR) · Collaborative learning · User acceptance · Ease of use · Task-technology fit

## 1 Introduction

Extended Reality (XR) technologies allow to visualize learning material as virtual augmentations of the real world (Augmented or Mixed Reality) as well as in completely computer-generated environments (Virtual Reality). Various interaction modalities are offered by sensors capturing gestures, gaze, or voice that are integrated in XR technologies such as head-mounted displays. Leveraging this variety of visualization and interaction techniques, students and teachers could be provided with a customized access to a joint learning space. Thus, XR technologies hold great potential to support co-located as well as distributed learning and teaching.

While in theory the combination of different devices, visualization, and interaction techniques to enhance educational settings appears very promising, the practical application of such systems is still limited. In order to detect the barriers that are preventing


Published by Springer Nature Switzerland AG 2022
C. Ardito et al. (Eds.): INTERACT 2021, LNCS 13198, pp. 443–452, 2022.
https://doi.org/10.1007/978-3-030-98388-8_40

the adoption of XR technologies in educational settings, the respective systems and their single features such as visual representations of learning contents need to be evaluated in real-world conditions throughout the development process. However, existing evaluation tools such as questionnaires, observations, and performance measurements restrict evaluations to controlled experiments and artificial use cases. This makes them insufficient for evaluating long-time, exploratory, and collaborative tasks as typical in educational contexts.

Thus, there is a high need for advanced tools that allow evaluating collaborative XR spaces quantitatively and objectively under real-world conditions. Since many wearables are developed for capturing physiological and behavioral data under real-world conditions, they appear well-suited for this purpose.

As a first step, we specify the parameters to be assessed by such advanced evaluation tools and discuss their operationalization considering wearable-based measuring instruments.

## 2 Background

### 2.1 XR Technologies

Extended Reality (XR) environments integrate virtual components to different extents. As such, the term XR fulfills two functions. First, it serves as an umbrella term for Mixed Reality (MR) environments consisting of real and virtual objects (i.e., Augmented Reality (AR) and Augmented Virtuality (AV)) as well as entirely virtual environments (VR), that are allocated along the so-called Reality-Virtuality continuum [21, 22]. Second, the term XR can be used to describe a new form of reality linking mixed and virtual realities to a joint XR space.

This joint space can be accessed with different devices such as head-mounted displays (HMDs) or handheld displays (HHDs) like smartphones and tablets. Further XR technologies such as Powerwalls or CAVEs (Cave Automatic Virtual Environment) [5] project virtual objects into a specific environment set up in the real world.

### 2.2 Benefits of XR-Supported Learning

Recent research has focused on the development of systems supporting collaboration of co-located as well as distributed people in joint XR spaces (e.g., [19]). As such, people that are actually located at different physical sites may meet in the same XR environment. In educational settings, such technologies could be applied to connect students and teachers to support distant and hybrid teaching which became particularly relevant during the Covid-19 pandemic.

MR technologies allow users to simultaneously interact with both real and virtual objects. Thus, contextual learning could be enhanced as students have necessary information at hand without having to shift their focus. Especially in natural sciences, XR could further foster the understanding of usually invisible processes and details as these could be visualized as virtual overlays. In the context of experiments, both MR and VR technologies offer crucial benefits: In MR, students could see processes evoking real-world phenomena and in VR, the whole experiment could be virtualized. As such, experiments would not have to be set up in reality but could be repeated several times in different environmental conditions without consuming material costs. Due to security issues, students are usually not allowed to conduct experiments on their own. In VR, these risks could be minimized, fostering independent practice and study. Eventually, students could be provided with a customized access to the joint XR space that allows to adjust their perspectives according to their individual needs.

### 2.3 Evaluating XR Environments

Today, XR environments are mainly evaluated via questionnaires, observation, and performance measurements. However, these techniques are not applicable for evaluations under real-world conditions.

Especially in long-time studies, data collected with questionnaires could be distorted by serial position effects. These include so-called primacy and recency effects: the tendency to remember first and last items better while recalling a previously presented list of items [23]. These effects may be prevented by posing questionnaires right after the single experimental conditions to be compared. Indeed, many studies interrupt the XR experience after each experimental condition (e.g., different input modalities). This interruption, however, restricts studies to very artificial use cases in laboratory settings and may decrease immersion which is considered one of XR's main benefits. Besides, data gathered with subjective evaluation tools like questionnaires may be distorted by participants rating with a central tendency or rating systematically too high or too low. Objective evaluation methods such as observation may overcome this issue but are highly time-consuming and thus limit the number of participants. Further, qualitative feedback impedes aggregating results to draw general conclusions. Although performance measurements such as task completion time and error rates provide quantitative results in an objective way, they are not applicable for exploratory tasks.

Considering collaborative settings, a further evaluation aspect comes into play. Current studies focusing on multi-user XR environments are mostly limited to two participants where the evaluation mainly focuses on each collaborator's individual performance or experience. Variables related to the actual collaboration such as the detection of collaboration patterns in [26] are considered very rarely. In [26] the respective data were collected via video-recording, taking notes, and semi-structured group interviews which again make data analysis time-consuming.

## 3 Increasing User Acceptance of XR Technologies

In order to increase future utilization and user acceptance (UA) of XR-supported learning systems, we discuss how sensors incorporated in wearables can support evaluating these systems in real-world conditions (i.e., during the performance of exploratory, collaborative tasks). To do so, we follow a top-down approach: Based on an existing model of UA, we specify the variables that are to be increased by HCI research and outline how wearables and sensors could be used to assess the respective parameters.

### 3.1 Modeling User Acceptance

Previous research proposed various models that aim to explain UA and future utilization behavior. A very popular model is the technology acceptance model (TAM) which was introduced by Davis in 1986 [7] and modified into various versions since then. According to TAM, ease of use and usefulness are the core factors to influence UA. Assuming that user acceptance is highly influenced by the degree to which the technology matches the demands of the task, Goodhue and Thompson [12] introduced the task-technology fit (TTF) model in 1995. In 1999, Dishaw and Strong [9] suggested to combine TAM and TTF due to the different acceptance behavior aspects captured by the two models. Regarding the prediction of UA, they found that integrating TTF in TAM explains a higher amount of variance than either of them alone.

HCI research is concerned about the development of visualization and interaction techniques that increase UA. However, UA is not solely affected by system design and hard to measure early in the development process. Hence, the impact of a particular interaction or visualization feature on UA cannot be measured directly by increases in UA. Instead, HCI research should focus on the optimization and evaluation of single variables that are contributing to UA.

In line with Davis [8], we specify ease of use as TAM's core latent variable to be increased and therefore evaluated by HCI research. Further, it needs to be assessed which visualization and interaction techniques are suited best for different tasks in collaborative learning settings. For these reasons, we propose that HCI research should focus on measuring and optimizing the latent variables TTF and ease of use. To assess whether or not a system increases ease of use or TTF, the two variables need to be operationalized with advanced evaluation tools.

### 3.2 Operationalizing *Ease of Use* and *TTF* with Wearable-Based Measuring Instruments

**Ease of Use.** A technology's ease of use is associated with the absence of effort [8]. Today, effort is mainly assessed by questionnaires that are posed during or after the XR experience. However, as described above, this approach may result in distorted data. Thus, instead of assessing effort subjectively at certain points in time, we suggest to assess different kinds of effort such as temporal, cognitive, and physical effort individually for each student and throughout the experience. While temporal effort is usually measured by time, assessing cognitive and physical effort requires more sophisticated tools. Based on findings of previous research, we suggest to use sensors incorporated in wearables to capture cognitive and physical effort throughout XR experiences.

*Cognitive Effort.* Indicators of cognitive effort that could be measured with wearables include changes in the pupil diameter (e.g., [13]), heart rate (e.g., [4]), and heart rate variability (e.g., [14]).

Research on the influence of cognitive effort on the pupil diameter dates back to 1964 when Hess and Polt [13] found, that the pupil diameter increases with problem difficulty. In subsequent papers such as [1] and [16] the assumption of the pupil diameter to indicate cognitive effort was supported further.

However, outside controlled laboratory conditions, a major challenge in assessing cognitive effort via pupil dilation concerns the separation of pupil dilation evoked by cognitive effort from the one evoked by light. Assuming that an increase in cognitive effort leads to changes in the pupil diameter signal that occur in an abrupt manner and are larger than those caused by light, Marshall [20] introduced the index of cognitive activity (ICA). Due to the lack of complete documentation of the ICA, Duchowski et al. [11] developed the index of pupillary activity (IPA) which is based on the general idea proposed by Marshall [20]. To assess cognitive effort, both algorithms measure how frequently abrupt changes occur within a pupil diameter signal. To do so, a wavelet transformation is applied to the pupil diameter signal. After the removal of wavelet coefficients below a certain threshold, the number of remaining wavelet coefficients is considered to distinguish time sequences of low and high cognitive effort.

Existing eye tracking technology includes head-mounted as well as remote systems. To maintain the user's mobility, head-mounted solutions should be applied in XR environments rather than stationary remote eye trackers. For example, Lindlbauer et al. [18] equipped an HMD with eye trackers for continuous calculation of the IPA and introduced a system that adapts itself in a dynamic fashion according to the current environmental conditions, task, and internal state of the user.

Besides the pupil diameter, cognitive effort may also be assessed based on heart beats. Both, the heart rate and heart rate variability (HRV) are determined by sequences of heart beats that are usually captured by electrocardiograms. In XR settings, the respective data could be obtained using photoplethysmography (PPG) sensors that are incorporated in wristbands: PPG sensors constantly emit green light and detect pulse waves by measuring the amount of reflected light. In this context, the HRV describes how strong the heart rate varies and thus indicates to what extent the organism is able to adjust its heart rate according to its current state and activity. Hence, a decreasing HRV could be associated with increasing cognitive effort (e.g., [14]), while the heart rate was found to generally increase with cognitive effort (e.g., [4]).

*Physical Effort.* Concerning physical effort, we distinguish between effort related to active motion of different body parts and constant muscle activity resulting in fatigue.

In order to minimize the physical effort that is required to reach and interact with learning contents, the motion of different body parts could be tracked by accelerometers, gyroscopes, and magnetometers (also referred to as inertial measurement units (IMUs)) that are for instance attached to the legs, arms, or upper body. An example of human motion assessment using IMUs that are attached to different parts of the body was given by Saggio et al. [25].

In order to lower the physical effort caused by interaction techniques, especially in-air gestures should be evaluated with respect to the physical fatigue they are causing. Muscle activity and fatigue in the arm may be assessed with electromyography (EMG) sensors such as presented by Papakostas et al. [24] who attached wearable EMG sensors to triceps and deltoid and applied machine learning to the data collected in order to detect physical fatigue as reported by participants.

*Flow.* Following the theory of flow [6], the design of XR learning environments should not aim to reduce effort to zero but rather to achieve a balance between task demands and the students' abilities throughout the experience. Hence, insights on changing levels of effort should be used to adjust the learning environment according to the users' needs. To do so, it needs to be researched how someone's optimal level of cognitive effort can be identified and tracked throughout the task. A model for the evaluation of flow based on different physiological indicators in VR was presented by Bian et al. [2].

Since levels of effort may change over time, we further encourage the consideration of learning effects (i.e., the speed at which effort decreases) to estimate future effort.

**TTF.** The extent to which a technology supports the completion of a task is referred to as TTF [12]. In [9], UA was assessed via questions and TTF was computed as the interaction of task and technology characteristics. However, this approach is not applicable for assessing TTF of single system features early in the development process. In fact, we aim at predicting a technology's contribution to UA without measuring UA.

Although TTF is associated with the support of performance, common indicators of performance such as task completion time and error rates cannot be considered to assess TTF for exploratory, collaborative tasks for which it is hard to define start and end points as well as (in)correct outcomes. Instead, the collection of data describing the students' individual and group behavior could be considered to assess TTF in XR environments. The respective data could be collected using different sensors incorporated in wearable devices such as gyroscopes, accelerometers, magnetometers, as well as eye tracking and event logging.

Apart from measuring the pupil diameter, eye trackers can be used to capture gaze patterns consisting of so-called fixations and saccades: A fixation describes a state in which the gaze is fixed on a certain area of interest, whereas shifting the gaze between two fixations is referred to as a saccade. In order to identify fixations and saccades, the single gaze points returned by eye trackers are analyzed with respect to their position and timestamp such that subsequent gaze points that are close to each other are grouped to a fixation [10]. In educational environments the analysis of students' gaze patterns and features such as fixation duration, saccade length, or number of fixations and saccades could provide valuable insight on their understanding. For instance, Ishimaru et al. [15] found that students with different levels of comprehension pay attention to different parts of a physics textbook while completing different task types.

As user behavior in XR environments is not only characterized by the small-scale behavior captured by gaze patterns, but also by large-scale behavior including movements in space and interactions with virtual objects, the evaluation of XR spaces should consider this behavior as well.

Recent research captured behavioral data in VR [17] and MR [3] scenarios to support the evaluation of user behavior on-site. Kloiber et al. [17] tracked the motion of HMDs and controllers used by single participants completing an assembly task in VR. In order to facilitate the detection of anomalies in task solving and behavioral changes after repetition, they visualize the respective head and hand movements as 3D trajectories in the VR environment. Similarly, Büschel et al. [3] visualize motion trajectories of tablets and HMDs of multiple collaborators during tablet-based spatial interaction and a multi-player game in MR. Further, they augment the MR scene with 2D event timelines, scatterplots, and heatmaps to support the visual analysis of user interactions and behavior.

While these approaches allow the automated collection of data throughout the experience, the analysis of the behavioral data is still highly time-consuming. In order to efficiently compare how well different XR environments are suited for different educational tasks, the approach should be extended with advanced data analysis techniques that allow computing TTF scores according to task-specific quality criteria. The respective task taxonomies and quality criteria remain to be defined by future research.

### 3.3 Future Research Directions

As described above, the evaluation of XR environments could be enhanced by several wearables and incorporated sensors. Before applying these tools to complex real-world scenarios, further research should address the following issues:

**Task Taxonomy.** In order to leverage the variety of visualization and interaction techniques offered in XR environments, it needs to be investigated which technologies are suited best for different educational settings and tasks. To research which devices (e.g., HHDs or HMDs), which degree of virtuality (e.g., MR or VR), and input modalities should be considered for which educational setting, a task taxonomy needs to be established describing XR-supported learning scenarios with respect to their social form (e.g., group or individual work) and task type.

**Quality Criteria.** Based on this taxonomy, the suitability of different XR environments should be assessed. Respective quality criteria are required to evaluate whether certain technologies support the different task categories of the taxonomy. These quality criteria should be based on quantitatively measurable parameters that indicate whether the application of certain XR technologies is supportive or not.

**Validation.** The wearables and sensors presented in this paper offer great potential to support the quantitative evaluation of collaborative XR spaces. Before such advanced evaluation tools can be applied in real-world conditions, they need to be validated extensively against existing, well-validated tools in controlled experiments. In this context, it should be investigated whether the results of existing and new evaluation tools correlate. Further, available wearables and sensors should be compared with respect to sensitivity and accuracy.

**Implementation.** As outlined above, a key benefit of XR-supported learning concerns the customized access students and teachers could be equipped with. In order to provide users with optimal experience, support features should be added and removed dynamically according to their individual needs. To evaluate the effectiveness of such features, data captured by various sensors need to be accessed and sent to the XR application in real time. Future research should further aim at facilitating the pre-study calibration of respective wearables and sensors for different users to reduce time overheads in large-scale studies.

**Data Analysis.** Another crucial research question refers to the analysis and interpretation of data captured with different devices. Physiological data are expected to vary highly among users. To ensure the comparability of measurements, the data must be normalized and analyzed with appropriate methods subsequent to the elimination of sensor noise.

## 4 Conclusions

In this paper we outline the potential of wearable-based measuring instruments to quantitatively evaluate collaborative XR spaces in real-world conditions. As such, our work is a first step towards investigating HCI-related impediments to the application of XR technologies in real-world settings such as educational environments.

Starting from the integrated TAM/TTF model, we specify ease of use and TTF to be the variables that are to be optimized by new visualization and interaction techniques. Due to the lack of evaluation techniques that are able to assess these variables in real-world conditions, we explore the operationalization of these variables with advanced assessment tools considering wearable devices.

In order to assess ease of use via the absence of effort, we distinguish between physical and cognitive effort. Based on previous research we encourage the usage of eye trackers and PPG sensors to capture cognitive effort via pupil diameter and heart beats. Physical effort could be assessed via motion that is captured by IMUs placed on different parts of the body as well as with EMG sensors capturing muscle activity. To assess TTF via user behavior during task performance, we consider both small-scale user behavior such as gaze patterns and large-scale user behavior like interactions and motion patterns captured by eye-trackers, IMUs, and event logging.

**Acknowledgements.** Funded by the Deutsche Forschungsgemeinschaft (DFG, German Research Foundation) – 252408385 – IRTG 2057.

## References

1. Beatty, J.: Task-evoked pupillary responses, processing load, and the structure of processing resources. Psychol. Bull. **91**(2), 276–292 (1982). https://doi.org/10.1037/0033-2909.91.2.276
2. Bian, Y., et al.: A framework for physiological indicators of flow in VR games: construction and preliminary evaluation. Pers. Ubiquit. Comput. **20**(5), 821–832 (2016). https://doi.org/10.1007/s00779-016-0953-5
3. Büschel, W., Lehmann, A., Dachselt, R.: MIRIA: a mixed reality toolkit for the in-situ visualization and analysis of spatio-temporal interaction data. In: Proceedings of the 2021 CHI Conference on Human Factors in Computing Systems, pp. 1–15. ACM (2021). https://doi.org/10.1145/3411764.3445651
4. Cranford, K.N., Tiettmeyer, J.M., Chuprinko, B.C., Jordan, S., Grove, N.P.: Measuring load on working memory: the use of heart rate as a means of measuring chemistry students' cognitive load. J. Chem. Educ. **91**(5), 641–647 (2014). https://doi.org/10.1021/ed400576n
5. Cruz-Neira, C., Sandin, D.J., DeFanti, T.A.: Surround-screen projection-based virtual reality: the design and implementation of the CAVE. In: Proceedings of the 20th Annual Conference on Computer Graphics and Interactive Techniques, pp. 135–142. ACM (1993). doi: https://doi.org/10.1145/166117.166134

6. Csikszentmihalyi, M.: Flow and the Foundations of Positive Psychology. The Collected Works of Mihaly Csikszentmihalyi. Springer, Dordrecht (2014). https://doi.org/10.1007/978-94-017-9088-8
7. Davis, F.D.: A technology acceptance model for empirically testing new end-user information systems: theory and results. Ph.D. dissertation, MIT, Cambridge, MA, USA (1986)
8. Davis, F.D.: On the relationship between HCI and technology acceptance research. In: Zhang, P., Galletta, D. (eds.) Human-Computer Interaction and Management Information Systems: Foundations. Advances in Management Information Systems, vol. 5, pp. 395–401. M.E. Sharpe, Armonk, NY, USA (2006)
9. Dishaw, M.T., Strong, D.M.: Extending the technology acceptance model with task–technology fit constructs. Inform. Manage. **36**(1), 9–21 (1999). https://doi.org/10.1016/S0378-7206(98)00101-3
10. Duchowski, A.T.: Eye Tracking Methodology. Theory and Practice. 3rd edn. Springer, Cham (2017). https://doi.org/10.1007/978-3-319-57883-5
11. Duchowski, A.T., et al.: The index of pupillary activity: measuring cognitive Load vis-à-vis task difficulty with pupil oscillation. In: Proceedings of the 2018 CHI Conference on Human Factors in Computing Systems, pp. 1–13. ACM (2018). https://doi.org/10.1145/3173574.3173856
12. Goodhue, D.L., Thompson, R.L.: Task-technology fit and individual performance. MIS Q. **19**(2), 213–236 (1995). https://doi.org/10.2307/249689
13. Hess, E.H., Polt, J.M.: Pupil size in relation to mental activity during simple problem-solving. Science **143**(3611), 1190–1192 (1964). https://doi.org/10.1126/science.143.3611.1190
14. Hillmert, M., Bergmüller, A., Minow, A., Raggatz, J., Böckelmann, I.: Psychophysiologische Beanspruchungskorrelate während kognitiver Belastung. Zentralblatt für Arbeitsmedizin, Arbeitsschutz und Ergonomie **70**(4), 149–163 (2020). https://doi.org/10.1007/s40664-020-00384-9
15. Ishimaru, S., Bukhari, S.S., Heisel, C., Kuhn, J., Dengel, A.: Towards an intelligent textbook: eye gaze based attention extraction on materials for learning and instruction in physics. In: Proceedings of the 2016 ACM International Joint Conference on Pervasive and Ubiquitous Computing: Adjunct, pp. 1041–1045. ACM (2016). https://doi.org/10.1145/2968219.2968566
16. Kahneman, D., Beatty, J.: Pupil diameter and load on memory. Science **154**(3756), 1583–1585 (1966). https://doi.org/10.1126/science.154.3756.1583
17. Kloiber, S., et al.: Immersive analysis of user motion in VR applications. Vis. Comput. **36**(10–12), 1937–1949 (2020). https://doi.org/10.1007/s00371-020-01942-1
18. Lindlbauer, D., Feit, A.M., Hilliges, O.: Context-aware online adaptation of mixed reality interfaces. In: Proceedings of the 32nd Annual ACM Symposium on User Interface Software and Technology, pp. 147–160. ACM (2019). https://doi.org/10.1145/3332165.3347945
19. Marks, S., White, D.: Multi-device collaboration in virtual environments. In: Proceedings of the 2020 4th International Conference on Virtual and Augmented Reality Simulations, pp. 35–38. ACM (2020). https://doi.org/10.1145/3385378.3385381
20. Marshall, S.P.: The index of cognitive activity: measuring cognitive workload. In: Proceedings of the IEEE 7th Conference on Human Factors and Power Plants, pp. 7–5–7–9. IEEE (2002). https://doi.org/10.1109/HFPP.2002.1042860
21. Milgram, P., Kishino, F.: A taxonomy of mixed reality visual displays. IEICE Trans. Inf. Syst. **77**(12), 1321–1329 (1994)
22. Milgram, P., Takemura, H., Utsumi, A., Kishino, F.: Augmented reality: a class of displays on the reality-virtuality continuum. In: Das, H. (ed.) Telemanipulator and Telepresence Technologies, vol. 2351, pp. 282–292. SPIE (1995). https://doi.org/10.1117/12.197321
23. Murdock, B.B.: The serial position effect of free recall. J. Exp. Psychol. **64**(5), 482–488 (1962). https://doi.org/10.1037/h0045106

24. Papakostas, M., Kanal, V., Abujelala, M., Tsiakas, K., Makedon, F.: Physical fatigue detection through emg wearables and subjective user reports – a machine learning approach towards adaptive rehabilitation. In: Proceedings of the 12th ACM International Conference on PErvasive Technologies Related to Assistive Environments, pp. 475–481. ACM (2019). https://doi.org/10.1145/3316782.3322772
25. Saggio, G., Tombolini, F., Ruggiero, A.: Technology-based complex motor tasks assessment: a 6-dof inertial-based system versus a gold-standard optoelectronic-based one. IEEE Sens. J. **21**(2), 1616–1624 (2021). https://doi.org/10.1109/JSEN.2020.3016642
26. Wells, T., Houben, S.: CollabAR – investigating the mediating role of mobile AR interfaces on co-located group collaboration. In: Proceedings of the 2020 CHI Conference on Human Factors in Computing Systems, pp. 1–13. ACM (2020). https://doi.org/10.1145/3313831.3376541

# Ears on My Back - Experiencing the Soundscape Without Hearing

Danzhu Li[1,2](✉) and Gerrit van der Veer[1,2,3](✉)

[1] Luxun Academy of Fine Arts (LAFA), Liaoning, China
lidanzhu@me.com, gerrit@acm.org
[2] University of Twente, Enschede, Netherlands
[3] Vrije Universiteit Amsterdam, Amsterdam, Netherlands

**Abstract.** This paper analyses the artistic dimensions of fine art, focusing on film and performances, and the aspects of experience by the audience of this type of art. We analyze the contribution of sound, and consider a way to, either translate relevant aspects of sound to other modalities, or use other modalities to artistically enhance the experience. We provide a conceptual framework of dynamic and interactive types of art and we discuss the development of the relation between visual art and sound and the concept of experience of art. We discuss the problems of experience if sound is not available and consider the translation of sound to other modalities. We propose an experimental design, "Ears on my Back" and show the initial development of a garment that aims at experiencing relevant sound aspects in alternative modalities. Finally, we show the challenges and opportunities of multidisciplinary collaboration in this domain.

**Keywords:** Fine Arts · Experience · Soundscape · Translating modalities · Interdisciplinary creation · Practice-triggered research · Stakeholders

## 1 Introduction

We teach artists. Many of our students focus on visual arts. They aim to create dynamic pieces of art (e.g., film, animation, digital video, drama, or multimedia art) or interactive art (VR art, dynamic installation art, participative performances). Generally, a dynamic artwork may include the following main elements, intended to develop an audio-visual world for the audience to live in [1]:

- Story (script, storyboard);
- Production and direction;
- Photography (camera position, composition, golden ratio, 3D means to increase the visual dimension and the depth of the picture, equipment, etc.);
- Movement (camera motion, screenage dynamics, multi-camera body tracking, frame rate);
- Art design or Mise-en-scène (scene design and selection, space, lighting, set dressing, wardrobe, makeup, props, visual effects, etc.);


Published by Springer Nature Switzerland AG 2022
C. Ardito et al. (Eds.): INTERACT 2021, LNCS 13198, pp. 453–473, 2022.
https://doi.org/10.1007/978-3-030-98388-8_41

- Sound and music (transmitting information, rendering emotion, actor characteristics);
- Acting and performance (voice, lines, expression, and performance of the actor or character);
- Editing and postproduction (rhythm control, special effect production, etc.).

Cinema film usually elaborates these important elements in detail, and there is a professional team responsible for the special work [2]. But in art schools, due to the limited conditions, we tend to simplify the team and try to shoot and perform by means of experiment and practice. Simple backgrounds and props express the plot. For example, in Fig. 1, the performers wear different masks to tell the audience that they play animals. In Fig. 2, an iron fence symbolizes the prison, separating the two worlds of freedom and imprisonment. Similarly, theaters often use simplified, and even exaggerated artistic treatment, such as drama, opera, ballet and so on. They use media that support their visuals, often sound, to match/support/explain Context and Story.

**Fig. 1.** Performance by LAFA students

Sound montage in film is an organic combination of various forms and relations between sound and picture. The use of sound montage both as an editing technique and as a theory has been present in filmmaking for nearly 100 years [3]. The application of sound composition in movies requires attention to various aspects [4]:

- The relationship between sound and picture (unity of sound and picture, separation of sound and picture, antithesis of sound and picture);
- Mixed use of sound (the sound of multiple sound sources is interwoven with the picture);
- The subjective use of sound (including subjective sound, pure subjective sound, and pure freehand sound)
- Sound editing.

**Fig. 2.** Scene from the drama school, Dalian University

## 2 Film and Sound

The function of the film score is to control the rhythm of stories, render emotions and transitions (connecting the preceding and the following), and symbolic significance. The audience's experience is manipulated by sound as well as images. The volume, pitch and rhythm of the soundtrack will affect the story and the audience's experience. This is how sound works [5].

In the silent film era, filmmakers did try to tell stories in lens language (visual montage). Since the sound film, the function of soundtrack has been developed by artists. Sound montage provides endless possibilities. For artistic creation, the director will no longer solely focus on the lens to convey some basic facts. E.g., actors can directly reveal class attributes, religion, occupation, prejudice, and other information with their line's performances that include rhythm, melody, dynamics, pitch, and other non-textual aspects [6].

However, people who can't hear will lose important experiences. And this experience is an aesthetic set up, designed by artists or directors. They even use audience's response to test and verify their intuitions or predict. An early classic case: Eisenstein's belief in his ability to predict the collective viewing behavior of his audience is staggering. At the time (1938) he was making "Alexander Nevsky", the scientific investigation of eye movements was still very much in its infancy. He predicted that viewer gaze should exhibit attentional synchrony during the sequence, where viewers would fixate and whether their gaze followed the patterns transcribed in his diagram (Fig. 3). Eisenstein's predictions sequence is unique for the time, as he emphasizes the role played by audio in guiding visual attention [7].

Sound montage in modern filmmaking means the use of sound clips from multiple sources to create a single sound or audio track. Sounds from a variety of sources, when

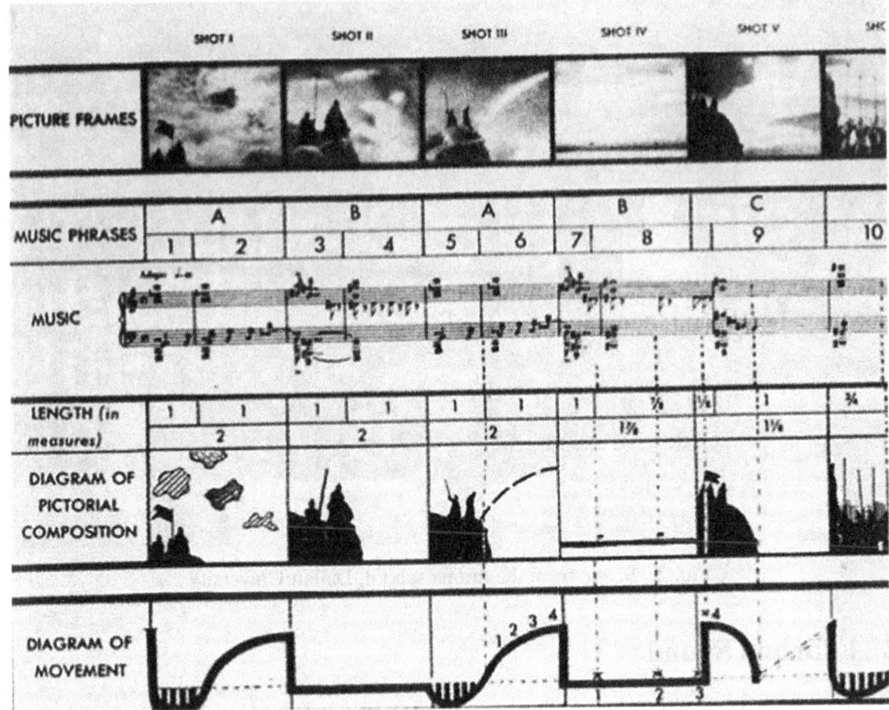


**Fig. 3.** Diagram of audiovisual correspondences in Sergei Eisenstein's Alexander Nevsky (1938). Content of each row, from top: Picture frames, music phrases, musical score, duration (in measures), diagram of pictorial composition, and diagram of eye movement. https://engagger.wordpress.com/2016/12/31/sergei-eisenstein-alexander-nevsky/

layered together, may create various moods or effects or even immersive experiences. Creative sound design is the key to both the score and the film, enlarging the potential multidimensionality and supporting meaningful and memorable audience perception [8].

Understanding the soundtrack is not a necessary skill mainly for directors, but the cooperation with soundtrack masters is an important factor in the film. For example, the cooperation between Italian soundtrack master Ennio Morricone and his high school classmate, director Sergio Leone: "Once upon a Time in America". Audiences experience the accurate marriage of picture and music. The scene and the soundtrack complement each other and depict the characters' emotions and intentions delicately. Some film critics even gave such praise that the classic soundtrack has increased the fame of the film itself. In particular, the use of the musical instrument Panpipe is acknowledged to be impressive of Once upon a Time in America.

In summary, sound and music play a connecting role in the structure of dynamic visual works. And the supplement, deepening, contrast and rendering of sound to the picture are indispensable parts of film and drama. We consider relation between the story and concepts we represent in fine arts, and the experience of the intended audience.

### 2.1 Story and Context

Film appreciation is a compulsory course in art colleges. Studying and analyzing classic works can inspire students' creation and inspiration. They will consciously value collaboration in their future careers. The authors regularly analyze and discuss masters' works with students in teaching. We teach them to consider aspects of a work of art in relation to the audience:

- The **Story** of the artwork. This often includes, either or bothl:
  - One or more **Actors** (human actors, puppets, animated objects, or embodiment) with distinctive appearance (posture, face, clothing), and character (movement, interactions, intentions or tendencies, and speech or other types of communicating);
  - A **Plot**, being a story line, or a set of patterns or a grammar of events, or a game with interaction rules.

- The **Context,** the **Background** against all is positioned. This aims at creating a general atmosphere and a background for the story. Often, the context is ornate with **Props,** elements that may be moved or used in actions, or potential agents in the story when we want to trigger an unexpected event.

  Both the story and the context often area mixture of visual and sound elements.

### 2.2 Experience

- Based on Vyas [9] we consider the audience's experience as consisting, in a holistic way, of four aspects. We are aware of, and the artist aims at, the audience of artworks will:
- Attribute **meaning** to the work of art as a whole and to elements like progress in the story and actions of the agents, and the background with any changes and the props including events caused by their use and by their actions;
- Feel being **attracted** (or not) to elements in the story or in the con text, resulting in focusing to these, or turning away;
- Understanding **emotions** in elements of the story and the context, and being moved by these themselves;
- Will develop a **tendency to act**, resulting in focusing on a location or movement in the context or a prop, on a specific agent or its action, on an element in the activities (a pattern, a communication exchange), or on the audience or a specific person or group in the audience. Focusing may exist in directing (or focusing) eyes or ears, turning the head or body, speaking of applauding, etc.

For each individual member of an audience, all of this occurs a single event or state of experience.

## 3 If Sound is not Available

Sometimes, the intended audience of our art is a context where sound is not an option (e.g., watching a video without disturbing others, being engaged in another activity where audio signals should be received undisturbed), sometimes a member of the audience has hearing problems.

The artist may not be able to provide audio: one of our students is deaf from birth. He exchanges verbal communication with non-deaf others, including the clients and audience of his art, by texting. He is fully aware of the modality he misses, both in experiencing the art of his colleagues, and in creating his own work.

In fact, working with him triggered our analysis of the role of the sound modality in fine arts production and experiencing, and provided cues for a translation approach of which this paper is the first expression. This are the first steps of a work in progress. The translation does not only aim at replacing sound though: it allows new artistic opportunities: to highlight sound (even literally), to provide speaking actors and musicians with novel colors to their creation (again, even literally) [10].

## 4 A Challenge: Translating the Sound of Art

Sound often is an important aspect of an artistic creation or performance:

- Regarding the **Context** – **Background** sounds of weather and physical environment (waves of water, wind in trees, rain showers) support the experience of meaning and emotions. Sound related to **Props** (background traffic, a ticking clock, voices of people in the crowd, noise of walking, moving doors, and window shutters) support awareness of "other" things going on.
- The **Story**, the intended focal part of the creation, is often mainly based on the behavior of **Actors.** Speech is a base of the story line, conveying meaning (mainly through the text, but additional through patterns in pitch and dynamics), and emotions (rhythm, dynamics, and pitch). Sounds that trigger the awareness and experience of a relevant event in the **Plot** may be generated by, or through, props.

### 4.1 Promising Alternative Modalities

For translating sound, we need to consider, both, the aspects of experience that we want to preserve (especially meaning and emotions), and the role of a sound in the artistic creation (the story, the context). At each moment in time, the elements of sound in a performance for an individual member of the audience can be characterized by the following elements:

- Perceived location of origin (3 dimensional for a member of the audience, plus the perceived distance as an extra dimension, like visual perception, for a freely moving individual);
- Loudness at the location of the listener, measurable in Decibels (Db);
- Pitch characteristics of the sound, measurable in a standard scale of frequency ranges Hertz (Hz).

Together this characterization is labeled the **Soundscape** [11]. In Marine Biology, this concept is shown to represent the most important perception space for deep sea animals, who mainly live in an environment where visual information is scarce and less relevant [12].

Of the modalities to consider translating the soundscape, **Vision** seems the first option. However, we would not like to spoil the experience that is triggered by the original visual part of a performance. Translating speech to **subtitles** below the main area of the visual performance is a standard addition, used when movies are created for an audience that might not be fully understanding the original language. However, as we have shown above, subtitling loses all information about rhythm, dynamics, and pitch. Providing vague **visual cues alongside** the main area are already applied when a visual screen format deviated from the golden ration that fits the standard area of human vision, e.g., when a vertical (smartphone generated) image is the source of the image. We consider this as an additional possibility and even an artistic opportunity, not a complete replacement for elements of sound to sufficiently provide triggers for the whole experience as possible by the soundscape [13].

The other modality that seems doable is **Tactile** stimulation. If we apply this stimulation at different positions on the audience's body, we may provide information on frequency in Hz (not as precise as the human ear can do it, but at least in a small number of frequency ranges), loudness in Db, and location (in the same as the ears would).

## 5 An Artistic Experimental Design: Ears on My Back

Based on the above, we designed "Ears on my Back", a wearable device, first aiming to construct a simulated soundscape to support the experience of deaf people to perceive the changes of sound in pitch, orientation, and strength with tactile perception. See Fig. 4. Figure 5 provides a description of the basic hardware that is tentatively location in the jacket sketched in Fig. 4.

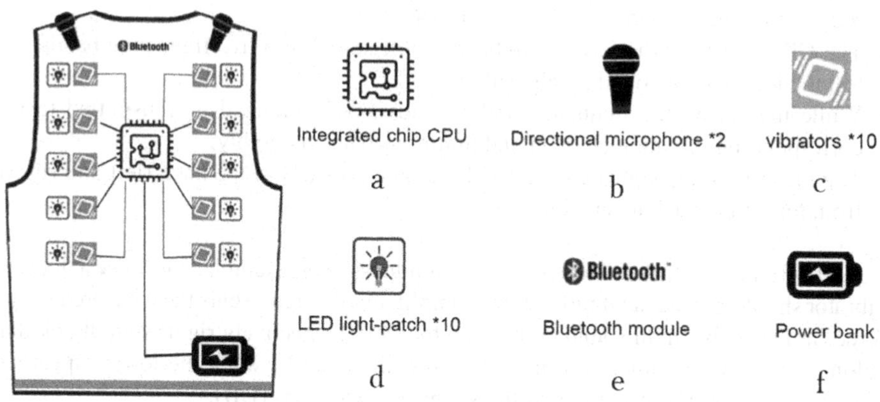


**Fig. 4.** Design sketch of ears on my back jacket, with indicators of the basic hardware: a–f

Specifications of the basic hardware:

a. Integrated chip CPU: Filtering the audio source of the left and right soundtracks into 5 different frequency bands (0–150, 150–200, 200–250, 250–500, 500- 2000Hz). Processing and measure the loudness of each frequency band (dB). Sending instructions to the corresponding LED light-patch, as well as vibrator, trigger vibration and light-emitting.
b. Directional microphones (2): We use BOYA MM1 directional noise reduction microphone. Two microphones on the left and right resemble human ears. They are connected to CPU chips and transmit sound information to chips.
c. Vibrators (10): Vibrators send out vibration signals of strength and speed of vibration according to loudness of sound (dB).
d. LED light-patches (10): We use LED light-patch to display signal indication of different frequency bands. We set five colors to distinguish different frequency bands and loudness (From low to high, red, orange, yellow, green, blue).
e. Bluetooth Module: To detect the change of data, and for the user to be able to read audio information more intuitively, we integrate Bluetooth module on CPU and write a program software. Through the APP of mobile terminal (Android system), the change of decibel value can be observed.
f. Power Bank: The 20,000 mA portable power supply can support all programs from a few hours to a day (power consumption varies depending on the audio source signal), and the power bank is friendly and convenient to use and can be connected to the fixed power supply when needed (to use it continuously for a long time).

The working principle is as follows:

- When the power is turned on, the device will transmit the sound source to the central processing chip through two directional microphones, located in a way that they receive the same sound as the ears would do;
- The CPU can filter the left and right tracks of sound into five frequency bands and test the loudness of sound by algorithm;
- While measuring the frequency and loudness, the command is transmitted to the corresponding vibration element and luminous patch assembly;
- The location of the signal emitters will be on both sides of the back (left and right), from low at the back to shoulder level;

All vibrators give feedback based on loudness. For example, the lowest located vibrator should provide a vibration force (amplitude) that represents the measured sound force (in Decibels) of all sound emitted by the (left, respectively right) soundtrack that belongs to the video, filtered to measure only all sound between the lowest specified range, e.g.: 0–150 Hz; categorizing the strength in Decibels (DB):

i. 0–20 DB;
ii. 20–40 DB;
iii. 40–and over 60 DB.

The CPU will translate decibel ranges in levels to vibration force,

i. → 0 force;
ii. → just noticeable;
iii. → maximum acceptable force.

The actual decibel ranges need to be experimented to make sure these levels can be distinguished by people, and these are not experienced as hurting or annoying.

1) 0–150 Hz;
2) 150–200 Hz;
3) 200–250 Hz;
4) 250–500 Hz;
5) 500–2000 Hz.

We will experiment with changing the borders of the 5 frequency ranges depending on the type of sound that is relevant for a certain example. At the same time, the indicator light will change with the same levels as the vibration element. We use 10 LED light-patches to display signal indication of different frequency bands (left and right separately, for 5 different lights each side). We set five colors to distinguish different frequency bands and loudness (From low to high: red, orange, yellow, green, blue):

1) 0–150 Hz → red
2) 150–200 Hz → orange
3) 200–250 Hz → yellow
4) 250–500 Hz → green
5) 500–2000 Hz → blue

To be able to change ranges to enable to experience translated audio information more intuitively, we integrate Bluetooth modules on CPU and write program software. Through the APP of a mobile terminal (Android system), the change of decibel value can be done. See to the mobile phone interface in Fig. 5. When the experimenter enters the Ears on My Back program, the real-time frequency and loudness measurement data can be read.

Vibrators at location 1), 2), 3), 4), 5), should provide a vibration force (amplitude) that represents the measured sound force (in Decibels) of all sound emitted by the (left, respectively right) soundtrack that belongs to the video, filtered to measure only all sound between a specified range. Since the stories in our films or performances often feature human communication consisting of speech and/or music, we will start by trying suitable ranges based on [14].

### 5.1 Experimental Video Footage

We developed a setup combined with a series of video footage. To investigate the experience of our target audience, the hearing impaired, we have prepared a series of edited video materials (Fig. 6):

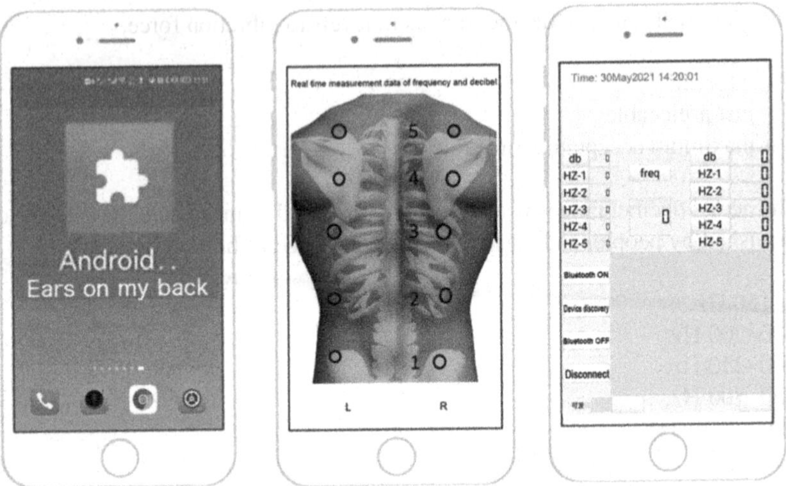


**Fig. 5.** APP interface design. Bluetooth connection to mobile terminal

**Fig. 6.** Testing video footage (first author's work "Tomorrow 2012"). Left picture without subtitles, right one with subtitles.

- A video with text as part of the story line and with some audible elements in the context;
- The same video without any sound and subtitles, to experience the reaction of deaf people when watching this video, and to find out what would be missing/changing the meaning of the text for a hearing audience;
- The same video without subtitles, where the user puts on the device to give vibration signal and/or alternative light signal stimulation outside the center of vision.
- The same video with Chinese or English subtitles, where at the same time, the experiencer is stimulated by vibration signals and light signals, translated to support experience and interpretation of the "sound".

The video materials we expect to select cover some scenes that a deaf artist hopes to experience in his life and work (according to our interviews with specific target characters). Our deaf students put forward that dubbing, and music are the most difficult to grasp when making a film. Based on this appeal, we chose a sample of a drama play with rich and varied sound clips, even including the interaction between the audience and the artist in the curtain call, and applause. We expect that our device may be able to give deaf people an alternative perception of soundscape, which we temporarily may call a Soundscape Perception Assistance, especially when allowing to feel the sound or combination of sounds formed or produced in live performance and similar immersive environment.

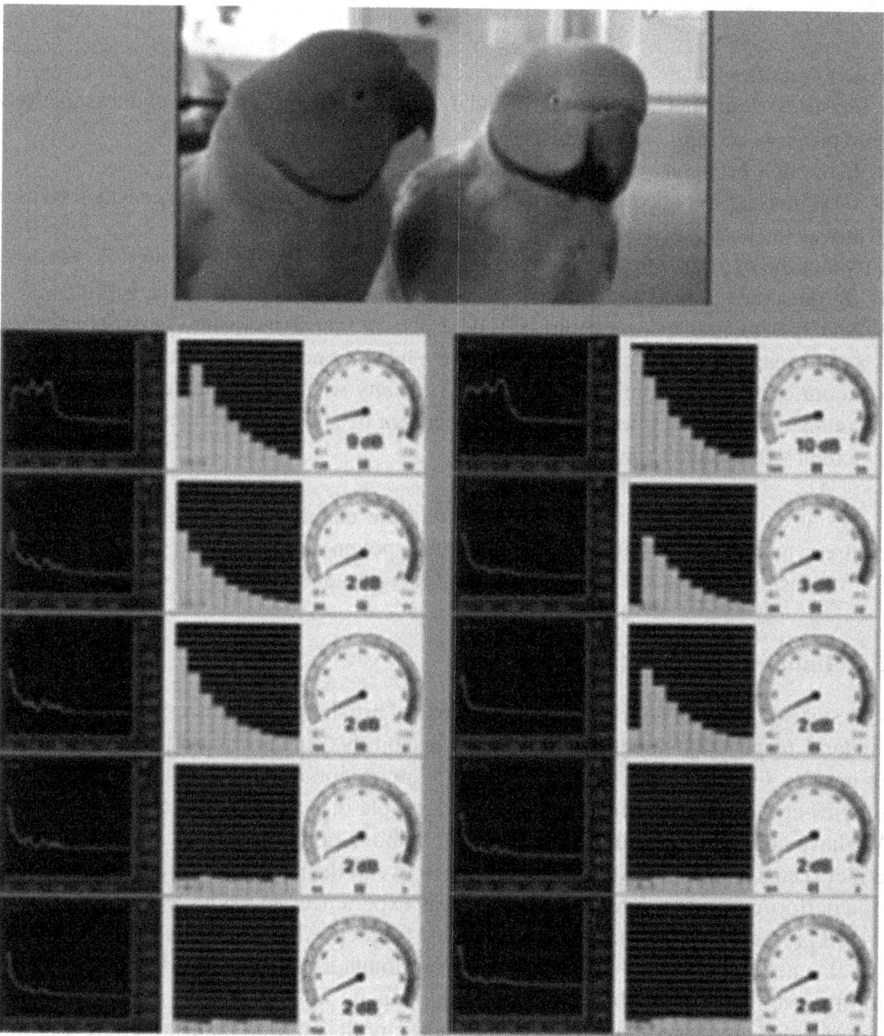

**Fig. 7.** Testing demos for volume and frequency of Parrot Dialogue.

In addition, we also focus on some specific acoustic environment and specific sounds of an acoustic environment. For example, the conversation between two cats, the communication between parrots, the passing of fire engines (Fig. 7). In recent years, many artists use various art forms to attack noise pollution. Our acoustic experience equipment has a special interpretation of these special acoustic environments. In a sense, when we wear "Ears on my Back" in some special acoustic environment, it seems that our auditory cognition is equal to that of the deaf, which is certainly interesting. We expect we will be able to discover the way that the various aspects of sound translation contribute to the experience:

- text (subtitles);
- emotions (loudness in Db, rhythm, and dynamics in the progress of loudness, melody in progress of frequency in Hz);
- distinction between voices (in Hz range);
- 3D soundscape context experience (in stereo, allowing 3D plus distance when the user moves the head / body).
- About the experimental subjects we intend to invite for or experiments:
- We presume subjects can view a video and to read and understand the subtitles.
- An experimental subject could be a deaf person that is motivated to experience the sound scape or a not deaf person wearing a headphone that mutes all sound;
- In our experiments, subjects should not hear any sound or be prevented to hear any sound (either by completely covering the ears or by showing the video on this person's screen without the sound transmitted).

Control groups my consist of people who are enabled to hear all sound. We will compare people who are able to understand the spoken dialogues and others who do not. For the last group we will investigate the effect of readable subtitling.

### 5.2 Initial Work Results and Summary

Our system has been developed in the context of artistic performances and in educating students (especially students with hearing disabilities) in showing artistic impressions in movies. Our focus is to make the artistic impression of sound of pieces of art (e.g., movies or theatre plays) intelligible to deaf people or people with hearing disabilities. We have conducted a preliminary test on the above process (see Fig. 10), and the test effect seems to work, though we will need to tweak the ranges: the applause at the end of a performance, translated to vibrators, was experienced in a pilot as "creepy".

At present, we need the best setting of test frequency band in terms of hardware, and we also need to get more feedback from experimenters after testing the whole process to improve. Next, we will integrate all the requisite modules to solve the problem of complicated circuit wires and occasional short circuit and power consumption. Then we will cooperate with the fashion designers of LAFA to make clothes. We want ears on my back to have a fashionable and attractive look, and we expect more viewers to try it.

## 6 Hardware Upgrade, Quantitative Testing and UX

After the first phase, we adjusted the hardware design. Figure 8 shows the Master Control Board (MPU) structure.

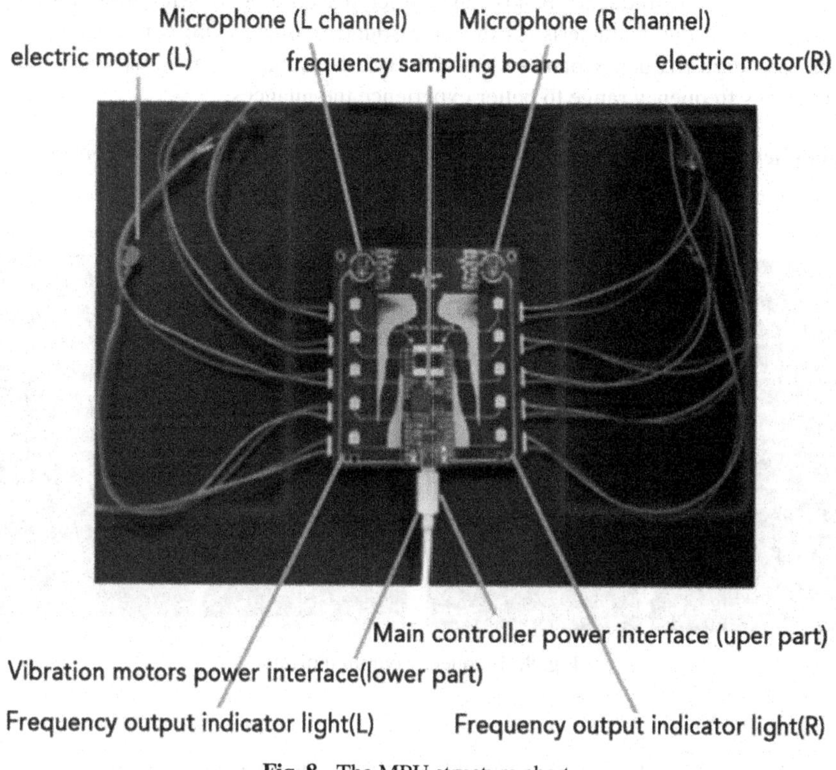


**Fig. 8.** The MPU structure chart

**The Upper Layer** is the core control board, which is mainly used in AI visual and auditory scenes. The built-in dual core 64-bit processor and a variety of hardware accelerators can easily carry out the preprocessing of voice direction scanning and voice data output.

**The Lower Layer** is the perceptual electric motor control and visual indication control board. With a built-in single core processor, power management and motor drive management unit. The data processed by the core control board is converted into electric motor control according to different decibels and frequency bands and displayed by corresponding indicator lights.

**Perception Electric Motor Controls,** 5 on the left and right sides, give vibration signal according to the decibel of different frequency band, to realize the perception of sound intensity.

**Microphones:** the directional microphone splits the sound source into left and right sound fields. Low power consumption, high SNR, high sensitivity, wide frequency response range, clear acquisition of sound source, accurate positioning.

**Frequency Acquisition:** mainly by the core control board built-in microphone array for acquisition. The frequency bands can be filtered according to different sound source. For example, if the characteristics of some sound frequency are concentrated in the middle and high frequency band (600–2000 Hz), the frequency band will be refined to adapt to this frequency range to better experience the nuances.

**Frequency Output Indicator:** 5 colorful LED on each side, flashing according to the frequency. The brightness and color can be adjusted flexibly (Fig. 9).

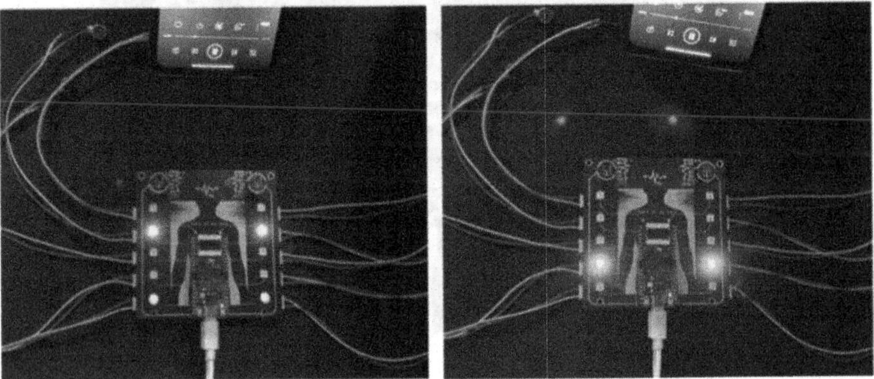

**Fig. 9.** Frequency output indicator

**Power Input** is divided into upper and lower layer. The upper layer is the power input of the core control board, and the lower layer is the input of the motor control board. The power supply voltage is 5 V. The common dual 5v2a output mobile power supply can supply power stably.

### 6.1 Principle Description

The core control board performs complex calculation and processing on the sound collected by the microphones on the left and right sides and the built-in microphone array on the core board, analyzes the time and frequency of the sound source by using Fourier transform algorithm, and then outputs it to the perceptual vibration motor on both sides of the main control board to realize the conversion of audio information to vibration signal, and indicator lights will display 5 corresponding filtered frequency bands. To show this clearly, we added an LED screen, so we can monitor the spectrum of different frequencies (Fig. 10).

### 6.2 Algorithm of Audio Processing: Fn = (n − 1) × Fs/N

FFT (fast Fourier transformation) is used in the audio processing system to convert the time domain signal into the frequency domain signal. In our work, the sound can be superimposed with multiple frequencies, but the signal cannot be directly processed to obtain the sound frequency without shunt mixed waveforms.

An analog signal, after ADC sampling, becomes a digital signal. Suppose the sampling frequency is FS, the signal frequency is f, and the number of sampling points is n. Then the result after FFT is a complex number with n points. Each point corresponds to a frequency point. The modulus of this point is the amplitude characteristic at this frequency value. The phase of each point is the phase of the signal at that frequency. The first point represents the DC component (i.e., 0 Hz), while the last point n (here is the assumed n + 1 point) represents the sampling frequency FS, which is evenly divided into N equal parts by n − 1 points, and the frequency of each point increases in turn.

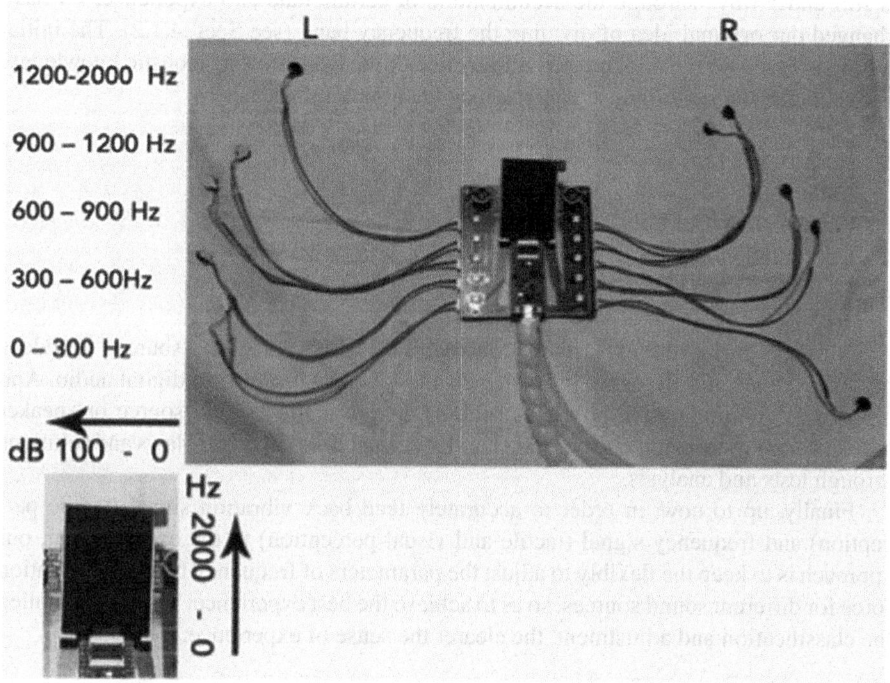


**Fig. 10.** MPU with the LED screen, and the display interface of frequency, loudness.

The formula **FN = (n − 1) x FS/n** shows that the frequency that FN can distinguish is FS/N. if the sampling frequency FS is 1024 Hz and the number of sampling points is 1024, 1 Hz can be distinguished. 1024 points are sampled at a sampling rate of 1024 Hz, which is exactly 1 s, that is, the signal for 1 s is sampled and FFT is performed, and the result can be analyzed to 1 Hz. If you want to improve the frequency resolution, you must increase the number of sampling points, that is, the sampling time. Frequency resolution and sampling time are reciprocal.

- The **Time domain** describes the relationship between mathematical function or physical signal and time. For example, the time domain waveform of a signal can express the change of the signal over time.
- The **Frequency domain** refers to analyzing the frequency related part of a function or signal, not the time related part. For example, Fourier transformation can convert a time-domain signal into the corresponding amplitude and phase at different frequencies, and its spectrum is the performance of the time-domain signal in the frequency domain, while inverse Fourier transformation can convert the spectrum back to the time-domain signal.

## 6.3 Quantification Testing and UX

We have repeatedly tested and compared the signal performance and perceptual feedback in the Frequency range of 0–20000 Hz, and Decibel range of 0–120 dB. In fact, this work is still under way. Through the accumulation of certain data and experience, we have changed our original idea of dividing the frequency band (see Sect. 4.1.2). The initial setting is based on the application and practice of the team's basic acoustic knowledge. For example, the performance of frequency in common sense is:

a) Low: 0–80 Hz
b) Male voice: 80–140 Hz
c) Female: 140–280 Hz
d) Child: 280–400 Hz
e) High 400–15000 Hz

however, during the experiment, we found that different sound sources or videos performed uneven differences in frequency and loudness, especially digital audio. And a series of comprehensive problems such as: audio quality, sound source or speaker location, test environment, noise, and other factors need to find certain laws and solutions through tests and analysis.

Finally, up to now, in order to accurately feed back vibration signal (tactile perception) and frequency signal (tactile and visual perception) to the experimenter, our approach is to keep the flexibly to adjust the parameters of frequency band and vibration force for different sound sources, so as to achieve the best experience. The more detailed the classification and adjustment, the clearer the sense of experience.

For example, we can set the demo whose frequency is concentrated in medium and low frequency as:

1) 0–100 Hz;
2) 100–300 Hz;
3) 300–500 Hz;
4) 500–700 Hz;
5) 700–2000 Hz.

while the demo whose frequency is concentrated in medium and high frequency can be:

1) 0–300Hz;
2) 300–600 Hz;
3) 600–900 Hz;
4) 900–1200 Hz;
5) 1200–2000 Hz.

The parameters of the variation with loudness are the same. With this work plan, the student volunteers of LAFA and the staff of our cooperative technical development team are experimenting. In practice, the technical team has to do most of the problem solving.

## 7 Challenges of Interdisciplinary Collaboration

The development of Technology, Art and Design constantly changes. Interdisciplinary collaboration between design-related disciplines like: Sonology; Visual Art; Drama; Costume Design; Information and Communication Technology; Perception- and Experience Psychology, and Interdisciplinary Education, brings unprecedented opportunities and unknown challenges in how we design, obtain information, and operate tools. Participants in our research and design come from different disciplines, learn from each other, and develop cooperative thinking in practice [15].

### 7.1 Ready-to-wear: Collaborations with Fashion Designers

We cooperated with LAFA's Fabric and Fashion Institute from the initial conception stage and completed the garment with them after the hardware development (Fig. 11).

In this process, participants held many online meetings to communicate and discuss the problems (cultural context, application scenario, audience perspective, function, and aesthetic dialectics) and finally determined the scheme agreed by everyone.

From the resulting sketches, we chose Fig. 12. The design is concise and considers the functionality and wearability. Elastic bands are used to fix the vibration elements, and large-area fasteners are used to replace the sewing thread, so that is gender friendly, and people of different heights and weights can wear it comfortably. In the actual production, we considered adopting new material and fabrics.

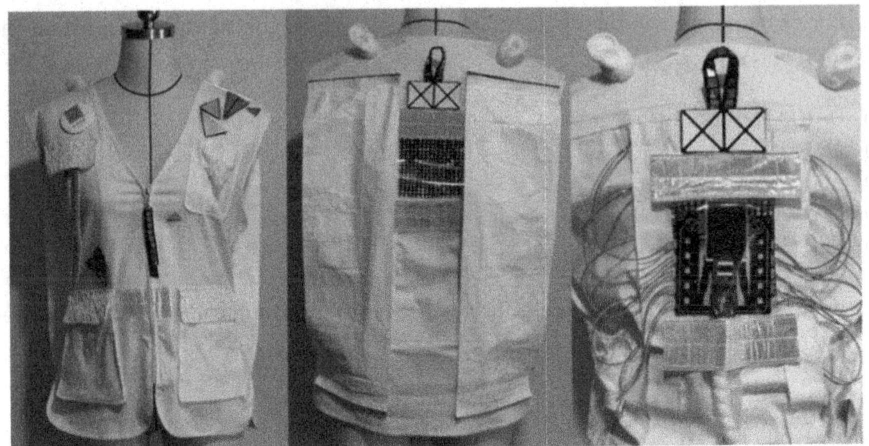

**Fig. 11.** Initial hardware – first version of "Ears on my back"

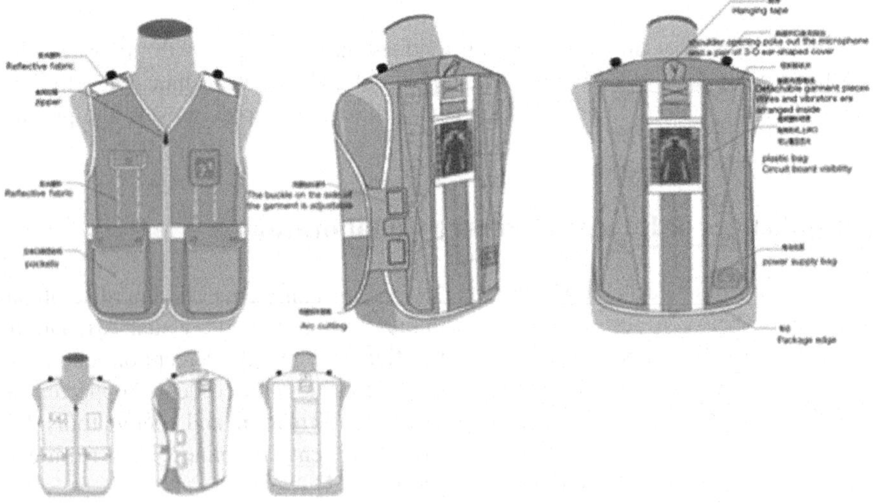


**Fig. 12.** Three views of garment.

We decided to use white as the main color to reflect the ambient lights. 3D printing technology and intelligent lighting hardware allowed us to render the intended sound translation to a colored visual atmosphere (Fig. 13). We invited professional tailors and students to participate in the design and usability testing.

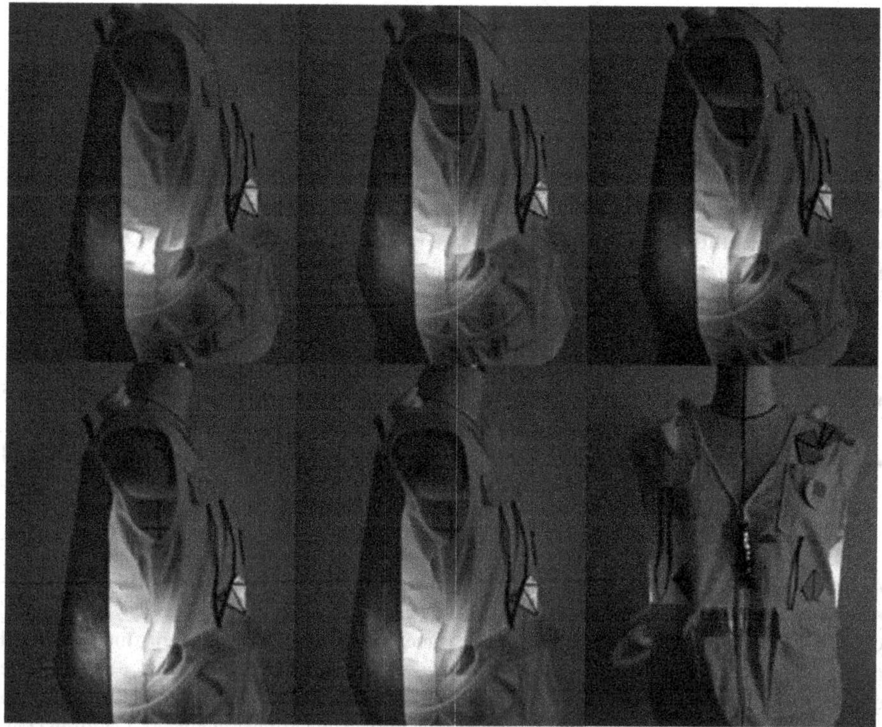

**Fig. 13.** Smart light-emitting components.

## 8 Work in Progress

We are planning an experimental study to discover the possibilities of translating relevant non-text sound to tactile and visual input. In most experimental conditions we will use muting headphones. We consider the following variation in subjects, for which we intend to aim at systematic **comparisons:**

- Gender (considering possible differences in sensitivity to tactile stimulation);
- Age (considering the loss of high frequency hearing related to age);
- Hearing (dis)ability;
- Cultural differences (considering variations in common meaning of non-textual sound, of colors, and of tactile stimulation).

We will compare **conditions** including:

- Dialogues with and without subtitles;
- Non-textual sound (and/or translations of this) providing:
  - Background noise;
  - Meaningful background queues like ticking clocks, machine noise, etc.;

- Informative sounds, like a clock beating, a ringing bell, a traffic signal;
- A sound event that indicates the displacement of a source of sound.

We will develop **measurement** for experience aspects of the conditions:

- Meaning (probably at least through open end questions);
- Being esthetically attracted/repelled (Likert scale)
- Emotions (multiple Likert scales);
- Tendency to act (attending/moving/focusing towards or away from …).

We hope the results of our experiments will feed two directions of application:

- We intend to support adequate replacement of relevant sound in artistic experience and appreciation for hearing impaired stakeholder of dynamic and interactive art.
- We aim at novel opportunities for arts where playful translation of sound may add new dimensions to the artistic design space.

**Acknowledgment.** Thanks to our collaborators: Lu Xun Academy of fine arts (LAFA): Multimedia and animation Collage Dalian campus, and Fashion and Fabric institute Shenyang campus, China. Shenyang Conservatory of music: Department of composition, and Department of vocal music. Shenyang, China. Northeastern University: Department of Computer science and software engineering, Shenyang, China. And our technical consultants. Dalian University: School of Drama and Performance, Dalian, China. Lun Xu and Changzhe Cai, electronics engineers. Geoffrey Donaldson Instituut, Noord-Scharwoude, Netherlands. And thanks to all faculty and student volunteers for their contribution to the project Ears on my back.

## References

1. Giannetti, L.: Understanding Movies, 14th edn. Pearson, USA (2017)
2. Boardman, A.A.: An Illustrated History of Filmmaking. Walker Books Australia, AU (2018)
3. Liu, J., Zhang, L.: Melody in Movies. Nanjing University Press, China (2017)
4. Tong, l., Han, k.: Creating Interactive Audio Applications with Pure Data. Post & Telecom Press, China (2018)
5. Academy of Motion Picture Arts: Motion Picture Sound Engineering: A Series of Lectures Presented to the Classes Enrolled in the Courses in Sound Engineering Given by the Research Council of the Academy of Motion Picture Arts and Sciences, Hollywood, California (Classic Reprint). Forgotten Books, London (2018)
6. Douglass, J.S., Harnden, G.P.: The Art of Technique: An Aesthetic Approach to Film and Video Production. Pearson Education, Peking (2004)
7. Smith, T. J.: Audiovisual correspondences in Sergei Eisenstein's Alexander Nevsky: a case study in viewer attention. In: Taberham, P., Nannicelli, T. (eds.) Cognitive Media Theory. AFI Film Readers, Taylor & Francis, Abingdon, UK (2014)
8. Millet, B., Chattah, J., Ahn, S.: Soundtrack design: the impact of music on visual attention and affective responses. Applied Ergonomics, (2021)
9. Vyas, D., van der Veer, G.: Experience as meaning: creating, communicating and maintaining in real-spaces. In: McCarthy, J., Wright, P. (eds) Tenth IFIP TC13 International Conference on Human-Computer Interaction - Rome, Italy (2005)

10. Gfeller, K., et al.: Musical backgrounds, listening habits, and aesthetic enjoyment of adult cochlear implant recipients. J. Am. Acad. Audiol. **11**(7), 390–406 (2000)
11. Warren, V.E., McPherson, C., Giorli, G., Goetz, K.T., Radford, C.A.: Marine Soundscape variation reveals insights into baleen whales and their environment. https://royalsocietypublishing.org/doi/https://royalsocietypublishing.org/doi/10.1098/rsos.201503. Accessed 31 May 2021
12. Schafer, R.M. : The Soundscape: Our Sonic Environment and the Tuning of the World. Destiny Books, Rochester (1993)
13. Hong, J.Y., et al.: Quality assessment of acoustic environment reproduction methods for cinematic virtual reality in soundscape applications. Build. Environ. **149**, 1–4 (2019)
14. Meyer, J.: Acoustics and the Performance of Music. Springer, Cham (2009). https://doi.org/10.1007/978-0-387-09517-2
15. Candy, L., Amitani, S., Bilda, Z.: Practice-led strategies for interactive art research. CoDesign. In: International Journal of Co-Creation in Design and the Arts. Taylor & Francis, UK, 24 April 2007, pp 209–223 (2007)

# Using Wearables to Optimize Learning at Home

Fiona Draxler(✉)

LMU Munich, Munich, Germany
fiona.draxler@ifi.lmu.de

**Abstract.** During the COVID-19 pandemic, there has been a shift from learning in classrooms to learning at home. However, currently applied learning methods are not optimized for learning at home. Therefore, we explore how the unique benefits of a home environment could be used to inform the design of learning experiences. In particular, we explore the applicability of wearables and IoT devices as flexible and affordable learning tools. Based on our findings, we present our prototype of an NFC-based learning application for mobile devices.

**Keywords:** Distance learning · Microlearning · Wearables · IoT

## 1 Introduction

Because of school closures during the COVID-19 pandemic, many students have had to continue their studies at home. Instructors have had to find ways to substitute classroom learning with alternatives that also function remotely. For example, they organize online meetings [2] and prepare task sheets that students work on individually. Thus, such strategies often imitate classroom setups and do not make use of the unique benefits that learning at home entails. For example, instead of watching a non-interactive video on a science experiment, students could use devices they already own or that are readily available in order to perform experiments themselves.

In particular, we explore how wearables and IoT devices could contribute to learning at home. First, we analyze what students can learn with such devices and how this can be realized. Then, we explore how this type of learning can be embedded into everyday life at home. In this context, we present "Tagged Revision", a prototypical Android app that presents questions for revision when an associated NFC tag is discovered. Finally, we discuss challenges such as the creation and distribution of learning material.

## 2 Learning in Home Environments

There are several key differences between learning in schools and at home, especially with respect to the social and time contexts. Typically, learning in schools is characterized by co-location of instructors and learners as well as synchronous teaching formats, while learning at home lacks physical contact with instructors and peers, but it can provide students with the flexibility to work independently and asynchronously [2, 4]. Additional


Published by Springer Nature Switzerland AG 2022
C. Ardito et al. (Eds.): INTERACT 2021, LNCS 13198, pp. 474–480, 2022.
https://doi.org/10.1007/978-3-030-98388-8_42

important factors that need to be considered when conceptualizing learning in home environments include the fact that not every child has access to a study room, and the availability of devices such as handhelds and computers [2, 6].

## 3 What and How to Learn with Wearables

Wearables are promising learning tools because of their sensing capabilities (e.g., location and motion sensing), but also their seamless usage in multiple environments. For example, they can be used for learning by binding learning resources to objects that are contextually related. For example, a smart speaker could start quizzing a student on nutrition while they are preparing food or on leverage when they move an object equipped with an IMU. Similar concepts have been explored in the past. In one project, Beaudin et al. equipped a home with RFID tags that triggered audio playback of the English word and its Spanish translation when users approached or interacted with a tagged object [1]. Similarly, Hautasaari et al. designed a system that presented context-relevant vocabulary via audio while walking, e.g., vocabulary regarding horticulture when they passed a garden [8]. In both systems, substantial exposure to vocabulary items was achieved.

Besides vocabulary learning, another possible application are physics concepts. For example, Garcia et al. utilized smartwatches to facilitated situated reflection on science topics via audio recordings [7]. In addition, current wearable or mobile devices already include a number of sensors that can be used to conduct physics experiments with relatively simple setups that are also possible at home [13]. For example, acceleration of falling objects can be measured with smartphone microphones, using sound signals triggered and registered at the start and end of the respective movement.

However, possible learning material is not limited to items available in a typical home. Humans are also good at creating links between items that were previously seen as unrelated. For example, when using the method of loci, learners associate specific locations with the items they want to remember [19]. Traditionally, the links to physical environments are imaginary only but there has also been work on visualizing them with augmented reality technology [22] and triggering the display of additional information with smart glasses, e.g. in a museum [15]. Similar strategies could also be employed with wearables and IoT devices by attaching tags to objects that are then connected to learning material.

For both contextual and associative content, suitable input and output modalities are an important aspect to be considered. Wearable devices are flexible and mobile but often have no or only small displays, which limits the amount of information that can be displayed as well as the possibilities of interaction. On the other hand, in home environments, voice interaction may be a viable alternative, as there are less privacy concerns in private spaces, i.e., homes.

## 4 When and Where to Learn

In addition to associations with learning material, tags and devices could also serve as study reminders by triggering short interactions (microlearning) when learners encounter them in their daily routine. For example, a tag attached to a bathroom mirror could cause a vibration on a smartwatch, which then displays or plays a short learning quiz. This idea is based on the (non-digital) practice of attaching sticky notes that serve as study reminders to furniture and other objects. Past research in similar contexts has, for example, explored tags that trigger learning sessions while someone is waiting for an elevator to come [3]. One advantage of location-based triggers is the idea that if tags are strategically placed, this could also automatically lead to a spaced repetition effect, and thus, increase recall [11].

Besides location-based triggers, moments such as just after a finishing a phone call have been used to suggest activities [10]. When such actions are regularly repeated, they can also contribute to building habits.

Other projects have integrated microlearning directly into common activities performed on smartphones or computers. For example, Meurers et al. implemented a browser extension that creates cloze exercises by removing linguistic constructs such as determiners in websites and asks users to fill the gaps [17]. Another project periodically adds interactive vocabulary quizzes in Facebook feeds [12].

Overall, moving sticky notes and other study activities into the digital domain opens up new possibilities for interaction and the integration of multimedia contents. Thus, addressing multiple channels and working with learning material in multiple representations.

## 5 Tagged Revision: An App for NFC-Triggered Learning

In order to explore learning triggers for studying at home in more detail, we developed Tagged Revision[1], an Android app that scans NFC tags and presents a series of questions associated with the discovered tag (see the workflow depicted in Fig. 1). The idea is that learners distribute tags around the house and initiate microlearning sessions when they approach these tags. For example, questions on Java programming could be shown when a learner gets a coffee, and questions on interaction design when they put down their mobile device on their desk.

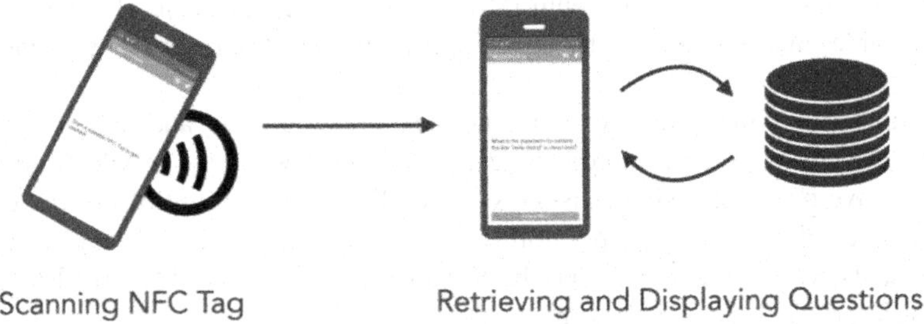


**Fig. 1.** Workflow of the Tagged Revision app

Hence, we approach the questions of "what and how to learn" by proposing short quizzing sessions on a topic that is physically tied to a location but not necessarily related

[1] https://github.com/fionade/tagged-revision.

to this location. Still, we expect learners to additionally form a mental association of the learning material and the respective tag location. And as in [3], we approach the questions "when and where to learn" as moments when learners perform a specific activity (e.g., getting coffee) or when they use a specific object.

The app was built for Android versions 6 and upwards and provides views for showing questions, adding questions, and adding locations to NFC tags, so that different tags can be created and distributed in a user's home.

Each location is associated to a set of questions in a local database. After a scan, the app displays the least recently viewed question and shows a button to reveal the stored answer (see Fig. 2). Once the answer has been revealed, users can pass on to the next question. New questions can be added and assigned to locations in a dedicated view. When an uninitialized NFC tag is detected, a new location can be added.

In order to correctly handle the NFC tags, we wrote two NDEF messages: a plain text record that solely contains an identifier of the associated location (e.g., "location: coffee machine") and an Android Application Record to make sure that the Android device reliably starts our app when the tag is scanned. This also means that it is not necessary to open the app first.

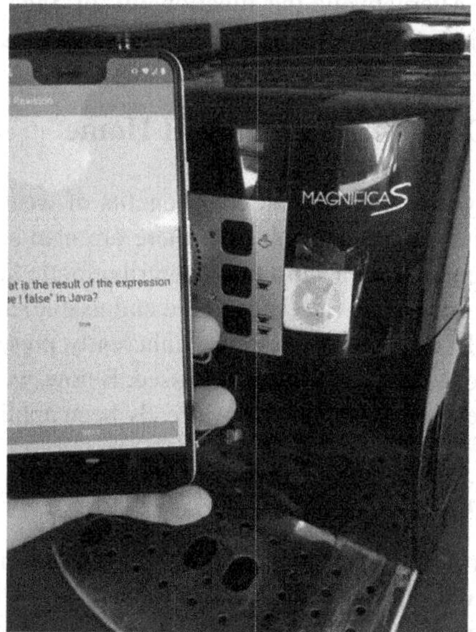


**Fig. 2.** A question is shown in Tagged Revision after the NFC tag attached to the coffee machine has been scanned

The Tagged Revision app is a first step towards integrating microlearning sessions into everyday activities at home. However, a number of technology-related challenges currently limit its seamless application. For example, we had initially planned to implement Tagged Revision for a smartwatch instead of a smartphone. However, despite the fact that NFC payment is possible with a number of smartwatches, the respective NFC APIs are not commonly exposed and developers cannot use them for other use cases (e.g., on the Huawei Watch 2). In addition, devices only scan an NFC tag when they are unlocked and positioned very close to the tag. This implies that in many cases, learners will need to make the first step (i.e., unlock, move closer) before the device picks up a signal and initiates a learning session. To avoid the necessity of user initiative, we recommend placing tags at locations where the probability of the phone being used while unlocked, for example, on their desk, on their device charger.

In sum, while NFC tags are promising because they do not require batteries, are cheap to produce, and because their limited storage capacity is perfectly sufficient for our purpose, an alternative such as Bluetooth Low Energy beacons may be a better option. In fact, by adding GPS-based triggers, the range of learning situations could be extended to include outdoor locations.

We envision several possible extensions for the Tagged Revision app, for the applied interaction paradigms as well as for the integration of learning content. As just mentioned, a first step will be the integration of alternative trigger methods such as Bluetooth beacons.

Further, question types could be extended to include interactive exercises and multimedia objects. New questions could be collaboratively created and shared within study groups; existing questions could be imported from decks created with the popular flashcard application Anki. Alternatively, the functionality of Tagged Revisions could be integrated into the Anki app itself, as the source code is openly available.

## 6 Challenges in Designing Learning at Home

Above, we have shortly summarized potential benefits of wearables and IoT devices for learning in home environments. However, there are also a number of challenges that need to be addressed to make a substantial contribution to home learning. Notably, technology needs to be accessible (i.e., affordable and usable) and content needs to be curated. In addition, while social interaction is inherently present in classrooms, in a remote setting, this needs to be specifically addressed. Below, we focus on the latter two aspects and list possible approaches that have already been applied in similar contexts.

### 6.1 Content Creation

A major limiting factor in the application of new technology for learning is the preparation and distribution of appropriate learning material [20]. If they previously taught in classrooms, instructors will need to adapt their teaching methods and rethink learner activities. Therefore, novel learning systems should provide authoring support, for example, by applying machine learning or crowdsourcing methods. In language learning, for example, possible solutions that have already been developed include the generation of English grammar exercises [21] and questions for text comprehension [9].

### 6.2 Peer Collaboration and Instructor Support

Further important aspects are collaboration and instructor as well as peer support, which have been found to facilitate learning, for example, in mobile learning [14]. Especially at a distance, collaborative and social aspects should not be neglected and individual needs should be catered to in order to sustain motivation and engagement. In the past, collaboration has been supported with frameworks such as Teachyverse, where a full classroom was imitated in VR [16], and collaborative problem solving in AR, where each participant holds a part of the necessary information [5]. In a study by Niemi et al., online pair assignments were found to be more helpful than online group work with several students [18].

## 7 Outlook and Conclusion

In this paper, we summarized how wearable and mobile technology can support learning in everyday environments, with a focus on possible learning content and opportune moments for learning. We presented examples of past projects focusing or learning at home and projects that included core ideas which could be translated to home environments. Based on this, we presented an exemplary Android app for revising learning material that is bound to NFC tags. Overall, we believe that such concepts are a promising approach for enabling learning at home, in addition to classroom learning or as an alternative when co-located learning is not possible.

## References

1. Beaudin, J.S., Intille, S.S., Munguia Tapia, E., Rockinson, R., Morris, M.E.: Context-sensitive microlearning of foreign language vocabulary on a mobile device. In: Schiele, B., et al. (eds.) Ambient Intelligence. AMI 2007. LNCS, vol. 4794, pp. 55–72. Springer, Heidelberg (2007). https://doi.org/10.1007/978-3-540-76652-0_4
2. Bond, M.: Schools and emergency remote education during the COVID-19 pandemic: a living rapid systematic review. Asian J. Distance Educ. **15**(2), 191–247 (2020)
3. Cai, C.J., Guo, P.J., Glass, J.R., Miller, R.C.: Wait-learning: leveraging wait time for second language education. In: Proceedings of the 33rd Annual ACM Conference on Human Factors in Computing Systems - CHI 2015, Seoul, Republic of Korea, pp. 3701–3710 (2015)
4. Daniel, S.J.: Education and the COVID-19 pandemic. Prospects **49**(1–2), 91–96 (2020). https://doi.org/10.1007/s11125-020-09464-3
5. Dunleavy, M., Dede, C., Mitchell, R.: Affordances and limitations of immersive participatory augmented reality simulations for teaching and learning. J. Sci. Educ. Technol. **18**(1), 7–22 (2009). https://doi.org/10.1007/s10956-008-9119-1
6. Fontanesi, L., Marchetti, D., Mazza, C., Di Giandomenico, S., Roma, P., Verrocchio, M.C.: The effect of the COVID-19 lockdown on parents: a call to adopt urgent measures. Psychol. Trauma Theory Res. Pract. Policy. **12**(S1), S79–S81 (2020). https://doi.org/10.1037/tra0000672
7. Garcia, B., Chu, S.L., Nam, B., Banigan, C.: Wearables for learning: examining the smartwatch as a tool for situated science reflection. In: Proceedings of the 2018 CHI Conference on Human Factors in Computing Systems, Montreal, Canada, pp. 1–13, April 2018
8. Hautasaari, A., Hamada, T., Ishiyama, K., Fukushima, S.: VocaBura: a method for supporting second language vocabulary learning while walking. In: Proceedings of the ACM on Interactive, Mobile, Wearable and Ubiquitous Technologies, vol. 3, no. 4, pp. 1–23, December 2019. https://doi.org/10.1145/3369824

9. Heilman, M., Smith, N.A.: Extracting simplified statements for factual question generation. In: Proceedings of the 3rd Workshop on Question Generation (2010)
10. Kang, B., et al.: Zaturi: we put together the 25th hour for you. Create a book for your baby. In: Proceedings of the 2017 ACM Conference on Computer Supported Cooperative Work and Social Computing - CSCW 2017, Portland, Oregon, pp. 1850–1863 (2017)
11. Kornell, N.: Optimising learning using flashcards: Spacing is more effective than cramming. Appl. Cogn. Psychol. **23**(9), 1297–1317 (2009). https://doi.org/10.1002/acp.1537
12. Kovacs, G.: FeedLearn: using Facebook feeds for microlearning. In: Proceedings of the 33rd Annual ACM Conference Extended Abstracts on Human Factors in Computing Systems - CHI EA 2015, Seoul, Republic of Korea, pp. 1461–1466 (2015)
13. Kuhn, J., Vogt, P.: Physik ganz smart: Die Gesetze der Welt mit dem Smartphone entdecken (2020)
14. Kukulska-Hulme, A., Viberg, O.: Mobile collaborative language learning: state of the art: mobile collaborative language learning. Br. J. Educ. Technol. **49**(2), 207–218 (2018). https://doi.org/10.1111/bjet.12580
15. Leue, M.C., Jung, T., Tom Dieck, D.: Google glass augmented reality: generic learning outcomes for art galleries. In: Tussyadiah, I., Inversini, A. (eds.) Information and Communication Technologies in Tourism 2015, pp. 463–476. Springer, Cham. https://doi.org/10.1007/978-3-319-14343-9_34
16. Marky, K., et al.: Teachyverse: collaborative e-learning in virtual reality lecture halls. In: Proceedings of Mensch und Computer 2019 on – MuC 2019, Hamburg, Germany, pp. 831–834 (2019)
17. Meurers, D., et al.: Enhancing authentic web pages for language learners. In: Proceedings of the NAACL HLT 2010 Fifth Workshop on Innovative Use of NLP for Building Educational Applications, pp. 10–18 (2010)
18. Niemi, H.M., Kousa, P., et al.: A case study of students' and teachers' perceptions in a Finnish high school during the COVID pandemic. Int. J. Technol. Educ. Sci. **4**(4), 352–369 (2020)
19. O'keefe, J., Nadel, L.: The Hippocampus as a Cognitive Map. Clarendon Press, Oxford (1978)
20. Oliveira da Silva, M.M., Alves Roberto, R., Radu, I., Smith Cavalcante, P., Teichrieb, V.: Why don't we see more of augmented reality in schools? In: 2019 IEEE International Symposium on Mixed and Augmented Reality Adjunct (ISMAR-Adjunct), Beijing, China, pp. 138–143, October 2019
21. Perez-Beltrachini, L., Gardent, C., Kruszewski, G.: Generating grammar exercises. In: Proceedings of the Seventh Workshop on Building Educational Applications Using NLP, Stroudsburg, pp. 147–156 (2012)
22. Raso, R., Lahann, J., Fettke, P., Loos, P.: Walkable graph: an immersive augmented reality interface for performing the memory palace method. In: AMCIS 2019 Proceedings, Cancún (2019)

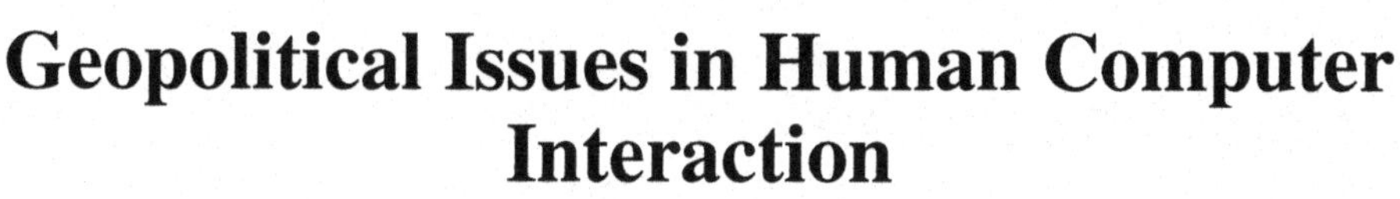

# Geopolitical Issues in Human Computer Interaction

# Micro-politics, Semiotic Power and Infrastructural Inversion: Theoretical Lenses for Geopolitical HCI

José Abdelnour Nocera[1,2](✉) and Ali Gheitasy[1]

[1] University of West London, London, UK
Jose.Abdelnour-Nocera@uwl.ac.uk
[2] ITI/LARSyS, Funchal, Portugal

**Abstract.** An argument is presented for the use of the concepts of Micro-Politics and Semiotic Power by Bijker, and Infrastructural Inversion by Bowker to understand the geopolitical dynamics of career-building, knowledge and value creation in the field of human computer interaction (HCI). This is illustrated with brief references to examples of HCI academic and professional practice and dissemination in local and global contexts. It is shown how local and global micro-politically dominant groups in the HCI field can construct scripts that define quality, impact and relevance. These scripts in turn have a direct effect in career-building and what is considered valid and useful knowledge and practice. The political leverage of these scripts is therefore embedded in artefacts used for different types of transactions in the HCI field. Infrastructural inversion is finally presented as a possible framework to deconstruct and make visible these scripts and the different types of historical and political tensions inscribed in them at disciplinary, local, national, regional and global level.

**Keywords:** Geopolitical HCI · Technological frames · Infrastructural inversion · HCI research · HCI practice

## 1 Introduction

The geographical diffusion of human computer interaction (HCI) as a field of knowledge and practice is underpinned by political and post-colonial discourses that pervade local indigenous and global knowledge networks shaping what is considered useful and relevant research and practice [1, 2]. Post-colonial analyses of HCI diffusion are fundamentally framed as set of intercultural and potentially uneven power relations encountered in design situations [1]. However, these analyses miss local and indigenous HCI concepts and methods [2] that are often invisible to professional and academic spaces of knowledge exchange [3]. The potential contribution of explicitly local or indigenous perspectives, approaches, and experiences with HCI tends to remain unknown, e.g. [4], and, it is argued, subject to political forces that make them remain largely invisible.


Published by Springer Nature Switzerland AG 2022
C. Ardito et al. (Eds.): INTERACT 2021, LNCS 13198, pp. 483–489, 2022.
https://doi.org/10.1007/978-3-030-98388-8_43

There are attempts to understand HCI maturity and diversity levels through origins, frequencies and levels of participation in conferences such as CHI or CSCW, e.g. [5]; through organizational adoption, e.g. [6, 7] or through regional institutionalizing efforts, e.g. [8]. The problem with these attempts and the discourses surrounding them is that HCI's maturity and diversity is placed on a scale underpinned by western models of value, quality and participation reinforcing geopolitical configurations of exclusion and inclusion, which regulate human and knowledge mobility in the field. Thus, limiting the potential to integrate other views, forms of being, living, understanding and succeeding in the world and in the HCI field itself.

An argument is presented for the use of the concepts of Micro-Politics and Semiotic Power by Bijker [9], and Infrastructural Inversion by Bowker [10] and Simonsen et al. to understand the geopolitical dynamics of career-building, knowledge and value creation in the field of HCI. These concepts enable political analyses of this field at local, national, regional and global level.

## 2 Background

### 2.1 Power and Politics in Information Technology Disciplines

The significance of power and politics have been studied in disciplines such as information systems and requirements engineering [11, 12]. Power considered as a complex concept and its role depends on the perspective of the research [13]. In the social context, it is considered as characteristic of an individual within a relationship or interaction of two or more people [12]. Power enables individual to have influence on the others' behaviour [14]; or convincing others to act accordingly [15]. In the social interactions, politics is considered as the directing of the individuals' power into actions and acting according to it [16]. In a social group power can be practiced in accordance with the structure of relationship amongst individuals and the politics is perceived within the decision-making actions and processes within individuals [11].

Within literature examining design and implementation of information systems the focus on political issues concentrated more on the organizational change, managerial practices, and political tactics to resist change [17, 18]. In software engineering some research has been carried out to investigate power and politics in different areas such as requirements engineering [11, 19], and software eco-systems [20, 21]. In a study by Bano, Zowghi, and Ramini, [16] the political aspects of the relationship between user involvement and system success has been studied. Their findings highlight the significance of politics used to exert power and impact in the decision-making processes. The manipulation of communication channels for political purposes caused users' dissatisfaction and negatively influenced the project outcome.

Rowlands and Kautz [22] study the relationship of different forms of obtrusive and unobtrusive power [23] in systems development methods. Obtrusive power is a hierarchy-based or economic-based form of power. Whereas unobtrusive power is the ability to give meaning to events and actions, and to have an impact on the perceptions of other individuals. Their results highlighted the obtrusive power of clients due to the controlled critical resources and funding through approval and sign-off on documentation process.

Developers were subject to the unobtrusive power embedded in the software development method in the form of habitual work practices and discipline.

All in all, the brief review of previous research in this area exposes a number of political tensions and power relations that tend to be asymmetric, dynamic and symbolically inscribed in artefacts used to develop and implement knowledge in these fields. The next two sections introduce theoretical frameworks and concepts that can be used to make sense and study this type of tensions.

## 2.2 Technological Frames, Micro-politics of Power and Semiotic Power

The concept of technological frame (TF) was developed by Bijker [9] to make sense of the social shaping of technology and the technological shaping of society. Bijker's TF places an important focus on the political processes influencing socio-technical change. This concept was first developed by Bijker in trying to understand the socio-technical processes that guided the interactions of groups of scientists and technologists in the invention and development of bakelite and the fluorescent lamp. A TF is constituted by knowledge, assumptions, expectations, practices, workarounds and other tools shared in a community that influence how meanings are attached to technology and how it evolves within that community. HCI in this case is a technological field around which TF revolve associated with different types of community therefore leading to different frames shaping the socio-technical change and evolution of this field.

TF have already been used in previous research to understand the political processes involved in the definition and diffusion of technology and IS design practices within different types of communities, organisations and cultures [15, 24, 25]. According to Bijker [9] the exercise of power in TF occurs through two political processes take place: one referred to the 'micro-politics' of creation, transformation and negotiation of meanings attributed to technology, in which powerful groups tend to impose their own perspectives [e.g. 26, 27]; and other referred to as 'semiotic power', in which meanings, once fixed in diverse elements of a TF by dominant stakeholders (e.g. artefacts, accepted practices, norms, etc.) in turn constrain and structure the actions and transactions of the communities associated with the technology in question [e.g. 28, 29]. The idea of semiotic power is derived from semiotic approaches in the Sociology of Technology, which study processes of user and producer configuration [30–32]. This coincides with the concept of unobtrusive power already discussed in the previous section [22].

The use of TF to analyse power structures and dynamics is not uncommon with IS research [24, 33, 34]. The study of the discipline of Requirements Engineering has also been subject to analysis of power dynamics shaping the TF of relevant actors and their decision making in the process of systems design [11]. And more recent research highlights the importance of the political forces of TF in defining the HCI profession and job roles [35] where it is recognized that the involvement of powerful or influential stakeholders and the influence of organisational and intra-organisational cultures and politics can influence the interpretative processes and affect the framing and reframing process, and this in turn may influence the formation of a dominant frame, both in terms of content and direction [24, 36].

### 2.3 Infrastructural Inversion

The notion of information infrastructure [37] can cover the HCI discipline as a sociotechnical assembly of relations between humans and the realities they create including the technologies that enable and support these practices. The concept is fundamentally grounded on a situated and relational view that infrastructure happens in practice and when connected to some concrete activity. The emphasis on context as the maim medium through which infrastructures exist allow the identification of gaps and issues at different levels of learning using Bateson's categories [38]: (1st level) know-how, (2nd level) social/organisational, and (3rd level) political/paradigmatic. It is at this last political level that an infrastructural analysis enables the understanding of the geopolitical tensions underpinning career-building, knowledge, and value creation in relation to the lower clearer levels of overt communication and transactions in the field of HCI.

Simonsen et al. [39] propose infrastructural inversion as defined by Bowker [10] to analyse infrastructures by turning invisible relations into visible entities. This is achieved according through conceptual-analytic, empirical-ethnographic, and generative-designerly strategies. A typical "way into" the inversion is through the identification of breakdowns in the infrastructure [37, 40, 41], which is an empirical-ethnographic route. In a co-design project aimed at the implementation of electronic whiteboards in a hospital pre-surgery ward Simonsen et al. [39] demonstrate how invisible relations can be identified thorough initially conceptual-analytical strategies moving onto a designerly ones with the help of local participants in co-design workshops. The identification of these relations in turn facilitated the implementation of whiteboards to achieve the desired effect of optimum management of fasting times.

## 3 Towards a Geopolitical Analysis of HCI

It is argued that the above theoretical lenses can enable an analysis of geopolitical tensions in the field of HCI.

For instance, a TF analysis of political dynamics driving HCI communities can identify how powerful groups frame actions and artefacts defining scientific rigour or professional value and utility. Typical tensions that could be analysed through this approach include practice (e.g., UXPA) versus research (e.g., SIGCHI, IFIP) globally; the local HCI versus the BigTech HCI; or the emergence of national and regional HCI communities as geopolitical entities in HCI research. A semiotic power analysis of tensions could deconstruct the scripts embedded in transactions in the field. These deconstructions can focus, for instance, on the semantics of HCI, e.g., user-centric versus people-centric; or on the technical program of HCI conferences reflecting geopolitical controversies and imbalances.

An infrastructural analysis of HCI will necessary highlight second and third level issues, using Bateson's categories, to identify and map invisible relations in social and organisational arrangements and configurations with their own political models and worldviews. Good candidates for infrastructural inversion in HCI can be the tension between the emancipatory and military motivations originating this field, or conflicting forms of participation in design in liberal, deliberative or Marxist democracies.

Infrastructural inversions help us visualise local and indigenous HCI concepts and methods [2] that are often invisible to professional and academic spaces of knowledge exchange [3]. The potential contribution of explicitly local or indigenous perspectives, approaches, and experiences with HCI tends to remain unknown, e.g. [4]. The literature reviewed so far reports on case studies where user involvement and developer-client relations are shaped by invisible power relations embedded in artefacts and transactions scripted in design and development methods and how situations of breakdown or empirical [e.g, 18, 19].

It is relevant to note that much of the knowledge production and mobilisation in HCI have taken place within developed countries. Political, Economic, Socio-cultural, Technological, Environmental, Legal, Managerial and Organisational analysis methods and concepts are needed for contextualising towards effective and meaningful HCI knowledge production in developing regions [42].

## 4 Conclusion: Theoretical Lenses for a Geopolitical HCI Research Agenda

This paper introduced three well-known concepts in the discipline of science and technology studies that enable a geopolitical analysis of HCI: TF [9] and Infrastructural Inversion [39]. The concepts have been briefly introduced and described illustrating how they can be used to research, identify and articulate typical geopolitical dimensions and contradictions present in the field of HCI. The scope of such research should span the political and historical forces, agendas and scripts underpinning professional and academic practice in HCI.

It is hoped these concepts can be used as analytical tools to help develop a research agenda for geopolitical HCI. Such an agenda should have as its main objective to offer a frame of reference for practitioners and researchers to mobilise knowledge [43] to reflect, plan and assess their own geopolitical position and assess the type of tensions embedded between theory, practice and the ideologies and worldviews underpinning them.

## References

1. Irani, L., Vertesi, J., Dourish, P., Philip, K., Grinter, R.E.: Postcolonial computing: a lens on design and development. In: Proceedings of the SIGCHI Conference on Human Factors in Computing Systems, pp. 1311–1320. ACM, New York, NY, USA (2010). https://doi.org/10.1145/1753326.1753522
2. Abdelnour-Nocera, J., Clemmensen, T., Kurosu, M.: Reframing HCI through local and indigenous perspectives. Int. J. Hum. Comput. Interact. **29**, 201–204 (2013). https://doi.org/10.1080/10447318.2013.765759
3. Suchman, L.: Located accountabilities in technology production. Scand. J. Inf. Syst. **14**, 91–105 (2002)
4. Kurosu, M., Kobayashi, T., Yoshitake, R., Takahashi, H., Urokohara, H., Sato, D.: Trends in usability research and activities in Japan. Int. J. Hum. Comput. Interact. **17**, 103–124 (2004)

5. Sturm, C., Oh, A., Linxen, S., Abdelnour Nocera, J., Dray, S., Reinecke, K.: How WEIRD is HCI? Extending HCI principles to other countries and cultures. In: Proceedings of the 33rd Annual ACM Conference Extended Abstracts on Human Factors in Computing Systems, pp. 2425–2428. Association for Computing Machinery, New York, NY, USA (2015). https://doi.org/10.1145/2702613.2702656
6. Guidini Gonçalves, T., Marçal de Oliveira, K., Kolski, C.: HCI in practice: an empirical study with software process capability maturity model consultants in Brazil. J. Softw.: Evol. Proc. **30**, e2109 (2018)
7. Lacerda, T.C., von Wangenheim, C.G.: Systematic literature review of usability capability/maturity models. Comput. Stand. Interf. **55**, 95–105 (2018). https://doi.org/10.1016/j.csi.2017.06.001
8. Smith, A., Joshi, A., Liu, Z., Bannon, L., Gulliksen, J., Li, C.: Institutionalizing HCI in Asia. In: Baranauskas, C., Palanque, P., Abascal, J., Barbosa, S.D.J. (eds.) INTERACT 2007. LNCS, vol. 4663, pp. 85–99. Springer, Heidelberg (2007). https://doi.org/10.1007/978-3-540-74800-7_7
9. Bijker, W.E.: Of Bicycles, Bakelites, and Bulbs: Toward a Theory of Sociotechnical Change. MIT Press, Cambridge, MA (1995)
10. Bowker, G.C., Geoffrey, C., Carlson, W.B., et al.: Science on the Run: Information management and Industrial Geophysics at Schlumberger, pp. 1920–1940. MIT press (1994)
11. Milne, A., Maiden, N.: Power and politics in requirements engineering: embracing the dark side? Require. Eng. **17**, 83–98 (2012). https://doi.org/10.1007/s00766-012-0151-6
12. Sabherwal, R., Grover, V.: A taxonomy of political processes in systems development. Inf. Syst. J. **20**, 419–447 (2010)
13. Sillince, J.A., Mouakket, S.: Varieties of political process during systems development. Inf. Syst. Res. **8**, 368–397 (1997)
14. Bachrach, P., Baratz, M.S.: Two faces of power. Power: Crit. Concepts. **2**, 85 (1994)
15. Sarkkinen, J.: Examining a planning discourse: how a manager represents issues within a planning frame and how the other could do the same. In: Participatory Design Conference. ACM, Toronto, Canada (2004)
16. Bano, M., Zowghi, D., da Rimini, F.: User involvement in software development: the good, the bad, and the ugly. IEEE Softw. **35**, 8–11 (2018)
17. Grover, V., Lederer, A.L., Sabherwal, R.: Recognizing the politics of MIS. Inform. Manage. **14**, 145–156 (1988)
18. Bjerknes, G., Bratteteig, T.: User participation and democracy: a discussion of Scandinavian research on system development. Scand. J. Inf. Syst. **7**, 1 (1995)
19. Johann, T., Maalej, W.: Democratic mass participation of users in requirements engineering? In: 2015 IEEE 23rd International Requirements Engineering Conference (RE), pp. 256–261. IEEE (2015)
20. Valença, G., Alves, C., Heimann, V., Jansen, S., Brinkkemper, S.: Competition and collaboration in requirements engineering: a case study of an emerging software ecosystem. In: 2014 IEEE 22nd International Requirements Engineering Conference (RE), pp. 384–393. IEEE (2014)
21. Poo-Caamano, G.: Release management in free and open source software ecosystems (2016)
22. Rowlands, B., Kautz, K.: Power relations inscribed in the enactment of systems development methods. Inform. Syst. J. **32**(2), 278–309 (2021)
23. Hardy, C.: The nature of unobtrusive power. J. Manage. Stud. **22**, 384–399 (1985)
24. Lin, A., Silva, L.: The social and political construction of technological frames. Eur. J. Inf. Syst. **14**, 49–59 (2005)
25. Pellegrino, G.: Thickening the frame: cross-theoretical accounts of contexts inside and around technology. Bull. Sci. Technol. Soc. **25**, 63–72 (2005)

26. Kaplan, S., Tripsas, M.: Thinking about technology: applying a cognitive lens to technical change. Res. Policy **37**, 790–805 (2008). https://doi.org/10.1016/j.respol.2008.02.002
27. Wolf, C.T.: Narrative Assembly: Technological Framing, Storytelling, and the Situating of "Data Analytics" in Organizational Life (2017)
28. Hsieh, M.F.: Learning by manufacturing parts: Explaining technological change in Taiwan's decentralized industrialization. East Asian Sci. Technol. Soc.: Int. J. **9**, 331–358 (2015)
29. Alnesafi, A.: Blended learning and accounting education in Kuwait: an analysis of social construction of technology. Acad. Account. Finan. Stud. J. **22**, 1–19 (2018)
30. Mackay, H., Carne, C., Beynon-Davies, P., Tudhope, D.: Reconfiguring the user: using rapid application development. Soc. Stud. Sci. **30**, 737–757 (2000)
31. Woolgar, S.: Configuring the user: the case of usability trials. In: A Sociology of Monsters: Essays on Power. Technology and Domination, pp. 58–100. Routledge, London (1991)
32. Akrich, M.: The description of technical objects. In: Shaping Technology, Building Society Studies in Sociotechnical Change. MIT Press, Cambridge, MA (1992)
33. Azad, B., Faraj, S.: Using signature matrix to analyze conflicting frames during the IS implementation process. Int. J. Account. Inf. Syst. **14**, 120–126 (2013). https://doi.org/10.1016/j.accinf.2011.06.003
34. Orlikowski, W., Gash, D.C.: Technological frames: making sense of information technology in organisations. ACM Trans. Inform. Syst. **12**, 174–207 (1994)
35. Austin, A.: The differing profiles of the human-computer interaction professional: perceptions of practice, cognitive preferences and the impact on HCI education (2018)
36. Davidson, E.: A technological frames perspective on information technology and organizational change. J. Appl. Behav. Sci. **42**, 23–39 (2006). https://doi.org/10.1177/0021886305285126
37. Star, S.L., Ruhleder, K.: Steps toward an ecology of infrastructure: design and access for large information spaces. Inf. Syst. Res. **7**, 111–134 (1996)
38. Bateson, G.: Steps to an Ecology of Mind: Collected Essays in Anthropology, Psychiatry, Evolution, and Epistemology. University of Chicago Press (2000)
39. Simonsen, J., Karasti, H., Hertzum, M.: Infrastructuring and participatory design: exploring infrastructural inversion as analytic, empirical and generative. Comput. Supp. Cooper. Work **29**(1–2), 115–151 (2019). https://doi.org/10.1007/s10606-019-09365-w
40. Ribes, D., Lee, C.P.: Sociotechnical studies of cyberinfrastructure and e-research: current themes and future trajectories. Comput. Supp. Cooper. Work **19**, 231–244 (2010)
41. Dreyfus, H.L.: Being-in-the-World: A commentary on Heidegger's Being and Time. MIT press, Cambridge, MA (1991)
42. Mkude, C., Wimmer, M.: Using PES$^{TEL}$MO to frame HCI contextual development in developing countries. In: International Conference on Social Implica-tions of Computers in Developing Countries, pp. 326–333. Springer, Cham (2019). https://doi.org/10.1007/978-3-030-19115-3_27
43. Ward, V.: Why, whose, what and how? A framework for knowledge mobilisers. Evid. Policy: J. Res. Debate Pract. **13**, 477–497 (2017)

# Africanization of HCI Teaching and Learning

Jan H. Kroeze(✉)

School of Computing, University of South Africa, Pretoria, South Africa
kroezjh@unisa.ac.za

**Abstract.** Most software interfaces are designed in the Western world. Western metaphors (such as the concept of menus to organize functions) are implicitly built into these designs. This may affect users in other parts of the world, in that they lack an intuitive feeling of how to use these interfaces and applications, causing a disappointing user experience, low efficiency and even unsatisfactory usability. This is the case in many parts of Africa, including South Africa. The situation is exacerbated by the fact that tertiary Human-Computer Interaction (HCI) curricula at undergraduate level are usually based exclusively on international textbooks. This article discusses the need for research on the Africanization of HCI teaching and learning. Some international and local work that has been done on the decolonization of HCI and the localization of Information Systems is acknowledged. Emic (intra-cultural) and etic (cross-cultural) aspects that influence the decolonization of HCI, such as Ubuntu and the hacker ethic are discussed in addition to geopolitical tensions and powers that encourage or counteract this endeavor. The paper argues that indigenous perspectives should enrich the HCI discipline at theoretical and practical levels. A few practical pointers are provided to make the ideal of Africanization relevant for and feasible within HCI.

**Keywords:** Human-Computer Interaction · Geopolitics · Africanization · Decolonization · Information systems · Teaching · Learning · Research · Community engagement

## 1 Introduction

Most software interfaces are designed in the Western world. Western metaphors such as the concept of menus to organize functions are implicitly built into these designs. This may affect users in other parts of the world, in that they lack an intuitive feeling of how to use these interfaces and applications, causing a disappointing user experience, low efficiency and even unsatisfactory usability. This is the case in many parts of Africa, including South Africa. The situation is exacerbated by the fact that tertiary Human-Computer Interaction (HCI) curricula on the undergraduate level are usually based exclusively on international textbooks.

Although promising work has been done in the area of decolonizing HCI in various countries in the world [cf. 1], little has been done in South Africa, and the outcomes and recommendations of such studies have not been integrated sufficiently into undergraduate


Published by Springer Nature Switzerland AG 2022
C. Ardito et al. (Eds.): INTERACT 2021, LNCS 13198, pp. 490–502, 2022.
https://doi.org/10.1007/978-3-030-98388-8_44

syllabi. This results in the delivery of tertiary students who are well-trained to compete on an international level but who lack understanding of the challenges facing software users in the country. Consequently, the students may have little attunement to the frustrations of local users with low levels of computer literacy. This may not be a major problem for the tertiary students themselves because they are usually taught computer literacy in the first year of their studies and quickly become citizens of the digital world. However, they move into the realm of practice, forgetting that software affordances are not intuitive for large sections of the local population and assuming that the users for whom they write software are living in the same cyber bubble. This includes the use of electronic devices by older people who have never had the opportunity to own a desktop, laptop or smartphone, or to receive structured training to use these devices efficiently. To merely teach this vulnerable group of citizens how to use current versions of applications would not be sufficient. Instead, researchers should find ways to redesign interfaces that afford older people in Africa the ability to use digital technology in an intuitive way. This will ensure that they are not left behind in a world where computing devices have become ubiquitous.

There is, therefore, a need to do more research on ways to Africanize tertiary undergraduate HCI curricula in order to stimulate a sensitivity among Information Systems (IS) students towards these stumbling blocks and to equip them with the necessary skills to address these issues when they start working in the industry as software analysts and programmers. [Note: In this article, 'information systems' with lowercase first letters refers to applications (software), while 'Information Systems' (IS) with uppercase first letters refers to the related academic discipline or study field.] The HCI research approaches themselves can (and should) also be Africanized. Furthermore, software trainers should reflect on the teaching and learning approaches being used to educate undergraduate students and to teach software users how to use applications. Africanizing tuition methods may also significantly assist in addressing the challenges of usability, efficiency and user experience. An Afrocentric HCI curriculum could broaden the horizons of researchers, teachers and designers and their capacity "to bring marginalized local voices forward in technology design" [18].

A comprehensive literature review is needed to identify relevant work that has been done in terms of the Africanization of the IS discipline, with specific reference to HCI tuition and the improvement of computer literacy in older people in Africa. Kroeze [16] conducted some conceptual research in terms of the scope of an IS Africanization project. Empirical work is needed to design alternative approaches to HCI syllabi and literacy training programs and to evaluate interventions based on this research. Qualitative work is necessary to gain a deep understanding of the challenges that African users experience when they start using software that is built on a Western thought paradigm and to formulate hypotheses for research to deal with these issues. Quantitative work is necessary to validate and test these hypotheses in order to ensure generalizability of the findings [cf. 7]. Mixed-method research would also be an appropriate approach to determine design requirements and to validate the usefulness of the proposed artefacts addressing these needs.

## 2 The Status Quo of Africanization in IS Research

The debate on decoloniality and Africanization has not yet received sufficient attention in IS circles, although there are some indications that investigations in this area are gaining momentum. As of 6 April 2021, the Association for Information Systems Electronic Library (AISeL) (https://aisel.aisnet.org), provided only one paper containing the word 'Africanizing' in its title, while no papers contained the word 'Africanization'. However, in a basic search of all fields, 1801 hits were found. This may indicate that there is much interest in the general idea [cf. 28] but little research that engages directly with the concept. Searches for 'decolonization' in all fields resulted in a mere 15 hits, which seems to support this premise. The Computing field needs more African perspectives on IS decolonization with specific reference to HCI, for example, how African storytelling and visualization principles can be used in HCI data-gathering techniques to counteract Western biases in design [cf. 2].

Myers et al. [28] acknowledge the "othering process", the domination of Western theories and the persistent "Western gaze" in qualitative IS research. The authors [28] call for new research approaches to investigate software phenomena in indigenous contexts and to actuate a "decolonial turn" in the field, an issue that has rarely been discussed in the past. Earlier 'turns' in social science such as the phenomenological, linguistic and practice turns illustrate how paradigm shifts may also occur in IS research [15]. This implies that it is scientifically founded to allow for another – decolonial – turn in IS epistemology, as propagated above.

Chughtai et al. [6] call on scholars to diversify IS epistemology to overcome theoretical challenges in investigating humans' interaction with information and communication technology (ICT). The authors believe that indigenous communities can contribute to finding alternatives for traditional IS methodologies. Interdisciplinary research should be implemented to decolonize IS methodologies by challenging and amending traditional "orthodoxies, theories, and methods tethered to a colonial past" [6]. The IS field can indeed learn from other social science disciplines such as education on how to adjust its research methods. For example, Romm [33] suggests that "when focus group research is being conducted with indigenous participants, an endeavor should be made to introduce the sessions in a way that indicates that relational styles of knowing are being encouraged." According to Chughtai [6],

> "existing methodologies in the IS literature often lack Indigenous grounding – particularly if one applies them to marginalized Indigenous peoples. As for why, scholars developed many extant theories without considering (or at the expense of) worldviews and epistemologies outside colonial sanctioning's myopic gaze. As such, one cannot simply generalize and extrapolate the insights that emerge from such theories as though they can capture the nuances of marginalized peoples' experiences ... Simply put, we need new methodological and theoretical approaches to integrate decolonial perspectives into IS research and, thereby, amplify marginalized people's voice."

Therefore, the challenging question for IS researchers is not only how ICTs can be used to 'develop' emerging communities, which is the traditional focus of Information and Communication Technology for Development (ICT4D), but also how epistemological inputs of these communities can enrich IS and ICT, which can be regarded as the opposite side of the same relationship.

## 3 Ubuntu and More Examples of Localization in IS and HCI

Within the context of Africanization, Tsibolane [38] uses the Ubuntu concept to enrich critical research by incorporating collective capabilities into the epistemology. His theoretical point of departure replaces the conventional approach that emphasizes individualistic aspects. 'Ubuntunized' critical research in IS serves as a good example of how principles of African ways of knowing can be used as driving principles [cf. 23, 39]. However, it should be noted that the conceptualization of Ubuntu in science comes with its own challenges [cf. 30]. Furthermore, a systematic discussion of African exegetical methods used in the IS discipline could not be found. This calls for further research regarding hermeneutics and exegesis from an African point of view. The work of Boland et al. [4] serves as an international example of how constructs borrowed from the humanities such as hermeneutic methods can be used in IS theory.

The concept of 'emic' is defined as the "analysis of cultural phenomena from the perspective of one who participates in the culture being studied" [24]. In HCI circles, culture is increasingly seen as a generative force towards new syntheses [34]. In this regard, Ubuntu may be regarded as a strong African example of a relevant indigenous cultural phenomenon. However, it is also acknowledged that there is a significant diversity on the continent and that Africa does not represent a single, homogenous culture [14].

Taylor [35] brings us closer towards practically applying these philosophical constructs in the IS field. He applies the concept of Ubuntu in business ethics using the following derived principle: "An action is right insofar as it promotes cohesion and reciprocal value amongst people. An action is wrong insofar as it damages relationships and devalues any individual or group" [35]. Following his example, interaction designers could, for example, ask the following questions to ensure ethical, viable and practical designs in an African context:

- Does the proposed software design enable cohesion of the community for whom it is developed?
- Does the proposed software promote reciprocal value between the software company and its customers?
- Does the software damage any relationships within the community for whom it is developed?
- Does the software devalue the company's employees or customers?

According to Jack and Avle [11], feminist geopolitics of technology can be used as a lens to question interaction designs originating in the West and disseminated unilaterally to so-called 'developing' countries. A unique feminist lens would emphasize personal and embodied issues in HCI more than national and corporate issues. This lens also values the diversity of cultures and languages in addition to alternative epistemologies.

Such an emic approach can be regarded as the epitome of the localization of the HCI discipline since it operates at the intersection of geopolitics, digital technology, HCI and cultural diversity.

Other enabling forces that may be regarded as emic are decolonization and internationalization if we define internationalization as an attempt to diversify academia [cf. 16, 20]. It should be noted that internationalization is sometimes considered a synonym for globalization [cf. 20]. With reference to HCI, decolonization refers to, inter alia, a "deeper teaching agenda that goes beyond user interface guidelines". Such a broadened scope should include scholarly areas that intersect with relevant constructs in the humanities disciplines [17]. These include the incorporation of cultural principles to ensure software malleability and to inform students on how gender differences in non-Western cultures may influence user acceptance and user experience. This is in addition to alternative approaches for recruiting research participants and the careful adjustment of research approaches to align them with local customs [17]. The internationalization of the HCI discipline is a closely related – maybe even synonymous – concept that refers to the diversification of theoretical concepts and practical methods by enriching current bodies of HCI knowledge with indigenous knowledge systems [cf. 8, 20].

Emic forces that work against the Africanization of the HCI discipline could be the internalization of a colonial state of mind. For example, tertiary students from indigenous groups may not always appreciate lecturers' attempts to localize the syllabus, believing that the Western-dominated content of international textbooks is sufficient for their future careers as software designers.

The concept of 'etic' is defined as the "analysis of cultural phenomena from the perspective of one who does not participate in the culture being studied" [25]. The so-called 'hacker ethic' [10] may be an external force that runs parallel to the emic force of Ubuntu. The emphasis of the hacker ethic on social worth, open sharing of information, and caring (especially for the marginalized) seems to mirror the centrality of humaneness in Ubuntu. The altruistic intent of the hacker ethic is often realized in free and open-source software projects. These philanthropic inclinations of the hacker ethic resonate well with the ideal IS values of avoiding harmful design and striving for advantageous – and even pro bono projects that benefit communities and the world [32]. The laudable aim to advance the community shows a strong affinity with Ubuntu's prioritization of social coherence and communal well-being [cf. 26]. While the juxtaposition of the forces of Ubuntu and the hacker ethic may reveal important ethical similarities across cultures, it could probably also uncover divergent cultural values and work ethics that should be considered in interaction-design organizations. Metz [27], for example, compares Western and African moral principles and finds six similarities and six differences. His contribution provides a solid theoretical basis for IS researchers to amend HCI theory by exploring ways in which the six "moral intuitions" that are more typical of many African cultures can be embedded in software design. In turn, lecturers should consider how these principles can be taught to undergraduate students.

Other forces that may be regarded as etic are globalization and transnationalization if we define these two closely related terms as attempts to homogenize academia worldwide [cf. 16]. Transnational economic forces seem to weaken geographic and political boundaries, indirectly causing "the blurring of the differences between developed and developing countries" [5]. Note that transnationalization is sometimes used more or less as a synonym for localization and diversification, as discussed above [cf. 34]. While the hacker ethic is an etic force promoting the diversification of digital interfaces, globalization is an etic power counteracting it. According to Jaishankar [12], the past few decades were "the iPhone era". During this period globalization was fast-tracked by a drive to make digital technology faster, better and more accessible with the iPhone, which was the culmination of a homogenizing process that embedded Western values into hardware and software and disseminated these globally. However, in the new era, which Jaishankar calls the "Huawei phase", globalization is weakening again. The US paradigms are being replaced with European or Chinese approaches, for example, the monetization of user data (US) is replaced with the protection of customers' rights (Europe) and state control of data (China).

The homogenization of academia – a drive to promote and adhere to uniform syllabi that are internationally competitive – also works against the localization of HCI etically. The global emphasis on research productivity measured by quantitative measures such as authors' citation indexes and journals' impact factors [cf. 37] may further hinder the endeavor. The publish-or-perish drive forces researchers to follow stereotype, standardized research approaches (often positivist/quantitative in nature) to ensure that their research is produced and accepted for publications as fast as possible, thus leaving little room for more esoteric approaches.

An etic force within academia supporting the Africanization of HCI is a drive to decolonize research methodologies in the educational sciences. Khupe [14] provides practical guidelines for the indigenization of education research methods, which seem to be relevant for HCI education. Some principles include an emphasis on researchers in their relationships founded in Ubuntu, respect for the elders and the community, the request for permission to gain access to targeted research participants, and explicit acknowledgement for participation versus the stereotypical anonymous participation. Letsekha [20] advocates a conceptual shift in the debate on the Africanization of tertiary education, believing that endogenization should be considered rather than indigenization. This would imply that HCI scholars should grow the discipline from within the continent using its inherent strengths and resources.

> "Higher education must be made relevant to the material, historical and social realities of the communities in which universities operate. This can be done by drawing on the philosophical traditions and discourses in these communities for relevant concepts and theories" [20].

One example of endogenization is provided by Letseka [19] who argues that good normative values, strategic thinking, and creativity are crucial for interaction design and can be inculcated by Basotho indigenous educational principles. The call for endogenization is a strong etic force that could support Africanized HCI research and tuition.

Although localization and Africanization may be in its infancy in the IS discipline, the HCI field is somewhat exceptional in this regard. Current HCI approaches may overall still resemble Western methodologies, but some work has indeed been done to show how African ways of creating knowledge can and should be used to collect data in local communities in order to enhance software usability and user experience. Volume 29 of the *International Journal of Human-Computer Interaction* is dedicated to "Reframing HCI through Local and Indigenous Perspectives". Three of the seven articles focus specifically on Africa [1]. The volume contributes towards addressing the following problem: "[E]ven if some evidence and rules have been obtained to narrow the challenges in analyzing local and indigenous perspectives relevant for HCI, *the final analysis of the intercultural HCI design process and its relating cultural differences is still outstanding* [emphasis added]" [1]. This subfield of IS may, therefore, facilitate a deeper and more systematic reflection on the use of African ways of knowing in the IS discipline.

Winschiers-Theophilus and Bidwell [42] believe that a set of tools is necessary for interaction design that is rooted in epistemologies that are aligned with the community for whom the software is developed. For example, in an Afro-centric paradigm, the researchers should become part of the collective community by using a collaborative design approach. Heimgärtner [9] constructed a conceptual model to determine a community's cultural profile in order to assist software analysts and programmers in ensuring intercultural interaction design. The model consists of four dimensions (i.e. uncertainty, individualism, sensitivity and term duration indices). This model has not been validated sufficiently to be generalized. This leaves room for follow-up empirical research to test and revise the proposed dimensions for the African context.

Geopolitics refers to the "interdependent relationship between politics and geography, sociology, demography and economy" [5]. Geopolitical powers promoting the Africanization of HCI include some of the United Nations' strategic development goals (SDGs) [40], for example, Goal 4: "Ensure inclusive and equitable quality education and promote lifelong learning opportunities for all". While inclusiveness supports the idea that knowledge should be localized, lifelong learning stresses the importance of facilitating the digital literacy training of older people, as discussed above. One of the targets of this SDG involves the "appreciation of cultural diversity". However, the targets of this SDG primarily focus on the youth and should be amended to include the older and often left-behind age groups. Scholars of HCI could, for example, conduct interaction-design research to improve cultural inclusivity and age-related accessibility of digital educational systems. Other positive geopolitical influences are the targets and strategies of local governments and research bodies that influence tertiary teaching and learning. In South Africa, for example, the National Research Foundation (NRF) catalyzes research that is aligned with national priorities such as transformation and government strategies, for example, the grand challenges of promoting human and social dynamics, and cultivating indigenous knowledge systems [29].

Ironically, other United Nations SDGs may endorse geopolitical tensions working against the Africanization of HCI. Actions to curb climate change, to promote clean energy, to encourage responsible consumption patterns, etc., may slow down the development of emerging economies. Austerity measures may restraint projects that use dirty energy sources or that could be regarded by profit-driven companies as non-essential nice-to-haves such as localization initiatives.

## 4 The Practical Side of IS and HCI Africanization

In addition to the theoretical and methodological aspects, there is also a practical side to Africanization research in Computing. Chughtai et al. [6] believe that information technology (IT) and IS should be demarginalized. Not only the way in which indigenous communities use software but also how previously disadvantaged communities "shape digital technologies" should be investigated. This could facilitate the process to overcome the existing state of affairs in which mainly Western cultural constructs are deeply embedded in digital technologies. The task for developers of information systems in this regard is to build the perspectives of marginalized communities into the software that they use. Jack and Avle [11] propose the use of feminist geopolitics of technology to refocus digital technology on "the affective everyday practices of care on the ground". Biyela et al. [3] study how ICTs are 'domesticated' or 'appropriated' [cf. 34] by local African communities to serve their unique purposes, for example, the use of WhatsApp to manage small businesses or a Stokvel (an indigenous South African way of saving money). This is another, opposite side of the relationship between design and usability regarding the localization of HCI.

The need to Africanize software programs subsequently challenges IS lecturers in Africa to sensitize their undergraduate HCI students to the problems and challenges facing interaction designers. Academics should teach the learners how to gather information for system and interface analysis and design, and train them how to apply conceptual ideas about Africanization practically. Complementing the syllabus in this way may eventually enhance the usability and user experience of software in local communities. One could apply Naudé's [30] discussion of three decolonization models for business ethics to guide the Africanization of undergraduate HCI syllabi. Interaction designers should be taught to be cautious of using a transfer model (simply using Western-based interfaces in Africa without any cultural adaptation). Designers should rather consider at least a translation model (critically appraising Western concepts from African contexts and using local case studies), or even better, a substantive model (developing distinct African methods, approaches and interfaces). Information systems designers should realize that their software has an impact on society and thus, a strong sense of responsibility and morality is required to align these artefacts with "global common values *and local cultural differences* [emphasis added]" [32]. One area where this is especially important is the design of artificial intelligence systems where unrepresentative training models may lead to biased outcomes and inaccurate predictions [41]. According to Rogerson [32], popular IS textbooks exclude or underplay ethics topics in general. Educators of HCI should, therefore, be challenged to address this gap in IS training by including ethical thinking and value systems in their HCI curricula.

Another practical application of the research could focus on the computer literacy of older people in Africa. Martínez-Alcalá et al. [22] are concerned that older populations in many parts of the world are being left behind due to a lack of digital skills and internet access. They argue for research to gain insight into how older people use electronic technology in order to guide the development of appropriate digital solutions. Although they do not discuss HCI in depth, Martínez-Alcalá et al. [22] mention that these solutions should include appropriate design. Interfaces that can be learned easily and used intuitively will enhance interaction with software; for example, replacing text with symbols could enhance the chatbot experience of older people of diverse language groups [41]. This provides an opportunity to engage with the community and to carry out participatory research that could eventually lead to better adoption of information systems by older Africans.

## 5 African Value Systems and Fine Arts

Other aspects that could be covered in Africanized HCI syllabi include African ethical systems and fine arts. Similar to other scientific paradigms, ethical systems change incrementally until a revolution eventually occurs in which an outdated set of values is replaced by a new set. In the social sciences, this phenomenon often prevents the replication of previous studies, especially where experiments that were conducted on vulnerable communities in the past would violate current human rights systems [13]. Moreover, one has to admit that scientific paradigms often reflect Western values [13]. Tsey [37] calls for the incorporation of African (and other local) narrative techniques, value systems and participatory action research for data gathering in the social sciences. Lazem [18] agrees that participatory research is a good way to indigenize epistemology on a deep level. Metz [26] encourages the use of the Ubuntu concept of harmonious relationships as a foundation for morality and an African value system. He believes that such an Ubuntu-based moral theory could solve legal and business issues in a unique way [26]. In addition, it could possibly resolve ethical issues in computing and guide interaction design in Africa.

Although some work has been done in IS theory on ethics, very little, if any, has been done in terms of the use of African ethical systems within the discipline. If we acknowledge that researchers' cultural 'baggage' affects their approach to scientific endeavors (post-positivism), it becomes imperative that alternative value systems should be investigated to enrich the underlying theories in IS. The development of local IS and HCI theories is indeed an important requirement towards the decolonization of the disciplines. To avoid a superficial glossing over, Mamdani [21] makes it clear that decolonizing universities should be based on an African mode of reasoning and should develop and foster local scholarly traditions, use indigenous languages, and theorize the African reality. Lecturers also have a responsibility to introduce their undergraduate HCI students to African value concepts in order to avoid the mere transfer of embedded Western values in ICT.

In addition, there is a gap for extensive reflection on the use of the fine arts in IS theory. Oates [31] discusses the reciprocal enrichment between computer art and IS. In further research, her contribution to humanities-informed IS could be extended by investigating how African art could be used to augment IS theory and how the look and feel of information systems could be adapted to be more intuitive for African users. For example, a basket metaphor could be used instead of files and folders as digital containers for related computing objects [36]. IS scholars should also reflect on ways to include this knowledge in HCI syllabi.

## 6 Conclusion

Promoting a paradigm shift towards the decolonization of science by Africanizing the HCI discipline can be achieved by encouraging sensitivity towards the challenges that are created by Western concepts and that are deeply ingrained within many interfaces of information systems. The Ubuntu concept and related African value systems should be explored to enrich the leading Western epistemologies used in HCI. Proposals have been made to adjust the curricula of undergraduate HCI courses in order to train a new generation of interaction designers who are well equipped to analyze current design principles critically and to develop alternative interfaces that are more intuitive for African users. The essay reflects on how emic and ethic geopolitical forces can either promote or counteract attempts to Africanize the discipline (e.g. Ubuntu and the hacker ethic on the one hand versus an internalized colonial state of mind and globalization on the other hand). There is ample room for further research, including the relevance of issues such as feminist geopolitics of technology, localization, and decoloniality and internationalization versus transnational and homogenizing forces regarding this transdisciplinary field. Furthermore, the 17 SDGs should be studied in more depth to determine if and how they inspire or discourage the Africanization and decolonization of HCI.

Using African case studies for assignment questions could prompt students to apply theoretical HCI principles in local scenarios. In addition, the HCI theory may be enriched by borrowing concepts from African epistemology, ethics and arts. This may not only prepare students for their roles as software and interface designers in Africa but could also cultivate their higher order thinking and learning skills such as analysis and synthesis. Including these approaches in undergraduate HCI tuition should enable students to evaluate interaction designs critically from an African perspective and to suggest alternative designs that incorporate African metaphors. Applying these acquired skills in their careers in the industry could eventually lead to Africanized software and interfaces that reflect the diversity of cultures on the continent.

**Acknowledgements.** This article is an extended and revised version of a position paper read at the IFIP WG 13.8 Workshop on Geopolitical Issues in Human-Computer Interaction that was held online on August 30, 2021. The research was supported in part by the National Research Foundation (NRF) of South Africa (Grant Number 132180) and the Research Professor Support Programme of the University of South Africa (Unisa). The grant holder acknowledges that opinions, findings and conclusions or recommendations expressed in the article are that of the author and that neither the NRF nor Unisa accepts any liability whatsoever in this regard. I would like to acknowledge the valuable feedback received from the peer reviewers and workshop attendees that was used to improve and extend the original workshop paper for publication in the workshop proceedings.

## References

1. Abdelnour-Nocera, J., Clemmensen, T., Kurosu, M.: Reframing HCI through local and indigenous perspectives. Int. J. Hum. Comput. Interact. **29**(4), 201–204 (2013). https://doi.org/10.1080/10447318.2013.765759

2. van Biljon, J., Renaud, K., Chimbo, B.: Visualization of African knowledge to embody the spirit of African storytelling: principles, practices and evaluation. In: Proceedings of AfriCHI 2018, 3–7 December, Windhoek, Namibia (2018). https://doi.org/10.1145/3283458.3283496
3. Biyela, N., Tsibolane, P., Van Belle, J.-P.: Domestication of ICTs in community savings and credit associations (stokvels) in the Western Cape, South Africa. Commun. Comput. Inf. Sci. **933**, 35–47 (2019). https://doi.org/10.1007/978-3-303-11235-6_3(Springer, Heidelberg, IDIA 2018)
4. Boland, R.J., Newman, M., Pentland, B.T.: Hermeneutical exegesis in information systems design and use. Inf. Organ. **20**(1), 1–20 (2010). https://doi.org/10.1016/j.infoandorg.2009.09.001
5. Cătălina, L.: Geopolitics - a new framework of analysis: global challenges and perspectives. SEA – Pract. Appl. Sci. **III**(1), 437–443 (2015)
6. Chughtai, H., et al.: Demarginalizing interdisciplinarity in IS research: interdisciplinary research in marginalization. Commun. Assoc. Inf. Syst. **46**(13), 296–315 (2020). https://doi.org/10.17705/1CAIS.04613
7. Creswell, J.W.: Research Design: Qualitative, Quantitative, and Mixed Methods Approaches. SAGE, Thousand Oaks, CA (2009). https://doi.org/10.2307/1523157
8. Dzvimbo, K.P., Moloi, K.C.: Globalisation and the internationalisation of higher education in sub-Saharan Africa. South African J. Educ. **33**(3), 1–16 (2013)
9. Heimgärtner, R.: Reflections on a model of culturally influenced Human-Computer Interaction to cover cultural contexts in HCI design. Int. J. Hum. Comput. Interact. **29**(4), 205–219 (2013). https://doi.org/10.1080/10447318.2013.765761
10. Himanen, P.: The Hacker Ethic, and the Spirit of the Information Age (with prologue by L. Torvalds and epilogue by M Castells). Kindle edn. Random House Books, New York, NY (2001)
11. Jack, M., Avle, S.: A feminist geopolitics of technology. Glob. Perspect. **2**(1), 1–18 (2021). https://doi.org/10.1525/gp.2021.24398
12. Jaishankar, D.: From the iPhone to Huawei: the new geopolitics of technology. https://www.brookings.edu/blog/order-from-chaos/2019/07/31/from-the-iphone-to-huawei-the-new-geopolitics-of-technology/. Accessed on 11 Oct 2021
13. Kalelioğlu, U.B.: The contemporary critique of positivism: the issues of replicability and universality. In: Sönmez, S., Özçoban, E., Balkan, D., Karaku, H. (eds.) New Horizons in Social, Human and Administrative Sciences, pp. 509–559. Gece, New York, NY (2019)
14. Khupe, C.: Towards an African education research methodology: decolonising new knowledge. Educ. Res. Soc. Chang. **6**(1), 25–37 (2017). https://doi.org/10.17159/2221-4070/2017/v6i1a3
15. Kosaka, T.: The semantic web and turns of social science. In: Mola, L., Carugati, A., Kokkinaki, A., Pouloudi, N. (eds.) Proceedings of the 8th Mediterranean Conference on Information Systems. Verona, Italy (2014)
16. Kroeze, J.H.: A framework for the Africanisation of the information systems discipline. Altern. Interdiscip. J. Study Arts Humanit. South. Africa. **28**, 38–65 (2019). https://doi.org/10.29086/2519-5476/2019/sp28.4a2
17. Lazem, S., Saleh, M., Alabdulqader, E.: ArabHCI. Commun. ACM. **64**(4), 69–71 (2021). https://doi.org/10.1145/3447733
18. Lazem, S., Giglitto, D., Nkwo, M.S., Mthoko, H., Upani, J., Peters, A.: Challenges and paradoxes in decolonising HCI: a critical discussion. Comput. Support. Coop. Work, 1–38 (2021). https://doi.org/10.1007/s10606-021-09398-0
19. Letseka, M.: Educating for Ubuntu/Botho: lessons from Basotho indigenous education. Open J. Philos. **3**(2), 337–344 (2013). https://doi.org/10.4236/ojpp.2013.32051
20. Letsekha, T.: Revisiting the debate on the Africanisation of higher education: an appeal for a conceptual shift. Indep. J. Teach. Learn. **8**(1), 5–18 (2013)

21. Mamdani, M.: Decolonising universities. In: Jansen, J.D. (ed.) Decolonisation in Universities: The Politics of Knowledge, pp. 15–28. Wits University Press, Johannesburg (2019). https://doi.org/10.18772/22019083351.6
22. Martínez-Alcalá, C.I., et al.: Digital inclusion in older adults: a comparison between face-to-face and blended digital literacy workshops. Front. ICT. **5**(21), 1–17 (2018). https://doi.org/10.3389/fict.2018.00021
23. Menze, A., Tsibolane, P.: Online stokvels: the use of social media by the marginalized. In: CONF-IRM 2019 Proceedings, pp. 1–13 (2019)
24. Merriam-Webster.com Dictionary: Emic. https://www.merriam-webster.com/dictionary/emic. Accessed on 08 Oct 2021
25. Merriam-Webster.com Dictionary: Etic. https://www.merriam-webster.com/dictionary/etic. Accessed on 08 Oct 2021
26. Metz, T.: The motivation for "toward an African moral theory." South African J. Philos. **26**(4), 331–335 (2007). https://doi.org/10.4314/sajpem.v26i4.31490
27. Metz, T.: Toward an African moral theory. J. Polit. Philos. **15**(3), 321–341 (2007). https://doi.org/10.1111/j.1467-9760.2007.00280.x
28. Myers, M.D., Chughtai, H., Davidson, E., Tsibolane, P., Young, A.: Studying the other or becoming the other: engaging with indigenous peoples in IS research (report on panel discussion on the ethics and politics of engagement with indigenous peoples in Information Systems (IS) research at the 40th ICIS, 2019, Munich). Commun. Assoc. Inf. Syst. **47**, 382–396 (2020). https://doi.org/10.17705/1CAIS.04718
29. National Research Foundation (CSIR): National Research Foundation Strategy 2020. https://www.nrf.ac.za/sites/default/files/documents/NRFStrategyImplementation.pdf (2020). Accessed on 11 Oct 2021
30. Naudé, P.: Decolonising knowledge: can Ubuntu ethics save us from coloniality? (Ex Africa semper aliquid novi?). In: Jansen, J.D. (ed.) Decolonisation in Universities: The Politics of Knowledge, pp. 217–238. Wits University Press, Johannesburg (2019). https://doi.org/10.18772/22019083351.6
31. Oates, B.J.: New frontiers for Information Systems research: computer art as an information system. Eur. J. Inf. Syst. **15**(6), 617–626 (2006). https://doi.org/10.1057/palgrave.ejis.3000649
32. Rogerson, S., Miller, K.W., Winter, J.S., Larson, D.: Information systems ethics – challenges and opportunities. J. Inform. Commun. Ethics Soc. **17**(1), 87–97 (2019). https://doi.org/10.1108/JICES-07-2017-0041
33. Romm, N.R.A.: Conducting focus groups in terms of an appreciation of indigenous ways of knowing: some examples from South Africa. Forum Qual. Sozialforsch./Forum Qual. Soc. Res. **16**(1) (2014). https://doi.org/10.17169/fqs-16.1.2087
34. Shklovski, I., Vertesi, J., Lindtner, S.: Introduction to this special issue on transnational HCI. Hum.-Comput. Interact. **29**(1), 1–21 (2014). https://doi.org/10.1080/07370024.2013.823823
35. Taylor, D.F.P.: Defining Ubuntu for business ethics - a deontological approach. South African J. Philos. **33**(3), 331–345 (2014). https://doi.org/10.1080/02580136.2014.948328
36. Thinyane, H., Gavaza, T., Terzoli, A.: An investigation into culturally-relevant GUI components within marginalised South African communities. In: ICT for Development: People, Policy and Practice, IDIA2011 Conference Proceedings, pp. 177–190 (2011)
37. Tsey, K.: Making social science matter?: case studies from community development and empowerment education research in rural Ghana and Aboriginal Australia. Asian Soc. Sci. **6**(1), 3–12 (2010). https://doi.org/10.5539/ass.v6n1p3
38. Tsibolane, P.: Towards a conceptual framework for social wellbeing through inclusive frugal ICT innovation in postcolonial collectivist contexts. In: CONF-IRM 2016 Proceedings, pp. 1–12 (2016)

39. Tsibolane, P., Brown, I.: Principles for conducting critical research using postcolonial theory in ICT4D studies. In: Proceedings of the Ninth Annual Workshop of the AIS Special Interest Group for ICT in Global Development (SIG GlobDev 2016). Dublin, Ireland, December 11 (Reflecting on appropriate global development and the role of ICTs and digital innovation), pp. 1–27 (2016)
40. United Nations Department of Economic and Social Affairs: Strategic development goals (SDGs). https://sdgs.un.org/goals. Accessed on 08 Oct 2021
41. Wambsganns, T., Höch, A., Zierau, N., Söllne, M.: Ethical design of conversational agents: toward principles for a value-sensitive design. In: Wirtschaftsinformatik 2021 proceedings, pp. 1–18 (2021)
42. Winschiers-Theophilus, H., Bidwell, N.J.: Toward an Afro-centric indigenous HCI paradigm. Int. J. Hum. Comput. Interact. **29**(4), 243–255 (2013). https://doi.org/10.1080/10447318.2013.765763

# Subverting Divisive Geopolitical Issues in HCI Through Autonomous Design and Punk Narratives

David Naranjo-Romero[1(✉)] and Leonardo Parra-Agudelo[2]

[1] Department of Systems and Computer Engineering, Universidad de los Andes, Bogotá, Colombia
da-naran@uniandes.edu.co

[2] Department of Design, Universidad de los Andes, Bogotá, Colombia
leonardo.parra@uniandes.edu.co

**Abstract.** Nowadays, the field of Human Computer Interaction (HCI) can be seen as a contact zone where different cultures, paradigms and worldviews meet. A critical analysis of these encounters brings to light several contradictions, asymmetrical relations of power, and other geopolitical issues that discourage the open discussion of large-scale societal issues, due to the controversies and divisiveness that can be found in the intersection between HCI and public policy. In this paper, we explore some of the factors that contribute to this divisiveness, and examine different design practices that have been used in the HCI community for approaching wicked social problems. Then, we present Autonomous Design as a legitimate practice in HCI that tackles these divisive issues, and introduce Punk narratives and aesthetics as a tool for prototyping better futures where multiple worlds co-exist in a relational manner.

**Keywords:** Geopolitical issues · HCI knowledge · Autonomous design · Decolonial perspectives · Societal issues · Design futures

## 1 Introduction

Rapid technological advances have made our civilization more connected, and have shown the benefits and drawbacks of different governance models. The 1989 Tiananmen Protests, the 2011 Arab Spring, the 2019 Chile riots, and the 2019 and 2021 protests in Colombia are examples of social unrest due to governmental failure to address civic needs. For instance, the Colombian protests, which started as a result of a controversial tax legislation, provide a platform to express frustration about corruption scandals, the assassination of social leaders, police brutality, and a general lack of opportunities for local youth and underserved communities. The critical times we live in are currently being addressed by research that explores how to design better futures in the face of civilizational crisis [11], and how technology can assist humanity in coping with major societal problems [78], while taking into account the needs and context of traditionally


Published by Springer Nature Switzerland AG 2022
C. Ardito et al. (Eds.): INTERACT 2021, LNCS 13198, pp. 503–522, 2022.
https://doi.org/10.1007/978-3-030-98388-8_45

marginalized groups. To achieve these goals, the HCI community requires a critical examination of its theories and practices, as well as free discussion on topics that often transcend political, cultural, and geographical barriers.

To contribute on developing a frame of understanding of geopolitical issues in HCI [1], in Sect. 2, we examine the fragmentation of the field of Human-Computer Interaction and identify three areas of controversy and divisiveness. Then, in Sect. 3, we examine four design practices, as well as their criticisms for dealing with large-scale societal problems. Afterwards, in Sect. 4, we embrace the plurality of paradigms in HCI and introduce a nascent design practice, Autonomous Design, as a platform to rethink and subvert HCI and its traditional divisive and binary paradigms. Then, in Sect. 5, we examine the role of Speculative Fiction and Worldmaking in the development of future scenarios, and introduce the notion of Punk Narratives. We make an argument for using Autonomous Design and Punk Narratives to go beyond utopia-dystopia dichotomies, and focus on prototyping possible futures where multiple worlds could exist in a relational manner. Finally, we make some recommendations for collaboration and point to future research directions.

## 2 Global Issues and Divisiveness in HCI

There are prevalent issues on a global scale that we can no longer ignore in our respective practices: The ongoing geopolitical state of affairs of the world, the crescent risk of environmental collapse, the rupture of the social fabric in the face of a global pandemic, and the current levels of social unrest and distrust in public institutions and professionals. Nowadays, these issues are sparking rich debates in venues such as CHI, CSCW, ICEIS, and INTERACT, in journals such as *Interactions*, IJHCI, ToCHI, and many other publications as well.

However, this was not always the case: The scope and breadth of the field of HCI has expanded, starting from a techno-centric standpoint, and currently undergoing several changes of paradigms and assumptions. Sometimes, this growth has brought frictions among researchers, practitioners, and the communities that have been the target of studies. For this reason, it is critical to understand the historical forces that have kept the field fragmented [34], and examine the current sources of divisiveness when dealing with global issues.

### 2.1 Waves of HCI

The evolution of the field of HCI is often depicted as waves. Although there is a consensus on the presence of different 'waves', the definition and understanding of what constitutes each wave is far from settled. Nevertheless, there is a commonality in the sense of a gradual and considerable expansion of HCI's concerns, methodologies, and application areas [28]:

**First Wave.** According to Harrison et al. [38], this wave is an amalgam of engineering and human factors, seeing interaction as a form of man-machine coupling in ways inspired by industrial engineering and ergonomics. According to Bødker [8], this wave combined cognitive science and human factors. It was model-driven, and focused on the human being as a subject to be studied through rigid guidelines, formal methods, and systematic testing.

**Second Wave.** According to Harrison et al. [38], this wave is organized around a central metaphor of mind and computer as symmetric, coupled information processors. Grounded in cognitive science, HCI is understood in terms of information transfer and effective communication. To Bødker [8], research paid a lot of attention to cooperation, learning, and participation in work contexts. Situated action, distributed cognition, and activity theory were important sources of theoretical reflection. Proactive methods, such as a variety of participatory design workshops, prototyping, and contextual inquiries were added to the toolbox.

**Third Wave.** To Harrison et al. [38], there were several limitations of the second wave's approach to social interaction, user/ambient context, the role of emotion in cognition, and the values associated by technology. These issues paved the way to new approaches such as participatory design, value sensitive design, user experience design, ethnomethodology, embodied interaction, interaction analysis, and critical design. Bødker [8] concurs with Harrison et al.: The third wave challenged the values related to technology in the second wave, and embraced experience and meaning-making. It signaled a departure from workplace to our homes and everyday lives and culture. It embraced emergent use of technologies, and its presence in all aspects of our lives.

### 2.2 Controversy in HCI

When discussing social, political, ethical, and societal implications of computer systems, HCI researchers may approach areas that are controversial, as researchers may not share the same views or goals regarding issues at the intersection of HCI and policy [40]. While discussion is one of the tenets of academic research, recurring tensions inside the community can lead to community fragmentation and academic rivalry [34], selection and publication biases [7], and other unintended consequences. To illuminate the sources of this divisiveness, we have identified three broad areas where geopolitical tensions are likely to surface:

**Dominant Paradigms.** Pratt [69] introduced the term **contact zones** to describe social spaces where disparate cultures meet, clash, and grapple with each other, often in highly asymmetrical relations of domination and subordination. Nowadays, HCI can be seen as a contact zone where dominant paradigms clash with a myriad of alternate practices. Dominant HCI paradigms are deeply rooted in a western epistemology that inherits a certain bias through embedded assumptions, values, definitions, techniques, frameworks, and models [91]. In addition, most HCI papers are supported by research performed in western, educated, industrialized, rich and democratic (WEIRD) societies [55,80]. Western epistemologies and models of value, quality and participation reinforce political configurations of exclusion, and limit the potential of HCI to integrate other views, forms of being, living and understanding the world and the field itself [1]. Furthermore, it legitimates a division of labor where academics located in the North Atlantic produce theories while scholars around the world must bring local cases to complement or extend them [15].

**Social Justice and Global Democracy.** Democracy is often associated with universal values such as participation, fairness, and inclusion. In practice, however, these values are usually limited to those with access and trust in the system itself – those deemed eligible, law-abiding, righteous, and human [2]. This contradiction can also be found at a supra-national level: While international relations between states subscribe to idealized models of global democracy, in practice they are based on unequal power relations and principles inherited from colonial and imperial traditions [6]. Recently, Hayes [39] examined the issue of inclusion and participation in the SIGCHI community:

> *Critical reflection on ourselves as a community is not easy. The CHI community, in my experience, truly wants to be inclusive and wants technology to be "for good." Even so, it is hard to acknowledge systems of oppression that are largely invisible and beneficial for a subset of us. [...] It is easier to ignore those systems and pretend we are all equal. But when we do that, there is a great potential to become offended, saddened, or defensive in the face of critique.*

**Prevalent Dichotomies and Binary Futures.** Asymmetrical encounters between paradigms are usually expressed as dichotomies, i.e. *west/non-west*, *developed/developing*, *north/south*, giving preferential treatment to a dominant paradigm (e.g. west), while placing myriads of subordinate practices from all over the world under one label (e.g. non-west), thus deepening the cultural, technological, and social divides of our world. This binary view is also present in the ways that we envision the future: Slaughter [75] calls into attention our tendency to frame the future as a polar choice between optimistic utopias – full of unabated growth fueled by technology– and pessimistic dystopias placed amidst societal and environmental collapse. In order to emancipate from these dichotomies and analyze how HCI should shape and is shaped by different models of democracy and governance that shape our ideas of the future [1], HCI lacks a common ground where whole spectra of identities, values, ideologies, and governance models can be identified and freely discussed.

## 3 Design Practices for Addressing Societal Issues

A critical view on the dominant paradigms of Human Computer Interaction requires an examination of the different design practices that are currently used in HCI, the assumptions that they carry, and the benefits (or drawbacks) that they bring when addressing large-scale societal issues. We focus on four design practices that appear in HCI literature: *Design* and *Designerly Thinking* [37], *Speculative Design* [92], and *Value Sensitive Design* [30].

What do these practices have in common? They all start from the paradigm of *Wicked Problems* [71], and approach in their own ways the problem of designing for the future while taking into account the context, value systems, practices, and knowledge of the communities impacted by the design process. To have a balanced overview of these practices, we include a summary of each design practice accompanied by a critique, not as a way of undermining the practice in itself, but as a brief discussion of its shortcomings under the light of the divisive issues described in Sect. 2. Critique, delivered from a position of confidence in the value of these practices [56] is often an indication of the maturity of the practice [29], adds nuance to the discussion [52], and contributes to its enrichment.

### 3.1 Design Thinking

The mainstream use of the term Design Thinking usually refers to the approach created by Kelley et al. [49] as a label for exporting the design processes and methods of IDEO, a design and consulting firm. It takes several design practices and applies them outside the context of design, to be used by people without a background in design, e.g. managers, consultants, and educators. Design Thinking approaches Wicked Problems by suggesting general actions (e.g. Inspiration, Ideation, Observation) that drive creativity and innovation. It also offers a collection of tools and techniques (e.g. Brainstorming, Storytelling, Journey Map) for engaging with stakeholders.

**Critique.** This particular flavor of Design Thinking has received its fair share of criticism. As Laursen and Møller [52] explain, Design Thinking has been ultimately rejected by design scholars and practitioners, as it has little to do with the field of design and its research practice. Instead, it can be seen more as a creative approach for problem-solving in management theory [46]. This is because it provides a set of suggested actions that provide little guidance to non-designers when it comes to selecting and using design tools and techniques. Irani [42] goes further, arguing that Design Thinking articulates a racialized understanding of labor fueled by social anxieties and the desire of placing North American design at the apex of global hierarchies of labor and creativity.

### 3.2 Designerly Thinking

Design*erly* Thinking is a practice-based design approach for addressing Wicked Problems in a multidisciplinary manner. In this approach, the perspectives of customers, users, and stakeholders are welcome, as is their active participation in the design process [86]. While Designerly Thinking shares the same basic tenets of Design Thinking, e.g. applying abductive reasoning to wicked problems, it differentiates itself from the latter by providing concrete methodological approaches (e.g. Reflective Practice, Co-development of problem and solution, Framing) that can be adapted to different problem situations [52]. Furthermore, it goes beyond mere description, involving a constant reformulation of the problem, as well as the refinement of possible solutions in an iterative manner.

**Critique.** While Designerly Thinking is still a viable approach to addressing societal problems, Vermaas and Pesch [86] argue that current incarnations of Designerly Thinking are not well-equipped for addressing societal issues and overcoming the general sense of distrust in the role of the designer, as this practice does not resolve the three social dilemmas first identified by Rittel and Webber [71]: Defining societal goodness, dispelling the wickedness of societal problems, and achieving social equity.

This loss of confidence in the design profession is most problematic when applying conventional design practices to local and underserved communities, as these practices perpetuate and legitimize latent systems of oppression [84], and impose a western view of innovation and progress that clashes with local views [37], an effort in translation where those invested with authority interpret the practices, beliefs, and words of a group taken to be inherently less sophisticated, less capable of speaking on its own behalf [16].

### 3.3 Speculative (Critical) Design

Speculative Design is a design practice coming from Critical Design that questions current normative design practices in the wake of wicked societal problems and a globalized world, advocating for a democratic and open discussion into how science and technology is developed and directed [56]. This practice assumes that *"many of the challenges we face today are unfixable and that the only way to overcome them is by changing our values, beliefs, attitudes, and behavior"* [20]. Thus, instead of trying to predict the future, Speculative Design seeks *"to open up all sorts of possibilities that can be discussed, debated, and used to collectively define a preferable future for a given group of people: from companies, to cities, to societies"* [20].

Dunne and Raby argue that by exploring alternative future scenarios, reality will become more malleable, and increase the probability of more desirable futures happening [20]. To describe the likelihood of potential future scenarios, this practice introduces the notions of Possible, Plausible, Probable, and Preferable futures. When constructing such scenarios, the speculative designer employs satiric mechanisms of understatement, distortion, and allegory [56]. As sources of inspiration and methodological playgrounds, Speculative Design encourages the use of cinema, literature, science, ethics, politics, and art. For creating scenarios, this practice offers tools such as *fictional worlds, cautionary tales, what-if scenarios, thought experiments, conterfactuals, reductio ad absurdum experiments,* and *prefigurative futures* [20].

A future scenario is materialized by creating a fictional object, that despite being of the highest design quality, it is not intended for mass production. Instead, this object is destined for public display (e.g. in a museum, exhibition, or in media appearances). Similar to cinematic props, these objects embody the narrative of the future scenario, triggering an imaginative response in the viewer, and extending an invitation to examine the mundane implications of scientific and technological advances.

**Critique.** In his writings [83] and interviews [65], Cameron Tonkinwise, while acknowledging the potential value of the practice and its motivation, also points to multiple shortcomings and contradictions in the discourse and practice of Speculative and Critical Design, limiting the applicability of the practice:

> *"I do think that the working assumption of Speculative Everything has merit, at least for the late consumer capitalist economies of the North/West."* [83]

This onto-epistemic standpoint neglects cultural, geopolitical, and economic differences among populations:

> *"It is an epistemological error when Speculative (Critical) Designers at the Royal College of Art, for instance, imagine what they believe to be dystopian scenarios in a distant future, when in fact people in other parts of the world are already living versions of those lifestyles."* [65]

This only contributes further to the view of design as an elitist practice, and increases the distrust of communities that pursue non-eurocentric futures. To overcome this issue, Tonkinwise encourages designers to approach other cultures, not as examples of the past, but as plausible models for the future [65].

Another issue with Speculative Design is the idiosyncratic nature of the produced artifacts: Dunne and Raby suggest (or rather impose) concrete aesthetic choices that configure what is and what is not approved as Speculative Design [83]. Their emphasis on satire, and the exaggeration of certain features to suspend disbelief make of this practice an uncompromising approach: Despite its very valid aspiration to question our relationships with designed objects, Speculative Design focuses this critique on a purely aesthetic level [61], and produces objects with no function, i.e. the product does not address community context and needs.

Another point of contention is the predominance of grim dystopias in the formulation of possible/probable future scenarios in Speculative Design. This is a consequence of its critical approach, that seeks controversy and reflection on the direction that unabated technological advancements entail. While necessary, this discussion does not provide pathways that formulate positive actions as a society, it only shows us the dangers that lie ahead.

### 3.4 Value Sensitive Design (VSD)

This practice provides an overarching theoretical and methodological framework that accounts for **human values** in a principled and designed manner throughout the design process [29,31], making a distinction between stakeholder values, designer values, and a project's explicit values. It also provides a list of human values that are often implicated in the intersection of design and technology:

> *Human welfare, ownership and property, privacy, freedom from bias, universal usability, trust, autonomy, informed consent, accountability, courtesy, identity, calmness, and environmental sustainability.*

VSD also offers seventeen methods for identifying stakeholders, discovering value sources, eliciting and analyzing particular values, and uncovering complex social relationships among values, technology, and social structures. This practice has an *Interactional Stance*, which means that *"human beings acting as individuals, organizations, or societies shape the tools and technologies they design and implement; in turn, those tools and technologies shape human experience and society"* [29]. This stance recognizes that values do not exist in isolation, and tensions arise when there is a conflict between values (e.g. security versus privacy) among different stakeholders. When faced with such tensions, the authors offer two strategies: 1) Focus on shared action, and 2) Pause the design process and wait.

**Critique.** The main critique towards Value Sensitive Design regards its commitment to universal values. Friedman and Hendry recognize that there are inherent risks in providing a specific list of human values, as it would privilege certain stakeholder groups, either by including or excluding certain values; moreover, any list of human values would likely be incomplete [29].

Having acknowledged these limitations, they provide a list of thirteen values often found in System Design. These values are typical from a liberal and relatively privileged western perspective, and come from HCI work that has been done in such a context [10]. Indeed, with some notable exceptions [4], Value Sensitive Design has been largely employed in western and urban contexts, and needs to be applied to other sociocultural contexts [29]. This issue is more dire when addressing geopolitical and cross-cultural issues, as different governance models and cultures subscribe to these values in different degrees.

Another common criticism is the lack of an ethical commitment: While taking notions from deontological and consequentialist ethics [29], VSD lacks a complimentary or explicit ethical theory for dealing with value tensions, as well as distinguishing genuine moral values from mere preferences or whims [57]. Instead, designers are encouraged to introduce relevant theories when necessary. The problem with this suggestion is that there are too many theories to choose from: *Utilitarism, Deontological Ethics, Consequentialist Ethics, Care Ethics, African Ethics, Confucian Ethics, Libertarian Ethics, Virtue Theory, Feminist Ethics,* and so on.

Finally, another issue is the anthropocentric status of the practice, as VSD is focused on *human* values [29], neglecting other perspectives (e.g. nonhuman species, superorganisms, the Earth, and social robots):

> *"Yet the technologies we design and build reach far beyond human beings to implicate other nonhuman entities. How to account meaningfully for the values of nonhumans within value sensitive design remains an open question".*

## 4 Towards a Pluriversal HCI

The design theories and practices described in the previous section are just a sample of a multitude of legitimate approaches that have surfaced from the second and third waves of HCI, each of them counting with established communities of research and practice. However, more than fifteen years have passed since a third wave of HCI was identified: The landscape of technology has changed, with several fora in the digital grounds where people meet, interact, and collaborate (e.g. Social Networks, Communication platforms, Collaborative Whiteboards), as well as new applications enabled by Artificial Intelligence and Virtual Reality.

### 4.1 Breaking the Waves

This would make us wonder whether we are undergoing a *fourth wave* of HCI. However, in 2015, when asked this same question, Bødker [8] answered that the field is in the middle of a chaos of multiplicity in terms of technologies, use situations, methods, and concepts, and that there are multiple unaddressed issues from the second and third waves. Furthermore, the public is examining the role of HCI in issues such as digital addiction, fake news, social media abuse, increased surveillance and rampant data collection [72].

Perhaps this might be an opportunity for abandoning the 'waves' metaphor. While the numbered system of waves might suggest more sophistication and better ideas, it is better to see these waves as strands of HCI research that run in parallel [34]. Work has been done that cuts across the paradigms or that exists outside them entirely [38], and many practitioners are developing hybrid approaches and technologies bridging across the discursive terrains of the various waves [28]. The field as a whole is being more critical, rediscovering works coming from other perspectives, challenging preconceived notions and introducing social issues at the forefront of current research.

### 4.2 Post-colonialism and Decolonialism

> *"Do not trust elitist versions of history and science which respond to dominant interests, but be receptive to counter-narratives and try to recapture them"* [27]

In order to counter the asymmetrical focus of HCI in western contexts, there have been several efforts for understanding and designing technologies that address the needs of underserved and marginalized communities. Research areas such as HCI for Development HCI4D, Information and Communication Technologies for Development (ICT4D), and Computing at the Margins (CoM) are interested in applying user-centered design principles for designing and evaluating technologies for users in *developing regions* around the world [17,94].

However, Irani et al. [43] and Philip et al. [68] point to the problematic rhetoric and practice of the concept of **development**, as it does not consider the history of global dynamics of power, wealth, economic strength, and political influence, shaping contemporary cultural encounters. They introduce Post-colonial Computing as a set of tactics for approaching HCI design in cross-cultural contexts, supported by existing theory of Post-colonial studies, an area in the social sciences with origins that can be traced to the end of the second world war [14].

More recently, post-colonial theories have received much criticism in the literature [3,18,77,94]. While recognizing its motivation and possibilities, Ali [3] points to several shortcomings of post-colonial theories, such as its emphasis on cultural concerns over political-economic concerns, and their adoption of an *"Eurocentric critique of Eurocentrism"* grounded in the post-structuralism of Foucault, Lacan, and Derrida. Furthermore, the post-colonial discourse neglects racial issues and past injustices, and does not engage with the matter of reparations. To overcome these issues, Ali proposes the adoption of a **decolonial perspective** grounded in a non-Eurocentric standpoint and including the perspectives and local knowledge associated with figures located at the margins/borders/periphery of the racial, political, and economic world system.

Recently, decolonization has been influencing HCI theory and practice [39] [12,25], and researchers are questioning the effectiveness of applying traditional design methods (e.g. Design Thinking) to engage underserved communities [18]. However, as Smith et al. [77] underscore, the decolonizing discourse, while present in the field of HCI, has not yet fundamentally affected current theories, concepts, models or practices.

### 4.3 Designs for the Pluriverse

> *"If we start with the presupposition, striking perhaps but not totally far-fetched, that the contemporary world can be considered a massive design failure, certainly the result of particular design decisions, is it a matter of designing our way out?"* [24]

In his book *Designs for the Pluriverse* [24], Arturo Escobar reflects on the design practice, and proposes a radical approach to design that encapsulates a multitude of theories, visions and practices that offer a different way of engaging with others and the world at large. This approach, *Autonomous Design*, stems from the postcolonial stance that the author has articulated in previous work

[21,22], and addresses the need of a framework for design that is conceived for/by/from the 'global south' [23,32].

Escobar starts by examining the historical and cultural background from within which the design practice enfolds, advocating for a conception of design *"as user centered, situated, interactive, collaborative, and participatory, focused significantly on the production of human experience and life itself"*. In order to uncover and question dominant western onto-epistemologies, and pave the way for other discourses that have been historically marginalized, Escobar explores the rationalistic and universalistic tradition of western modernity – the *One World World* (OWW), a term coined by John Law [53] – which approximates reality by posing ontological dualisms (e.g. mind/body, self/other, subject/object, nature/culture, matter/spirit, reason/emotion). This tradition is founded in a definition of cognition and the self deeply grounded on the notion that we exist as separate individuals, discrete minds that represent the world as a preexisting, separate entity.

This OWW establishes hierarchical and reductionist systems of classification based on difference, where a dominant paradigm suppresses, devalues, subordinates, or destructs other forms of knowledge and being that do not conform to the dominant form of modernity. As Escobar underscores, the discourse of this tradition is grounded on these systems of classification for bringing 'civilization', 'modernity', and, later on, 'development' to much of Asia, Africa, and Latin America. Escobar contrasts this traditional view with indigenous and oriental paradigms that do not conform to western notions of the self, holding a more embodied view where all the dualisms and dichotomies dissolve: *"mind is not separate from body, and both are not separate from the world, that is, from the ceaseless and always-changing flow of existence that constitutes life"*. A consequence of this worldview is that we necessarily co-create (co-design) with all other beings (humans and nonhumans) that co-exist with us in this world.

**Ontological (re)design.** To escape the *One World World*, Escobar proposes an ontological approach to design, based on the cognitive theory of Winograd and Flores [90] where *"the observer is not separate from the world she or he observes but rather creates the phenomenal domains within which she or he acts"*. This approach promotes futuring practices, particularly those that embrace relationality, and takes into account the entire range of design traditions, not just eurocentric ones. While Escobar underscores that some design practices (e.g. Design Thinking, Speculative Design) resonate with this futuring approach, they fall short in designing functional, relational, and sustainable versions of the future.

**Transition Design.** Instead of employing these design practices, Escobar navigates among multiple discourses of transition, such as the Transition Town Initiative [41], the Great Transition Initiative, Degrowth communities, the commons [9], *Buen Vivir* [73], and communalization, postdevelopment and postextractivism perspectives. These transition discourses posit a radical cultural and institutional transformation that goes beyond the modern dualist, reductionist, economic, anthropocentric, and capitalistic age. They promote values such as solidarity, well-being, human dignity, de-centering, social justice, ecology, and sustainability. Then, Escobar introduces the Transition Design framework from the School of Design at Carnegie Mellon University (CMU) [44,45] as a design approach for the creation of visions of more sustainable futures by applying an understanding of the interconnectedness of social, economic, political and natural systems for addressing wicked societal problems that exist at all scales (household, village, city, region, and planet) in ways that improve quality of life and tackle poverty, the loss of biodiversity, the decline of community, and environmental degradation. As ethical commitment, Transition Design employs relational ethics to escape the dualist ways of thinking, being, and doing that are entrenched in our capitalistic everyday lives.

**Autonomous Design.** In the last part of his book [24], Escobar outlines the approach of *Autonomous Design*, best described as "a theory and practice of interexistence and interbeing, a design for the pluriverse". Its central concept, *Autonomía*, is inspired on the notion of *autopoiesis* from Maturana and Varela [62]. Instead of examining living systems (and their sub-systems) in terms of their functions, inputs and outputs (the traditional view), autopoiesis is a form of biological autonomy of all living beings, seen as systems of self-contained components whose continued interaction produces the system itself as a unit. In this manner, *"living systems can undergo structural changes in response with interactions with the environment, but they have to maintain a basic organization in order to remain as the units they are"*.

Escobar translates this vision of autonomy to the social domain: A socio-economic system is autonomous when the conditions exist for changing its norms from within, not imposed from its external environment. Autonomous communities interact with each other and to other systems (e.g. the State) through the internal organization – and autonomy – of their members. Autonomy is a cultural, ecological, and political process that involves autonomous forms of existence and decision-making, and embraces a pluriverse of visions and practices. It embodies a communal form of existence that allows genuine interculturality without establishing dominant-subordinate relationships: *"The proposal is not a call for a new hegemony but for an end of any system, for taking leave of the universals of modernity and moving into the pluriverse of interculturality"*. Escobar explains autonomous design as a design praxis with communities that follows the following tenets:

- Every community practices the design of itself.
- People are practitioners of their own knowledge, and design practices must align to their understanding of reality.
- The community designs an inquiring system about itself.
- The result of every design process should be a series of scenarios and possible paths for the transformation of practices (or the creation of new ones).
- The statement of problems and possibilities involves building a model of the system that generates the problem of communal concern.

### 4.4 Autonomous Design in Human-Computer Interaction

Autonomous Design presents an alternative approach that addresses the geopolitical issues that introduce controversy and divisiveness to the field of HCI (see Sect. 2.2). Despite its novelty, it has already been adopted by a number of members of the CHI community [25,67,77,93]. A pluriversal perspective of HCI provides an opportunity for collaboration where researchers and participants from western societies can engage in a horizontal manner with members of the global south [93], and where both can draw from each other's vast production of knowledge. However, there is much work ahead: As pointed by Smith et al. [77], how such visions translate into concrete research practices and strategies for pluriversal participation and knowledge production is still an open question.

## 5 HCI, Literature, and Punk Narratives

> *"Distrust everything I say. I am telling the truth. The only truth I can understand or express is, logically defined, a lie. Psychologically defined, a symbol. Aesthetically defined, a metaphor."* [48]

There is little doubt about the strong (and sometimes conflicted) relationship between Science Fiction (SF) and Human Computer Interaction. On the one hand, movies adopt current HCI research and translate it to a future setting, expanding its possibilities [74]. On the other hand, SF is a fertile source for new metaphors for Visualization and Interaction in HCI [51]. Growing in recognition and adoption, SF is currently a serious research topic in Computer Science, HCI and Design Research [47,59,60]. Most emphasis has been given to SF movies and television, where interaction design is the most visible part [74].

However, these media, Dunne and Raby [20] explain, while capable of delivering a very powerful story and immersive experience, require a degree of passivity in the viewer, often reinforced by clichés and visual cues. Conversely, SF Literature makes us construct all the details of a fictional world inside our heads [20]. Dunne and Raby also highlight the power of ideas as stories, and suggest the use of utopias and dystopias in design. Utopias can be used as a stimulus to keep idealism alive, and dystopias can be seen as cautionary tales warning us of what might lay ahead if we are not careful. Nevertheless, these two narratives introduce another dichotomy: Every utopia contains within the seeds of another's dystopia [88]. Furthermore, bleak landscapes of the future are more prevalent in this purview, making it difficult to construct shared imaginaries [67].

### 5.1 Punk Narratives

The problem with SF is that it encompasses under the same umbrella a multitude of genres and visions of the future. Several SF authors feel uncomfortable when associated with the popular conception of SF (spaceships and aliens), and try to position their work under other labels: For instance, Margaret Atwood places herself under *Speculative Fiction*, i.e. a more plausible Science Fiction "without the aliens" [20]. Originated in the *Cyberpunk* movement, the **punk suffix** has been used for referring to several genres of alternate reality narratives and aesthetics that renounce to consensus reality. Some of these genres forego the assumption of a dystopia (Post-cyberpunk, Solarpunk, Lunarpunk), others are based on particular technological advances (Biopunk, Nanopunk), retro-futuristic reimaginations of particular periods (Atompunk, Steampunk, Dieselpunk), or place the story in a contemporary setting (Nowpunk).

**Cyberpunk** narratives can be seen as cautionary tales of our future, and have influenced how designers envisioned a digital realm that today we largely take for granted [13]. By usually taking a post-colonial lens, Cyberpunk shows how and why dominant ideologies marginalize underserved groups [13], whilst including geographical and cultural locales that include not only non-western [54] and indigenous [19] perspectives, but also perspectives coming from social justice movements [82], e.g. black, feminist, and queer perspectives [63]. **Solarpunk** narratives describe idealized futures where current environmental and social problems have been solved in a sustainable manner, transcending cultural, race, and gender divisions. Solarpunk futurism is not nihilistic (like cyberpunk) and it avoids steampunk's potentially quasi-reactionary tendencies: it is about ingenuity, generativity, independence, and community.

### 5.2 Towards Functional Futures

Punk narratives – not just *Cyberpunk* – can serve as inspiration for envisioning more pluriversal future visions. This is more critical in today's world, where the *Metaverse*, a concept developed in a dystopic cyberpunk novel [79] is now presented as "the next evolution of social connection" [64]. The problem with this view is that it imposes the particular vision of social connection championed by Silicon Valley, effectively colonializing the digital experience. Escobar [24] underscores that this kind of virtual experience is not desirable, as it removes agency and autonomy from all of us:

> *"Yet as we plug in to our various interfaces and engage in tele-existence, as we become citizen-terminals of sorts, our bodies are deterritorialized, as in the cyberpunk fantasies of the 1980s, when cyberspace became a metaphor for anything that was cool."*

Members of the HCI community are starting to make explicit use of punk narratives, e.g. *Cyberpunk* [50], *Steampunk* [81], and *Afropunk* [70,89]. However, there is an urgent need of developing new ways of translating these narratives and aesthetics to more inclusive inter-cultural contexts. For this purpose, Vervoort et al. [87] propose worldmaking as a framework for pluralistic, imaginative scenario development. Worldmaking is a concept introduced by Nelson Goodman [33], where *"there is no singular, objective world (or "real reality"), and instead worlds are multiple, constructed through creative processes instead of given, and always in the process of becoming"*.

Approaches to Worldmaking, Futures Literacy [58] and Design Fictions [36,66] can help to bring stories to local contexts [26], while considering young people's imagining of the future [5] and multispecies cooperation [85]. Of interest is *design anthropology futures* [35,76], a community focused on offering a decolonizing approach to the situated values, ethics, and politics of future making [77].

## 6 Conclusion

Interrogating assumptions reproduced by dominant HCI paradigms paves the way for establishing new methods, and indeed, new theories on HCI in general [91]. In this paper, we identified three critical geopolitical issues that cause divisiveness in the field, and examined four mainstream paradigms in design that try to address large-scale geopolitical and societal issues. We underscore that these practices, while legitimate and valuable, have some issues in their applicability to non-western contexts. Thus, rather than proposing another theory to displace all others, we point to the work of Arturo Escobar and his proposal of an all-encompassing and inclusive – pluriversal – reorientation of design. Then, we introduce Punk narratives, that coupled with approaches such as worldmaking and design fiction, can produce more plausible future scenarios in a pluriversal and autonomous manner.

We think there are several views in common in all these research communities, and bridges must be build between different venues (e.g. CHI, INTERACT, CSCW) to co-create a pluriversal Human-Computer Interaction, as well as designing **functional fictions**, rather than just **science fiction** [24]. We also consider that there is a whole breadth of future directions for this nascent line of research, which presents an opportunity for designing our way out of our current dystopic reality.

**Acknowledgment.** This work was supported by the COLCIENCIAS grant 727 for doctoral studies.

## References

1. Nocera, J.A., et al.: Geopolitical issues in human computer interaction. In: Ardito, C., et al. (eds.) INTERACT 2021. LNCS, vol. 12936, pp. 536–541. Springer, Cham (2021). https://doi.org/10.1007/978-3-030-85607-6_73. https://doi.org/10/gngf9d
2. Abdurahman, J.K., Ghoshal, S., Rosner, D., Taylor, A., Wiberg, M.: (Un)making democracy. Interactions **28**(6), 6–7 (2021). https://doi.org/10/gngfwk
3. Ali, M.: Towards a decolonial computing. In: CEPE 2013: Computer Ethics: Philosophical Enquiry, pp. 28–35. International Society of Ethics and Information Technology, Lisbon (2014). http://oro.open.ac.uk/41372/
4. Alsheikh, T., Rode, J.A., Lindley, S.E.: (Whose) value-sensitive design: a study of long- distance relationships in an Arabic cultural context. In: Proceedings of the ACM 2011 Conference on Computer Supported Cooperative Work - CSCW 2011, Hangzhou, China, p. 75. ACM Press (2011). https://doi.org/10/c7zvkr
5. Angheloiu, C., Sheldrick, L., Tennant, M.: Future tense: exploring dissonance in young people's images of the future through design futures methods. Futures **117**, 102527 (2020). https://doi.org/10/gjndn8

6. Archibugi, D., Koenig-Archibugi, M., Marchetti, R. (eds.): Global Democracy: Normative and Empirical Perspectives. Cambridge University Press, Cambridge (2012)
7. Besançon, L., Dragicevic, P.: The continued prevalence of dichotomous inferences at CHI. In: Extended Abstracts of the 2019 CHI Conference on Human Factors in Computing Systems, CHI EA 2019, pp. 1–11. Association for Computing Machinery, New York, May 2019. https://doi.org/10/ghs8mh
8. Bødker, S.: Third-wave HCI, 10 years later–participation and sharing. Interactions **22**(5), 24–31 (2015). https://doi.org/10/gdqdv6
9. Bollier, D.: Think Like a Commoner: A Short Introduction to the Life of the Commons, 1st edn. New Society Publishers, Gabriola Island (2014)
10. Borning, A., Muller, M.: Next steps for value sensitive design. In: Proceedings of the SIGCHI Conference on Human Factors in Computing Systems, Austin Texas USA, pp. 1125–1134. ACM, May 2012. https://doi.org/10/gm84qf
11. Bowden, M.: Deepening futures methods to face the civilisational crisis. Futures **132**, 102783 (2021). https://doi.org/10/gngfqr
12. Cannanure, V.K., et al.: Decolonizing HCI Across Borders. In: Extended Abstracts of the 2021 CHI Conference on Human Factors in Computing Systems, pp. 1–5, no. 106. Association for Computing Machinery, New York, May 2021. https://doi.org/10.1145/3411763.3441348
13. Cavallaro, D.: Cyberpunk and Cyberculture: Science Fiction and the Work of William Gibson. The Athlone Press (2000). https://doi.org/10.5040/9781472545558
14. Césaire, A.: Discours Sur Le Colonialisme. Editions Présence Africaine (1955)
15. Chakrabarty, D.: Provincializing Europe: Postcolonial Thought and Historical Difference, 1st edn. Princeton University Press, Princeton (2007)
16. Crooks, R.: Between communication and violence. Interactions **27**(5), 60–63 (2020). https://doi.org/10/gnj7fs
17. Dell, N., Kumar, N.: The ins and outs of HCI for development. In: Proceedings of the 2016 CHI Conference on Human Factors in Computing Systems, CHI 2016, pp. 2220–2232. Association for Computing Machinery, New York, May 2016. https://doi.org/10/gnj37r
18. Dillahunt, T.R., Erete, S., Galusca, R., Israni, A., Nacu, D., Sengers, P.: Reflections on design methods for underserved communities. In: Companion of the 2017 ACM Conference on Computer Supported Cooperative Work and Social Computing, CSCW 2017 Companion, pp. 409–413. Association for Computing Machinery, New York, February 2017. https://doi.org/10/gnj3v3
19. Dillon, G.L. (ed.): Walking the Clouds: An Anthology of Indigenous Science Fiction, 1st edn. University of Arizona Press, Tucson (2012)
20. Dunne, A., Raby, F.: Speculative Everything: Design, Fiction, and Social Dreaming. The MIT Press, Cambridge (2013)
21. Escobar, A.: Reflections on 'development': grassroots approaches and alternative politics in the Third World. Futures **24**(5), 411–436 (1992). https://doi.org/10/bhf59h
22. Escobar, A.: Encountering Development: The Making and Unmaking of the Third World, Revised edn. Princeton University Press, Princeton (2011)
23. Escobar, A.: Response: design for/by [and from] the 'global South'. Des. Philos. Papers **15**(1), 39–49 (2017). https://doi.org/10/gj8qqz
24. Escobar, A.: Designs for the Pluriverse: Radical Interdependence, Autonomy, and the Making of Worlds. New Ecologies for the Twenty-First Century. Duke University Press, Durham (2018)

25. Escobar-Tello, M.C., Ruette-Orihuela, K., Gough, K.V., Fayad-Sierra, J.A., Velez-Torres, I.: Decolonising design in peacebuilding contexts. Des. Stud. **73**, 101001 (2021). https://doi.org/10/gk4j75
26. Facer, K., Sriprakash, A.: Provincialising Futures Literacy: a caution against codification. Futures **133**, 102807 (2021). https://doi.org/10/gk4j75
27. Fals-Borda, O., Gaventa, J.: Research for social justice: some north-south convergences. Sociol. Imagin. **33**(2), 154–163 (1996)
28. Filimowicz, M., Tzankova, V. (eds.): New Directions in Third Wave Human-Computer Interaction: Volume 2 - Methodologies. Human-Computer Interaction Series. Springer, Cham (2018). https://link.springer.com/10.1007/978-3-319-73374-6
29. Friedman, B., Hendry, D.G.: Value Sensitive Design: Shaping Technology with Moral Imagination, Illustrated edn. The MIT Press, Cambridge (2019)
30. Friedman, B., Hendry, D.G., Borning, A.: A survey of value sensitive design methods. Found. Trends® Hum.-Comput. Interact. **11**(2), 63–125 (2017). https://doi.org/10/ggzfcj
31. Friedman, B., Kahn, P.H., Borning, A., Huldtgren, A.: Value sensitive design and information systems. In: Doorn, N., Schuurbiers, D., van de Poel, I., Gorman, M.E. (eds.) Early engagement and new technologies: opening up the laboratory. PET, vol. 16, pp. 55–95. Springer, Dordrecht (2013). https://doi.org/10.1007/978-94-007-7844-3_4
32. Fry, T.: Design for/by "The Global South". Des. Philos. Papers **15**(1), 3–37 (2017). https://doi.org/10/gfsqdf
33. Goodman, N.: Ways of Worldmaking. Hackett Publishing Company Inc., Indianapolis (1978)
34. Grudin, J.: Is HCI homeless? In search of inter-disciplinary status. Interactions **13**(1), 54–59 (2006). https://doi.org/10/dt2pdk
35. Gunn, W., Otto, T., Smith, R.C. (eds.): Design Anthropology: Theory and Practice, 1st edn. Routledge, London (2013)
36. Hales, D.: Design fictions an introduction and provisional taxonomy. Digit. Creat. **24**(1), 1–10 (2013). https://doi.org/10/gd4q6g
37. Harrington, C., Erete, S., Piper, A.M.: Deconstructing community-based collaborative design: towards more equitable participatory design engagements. Proc. ACM Hum.-Comput. Interact. **3**(CSCW), 216:1–216:25 (2019). https://doi.org/10/ghzbng
38. Harrison, S., Tatar, D., Singers, P.: The three paradigms of HCI. In: Proceedings of the 2007 CHI Conference on Human Factors in Computing Systems, San Jose, USA, p. 18. ACM (2007)
39. Hayes, G.R.: Inclusive and engaged HCI. Interactions **27**(2), 26–31 (2020). https://doi.org/10/gnj7wd
40. Hochheiser, H., Lazar, J.: HCI and societal issues: a framework for engagement. Int. J. Hum.-Comput. Interact. **23**(3), 339–374 (2007). https://doi.org/10/bv6w5n
41. Hopkins, R.: The Transition Handbook: From Oil Dependency to Local Resilience. Green Books, Place of publication not identified (2014)
42. Irani, L.: "Design Thinking": defending silicon valley at the apex of global labor hierarchies. Catalyst Feminism Theory Technosci. **4**(1), 1–19 (2018). https://doi.org/10/gmk84t
43. Irani, L., Vertesi, J., Dourish, P., Philip, K., Grinter, R.E.: Postcolonial computing: a lens on design and development. In: Proceedings of the SIGCHI Conference on Human Factors in Computing Systems, CHI 2010, pp. 1311–1320. Association for Computing Machinery, New York (2010). https://doi.org/10/cv6vsj

44. Irwin, T., Kossoff, G., Tonkinwise, C.: Transition design provocation. Des. Philos. Papers **13**(1), 3–11 (2015). https://doi.org/10/ggb5hs
45. Irwin, T., Kossoff, G., Tonkinwise, C., Scupelli, P.: Transition design 2015. Technical report, CMU School of Design (2015). https://www.design.cmu.edu/sites/default/files/Transition_Design_Monograph_final.pdf
46. Johansson-Sköldberg, U., Woodilla, J., Çetinkaya, M.: Design thinking: past, present and possible futures. Creat. Innov. Manag. **22**(2), 121–146 (2013). https://doi.org/10/f22xmp
47. Jordan, P., Silva, P.A.: Science fiction—an untapped opportunity in HCI research and education. In: Soares, M.M., Rosenzweig, E., Marcus, A. (eds.) HCII 2021. LNCS, vol. 12779, pp. 34–47. Springer, Cham (2021). https://doi.org/10.1007/978-3-030-78221-4_3. https://doi.org/10/gngfhf
48. Le Guin, U.K.: The Left Hand Of Darkness. Hachette UK, London (1969)
49. Kelley, T., Littman, J., Peters, T.: The Art of Innovation: Lessons in Creativity from IDEO, America's Leading Design Firm, Hardcover edn. Currency, New York (2001)
50. Kong, B., Liang, R.H., Liu, M., Chang, S.H., Tseng, H.C., Ju, C.H.: Neuromancer workshop: towards designing experiential entanglement with science fiction. In: Proceedings of the 2021 CHI Conference on Human Factors in Computing Systems, pp. 1–17, no. 625. Association for Computing Machinery, New York, May 2021. https://doi.org/10.1145/3411764.3445273
51. Averbukh, V.L.: Sources of computer metaphors for visualization and human-computer interaction. In: Silvera-Roig, M., López-Varela Azcárate, A. (eds.) Cognitive and Intermedial Semiotics. IntechOpen, June 2020
52. Laursen, L.N., Haase, L.M.: The shortcomings of design thinking when compared to designerly thinking. Des. J. **22**(6), 813–832 (2019). https://doi.org/10/gf9rnf
53. Law, J.: What's wrong with a one-world world? Distinktion J. Soc. Theory **16**(1), 126–139 (2015). https://doi.org/10/ggf2fs
54. Lee, G.B., Lam, S.S.K.: Wicked cities: cyberculture and the reimagining of identity in the 'non-Western' metropolis. Futures **30**(10), 967–979 (1998). https://doi.org/10/cqxdkk
55. Linxen, S., Sturm, C., Brühlmann, F., Cassau, V., Opwis, K., Reinecke, K.: How WEIRD is CHI? In: Proceedings of the 2021 CHI Conference on Human Factors in Computing Systems, no. 143. Association for Computing Machinery, New York, May 2021. https://doi.org/10.1145/3411764.3445488
56. Malpass, M.: Critical Design in Context: History, Theory, and Practices. Bloomsbury Academic, London (2017)
57. Manders-Huits, N.: What values in design? The challenge of incorporating moral values into design. Sci. Eng. Ethics **17**(2), 271–287 (2011). https://doi.org/10/d4m6ch
58. Mangnus, A.C., Oomen, J., Vervoort, J.M., Hajer, M.A.: Futures literacy and the diversity of the future. Futures **132**, 102793 (2021). https://doi.org/10/gngfqj
59. Marcus, A.: The history of the future: sci-fi movies and HCI. Interactions **20**(4), 64–67 (2013). https://doi.org/10/gngfvk
60. Marcus, A.: The past 100 years of the future: HCI and user-experience design in science-fiction movies and television. In: SIGGRAPH Asia 2015 Courses, SA 2015, pp. 1–26. Association for Computing Machinery, New York (2015). https://doi.org/10/gngfsm
61. Martins, L.P.d.O.: Privilege and oppression: towards a feminist speculative design. In: DRS Biennial Conference Series, June 2014. https://dl.designresearchsociety.org/drs-conference-papers/drs2014/researchpapers/75

62. Maturana, H.R., Varela, F.J.: De máquinas y seres vivos: autopoiesis, la organización de lo vivo. Editorial Universitaria, Santiago de Chile (2006)
63. McFarlane, A., Murphy, G.J., Schmeink, L. (eds.): The Routledge Companion to Cyberpunk Culture. Routledge, Taylor and Francis Group, New York (2020)
64. Meta: Meta Keynote Mark Zuckerberg explaining metaverse, October 2021. https://www.youtube.com/watch?v=YJQ6z1EsLbg
65. Mitrović, I., Šuran, O. (eds.): Speculative – Post-Design Practice or New Utopia? Ministry of Culture of the Republic of Croatia & Croatian Designers Association, Zagreb (2016). http://speculative.hr/wp-content/uploads/pdf/speculative_triennale.pdf
66. Morrison, A., Tronstad, R., Martinussen, E.S.: Design notes on a lonely drone. Digit. Creat. **24**(1), 46–59 (2013). https://doi.org/10/gmz4kk
67. Pansera, M., Ehlers, M.H., Kerschner, C.: Unlocking wise digital techno-futures: contributions from the Degrowth community. Futures **114**, 102474 (2019). https://doi.org/10/ghj2dv
68. Philip, K., Irani, L., Dourish, P.: Postcolonial computing: a tactical survey. Sci. Technol. Hum. Values **37**(1), 3–29 (2012). https://doi.org/10/bkgzfj
69. Pratt, M.L.: Imperial Eyes: Travel Writing and Transculturation, 2nd edn. Routledge, London (2007)
70. Reynolds, K.: Black literary technoculture and afrofuturist rupture. Interactions **28**(6), 8–9 (2021). https://doi.org/10/gngfv4
71. Rittel, H.W.J., Webber, M.M.: Dilemmas in a general theory of planning. Policy Sci. **4**(2), 155–169 (1973)
72. Rogers, Y., Brereton, M., Dourish, P., Forlizzi, J., Olivier, P.: The dark side of interaction design. In: Extended Abstracts of the 2021 CHI Conference on Human Factors in Computing Systems, pp. 1–2, no. 152. Association for Computing Machinery, New York (2021). https://doi.org/10.1145/3411763.3450397
73. Santos, B.d.S.: Epistemologies of the South: Justice Against Epistemicide, 1st edn. Routledge, London (2014)
74. Schmitz, M., Endres, C., Butz, A.: A survey of human-computer interaction design in science fiction movies. In: Proceedings of the 2nd International Conference on INtelligent TEchnologies for Interactive enterTAINment. ICST, Cancun (2008). https://doi.org/10/d98jtk
75. Slaughter, R.A.: Futures beyond dystopia. Futures **30**(10), 993–1002 (1998). https://doi.org/10/dnw2r4
76. Smith, R.C., Vangkilde, K.T., Kjaersgaard, M.G., Otto, T., Halse, J., Binder, T.: Design Anthropological Futures. Taylor & Francis (2016)
77. Smith, R.C., et al.: Decolonizing design practices: towards pluriversality. In: Extended Abstracts of the 2021 CHI Conference on Human Factors in Computing Systems, pp. 1–5, no. 83. Association for Computing Machinery, New York (2021). https://doi.org/10.1145/3411763.3441334
78. Stephanidis, C.C., et al.: Seven HCI grand challenges. Int. J. Hum.-Comput. Interact. **35**(14), 1229–1269 (2019). https://doi.org/10/ggpwdz
79. Stephenson, N.: Snow Crash. Random House Publishing Group, New York (2000)
80. Sturm, C., Oh, A., Linxen, S., Abdelnour Nocera, J., Dray, S., Reinecke, K.: How WEIRD is HCI? Extending HCI principles to other countries and cultures. In: Proceedings of the 33rd Annual ACM Conference Extended Abstracts on Human Factors in Computing Systems, CHI EA 2015, pp. 2425–2428. Association for Computing Machinery, New York, April 2015. https://doi.org/10/gkcmbq

81. Tanenbaum, T.J., Tanenbaum, K., Wakkary, R.: Steampunk as design fiction. In: Proceedings of the SIGCHI Conference on Human Factors in Computing Systems, CHI 2012, pp. 1583–1592. Association for Computing Machinery, New York, May 2012. https://doi.org/10/gjpwbd
82. Thomas, S.R.: Octavia's Brood: Science Fiction Stories from Social Justice Movements, 1st edn. AK Press, Oakland (2015)
83. Tonkinwise, C.: How we intend to future: review of Anthony Dunne and Fiona Raby, speculative everything: design, fiction, and social dreaming. Des. Philos. Papers **12**(2), 169–187 (2014). https://doi.org/10/gfsp66
84. Tran O'Leary, J., Zewde, S., Mankoff, J., Rosner, D.K.: Who gets to future? Race, representation, and design methods in Africa town. In: Proceedings of the 2019 CHI Conference on Human Factors in Computing Systems, pp. 1–13. Association for Computing Machinery, New York (2019). https://doi.org/10.1145/3290605.3300791
85. van Gaalen, S.: Functional fictions for multispecies cooperation. Interactions **28**(2), 14–15 (2021). https://doi.org/10/gngfxf
86. Vermaas, P.E., Pesch, U.: Revisiting Rittel and Webber's dilemmas: designerly thinking against the background of new societal distrust. She Ji J. Des. Econ. Innov. **6**(4), 530–545 (2020). https://doi.org/10/gh52n2
87. Vervoort, J.M., Bendor, R., Kelliher, A., Strik, O., Helfgott, A.E.R.: Scenarios and the art of worldmaking. Futures **74**, 62–70 (2015). https://doi.org/10/gcsmfw
88. Whitfield, D., Galpine, L., Ahlquist, D. (eds.): Imperfect Ideal: Utopian and Dystopian Visions. The Great Books Foundation (2015)
89. Winchester, W.W.: Afrofuturism, inclusion, and the design imagination. Interactions **25**(2), 41–45 (2018). https://doi.org/10/gnkdgj
90. Winograd, T., Flores, F.: Understanding Computers and Cognition: A New Foundation for Design. Intellect Books, Bristol (1986)
91. Winschiers-Theophilus, H., Bidwell, N.J.: Toward an afro-centric indigenous HCI paradigm. Int. J. Hum.-Comput. Interact. **29**(4), 243–255 (2013). https://doi.org/10/ghcm2x
92. Wong, R.Y., Khovanskaya, V.: Speculative design in HCI: from corporate imaginations to critical orientations. In: Filimowicz, M., Tzankova, V. (eds.) New Directions in Third Wave Human-Computer Interaction: Volume 2 - Methodologies. HIS, pp. 175–202. Springer, Cham (2018). https://doi.org/10.1007/978-3-319-73374-6_10
93. Wong-Villacres, M., et al.: Lessons from Latin America: embracing horizontality to reconstruct HCI as a pluriverse. Interactions **28**(2), 56–63 (2021). https://doi.org/10/gj7k56
94. Wyche, S.P., et al.: Learning from marginalized users: reciprocity in HCI4D, p. 2 (2012). https://doi.org/10/gh54tq

# Correction to: Extreme Citizen Science Contributions to the Sustainable Development Goals: Challenges and Opportunities for a Human-Centred Design Approach

Artemis Skarlatidou, Dilek Fraisl, Yaqian Wu, Linda See, and Muki Haklay

## Correction to: Chapter "Extreme Citizen Science Contributions to the Sustainable Development Goals: Challenges and Opportunities for a Human-Centred Design Approach" in: C. Ardito et al. (Eds.): *Sense, Feel, Design*, LNCS 13198, https://doi.org/10.1007/978-3-030-98388-8_3

Chapter "Extreme Citizen Science Contributions to the Sustainable Development Goals: Challenges and Opportunities for a Human-Centred Design Approach" was previously published non-open access. It has now been changed to open access under a CC BY 4.0 license and the copyright holder updated to 'The Author(s)'. The book has also been updated with this change.

---

The updated version of this chapter can be found at
https://doi.org/10.1007/978-3-030-98388-8_3



C. Ardito et al. (Eds.): INTERACT 2021, LNCS 13198, p. C1, 2022.
https://doi.org/10.1007/978-3-030-98388-8_46

# Author Index